AMERICA'S DREAM PALACE

America's Dream Palace

Middle East Expertise and the Rise of the National Security State

OSAMAH F. KHALIL

Harvard University Press

Cambridge, Massachusetts
London, England
2016

Second printing

Library of Congress Cataloging-in-Publication Data

Names: Khalil, Osamah F., 1971– author.

Title: America's dream palace : Middle East expertise and the rise of the
national security state / Osamah F. Khalil.

Description: Cambridge, Massachusetts : Harvard University Press,
2016. | Includes bibliographical references and index.

Identifi ers: LCCN 2016013981 | ISBN 9780674971578 (hardcover : alk.
paper)

Subjects: LCSH: Middle East—Study and teaching (Higher)—United
States. | National security—United States—History. | United States—
Foreign relations—Middle East. | Middle East—Foreign relations—
United States. | Research institutes—United States.

Classification: LCC DS61.8 .K47 2016 | DDC 956.0071/173—dc23

LC record available at https://lccn.loc.gov/2016013981

For Dalal and Laila

Contents

Abbreviations

ABCFM	American Board of Commissioners for Foreign Missions
ACE	American Council on Education
ACLS	American Council of Learned Societies
AEI	American Enterprise Institute
AIOC	Anglo-Iranian Oil Company
ARAMCO	Arabian-American Oil Company
ASTP	Army Specialized Training Program
AUB	American University of Beirut
AUC	American University in Cairo
BASR	Columbia University, Bureau for Applied Social Research
BNE	Board of National Estimates
BOB	Bureau of the Budget
CCF	Congress for Cultural Freedom
CFR	Council on Foreign Relations
CIA	Central Intelligence Agency
CMES	Harvard University, Center for Middle East Studies
COI	Coordinator of Information
CPD	Committee on the Present Danger
CSIS	Center for Strategic and International Studies
DCI	Director of Central Intelligence
DIA	Defense Intelligence Agency
DRN	Division of Research and Analysis for the Near East, South Asia, and Africa
ERS	State Department External Research Staff
FSI	State Department Foreign Service Institute

HEW	Department of Health, Education, and Welfare
INR	Bureau of Intelligence and Research
JCS	Joint Chiefs of Staff
MESA	Middle East Studies Association
NATO	North Atlantic Treaty Organization
NDEA	National Defense Education Act of 1958
NEA	Bureau of Near Eastern Affairs
NECA	Near East College Association
NIE	National Intelligence Estimates
NIS	National Intelligence Summaries
NSA	National Security Agency
NSC	National Security Council
NSRB	National Security Resources Board
ODM	Office of Defense Mobilization
OE	United States, Office of Education
OIR	Office of Intelligence and Research
ONE	Office of National Estimates
OPEC	Organization of the Petroleum Exporting Countries
ORE	Office of Research Evaluation
OSS	Office of Strategic Services
OWI	Office of War Information
PLO	Palestine Liberation Organization
PPS	State Department Policy Planning Staff
PWD	Psychological Warfare Division
R&A	OSS Research and Analysis Branch
SI	OSS Secret Intelligence Branch
SPC	Syrian Protestant College
SSRC	Social Science Research Council
UN	United Nations
USAID	United States Agency for International Development
VOA	Voice of America
WINEP	Washington Institute for Near East Policy

Note on Translation and Transliteration

Except where noted, all translations from Arabic are my own. Transliterations of Arabic are based on the standards of the *International Journal of Middle East Studies* with some minor modifications.

AMERICA'S DREAM PALACE

Introduction

The Crossroads of Empire

> It is no coincidence that the great world conquerors of history
> have fought in and over the Middle East. . . . Any power that has
> hoped to extend its domination over continents has learned that
> domination of the Middle East is an essential step. And any power
> trying to resist continental expansion by another has learned in turn
> that the Middle East must be protected at all cost.
>
> —KERMIT "KIM" ROOSEVELT JR.

The port of Aden was bustling when the USS *Iroquois* arrived in the summer of 1867. A thousand-ton corvette, the *Iroquois* departed New York in February bound for China and Japan. Aden was the midway point in the voyage. Alfred Thayer Mahan, the ship's executive officer, briefly visited the British-controlled port, which facilitated trade between the Indian Ocean and the Arabian Sea. Almost four decades later, Mahan recounted the details in his memoir. Although he was impressed by camels and reflected at length on the "ships of the desert," Mahan was less enamored with the people he encountered. The *Iroquois* left Aden for Muscat, near the entrance to the Persian Gulf. Away from the open sea, Mahan wrote, the heat confirmed "the association of the name Arabia with scorching and desert." He marveled at the water's green color and wondered if it inspired the lines in Thomas Moore's poem, "Araby's Daughter":

> No pearl ever lay under Oman's green water
> More pure in its shell than thy spirit in thee.[1]

Mahan's romanticism was exceeded by his admiration for Britain's military presence along the main maritime trade routes. "It is not that there is so much of him," he observed of British soldiers, "but that he is so many-where." Britain's empire, Mahan wrote, was not a "chance phenomenon, but an obvious effect of a noteworthy cause; an incident of current history, the exponent unconsciously to himself, of many great events." He added, "In our country we have wisely learned to scrutinize with distrust arguments for manifest destiny, but it is, nevertheless, well to note and ponder a manifest present, which speaks to a manifest past."[2]

Eighteen years after visiting Aden and Muscat, Mahan joined the newly established Naval War College as a lecturer of Naval Tactics and History. It was a fateful choice. Although Mahan was promoted to captain, he disliked the navy and was not viewed favorably by his superiors or subordinates. Quiet and reserved, Mahan enjoyed and was more adept at writing naval history than he was at ship duty. His books on sea power inspired dramatic changes in Britain and the United States. They also transformed Mahan into a celebrity strategist and advisor, the forerunner of today's national security academic. In spite of his rank, Mahan met with senior British military and political leaders eager for his insights. At home, Senator Henry Cabot Lodge and an ambitious Theodore Roosevelt promoted the captain's expertise, much to the chagrin of his naval rivals. As assistant secretary of the navy and later president, Roosevelt implemented Mahan's theories on naval power.[3]

Mahan's reputation as a naval strategist brought him back to the Persian Gulf in 1902. Writing in the *National Review,* he discussed the area's importance for trade in India and East Asia. Mahan advocated for continued British hegemony over the region, which he dubbed the "Middle East." Although Mahan did not specify boundaries to accompany the term, it was eventually adopted by the press and government officials, first in Britain and later the United States.[4]

Mahan was an American renowned in Britain, but his celebrity status was eventually surpassed by an Englishman. Thomas Edward (T. E.) Lawrence's exploits during World War I inspired subsequent generations on both sides of the Atlantic. The Oxford-educated British Army officer's wartime memoir, *Seven Pillars of Wisdom,* became an instant classic. That it exaggerated Lawrence's role and bordered on fiction was irrelevant. Long before he was immortalized in film, "Lawrence of Arabia" was a legend. "In these pages the history is not of the Arab movement," Lawrence wrote, "but of me in it." Yet he still proclaimed, "I meant to make a new nation, to restore a lost influence, to give twenty millions of Semites the foundations on which to build an inspired dream-palace of their national thoughts." Like

Mahan, Lawrence was another prototype: the classically trained scholar and expert whose carefully crafted image influenced academics and policy-makers in the United States. Lawrence became a shared reference point for American scholar-spies during World War II and counterinsurgency experts in the twenty-first century.[5]

The dream palace that Lawrence actually inspired, this book argues, was America's conception and construction of the Middle East. This is a story about missionaries, spies, soldiers, diplomats, and scholars and the dream palace they created. From the Palace of Versailles to Harvard Yard and from Foggy Bottom to Tahrir Square, this is a history of the "American Century" in the Middle East from World War I to the Global War on Terror. It is also a story about expertise and its relationship to America's national security interests in the Middle East. In the pages that follow, I discuss Orientalists and area experts, modernization theorists and national security academics, nervous liberals and neoconservatives. They all sought to make or remake the Middle East in America's image based on their hopes, fears, and illusions. It is also a history of governmental and nongovernmental institutions in the United States and the Middle East, from the State Department and intelligence agencies to prestigious American universities and leading academic societies, prominent philanthropic foundations, and influential think tanks. This book details how their actions and interactions have informed and been shaped by U.S. foreign policy.

America's Dream Palace explores the relationship between American power and the production of knowledge and expertise over the past century. It demonstrates how the Middle East has been constructed and reified by scholars, policymakers, and governmental and nongovernmental institutions. It examines the origins and expansion of Middle East studies against the backdrop of America's evolving and expanding foreign policy in the region. I contend that the emergence of Middle East expertise reflected U.S. national security interests in the region and globally. *America's Dream Palace* details how the mutually beneficial relationship between the U.S. foreign policy and national security establishments and academia influenced the creation and formalization of Middle East studies and expertise. It demonstrates that university-based Middle East studies programs were integral to expanding and enhancing Washington's knowledge of the region. Over time, however, the U.S. government developed its own methods for collecting and analyzing information on foreign areas as well as training personnel who benefited from but were independent of academia. By the late Cold

War period, area studies were perceived as a failure. Instead, think tanks garnered increased attention, access, and influence.

American Orientalism and American Exceptionalism

Like other invented geographic regions, the area now called the "Middle East" was the product of imperial interests and competition. Since Mahan offered a name for the region, its boundaries have varied reflecting British and American foreign policies. During the era of British hegemony, the "Middle East" encompassed India and its land and sea approaches, affirming London's geopolitical and economic interests. By the mid-twentieth century, the region's boundaries aligned with America's Cold War goals and stretched from Morocco to Pakistan. While the boundaries of the Middle East have been inconsistent over the past century, scholars and policymakers have consistently described the region as a source and site of tension, turmoil, and hostility. These characterizations also extended to the region's inhabitants. Thus, a region created by Britain and the United States was reproduced intellectually, ideologically, and geographically. *America's Dream Palace* contends that Middle East studies and expertise were a reflection of American power and hegemony over an area that Washington considered vital to its national security interests.[6]

The origins of Middle East studies and expertise can be traced to Orientalism, which emerged as a scholarly field in Europe during the late eighteenth century. Although there was European interest in and study of Islam and the present-day Middle East before this period, it was not always university-based. Usage of the term "Orientalism" to describe a scholarly field began in the nineteenth century. Orientalism was, and to an extent remains, largely based on the practice of philology and driven by the notion that textual analysis provides insights into the history and culture of different societies. The reliance on historical texts over contemporary knowledge implied that the regions and societies were static and unchanging. In addition, the analysis tended to contrast the perceived differences and inherent deficiencies of the "Orient" with the superiority of the modern and progressive West.[7]

As a scholarly discipline, Orientalism in America lagged behind that of Europe. Although the American Oriental Society was founded in 1842 and is the oldest learned society in the United States, the main centers of Orientalist scholarship were in Britain, France, and Germany. In addition,

American perceptions and representations of the "Orient" were generally of East Asia, not the territories of the present-day Middle East.[8]

Edward Said's seminal work *Orientalism* critiqued the discipline as well as the ideology it represented. Said argued that the notion of "the Orient" was an invention of the "Occident"—Europe and later the United States. He asserted that Orientalism reproduced and served to justify the imperial policies of Britain and France. This relationship to imperialism, Said explained, gave Orientalist discourse its power and ensured its durability. The production of knowledge about the Orient classified and represented who and what were (and were not) "Orientals." These definitions reflected the prevailing political order. Thus, the characterizations of the Orient's inferiority reaffirmed the superiority of the Occident and perpetuated its hegemony. Said argued that the United States not only inherited the imperial mantle from Britain and France, but adopted its Orientalist representations as well. European characterizations and study of the Orient were incorporated into and reproduced by American Orientalist scholarship and later area studies. As in Europe, it was also evidenced in American popular culture. In addition, the emphasis placed on the threat posed to Western civilization by the Oriental other was readily adopted by the United States.[9] Scholars have attempted to determine what influence, if any, Orientalism has had on U.S. foreign policy in the Middle East.[10] This book will demonstrate that Orientalism influenced the analysis, formation, and implementation of American policies in the region over the past century.[11]

The "othering" integral to Orientalism is also an essential aspect of American exceptionalism. Both have influenced U.S. foreign policy in the Middle East and the development of regional expertise. Even prior to the founding of the republic, the notion that the American colonies were unique with a divine mission was prevalent. The colonies were a second Promised Land, an American Israel, and Americans were a "chosen people."[12]

Exceptionalism and empire are intimately connected. Prior to the American Revolution, colonial intellectuals and pamphleteers claimed that Britain was the inheritor to the civilizations that began in Asia Minor and moved westward to Greece, Rome, and Britain. America, they argued, represented the ultimate and final destination of empire. Unlike Britain, it would be an empire of liberty and freedom.[13]

Continental expansion and dominance affirmed the notions of Divine Providence and manifest destiny that accompanied initial settlement. The United States was not just unique on earth, but was favored by heaven. Writing in 1811, John Quincy Adams, future president and secretary of state, proclaimed, "The whole continent of North America appears to be destined by Divine Providence to be peopled by one nation, speaking one language, professing one general system of religious and political principles, and accustomed to one general tenor of social usages and customs." The twin notions of Protestant exceptionalism and American exceptionalism inspired missionaries to travel overseas, including to the "Bible lands" of the present-day Middle East. Thus, Mahan's reflections on a manifest present and past in the early twentieth century were not only well rooted in elite American discourse and belief, but had already been tested and affirmed. By the time of Mahan's death in 1914, America was already an empire, and it was not a reluctant one.[14]

The emergence of the United States as a global superpower after the Second World War was yet another demonstration of its exceptionalism. Compared to Europe and Asia, the United States was relatively unscathed from the conflict. Its industrial production eclipsed that of prewar European economic rivals as well as the Soviet Union. Meanwhile, America's atomic monopoly affirmed its technological prowess. In addition, the shaping of the postwar economic and political order not only reflected American institutions, but extended and ensured the global power of the United States.[15]

An indicator of American power has been the different presidential doctrines announced in the postwar era declaring U.S. national security interests. Prior to World War II, the Monroe Doctrine and the Roosevelt Corollary were focused on the Western Hemisphere. Yet each doctrine from Harry Truman to George W. Bush was directly or indirectly related to the Middle East. The doctrines were informed by and reflected ideology, material concerns, and geopolitical strategy. These different factors have been reproduced in American interests in the Middle East, broadly defined as oil, regional security and stability, and Israel.[16]

Notions of exceptionalism and empire were incorporated into the American social sciences. Although the disciplinary traditions were borrowed from Europe, they were adapted to reflect American exceptionalism. American social science, according to historian Dorothy Ross, "has consistently constructed models of the world that embody the values and follow the logic of the national ideology of American exceptionalism." This continued with the postwar development of area studies.[17]

Area studies represented the intersection of the Cold War university and the American national security state. As I demonstrate, in creating and funding Middle East studies, the different governmental and nongovernmental institutions were united by shared goals and interests.[18] Their actions were driven in part by a desire to defend and protect the United States and to a lesser extent the region they believed was subject to Soviet influence and domination. When they differed, it was over how the United States could best maintain its predominance and secure its interests regionally and globally.[19] Although the National Defense Education Act (NDEA) of 1958 was deliberately linked to America's Cold War goals, Washington could not ensure that it would produce scholars aligned with its national security interests. The NDEA had the unintended consequence of diversifying Middle East studies.[20] A decade after its passage, American policymakers were prepared to abandon area studies. The increased prominence of think tanks and their close ties to the U.S. national security establishment, I argue, came at the expense of university-based Middle East studies programs. The post–September 11 period witnessed an expansion of both the national security bureaucracy and the influence of think tanks. Meanwhile, claims of anti-American bias and attempts to target government funding of Middle East studies served to further marginalize university-based centers and academics.[21]

Middle East studies were part of the broader professionalization of the social sciences in the United States. What scholars studied—and how and why they studied it, especially in the sciences and social sciences—was inextricable from Washington's efforts to shape the postwar global order.[22] The emergence of area studies in general, and Middle East studies in particular, were directly linked to the competition between Washington and Moscow. Although American research universities expanded dramatically during the Cold War, area studies struggled for academic recognition and resources. Meanwhile, U.S. government agencies and businesses sought a sustainable supply of potential candidates for employment in foreign areas. The State Department, fledgling intelligence agencies, and the Department of Defense also sought to develop tools and processes for research and analysis. This was particularly pronounced with the expansion of the national security bureaucracy as well as the creation of the United Nations (UN) and the North Atlantic Treaty Organization (NATO). Universities and academic societies developed programs aligned with America's goals at the outset of the Cold War. While philanthropic foundations provided early support for area studies, they also sought a commitment from Washington for sustained funding to ensure their future growth and development. As this book reveals, the link to U.S. national security interests was mutually beneficial for the different governmental and nongovernmental actors and contributed to the formalization of Middle East studies.

Although *America's Dream Palace* covers the past century of involvement in the Middle East, it is not a comprehensive history of Middle East studies, Orientalism, or U.S. foreign policy in the region. Nor is it an institutional analysis of their respective professional associations. Instead, this book examines how the United States developed expertise to match its increasing interests and involvement in the Middle East. Therefore, some institutions and individuals receive extensive attention while others are excluded. Similarly, there are debates that I only touch on briefly or not at all due to limitations of space and time. This book draws on sources from national, university, and foundation archives in the United States, the United Kingdom, Lebanon, and Egypt. I also conducted interviews with several scholars and former government officials to provide additional context. However, a number of scholars and former foundation officials I contacted did not respond to my interview requests. Similarly, several institutions were unwilling to provide access to their archives. Even though this book examines American actions and perceptions, I have attempted to use Arabic-language sources where possible and relevant. Finally, while acknowledging that the term "Middle East" is problematic, it is used throughout the book as are other appellations for the region (e.g., Western Asia, Levant, and the Near East) as they were applied by American policymakers and scholars. I have attempted to note the region's varying boundaries as they related to these terms and U.S. national security interests.

In the pages that follow, I examine how the Middle East became a site for the exercise of American power and hegemony. The development of Middle East studies, I contend, was an articulation of American power, Orientalism, and exceptionalism, as well as their limits. This is not merely a story of rise and decline. Rather, it demonstrates how U.S. foreign policy interests have had a predominant influence on the production of knowledge related to the Middle East and the development and cultivation of area expertise. Much like America's continued involvement in the region, it is a story that is still being written.

CHAPTER 1

Private Knowledge

American Missionaries, the Inquiry, and the First World War in the Middle East, 1917–1922

> You are, in truth, my advisers, for when I ask [for] information, I will have no way of checking it, and must act on it unquestionably. We shall be deluged with claims plausibly presented, and it will be your job to establish the justice or injustice of these claims, so that my position may be taken intelligently. . . . Tell me what's right and I'll fight for it, give me a guaranteed position.
>
> —PRESIDENT WOODROW WILSON to members of the Inquiry

The USS *George Washington* was the center of attention on December 4, 1918. Docked at Pier 4 in Hoboken, New Jersey, the *George Washington* was originally a German ocean liner seized by the United States and converted into a troop transport. It was refitted and restored with the tapestries, curtains, and rugs of other captured German vessels in order to carry President Woodrow Wilson to France. The *George Washington* also had a crew of a thousand officers and men, a naval brass band and string orchestra, and a marine company designated to serve as the president's honor guard. Wilson was the first sitting American president to make a trip to Europe. He was accompanied by First Lady Edith Wilson, Secretary of State Robert Lansing, Secretary of War Newton D. Baker, and other advisors and distinguished guests. Among the advisors was William Westermann, a classics professor from the University of Wisconsin and member of a team of American experts assisting with the negotiations.

"The departure was a great occasion," Westermann wrote in his diary. At 10:15 A.M., the *George Washington* left the dock and slowly made its way into New York Harbor. Cheering crowds gathered at the Manhattan and Staten Island waterfronts to watch the departure. "All the tugs and ferry boats whistled in one long and continuous deep base tone supporting the shrill whistles of the tugs. Two aviators flew over the ship coming close to the masts and waving their hands," Westermann recounted. As the *George Washington* passed the Statue of Liberty, it encountered the troop transport *Minnekhada* arriving from London. Soldiers on the *Minnekhada*'s crowded deck shared greetings and cheers with the president and first lady. After Liberty Island, the battleship USS *Pennsylvania* and four destroyers escorted the *George Washington* to Brest, France.[1]

Two years earlier, Westermann joined a group of American scholars known as the Inquiry. Organized by "Colonel" Edward M. House, Wilson's friend and advisor, the Inquiry assessed the different and competing territorial claims to be discussed at the postwar peace conference. However, little was known about the countries and territories outside of the Western Hemisphere or parts of Western Europe. The dearth of American expertise was particularly pronounced for the territories of the Ottoman Empire. Westermann led the Inquiry's Western Asia division, which encompassed the present-day Middle East. At its height, the Inquiry comprised over 150 scholars, but only twenty-three made the voyage to France. Although Westermann and other Inquiry members had limited access to Wilson in Paris, due to their position and status they were sought out by major figures hoping to influence the president. From T. E. Lawrence and Amir Faysal to Gertrude Bell and Chaim Weizmann, Paris was filled with hope and excitement largely inspired by Wilson's vision of a postwar world. Yet most were disappointed by the final treaty and the return voyage was not celebratory.

The Inquiry represented a significant early attempt by the U.S. government to develop foreign area expertise, albeit one that has largely been overlooked. It also revealed the intersection of privately held sources of knowledge of American missionaries abroad or university-based Orientalist scholars in the United States with government agencies. When we examine the activities and proposals of the Inquiry's Western Asia division, it is evident that Orientalist perceptions shaped their recommendations for the postwar disposition of the Ottoman Empire. In particular, members of the Inquiry concluded that Muslims and Arabs were incapable of self-rule. This argument was incorporated into the proposals made to President Wilson and were used to advocate for the establishment of European-ruled protectorates over the former Ottoman territories. At Versailles, Wilson endorsed the creation of League of Nations Mandates over the former Ottoman territories, contradicting his earlier support for self-determination and aligning the United States with the colonial expansions of Britain and France.[2]

Missionaries in the East

Prior to the Second World War, America's main interests in the Near East were religious and commercial. Beginning in the mid-nineteenth century, American missionaries began traveling to the region and eventually established schools, colleges, and hospitals. The State Department maintained a limited presence in the region. Missionaries, or their children, were some of the main sources of information about the Near East, which was further reinforced by their presence in the U.S. diplomatic corps. Their privately held knowledge created a base of expertise about the region and its inhabitants. Another source of expertise was from American business and commercial interests in the region, in particular oil companies. Although university-based knowledge was limited, as Bruce Kuklick demonstrates, the study of the ancient Near East through archeological expeditions also created a body of knowledge. Some archeologists joined the Inquiry, including in the Western Asia division. As discussed in Chapter 2, they were also recruited by the Office of Strategic Services (OSS) during World War II because of their field work experience.[3] Missionaries and their children have been described as more sympathetic toward the native populations where they resided than other Americans. However, such characterizations ignore the missionaries' paternalistic attitudes, which were often mixed with notions of racial and religious superiority.[4]

Founded in 1810, the American Board of Commissioners for Foreign Missions (ABCFM) eventually became the largest missionary organization in the United States. Emerging out of the New England Congregationalists, ABCFM members were firm believers in the notions of American exceptionalism and Divine Providence, of which they were to be the vanguard. Spurred on by the Second Great Awakening, the ABCFM dispatched missionaries across the North American continent to convert Native Americans. They also saw the rest of the world as ready for conversion. India, China, and the "Bible lands" of the present-day Middle East were prime destinations for the ABCFM's members. In the Ottoman Empire, however, early attempts at converting Muslims failed. In order not to anger the Ottoman Sultan, American missionaries focused largely on other Christian denominations. The second wave of missionaries, which emphasized educational institutions, had a more lasting impact.[5]

In May 1864, the Syrian Protestant College (SPC) in Beirut and Robert College in Istanbul were incorporated in New York. Over two years later, SPC opened its doors to sixteen students with limited course offerings and few instructors. By the turn of the century, however, the college boasted a student body from across the Ottoman Empire. Instruction was initially in Arabic, but English was adopted in 1884. The shift to English-language instruction was one of several controversies that gripped the SPC during this period. Two years earlier, there was a major split between administration, faculty, and students over teaching Darwinism that resulted in forced resignations and expulsions. The following year, SPC adopted a new policy that prohibited hiring Arab professors. In spite of these controversies, Britain's occupation of Egypt and increasing hegemony over the region coupled with the SPC's English-language instruction eventually benefited the college and its alumni.[6]

By the late nineteenth century, SPC had established a reputation across the region. Graduates of the college were key figures in the "Arab Awakening," a literary and political movement that contributed to the emergence of Arab nationalism. In addition, SPC alumni launched two influential Arabic-language journals based in Egypt, *al-Muqtataf* ("The Digest") and *al-Hilal* ("The Crescent").[7]

The college's relationship with the ABCFM ensured access to wealthy and influential American donors. Among the SPC's prominent supporters was the Dodge family, owners of the Phelps Dodge mining company. David Stuart Dodge was one of the SPC's founding donors and served as an English instructor. Dodge eventually became chairman of the board of trustees. His grandson, Cleveland, was close friends with fellow Princeton alum Woodrow Wilson. Cleveland Dodge was one of the major financial backers of Wilson's presidential campaign.[8]

The Reformer and the War

The missionary movement was part of the broader Progressive era in the United States. Emerging out of the post–Civil War Gilded Age, progressivism embodied a broad range of social issues from organized labor and women's suffrage to prohibition and antitrust. Wilson's victory in the 1912 presidential election reflected the increasing power and influence of progressivism in American politics and society. His reputation as a reformer was initially earned at Princeton and was reaffirmed as governor of New Jersey. Wilson attracted national attention after pushing a series of progressive laws through the New Jersey legislature, including electoral and education reform.[9]

Wilson's ascendancy to the White House benefited from internal strife within the Republican Party. Much of the campaign focused on domestic issues, particularly antitrust reform, with Wilson and former president Theodore Roosevelt offering contrasting policies. Foreign policy was largely absent from the discussion. After Wilson's victory, he confided to a Princeton faculty member that "it would be an irony of fate if my administration had to deal chiefly with foreign problems, for all my preparation has been in domestic matters."[10]

The outbreak of war in Europe during the summer of 1914 interrupted Wilson's hopes and plans for his first term. For foreign policy expertise he increasingly began to rely on Edward M. House. A fixture in Texas politics, House became a close confidant of Wilson during the 1912 campaign. Although he was referred to as "Colonel," he did not have a military background. House helped Wilson identify cabinet members during the transition period, but he refused an official post and served as an unofficial advisor. In January 1915, House left for Europe carrying Wilson's offer for the United States to mediate between the belligerents.[11]

While House was in Europe, relations between Wilson and Secretary of State William Jennings Bryan deteriorated. In May 1915, a German submarine sank the British cruise liner *Lusitania*, killing nearly 1,200 passengers, including over 120 Americans. Wilson and House wanted to adopt a tough line with Germany, a stance that Bryan feared would lead to war. Bryan eventually resigned, hoping to lead an antiwar campaign. Even though he did not become secretary of state, House's influence grew within the Wilson administration.[12]

In spite of the continuing German submarine attacks and American civilian casualties, the United States did not enter the war until after Wilson was elected to a second term. "The world must be made safe for democracy," Wilson pronounced before a joint session of Congress on April 2, 1917. Yet in declaring war on Germany, he claimed that the United States still sought "peace without victory." In spite of his rhetoric, Wilson had few illusions about America's allies. By the fall, he asked House to recruit experts to assist with preparations for the eventual peace conference.[13]

The Inquiry

During the 1912 campaign, Wilson derided Roosevelt's policy proposals. The former college professor and president said that he feared a "government of experts." Yet to help prepare America's negotiating positions for a postwar settlement, House assembled such a group from American academia. House's initial outreach was to Harvard president Lawrence Lowell and Herbert Croly, the progressive writer and cofounder of *The New Republic*. He also selected Sidney E. Mezes, then president of the City College of New York and his brother-in-law, to serve as director and manage the organization's daily activities. Based on Wilson's recommendation, House also recruited Walter Lippmann. Lippmann cofounded *The New Republic* with Croly and served as an assistant to Secretary of War Baker. He would later become one of the most influential newspaper columnists of the twentieth century.[14]

House's new organization operated independently of the State Department, an arrangement that contributed to bureaucratic infighting and competition. These tensions were exacerbated by Wilson's disdain for the State Department. Wilson not only edited and corrected diplomatic cables, but wrote and typed his own correspondence. He also reached decisions without the State Department's input, a practice he continued at Versailles.[15]

To prevent any false optimism on the part of the public, Wilson wanted the new body to operate in secrecy. However, rumors hit the press soon after it was initially formed, which the White House worked to squelch. The press frenzy subsided by the fall and the experts settled into their initial headquarters at the New York Public Library. Originally dubbed the "War Data Investigations Bureau," the name was replaced by a more nondescript moniker offered by James T. Shotwell, a Columbia professor and historian. The group was called "The Inquiry," and Shotwell later explained that the cryptic name was deliberately and appropriately chosen because it was "blind to the general public, but would serve to identify it among the initiated." A month later, the Inquiry relocated to the offices of the American Geographical Society (AGS), occupying the third floor. Isaiah Bowman, director of the AGS, initially served as secretary and eventually replaced Mezes as head of the group in Paris.[16]

Revelations in the press about the formation of the Inquiry were overshadowed by events in Russia. The reverberations from the Bolshevik Revolution were felt around the globe and were compounded by Russia's withdrawal from the war and the publication of secret agreements for the postwar disposition of the Ottoman Empire's territories negotiated with Britain and France. Britain's Foreign Secretary Arthur Balfour informed Wilson about the secret agreements before they were revealed by the Bolsheviks. Afterward, Wilson explained to House that he planned to use financial pressure to change Allied attitudes after the war. He requested that the Inquiry prepare a memorandum detailing the major questions to be resolved at the postwar peace conference. Led by Lippmann, the Inquiry's Directorate drafted a memorandum entitled "The War Aims and Peace It Suggests." Delivered to Wilson after the New Year, the Inquiry's memorandum served as an outline for his "Fourteen Points" speech.[17]

On January 8, 1918, Wilson addressed a joint session of Congress. Four days earlier, he adapted the Inquiry's memorandum into fourteen statements. Wilson declared that "the world be made fit and safe to live in; and particularly that it be made safe for every peace-loving nation which, like our own, wishes to live its own life, determine its own institutions, be assured of justice and fair dealing by the other peoples of the world as against force and selfish aggression." After reading the fourteen points in succession, he concluded with a powerful call:

> An evident principle runs through the whole program I have outlined. It is the principle of justice to all peoples and nationalities, and their right to live on equal terms of liberty and safety with one another, whether they be strong or weak. Unless this principle be made its foundation no part of the structure of international justice can stand. The people of the United States could act upon no other principle; and to the vindication of this principle they are ready to devote their lives, their honor, and everything that they possess. The moral climax of this the culminating and final war for human liberty has come, and they are ready to put their own strength, their own highest purpose, their own integrity and devotion to the test.[18]

Wilson's speech had an impact far beyond America's shores. The final point calling for the creation of a "general association of nations" was arguably the most groundbreaking part of the address. Yet it was the phrase he did not utter—self-determination—that became most associated with the Fourteen Points. Although implied in "Point V," the term "self-determination" was coined by British prime minister David Lloyd George. Lloyd George used the phrase in a speech while Wilson was finalizing his own address. The president was concerned that he had been upstaged by the prime minister. However, House reassured Wilson that his speech would "smother" that of Lloyd George. Wilson, House asserted, "would once more become the spokesman for the Entente, and indeed, for the liberals of the world." While House's prediction was accurate, Wilson would struggle with the implications of the term and the different and sometimes conflicting aspirations of those he inspired.[19]

Wilson inched toward self-determination. In his subsequent "Four Points" address to Congress on February 11, Wilson declared that self-determination was "not a mere phrase. It is an imperative principle of actions which statesmen will henceforth ignore at their peril." Wilson again offered hope to those living under colonial rule. "Each part of the final settlement must be based upon the essential justice of that particular case," Wilson asserted, "peoples and provinces are not to be bartered about from sovereignty to sovereignty as if they were mere chattels and pawns in a game." Yet his last point created a standard and conundrum that would hang over the Paris Peace Conference. "All well defined national aspirations" would be considered and fulfilled, Wilson stated, "without introducing new or perpetuating old elements of discord and antagonism." At Versailles, however, this final goal was not achieved.[20]

Wilson's support for self-determination was tenuous. He was more comfortable with self-government, or political participation within a given polity, than the creation of ethnic nation-states.[21] In 1885 he explained, "Democracy is poison to the infant but tonic to the man" and was only possible for a nation "in the adult stage of its political development."[22] Yet this distinction was not clear to the members of the Inquiry or to the rest of the world. As demonstrated in the specific and deliberate phrasing of the Fourteen and Four Points speeches, Wilson sought to raise the hopes of war-weary globe and counter the influence of the Bolshevik Revolution. The Fourteen Points speech influenced burgeoning nationalist movements to pursue their claims of independence.[23] Yet Wilson's notions of ethnic and racial nationalism, as well as those of his advisors, would complicate, if not undermine, his lofty rhetoric. Wilson's apathy on domestic race issues was another reflection of his political philosophy.[24] Thus, it was Wilson who proved to be unprepared for the implications of self-determination, not the world.

Wilson's rhetoric created an additional burden for the Inquiry. The group viewed itself as an impartial referee of the different and competing claims that would be presented at the conference. This was detailed in the memorandum titled "Report on the Inquiry: Its Scope and Method." Because the peace conference would be an open discussion," the memorandum explained, "a command of fact totally unnecessary in secret negotiations is required." "The whole world is to be the critic of the debates, the American influence will be in proportion to the depth and incisiveness with which just principles are applied to particular cases," it added. Therefore, the "American negotiators must be in a position to judge whether a claim put forth by a power is supported by the democracy at home, or whether it is merely a traditional diplomatic objective or the design of an imperialistic group." In the "fiercely disputed areas," the memorandum stated that American negotiators "must be prepared freely to offer friendly suggestions either of compromise or of constructive experiment" backed by "a body of reliable fact" that "must be presented tersely and graphically so as to carry conviction." The memorandum explained that American negotiators were expected to be well versed in a variety of topics ranging from trade to minority rights and should also "command various well-tested programs of reform and reconstruction for the historically embittered areas."[25]

Recruiting the required expertise, however, proved to be more difficult than House or his aides imagined. Writing to Secretary of War Baker, Lippmann confided, "On many of the problems we face of first-rate importance there is a real famine in men and we have been compelled practically to train and create our own experts." He added that this was particularly true of Russia, Southeastern Europe, the Ottoman Empire, and Africa, which he declared were "intellectually practically unexplored." "What we are on the lookout for is genius-sheer, startling genius and nothing else will do because the real application of the President's idea to those countries requires inventiveness and resourcefulness which is scarcer than anything," he wrote.[26]

Yet political connections were more important than intellectual prowess. Like the choice of Mezes as director, nepotism trumped knowledge. Most of the experts were drawn from elite eastern universities, in particular Harvard, Yale, and Princeton. In addition, scholars with ties to the American missionary community were favored. However, American expertise, even from elite universities, was limited. The Inquiry's Western Asia division compounded this dearth of knowledge by seeking and reinforcing a particular form of expertise. Initially led by Princeton's Dana C. Munro, the Western Asia division was populated with experts in ancient history and literature who had little or no knowledge of the contemporary issues of the region. When Arthur Andrews, a history professor at Tufts and a Harvard alum, joined the Inquiry he was informed of its lack of knowledge by Harvard historian Archibald Cary Coolidge. Coolidge explained to Andrews, "'You know one Mohammedan from another' i.e., from others." Munro, a medievalist with knowledge of the Crusades, was joined in the division by his son, Dana G., a Latin American specialist. Other members included Princeton's L. H. Gray, a scholar of Persian linguistics, and archeologist Howard Crosby Butler. One of the most prominent experts on the Ottoman Empire in the United States, Albert Lybyer of the University of Illinois, served in the Inquiry's Balkans division. Lybyer was only allowed to join the Inquiry after he was cleared of accusations of pro-Bulgarian bias. Other notable scholars were either excluded from the Inquiry's Western Asia division or chose not to participate, including Berkeley's William Popper and William Thomson of Harvard. The lack of contemporary knowledge for Western Asia was not replicated in other divisions.[27]

Orientalism as Policy

While the Inquiry's goal was to be objective in its assessments, its research reports and proposals demonstrated a consistently unfavorable view of the Western Asia region. In part this reflected the initial tasks requested of the group, which included creating a "racial map" of the region that displayed "boundaries and mixed and doubtful zones." In addition, Inquiry members were to provide studies of "the stability or instability of racial distribution" created by altering political boundaries as well as economic, religious, and cultural forces. The combination of limited, if any, contemporary information about the region with the racial and religious biases of the Inquiry members resulted in the construction of particular types of knowledge about Western Asia and its inhabitants.[28]

Leon Dominian authored several Inquiry reports related to the Ottoman Empire and Islam. A recent Armenian émigré from Anatolia, Dominian was a staffer at the AGS before joining the Inquiry. Originally assigned to the Balkans group, Dominian's assessments were dismissed by other members of the Inquiry due to their "Greek bias," which they argued prevented him "from any attempt to achieve scientific objectivity in his reports."[29]

In a May 1918 report, Dominian offered a scathing assessment of the "Mohammedan World." "Restlessness and a chafing of the Mohammedan spirit under non-Mohammedan rule or influence is observable everywhere," Dominian wrote. "As a rule the Mohammedan has shown a total want of compatibility with the spirit of modern progress. He is generally bigoted and inclined to be violent in word and deed against non-Mohammedans." This was due to general and inherent Muslim deficiencies, both psychological and moral, that "compelled European powers to control and police Mohammedan lands." However, Dominian cautioned that there was a difference in the rule of the European powers. Unlike the areas under German rule, "economic exploitation" by Britain and France was "accompanied by a cultural development of the native."[30]

Dominian's "Mohammedan World" report offered few specific policy recommendations other than maintaining the status quo. He acknowledged that the United States could have a greater role in affairs within the Muslim world, particularly by influencing its allies. However, Dominian warned that "the low stage of economic and cultural development of Mohammedan countries preclude placing too great resilience [sic] on Mohammedan sympathy for foreigners." He also cautioned that Muslim countries abandoned to self-rule quickly fell into anarchy.[31]

In a separate report on "The Arab Problem," Dominian again asserted that inherent deficiencies limited the prospects for self-rule in the Arab-majority provinces of the Ottoman Empire. He argued that "the exercise of a protectorate by one of the great powers is a requisite because in each region the majority of the population consists of Mohammedans who have proven themselves culturally inferior to either Jew or Christian and whose sympathy to the ideas of civilization upheld in Western lands is doubtful." He explained that Islam was a "bar to cultural contact with the occident, whereas intimate ties of material and moral interests bind the Jews and Christians to the west." Dominian added that independence for the majority Arab Muslim areas would be a "menace to unhampered intercourse between Europe and the regions of Southern Asia and the Far East."[32]

Dominian advocated for the establishment of British and French protectorates that would create an "Entente ring" around the Arabian Peninsula helping to contain any emerging pan-Arab movement. Although he acknowledged that a pan-Arab union was unlikely, Dominian reported that "already at this early stage of emancipation from Turkish rule, the signs are not wanting to indicate that the possibility of an all-Arab union from the

Mediterranean Sea to the Persian Gulf and southward to the Indian Ocean is not foreign to the thought of some ambitious Arab." In Palestine, he argued that the presence of a large Jewish population would "contribute an important shore in the development of" the territory and would result in closer relations with the West.[33] Dominian reiterated these arguments in a separate report on Arabia. "The Arabs are a primitive people with uncritical minds and hence are easily swayed by religious feeling," Dominian wrote.[34]

Although Dominian was removed from the Balkans group due to an apparent bias, a similar determination was not made regarding his analysis of the Ottoman Empire. Dominian was one of the few Inquiry members to attend the peace conference. While in France, he actively sought a greater role in decision making on the disposition of the Ottoman territories. However, his ambitions were frustrated by Westermann and Bowman.[35]

Other scholars in the Western Asia division attempted to offer more nuanced portraits of the region and its inhabitants. However, they reflected prevailing theories about race and religion. Writing in October 1919, E. H. Byrne claimed that Syria's population was comprised of Arabs, Christians, and Jews. Byrne conflated "Arabs" with Muslims and explained that except for the Armenian population, Christian Syrians were Semitic, spoke Arabic, and had "to a degree Arab manners and mode of thought." Yet he argued there was diversity in racial origins of Syria's Christian community. Byrne identified Christians in the villages and the cities of the interior as "Arabs." However, those along the coast were "a bastard race, the result of crossings of conquerors, crusaders and traders through thousands of years; they are not Arab, but fundamentally Semitic." He added that Jews in Palestine were "another racial element of disunion."[36]

Byrne noted that a Syrian national consciousness had developed despite Turkish and European efforts. Pointing to the influence of the SPC in Beirut among regional elites, he argued that education could help form a national ethos. However, he cautioned that the emphasis should be on "national unity," rather than a particular nation-state.[37]

In a separate report, Princeton archeologist Howard Crosby Butler examined the possibility of creating an independent Arab state or states. Butler had previously conducted several expeditions in Syria. However, he did not recommend self-rule. Butler argued that "it would be impossible to any theory of self-determination in this case because it would be impossible to discover what any large number of these peoples [*sic*] desire."

"Even if this were possible," he added, "it might easily turn out that they desired something which would soon be found to be disastrous to their well being."[38]

In Arabia, Butler offered two perspectives on how to approach the issue of self-determination. One possibility was a government that would not disrupt their social customs and allow for gradual improvements in living conditions and governance. The second option was the type of government based on what "more highly experienced experts in political institutions and social economics believe to be best for them in the long run, regardless of native customs and prejudices." Although Butler conceded that native inhabitants would not welcome a foreign protectorate, without such "foreign guidance and protection, the Arabs can not be guaranteed good government of any sort at the present time."[39]

Westermann replaced Dana Munro as head of the Western Asia division. He was a supporter of Wilson's political campaigns and had contacts with the missionary movement. These factors accounted for his prominent role in the Inquiry, rather than any contemporary knowledge of the region. Westermann concurred with the determination of other members that the Arab-majority territories of the Ottoman Empire were not prepared for self-rule. His report on the "Just and Practical Boundaries for Subdivisions of the Turkish Empire" drew on pseudo-scientific justifications to examine the religious, racial, and ethnic differences within the Empire and to advocate for the postwar establishment of protectorates. While in Anatolia "the 'Turkish' population preponderates over all other peoples," Westermann wrote, "throughout the rest of the Turkish Empire no large 'nations' exist in the sense of peoples of one blood, fairly pure from racial intermixture, who are massed in some one given area." The few exceptions he noted were Armenians, Jews in Palestine, and Arabia. Although the Armenians were a minority, Westermann argued they "may with more justice claim a real ethnographic distinction and a definite ethnographic area than most of the peoples of the Near East." In Palestine, Jews comprised a small minority of the population and Westermann explained that "in many of the states which may be suggested, including Anatolia, there will be scattered areas where people of other ethnogeographic groups appear in considerable numbers." One example was the Arabian Peninsula, where Westermann reported that the "desert Arabs" were a "people practically untouched by infiltration of foreign blood." He concluded, "For this and for other reasons Arabia must be treated in an entirely different manner from the rest of the Empire." Yet Westermann asserted that "the ethnographic factor" should not be the sole criterion for settling political issues and claims.[40]

Like other Inquiry reports, Westermann defined the different populations of the Empire. A Turk, he wrote, "is a man of Mohammedan religion who speaks the Turkish language." An "Arab is, generally speaking, a man of Mohammedan religion whose native tongue is Arabic." However, Westermann cautioned that the "Syrian Arabs are ethnographically distinct from the desert Arabs and have totally different political ambitions." Armenians were also categorized based on religious identification and language.[41]

Westermann depicted the different Christian and Muslim religious sects as irredeemably hostile. He asserted that peace was maintained only through "oppressive Turkish overlordship." In the absence of Turkish rule, the different religious and ethnic populations made the establishment of new states difficult. If a new power was to rule the area, he wrote, it must be sufficiently powerful and benevolent to maintain peace between and within the new states and ensure the welfare of their populations. Westermann prioritized religion and ethnicity and said they were "the greatest bond of unity which exists in the Near East." He also recommended basing boundaries on economic factors, topography, and trade routes.[42]

Westermann examined different boundaries for a new state of Syria or combination of states. Asserting that it was a "historic as well as a linguistic and economic unit," he warned that the population was "unused to anything more than a shadow of political rights" and total independence was "inadvisable." Divided by religion and ethnicity, the population needed to be "brought into a unified political system by some stronger agency than a purely native government and be instructed by what will necessarily prove a long course of training before they will govern themselves." Westermann also envisioned different forms of international protection over other areas of the Ottoman Empire, including Armenia, Kurdistan, Mesopotamia, and Anatolia.[43]

Palestine, then part of the Greater Syria province of the Ottoman Empire, was a special case. Westermann acknowledged that his proposed boundaries were "drawn with a view toward satisfying the aspirations of the Zionists for a national home." Indeed, the proposal referred to the territory as the "Jewish state." He explained that the boundaries were designed to ensure that the Jewish minority in Palestine would have "a larger percentage than they would in any other state defined in this region" while still ensuring the "legitimate economic interests of the inhabitants." Although the Zionist movement also sought the east bank of the Jordan River (present-day

Jordan), Westermann explained that it was excluded from the proposed state because a prior attempt by Zionist settlers to establish a colony in the area failed due to "the hostility of the native Arab population." He also noted that discussions of independence must take Palestine's religious significance to the three major monotheistic faiths into consideration.[44]

In contrast, he recommended independence for Arabia. Arguing that it was militarily impractical to impose a protectorate over the area, Westermann asserted that the different tribes that populated the peninsula should be allowed to decide their own traditional form of government. He also suggested that the Kingdom of the Hijaz could unify the different tribes and should be encouraged to do so, if a "legitimate plan" were developed.[45]

Britain, America, Palestine, and Zionism

During the late nineteenth century, competition over the Ottoman Empire's territories by the European powers threatened a wider war. Diplomats from London to Moscow were preoccupied by the "Eastern Question," or what to do about the so-called "sick man of Europe." Istanbul's wartime alliance with Berlin provided the opportunity for Britain and France to expand and formalize their presence in the Middle East and resolve the Eastern Question.[46]

London engaged in separate and contradictory negotiations and agreements that helped shape the modern map of the region. Hoping to create dissension within the Arab territories of the Ottoman Empire, Britain initiated a series of conversations with Sharif Husayn of Mecca. Husayn was the patriarch of the Hashemite family, direct descendants of the Prophet Muhammad and guardians of Islam's holiest shrines in the cities of Mecca and Medina. Beginning in July 1915, Henry McMahon, the British high commissioner in Cairo, and Sharif Husayn exchanged letters over the course of six months. Although he was granted relative autonomy over the Hijaz region by the Ottoman Sultan, Sharif Husayn had larger ambitions, which London was eager to encourage. The Husayn-McMahon correspondence prompted the Arab Revolt against the Ottoman Empire. In return for initiating the revolt, Husayn was promised support for an independent Arab state. However, the boundaries of the state were vaguely defined, particularly for Palestine. Backed by London and led by Husayn's sons, Faysal and Abdullah, the revolt opened a new southern front against Istanbul.[47]

During the period of the Husayn-McMahon correspondence, London and Paris also conducted secret negotiations over the territories of the Ottoman Empire. Negotiated by Sir Mark Sykes, a member of the British Parliament, and Georges Picot, a veteran French diplomat, the May 1916 Sykes-Picot Agreement divided the Ottoman Empire into areas of "direct rule" and "spheres of influence." British direct rule would be established over Egypt and the region of Mesopotamia in present-day Iraq. Britain's sphere of influence encompassed lower Palestine, the cities of Haifa and Acre, present-day Jordan, and eastern Iraq. French direct rule would be established over present-day Lebanon and eastern Anatolia and its sphere of influence encompassed present-day Syria. The region of northern Palestine, including Jerusalem, would become an international protectorate. Russia was also a party to the negotiations and its participation was revealed after the Bolshevik Revolution. While neither London nor Paris was satisfied with the final agreement, it served as the foundation for later arrangements.[48]

The Sykes-Picot Agreement contributed to Britain's third set of secret negotiations, this time with representatives of the Zionist movement. The Zionist movement emerged in the late nineteenth century and was largely based among Russian Jews, who suffered from a series of legal restrictions and *pogroms* under the tsar. Zionism called for the emigration to Palestine, the "ancient home of the Jews." Yet the movement had limited appeal among Western European Jews, where assimilation was preferred to emigration to Palestine. However, it did find prominent supporters who helped fund the initial settlements.[49]

Announced in November 1917, the Balfour Declaration promised support for a Jewish national home in Palestine. The declaration was based on negotiations between Chaim Weizmann, a former chemistry professor and activist with the World Zionist Organization, and Britain's Foreign Secretary Lord Arthur Balfour. Balfour detailed the terms in a brief letter to Lionel Walter Rothschild (Baron Rothschild), a wealthy and influential supporter of the Zionist movement in Britain. He also explained that it guaranteed the "civil and religious rights of existing non-Jewish communities in Palestine"—i.e., the Palestinian Arabs—who comprised roughly 90 percent of the population. However, the declaration did not explicitly guarantee their political rights. When its terms were incorporated into the League of Nations Mandate for Palestine after the war, the stage was set for future discord.[50]

British prime minister David Lloyd George and President Wilson had similar reactions to the Balfour Declaration. Lloyd George later explained his support for the Zionist movement by recalling, "I was taught in school far more about the history of the Jews than about the history of my own land. I could tell you all the Kings of Israel. But I doubt whether I could have named half a dozen of the Kings of England and no more of the Kings of Wales." Israeli journalist and historian Tom Segev notes that while Lloyd George appeared to profess an admiration for Jewish history and tradition, it was based on a deeply seated anti-Semitic fear of perceived "Jewish power" that was also prevalent among British officials and diplomats. He adds that Chaim Weizmann actively encouraged the impression that the Zionist movement had international support, especially in the United States, where Lloyd George believed it had influence in the White House.[51] Wilson expressed sympathy for the Zionist movement based on his own Presbyterian background. In 1916, Wilson confided to Rabbi Stephen Wise, a leading American Zionist leader, "To think that I, a son of the manse, should be able to help restore the Holy Land to its people." Unlike Lloyd George, Wilson's support for the Balfour Declaration was discreet and relayed to Whitehall through Colonel House.[52]

Following the announcement of the Balfour Declaration, Lloyd George ordered Jerusalem to be captured by Christmas. British troops under the command of General Sir Edmund Allenby entered the city on December 9, 1917. In response, Lloyd George remarked that Allenby had achieved "something which generations of the chivalry of Europe failed to attain."[53] Accompanied by French, Italian, and American representatives, Allenby formally accepted the city's surrender from Mayor Hussein Salim al-Husseini. The British Parliament was informed of Jerusalem's capture and the bells of Westminster Cathedral rang for the first time in three years. King George V also wrote a personal note of congratulations to Allenby.[54]

The Inquiry's reports and conclusions were sympathetic to the Zionist movement. In his report on Palestine, Princeton classics professor David Magie echoed Byrne's analysis of Syria. Like other Inquiry reports, Magie's description of Palestinian society was more revealing about American perceptions than a particular reality. Like Byrne, Magie considered "Muslims" synonymous with "Arabs" and "Christians" were classified as "Syrians." He argued that the Jewish population was represented by the "immigrant Zionist," which only comprised a small minority, and ignored the presence of the larger, non-Zionist Jewish population. He explained that neither Christians nor Muslims "would accommodate themselves readily to a Zionist State *at present*." However, Magie asserted that the native Palestinian Arabs lacked "any sufficient experience in self-government to offer a nucleus for autonomous control," overlooking the participation of leading families in the Ottoman parliament. Although he claimed that either British or American rule would be "welcome by all classes" in Palestine, Magie advocated for a British protectorate. He added that until self-government was achieved, a "Jewish chartered company" should be established to assist the country's development and "the settlement therein of the Jewish people," essentially describing the role filled by the Jewish Agency in British Mandate Palestine.[55]

At least one Inquiry report was revised to align with the goals of the Zionist movement. Westermann recorded in his diary that a report "related to the settlements for Western Asia had been badly altered by Dr. Mezes in certain places." In particular, a "statement entirely unfavorable to the 'Jewish state' idea, though granting an independent Palestine, had become entirely favorable." Westermann added that "many of the ideas are not mine at all and it reads like a valedictorian High School address." The altered report was provided to the British delegation for the creation of a joint document. Westermann wrote that he planned to reject the joint report when it was presented for consideration and discuss the incident with Mezes. However, it is uncertain if he did either.[56]

Paris

Inspired by Wilson's Fourteen Points speech, numerous dignitaries flocked to Paris from around the world to press their claims. Some sought independence from colonial rule or the establishment of new states, while others wanted political rights within the British and French empires. Few, however, would have their cases heard and even fewer achieved their goals. In January 1919, the Supreme Council (or Council of Ten) was established. Driving the proceedings were Wilson, Lloyd George, French Premier Georges Clemenceau, and Italian prime minister Vittorio Orlando. For the next two months, the Council convened daily at the French Foreign Ministry. The leaders were joined by their foreign ministers and advisors as well as two Japanese representatives. Although the Council meetings should have served as a forum for the advisors to provide expert opinion and analysis, they were utilized inconsistently, especially by Wilson.[57]

Secretary of State Lansing was skeptical of Wilson's lofty rhetoric and the implications for a postwar settlement. "When the President talks of 'self-determination' what unit has he in mind? Does he mean a race, a territorial area, or a community? Without a definite unit which is practical, application of this principal is dangerous to peace and stability," Lansing wrote in his diary. He viewed the different delegations with suspicion and was hostile to the embrace of self-determination. "The more I think about the President's declaration as to the right of 'self-determination', the more convinced I am of the danger of putting such ideas into the minds of certain races. It is bound to be the basis of impossible demands on the Peace Congress and create trouble in many lands," Lansing declared. He asked, "What effect will it have on the Irish, the Indians, the Egyptians, and the nationalists among the Boers? Will it not breed discontent, disorder, and rebellion?" Lansing added, "Will not the Mohammedans of Syria and Palestine and possibly of Morocco and Tripoli rely on it? How can it be harmonized with Zionism, to which the President is practically committed?" "The phrase is simply loaded with dynamite. It will raise hopes which can never be realized. It will, I fear, cost thousands of lives," Lansing wrote. He predicted that "in the end it is bound to be discredited, to be called the dream of an idealist who failed to realize the danger until too late to check those who attempt to put the principle in force. What a calamity that the phrase was ever uttered! What misery it will cause!"[58]

In Paris, Lansing and the State Department were eclipsed by Bowman and the Inquiry. During the voyage to France, members of the Inquiry had only one formal meeting with the president. The American delegation numbered over 1,200 and was led by five commissioners: Wilson, House, Secretary of State Lansing, General Tasker Bliss, and Henry White, a retired Republican diplomat. Only a small number of Inquiry members were part of the delegation and the State Department and the military were intent on reasserting their advisory roles. Upon arrival, however, Isaiah Bowman and Colonel House appealed to President Wilson to intervene. Wilson placed the Inquiry, and in particular Bowman, over the State Department and military personnel. Renamed the "Division of Territorial, Economic, and Political Intelligence," Bowman's staff swelled to over a hundred individuals across eighteen divisions.[59]

As America's expert on the Ottoman Empire, Westermann was called on to provide his opinion and that of the Inquiry. This included sharing the Inquiry's reports. In January 1919, General Bliss requested information on the Arab Revolt prior to a meeting with T. E. Lawrence. In response, Westermann dispatched Howard Crosby Butler's report on proposals for an independent Syria.[60]

Lawrence attended the Paris conference with Sharif Husayn's son, Faysal. Although his father initiated the revolt, Faysal emerged as its leader and was favored by London. After British and Arab forces captured Damascus, an independent Arab state was declared with Faysal's father initially named as king. As his father's representative at the conference, Amir (prince) Faysal spent early January meeting with French and American officials. He hoped to secure recognition of the kingdom based on Wilson's principles of self-determination. On January 20, he and his entourage met Colonel House. Faysal presented Arab demands, including a plebiscite to determine Syria's future status, and was pleased with the discussion. Yet Rustum Haidar, Faysal's secretary, recorded in his diary that the Americans were "ignorant" of the situation in Syria.[61]

Later that evening, Faysal and Lawrence met Bowman and Westermann for dinner. With Lawrence translating, Faysal entertained and lobbied his dining companions. He repeated his opposition to French rule in Syria and argued for the creation of an Allied Commission to travel to the region and determine the desires of the population. He impressed upon the Americans at dinner to support his initiative and said it was time for Arab independence. Westermann was impressed by Faysal. "This is a remarkable man really," he recorded in his diary. "Lawrence is not his brains as I thought. Lawrence says that he can help him on details, but when he starts on principles Faysal goes off like a 60 power car. . . . Great is Lawrence and great is Faysal, I am a convert!"[62]

Three days later, Faysal met Wilson and pressed his case for an independent Syria. However, Faysal returned from the meeting disappointed. Wilson had only agreed to "do the right thing."[63]

Westermann lobbied American representatives behind the scenes for a commission. He enlisted the help of Howard Bliss, president of the SPC, and William Bullitt of the State Department. Bliss was a respected figure among the American and British officials in Paris, including Lawrence. In his diary, Westermann wrote that Bliss was the "root of all good" in Western Asia and that American educational and missionary work in the region was "the highest form of modern Christianity." Faysal also praised Bliss and the SPC. He told an American reporter in Paris that because of the SPC, Daniel and Howard Bliss were the "grandfather" and "father" of Syria. "Without the education that [the SPC] has given," Faysal added, "the struggle for freedom never would have been won. The Arabs owe everything to these men."[64]

Over the first month of the conference, the Council began discussing drafts of the peace accord. This included the creation of the League of Nations and mandates for Germany's colonial territories in Africa and the Pacific. By February, the Council determined that the League of Nations mandates would be expanded to include the territories of the Ottoman Empire. The United States, Britain, France, Italy, and Greece began open and secret discussions of various proposals to carve up the Empire.[65]

On February 6, Faysal appeared before the Council and delivered his plea for Arab independence. Prior to arriving in Paris, Faysal dispatched a memorandum to the British Foreign Office detailing his proposal for a confederation of Arab states. A summary was distributed to the Council in late January with the added caveat that the proposal was based on Wilson's Fourteen Points. As Faysal spoke to the Council, Lawrence read an English translation and Clemenceau's aide simultaneously translated into French. He detailed Arab sacrifices during the war and Allied promises. Although Faysal conceded that the Arabs realized "how much their country lacked development," he added that their desire for help could not be at the expense of their independence. He called for the creation of a commission to investigate what the population of Syria wanted. Faysal also expressed a conciliatory attitude on the issue of Palestine, suggesting it not be included in the independent Arab state. Because of its "universal character," he argued that the disposition of Palestine should be discussed by all concerned parties.[66]

Wilson asked Faysal whether he preferred a single mandatory power or several. Faysal replied that he attended the conference "to ask for the independence of his people and for their right to choose their own mandatory." When the president pressed for his personal opinion, Faysal responded that he feared partition and favored "Arab unity."[67]

A week later, Howard Bliss appeared before the Council and reiterated many of the same points. Bliss presented a favorable but paternalistic portrait of the area and its population. He expressed a "deep interest in the people of Syria" and explained that they were "intelligent, able, hospitable and lovable, but with the sure defects of a long, oppressed race; timidity, love of flattery, indirectness." "They also have the defects characteristic of people who are face to face with civilization without having passed through the processes of modern civilization," Bliss added. Although they lacked "balance" and "political fairness," Bliss asserted that the people of Syria could "grow into [the] capacity for self-determination and independence." Like

Faysal, he urged the Council to send a commission to the region in order to determine the wishes of the population and framed its mission as consistent with Wilson's Fourteen Points. He cautioned the Council that unless the League's assigned mandatory power approached "its great task in the spirit of lofty service, her splendid opportunity to lead an aspiring people to independence will be forever lost."[68]

The Council members questioned Bliss about the political aspirations of Syrians. Bliss stated that press censorship by French and British authorities made it difficult to determine the true feelings of the population. In response, British Foreign Minister Arthur Balfour asked what opinions Syrians would express if they were free to do so. Bliss explained that Syrians were "very honest and childlike" and the new political situation had created great uncertainty. However, he demurred from offering his own opinion and requested the Council form a commission of inquiry.[69]

Bliss repeated these claims in private. He explained to Westermann that Syrians were "like children, pleased at notice, vain and superficial." Westermann wrote in his diary, "I judge that [Bliss] is right. But they are very gentlemanly and attractive, though all noisy eaters."[70]

Representatives of the Zionist movement also presented their claims in Paris. Unlike Faysal or Bliss, Chaim Weizmann embraced the idea of a British mandate and proposed expansive borders for the new state of Palestine. Weizmann's testimony in Paris was only part of his broader public and private efforts in Europe and the United States to ensure support for the Zionist movement's goals. Weizmann also conducted side negotiations with Amir Faysal. The Council was receptive to Weizmann's presentation, and he emphasized the potential benefits to the Arabs in Palestine and across the region.[71]

By late March, the Council of Ten was reduced to four. Wilson was able to convince Lloyd George and Clemenceau to dispatch an Inter-Allied Commission to Syria. Faysal celebrated the news and drank champagne for the first time. However, London and Paris were determined to undermine the effort. British experts with local knowledge of the region sought to minimize the Commission's importance. Westermann was informed by Gertrude Bell, the British writer and intelligence agent, "that no Oriental ever told what he actually thought about matters openly, and in a public way."[72]

Bell was one of an emerging clique of early twentieth-century British Middle East experts with ties to Whitehall's political and intelligence community.[73] She explained to Westermann that British authorities attempted a similar effort in Mesopotamia. Bell claimed that the leading figures in Baghdad and Mosul grew suspicious when asked if there should be a single Arab state and preferred to "have it settled for them." Bell and Westermann agreed that any delay in sending the Commission would result in nationalist unrest in the area. Westermann was also distressed that all decisions related to the Near East were on hold until the Commission returned, calling it "an extremely foolish decision." He wrote, "I have come to the conclusion that a wrong decision now will do less harm than a correct decision made in two months or five months."[74]

Westermann's fears of a delay proved to be unfounded. But the Council of Four, and Wilson in particular, did not make the decisions he hoped and advocated for. The Inter-Allied Commission was eventually led by Charles Crane, a wealthy confidant of President Wilson, and Henry King, the president of Oberlin College. Albert Lybyer served as the general technical advisor to the Commission and helped draft the final report. But the Commission did not arrive in the region until the summer. In the interim, Westermann advocated for an aggressive American role in the Anatolian Peninsula. He recommended sending American troops to secure an area for the creation of an Armenian state. However, he and other supporters of Armenian independence were disappointed by the decisions at Paris. Westermann's proposals for Armenia were rejected by Secretary of State Lansing and General Bliss, who explained that the United States was not at war with the Ottoman Empire and could not dispatch troops to the region. This was reinforced on May 13, 1919, when the American representatives working on the Ottoman Empire were informed that they were only to act in an "advisory capacity" on the final treaty, rather than as a party to the agreement.[75]

Four days later, Westermann and David Magie had a private meeting with Wilson. The president confirmed that the United States was interested in mandates for Constantinople (Istanbul) and Armenia and reiterated his opposition to secret agreements. As the outlines of the final treaty began to resemble the Sykes-Picot Agreement, Westermann lamented in his diary, "The Turkish Empire is the loot of the war."[76]

Although his role advising Wilson was limited, Westermann was approached by members of Faysal's entourage for assistance. Faysal left for Syria to prepare for the arrival of the King-Crane Commission. Several of his advisors returned to the conference, including General Nuri al-Said, the future Iraqi prime minister, and Dr. Amin Maalouf. In June, al-Said and Maalouf approached Westermann and Magie to assist with a proposal for

Syria and Mesopotamia to be considered a single economic unit. Faysal and his advisors hoped that an Arab state would be independent but benefit from foreign assistance, especially for education. The next best option, they believed, was an American or British mandate. Westermann asked if the Arabs in Syria and Mesopotamia could unite and avoid internal fighting. Maalouf conceded that they could not. However, he was staunchly opposed to French rule exclaiming, "For God's sake don't put the French over us!" In subsequent conversations with Westermann, Maalouf said the Syrians were not capable of establishing an effective and independent government at the time, confirming the assessments of the Inquiry and British experts.[77]

A Peace of Shreds and Patches

Wilson returned to Washington exhausted but triumphant. Although he was treated to a hero's welcome, the president soon found that the negotiations in Paris were only the beginning of his problems. The Treaty of Versailles and the League of Nations hardly resembled the "new international order" that Wilson spoke about in February 1918. Instead, they represented the "peace of shreds and patches" he warned against. Even self-determination, the phrase he was most associated with, was absent from the League's covenant. Wilson's health deteriorated after his return from Paris, providing Republican opponents of the Treaty and the League with the opportunity to block ratification. In addition, former supporters who hailed Wilson's vision for the postwar world were disappointed by the Treaty and the raw power politics on display in Paris. The hope and celebration that accompanied Wilson's departure for France eventually died on the Senate floor.[78]

Although the U.S. Senate did not ratify the Treaty of Versailles or join the League of Nations, Britain and France used both to consolidate their wartime gains. The League of Nations mandates were intended to be temporary. London and Paris were to assist the territories under their control in forming the necessary political, economic, and social structures and institutions for democratic self-governance. In reality, the mandates legitimized British and French imperial interests. The majority Arab areas of the Ottoman Empire were divided into new nation-states that were designated class "A" mandates. This signified that their provisional independence could be recognized and their populations would have input into the selection of a mandatory power. Instead, British and French plans were finalized at the April 1920 San Remo Conference, without the consent of the inhabitants.

Britain imposed mandates on the new states of Palestine, Transjordan, and Iraq. Meanwhile, France established mandates over Lebanon and Syria. In the case of Palestine, the Balfour Declaration was incorporated into the mandate's preamble, firmly establishing the creation of a Jewish national home as British policy.[79]

The decisions at the San Remo Conference also ignored the findings of the King-Crane Commission. After conducting interviews in Palestine, Syria, and Lebanon, the Commission had a far different understanding of the region, its inhabitants, and their wishes than the leaders in Paris. Although the Commission determined that the areas were not ready for self-rule, it found strong resistance to British and French rule as well as the Zionist movement. The interviews conducted by the Commission revealed a desire for an independent and united Syria that would also encompass the new states of Lebanon, Palestine, and Transjordan. Moreover, if a mandate was to be established, the inhabitants wanted it to be administered by the United States. In its initial report, the King-Crane Commission warned that the Palestinian Arabs were resistant to the program and aims of the Zionist movement and recommended limiting Jewish immigration to Palestine. However, the Commission's final report was not completed until 1922 and was a dead letter.[80]

In March 1920, an independent Syria was declared and Faysal was named king. Three months later, French forces invaded and imposed their mandate. Faysal was a king without a kingdom. Although Westermann had a favorable view of Faysal, the Amir's demands for independence found an unwelcome audience. Colonel House later described Faysal's appearance before the Council:

> Of the visiting chiefs and potentates from far-off lands, none made a more profound impression than the Emir Feisal, son of the king of the Hedjaz [*sic*]. He spoke Arabic only, but he had an able friend and interpreter in Colonel Lawrence, who himself was one of the unique characters of the war. The Arabian prince, in his native dress, was a striking figure. He looked not unlike the accepted pictures of the Christ, but there the resemblance ended, for Feisal had proved himself a dangerous foe on many fields of battle, and at Paris asserted himself in a way in which no signs of humility were apparent. He came less like a suppliant than any of the others, for he bore himself with a kingly air and was imperious in his demands. This attitude finally brought about his undoing and landed him in exile.[81]

Faysal was eventually rescued by his British patrons and installed as the monarch over the newly established mandate territory of Iraq. His brother Abdullah was expelled from the Arabian Peninsula by the forces of Abd al-Aziz Ibn Saud, the founding monarch of Saudi Arabia. Like his brother, Abdullah was also saved by London and eventually became the King of Jordan.[82]

The Entente powers also planned to partition the remainder of the Ottoman Empire. However, a nationalist insurgency led by Mustafa Kemal, a former diplomat, thwarted plans to carve up the Anatolian Peninsula. Later known as Atatürk, or "Father of the Turks," Kemal's nationalist forces also prevented the emergence of Armenian and Kurdish states. The establishment of the Turkish Republic marked the end of the Ottoman Empire after nearly six centuries.[83]

The Legacy of the Inquiry

What was the Inquiry's influence on the Paris Peace Conference and the Treaty of Versailles? The Inquiry was the focus of media attention, had access to Wilson, and was instrumental in the drafting of the Fourteen Points. In Paris, Bowman was elevated to a position of authority above the State Department and the U.S. military. Although the final decisions rested with President Wilson, he consulted the collected team of experts, especially Bowman, on a range of territorial issues. While the Fourteen Points speech served as the basis for the American position at Paris, other policy recommendations advanced by the Inquiry were also adopted. In the case of Western Asia, their proposals were modified into the mandate system. But for the intervention of Mustafa Kemal, the remainder of the Ottoman Empire would have been further segmented into small states administered by different European powers.

Yet in many respects the Inquiry was underutilized. Wilson deliberately limited the input of his advisors, especially when the Council of Ten became the Council of Four. This was also a misnomer, since Wilson, Lloyd George, and Clemenceau were the key decision makers. At one point Wilson and Lloyd George clashed over the need to solicit expert opinion, with the president remarking that it was "only useful in the consideration of established facts."[84] After Paris, some key participants like Secretary of State Lansing attempted to downplay the Inquiry's influence on the final decisions.[85]

One of the Inquiry's most ambitious undertakings was the development of maps for the different regions under consideration. This reflected the influence of the AGS on the Inquiry, in particular Bowman. Yet Inquiry Director Sidney Mezes observed afterward that the maps were "hardly used at all" and that "some of the cases containing them were not opened."[86]

Some prominent members of the Inquiry attempted to defend their role as well as the outcome of the conference. For example, Mezes explained that unlike the European powers, the United States had no permanent consular services in many of the areas that were discussed at the conference. "It was only recently that our diplomatic and consular services had been organized on a permanent basis with secure tenure, and the incumbents in these services had dealt chiefly with governments and with business agencies, and had little training or interest in questions of geography, history, ethnology, economics, strategy, etc., that would be the chief considerations at the Peace Conference," he wrote. While Europeans often traveled to these different areas, Mezes noted that "few of these regions had been visited more than casually, or studied with any thoroughness by American travelers, traders, or scientists."[87]

Isaiah Bowman was cautiously optimistic about the conference and the mandate system. Writing a few years after the conference, he claimed that if successfully implemented, the mandates could be "one of the most powerful elements of international justice."[88] In later years, Bowman defended the Inquiry and its role at the conference. According to Neil Smith, he was "proud and possessive" of the group's activities and was "ever vigilant in correcting others about the true history."[89]

Colonel House offered the most strident defense of the conference. Before Paris, House and Wilson had a strong relationship. However, their friendship became strained when Wilson learned that House was conducting side negotiations and offering concessions. After returning from France, the two men never saw each other again.[90] House claimed that despite public expectations, which he and Wilson had helped set, "It is doubtful whether more could have been done, considering the conditions after the armistice was signed." Like Wilson, he saw the creation of the League of Nations as the major outcome of the conference. House extolled the "sincere effort to give racial entities self-determination" and the creation of the mandate system. He argued that "these parts of the treaty mark a distinct advance in international morals, and if they fail of their purpose it will be because of the refusal of the United States to accept the treaty in good faith and to give it her powerful support—a support which is essential to success." He added that the League of Nations was "the only instrument which has been devised to save us from the destruction another world war would bring. It is a melancholy reflection upon our right to exist."[91]

Yet other Inquiry members criticized the Treaty and Wilson's actions. Westermann assailed the abandonment of American principles and responsibilities, particularly toward the Armenians. He argued that the few gains achieved in the treaty were meager in comparison with "the hopes that men set their hearts upon at Paris."[92]

In January 1919, the Inquiry ceased operations as an independent functional body. The small group that went to Paris and became the Division of Territorial, Economic, and Political Intelligence returned with Wilson. While most members went back to academia, others joined the State Department. Westermann was able to draw on his new political connections and experience to leave Wisconsin for Cornell and eventually Columbia. Dana G. Munro joined the State Department, where he remained for twelve years, including as head of the Latin America division. After returning to Princeton, he led the School of Public and International Affairs. When the Second World War broke out, both Westermann and Munro were recruited by the State Department.[93]

Before returning to New York, Isaiah Bowman helped establish a new organization to address the personal and structural failings of the Paris Peace Conference. A series of meetings was arranged between disgruntled American and British advisors who were frustrated by Wilson's behavior during the conference. Although Bowman missed the initial meetings in Paris, he helped found the Council on Foreign Relations (CFR). While the initial vision of establishing an Anglo-American organization to address important issues of world affairs did not materialize, the CFR maintained close relations with its British counterpart, the Royal Institute for International Affairs. By its first year, the CFR had nearly 300 members. According to Bowman, its main goal was to "change the opinion of our government."[94]

Twenty years later, as another conflict was sweeping Europe, Walter Lippmann met with Colonel William "Wild Bill" Donovan in Washington. Donovan was selected by President Franklin D. Roosevelt to lead the Office of Coordinator of Information (COI). Like the Inquiry, the COI was a vague title that offered little insight into its true purpose: a centralized intelligence agency. Lippmann discussed his experience with the Inquiry and provided Donovan with the names of several scholars who could assist with gathering information on foreign areas, including Bowman.[95]

The creation and operation of the Inquiry mirrored the hopes, frustrations, and disappointments of Woodrow Wilson's presidency. To help determine the best course of action at the peace conference, Wilson sought expertise from outside the U.S. government. In spite of their intelligence, individual and collective, Wilson's experts had little if any first-hand knowledge about the areas they were researching. Moreover, their research and policy proposals were marked by Orientalist sentiments and notions of racial and religious supremacy. The characterizations of Muslims and Arabs as well as their perceptions of different societies in the region contributed to the justifications for British and French rule in the former territories of the Ottoman Empire. While it is questionable whether the United States could have imposed its will on London and Paris, as Wilson learned to his frustration, the Inquiry's claims that establishing protectorates in order to assist the native populations with self-governance were dubious at best.

Nor did America's lack of expertise in foreign areas at the time justify the shortcomings of the Inquiry's reports. The establishment of the Inquiry was a political decision and its composition and assignments were similarly based on political and social connections, shared ideology, and some nepotism. In addition, those experts outside of the Inquiry who provided information to the group often reinforced their own ideological predispositions and prejudices. This was also true of the American missionaries and British agents whose expertise was sought after and respected because of their experience in foreign countries. Indeed, the missionaries' paternalistic attitudes toward the natives of the countries where they served were evident in the Inquiry's final reports and recommendations as well as testimony before the Council of Ten.

Yet Amir Faysal's advisors confirmed the assertions made by the American and British experts. While this validated the Inquiry's recommendations it also reflected the political fears and biases of Faysal and his advisors, who benefitted directly and exclusively from London's support and sponsorship. The role of "native informants," particularly those tied to centers of power in London and Washington, would only grow over the next century as the Middle East became more important to Britain and the United States. Indeed, their insights would remain remarkably consistent over time.

The Inquiry was an early attempt by Washington to develop contemporary expertise on foreign areas. It was also a reflection of the reformist trend sweeping American society, including in the social sciences. Based on the principles declared by Wilson in his Fourteen Points address and subsequent speeches, the members of the Inquiry believed they were utilizing their knowledge to help create a better world. Some of those who traveled to Paris were dismayed by the negotiations and subsequent treaty, which they viewed as an abandonment of the principles and cause they served. Moreover, it was the perceived failure to achieve their goals that led Inquiry members to establish the CFR upon returning from France.

The Inquiry left an uncertain legacy. While it successfully produced voluminous reports on different geographic areas and key issues to help Wilson prepare for the peace conference, they were not fully utilized. Indeed, their limited role at Versailles revealed the tensions between expertise and Presidential diplomacy. When the war in Europe began, Washington had few scholars in academia to consult for foreign area expertise. This situation did not improve over the next two decades, especially for areas outside of Europe and the Western Hemisphere. Moreover, those scholars with knowledge and experience in the Western Asia division were predominantly Orientalists who could offer little insight into the contemporary affairs of the areas they studied. With the outbreak of World War II, the United States sought to create a new organization to provide research and intelligence on foreign areas. Although the founders of the OSS were aware of the Inquiry, they chose not to adopt it as a model. Yet other efforts over the next century resembled the Inquiry. From modernization theorists to terror experts, scholars with ties to the foreign policy and national security establishments with shared ideological predispositions would attempt to represent and shape the Middle East.

CHAPTER 2

Wartime Expertise

The Office of Strategic Services, the Army Specialized Training Program, and World War II in the Middle East, 1940–1945

> It is permitted to walk with the devil until you have crossed the bridge. The OSS was in a death struggle with the Gestapo and, like Churchill, allied itself with devils to survive. We deserve to go to hell when we die. . . . The OSS had no conscience. . . . It is still an open question whether an operator in OSS or in CIA can ever again become a wholly honorable man.
>
> —WILLIAM A. EDDY

Harvard's campus was a flurry of activity the weekend of November 22, 1941. A variety of formal and informal functions, from the Yale-Harvard Ball to joint performances by the Red and Blue Glee Clubs, were held leading up to the sixtieth playing of "The Game." Next to stories describing the weekend festivities, the *Harvard Crimson* published ominous signs of the conflict abroad and sentiments at home. Under the headline "Yale 'News' Poll Reveals Bulldogs Swing Toward War," the paper reported that 67 percent of Yale students favored increased aid to opponents of Nazi Germany and 21 percent advocated full participation—a dramatic increase from just 6 percent in February. Another article warned that the Axis powers were advancing against the Soviet Union and were countering a British offensive in North Africa. It was the North African Front that brought Wallace Phillips to Cambridge that weekend.[1]

Dressed in a blue serge suit and walking among the large crowds in Harvard Square, Phillips had a different purpose from the other visitors. A naval officer, Phillips recently accepted a post with the newly created Office of the Coordinator of Information (COI) and was the director of its Special Information Service.[2] In spite of its generic title, the COI was America's first attempt to create a centralized intelligence agency and Phillips was in town to recruit a spy.[3] He appeared at the office of anthropology professor Carleton Coon without an appointment. Coon had previously conducted research in North Africa, spoke local Arabic dialects, and was familiar with the regional tribes. "First he swore me to utter secrecy," Coon recalled, "then he told me more about myself than I had dreamed anyone else could know. He asked me if I wanted to serve my country." After Coon explained that he was already in the Massachusetts State Guard, Phillips replied that it "was not enough."[4]

Phillips discussed the Nazi threat to North Africa and the Middle East. Coon, he explained, "had been chosen to be the Lawrence of Morocco." T. E. Lawrence's legacy hung over the scholar-spies assigned to the North African and Middle Eastern theaters of operations. Some scholars were approached by the COI with the promise of becoming the Lawrence of their generation, while others privately hoped that would be the case.[5]

Like other scholars recruited for the COI and its successor agency, the Office of Strategic Services (OSS), Coon was approached with great secrecy. However, after Japan's attack on Pearl Harbor less than three weeks later, scholars volunteered to assist the American war effort. The United States entered the war as an industrial power with limited political influence on the world stage and negligible military forces, but it emerged as a global superpower. During the war, key agencies were established to provide the U.S. government and military with area expertise and intelligence as well as language training.

The OSS and the Army Specialized Training Program (ASTP) were influential precursors of university-based area studies. Several prominent scholars served in the OSS as spies or as analysts and others were active with the ASTP. Although the wartime experience provided the U.S. government with contemporary expertise, the knowledge produced by the OSS's scholar-spies was heavily influenced by and reflected their Orientalist training. In addition, government service also influenced—or at least reinforced—how academics viewed America's role in the world and in the Middle East. The personal and institutional linkages established during the war later served as reference points for scholars, universities, and the U.S.

government for the development of area studies and language training programs as well as conducting and analyzing foreign area research. Moreover, the close collaboration between the U.S. government and academia deemed essential during the war transitioned seamlessly to postwar planning before hostilities ended.

The Coordinator of Information

In July 1941, five months before Pearl Harbor was attacked, President Franklin D. Roosevelt established the COI. He selected Colonel William "Wild Bill" Donovan, a corporate attorney with a private practice on Wall Street, to lead the organization. Donovan was a one-time Republican Party nominee for governor of New York. On previous trips abroad he gathered foreign intelligence and reported it back to FDR. This included a 1935 trip to Italy and Ethiopia, where he was able to assess the capabilities and effectiveness of Italian forces fighting in Africa. Donovan's report was also shared with the British Foreign Office. During the war, Donovan's personal relationship with the Foreign Office helped facilitate intelligence sharing and cooperation between London and Washington.[6]

While the origins of the COI are well known, less recognized is the importance of the Middle East in shaping its creation. A year before the COI was created, Roosevelt asked Donovan to travel to England. His mission was to evaluate British defensive capabilities against a German invasion and Nazi saboteurs. This was followed by a tour of the Mediterranean region and the Middle East from December 1940 to March 1941. After his trip, Donovan was convinced that the Middle East and southeastern Europe "should be utilized to the utmost in British military strategy and in American political strategy." Donovan's travel abroad also convinced him of the important role that strategic intelligence would play in modern conflicts.[7]

In June 1941, Donovan submitted his proposal for creating a "service of strategic information." He stated that its basic purpose would be to provide the president and his military and political advisors with "available and complete enemy intelligence reports upon which military operational decisions could be based." Donovan argued that existing military intelligence efforts were inadequate for wartime strategic planning and assessment. He believed that valuable intelligence regarding the Axis powers already existed in different government departments. Drawing on specialized personnel trained in research techniques and languages, the relevant information could be identified, collated, and analyzed. Although he did not specifically advocate for their recruitment, Donovan was essentially describing scholars trained in the social sciences and other disciplines as his ideal analysts.[8]

Donovan also approached Archibald MacLeish, the Librarian of Congress, about assistance for the COI. MacLeish responded that the Library needed additional funding in order to provide the necessary support.[9] Later that summer MacLeish organized a meeting at Boston's Tavern Club to identify individuals for the COI. Attended by representatives of the American Council of Learned Societies (ACLS), the Social Science Research Council (SSRC), the National Archives, and scholars from major universities, the goal was to identify a "board of analysts" to oversee experts on different foreign areas. This group became the governing board of COI's Research and Analysis Branch (R&A).

R&A was initially led by James Phinney Baxter III, the president of Williams College. Baxter recruited Harvard's William Langer to serve as chairman of the board of analysts and director of research. Langer replaced Baxter as the head of R&A in September 1942 and remained in the post until the division was absorbed into the State Department's Office of Intelligence and Research (OIR) four years later.[10]

Originally based in the Library of Congress, R&A's scholars were first tasked with examining the Library's published works for potential intelligence. Langer later explained that this approach was based on Donovan's "hunch" that valuable intelligence could be gleaned from published works, including older books. While the "cloak and dagger" of the OSS's Secret Intelligence (SI) branch was later glorified in the press and films, Langer asserted that it "never became a major source of intelligence for [R&A] studies." However, SI procured a variety of published material from Germany and the Soviet Union that proved to be useful. Although not as exciting as SI, the R&A's strength "lay in the research training and experience of its personnel." Langer added that Donovan's instinct was "proved altogether correct," as the analysis of disparate published materials and diplomatic cables demonstrated the branch's effectiveness to the military services.[11]

While Donovan's office was based in New York, R&A was located in Washington. In spite of the presidential authorization, the COI immediately encountered bureaucratic hostility from other governmental agencies. This was compounded by the COI's vague charter of operations. Langer later admitted that "we were badly hampered by our own ignorance about the details of our mission. No one would or could enlighten us as to what we should do and how to go about it."[12] As they attempted to overcome Washington's entrenched interests and resentments, Langer recruited an elite group of scholars for R&A, including a number of his Harvard colleagues. The composition of the OSS's personnel led others in Washington to dismiss it as "Oh-So-Special." Like Langer, a number of these scholars alternated between government service and academia in the postwar era.

Following America's entry into the war, Roosevelt authorized the COI's transformation into the OSS. Now reporting to the Joint Chiefs of Staff (JCS), Donovan was given the new title of director of OSS and was eventually promoted to general. The OSS was enhanced and expanded to gather and analyze information required by the JCS, as well as to organize and implement "special services" or covert operations.[13]

In Washington, the R&A's Near East section was part of the broader Europe-Africa division led by Sherman Kent. Like fellow historian Langer, Kent played an influential role in the postwar development of the intelligence establishment. While Kent led the division throughout the war, the Near East section had several different heads over time. It was initially led by Walter E. Wright Jr., former president of Istanbul's Robert College. After Wright was ordered to Turkey, John Wilson of the University of Chicago was his initial replacement. Wright's deputy, Ephraim Avigdor (E. A.) Speiser, an expert in Semitic languages at the University of Pennsylvania, was the third head of the Near East desk and remained in the position for most of the war. R&A's Near East section initially focused on the Muslim world and covered territory ranging from Palestine to Afghanistan, including Turkey and the Arabian Peninsula.[14]

The Near East desk had a mixture of elder Orientalists and younger scholars, including historians Edwin Wright and Lewis Thomas, political scientists Jacob Coleman (J. C.) Hurewitz and Harvey Hall, archaeologist William F. Albright, and linguists Harold Glidden and T. Cuyler Young. Hurewitz was a history doctoral student at Columbia drafted into the Army Signal Corps. After publishing an article entitled "Arab Politics in Palestine" in the *Contemporary Jewish Record*, he was recruited by Speiser into R&A. Hurewitz was assigned to cover British Mandate Palestine and Transjordan. When he joined the division, Hurewitz found that its contemporary information on Palestine was limited to two published articles on Arab nationalism and Zionism. Before being assigned to the Cairo office,

Glidden was responsible for Egypt, Sudan, and the Arabian Peninsula. He was replaced by Franz Rosenthal, who later became a scholar of Islamic history at Yale. T. Cuyler Young, later of Princeton, was responsible for Iran. Young had lived in Iran for eight years as a member of the Presbyterian Board of Foreign Missions. He was eventually appointed deputy chief of R&A's Near East section. Meanwhile, Harvey Hall covered Turkey.[15]

Over fifty years later, Hurewitz reflected on his time in the OSS. "It did not take long to appreciate that I had been invited to join a unique and uninterrupted scholarly seminar on the Near East at war," he wrote, "for which at government expense I was ordered to update my familiarity with the contemporary history of Palestine and keep abreast of unfolding developments with the support of the best evidence available to Washington." Hurewitz added that E. A. Speiser "infused in our work a 5,000-year perspective on the overall region." As Near East chief, Speiser combined his training in biblical Mesopotamia with contemporary knowledge of Iraq's political leaders based on his trips to the country to conduct archeological digs.[16]

Speiser offered a similar assessment after the war. "It was not unusual for an Egyptologist to serve as an analyst on Arab affairs or for a cuneiformist to investigate the manifold problems of Afghanistan," he wrote. Speiser continued to advocate for a similar approach, stating that "we realize now more than we ever could before that in this region of immemorial and persistent cultural traditions it is impossible to splinter off the modern phase from its antecedent periods."[17]

While most of the scholars remained in Washington as analysts, other scholars were assigned to the region. Some used their academic credentials and networks as cover for their espionage activities. This included archaeologist Nelson Glueck, anthropologist Carleton Coon, and historian Richard Frye.

Princeton at War

As the OSS gathered scholars for the war effort, university campuses were converted to provide area and language training to military personnel. Princeton became the ASTP's major center for Arabic language instruction. Led by Philip K. Hitti, Princeton's ASTP program offered a model for area training programs.

Hitti was born in the tiny farming village of Shimlan in the Mount Lebanon region outside Beirut on June 24, 1886. One of six boys in a large family of eight children, he was nearly killed in an accident at the age of nine. After several surgeries and months recuperating, Hitti's family and the village elders decided he could not be a farmer. Instead, he was sent to school run by American missionaries in a neighboring village to become a teacher. After teaching for a year, Hitti enrolled in the Syrian Protestant College (SPC). He graduated in 1908 and received his doctorate from Columbia eight years later. Hitti was forty years old when he joined Princeton's faculty and would become a leading Near East scholar in the United States.[18]

In May 1942, an urgent request came from Washington. Princeton president Harold W. Dodds notified Dana Munro, director of the School of Public and International Affairs, about the government's need to train men for the Near East. A former member of the Inquiry, Munro established Princeton's Latin American studies program. "The need in the war emergency," Dodds explained, "and for the reconstruction to follow of men with knowledge of the languages and culture of the Near East is being brought to our attention constantly by various agencies of the Government." While the university was offering an "emergency course" in colloquial Arabic, it did not have similar offerings in Turkish or Persian. Dodds recommended that Hitti develop a proposal for course work that combined language training in Arabic, Persian, and Turkish with studies in the social sciences. "We should consider our responsibilities and opportunities as a University in this area," he wrote.[19]

Hitti's Near East program was quickly established in the fall 1942 semester. Munro notified students that the program was "planned with the idea that men with a knowledge of the language and civilizations of specific regions in which military operations are being carried out will be particularly useful in the Army or Navy and may have opportunities for interesting and important specialized services during the war or in the period of reconstruction afterward." Princeton's ASTP program in Arabic and Turkish had several components. Area study focused on the history and culture of the region, as well as geography, economics, and current issues. Language classes consisted of six hours of class work and ten hours of conversation per week. In addition, the trainees participated in preceptorials, a Princeton tradition where topics from the readings and lectures were discussed in small groups of eight to ten trainees with a moderator.[20]

The university identified a need to train military personnel for combat and post-combat operations. A 1942 memorandum produced by the School of Public and International Affairs noted that advanced training was important for the Near and Far East, "where social conditions and points of view are so different from our own." In listing the different departments and programs that could be drawn upon to help train Army and Navy personnel, Princeton offered an interdisciplinary model for postwar area studies programs.[21]

However, a concern developed within the ASTP program about the trainees. An undated internal memorandum stated that a majority of the seventy-five men assigned to Princeton for Near East training were Jews. It cautioned that those returning from official missions to the region reported that "the rising tensions between Jews and Arabs is a serious problem in the whole area from Morocco to India," with the threat of violence breaking out in Syria and Palestine. Axis propaganda in the region warned that an Allied victory would strengthen the position of the Zionist movement in Palestine. The memo argued that "this propaganda could obviously become more effective if most of the men showing up in the Near East for military government or liaison work turned out to be Jews, or even if reports that we were training Jews for this work were disseminated by Axis propaganda." It noted that a number of the trainees "were beginning to understand the seriousness of this problem" and were concerned that they would not be useful in the region. As a solution, the university proposed assigning some of the Jewish trainees to the Far East and others to be trained in Greek or Italian or possibly Turkish or Persian. It specifically stated that not all of the Jewish trainees should be transferred and added that "a reasonable proportion of Jewish officers in military government in the Near East might do no harm. What must be avoided is the impression that most of the men being trained for this work are Jews."[22]

Hitti also assisted the COI and later the OSS with intelligence and translation of Arabic publications. In November 1941, he provided the COI with detailed information about Arabic-language publications in the United States, South America, and the Middle East. He also identified and offered brief biographies of Arab literary and political figures. These contacts continued throughout the war and into the postwar period.[23]

Orientalism as Area Intelligence

As Princeton's ASTP implemented language training, the R&A division developed country guides for military personnel ordered to the Middle East and North Africa. By early 1942, three country guides were completed and distributed detailing life in the Persian Gulf, Egypt, and Eritrea. Offering a mixture of practical travel advice and information with stereo-typical and contradictory observations about the different areas, the guides provide a revealing insight into the influence of Orientalism on the production of intelligence.[24]

This was evident in the "Hints on Life in Egypt" guide. A crude illustration on the guide's cover depicted a presumably Western male riding a donkey in the desert while flogging (or threatening to flog) an Egyptian with the pyramids of Giza in the background (see Figure 1). The guide cautioned that Egypt was "a more or less medieval country" until the end of the nineteenth century. Following the British occupation in 1882, however, the guide claimed it was "being modernized fairly rapidly." As the U.S. military remained segregated and servicemen were dispatched from across the United States, including the Jim Crow South, the guide informed its readers that "many Egyptians are very dark, but this does not necessarily mean that they are Negroes, any more than Hindus or Hawaiians are." It added that Egyptians "don't like to be called 'natives', because this word makes them think you are comparing them with inhabitants of uncivilized or backward countries." Moreover, as Americans would encounter troops from across the British Commonwealth, including South Africa, the guide stated, "Don't forget that the South Africans have Negroes in their country too, and feel about the same toward them as we do in the South." In describing Egyptian society, the guide explained that members of the upper and middle class "are more or less westernized in dress and home life and speak English and French." However, it also warned, "If you have to deal with upper-class Egyptians; you should dress carefully; nowhere is a man more judged by his clothes than in the East."[25]

The Near East section coordinated with the Psychology Division to produce a series of booklets for the War Department. Intended for American servicemen deployed to the region, booklets were created for North Africa, Syria, Iran, and Iraq. Adorned with a number of illustrations, the guides were designed to provide brief introductions to the different areas. The Iraq and Syria booklets shared a number of features, including illustrations.[26]

Although the Syria guide discussed the cosmopolitan nature of cities like Beirut and Damascus, the illustrations offered a different image of the area and its inhabitants. This included men dressed in traditional grab and herding sheep, a bazaar, and a Bedouin male. Under a drawing of a camel caravan, it explained the apparent historic importance of the U.S. mission:

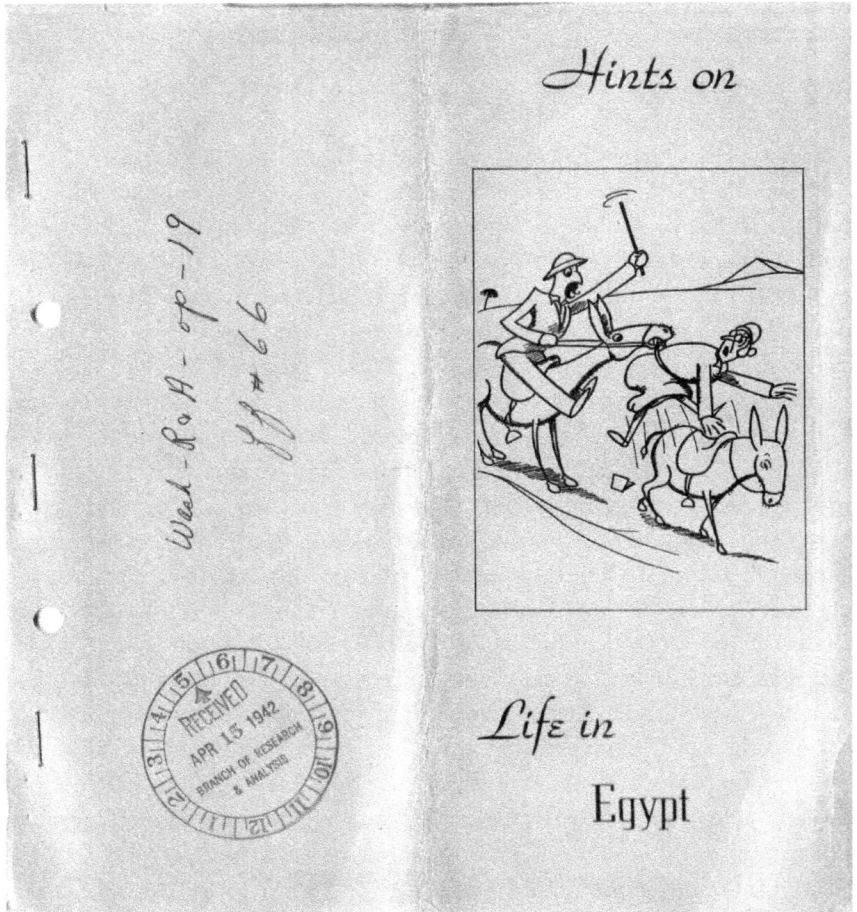

Figure 1. Cover of R&A's *Life in Egypt* booklet. (Courtesy of the U.S. National Archives, College Park, MD)

Your unit has been ordered to Syria. Soon you will be standing on the shores of the sea or on a desert which has played a great part in world history. You, an American soldier, are now one of the countless fighting men, over the past two thousand years, who have tramped across this neck of land connecting Europe and Asia. Alexander the Great, Caesar, Napoleon—all have struggled on this land for world domination.

You are in Syria to fight for—and to win—against Hitler, who seeks world domination. And a big part of your job is to make friends for your cause—because this is a war of ideas, just as much of tanks, planes and guns.

The guide stated that Syria was a "friendly country" that would welcome American troops. It noted that Syria once sought an American mandate from the League of Nations at the end of World War I and that many Syrians were educated at the American University of Beirut (AUB). Although it was not hostile territory, the guide cautioned the servicemen that they needed to use "ordinary horse sense" in their "dealings with the people of this land." While it offered some practical advice, including navigating local customs and understanding religious practices, the guide also contained several curious warnings:

Shake hands with Syrians; otherwise don't touch them or slap them on the back [see Figure 2].[27]

Remember Syrians are very modest people and avoid any exposure of the body in their presence.

When you see grown men walking hand in hand, ignore it. They are not "queer."

Be kind and considerate to servants. The Syrians are a very democratic people.

Avoid any expressions of race prejudice.

Shake hands on meeting and leaving.

On meeting a Syrian, be sure to inquire after his health.

Be polite. Good manners are essential among the Syrians. Be hospitable to Syrians whenever possible.

Above all, use common sense on all occasions. And remember that every American solider is an unofficial ambassador of good will.[28]

Although the Iraq guide offered similar advice, it also provided different observations of the population with T. E. Lawrence as a reference point. Accompanying a picture of a bearded man in traditional garb and headdress, the guide stated:

That tall man in the flowing robe you are going to see soon, with the whiskers and the long hair, is a first-class fighting man, highly skilled in guerilla warfare. Few fighters in any country in fact, excel him in that kind of situation. If he is your friend, he can be a staunch and valuable ally. If he should happen to be your enemy—look out! Remember Lawrence of Arabia? Well it was with men like these that he wrote history in the First World War.[29]

GETTING ALONG WITH THE SYRIANS

Figure 2. Image from a "Short Guide to Syria," 1942. (Courtesy of the U.S. National Archives, College Park, MD)

While the guides demonstrated the benefit of combining regional expertise with contemporary knowledge of conditions and customs, they also demonstrated the patronizing and paternalistic nature of American and European scholarship on the Middle East at the time. The booklets were produced in the COI's early months of operation when the United States was largely reliant on its British allies for intelligence from the region as well as published works, which were often written by American and European Orientalist scholars. By the time the guides were distributed to the War Department, the OSS's first secret mission in the area was underway.

The OSS in Cairo

Building on Donovan's 1941 trip to the region, the OSS established its Cairo office in the spring of 1942. A Nazi offensive threatened British forces in Egypt and Donovan explained to the JCS that "the importance of holding the Near East area is increasingly obvious." Allied goals included preventing the linkage and unification of Axis offensives in North Africa and the Caucuses, ensuring Allied control of the region's oil resources, and preventing German and Japanese forces from joining in Central Asia. Even though the region was under British hegemony, Donovan believed that the United States could assist because "American prestige and influence in the Near East is still probably as high as ever." The Cairo mission had three objectives. First was to establish a base for the OSS's SI branch to coordinate with existing British intelligence organizations. Second was to counter German espionage and sabotage activities. Finally, the Cairo office would organize resistance activities if British forces were defeated.[30]

Donovan discussed his plans at a subcommittee meeting of the Joint Psychological Warfare Committee in late July 1942. Also attending the meeting was Lieutenant Colonel Harold Hoskins, one of President Roosevelt's most trusted advisors. Hoskins was born in Beirut to missionary parents and was the vice president of the American University of Beirut's Board of Trustees (formerly the SPC). Donovan explained to the subcommittee members that Hoskins's background qualified him as an expert on the region. The OSS chief also wanted Hoskins to head the organization's Cairo office. In discussing the creation of a subversive military unit based in the region, the JCS's representatives argued that the head should be a uniformed military officer because "the only thing that reaches the Arab mind is power. The only other thing that reaches them is money." Hoskins confirmed these points and added that "power, money, and independence" were the keys to influencing Arab leaders. Although he was not chosen to oversee operations in Cairo, as Chapter 4 demonstrates, Hoskins actively promoted relations between American educational institutions in the Middle East and Washington during and after the war.[31]

Drawing on Donovan's relationship with Britain's political and military leadership, the OSS's Cairo office quickly developed a rapport with the British Secret Intelligence Service (SIS) and other Allied intelligence agencies. Among the first actions taken was to establish a radio station to counter Nazi propaganda in the region. The SIS also began sharing intelligence from the Middle East and southeastern Europe regions with their OSS liaison officer and, in an unprecedented manner, also allowed the information to be distributed to Washington without restrictions.[32] As the United States lacked sources of intelligence in the region, the SIS reports were welcome. Although there were already several American agents operating in the region, due to security concerns they did not have contact with the Cairo office and some of the agents did not have the appropriate security clearance for their activities with the British authorities. One of the first agents in the field was archaeologist Nelson Glueck.[33]

The New Lawrence?

Nelson Glueck was interviewed by COI representatives in Washington on December 2, 1941. An archaeologist fluent in German and Hebrew and conversant in colloquial Arabic, Glueck was an ideal candidate for the fledgling organization. The previous summer, he completed his term as director of the American School of Oriental Research (ASOR) in Jerusalem. A professor of biblical archeology at Hebrew Union College in Cincinnati, Glueck had conducted several expeditions in Transjordan over the previous decade and led ASOR for five years. However, he demurred after meeting with Walter Wright Jr., the head of the State Department's Near Eastern Affairs (NEA) division, and Wallace Phillips. Five days later, Japan attacked Pearl Harbor. Writing separately to Phillips and Wright on December 12, Glueck restated his credentials and his new willingness "to offer my services to the Government under any conditions, anywhere."[34]

In a subsequent correspondence, Glueck offered further evidence of his suitability for covert activities. "Transjordan is a vital pathway between the Red Sea and Syria, between Palestine and Iraq. I believe that an American with my knowledge of the Near East in general, and particularly of Transjordan could be of use to my government," he wrote. He explained that over the previous five years he had surveyed two-thirds of the country, adding, "I do not believe that there are five men in the world, European or Arab, who know the country as well as I do." Glueck asserted that he was "the only non-Governmental official who was allowed to enter Transjordan at will." He further wrote, "For years, I have wandered far and wide in the Transjordan desert, unarmed, and accompanied by only one Arab companion, and never suffered any harm, where others were not allowed or did not dare to go, or were killed when they went. I had learned how to get along with the Arabs. All of my contacts in Transjordan were with Arabs only."[35]

Glueck also promoted his close relations with British Mandate officials in Transjordan. "There was never a reasonable request which I addressed to them, with which they did not immediately comply," Glueck explained. He added, "They provided me with everything from armored cars, when once I went into the Arabian desert, to cavalry horses, to airplanes put at my disposal. The work I was doing was work they wanted done." "The Transjordanian Government is controlled by a British Resident, Mr. [Alec] Kirkbride (known as Kirk to his friends)," he confided. "Emir Abdullah the titular head of Transjordan, is advised by Mr. Kirkbride, and has thus far acted in accordance with that advice," Glueck added. He was also well acquainted with Major John Bagot Glubb, the British officer in charge of Transjordan's Arab Legion.[36]

Glueck's knowledge and contacts were not limited to sparsely populated Transjordan. His time in the region coincided with the "Great Arab Revolt" in Palestine, a three-year uprising by Palestinian Arabs against the British Mandate. Glueck claimed that he was able to travel extensively and conduct his work during the revolt without incident, even though heavily armed convoys were "frequently attacked" on the same roads. Although ASOR was located in Jerusalem's Arab quarter, "no harm every came to any of us at the School because of the personal relations which I had with the Arabs of the area." Moreover, under his tenure as director, ASOR was "about the only place where Arabs and Jews and others could or would come together for meetings." Glueck offered to be affiliated with ASOR as a cover, "at no expense to the Government."[37]

Glueck did not believe that his proposal was unethical or improper. During an expedition seven years earlier, he encountered Fritz Frank, "the notorious German spy" who was based in Palestine during World War I. "At least, I could do, on behalf of my government, or on behalf of the British government, what he has been doing," Glueck wrote, "and I should be glad to do it." He added, "If I were sent back to Transjordan, I believe I am one of the few capable of really knowing what is really going on among the Arabs of the country." In addition to the letter and a copy of his curriculum vitae, Glueck provided a memorandum on the strategic importance of Palestine and Transjordan.[38]

The OSS coordinated with Britain's SIS to facilitate Glueck's mission. Glueck arranged to be reappointed director of ASOR and obtained funding to conduct an expedition as his cover. He also received an OSS salary of $400 per month.[39] Apparently hoping to emulate or surpass T. E. Lawrence, Glueck sought the rank of army colonel, which was denied. His mission orders were also tightly restricted. While in Palestine and Transjordan, Glueck was to use his archeological operation as a cover to establish a network of informants. He was also notified that if British officials sought to utilize him "in a role parallel to that played by Colonel Lawrence in the last war," different arrangements were to be made and that "a very long and arduous preparation for such operations would have to be made in Washington, London, Cairo, Palestine and other central points."[40]

Glueck arrived in Jerusalem at the end of April and spent most of the war in Palestine and Transjordan. Signing his dispatches to Washington as "William Hicks," Glueck relayed information ranging from the state of Arab-Jewish relations in Palestine, to the level of Soviet activity, to suggestions for reshaping the region after the war. He repeatedly warned Washington of the dangers of the "Palestine problem" in fostering conflict and instability across the region. Glueck argued that the region should remain under direct rule from Britain, asserting that the Arab world "does not understand this business of running a country by committee."[41] He maintained his cover as director of ASOR throughout his stay and even convened a two-day conference in July 1943 on postwar archeology in the region. The participants included American, European, Egyptian, and Palestinian Arab and Jewish academics. Alec Kirkbride, Britain's resident minister in Transjordan, also participated. Materials from the conference, including copies of the agenda, list of attendees, and detailed meeting minutes were sent to Washington.[42]

In May 1943, Glueck reported on British attempts to establish a training program in Jerusalem. Developed in conjunction with Britain's intelligence services and the Colonial Office, the program's goal was to "train advanced students in the affairs of the Middle East, languages, politics, literature, etc., who will be able to function in this part of the world no matter what changes in boundaries and governments may take place after the war, and who will form a permanent source for recruits for particular kinds of services in case of need." He advocated that the OSS pursue a similar training program. Glueck qualified the suggestion stating, "I need not assure you that I have no personal interest in any of these things other than assisting our cause to the best of my abilities. As soon as is possible in consonance with my duty to my country I want to return completely to my private academic life, and pursuits." Back in Washington, the R&A division began assisting military preparations for invading North Africa.[43]

Operation Torch

Dubbed "Operation Torch," the Allied invasion of North Africa offered the R&A Branch an opportunity to demonstrate its value. Scheduled for November 1942, R&A scholars spent much of August and September rapidly producing detailed reports on Morocco, Algeria, and Tunisia. The initial Morocco report was finished in fifty hours, and within the next month similar reports were produced for Algeria and Tunisia. Based on published information, the massive reports detailed the relevant demographic, historical, and sociopolitical information for each North African country. R&A's efforts earned the thanks of Army Chief of Staff George C. Marshall. Donovan informed the branch that the military leadership was surprised and impressed by the level of detail and the speed at which the information was produced and called it "the first victory" for the R&A concept.[44]

As part of the Torch preparations, the Near East section also developed psychological warfare plans. One of the key concerns was the impact of the North African invasion on the rest of the region and the broader Muslim world. In detailing the potential effectiveness of propaganda, the report stated, "Most loyalties in the Moslem world are based on direct, personal relationships, not on abstract ideas or distant propaganda." It added, "In general Moslems are impressed by force only. This also has come to be true of Frenchmen." Among the complicating factors for the Allied mission was the "Jewish problem." The report asserted that "Moslems are Anti-Semitic" and "the support of 400,000 Jews is not worth the antagonism of 15,000,000 Moslems." It claimed that in "ideological terms: Democracy and freedom in the American and British sense of the word are not understood. There is no Arab word for democracy. Natives follow the leaders they respect for their force and wealth." The report criticized the French as well, stating that they only believed in democracy "for themselves, not for the population as a whole." "Freedom is interpreted as freedom to do what you please. Freedom to the natives is freedom to loot and persecute enemies. Freedom to Frenchmen is freedom to exploit North Africa economically for their own and not the natives' benefit," it stated.[45]

For propaganda to be effective, the report asserted, the Allies must defeat the Axis powers and demonstrate that they had no interest in the acquisition of territory. Moreover, the Allies could ensure the friendliness of the local population through the prior deployment of agents. These agents "should have absolute control and directive power over all propaganda. Agents should always be men intimately familiar with North African conditions." Among their activities was maintaining relationships with local leaders and producing materials for dissemination to the population. One of the most prominent men sent to North Africa in preparation for Torch was anthropologist Carleton Coon.[46]

Lawrence of Morocco

Nearly seven months after he was visited on the Harvard campus, Carleton Coon was dispatched to Tangier. Phillips wanted Coon to obtain a naval commission and travel under navy cover. However, he failed the physical because of "obesity and gross overweight, and hypertension." After the war, Coon was quick to point out that "none of these conditions exists today."[47] Instead, Coon was assigned to the American Legation in Tangier as a "Special Assistant." However, the position came with no associated responsibilities and Coon quickly clashed with the chargé d'affaires, J. Rives Childs. Among the issues between the two men was Coon's lack of fluency in written and spoken Arabic. They also quarreled over a large report on "Propaganda in Morocco" produced by Coon and based on his book *Principles of Anthropology*. Coon explained that the report incorporated "enough technical words to make it ponderous and mysterious, since I had found out in the academic world that people will express much more awe and admiration for something complicated which they do not quite understand than for something simple and clear." Although Childs was impressed by the report he refused to allow Coon to send it to Washington. Coon ignored the order, however, and secretly dispatched the report. Unaware of Coon's actions, Childs asked him to revise the document and then sent it to the State Department with his own introduction. Upon leaving North Africa, Coon was under the mistaken impression that he and Childs had developed a mutually amicable and beneficial relationship. After the war, Coon sought and was denied approval by the U.S. Embassy in Saudi Arabia to conduct research in the country, where Childs was now ambassador.[48]

Coon's duties in North Africa included coordinating agents in the area and conducting sabotage raids against Axis targets. In addition, he was to assist with the production and dissemination of propaganda throughout the theater of operations. Although he was ordered to the region, Coon was unaware that the Allied invasion had been set for November. He was not informed until two weeks before the landing. Coon later explained, "I did know that I was there to prepare for military eventualities and that my probable job was to make things hot for the Germans if and when they should move westward from Egypt and Tripoli."[49]

In Tangier, Coon joined Colonel William A. Eddy. Like his cousin Harold Hoskins, Eddy was the son of American missionaries. Born in present-day southern Lebanon, he spoke fluent Arabic. He served in the

Marine Corps and was a highly decorated veteran of World War I. After the war, he received his doctorate from Princeton and was briefly the head of the American University of Cairo's English department. Prior to America's entry into the Second World War, Eddy was president of Hobart College in Geneva, New York. Coon and Eddy met in Washington before they were ordered to North Africa. Coon later wrote that Eddy was "one of the greatest men I have ever met, one of the happiest associations of my life." Eddy not only spoke perfect Arabic, Coon explained, but could also "think like an Arab."[50]

As part of Coon's propaganda efforts, he helped to translate President Roosevelt's Flag Day speech into Arabic. However, he did not believe a literal translation was suitable and with the assistance of two other OSS agents revised the speech. Coon stated that "every time Mr. Roosevelt mentioned God once, we named Him six times; and the result was a piece of poetry which might have come out of the Koran." Although the actual translation of the text was less ornate than Coon described, it was still steeped in an Orientalist imagination of what would appeal to a Muslim audience:

> Praise be unto the only God. In the name of God, the Compassionate, the Merciful. O ye Moslems. O ye beloved sons of the Moghreb [sic]. May the blessing of God be upon you. This is a great day for you and for us, for all the sons of Adam who love freedom. Behold. We the American Holy Warriors have arrived. Our numbers are as the leaves on the forest trees and as the grains of sand in the sea. We have come to fight the great Jihad of Freedom. We have come to set you free.[51]

The translation of Roosevelt's statement was produced as a leaflet and dropped into the Spanish North African zone and accidentally into the French zone. It was also read over Rabat radio several times after the Allied invasion. Coon claimed afterward that the leaflet helped convince many North Africans to support the Allied effort, "particularly those who had been wavering in an Axis direction." "It was very hard to explain to these natives, after the landing, why their condition had not immediately changed for the better," he added.[52]

With the success of Operation Torch and the Soviet Union's defeat of German forces at Stalingrad, the Middle East and North Africa were no longer a priority for military planners. As the Allies began preparing for the invasion of Europe, SI transferred Coon to the Near East theater. He was ordered to conduct sabotage and subversive operations in southeastern Europe. Meanwhile, R&A's Near East section was no longer focused on supporting military operations. Instead, the staff in Washington and Cairo began planning for the postwar.

Preparing for the Future

Allied success on the battlefield inspired Glueck to question anti-British sentiment prevalent throughout the region. In August 1943, he reported on an initiative by the British Council, the Foreign Office's cultural and educational outreach division, to enhance and expand cultural activities across the region. "The real purpose, however, it seems to me, is more than to spread just a knowledge of British culture among the Arabs in the Near East. It is rather to strengthen the entire British position as such," Glueck wrote. However, he argued that the United States should not follow suit and that the work and reputation of American educational institutions in the region surpassed any superficial and belated British attempts at cultural outreach. "These [American] institutions," he explained, "perform an excellent task of representing America without posing like a kind-hearted uncle giving away gifts. The Arab always asks himself when gifts are given 'Well, what are we expected to do in return?' "[53]

Less than year later, however, Glueck argued for an even more robust American presence in the region. In a letter detailing Britain's plans for its Jerusalem-based training center, he wrote, "The purpose, I take it, is to strengthen the British hold on the Middle East. Ought we Americans not methodically plan to do something of the sort." Yet as American intelligence activity increased, Glueck became uncomfortable with his role.[54]

There were also attempts to influence the use of OSS agents in the field. In November 1943, the White House requested that Donovan send Glueck to Northern Syria and Iraq to evaluate "irrigation and consequent settlement possibilities." However, Glueck's SI superiors objected. They argued that the new mission was unnecessary and an "obviously Zionist inspired" attempt to examine possibilities for Jewish resettlement that would endanger Glueck's cover.[55] It is unclear if Glueck was informed of the request, but he would raise his own objections to Washington's increased interest in Palestine. In May 1944, Glueck assailed the different individuals and officials traveling to Palestine to understand the political situation. "If it were within my power I should prevent all the sob-sisters and wise-acres, whether they are dressed in skirts or pants, in civilian clothes or military uniform from coming into the country at all, until the end of the war, at least, and quit stirring up trouble by asking questions, or what is worse, by trying to use their influence, such as it may be, to formulate policy in their home countries," he wrote. Glueck wished "that all of the amateur strategists and amateur spies and amateur soldiers and amateur statesman would stay away for a while, and give the country a chance to breath." These sentiments were eventually excised from his report to Washington. Although Glueck objected to the changing mission parameters, he continued reporting on internal politics in Palestine before ultimately returning to Ohio and academia.[56]

The shifting focus on Palestine mirrored Washington's more prominent role in the region. In March 1944, President Roosevelt informed James Landis, the American Director of Economic Operations in the Middle East, that "it was an area in which the United States has a vital interest."[57] Roosevelt's declaration built on a similar determination the previous February that Saudi Arabia's oil reserves were vital to U.S. interests. Although the determination was ostensibly for providing Saudi Arabia with Lend-Lease aid, by the summer the JCS informed Roosevelt of the need to identify and secure crude oil reserves for the war effort.[58]

In April, R&A's Near East section chief argued that the United States needed to begin planning for the postwar era. Writing to Langer, E. A. Speiser asserted that since the military threat to the region had largely passed, it was time to assess its "broader strategic and economic importance." He noted the interest of the Soviet Union and Britain in the region as demonstrated by the increasing number of Soviet legations that had been established. Speiser made particular note of the new U.K. training center established in Jerusalem, which added "to the already formidable British representation throughout the region." He referenced the mission of then under secretary of state Edward R. Stettinius, who went to London to begin planning for the postwar. The London meeting included a discussion of the postwar disposition of the British and French mandate territories in the Middle East. Speiser stated that the meeting confirmed the area's importance and that there was "no doubt as to the potential scope and magnitude of the stakes involved." "The political implications," he wrote, "are without precedent in U.S. foreign policy."[59]

Due to the region's importance, Speiser asserted that the United States needed to collect intelligence independent of its British allies. He explained that "we need research and analysis material of our own not rationed or predigested by our allies, who in this area may be, and in some respects actually have proved to be, our determined rivals." Moreover, the intelligence would need to be gathered across the whole area, due to what Speiser claimed were "the peculiar interplay of local interests, especially in the Arab World, whereby a matter affecting Saudi Arabia or Palestine will produce immediate reactions on Iraq, the Levant States or Egypt." He wrote, "With the existing close interconnection of the local economic, cultural, and political factors, an accurate appraisal of Turkish or Iranian sentiment is apt to be a prerequisite to the success of a given enterprise in any one Arab state."[60]

Speiser argued that the OSS's Cairo office needed to be enhanced and formalized. From the "standpoint of our national needs," he explained, it was irrelevant which agency was responsible for collecting and analyzing information. However, Speiser claimed that "R&A alone has the nucleus for doing this work adequately" and the State Department's Near East personnel were not up to the task, especially when compared to their British counterparts. In order for R&A to succeed, he recommended the "intensification in the direction of up-to-date direct contacts with the area." While the OSS was already based in Cairo, a "proper Near Eastern outpost" needed to be established. "What is wanted there is a small but hand-picked group of experts capable of commanding the respect of the British officials and native leaders while fully alive at the same time to our quickening requirements. In selecting such men we cannot aim our sights too high," Speiser wrote.[61]

Five months later, Speiser proposed an overhaul of SI efforts in Cairo. He explained to Sherman Kent that the Near East section had four main sources of intelligence: British, U.S. military, the U.S. State Department, and OSS agents. However, the majority of reports produced by the OSS were duplicative of the other three sources. He stated bluntly that "what independent residue there is, generally fails to meet our present needs. The exceptions serve by their very excellence to bring out the insignificance of the rest." Speiser asserted that continued OSS effort in the region was "essential" as "indications are multiplying that the Near East is destined to supplant and outdo the Balkans as a center of political gravity." Based on its geographic location and oil wealth, the area was "certain to command increasing attention on the part of the world powers," including the United States, which had already demonstrated its interest. Reiterating his previous argument, Speiser stated that "the task before us is to concentrate more and more on independent, rather than pooled intelligence, since in the Near East our Allies of yesterday are at best the fence-sitters of today and will be our rivals of tomorrow."[62]

Speiser maintained that the Near East section should pursue the "sort of intelligence that is calculated to meet our prospective future needs in the area." This required a shift from gathering intelligence for immediate military needs, "which is scarcely suitable for coping with the subsurface developments in so complex a region as the Near East." He claimed that the "tid-bits and handouts for which we might have been grateful in 1942 will not satisfy our requirements in 1945." "The kind of information that we shall need," Speiser explained, "is not likely to be on tap to secret operatives, who of necessity are restricted in their contacts." He suggested that "the required background intelligence be accessible to those who combine an intimate knowledge of the local scene—social, political, historical, and linguistic—with a keen analytical sense, in other words experts who can hold their own with the native foreign and political leaders while keeping their own counsel and forming their own conclusions."[63]

The best reports from the Middle East were prepared by R&A staffers recently assigned to the region. Since Operation Torch was completed, Speiser reported that SI personnel had not displayed an adequate understanding or knowledge of the R&A's needs or the situation on the ground. He added that "they have not shown, and could not be expected to show, the foresight and initiative needed to foreshadow trends and sift out possibilities." Speiser concluded by calling for an integration of the objectives and resources of SI and R&A. "Our future needs are certain to be greater and far more complex than they have been so far," he wrote, and would "lean heavily in the direction of expert research and analysis."[64]

Langer repeated Speiser's arguments in a memorandum three days later. Discussing the future of R&A's Cairo section, he confirmed the region's postwar potential and America's increasing interests. Like Speiser, Langer argued that new and independent intelligence and different types of analysts were needed for the future. He also identified staff members of R&A's Cairo office whose area competence or functional expertise qualified them for future intelligence work in the region. One of the men he mentioned was Harold Glidden, who remained in government service for the next two decades. Langer detailed the Cairo office's new responsibilities, which included collecting important publications, reporting on key figures and "potential leaders," and monitoring political, economic, and social trends. In addition, it would provide "judicious reports on the interests, moves, and prospects of the foreign powers interested in the area."[65]

While Speiser was arguing for what would eventually become the template of future area studies training, one of the leading figures in the creation of Middle East studies was putting theory into practice. In the fall of 1941, Richard Frye was completing his dissertation at Harvard when he was contacted by Walter Wright, his former Turkish instructor. Then head of R&A's Near East section, Wright asked Frye to serve as an analyst for Afghanistan. Fluent in multiple languages, including Arabic, Turkish, Persian, German, and Russian, Frye was also trained in Chinese and Japanese. Upon arriving in Washington, he was given an initial task to compile a bibliography on Afghanistan. However, after the attack on Pearl Harbor, he was ordered to Kabul, where the OSS believed the Japanese and German embassies had relay stations for Nazi radio broadcasts. Under cover as a teacher, Frye made the long trek to Kabul in August 1942, first by boat and then over land by train, plane, and bus.[66]

During his tenure in Kabul, Frye traveled throughout Afghanistan and India, including present-day Pakistan. Frye dispatched his observations to the Cairo office. When he wasn't attempting to gather information on German and Japanese activities in the region, Frye spent his days teaching. By December 1943, Frye was preparing to leave Kabul—he thought for good. Shortly after arriving in Cairo he was sick with dysentery and spent most of the winter convalescing. Although he was reluctant to return to Afghanistan, Frye was back in Kabul by the spring.[67]

OSS Cairo asked the American Legation in Kabul to support Frye's activities. While he was still operating undercover as a teacher, the Cairo office explained, "We want him to send us reports from time to time on the state of mind existing in that country, any occurrences of strategic, economic and other importance." Frye's reports were to be dispatched to Cairo by the Legation's diplomatic pouch. The letter added that Cornelius Van H. Engert, the American minister in Kabul, was free to correct the reports for accuracy and to avail himself of Frye's services if needed. It concluded by stating, "Naturally we are anxious to conceal his relationship with our organization, so we hope his communications to us and ours to him and any remittance of funds to him may be handled as discreetly as possible."[68]

Engert, however, was not as cooperative as the OSS Cairo office had hoped or its Kabul operative would have liked. Mirroring Coon's experience in Tangier and the bureaucratic infighting in Washington, the American

Legation in Kabul limited OSS operations as much as possible. As he prepared to depart Kabul for the second and last time, Frye detailed the problems of serving as a teacher for undercover operations. He explained that
American teachers paid by the Afghan government were not entitled to any of
the privileges afforded to the American Legation staff or military attachés.
This impacted everything from travel to obtaining basic supplies, which were
rare and expensive. Foreigners were prohibited from traveling within Afghanistan without special permits, which were difficult to obtain without
diplomatic intervention. In addition, teachers were forbidden to discuss
internal politics and there were no libraries in Kabul, except for a small
collection at the British Legation.[69]

After Kabul, Frye spent the rest of the war in Iran and Istanbul. His reports often mixed the political with the mundane, including information
about tensions between Iran's Provisional Government and British advisors.[70] In Istanbul, Frye's Russian language skills were essential and he
helped the OSS prepare for the postwar. Like Glueck, Frye demonstrated
the transition from wartime espionage to establishing postwar intelligence
networks and the tension between coordinating with Allies and spying on
potential competitors.[71] Indeed, the OSS produced reports in the spring
and summer of 1944 that focused on Iran's oil concessions and the potential
for great power conflict. These reports drew on the intelligence provided by
Frye and other OSS agents.[72]

Glueck and Frye were part of a larger effort to expand America's intelligence operations. In June 1943, Donovan discussed the expansion of the
OSS's covert operations in Saudi Arabia with Carleton Coon. Coon delivered his proposal fifteen months later. He argued that intelligence on Saudi
Arabia would be of the "greatest value" to Washington only if it was "a part
of intelligence from the Moslem world as a whole." Although his proposal
appears to have been developed independently, Coon echoed the statements
by Speiser and Langer of the benefits to Washington in establishing independent sources of intelligence. He identified three major U.S. interests in
Muslim countries: oil, air bases, and future markets. Coon called for the creation of a "special Moslem intelligence service" that would provide the United
States with advance notice of future conflicts and assist with preventing or
minimizing hostilities.[73]

The proposed intelligence service also required sufficient cover stories,
including from other OSS personnel. Donovan had previously suggested an
archaeological expedition, but Coon did not believe it would be advisable.

He claimed this was because European archaeologists dispatched to the region during the interwar period were suspected (or were in fact) agents and American archaeologists were subjected to travel restrictions during the war. "No foreigner," Coon wrote, "could believe that the American scholars were there for scholarly work alone." After the war, however, "we must use every kind of mission that sends Americans to the Moslem countries as cover. We must penetrate every expedition, every business concern, every government department that brings men into possible contact with Moslems." Coon also called for dispatching "genuine Moslems" to the region, arguing that without them the United States could not "do a complete job of penetration." Although the Syrian and Lebanese immigrant communities were "unreliable," Coon believed "a few trustworthy individuals" could be identified. Similarly, he identified a small group within the OSS "who speak some kind of Arabic to some degree; who have lived among Moslems and like them; whom Moslems almost always like and trust; who are full-blooded old time 100% Americans and who have no personal reasons for any loyalty to any other nation." He called for recruiting undergraduate and graduate students from leading universities, including Harvard, Princeton, Columbia, and the University of Pennsylvania trained in "Moslem languages, culture, and attitudes." Once recruited, supplemental training could be provided by OSS instructors undercover at the academic institutions.[74]

Coon volunteered for the proposed service and recommended that planning begin immediately. Because he was well known to British SIS agents, Coon explained "it might be more useful for me to return to Harvard on completion of my present duties, and get this thing moving under academic cover, than inexplicably to leave the best job in Anthropology in the United States to do field work that I would normally delegate to a graduate student."[75]

Although Coon's proposal was not implemented, he continued advocating for similar efforts. His report on OSS operations in North Africa offered a recommendation for a postwar organization, which he dubbed "the Invisible Empire." The new organization, he explained, would be comprised of a "third class of individuals aside from the leaders and the scholars." Like his proposal for a special intelligence service, members of the Invisible Empire would be tasked with "thwarting mistakes, diagnosing areas of potential world disequilibrium, and of nipping the causes of potential disturbance in the bud." "There must be a body of men," Coon wrote, "whose task it is to throw out the rotten apples as soon as the first spots of decay appear." He explained that if such a group existed in 1933, the Nazi Party could have been eliminated before it came to power. Like his previous proposal, Coon advocated that the new group would be an undercover organization that "must either be a power unto itself, or be given the broadest discretionary powers by the highest human authorities." Drawn from veterans of the OSS and the British Special Operations Executive, Coon believed that the new organization could be comprised of "a group of men, sober-minded and without personal ambition, men competent to judge the needs of our world society and to take whatever steps are necessary to prevent this society from permanent collapse."[76]

Eddy in Arabia

While Donovan and Coon explored possibilities for covert operations in Saudi Arabia, an OSS agent was already in the kingdom. William Eddy was ordered to Saudi Arabia following Operation Torch. His new assignment reflected the Roosevelt administration's growing recognition of the importance of Saudi Arabia's immense petroleum reserves. Serving initially as the special assistant to James Moose, the American minister resident, Eddy arrived at the American Legation in Jidda in February 1944. His first task was to travel throughout the region making contacts with local leaders and gathering intelligence. By August, Eddy replaced Moose and became the main U.S. diplomat in Saudi Arabia.[77]

Over the previous seven months, Saudi Arabia's importance to the U.S. war effort and the postwar reconstruction was discussed at the highest levels in Washington. In June 1943, the JCS informed Roosevelt that because domestic supplies of oil were insufficient to meet the needs of civilians and the armed services, the United States needed to secure adequate foreign reserves. In particular, the JCS recommended that Washington acquire a "controlling interest" in Saudi Arabia's oil concession. By April 1944, the State Department recommended economic assistance to the kingdom through Lend-Lease funds. Yet even before these determinations, Roosevelt made America's interest in Saudi Arabia clear to potential competitors. He informed Lord Halifax, Britain's Ambassador to the United States, that Persian oil belonged to Britain and the Anglo-American allies shared oil from Iraq and Kuwait. "As for Saudi Arabian oil," FDR explained, "it's ours."[78]

In December, Secretary of State Edward Stettinius Jr. informed Roosevelt that "an American national interest, basically strategic in character exists in Saudi Arabia." As a result of this determination, Stettinius proposed extending long-term financial aid to the kingdom. He asserted that the assistance would help strengthen the Saudi government against possible aggression as well as protect and develop the oil concession. U.S. military advisors in the country also believed that establishing air bases and flight privileges would assist with the Pacific Front. Stettinius reported that King 'Abd al-'Aziz Ibn Sa'ud "indicated that he prefers to rely upon the United States for the assistance his country needs and that he would adopt a much more independent attitude toward third countries if he were assured that this Government will extend adequate aid on a long-range basis." Stettinius's proposal, which was also backed by the secretaries of war and the navy, requested roughly $43 million over five years until the kingdom's budget deficit was resolved.[79]

As the U.S.-Saudi relationship developed, Eddy's relationship with 'Abd al-'Aziz also blossomed. The king was impressed that Eddy spoke Arabic and was concerned about the impact of a recent drought. Eddy also accompanied the king on frequent excursions to visit different tribes. As Stettinius was advocating for aid to the kingdom, 'Abd al-'Aziz was making his annual trip to Mecca in a massive caravan of American-made cars. While Washington was discussing how to resolve the problem of the kingdom's deficits, the royal family, and in particular the king, did little to contain their profligate spending.[80]

Saudi Arabia's key role in the postwar political and economic order was on display in a February 1945 meeting between 'Abd al-'Aziz and Roosevelt in the Suez Canal's Great Bitter Lake. Eddy accompanied the king on a voyage up the Red Sea on the USS *Murphy* to meet Roosevelt. The meeting was scheduled during a stopover as Roosevelt returned from the Yalta conference. In addition to 'Abd al-'Aziz, Roosevelt was also scheduled to meet Egypt's King Farouk and Ethiopian Emperor Haile Selassie on board the USS *Quincy,* anchored near the Egyptian city of Ismailia.

The trip up the Red Sea took a day and a half. Eddy described the interactions between the American sailors and their guests in *FDR Meets Ibn Saud.* He stated that "the sailors were much more impressed and astonished by the Arabs and their ways than the Arabs were by life on the U.S. destroyer." Eddy explained:

Neither group had seen anything like their opposites before, but the difference is that any such violent break with tradition is news on board a U.S. destroyer; whereas, wonders and improbable events are easily accepted by the Arab whether they occur in the Arabian Nights or in real life. The Arab is by nature a fatalist and accepts what comes as a matter of course and as a gift from Allah, all of whose gifts are equally wondrous, undeserved and unexplained. The Arab gets off a camel and climbs into an airplane without any special excitement even though he has skipped all the intervening stages of the horse and the buggy and the automobile. Allah gave the camel the proper equipment to walk on the sand and he gave the airplane wings with which to fly like a bird. There is, therefore, no reason to be astonished at the airplane any more than to be astonished that camels can walk or birds fly.[81]

Demonstrating the burgeoning relationship between the countries and between the American diplomat and the Saudi king, Eddy served as a translator for both Roosevelt and 'Abd al-'Aziz. The meeting on the *Quincy* lasted nearly five hours and the discussion ranged from Palestine and Zionist immigration to Saudi Arabia's development and the postwar status of Arab countries under British and French rule. According to Eddy, 'Abd al-'Aziz asked for and received Roosevelt's "friendship and support."[82]

Preparing for Postwar Area Studies

While the R&A division began preparations for the postwar, one major foundation was interested in replicating the wartime programs for academia. During the war, representatives from the Carnegie Corporation visited William Langer in Washington. In coordination with the SSRC and the ACLS, the Carnegie Corporation funded early university-based area studies programs and believed that R&A could offer an example for future endeavors. Describing the meeting in his autobiography, Langer recalled that "my visitors were impressed by the R and A approach to the analysis of complicated situations" and were curious if it could be applied to a university setting. "I gave them what encouragement I could," he wrote. Carnegie eventually funded the establishment of Columbia's Russian Institute and Harvard's Russian Research Center.[83]

The SSRC also recognized the increasing importance of planning for the postwar period. In June 1943, the SSRC informed Langer that it was establishing a committee on world regions. Chaired by Guy Stanton Ford, president of the American Historical Association and former president of the University of Minnesota, the committee report stated "the present war has focused attention as never before upon the entire world." It added, "The immediate need for social scientists who know the different regions of the world stands second only to the demand for military and naval officers familiar with the actual and potential combat zones." "Our need," the report explained, "for comprehensive knowledge of other lands will not end with the armistice or reconstruction." Moreover, it asserted that for the United States to fulfill its postwar role as a member of the United Nations, "our citizens must know other lands and appreciate their people, cultures, and institutions."[84]

The SSRC Committee discussed different European examples and how their experience could benefit the U.S. government, academia, and business. It noted that because of its "world-wide interests and age-old political wisdom," the British example was "particularly important." This included funding by the British government for the School of Oriental Studies at the University of London. To address the dearth in American expertise, the SSRC report called for the establishment of university-based area studies centers focused on research and graduate training as an initial step. It asserted that the primary goal should be to supply experts for government service and employment in the business sector and secondarily to train instructors and develop teaching materials. The report recommended the establishment of initial centers for "broad areas of great economic, political, or cultural importance" to the United States.[85]

Less than a year later, the Rockefeller Foundation in conjunction with the SSRC and the ACLS organized a two-day area and language program conference in Philadelphia. Led by the ACLS's Mortimer Graves, the conference gathered some of the leading American scholars, including Princeton's Philip Hitti. The hastily planned conference attempted to build on the SSRC Committee report in preparation for the end of the Army Specialized Training Program on April 1, 1944. Although the attendees were generally supportive of the area studies approach, their main concern was how it could be sustained by universities after the war. Graves asserted that there was "no necessary connection" between selecting the areas for study and those that were developed during the war. "There is no particular reason why the training technique should carry over in place of an educational technique," he added.[86]

Hitti supported Graves's statement and argued that the ASTP would not be an appropriate model for university-based areas studies, especially for Arabic-speaking countries. He added that the key characteristic for each area should be linguistic rather than geographic or political units. However, he emphasized the importance of literary Arabic to area programs. Hitti was careful to point out that defining an area by language would exclude countries with religious, historical, and cultural ties. For example, defining a region by the Arabic language would exclude Turkey, Iran, and parts of East Africa. He added that area programs should be prioritized based on the lack of existing resources and knowledge as well as perceived importance (e.g., Russia, China, "Arab world") rather than reinforcing existing strengths (e.g., Western Europe, Britain). Although not all attendees agreed with Hitti's suggestions, they found consensus by prioritizing particular areas due to their relative importance to the United States.[87]

The conference attendees agreed that area programs required cooperation across disciplines and university departments. However, they believed that this would be difficult to sustain due to bureaucratic constraints within universities as well as the need for a different approach that corresponded with the new discipline. In describing the ideal individual to teach an Arabic area program, Hitti stated that the "new type of professor" would be one who was a "cross between a political scientist and a social scientist and an anthropologist." "If we can find such a creature and train him," Hitti explained, "we may have to find a new designation for him." Other participants, however, were unsure whether the new scholar would be a "Superman" or a "Superficial-man." Hitti argued that since area programs were different from existing practices, it was a "golden opportunity" for experimentation. "A new discipline is being introduced into our curriculum," he asserted, "Let's develop new personnel, if we can."[88]

In order to meet the new challenge of establishing area programs and developing new personnel, some attendees believed that "native informants" could fill a short-term need for expertise. These native informants could either be living in the United States or individuals recruited from abroad for a short period of time to assist with training. The ACLS's Milton Cowan, who was also an OSS member, argued that these individuals could serve "as a storehouse of information" and did not require formal training. However, other attendees believed that native informants were of limited value. William Fenton representing the Bureau of American Ethnology argued that unlike trained scholars, the native informant was "a little naïve about his culture, as all good informants are." Fenton argued, "The native of the culture, even though he may be trained, has an inevitable bias in terms of one pressure group, one class group or another, and needs the unbiased perspective of the student of society," to assist with identifying the relevant information to be imparted.[89]

The attendees agreed that native informants were useful in language training. At Princeton, Hitti explained, native Arabic speakers were recruited to teach classes in colloquial Arabic. Another option was to recruit Americans living abroad who were educated in the United States but fluent in the language and culture of the region and therefore knew "the East and the West." A number of these Americans, he said, were children of missionaries or were missionaries themselves working in the Near and Far East, and some were involved in American educational institutions overseas.[90]

The Future National Good

Two months after Imperial Japan surrendered, the U.S. Senate Committee on Military Affairs began holding subcommittee hearings on the future mobilization of national resources. Among those giving testimony during the four days were representatives from academic associations and universities, professional organizations, major corporations, and government agencies, including the OSS. Brigadier General John Magruder appeared before the subcommittee on October 31. Magruder was Donovan's deputy director for intelligence and was recently named director of the Strategic Services Unit (SSU), the initial successor agency for the OSS's SI branch.[91]

Magruder cautioned the subcommittee members that national strength was not merely a function of military might. "This war," he explained, "has demonstrated that the role in wartime of the nonmilitary instrumentalities of strategy is only slightly less important than in peace." Magruder cited the wartime efforts of the Allied and Axis powers to utilize the "forces of political, economic, and psychological warfare and the large strategic advantages which came to those who used them with skill and with a knowledge of their power." Citing Prussian military philosopher Carl von Clausewitz, Magruder claimed that war was economics and psychology as well as politics. The general stated that during the war, political, economic, geographic, and psychological factors were "extraordinarily important" in the development of military strategy and that "estimates of enemy capabilities—a prime determinant in strategic planning—must be based on something more profound than knowledge of front line strength."[92]

Magruder asserted that a "strategy of peace" was needed. Such a strategy, he explained, must be based on the "knowledge of the geography and history of other countries, their political, social, and economic structures, their national psychology without which no analysis of their capabilities, aspirations and probable intentions can be made." Magruder called for the U.S. government to "do all in its power to promote the development of knowledge in the field of social sciences." Without government support he feared that the "best minds" would be diverted into "fields of less value to the future national good," handicapping American intelligence agencies. "The research of physical scientists is essential to the nation's industrial strength, so is research of social scientists indispensable to the sound development of national intelligence in peace and war," Magruder concluded. As part of his testimony, Magruder submitted a chart that illustrated how the OSS developed intelligence from the social sciences (see Figure 3). Senator Harley Kilgore, the chairman of the subcommittee, noted that Magruder's statement was particularly important because of the "sad lack of public understanding of the social sciences and what they do."[93]

Magruder's emphasis on the need for social scientists was echoed by other witnesses. Appearing on the first day of testimony, Wesley Clark Mitchell, president of the Social Science Research Council, said the U.S. government should "for purposes of the national interest" support research in the natural and social sciences. Mitchell added that "every problem of national concern has its human as well as its material aspects" and noted that the military services recognized the benefits social scientists could provide during the war. "The need for the best research obtainable on the human aspects of innumerable matters of national interest and welfare is no less in times of peace," he explained.[94]

The SSRC called for both direct and indirect federal funding of research. Mitchell explained that in addition to the research conducted under government oversight, funds should also be made available to nongovernmental and academic institutions to conduct research that would "advance mutually advantageous objectives." However, he cautioned that the SSRC was concerned that participation of social scientists within a government-run agency would make them subject to government control or bias the outcomes of their research. He argued that this problem could be overcome through contract work between governmental and nongovernmental agencies, which would include the "definition of suitable areas of work involving matters of national interest, and the specification of proper and effective terms governing the conduct of the work to be done." A more problematic issue for Mitchell was ensuring that enough students were trained in the social sciences, which

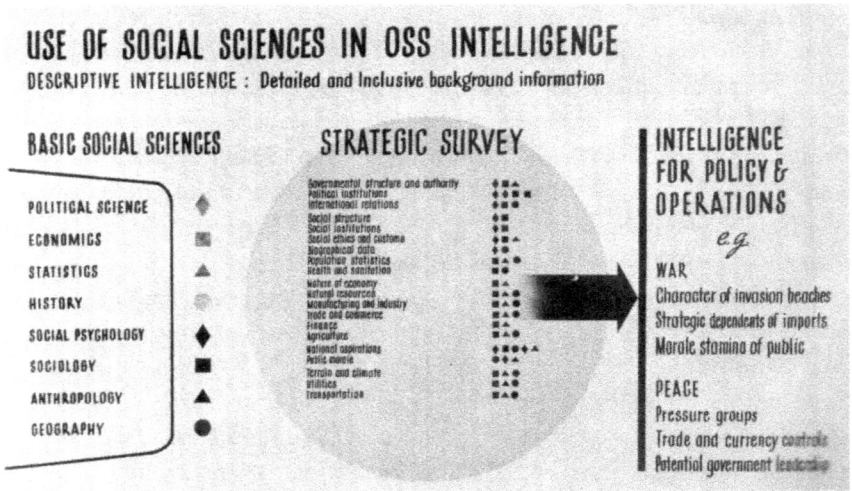

Figure 3. "Use of Social Sciences in OSS Intelligence" chart, presented as part of General Magruder's testimony to Congress. (Courtesy of the U.S. National Archives, Washington, DC)

he maintained was not possible due to the prohibitive cost of undergraduate education.[95]

Dramatically increased enrollment in colleges and universities after the war helped to address some of the concerns expressed by the SSRC and the intelligence community. The growth was due largely to the 1944 Servicemen's Readjustment Act (the G.I. Bill). However, the surge in student enrollment only addressed part of America's need for social science knowledge to match its increased global commitments in the postwar era. In the early Cold War period the State Department and nascent intelligence establishment actively sought partnerships with American universities to produce and analyze foreign area research.[96]

The End of the OSS

The end of the war also saw the end of the OSS. Although Donovan advocated for the creation of a postwar centralized intelligence agency with him as chief, a conflict with Roosevelt and enemies within the Washington bureaucracy ensured that would not occur. Donovan's influence experienced a sharp decline after Roosevelt's death.[97]

R&A was transferred to the State Department in 1946, where it was initially led by William Eddy. Although it collected a large number of preeminent scholars, R&A's impact on wartime planning is difficult to discern. It collected a vast quantity of documents and maps that were used to create country handbooks and regional surveys that military planners valued. However, R&A's final intelligence summaries and reports—"cooked intelligence"—were either disregarded by military and political leaders or were simply irrelevant.[98]

A State Department memorandum written by Near East Chief Gordon Merriam after the war discussed the benefits and limitations of R&A's analysis. "While a great deal of winnowing of wheat from chaff was necessary with regard to OSS reports, it must be said that on the whole they were of great value to us during these past two years," Merriam wrote. In particular, he cited reports from Greece as well as those on minority groups in the Near East. Merriam noted, "For the first year, reports from the field were practically worthless because sources were hidden and evaluation was impossible." However, after the State Department complained to OSS leadership, "a considerable improvement resulted." In spite of this mixed legacy, R&A's example and its alumni would have a far greater impact on academia and the U.S. government in the postwar era than their activities during the conflict.[99]

The end of the Second World War found some scholars returning to their universities while others chose to stay within government service. Although he volunteered for clandestine work at the beginning of the war, by 1944 Nelson Glueck was increasingly uncomfortable with orders for continued spying inside Palestine and Transjordan and eventually resigned. After the war, William Langer, Carleton Coon, and Richard Frye returned to Harvard, but over the next decade they maintained their contacts with the U.S. national security establishment. After briefly returning to Yale, Sherman Kent went back to Washington and became one of the key figures in defining the role of America's postwar intelligence services. William Eddy eventually left the State Department's OIR for the Saudi-based Arabian-American Oil Company (ARAMCO), but he continued spying for the United States and its newly established Central Intelligence Agency while in the kingdom.[100] Although he did not achieve T. E. Lawrence's notoriety, Eddy was perhaps the only scholar-spy of the war to replicate the British colonel's access and trust among regional leaders during and after the conflict. However, Eddy died before his memoirs were published and in spite of Coon's best efforts, the World War II generation had no literary equivalent to Lawrence's *Seven Pillars of Wisdom*.

Like the Inquiry, the OSS's R&A branch relied on American academia for research and analysis about different foreign areas. Although there were major differences in the sources and quantity of intelligence produced during the two conflicts, the analysis was still marred by racial and religious stereotypes and a paternalistic attitude toward the inhabitants of the areas that the United States sought to liberate or keep free. Most, if not all, of the scholars were trained in or influenced by the Orientalist tradition, and this was reflected in the country guides that were produced for American soldiers or the analysis to assist Allied policymakers and military strategists. While the influence and biases of the British Foreign Office and intelligence services was clearly present and transferred to American agencies, as was some of their research, American scholars brought and applied their own preconceived notions to the Middle East and North Africa. These perceptions were reintroduced into the academic study of the region after the war. In addition, Washington adopted London's commitments in the region and endorsed continuing British and French colonial rule while enhancing its intelligence network and posts. The Americans may have been liberators but they were hardly innocents.

World War II offered an extensive demonstration of the intersection of scholars and national security. After the war, scholars defended their decision to serve in the OSS and other government and military agencies because of the fundamental threat of fascism to the American way of life and the justness of the cause. Yet once the threat to the Middle East and North Africa was over, scholars began planning for intelligence operations in the postwar. While not all scholars agreed with this approach, a significant number of influential scholars from major universities drew on their OSS connections and operated in both academia and government intelligence, raising the question of where the line was drawn between the two.

Almost two decades after World War II ended, McGeorge Bundy, national security advisor to Presidents John F. Kennedy and Lyndon B. Johnson and later president of the Ford Foundation, asserted that "the first great center of area studies in the United States was not located in any university but in Washington . . . in the [OSS]."[101] During and after the conflict, the government and academia sought to evaluate the different wartime programs and determine what aspects, if any, could be retained for university-based area studies. This included an examination of the OSS. However, it was the OSS's veterans rather than its model that proved to have the greatest influence on the creation and expansion of area studies, especially for the Middle East.

CHAPTER 3

A Time of National Emergency

The National Security Establishment,
Academic Institutions, and the Origins
of Middle East Studies, 1947–1957

> If [educational leaders] recognize the many ways in which the
> resources of their institutions can help to save the nation by
> building programs in the humanities and sciences which serve
> national security as well as military defense, the nation will be
> safer—and so will our educational institutions.
>
> —CHARLES E. ODEGAARD, executive director, American Council
> of Learned Societies

Standing before a joint session of Congress on March 12, 1947, President Harry S. Truman called for the United States to support the governments of Greece and Turkey. Reading from an open notebook, Truman declared, "I believe that it must be the policy of the United States to support free peoples who are resisting attempted subjugation by armed minorities or by outside pressures." He recommended providing economic and military assistance to both countries. Truman warned that the implications were stark, "Should we fail to aid Greece and Turkey in this fateful hour, the effect will be far reaching to the West as well as to the East."[1]

The Truman Doctrine publicly enunciated Washington's strategy of containment toward the Soviet Union. Two months later, the Marshall Plan to rebuild Western Europe was announced. While the Truman Doctrine was an open declaration of support for the regimes in Greece and Turkey, it was also intended to covertly bolster the governments of Iran and Italy. Washington believed that its support would create a barrier to Soviet influence in Western Europe and the Middle East.[2]

Containing the Soviet Union and promoting economic development in Europe and the Middle East required trained specialists. However, by 1947 the wartime efforts to establish foreign area expertise were either orphaned or absorbed into existing bureaucracies. Yet their example and their alumni served as the foundation for the creation of Middle East studies in the United States. In the initial postwar period, the foreign policy and national security establishments were transformed in order to match America's new superpower status. Similarly, academic societies, universities, foundations, and the U.S. government struggled to create Middle East expertise to match America's growing interests and commitments in the region. These declared interests, coupled with rising tensions with Moscow, drove Washington's need to formalize area and language training. The overriding goal of these efforts was to create a sustainable supply of candidates for the State Department and the intelligence agencies. The interactions between the U.S. government and academic societies, universities, private foundations, and corporations were far deeper and more involved than previously conceded by the participants. Although they were influenced by wartime agencies, they were not simply a continuation of those programs.

The relationship between academia and the national security establishment was more complex and dynamic than its portrayals would suggest. During the early Cold War period, government agencies actively sought to collaborate on foreign area research and to recruit personnel from major universities and academic societies. Far from rejecting these overtures, academic institutions and scholars embraced and encouraged collaboration with the U.S. government to help guide and shape their research agendas and programs. In addition, government agencies and personnel played key roles in the production of influential reports on area studies by the leading academic councils. As the United States settled into its role as a global superpower, the federal government and academia were bound in a mutually beneficial relationship based on shared interests and ideals. At the center of these discussions were "national security academics," influential scholars who alternated between government service and academia and were instrumental in shaping both to reflect America's Cold War policies.[3]

Establishing the National Security Bureaucracy

The dissolution of the Office of Strategic Services (OSS) at the end of World War II and the transfer of the Research and Analysis (R&A) branch to the State Department was part of a larger transition toward the creation of a centralized intelligence body. President Truman proposed the unification of the armed services in a message to Congress on December 19, 1945. Truman's proposal led to the development and eventual passage of the National Security Act in July 1947. The Act created the position of Secretary of Defense and placed the different military branches under civilian control. It also established the Central Intelligence Agency (CIA) and the National Security Council (NSC), a coordination council to advise the president on all "domestic, foreign, and military policies relating to the national security."[4] The Truman Doctrine and the European Recovery Program (Marshall Plan) dedicated funds to support the CIA's intelligence gathering and covert operations. While the State Department operated under tight budget constraints in the early Cold War period, the CIA benefited from $685 million in Marshall Plan funds.[5]

By early 1948, a series of NSC directives were authorized for intelligence collection and analysis. NSC Intelligence Directives Numbers 2 and 4 identified the governmental agencies responsible for collecting, distributing, and producing foreign area intelligence. A subsequent directive, Number 7, authorized the "domestic exploitation" of foreign intelligence resources, which included initiating contacts with nongovernmental organizations for technical information and foreign intelligence. It also called for identifying and contacting American citizens with "high foreign intelligence potential" who were leaving or returning to the country for "briefing or interrogation."[6]

These directives instigated an unprecedented level of discussions and agreements between U.S. government agencies and universities, academic councils, and private foundations. To date, these interactions have only received minimal attention by scholars.[7] In addition, they reveal the importance of a governmental department, the External Research Staff, whose activities have been overlooked in the scholarship on the national security bureaucracy.

The NSC Intelligence Directives were finalized in the wake of talks held between the Anglo-American allies in the fall of 1947. Known as the "Pentagon Talks," London and Washington agreed to coordinate policies in the Eastern Mediterranean and the Middle East. Subsequent policy statements affirmed that the region was "vital" to American security. While Washington was implementing these policies, Princeton University established a program to assist government agencies in developing expertise for the region.[8]

Princeton in the Nation's Service

In spite of the determination that the Eastern Mediterranean and the Middle East were vital to U.S. national security, only one formal multidisciplinary area studies program existed for the region. Located at Princeton under the supervision of Philip Hitti, the Near Eastern Studies program attempted to build on the university's wartime activities. Walter Wright, former president of Robert College in Istanbul and one-time head of the R&A's Near East division, joined Princeton's faculty after the war. The combination of these individuals, resources, and ties to Washington made Princeton the ideal collaborator for the foreign policy establishment.

In April 1947, Princeton announced the creation of its Near East studies program. It cited the "rapid emergence of the Near East as an area of vital interest to the United States." Beginning in the fall, the university would begin training "men for eventual service in government, business, and teaching posts." Princeton boasted that this was first program to be established in the United States and emphasized the university's history of Arabic and Islamic scholarship as well as its wartime Army Specialized Training Program (ASTP). Organized through the Department of Oriental Languages and Literatures, the program was geared toward undergraduate education and offered interdepartmental course work on the "culture, religion, history and institutions of the Near East area" combined with language training in Arabic, Persian, and Turkish. Princeton also offered master's and doctoral degrees. The press release reiterated that "one of the objectives of the program was training men for government service or business positions in the region" and for "teaching and missionary work." It noted that the students would receive the benefits of a liberal education "irrespective of whether or not they pursue careers in the Near East."[9]

The State Department embraced Princeton's new program. Harry Lee Smith Jr., then assistant director of the State Department's Foreign Service Institute (FSI), informed Hitti that Princeton's announcement was "most enthusiastically received" in Washington. Smith added that a formal letter would be forthcoming to "express officially the interest of the Foreign Service and the Department in your program." Although the FSI welcomed the Near East studies program, it also recognized that language training was limited to writing not speaking. Those Foreign Service Officers (FSOs) without prior knowledge of Arabic or Turkish would receive initial training at the FSI before attending Princeton's program.[10]

Christian Ravandal, director general of the Foreign Service, wrote to Princeton's president, Harold Dodds, a month later. Ravandal welcomed the new program "since so few universities have taken an adequate interest in this important area." "For many years," he explained, Princeton has "been the source of rich talent for the Foreign Service and the Department of State. We shall follow with interest the development of your Near East studies and trust that you will have many able students preparing for the public service who will take advantage of them."[11]

Princeton, however, was unwilling to wait for the State Department's developing interest. In July, Gordon Merriam, chief of the Near Eastern Division, informed Loy Henderson, then director of Near East and African Affairs, that "Princeton let us know in strong terms that they have gone to great trouble and expense in creating facilities for advanced study in languages, history, and institutions of the Near East and that we ought to support them by utilizing these facilities more than we have."[12]

Establishing a pattern for future Middle East studies centers, Princeton's program was supported by philanthropic foundations and major oil companies. Initial funding was provided by both the Rockefeller Foundation and the Carnegie Corporation. Three years later, this was augmented with support from ARAMCO, the Gulf Oil Company, and California-Texas Oil Company (Cal-Tex).[13]

As part of its bicentennial celebration in 1947, Princeton hosted a three-day conference in April on "Near Eastern Culture and Politics." Under the broad title of "The Arab and Moslem World: Studies and Problems," the conference demonstrated the university's commitment to the new program and brought together leading scholars with the major benefactors and supporters of Middle East studies in the United States. Under the general theme of "new approaches in research," the topics ranged from Islamic art and architecture to international relations. In addition to Hitti and Wright, the presenters and commentators included Oxford's Sir Hamilton Alexander Rosskeen Gibb, Gustave von Grunebaum and John Wilson of the University of Chicago, and Charles Malik and Constantine Zurayk of the American University of Beirut (AUB). Attendees included representatives from ARAMCO, the Rockefeller Foundation, the Carnegie Corporation, the American Council of Learned Societies (ACLS), the State Department, and the newly established Middle East Institute (MEI).[14]

MEI was founded a year earlier, and like Princeton's program it signified America's growing interest in the region. Based in Washington, MEI was initially sponsored by the School of Advanced International Studies (SAIS). SAIS cofounder, congressman and future secretary of state Christian Herter, helped establish MEI. The institute maintained ties to government officials and major corporations active in the region, especially oil companies. Through its *Middle East Journal* and sponsored conferences, MEI promoted the study of contemporary events in the region. In addition, its leadership was drawn largely from the State Department and other government agencies.[15]

Princeton established a special program to train government and military personnel. The university provided area studies and language courses to members of the armed services, the State Department, and the intelligence agencies. In 1951, Princeton reported to the Rockefeller Foundation that it was "meeting a national need," due to "the continuing and increasing demand on it by the Armed Forces, the Department of State, the educational institutions operating in the Near East—both American and native—the industries and the general public."[16] On the program's fourth anniversary, Hitti declared that the university's emphasis on preparing graduate students for careers in government or business in the region was "further testimony to the continuing vigor of Woodrow Wilson's ideal, 'Princeton in the nation's service.'" He claimed that with international students joining the program and American alumni going abroad, the university's purpose was broadened to "Princeton in the world's service."[17]

Evaluating Wartime Programs

As Princeton was preparing to launch its Near East studies program, leading educational societies produced evaluations of wartime training programs. The American Council on Education (ACE) published an examination of the ASTP by the Smithsonian's William Nelson Fenton. Fenton, an ethnologist, defined integrated area studies as the concentration of "all the disciplinary competences (geography, history, economics, language, and literature, philosophy, political science, and the like) upon a cultural area for the purpose of obtaining a total picture of that culture." Fenton favored the establishment of area programs, even though they would encounter resistance and challenge existing university departmental structures.[18]

In a pattern that would be consistent over the next decade, Fenton argued that the areas to be studied should be based on "their importance to education and in international relations at the time." He ranked "the Arabic World" and "the Indic World" fourth.[19] "The Near East is a center of culture crisis and India has reached a climax in her long history," Fenton wrote, "Americans cannot afford to be ignorant of the potentiality for future history in the Moslem and Hindu worlds." To expand Near East studies programs, Fenton recommended relying on American relief and educational institutions operating in the region. He identified Princeton's Near East program as a model for future area studies because of its faculty and interdisciplinary courses. Unlike European area programs, Fenton claimed that Princeton managed to avoid interdisciplinary squabbles and competition.[20]

In May 1947, the Social Science Research Council (SSRC) published Robert Hall's evaluation of existing area studies programs. Hall was a political scientist at the University of Michigan and chairman of the SSRC's Committee on World Area Research. A specialist on modern Japan, Hall served on the Ethnogeographic Board during the war. The Ethnogeographic Board was created by the SSRC, the Smithsonian Institute, the ACLS, and the National Research Council (NRC) to collect information needed by the military services and intelligence agencies for overseas operations. Hall's evaluation was the first of two landmark reports on area studies produced by the SSRC in the early postwar period.[21]

The SSRC report detailed the positive and mostly negative implications of the wartime area studies programs. "World War II was not the mother of area studies," Hall wrote, "In fact, a strong case can be made that a healthy prewar development was not only retarded but, at least temporarily, warped in direction by wartime developments."[22] Thanks to wartime programs like the ASTP and the Civil Affairs Training Schools (CATS), Hall explained that there was an "acceleration in and enthusiasm for area studies." Because research by government agencies was organized by regions during the war, it served to introduce some scholars to the area approach. Yet he argued that this makeshift approach to instruction in area studies and languages was actually detrimental to the field's development. Although languages were generally well taught, Hall stated bluntly that "the wartime program is certainly not to be taken as the model for a liberal education or for training for research." "No campus was found in the course of this survey," he observed, "where any important residue of personnel or materials remains from the war programs relating to special areas."[23]

Hall reported that there was a legacy of bitterness and opposition to area studies on some campuses because of the wartime programs. This was particularly true of those universities with existing programs, as they lost a significant number of faculty members to government agencies and the military. These losses were compounded by government awards to the same institutions to administer ASTP and CATS programs. The dearth of instructors meant that many wartime programs were taught by instructors without the appropriate qualifications. In addition, a large number of faculty members were either killed during the war or decided to continue working for the government, leaving a significant gap in skilled faculty available to establish and direct area programs. As a result, Hall reported that "some of the opposition to postwar area programs is traceable" to the wartime experience.[24]

The loss of personnel was exacerbated by the lack of institutional support within the universities for area studies. Hall claimed that many of the prewar area programs were operated as a "labor of love," where faculty members were "convinced of the inherent value of the area approach" and "learned to work together and to benefit from each other's experience and knowledge." However, in these programs, "no one person had the responsibility or authority to make good the losses as they occurred, or to plan and provide for the future."[25]

Hall recommended establishing a national area studies program that would incrementally achieve global coverage. "In terms of the national good, we must not gamble," he wrote. Not only was it uncertain where America would face the "next great crisis," but world coverage would also benefit academia. However, since consistent quality across all regions could not be developed, Hall echoed Fenton's recommendation that the "critical" areas should be targeted first. Classification of areas would be based on several considerations, such as their "relative power" and "level of culture existing in an area." He noted that once coverage of "important areas" was achieved the United States should "move rapidly toward filling out the map."[26]

The SSRC report provided a cursory overview of existing area programs by region. Hall found that the Near East was "completely neglected," with a small number of scholars who had relevant language skills but were not knowledgeable about the region. He noted, however, that Princeton had "both plans and some resources" for the Near East.[27]

To help coordinate area research nationally, Hall called for the creation of a national organization affiliated with a quasi-governmental body. The proposed arrangement would be similar to that wartime relationship between the Smithsonian Institution and the Ethnogeographic Board. He argued that it could serve as a "recording center" that would maintain a list of area research being conducted in the United States and a current list of experts as well as existing centers for area studies. Hall also wanted the center to distribute "certain limited types of area information," similar to what was readily available in Washington.[28] Instead of a quasi-governmental organization, the national security establishment was already in the process of developing an agency to serve as a coordinating body for research on foreign areas.

Foreign Area Intelligence and Academia

In late 1947, the External Research Staff (ERS) was established to coordinate between the State Department and universities, foundations, and research organizations. Housed in the State Department, the ERS was a joint effort between Foggy Bottom and the CIA. Over the next few years, as the State Department faced budget constraints, the CIA and the Pentagon helped fund ERS. Yet it remained a division of the State Department.[29]

By 1952, the ERS had six major responsibilities. First, it arranged research contracts for the CIA and the State Department with organizations and individual scholars. Second, it maintained and produced a report listing all research contracts related to psychological warfare. Third, it coordinated the research programs of State and CIA with other federal agencies. Fourth, in keeping with NSC Intelligence Directive Number 4, it monitored and collected foreign area research from different scholars, organizations, and research institutions. Fifth, it developed "close and effective relationships on research of intelligence value with private foundations, professional associations, and private organizations." Finally, it collected and distributed external research products to interested government agencies.[30] In promoting its activities, the ERS explained to universities and private research organizations that its purpose was to draw on the "great deal of valuable research on foreign areas" conducted outside the federal government. It also sought to "provide all possible assistance to scholars in the social sciences working on foreign areas." The parameters of that assistance and much of the ERS's activities, however, are still unclear.[31]

Although the ERS had minimal staffing, it quickly established contacts with other relevant government agencies and departments.[32] It was initially led by Evron Kirkpatrick, an OSS veteran and former political science professor at the University of Minnesota. Kirkpatrick later served as the executive director of the American Political Science Association for almost three decades and married Jeane Duane Jordan (Kirkpatrick), Ronald Reagan's ambassador to the UN. Within weeks of the creation of the ERS, its staff met with the leading foundations, academic societies, and professional organizations.[33] This included the Rockefeller and Mellon Foundations, the Carnegie Corporation, the SSRC, the ACLS, the American Political Science Association, and the NRC. It continued expanding these contacts over the years, in particular with the Ford Foundation by the early 1950s. ERS staff also made contact with a number of former OSS members, including Allen Dulles, the future CIA director, and A. W. Schmidt and Alan Scaife, part of the extended Mellon family.[34]

In the fall of 1948, ERS staff visited almost a dozen prestigious universities. Kirkpatrick and Howard Penniman traveled to Yale, Harvard, Georgetown, and Columbia. While the conversations with university faculty and administrators focused initially on obtaining research related to Europe and the Soviet Union, Kirkpatrick and Penniman were also interested in other foreign areas. In addition to providing the State Department and associated intelligence agencies with the requested research, the universities asked for help in identifying topics and areas for future research programs and projects.

At Yale, Penniman met with a number of influential faculty members, including Frederick Dunn, director of the Institute of International Studies, and William T. E. Fox, then editor of *World Politics.* Percy Corbett, head of the Political Science Department, and S. B. Jones, the director of Graduate Studies in Foreign Areas, also attended the meeting.[35] During World War II, Yale's Institute of International Studies established ties with the American foreign policy establishment. Professors Dunn and Corbett were members of a luncheon group, organized by political science professor Arnold Wolfers, that included other prominent Yale scholars and visiting fellows. Wolfers served as Yale's main conduit to Foggy Bottom. He visited Washington every two weeks and communicated regularly with Dean Acheson, then assistant secretary of state, and traveled abroad on behalf of the State Department. The luncheons eventually expanded into a faculty seminar entitled "Where Is the World Going?" that discussed important foreign policy issues. From the seminar, Wolfers created study groups to address problems the State Department was attempting to resolve.[36]

The ERS initiative was well received at Yale. Penniman reported that "all who attended the meeting supported the [ERS] program." He added that

Professor Jones offered to "do research of value to the intelligence offices if the Branch and Division chiefs" provided "a list of topics to the agencies" through the ERS. Like Jones, other attendees sent copies of their manuscripts and graduate student papers, while Professor Fox offered to give the ERS manuscripts submitted to *World Politics* or other journals for publication.[37]

Established in 1943, the School of Advanced International Studies (SAIS) was another institution that had a preexisting relationship with the State Department. After meeting with ERS staff, SAIS agreed to expand these contacts, including providing the group with a biographical statement of each student, a list of a current research underway at the school, and copies of completed research papers. In return, SAIS "expressed a strong desire to have lists of basic research desired on various foreign areas to serve as a guide in the direction of their program." The papers received from SAIS covered a broad range of topics from "Wool as a World Problem" to "Trans-Jordan from 'mandate' to 'independence' 1918 to 1947."[38]

Georgetown and Harvard's Russian Research Center were also eager to cooperate with the ERS. Father Gerard F. Yates, then chairman of Georgetown's Political Science Department and acting dean of the Graduate School, agreed to help "in any way he could." This help included making all PhD and MA theses available to "the intelligence agencies" through the ERS. Father Yates also requested that research topics be provided when not prohibited by "security needs." In addition, Georgetown provided a report on all foreign area research conducted at the school in 1948.

Clyde Kluckhohn, director of Harvard's Russian Research Center, agreed to cooperate on "basic research" and requested a list of topics from the ERS. According to declassified but redacted FBI reports, Kluckhohn would "within limits, shape the research program of the [Russian Research] Center to the needs of the United States." This included guiding graduate students to perform dissertation research on areas or subjects, but without indicating the State Department's interest. "Subsequently the results of the individual research could be brought to the attention of the State Department," the report noted.[39]

Within a few years, however, Kluckhohn apparently had a change of heart. He resigned from Harvard's Russian Research Center in 1954. Laura Nader writes, "I never heard why he resigned and he never spoke of his resignation. No other anthropologist subsequently joined the center." Peter Mandler suggests that Kluckhohn reluctantly agreed to head the Center because he was "being sexually blackmailed by the FBI."[40]

The ERS distributed information it collected from the universities and produced on its own to the State Department's OIR and the Office of Research Evaluation (ORE). Among the initial items was a listing of area programs at universities and research institutes in the United States, including a report for the Near East. As part of its coordination with universities and private foundations, the ERS arranged for the OIR and ORE to interview scholars returning from research trips abroad. These interviews were partially based on a list of scholars with research projects funded by the SSRC. At least one Yale professor, Kirkpatrick noted, was not only debriefed after returning from an SSRC-funded research project in the Philippines, but "loaned extensive notes" to the ERS and agreed to provide it with a draft of his study before publication.[41]

Information collection was not one-way. The ERS supplied declassified reports to universities, research libraries, and scholars. It also provided a bibliography service "on special subjects for research workers engaged in projects of interest to the intelligence agencies." Kirkpatrick noted that "these services, as well as other aid and assistance given to scholars, not only creates good will but serves to improve the character of research done and to make the product more useful."[42]

The ERS deliberately sought to replicate the OSS's ties to universities and scholars. Evron Kirkpatrick later explained to journalist Christopher Simpson that the State Department and "foreign policy in general did not make as much use as they should have of scholars and foundations on the outside." Among the scholars the ERS sought for consulting work were European émigrés, Eastern European political figures and defectors, and former Nazis. In addition to obtaining information about the Soviet Union and the Eastern European states, the ERS helped secure university positions for its émigré consultants.[43]

The attempt to recreate the OSS experience was also demonstrated in the proposed Eurasian Research Institute. In ERS's first year, Kirkpatrick reported that he spent roughly a third of his time on the Institute. Although the Eurasian Institute was never established in the United States, the proposal demonstrates yet another example of attempts by the national security establishment to identify sources of foreign area knowledge and expertise during the early Cold War period, as well as their limits. Kirkpatrick developed the proposal with feedback from the State Department's George Kennan and General Donovan. Two years earlier, Kennan was the chargé d'affaires at the U.S. Embassy in Moscow and his February 1946 "Long

Telegram" informed America's policy of containment. Secretary of State George Marshall brought Kennan back to Washington to lead the State Department's new Policy Planning Staff (PPS). After the OSS was disbanded, Donovan returned to civilian life and private law practice, but maintained his contacts with the fledgling CIA. Donovan attempted to secure funding for the Eurasian Institute through the Rockefeller Foundation and Carnegie Corporation as well as wealthy OSS veterans. However, the effort was ultimately abandoned.[44]

By 1952, the ERS produced several reports for policymakers, including "External Research," an unclassified compilation of social science research on foreign areas that served as "a quid pro quo for scholars" who provided the ERS with "considerable intelligence information through the External Research program." The collected information was shared within the government as well as with individual scholars, university libraries, and faculty members. A second report of "External Research Papers" included reproductions of scholarly research made available to State Department officials. Depending on the information, these reports were either classified as "Official Use Only" or unclassified. The ERS also produced and distributed a third report, "External Research Papers and Memorandum," which provided officials with an unclassified summary of academic conferences and other relevant events in the social sciences. Finally, ERS developed a report entitled "Government-Sponsored Research on Foreign Areas." Classified as "Secret" and distributed to different intelligence agencies, these reports detailed government-funded research "on foreign areas and with psychological and unconventional warfare" and were designed to "facilitate the planning and utilization" of the research. The CIA eventually developed its own code for intelligence from academia: P-Source. Yet Washington's early efforts to identify research on foreign areas revealed the dearth of expertise within American academia, especially for the Middle East.[45]

Planning Near East Studies Programs

Writing from Beirut on a cold April morning in 1949, Mortimer Graves was struggling with the best way to create a program for Near East studies and language training in the United States. Graves, the administrative secretary of the ACLS, was in Lebanon to conduct an examination of the region's existing educational institutions and the possibility of collaboration with their American counterparts. His trip was funded by the Rockefeller Foundation, an early supporter of area studies. Graves wrote to John Marshall, the Foundation's associate director of the humanities, about the challenges facing the field. "Every suggestion for the stimulation of Near Eastern studies begins with the demand for more and better language teaching," he explained, "and we simply do not have the materials for such teaching."[46]

Graves's interest and involvement with Near Eastern studies predated World War II. In the late 1930s, he was a key figure at the ACLS attempting to reform and revise Oriental studies in America. As discussed in Chapter 2, Graves began coordinating with leading scholars in order to plan for postwar area studies programs in 1944. Four years later, Graves and the ACLS were collaborating with the SSRC to develop a multidisciplinary, long-range program focused on the modern Near East.[47]

The ACLS's newly formed Committee on Near Eastern Studies was comprised of the leading American figures in the field, a number of whom served with the OSS in the region. This included Harvard's Richard Frye, Nelson Glueck of the American School of Oriental Research (ASOR) and Hebrew Union College, the University of Pennsylvania's E. A. Speiser, and Princeton's Walter Wright. The Committee also had several representatives from the State Department, including Harold Glidden, Sidney Glazer, Edwin Wright, and Halford Hoskins.[48] Other prominent members were Princeton's Hitti, Chicago's John Wilson, and William F. Albright of Johns Hopkins and ASOR. Tasked with surveying and evaluating existing American facilities and recommending improvements, the Committee's final report was published in 1949. Although it boasted an illustrious panel of scholars, the Committee's report was drafted by Glazer and Hoskins of the State Department, as well as Myron Bement Smith, acting secretary of the ACLS and Fellow of the Library of Congress in Islamic Archeology and Near Eastern History.[49]

The ACLS report stated that the Near East was important not only for its rich historical past, but the modern geopolitical realities of the Cold War. Its proximity to the Soviet Union, vast oil deposits, and key transportation routes ensured "that Americans will have to make many decisions affecting the peoples of that area." "Without widely diffused knowledge of the Near East, public understanding of the issues involved is impossible," the report asserted, "Without competent experts in universities, in the professions, and in government, there will be no way to enlighten the public." It added that there was a lack of area and language expertise for the region stretching from Central Asia to North Africa.[50]

The ACLS's long-term goal was for American universities to surpass their European counterparts and become the world leader in Near Eastern scholarship. It called for a coordinated effort between academia, government, private foundations, and business interests to achieve this goal in ten years. Rather than create separate Near East departments, the ACLS recommended that scholars of the region be integrated into relevant university departments in the short term. It also advocated for the creation of university centers for area training and research, establishing American research centers in the region, and education outside of the university setting. The ACLS argued that establishing university-based centers was vital to advancing American scholarship. Similarly, overseas research centers were seen as benefiting both the United States and the host countries, where they might one day be absorbed into the national universities.[51]

Although the ACLS had ambitious goals, its proposed program was modest. The ACLS did not explicitly advocate for direct government funding of Near East studies. Instead, it recommended the creation of new language and field training programs and associated fellowships. It argued that new fellowships were needed for an "understanding of the problems of the modern Near East, their historical developments, and—most important of all—what the best Near Eastern minds are thinking about their problems and the world's." Building on Graves's suggestions to the Rockefeller Foundation, the ACLS proposed that it should have a central role in the language program, including the preparation of the Arabic, Persian, and Turkish training materials.[52] A year later, Graves participated in a conference at Harvard. He argued that government intervention was required if American universities were to reorient from a Western European perspective to one focused on the entire world. While Graves acknowledged the contribution of private foundations, he argued they could not achieve the task alone.[53]

In spite of Washington's determination about the region's strategic importance, the need for Middle East expertise remained a secondary priority. Although attention was focused primarily on thwarting Soviet influence in Western Europe, the Korean conflict spurred crisis planning between academia and the fledgling national security establishment for the entire globe.

Korea and the National Emergency

Early Sunday morning on June 25, 1950, an artillery barrage across the 38th parallel initiated the Korean War. Initially a civil war between North and South Korea, it became an international conflict after the United Nations authorized the creation of a U.S.-led force to intervene. As UN forces advanced up the Korean peninsula in September, the State Department began addressing its dearth of area expertise.[54]

Led by the FSI, Foggy Bottom's overriding concern was maintaining the small number of language and area specialists if President Truman ordered a full mobilization. The FSI organized meetings with representatives of the National Security Resources Board (NSRB), the armed services, and universities to "discuss the unanimous concern over the critical shortage of qualified specialists who would be needed to conduct cross cultural (language and area) training, especially for Asia and Eastern Europe, in the event of a national emergency." Because the NSRB had yet to classify language and area specialists on the list of "critical occupations," the State Department feared that they could potentially be assigned to "unrelated or less crucial work." If a national emergency was declared, the State Department argued that a unified language training program—likely under the Pentagon's auspices—would be needed. In the interim, existing programs would remain intact, including the FSI's courses and those at university-based programs for foreign service and intelligence officers. The State Department asserted that it was "important that all of these groups be left intact because they are already serving the national defense and because they should be available as functioning units to be taken over by the military" during a national emergency.[55]

By late October, UN forces crossed the 38th parallel and captured Pyongyang. After repeated warnings that they would intervene, Chinese forces crossed the Yalu River on November 2. Only two months earlier, Truman approved NSC 68, which advocated for a more aggressive containment policy. China's entry into the Korean conflict convinced the American policymakers behind NSC 68 that their description of the Soviet Union as an expansionist power with designs for world domination was accurate. To thwart the Kremlin, NSC 68 called for a dramatic increase in military spending coupled with a robust global containment effort.[56]

On December 16, Truman declared a national emergency. He warned of the "increasing menace of the forces of communist aggression." As UN coalition forces retreated back across the 38th parallel, the State Department began addressing the anticipated need for area experts once the Cold War turned hot across multiple fronts. However, it needed to determine what training resources and materials were available. This included evaluating existing programs and planning for a central agency to coordinate with the universities for their expansion. Foggy Bottom proposed a conference on language and area training to assist government planning and coordination. Representatives of government agencies, universities, research councils, and foundations were invited to participate in the conference.[57]

In response to the national emergency declaration and to assist the State Department's planning, the ERS produced a special report that detailed its existing contracts with researchers as well as contacts with universities and foundations. The report stated that the ERS maintained contact with the social science departments of over ninety universities and colleges. It noted that "cooperation between ERS and Area research programs and special research groups is of particular value to the State Department." ERS also reported that it maintained "continuing and close contact" with forty-eight foundations and research councils and institutions, including Ford, Rockefeller, the Near East Foundation, the ACLS, the SSRC, the Brookings Institution, and the RAND Corporation.[58]

American universities used the opportunity to remind Washington of their value. Writing from Princeton, Hitti informed the State Department that "our department stands ready in this national emergency to cooperate to the utmost limits of its resources with any agencies in Washington, civilian and military, in providing basic training in the languages and areas of the Arab Moslem world."[59] Two months later, the University of Michigan sent a similar letter. University Provost James Adams called attention to "the contribution the University could make in the present emergency." Accompanying the letter was a report entitled "The University of Michigan Is Ready to Serve in the National Emergency." The report detailed the different ways the university could assist the U.S. government and emphasized its area training programs.[60] The initial outreach by these universities was just the beginning of extensive contacts between academia and U.S. government agencies that expanded over the next few years.

The National Need

By February 1951, the State Department was considering an informal SSRC proposal for expanding university-based area studies programs. Under a heading proclaiming "THE NATIONAL NEED," the proposal stated that "in the present crisis," America was "faced with the urgent need of specialists with knowledge of the languages and peoples of major world areas and competent to work on economic, political or social problems of these regions." Trained personnel were needed in key government departments, including State, Defense, and the CIA. Existing university-based programs, the SSRC argued, could be doubled in size and "put to more intensive use" in order to meet this need. However, because existing area specialists were likely to be recruited by government agencies they would be unavailable to train a larger and younger cohort.[61]

The SSRC proposed government funding for the training of 1,000 area specialists over three years. The SSRC would serve as the coordinating body and establish an eight-man board of leading specialists from participating universities to set standards and coordinate activities. This included assigning the number of seats per training class at each participating university and selecting the trainees. Training was to be modeled on doctoral programs with two years of university-based course work and a third year in the field. Course work would range from language training and general area background to specialized classes and research. Depending on their status, students would require a deferment during the training period.[62]

Although the State Department considered the SSRC proposal to be "highly desirable and in the national interest," it had reservations. Foggy Bottom shared the SSRC's fears that the existing cohort of university-based language and area training personnel would be "dissipated" by the national emergency unless existing centers received a "reasonable flow of students or trainees." However, the proposed military deferments for graduate study were deemed unlikely and required the support of the Pentagon and the Selective Service. Moreover, in the absence of a national policy on deferments, the State Department asserted that language and area studies would be competing with the physical sciences, which were perceived to have stronger support in the military and Congress.[63] To bypass the deferment issue, Foggy Bottom proposed expanding language and area training for existing government employees, rather than adopting the SSRC's focus on university students.

Congressional funding was a key requirement and second major obstacle. In discussing the SSRC proposal, the State Department acknowledged that Congress had "traditionally been conservative with respect to Federal grants for education." A State Department staff study asserted that those representing the program before Congress "must be able to refute successfully the charge that the program is designed to foster an 'aristocracy of brains' at the taxpayer's expense while the average young American is required to don a uniform." Regardless of federal funding, the State Department emphasized that "full use should be made of funds supplied by foundations," in particular the Ford Foundation.[64]

To obtain the necessary funding, Foggy Bottom emphasized the national security implications. Under Secretary of State James Webb explained to the Bureau of the Budget (BOB) that the proposed training program was "designed to meet the urgent need for specialists" by key national security agencies "for work essential to the national interest." "With its responsibility for effective diplomacy in the present 'cold war,'" Webb stated that the State Department "must have in the universities educational programs which will produce the kinds of trained specialists needed for work in critical areas of the world." Area specialists, he argued, were "no less vital to the national interest than highly trained physical scientists." To "meet this national need," Webb called for maintaining and strengthening existing programs for language and area instruction.[65]

The State Department staff study reinforced the SSRC's proposal. America's leadership in the Cold War and its increased global commitments, the study explained, "placed a high premium on persons who can speak and read the difficult languages involved, who possess expert knowledge about the critical areas of the world, and who can interpret the interrelated facts of economics, politics, culture, and geography." The study added, "It must be assumed that the Soviet Union has placed as much importance on this vital cog in its foreign affairs machine as it has on machinery for disseminating propaganda."[66]

Internal State Department discussions also took place under the cloud of Wisconsin Senator Joseph McCarthy's accusations that communists had infiltrated the U.S. government. Although State Department personnel were subjected to a loyalty review in the initial postwar period, Foggy Bottom was one of McCarthy's targets. The staff study insisted on "adequate provisions" to verify the "security and loyalty fitness" of students receiving government funds. It also recommended greater departmental input into the students selected for training to ensure that they would meet the different employment requirements of the various agencies invested in the program. For employment in the State Department, "a premium would be placed on securing well-rounded individuals willing to serve abroad and able to represent the United States in its foreign relations."[67]

Ensuring the loyalty of future employees was one concern, training them was another obstacle to overcome. As part of the national emergency declaration, Truman created the Office of Defense Mobilization (ODM). Tasked with overseeing industrial mobilization, the ODM interfaced with the NSC and the NSRB. In March 1951, Robert Clark, the director of the NSRB's Manpower Office, assessed the state of area expertise. Clark wrote Arthur Flemming, then assistant to the director of ODM, that the U.S. government suffered from a lack of experts on the Middle East and East Asia, including Korea. "Our manpower resources in understanding and dealing effectively with Middle Eastern countries are inadequate in the extreme," Clark reported. He explained there were only eight to ten universities in the United States that offered area and language training and they were "staffed with a bare minimum of competent specialists." This concern was compounded by the fact that many of the specialists were foreign born and could not qualify for the appropriate security clearances.[68]

The lack of expertise was further exacerbated by the even greater dearth of knowledge about the actual requirements of the government agencies and the availability of resources nationwide. Clark explained that the most thorough estimates were those of the ACLS's Graves, who believed that Washington would need a minimum of 1,200 language specialists to cover all world regions. Even though Graves conceded that the estimates were arbitrary, Clark explained that they benefited from his knowledge and "extensive contact with the departments of government using such personnel." In short, they were the best guess available. Clark echoed Graves's assessment that the United States did not have "even an approximation of this minimum." "In contrast with the bleak resource outlook in this highly important field," Clark warned, "our requirements are already pressing and growing rapidly." In addition to the key national security agencies, he noted that area specialists were also needed at the UN, NATO, and for Marshall Plan–related programs, as well as in the private sector. "As our broad security programs develop," Clark advised, the "need for specialists in foreign languages and cultures will be more urgently needed as advisors in policy formulation and execution, as administrators, as technicians in special problems, and as observers."[69]

Even though the State Department was exploring how to expand language and area training, its own center was underutilized. By 1951, there were only thirty FSOs enrolled in the FSI's year-long language and area training program. According to the State Department staff study, the actual number should have been 200 FSOs enrolled each year for the next four to five years. However, it warned that this number could be achieved only "at the expense of crippling essential operations." Moreover, FSI staff acknowledged that the institute could not meet the expected demand for specialists without an infusion of funding, additional support, and expansion of existing university-based centers.[70]

The FSI's training program was deteriorating. Frank Hopkins, the FSI's acting director, reported that it was "difficult to get sufficient officers to express an interest in Asian specializations, and it is very difficult to make them available for training even when they display interest." Hopkins believed that one benefit of an expanded government training program would be to reassure the universities, which were considering abandoning their Asian area studies programs due to a dearth of students.[71]

Hopkins offered his own training proposal. Although less ambitious than the SSRC, it would still "give the universities assurance that they could stay in the area training business." Hopkins argued that existing university-based training and research centers needed to be maintained in order to "handle large volumes of important area research" on behalf of the key national security and governmental agencies that lacked the appropriate personnel. In addition, the State Department was securing authorization from President Truman to lead an interdepartmental effort that would "mobilize the various agencies for immediate joint action to utilize the university centers while they are still in existence, and thereby to preserve and maintain them in operation throughout the entire emergency period."[72]

Negotiating a Gentleman's Agreement

On March 20, 1951, the FSI hosted an "informal meeting" between representatives of key government agencies and academia. Chaired by Elmer Staats, assistant director of BOB, the meeting's agenda was largely based on the SSRC proposal and the State Department staff study. The discussion largely centered on identifying trainees, priorities for their assignment, and coordination between governmental and nongovernmental institutions.[73]

Arguably the most influential figure attending the meeting was E. Pendleton Herring. Herring was the president of the SSRC and the first dean of

Harvard's School of Public Administration. Although there were vastly more powerful agencies in the room, many of the government representatives were mid-level officials. In contrast, Herring helped shape the postwar national security bureaucracy. Herring's *The Impact of War: Our American Democracy under Arms* was published several months before the Japanese attack on Pearl Harbor and examined the tenuous balance between democratic governance and national security during wartime. Herring was given the opportunity to adapt his theory into policy while serving on a government committee that developed a plan for unifying the armed services. Under the leadership of Ferdinand Eberhardt, the former vice chairman of the War Productions Board, the committee's plan eventually became the National Security Act of 1947.

The SSRC proposal bore all of the hallmarks of Herring's corporatist philosophy. Herring believed that in a time of total war the national security institutions should be managed by governmental, business, and academic elites. During wartime these groups would act as "national symphony," balancing out their different and at times competing interests to achieve victory.[74] Herring was joined by Yale professor Wendell C. Bennett, an anthropologist who served on the Ethnogeographic Board during the war. Over the previous two years, Bennett conducted a follow-up to the SSRC's 1947 area studies report authored by Robert Hall. Bennett's findings served as the basis for the SSRC's area studies proposal to the State Department.[75]

The most enthusiastic support for the SSRC's proposal came from the State Department and the CIA. FSI's Frank Hopkins endorsed the proposal and advocated for coordination between the different government agencies. Matthew Baird, the CIA's director of training, explained there was "tremendous demand for the type of 'end product' envisaged in the SSRC proposal." However, both Hopkins and Baird wanted to make some changes, particularly to the fellowships and military deferments. Although the armed services hoped to benefit from an eventual area studies program, their representatives at the meeting indicated they did not want to be involved in the planning effort.[76]

Herring and ACLS director Charles Odegaard warned the participants of the need to act quickly. Government coordination was essential, Odegaard explained, as the foundations that provided the initial funding for area centers were unable to finance their expansion. "The point had been reached where private foundations might turn away from this field," he cautioned, and to "retain interest on the part of the foundations, some indication of government interest must be shown."[77]

The participants, led by the CIA's Colonel Baird, agreed that a long-term plan was essential. BOB's Elmer Staats explained that a presidential letter was required to authorize the State Department to lead the initiative and coordinate with the other agencies present at the meeting. In addition, Congress needed to consider legislation for the creation of a fellowship program for graduate students and government personnel. Pending congressional approval, the interagency group was to assess how much training could be completed under existing authorizations. "The whole program," Staats suggested, "should be looked at in terms of a long-range plan of research in the interests of our national security."[78]

Until a program was created, however, the academic councils feared that government agencies would poach faculty from different area studies centers. Baird suggested that the agencies represented at the meeting adopt a "gentleman's agreement" not to raid faculty. Staats supported the proposal and said it would be incorporated into the presidential letter. Until Truman signed the letter, Staats recommended that the State Department convene informal meetings to coordinate between the different parties.[79]

Two days later, the FSI convened the first informal interagency meeting. Although the government agencies believed the SSRC proposal was insufficient, the national emergency declaration provided a unique opportunity to resolve, through a single program, the related problems of an inadequate number of specialists and training facilities. However, implementing the program would not be a trivial task. In spite of the hopes of a "gentleman's agreement," the attendees agreed it would be difficult to prevent government agencies from raiding existing faculty at university area centers. FSI's Frank Hopkins noted on his copy of the meeting agenda that "[the] State [Department] won't raid but can't be sure." The attendees also believed it would be difficult to prevent reserve officers or area center faculty from being activated for military service. This latter issue was further complicated by a number of different groups attempting to make special arrangements to retain their staff.[80]

The participants expected that the legislation would be delayed. In the interim, the academic councils were encouraged to approach the Ford Foundation and other private foundations for funding. This would allow the universities to begin planning for expanded enrollment. FSI director Hopkins argued that funding from Ford was necessary for both the interim and a "nationwide buildup," with "some subsidies from Congress or FSI and other agencies."[81]

A follow-up meeting was hosted by the SSRC a week later.[82] Although the letter from President Truman was still pending, based on a circulated draft the attendees were aware that it would likely empower the State Department to lead the government's effort in defining requirements and training needs. FSI director Hopkins informed the committee that the State Department was interested in the SSRC's proposed program as well as area training for its own employees. The CIA and ECA, however, were only interested in area training. This combination of agencies required 500 specialists per year for the next several years, with the interdepartmental committee determining the need by area and specialty. Hopkins explained that the agencies would provide grants-in-aid to universities to support the expansion of their area studies facilities but would not underwrite student scholarships because they "could not be certain of securing the services of the students at the end of the training period."[83]

The inability to secure funding for graduate students made the SSRC proposal unfeasible. Representing the SSRC, Wendell Bennett stated that there was still a need for highly trained area specialists "both for the advancement of knowledge and the training of additional government personnel." Bennett offered two possible alternatives. First, to train new PhD's in the social sciences with the government agencies. After serving with a government agency they could then staff a university area center. The second proposal would "permit the employment of graduate students on research projects financed by contracts between government agencies and area centers." Hopkins thought that the proposals "might be feasible" and suggested that the ERS's Evron Kirkpatrick serve as liaison for research contracts with the Department. After he was briefed on the proposals, Kirkpatrick stated that they were "right in line with our needs and with conversations that I have been having with the SSRC and university people."[84]

Yet representatives from the universities warned their government colleagues of the risk of relying on recent college graduates. Philip Mosely, an OSS veteran and professor of international relations at Columbia University, was skeptical about the plans for training government employees. He warned that "there would be many misfits" if the agencies hired college seniors and that the program would be more expensive, as the government would be paying full salaries rather than fellowship stipends. Mosely also believed a fellowship program could be implemented faster than a program for training government employees and urged the attendees not to abandon the SSRC proposal.[85]

Mosely was another national security academic whose influence extended beyond Columbia, where he was also head of the Russian Institute. According to historian Bruce Cumings, Mosely was "one of the most important figures in Russian studies and U.S. foreign policy in the 1950s." David Engerman notes that Mosely was "the best connected Sovietologist of his generation," serving as a gatekeeper for joint university-government research projects.[86]

While the other university representatives concurred with Mosely's assessment, they argued that research contracts could serve a similar purpose as fellowships. In addition, the government agencies believed that if selection for training programs was similar to the process for entering the Foreign Service, the risk of recruiting poor candidates directly from college would be mitigated.[87]

The Bennett Survey of Area Studies in America

Before the discussions between the SSRC and the State Department were held, Yale's Wendell Bennett was conducting a detailed examination of area studies in the United States. Bennett's study was near completion by the spring of 1951, but additional data was collected after the government's ad hoc committee meetings were initiated. In May 1951, Bennett compiled census data from forty area centers in twenty-four universities and distributed the information to committee members.[88]

Published a month later, *Area Studies in American Universities* was a landmark report on area studies. It was also deeply influenced by the U.S. government's ad hoc committee, whose members were acknowledged in the preface. The published report contained revised versions of the information presented to the committee. However, the data was generalized and Bennett did not publish the university-specific information shared with the ad hoc committee. Instead, he noted in the report's preface that the detailed census information was on file in the SSRC's Washington office.[89]

Government influence on the study reflected the SSRC's involvement in area studies dating to World War II. Bennett explained that the SSRC's Committee on World Area Research "has given continuing consideration to the government's interests in area-trained personnel for the execution of its numerous, large scale international programs." He wrote, "The principal problem which faces the universities is how they can serve the government's expanding need for personnel and the requirements for specialized area training programs without disrupting the highly important function of training research scholars."[90]

Although the Bennett report did not specifically define the criteria for area specialists, the SSRC provided a detailed description to the ad hoc committee. It defined an area specialist as a "person possessing competence in any one of a large number of professional fields, such as agronomy, economics, or engineering, and who in addition has a special knowledge of the social, physical and linguistic features of a foreign country or region." The SSRC differentiated specialties into two general categories. First were scholars with a doctoral degree in a discipline with regional specialization, the ability to read and speak in local languages, and experience conducting field research in the area. The second category was comprised of individuals with two years or less of graduate training and the ability to read the local language and obtain spoken language competence. In addition, the SSRC noted a third category of individuals who had some level of area training, including a military program or prior language instruction.[91]

The SSRC focused on "integrated area programs" that relied on interdisciplinary faculty, research, and training. Their key features included intensive language instruction, joint seminars, group research, compiling and using specialized research materials, and drawing on foreign instructors and students for language training and cultural insights. In addition, the programs combined elements of the humanities and social sciences for the "full comprehension of the life of peoples of another culture."[92]

By June 1951, Bennett reported that Princeton and Michigan were the only universities with integrated area programs dedicated to the Near East. He identified five "potential area programs" at the University of Chicago, Columbia, Dropsie College, Johns Hopkins, and the University of Pennsylvania.[93] However, none of these programs was determined to be "adequate to meet the anticipated demand for specialists in the area." In addition, the continued emphasis on ancient rather than modern history was problematic. Bennett noted that inadequate language instruction was particularly acute for the Near East and that expertise needed to be expanded in the social sciences and economics.[94]

Preparing for the Future

Led by Robert Ramspeck, a former congressman and the chairman of the United States Civil Service Commission, the interagency committee convened in April 1951. It was tasked with identifying the short- and long-term needs of key departments and developing a plan that would not impact existing university centers and faculty. The committee's final report was delivered four months later and concentrated on the government's long-term requirements. It adopted the SSRC's definition for area specialists and stated that 1,500 specialists were needed over the next five years. Drawing on the Bennett study, it noted that certain areas were expected to have a "critical shortage," particularly Western and Eastern Europe, the Near East, and Southeast Asia.[95] Although the majority report acknowledged an "urgent need" for area specialists to "serve the interest of the United States in its international relations," it deferred making recommendations for the best course of action.[96]

Instead, the Ramspeck report recommended establishing a permanent interagency committee to address the issue and implement a solution. The committee would serve as the main interface between the government, the universities, and academic councils and replace any existing arrangements. In spite of the apparent urgent need for specialists, the permanent committee was not established until a year later.[97]

Meanwhile, a second survey committee was created to determine the needs of American businesses and higher education in relation to those of the government. Chaired by Lawrence Carmichael, president of Tufts University, the second survey committee did not hold its first meeting until February 1952. Although given different charters, both the Ramspeck and Carmichael committees assisted in finalizing area training requirements.[98]

Ironically, the interagency and special survey committees both sought to reduce the duplication and inefficiencies that plagued interactions between the U.S. government agencies and universities during World War II. The most notable difference between the two was the presence of, and discussion about, the needs of American business interests in the Carmichael committee. Represented initially by Standard Oil of New Jersey, the special survey committee determined that there was a sharp difference between industry's "on-the-job-training" approach for recent college graduates and that of the State Department and other governmental agencies. However, the committee members agreed that Standard Oil and other companies would benefit from graduates of area training programs. Building on the discussions with Standard Oil, the Carmichael committee authorized the creation of a survey to determine industry needs. In addition, it invited the SSRC, ACLS, Carnegie Corporation, and the Rockefeller and Ford Foundations to appoint representatives for future meetings and share insights from their experiences to date.[99]

The SSRC and Near Eastern Studies

While the government considered the broader issue of area studies training during early 1951, the SSRC and the ACLS formed committees devoted to Near Eastern Studies. The SSRC sponsored a conference in January 1951 attended by leading academics and government officials, including OSS veterans Carleton Coon from the University of Pennsylvania and J. C. Hurewitz, then of Dropsie College. Invited but unable to attend was another OSS veteran, Harvard professor Richard Frye. W. Wendell Cleland of the State Department's OIR division and an American University in Cairo trustee also participated.[100] The attendees agreed that the conference was convened at an opportune time and confirmed the government's need for Near East specialists. They unanimously supported the establishment of a committee devoted to Near Eastern studies and developed an initial program for the committee to pursue.[101]

A few weeks later, the SSRC's Committee on the Near and Middle East held its inaugural meeting in New York. The Committee's goal was to "contribute to a more complete understanding by the Government, people and scholarship of the United States about the area of the Near East." Illustrating the influence of the wartime experience on the committee members, they asserted that an "over-all area program" should be developed similar to "that attained by the OSS during World War II." The Committee members hoped to adapt the OSS's ability to pool resources for a better understanding of the entire region. They also determined that none of the universities had developed the ideal Near East program, including Columbia, Harvard, Michigan, and Johns Hopkins.[102] The SSRC Committee eventually selected "forces and factors of tension in the Near East" as its main research area because it was "related to [the] policy concerns of the United States Government." Committee members also believed that the topic would enable broad participation of scholars interested in the region and maximize existing university resources, including faculty already engaged in related research.[103]

By the summer, as the government's interagency committee report was finalized, the SSRC's Near and Middle East Committee prepared a draft of its own research program. Renamed "Dynamic Forces in the Near East," the program proposed a broad-based examination of the social, political, and cultural forces in the region. It tentatively approved ten projects to be conducted by committee members and nonmembers. To fund the research program, the SSRC committee approached the Ford Foundation.[104]

The Foundations

Prior to the National Defense Education Act, university-based area studies in the United States were largely underwritten by private foundations. Initially, the most prominent organizations were the Rockefeller Foundation and the Carnegie Corporation. Both foundations funded Princeton's Near East program. However, their involvement in higher education was eclipsed by the Ford Foundation. Inderjeet Parmar argues that the "Big 3" foundations served to "strengthen and mobilize" academe in support of American foreign policy goals. The foundations, he writes, "were directly engaged in extending and consolidating U.S. hegemony around the globe, especially during the Cold War."[105]

Established in 1913 and 1936, respectively, the Rockefeller and Ford Foundations followed different paths to funding educational programs. Almost from its inception, one of the Rockefeller Foundation's main goals was to support medical education and public health at home and abroad, including the American University of Beirut's medical school and hospital. During the 1940s, the Rockefeller Foundation was actively involved in promoting area studies with the ACLS. From 1946 to 1949, the Rockefeller Foundation provided over $3.2 million in funding for area studies, $2.4 million of which was for the humanities and $830,000 for the social sciences. By the 1950s, however, the Rockefeller Foundation began to question how and if it should continue supporting area studies.[106]

The Ford Foundation's reorganization and new purpose emerged after Henry Ford's death. In 1949, the Foundation expanded its mission toward the "advancement of human welfare," which included education. Acknowledging the threat posed by communism, the Ford Foundation sought to influence domestic and foreign policy and broader public discourse through direct engagement with policymakers. By 1951, it was poised to be the leading private funder of educational initiatives, and the Middle East was a top priority.[107]

As agreed during the March 1951 ad hoc committee meetings, the SSRC dispatched a draft proposal to the Ford Foundation. In the accompanying letter, SSRC president Herring informed Bernard Gladieux, assistant to the president of the Ford Foundation, that it was not a formal submission but rather "the basis for further discussions." Divided into two phases, the proposal mirrored the discussions of the ad hoc committee. It called for area centers to be expanded and a greater number of students recruited in the first stage. "This move," the proposal declared, "is of the utmost immediate importance if a beginning is to be made in meeting governmental needs and if the faculties of the existing training centers are not to be dispersed."[108]

The second phase would be initiated after the government program was created. Government funds would be allocated for the training of "substantial numbers of men from the Central Intelligence Agency and the Department of State." Herring explained that negotiations were underway and "it seems not unlikely that within six to eight months Federal funds may be available to pay for the training of officials and prospective Federal employees who are to be sent to foreign areas." The SSRC proposal asserted, "Existing area centers must be greatly strengthened if they are to be able to bear the increased load. Once the present crisis is met by holding the area centers together and getting a good flow of trainees started, the second phase of the program becomes of major importance."[109]

Echoing its original proposal to the State Department, the SSRC offered to administer the program. An advisory committee of leading specialists would be created for planning and coordination with the participating universities, but "final authority on major policy and fiscal questions would be vested in the [SSRC]." The SSRC requested $4 million over three years to support existing centers at fifteen universities and underwrite fellowships to train 400 specialists, with a particular focus on neglected areas including the Near and Middle East.

The SSRC's proposal arrived as the Ford Foundation began exploring opportunities for funding initiatives in the Middle East. In May 1950, a Ford Foundation delegation visited eight countries in the region. The delegation coordinated closely with the State Department and shared its report with U.S. government officials.[110] The trip was part of a growing alignment between the Ford Foundation and the State Department. In January 1951, Assistant

Secretary of State George McGhee wrote to Ford Foundation president Paul Hoffman to encourage "the Foundation's activities in the countries coming within the purview of the Bureau of Near Eastern, South Asian, and African Affairs." Noting the "areas of action" identified in the Ford Foundation's September 1950 Trustees Report, McGhee explained that "these areas indicate problems of special concern and interest to the [State] Department." He encouraged the Ford Foundation to support research on population growth and migration patterns, agrarian reform and food resources, and the social structure of rural villages. McGhee also encouraged research on "the impact of Western technology and capital development on traditional cultures and patterns of behavior," as well as labor-management relations in the petroleum industry. Although unstated, these suggestions reflected Washington's fears of the potential sources of instability in the developing world in general and the Middle East in particular. McGhee also sought financial support for American educational institutions in the Middle East. "In general," he wrote, "we can think of no more important sphere of activity and interest for private American support, and no better or more useful field for the Foundation to examine." Chapter 4 details how McGhee's suggestions aligned with the goals of the Truman administration's Point IV program and support of American educational institutions in the region.[111]

Two months later, Secretary of State Dean Acheson invited nineteen leading foundations to Washington. The meeting occurred as the interagency committee was discussing the development of an area and language training program. Hosted at the State Department, the two-day meeting discussed the domestic and foreign policy challenges created by the Cold War. While Foggy Bottom was concerned with the attitudes of Americans toward their new global responsibilities, it also sought to promote research on certain topics, including the impact of nationalism and independence movements and the requirements for long-term development programs.

During the meeting, Acheson focused on the importance of American perceptions. He told the participants that it was "the most difficult of all questions" related to foreign policy. Educating the American public, particularly about supporting key Cold War allies, was his primary concern. Acheson sought the support of foundations, universities, and associations in the public education effort, calling it "one of the most vital problems which faces this democracy."[112]

Although the SSRC's area studies proposal reflected the State Department's concerns, the Ford Foundation did not support the initiative directly.

Instead, it announced another mechanism to fund research in the region the following year.[113] The Foreign Study and Research Fellowship Program supported research in Asia and the Middle East, funding eighty-three fellowships in its first year.[114] While there were other research fellowships available, including those sponsored by the SSRC and ACLS, they were not exclusive to the Middle East or Asia. The Ford Research Fellowship became integral to scholarly research overseas; however, it also provided U.S. intelligence agencies with sources of information on other countries. Within five years, the State Department's OIR was providing some Ford Fellows with orientation before their departure, and the ERS and the CIA were debriefing them on their return.[115]

As the Ford Foundation dramatically increased its presence and influence in area studies, the Rockefeller Foundation began questioning its involvement. In a 1954 report to the Foundation's Board of Trustees, Director of Humanities Charles B. Fahs argued for a reassessment of how the organization funded area studies. Although Fahs reaffirmed that America had a long-term need for area studies, he stated that the Rockefeller Foundation could not "continue indefinitely as a nursemaid in these fields." He argued that an alternative would be a limited number of large capital grants to provide long-term support and stability to a few institutions where the Rockefeller Foundation had previously provided funding, including Princeton and Columbia. Chapter 5 details how Fahs's recommendations were implemented by the end of the decade.

Fahs also presented the Board of Trustees conflicting data on the state of area studies and the national need. He reported that there was an overproduction of doctorates for some areas and that some graduates with area specialization were unemployed. Moreover, the U.S. government had dramatically reduced its employment of area-trained graduates. By 1953, the national emergency had passed.[116]

Collaboration and Its Challenges

While running for president, Dwight D. Eisenhower declared he would "go to Korea" if elected, but not what he would do there. Eisenhower's victory at the ballot box appeared to portend an escalation in the Korean conflict. Instead, the death of Soviet premier Joseph Stalin less than two months after Eisenhower's inauguration instigated movement by China and North Korea at the negotiating table. Signed on July 27, 1953, the Korean armistice marked the end of crisis planning for area studies.

Washington's failure to fund area and language training led to greater reliance on existing programs. The relationship between Princeton's Near East studies program and the State Department was tested over the type of language instruction and the training of female employees. While the FSI was satisfied with the area course work, it was less pleased with language instruction. Princeton's language classes were designed to train doctoral students for research rather than government employees. Course materials ranged from translations of Islamic legal essays to classic Persian poetry. Foggy Bottom, however, needed materials that would prepare FSOs for assignments in the region, in particular translating media publications. The FSI and Princeton attempted to find an arrangement that met the needs of the university and the foreign policy establishment. When the FSI wanted a separate course created for government employees, Princeton sought to assuage its concerns by hiring an additional instructor and modifying the existing language course.[117]

The State Department also required a special accommodation for female employees. Prior to 1961, Princeton did not accept female students for either graduate or undergraduate degrees. During World War II, women affiliated with different government agencies attended area and language courses at Princeton but were not formally admitted or enrolled as students. When the university offered a similar arrangement to the FSI in 1953, it did not believe the State Department would find it appropriate. However, Foggy Bottom's apparent desperation for appropriate language training led the FSI to accept the informal arrangement.[118]

In spite of these issues, the State Department continued exploring possibilities for collaboration with the universities. The development of the National Intelligence Summary (NIS), the forerunner to the National Intelligence Estimate (NIE), was intended to provide policymakers with an assessment of key political, military, and economic trends and indicators by country. Tasked to the Director of Central Intelligence in 1947, the NIS was developed in collaboration with other government agencies, in particular the State Department's OIR. As observed with the External Research Staff, CIA funding also underwrote the State Department's analysis and development of the NIS.[119]

By May 1954, the OIR division initiated contacts with major universities for assistance with developing the NIS. After visiting Yale, Harvard, Princeton and MIT, OIR's Cyrus Peake determined that research conducted at the universities was of "direct interest and value to the NIS program."

Peake recommended that OIR adopt an experimental program in the fall, in which personnel would be retrained in research techniques used by political scientists and sociologists at the different universities. He added that the personnel would also "reap the benefits of research underway for strengthening the NIS basic research program." Peake reported that he "received a hearty response" from Harvard and Princeton to his request for office space and permission for OIR staff to attend and participate in classes. He added that "our people would be welcome and [the universities] would do everything they could to make the stay of OIR personnel profitable."[120]

Peake singled out Princeton as a definite site for training and collaboration. He found the university's research was "most interesting and suggestive in so far as future NIS needs are concerned." In particular, the research approach and interests of Princeton's centers were similar to the sections of the NIS related to the foreign and domestic policies of different countries, especially for the Near East and Latin America. He explained that NIS staff could benefit from their association with different research projects conducted by the centers as well as contribute to the development of future analytical tools and methods. Peake identified Dana Munro, director of the Woodrow Wilson School of International Affairs, and Fredrick Dunn of the Center for International Studies as potential collaborators. He wrote that Munro's background as a former State Department officer for Latin America enabled him "to appreciate readily the research needs of the [State] Department." As discussed in Chapter 5, the NIS and its successor the NIE, led to even greater collaboration between the U.S. government and national security academics.[121]

When the Soviet Union launched the *Sputnik* satellite, university-based area studies in the United States were still small and underfunded. Although the wartime intelligence and training programs provided an example, they were not a model adopted wholesale by American universities. Instead, they served as a reference point for scholars. Indeed, how scholars perceived the effectiveness of the wartime programs was largely dependent on which wartime agency they were affiliated with, as they ranged from one of the military branches to the OSS to the Ethnogeographic Board. Moreover, even when universities had wartime relationships and training programs with government agencies like Princeton, their new area programs still encountered problems in the content and focus of their curriculum. More than five years after it was founded, Princeton's Near East program had yet to change its focus to the modern history of the region.

While there were significant discussions and planning for federal funding for area studies driven by the Korean War, the crisis planning ended when the threat of a broader conflict with the Soviet Union passed. Yet these discussions served to formalize the network around which university-based area studies would be built: government agencies, academic councils, universities, private foundations, and major corporations. They also demonstrated the central role occupied by the two major academic councils: the Social Science Research Council and the American Council of Learned Societies. While the SSRC and ACLS collaborated on developing Middle East studies, they both sought a central role in the administration of a future government-backed area studies program. Although there was clearly an ideological component to the SSRC's initial proposal that was based on E. Pendleton Herring's writings and public policy experience, its motives were not purely altruistic or patriotic. Similarly, even though the U.S. foreign policy establishment, especially the State Department, was sympathetic toward the goals of the academic councils and universities to expand area studies, its primary mission was to effectively train its employees. All other considerations were secondary.

Without federal funding the potential growth of area studies was severely restricted. Although philanthropic foundations could provide the seed funding to begin programs, without governmental support the institutions were unlikely to expand their course offerings, faculty, or even the development of new teaching materials. In addition, the bilateral arrangements between various government agencies and different universities served to restrict rather than promote Middle East studies. Indeed, one implication of universities tailoring their research programs to the needs and interests of the U.S. government was that it ensured there was little diversity in the approach or analysis of the region. Moreover, as observed at Princeton, government agencies gravitated toward the university centers where the research, analysis, and experience reflected that of the national security establishment.

What stands out about the pre-NDEA period is the enthusiasm in which universities, academic councils, and individual scholars pursued interactions with U.S. intelligence agencies and major corporations. Rarely was there a concern about compromising academic inquiry due to these relationships or their potential for influencing scholarly analysis. Instead, the actions and reactions of the different institutions reaffirmed the notion that in a time of national emergency, a "national symphony" of different organizations with similar interests was required to work in harmony to achieve victory. However, on closer inspection, as these relationships were largely initiated before and continued after the Korean War, how the "national need" was defined by different groups appeared to be influenced as much by opportunity as necessity. Moreover, the planning discussions revealed that the scholars and institutions involved shared an affinity with the stated interests of the U.S. government and the belief that their activities would assist in achieving those goals. Yet federal funding for area studies had an unintended consequence. Within a decade, these relationships were called into question and ultimately frowned on within segments of academia.

CHAPTER 4

America's Sheet Anchors

Creating Cold War Universities
in the Middle East, 1922–1962

> [The U.S. Government] is trying to maintain American good will
> and prestige. They've found that the university does more than
> anything else to keep up good will for the people of the country
> towards America. It's a counter-irritant to some of the things the
> Arabs don't like. The Arabs don't like U.S. Government policy,
> but they really do like Americans.
>
> —BAYARD DODGE, former president of the American University
> of Beirut

In the spring of 1942, Washington was closely monitoring an offensive by Nazi Germany's *Penzarmee Afrika*. Led by Field Marshal Erwin Rommel, German forces threatened to oust Britain from Egypt and capture the vital Suez Canal waterway. As discussed in Chapter 2, William Donovan, head of the Office of Strategic Services (OSS), developed a plan to organize resistance activities if British forces were defeated. To prevent competition or redundancy with existing British efforts, Donovan informed the Joint Chiefs of Staff (JCS) that the OSS's newly established Cairo office would focus its activities on the students and alumni of the American educational institutions in the region. He explained that the students were the "mental and physical elite of these countries," while the alumni were "naturally the political and business leaders." Donovan claimed that the students and alumni would serve as "the backbone for sabotage and guerilla work" or simply support Allied wartime activities.[1]

Although Rommel's offensive failed, Donovan's proposal offers an insight into how American officials viewed the mission of the educational institutions in the Middle East and their students and alumni. Prior to World War II, the educational institutions founded by American missionaries were arguably Washington's most important interests in the region. Indeed, Donovan informed the JCS that America's influence in the region was due "mainly to a century of American missionary, educational, and philanthropic efforts that have never been tarnished by any material motives or interests." The United States emerged from the war as a global superpower with greater interests and commitments in the region. As tensions mounted with Moscow, Washington's view of American educational institutions in the Middle East also began to change.[2]

American educational institutions in the Middle East were viewed by the U.S. government as vanguards of American ideals and policies. The American University of Beirut (AUB) and the American University in Cairo (AUC) were the most prominent American universities in the region. During the early Cold War period, AUB and AUC—like their counterparts in the United States—drew on and benefited from their ties with Washington. Support for the universities reflected and was at times hindered by American policies in the region and globally. In addition, AUB and AUC were highly regarded by political and business elites in the Middle East. The universities emphasized their transnational identities to secure bases of financial and political support in the United States and the Middle East.[3]

American Missionaries and Education

While the Paris Peace Conference was underway, a new university was founded in Cairo by American missionaries. Led by Charles Watson, then the corresponding secretary of the Presbyterian Board of Foreign Missions, the missionaries conducted negotiations with British officials for several years. Britain's Colonial Office was initially unsupportive of the effort, but finally relented in 1917. It took an additional two years to raise the funds and the "American University at Cairo" was incorporated in Washington, D.C. in July 1919. Its doors opened to students a year later with an initial class of 142 students. Although AUC expanded over the next several years, it struggled with attracting permanent faculty members from the United States and experienced the typical growing pains of enrolling qualified students.[4]

Watson was the ideal founder for such an effort. The son of missionaries, he was born in Cairo and later educated at Ohio State University and Princeton. He was joined by fellow Princeton alum Wendell Cleland and Carl McQuinston, also a graduate of Ohio State. Watson spent World War I working with the Red Cross in Palestine and represented the interests of German missionaries in the region at the Paris Peace Conference.[5]

Like other American educational institutions in the region, AUC struggled to find the balance between its missionary heritage and an interdenominational student population. The university was originally envisioned as a training ground for new missionaries in Egypt and neighboring countries and its School of Oriental Studies was intended for instruction in Arab history and Islamic history and theology. AUC's early promotional materials reflected this emphasis. The university was portrayed as the "fulcrum" on which the "lever" of Christianity would overturn the "rock" of Mohammedanism (see Figure 4). Similarly, AUC placed an advertisement in *The Christian Intelligencer* in February 1919 that hailed the "retreat of the Turk." The advertisement noted Britain's predominant influence in Egypt and Persia and stated: "Jerusalem is in Christian Hands—GOD DID IT." This statement was reinforced with the claim that the Near East was the area where "God is working most actively," and that donations to AUC would further God's work (see Figure 5).[6]

By the 1930s, however, a rift developed between the university and American missionary organizations. Missionary groups argued that AUC's interdenominational approach was contrary to its original goals. Many of the organizations originally supported AUC with the understanding that it would assist their efforts in the region. Although Watson and other staff members claimed the university was interdenominational, in reality it had quickly evolved into an independent, nondenominational institution. Over time, fewer faculty members were selected from the ranks of the United Presbyterian Church and a greater number of Muslim and Jewish students enrolled in the university.[7]

In Beirut, the influence of the Syrian Protestant College (SPC) grew during the interwar period. Renamed the "American University of Beirut" in 1920, the institution was evolving from its missionary origins. The new name signified a change in the university's mission and goals toward an ecumenical approach to education. Writing in the *Atlantic Monthly* in May

IT IS A UNION PROJECT. In these days of petty bicker-ings, an interdenominational work which gives me a chance to work side by side with my friends in other denominations, gets my vote. In a proposition like this, it is right that we put up a great American University at Cairo, of which all Protestant Christianity can be proud.

Figure 4. AUC promotional pamphlet (undated, circa 1921–1922). (Courtesy of the American University in Cairo Archives)

1920, AUB president Howard Bliss argued that "modern" missionaries must not only retain their Christian convictions, but also demonstrate religious tolerance toward other faiths.[8]

AUB was concerned that the French Mandate authorities would interfere with its operations; however, the fears proved to be unfounded. The university was able to attract European, American, and Arab faculty members. Meanwhile, its student body grew and diversified. AUB's graduates were soon found in the government ministries and parliaments of the British and French Mandate territories. The university's expansion was aided by dona-tions from the Rockefeller Foundation, which were geared toward the basic and medical sciences. AUB was awarded grants to establish a medical school and hospital as well as funds to hire faculty. By 1938, the Rockefeller Foundation promised another major grant to support AUB's expansion. Al-though World War II delayed AUB's plans, it contributed to a closer rela-tionship with Washington.[9]

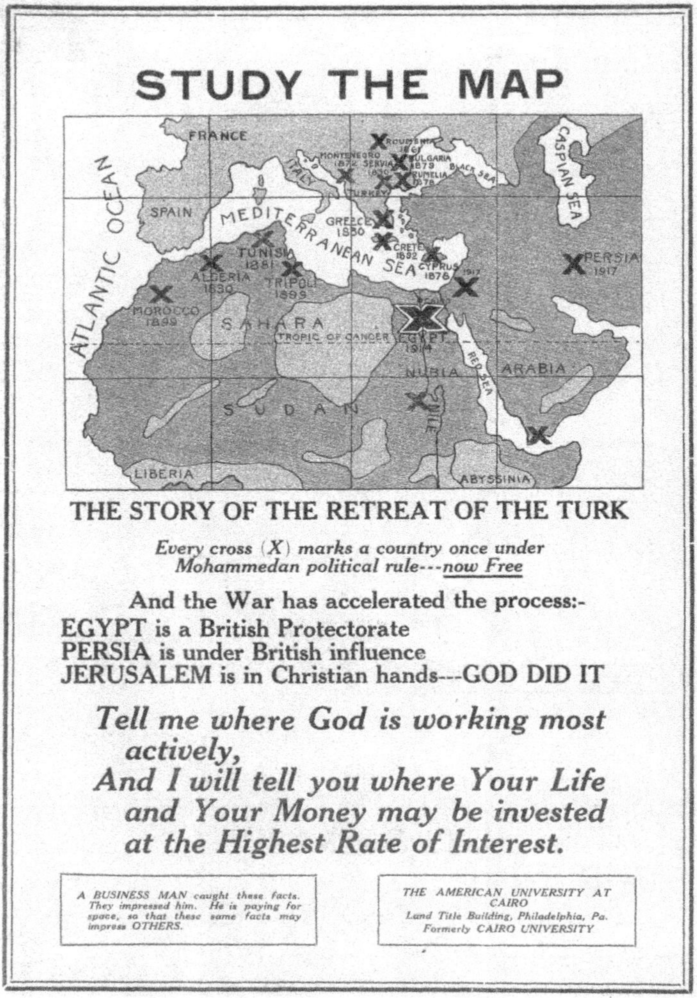

Figure 5. AUC advertisement, *The Christian Intelligencer*, February 19, 1919. (Courtesy of the American University in Cairo Archives)

The Sheet Anchor

Faculty and administrators from the different American educational institutions in the Middle East actively contributed to the Allied war effort. Stephen Penrose, a member of AUB's Board of Trustees, was the chief of the

OSS's Secret Intelligence (SI) Branch in Cairo. Similarly, Wendell Cleland, an AUC founder and faculty member, worked for the Office of War Information (OWI). After the war, Cleland shifted to the State Department's Office of Intelligence and Research (OIR) and remained actively involved with AUC. John Badeau, Cleland's colleague at AUC, also served in the OWI. However, Badeau declined an invitation to join the OSS. Then the dean of the College of Arts and Sciences, Badeau served as AUC's president after the war and later became U.S. Ambassador to Egypt during the Kennedy administration.[10]

Badeau explained his reasoning in a letter from September 1942. While he understood the need for the clandestine services and was "entirely in sympathy with its objectives," Badeau wrote, "I also believe that the work we are doing at the University is making a unique contribution toward winning the loyalty and cooperation of the Arab world for the United Nations." He added that the "contribution rests in part upon the fact that we are accepted in Egypt as a non-official American agency." "What I fear, both for the present and the future is that to engage in the activity you suggest *in the Near East* (i.e. where one is known) would be to rob the University of this influence," Badeau said. He added, "Even the State Department has said to us that we were doing [the] work that they, because of their official status, could not do. I do not want to imperil that kind of work nor the influence for American sympathy that it brings."[11]

Bayard Dodge, AUB's president, shared Badeau's assessment of the importance of American universities and colleges in the region. In a letter to the State Department's Near Eastern Affairs (NEA) division, Dodge explained that "what the Arab lands need, if they are to become stable, progressive and contented enough to withstand Communism and other dangerous influences, is a greater enlightenment of the people as a whole." He argued that this could be achieved through improvements in education, agriculture, science, as well as medicine and public health. Dodge recommended establishing a fellowship program that would fund promising Arab students to study in the United States and train future leaders. Before students were issued a visa to study in the United States, preliminary studies would be completed at one of the American educational institutions in the region. This would allow the students to learn English, demonstrate their aptitude, complete required coursework, and gain "an understanding of western ways of doing things."[12]

Dodge claimed that the American educational institutions, in particular AUB, were essential to Washington's goals in the region. "In order to make the Arab respect American culture," he wrote, "it is very important that such American institutions as exist, should maintain high standards and be worthy in every way of the names which they bear and of the announcements, which they publish." Of the existing institutions, Dodge asserted that AUB was the only one able to meet the preliminary requirements for training students. "The future of these Arab states depends to a great extent upon the efficiency of" AUB, he claimed. However, Dodge cautioned that additional funding was needed to improve and expand the university's facilities. "The Arab World is at a crossroads," he warned, "Whether it becomes sympathetic with our democratic Anglo-Saxon civilization, or is dominated by some other culture, like Pan-Islamism or Communism, will depend largely upon the coming generation." He concluded that "unless America does her part at this time, the Arab World cannot hope to have commercial stability or political peace."[13]

Dodge's letter was written at the request of Harold Hoskins. As discussed in Chapter 2, Hoskins's insights and assertions about the region and its inhabitants influenced the decision to establish the OSS's Cairo office. Although he was not selected to lead the Cairo office, Hoskins remained active during the war. In early 1943, he traveled to Lebanon twice. The purpose of these trips, according to Bayard Dodge, was to "initiate negotiations" for Washington to "subsidize American cultural activities in the Middle East."[14]

After returning from Lebanon, Hoskins promoted AUB to the State Department. He argued that recent immigration from the Near East combined with the Palestine question made the region more important to Washington. Hoskins added that American missionary and educational activities were more valuable to the United States than its limited commercial interests in the region. Because the educational institutions were backed by missionary societies and philanthropic foundations and not the U.S. government, he explained, they "added to the prestige that America gained from these efforts. As a result, American standing and influence have for many years been extremely high throughout the whole Near East."[15]

Hoskins warned, however, that American prestige had declined over the previous two decades. He argued that this was due to American isolationism after World War I, support for the Zionist movement, and Washington's association with British and French colonialism in the region. Meanwhile, Nazi propaganda emphasized these issues while also promising "complete independence."[16]

Hoskins asserted that the existing American educational institutions should serve as the backbone of Washington's efforts to restore its position in the region. "Higher education along American lines is the soundest form of cultural contribution to this area," he wrote. The universities and colleges, however, needed additional funds but feared that direct government subsidies would affect how they were perceived by the host countries. Indeed, this issue persisted over the next two decades. Hoskins proposed indirect funding for the colleges through private foundations or the Near East College Association (NECA) tied to a combination of short- and long-term projects, with an emphasis on agricultural programs and economic research. However, he warned against "short-range political or propaganda efforts." Instead, Hoskins emphasized that programs that helped raise the standard of living would "prove to be the soundest form of propaganda and political policy for the United States."[17]

Less than a year later, AUB received its first funds from the U.S. government through the NECA. A total of $175,000 was provided for student scholarships and for training rural extension workers by the Agriculture and Engineering Department. The State Department also provided over $10,000 for an Arabic-language history of the United States.[18]

As the war neared its end in February 1945, Bayard Dodge reiterated the importance of the universities in the region. Writing to Washington, Dodge asserted that American educational institutions could play a vital role in training the future leaders of the newly independent states. "The task of providing cultural leadership for the states of the Near East will not end but will really begin in earnest, when the war terminates," he wrote. "Subversive influences cannot be guarded against by neglect, but rather by the consistent and positive pressure of intellectual and cultural guidance," Dodge explained.[19]

After the war, Dodge believed that the existing educational institutions would need to be expanded and modernized for expanded enrollment. Although the universities did not receive significant assistance from the U.S. government before the conflict, Dodge argued that such support would benefit the people of the region and the United States. He explained that it would assist with the "establishing of stability and order, so as to add to the security and wealth of the world as a whole, America included," assuring "loyalty to the United States, in case there should be conflicts in the future."[20]

However, Dodge cautioned that the propaganda benefits of any support should be indirect. Any assistance from Washington, he argued, must be free of political pressure or religious influence. Dodge feared that overt propaganda efforts would "cheapen" the United States "in the eyes of the natives." Rather than building new institutions, he proposed that existing universities should be expanded and enhanced. He emphasized the importance of trade work and agriculture, which were lacking in the region. "From the point of view of propaganda, work of this sort is especially valuable," Dodge suggested.[21]

American educational institutions in the Middle East also had supporters within the State Department, particularly among former instructors and the children of missionary parents. This was reflected in a May 1946 memorandum by Gordon Merriam, chief of the Near East Division and a former instructor at Robert College in Turkey. Writing to Dean Acheson, who was then under secretary of state, Merriam argued that "our policy toward, interests in, and relations with the various Arab countries in the Near East, chiefly Egypt, Syria, Lebanon, Iraq, and Saudi Arabia, are of an importance which is certainly commensurate with our interest in the future of the occupied zones of Europe." He added, "We have many political, economic and educational interests in these countries. Our educational institutions, for example, have taken more than a century to build up, and they constituted a sheet anchor in the Middle East when we were militarily weak. These American schools and colleges require Arab good will for their continuance and effectiveness."[22]

Merriam's use of the term "sheet anchor" had religious and political significance. In nautical terms, the sheet anchor is the largest of a ship's anchors and typically only used during emergencies. However, it also has a religious connotation and symbolism. As historian David Hackett Fischer explains, the sheet anchor became a religious symbol during the English Reformation—"the sheet anchor of salvation"—and was adopted by Oliver Crowell's New Model Army during the English Civil War. Fischer argues that these Puritan symbols "became part of New England's complex imagery of liberty and freedom." Thus, when Rhode Island was initially formed, the sheet anchor became its emblem and was eventually adopted by Rhode Island regiments during the American Revolution. It still graces the Rhode Island state flag today. As a native of New England and former Robert College instructor, Merriam would have been familiar with both usages of the term.[23]

Merriam's comments were part of a broader discussion and complaint about the U.S. government's emerging policy toward Palestine and the Zionist movement. His memorandum to Acheson was in response to the recommendations of the Anglo-American Committee of Inquiry that called for the immigration of 100,000 European Jewish displaced persons to British Mandate Palestine. Even though London rejected the recommendations, President Truman publicly endorsed their implementation, creating a rare moment of public acrimony between the Anglo-American allies. In his memorandum, Merriam warned Acheson of the implications. He stated that "the Arab reaction to the Committee's recommendations has been swift and alarming" and "they give every indication of the intention to resist."[24]

Palestine and the American Universities in the Middle East

In spite of their strong relations with the State Department, tensions existed between universities in the region and Washington. Both AUB and AUC felt the direct repercussions of U.S. policy toward Palestine but they approached the issue differently. In response to Truman's statement on displaced persons, AUC president John Badeau attempted to gather support for an open letter of protest signed by the presidents of other American educational institutions in the region. In a letter to Dodge, Badeau explained that AUC had a policy of refraining "from taking any official stand on political issues—either Egyptian or American." However, because "the present situation causes such grave concern," AUC's University Council believed that "some step ought to be taken which would on one hand call the attention of American authorities to our position and interest here, and on the other hand give evidence to our constituency in the Middle East that we are not merely acquiescent in the face of a questionable American policy," he wrote. Badeau added that "such a letter would still maintain our official neutrality so far as the *actual* policy towards Palestine is concerned, and yet its implications would be clear to our constituency here."[25]

In his reply to Badeau, Dodge explained that it was a "fixed policy" at AUB to "keep out of political matters." He added that "if members of the faculty mix into politics, it makes it impossible to keep students from doing the same." "It is also true that we have a good many Jews on our staff and in our student body, so that it is very delicate for us to enter into the Zionist question," Dodge wrote. He cautioned Badeau that "anything which is done through the State Department will have little effect, as I am sure that the State Department is doing all that it can to keep the White House from being unreasonable." Yet Dodge was hopeful that "after election day the politicians will leave foreign affairs to the Department of State."[26]

Badeau responded eight days later. "Such a statement will probably receive little attention at home," he wrote, "but my hope was that it might be useful here." Badeau conceded, however, that the U.S. ambassador to Egypt was opposed to such a move and it no longer had support in the University Council.[27]

Although Badeau was unable to convince the other universities to join him in protesting the Truman administration's policies on Palestine, he reached out personally to regional leaders to distance AUC from Washington. Writing to Abdel Rahman Azzam, the general secretary of the Arab League, Badeau enclosed a lecture delivered at Princeton by his predecessor Charles Watson. Watson's lecture, he explained, "was prepared for Americans and seeks primarily to correct the misinformation they have received through Zionist propaganda." Badeau added that while AUC was an educational institution that was apolitical and nonpartisan, there were "opportunities for individual members of the staff while in the United States to correct some of the misunderstandings regarding the situation in the Middle East." He noted that as a recently retired member of the AUC administration, Watson felt that "he could speak on the topic of Palestine without prejudicing the nonpolitical character" of the university. "We are glad that he has delivered this lecture for as individual American citizens living in the Middle East, we are all gravely concerned for American-Arab relationships," Badeau wrote.[28]

In February 1947, Britain announced it was terminating its mandate and referring the "Palestine Question" to the UN. At the end of November 1947, the UN General Assembly voted to partition Palestine into two states: one majority Jewish and one largely Arab. The result was civil war with regional and international implications. By April 1948, the Zionist movement's militias had largely defeated rival Palestinian Arab forces. The capture of major urban areas in Palestine was accompanied by the forced expulsions and flight of the civilian population. Sheltered in other towns and villages within Palestine as well as the neighboring states, the Palestinian refugee crisis heightened the pressure on the governments of Syria, Egypt, Transjordan, and Lebanon to intervene. On May 14, the British Mandate of Palestine ended. The State of Israel was declared and quickly recognized by Washington. Although the Arab League authorized an invasion of Palestine, the member states had their own agendas. Divided by competition, undermined by secret agreements, and outnumbered and outgunned by the better equipped and trained Zionist militias, the 1948 Palestine War resulted in a re-sounding defeat for the Arab states. By the end of 1948, the State of Israel had expanded its borders beyond those called for in UN General Assembly Resolution 181, the remaining territories were controlled by Egypt and Transjordan, over 750,000 Palestinians had become refugees, and Palestine ceased to exist.[29]

Although the leadership of both universities appeared to disagree with the Truman administration's overt support for the Zionist movement, they continued to adopt different approaches to express their dissatisfaction. AUC and Badeau maintained an open political stance. In contrast, Dodge attempted to sway opinion in Washington through private meetings with the State Department and Army Intelligence. After Israel was created, Dodge was actively involved in relief efforts and ongoing humanitarian assistance for the Palestinian refugees scattered across the region.[30]

In a scathing telegram, AUC's Badeau criticized Truman's recognition of Israel. Dispatched to Washington on May 17, 1948, Badeau protested "on behalf of my colleagues and myself." He explained that it would hurt American interests in the region, cause the deaths of innocent Palestinian Arabs and non-Zionist Jews, and undermine the United States' "long record of interest in freedom and justice." Badeau's telegram concluded by stating that "as American citizens long resident in the Middle East and devoted to the best interests both of Middle Eastern peoples and the United States we are humiliated by the action of our government and strictly repudiate it. We urge that this action be immediately reviewed and altered by our government."[31]

Badeau's letter received wide coverage and praise in the Egyptian press, including newspapers published in English and French. In an interview with the Arabic-language newspaper *al-Assas*, Badeau explained that AUC was independent of the U.S. government and claimed that a majority of Americans favored the "just cause" of the Arabs. He also criticized Truman's decision to recognize Israel as driven by electoral politics. Egyptian prime minister Mahmoud an-Nukrashi visited the AUC campus two days later and thanked Badeau and the university for their "noble character and feelings."[32]

Arab League general secretary Azzam also wrote Badeau a letter of thanks. In his reply, Badeau reiterated his opposition to America's Palestine policy. He explained that "this decision of Mr. Truman made it impossible for us longer to keep still. I only hope that such protests will help in changing our present policy." "We are looking forward eagerly to the success of the Arab armies in finally liberating Palestine from political Zionism," Badeau wrote, "Only then can a new era of peace begin."[33]

A year later, Azzam was a commencement speaker at AUC's graduation ceremony. He praised and thanked the university and Badeau for their stance on Palestine. Azzam declared, "They rose in opposition to the unjust decision taken by their fellow citizens in authority. They protested against the action of the President of their country." Azzam's statement was reported by English, French, and Arabic-language newspapers in Egypt.[34]

Student protests erupted at AUB and AUC over the UN's partition resolution. The U.S. embassies in Beirut and Cairo monitored the situation on both campuses. After the initial uproar subsided, the U.S. Embassy in Beirut continued to track student activism on the AUB campus for the next three decades. Washington's support for partition also affected AUB's ability to recruit a new university president. After the UN General Assembly's partition resolution, the AUB Board found it difficult to attract candidates for the position. For example, the university actively pursued John Wilson for the position. Wilson was a noted Orientalist scholar at the University of Chicago and an OSS veteran with ties to the missionary community, but he repeatedly declined AUB's offer. AUB eventually settled on Stephen Penrose, the former head of OSS-SI Cairo, whose family had close ties to the university. Commenting on behalf of the Board's Executive Committee, Harold Hoskins noted that Penrose was selected in part to demonstrate to "the Arabic speaking population the unselfish purpose of [AUB] and the perpetuation of its instructive tradition."[35]

Cold War Universities in the Middle East

The Palestine conflict was only one issue that Washington grappled with in the early Cold War period. As discussed in Chapter 3, the announcement of the Truman Doctrine was followed by public and covert efforts to contain real or perceived Soviet influence in the Middle East. Seven months later, during the "Pentagon Talks," British and American military discussed "raising living standards." Among the British objectives was "to encourage the Middle East countries in all fields—technology, medicine, etc.—to look to the West." London argued this could be achieved by providing advisors in different fields and "by gradually linking Middle Eastern institutions" with those in Britain and the United States.[36]

British officials noted the importance of the "traditional link" that Syria and Lebanon "constituted between the Arab world and Western thought." Denis A. Greenhill of the Foreign Office's Middle East Secretariat asserted that it was "fortunate that American traditions of education and thought had played a part." However, he cautioned his State Department counterparts of the "possibility of communist influence infiltrating AUB" and described Beirut as "the center of communist activity in the Middle East." Greenhill explained that London "favored the extension of Anglo-Saxon cultural activity to prevent the spread of communism" and recognized that the British Council and AUB were "active in this respect."[37]

The State Department rejected Greenhill's claims of communist activity in American educational institutions. Joseph C. Satterthwaite, director of the Division of Research and Analysis for the Near East, South Asia, and Africa (DRN), argued that AUB could be "of considerable help in combating communism." W. Wendell Cleland of the State Department's OIR division added that "with only one or two exceptions," AUC's students had not been influenced by communism.[38]

A year later, the Central Intelligence Agency (CIA) identified potential threats to American security from the dissolution of the British and French empires. "Friction engendered" by anticolonial movements and economic nationalism in the Middle and Far East, the agency warned, could "drive the so-called colonial bloc into alignment with the USSR." The assessment called for the United States to adopt a policy toward the colonial territories independent of, but in consultation with, its European allies. It recommended that the colonial powers adopt comprehensive reforms in their territories and promote political, economic, and social development. This would "neutralize the more violent aspects of native nationalism and to substitute orderly evolution toward the inevitable goal of independence for the violent upheavals characteristic of the present situation." The CIA asserted that Washington's support for the economic self-sufficiency of the colonial territories would have "a great effect on their good will." Otherwise, it predicted that an American policy influenced by the colonial powers would "alienate the dependent peoples and other non-European countries, lay the ground work for future disruption, and in the long run weaken the power balance of both the U.S. and the Western European nations vis-à-vis the USSR."[39]

President Truman built on the CIA's assessment in his January 1949 inaugural address. Truman proposed a "Fair Deal" to the American public, while also warning of an ominous threat beyond America's borders. To counter the danger, he called for a "bold new program" that would assist the "underdeveloped areas of the world." "More than half the people of the world are living in conditions approaching misery. Their food is inadequate. They are victims of disease. Their economic life is primitive and stagnant. Their poverty is a handicap and a threat both to them and to more prosperous areas," Truman declared. American scientific and technical expertise, he explained, could "relieve the suffering of these people" and "help them realize their aspirations for a better life." Eventually named the Point IV program, the press dubbed it a "'Fair Deal' Plan for the World."[40]

Nine months after Truman's inauguration, AUB president Stephen Penrose wrote Assistant Secretary of State George McGhee. Penrose promoted AUB's ability to support the new Point IV program. In response, McGhee noted that the university had "many 'partisans' who would like to see it maintain its high standards and expand its services." A number of the AUB "partisans" were connected to Point IV's Near East division, McGhee explained, and "know of the work that [AUB] has done, [and] will give warm support to make full use of the facilities of the American University of Beirut when the Point IV plans are formulated."[41]

The partisans were vocal advocates within the State Department's NEA division, often with direct ties to American educational institutions in the region. They argued that the universities and colleges were vital to American interests in the emerging Cold War. Shortly after Point IV was announced, DRN's Joseph Satterthwaite attempted to link the educational institutions more firmly with American policy. "It would be difficult to exaggerate the importance of the American philanthropic educational institutions to our relations with the countries of the Near East," Satterthwaite declared. "These colleges, and related organizations like the Near East Foundation," he wrote, "are far and away the most effective representatives of America and the most effective demonstrations of what America is and stands for." Satterthwaite asserted that they played a vital role in educating the leaders of the region and were the source of the remaining goodwill toward the United States even after the "Palestine controversy." "Any impairment" to their status, he added bluntly, "would be an absolute disaster from the point of view of American foreign policy in the Near East."[42]

To support the universities, Satterthwaite proposed immediate and long-term actions, including federal aid. In a separate letter to Willard Thorp, assistant secretary of state for Economic Affairs, Satterthwaite suggested that the American colleges could assist with the Point IV program in the region. By using Point IV funds to pay the salaries of the instructors involved in technical assistance and providing the colleges with new equipment, he explained, the U.S. government would help alleviate the financial pressure on the universities. This would ensure that the Point IV program benefited from their "prestige and facilities" and "get [the program] off to a flying start," Satterthwaite wrote.[43]

Satterthwaite's advocacy came during a difficult period for AUB and AUC. Although both universities were "American," they could not rely on state or federal funding. As private foreign institutions that valued and guarded their independence, they were similarly unable to rely on the governments of Lebanon or Egypt for funding. Both universities feared that they would be nationalized after their respective host countries achieved independence from colonial rule. Thus, their capacity to fund growth and ability to recruit talented faculty from the United States was limited. Instead, American foundations and private donors were the main source of funds. While both universities were founded by American missionaries, there was a distinct difference in their reputation and financial standing. By the 1950s, AUB's prominent alumni were government ministers and officials throughout the region. AUB was also the largest and most respected institution in the NECA, an organization that excluded AUC until the 1960s. AUC was smaller and lacked a consistent base of donors.[44]

In spite of the financial uncertainty facing the universities, other State Department partisans warned against overt support. After a discussion of the issue in a NEA staff meeting, OIR's Wendell Cleland argued that any assistance must be indirect in order to maintain the institutions' influence in the region. "If their high standing is to be preserved," Cleland wrote, "this fact of dissociation from national political policy must be maintained, even to the extent of exercising the liberty to criticize their own government's policies." "This liberty in fact gives them a great deal more influence than if they appeared to be subservient to government policy," he explained. If other members of the State Department agreed with his assessment, Cleland wrote, "then it is essential that whatever assistance of any kind is given to American institutions abroad, it must allow them to maintain their liberty of policy and action." Instead of direct government assistance, he recommended a combination of scholarships, donations of books, and loans of personnel and materials from American universities and government agencies. To maintain the appearance of independence, Cleland suggested that local boards and foundations should coordinate the activities. This is precisely the approach the State Department pursued in the short term.[45]

In April 1950, AUB president Stephen Penrose visited Washington and met with Assistant Secretary of State George McGhee. The purpose was to discuss some of his suggestions on how the United States could improve relations with the Arab world following the creation of Israel. During the meeting, Penrose asked for Washington's assistance in establishing an agricultural department at AUB and said the project was "one of the most worthwhile in the area."[46]

Less than a year later, McGhee encouraged the Ford Foundation to support American educational institutions in the region. As discussed in Chapter 3, McGhee wrote to Ford's president, Paul Hoffman, in February 1951 in response to the Foundation's September 1950 Trustees Report. A former oil company executive, McGhee explained that the State Department had "become increasingly concerned with the desirability of expanding private American activities throughout the whole area at the 'grass roots' level." He noted the work performed by AUB, AUC, and Robert College. "It is no exaggeration to say that the graduates of these universities, who come from many countries throughout the Near East, represent, by and large, the most important points of contact between the United States, on one hand, and the Near Eastern world, on the other," McGhee stated. "Graduates of these colleges speak to us in our own language; they are oriented to Western thinking; and they occupy important posts in the governmental, legal, commercial, and financial circles of the communities in which they live," he wrote. McGhee reported that all of the institutions had plans to expand but needed additional funds. "We can think of no more important sphere of activity and interest for private American support," he explained, "and no better or more useful field for the Foundation to examine."[47]

McGhee stressed the importance of countries emerging from colonial rule in the Near East and South Asia. However, he warned that "their futures depend on all too thin a layer of administrative capability at the top." The State Department believed that American assistance in developing administrative skills and expanding existing educational institutions was "most desirable." "Such help and guidance is often better received, and more effective," McGhee suggested, "if tendered by private interests rather than through governmental channels."[48]

By October 1951, Penrose received oral approval from the Ford Foundation for a $500,000 grant for the agricultural department. In addition, the Foundation expressed interest in a proposal submitted by AUB to strengthen its arts and sciences programs. The Ford Foundation's support for AUB was part of a larger effort to fund projects in the region closely aligned with the State Department's goals. Indeed, Ford and other foundations were key sources of funding for AUB and AUC in the early Cold War period and provided support when the U.S. government was unable to do so.[49]

The Foundations and American Universities in the Middle East

On July 1, 1952, a small delegation from the Ford Foundation boarded the *Île de France* bound for New York. Led by Dr. Raymond Moyer, deputy director of the Foundation's Division of Overseas Activities, the group recently completed a hasty tour of eight countries in the Middle East. The trip reflected the Foundation's new emphasis on the Near East and Asia. Priority was given to the newly independent countries in these areas due to their political and economic instability and proximity to the Soviet Union. Before arriving in the region, the Ford delegation met with British experts at London's Chatham House. The delegation reported that during the trip they "interviewed hundreds of people including most of the leading government officials and university teachers as well as businessmen." They also consulted with U.S. Embassy officials, representatives of the Point IV and Mutual Security Act programs, and UN representatives in the countries they visited.[50]

The Ford delegation's report provided a stark assessment of the region. "Every Arab government is insecure," it stated, "None is supported by a genuine patriotism." "The only possible exception," the report suggested, was Lebanon due to the "growing recognition that the Christian minority which is active in commerce and education should not be engulfed in a great Moslem state dominated by religious fundamentalism." It warned of the dangers of nascent pan-Arabism, "There is a widespread belief that, as in the past, and more recently in Saudi Arabia, the Arab of the desert moved by religious fervor, may sweep across the more modernized lands." Soviet influence was also a concern, particularly in the Palestinian refugee camps, where the delegation reported there was "virulent anti-Americanism." The political context was provided in order to explain the delegation's recommendations. It proposed granting $3.2 million in support of programs across five major areas rather than a single regional initiative. This included basic research, vocational education, village development, leadership training, and medical assistance. Nearly 70 percent of the funds were devoted to village development and leadership training programs, with Egypt and Iran receiving the largest share.[51]

The report argued that American educational institutions were "the most effective mechanisms" to promote the Foundation's goals in the region. In particular, the delegation recommended the establishment of a Social Research Institute at AUC and an Economic Research Institute at AUB. These institutes, the report explained, would have a regional impact. It also proposed establishing a Center for Arab Studies. "This is a gesture strongly urged upon us by all the leading foreign experts we consulted, designed to indicate our sense of the contribution which Arab scholarship can make to the solution of local problems and also to the west," the delegation stated. The report added:

> The impact of the western world has been largely destructive of Arab values and Arab ways of life. It has taken little account of the views or wishes of the Arabs themselves. Too often it has imposed its own values and desires and brushed aside with contempt or ignored those of the peoples concerned. The creation of Israel has deeply wounded the whole Arab world, but this is only one illustration of the manner in which Americans ignore, even when they patronize and do good to, the Arabs. The inevitable result is that the Arabs are cynically suspicious of even the best intentioned approaches of American goodwill. It seems important to us to do something which indicates that we have nothing to teach.[52]

The Ford delegation argued that Lebanon was a "special case." They found that it had "by far the most developed educational institutions in the Middle East and should be regarded as the intellectual and commercial center of the Near East." The report asserted that AUB was the "only institution in all the countries visited which in fact discharges true university functions." Its influence was not just limited to Lebanon, the delegation explained, but served the entire region. This was demonstrated by the programs AUB developed in conjunction with the Lebanese government, the U.S. Point IV program, and the Arabian-American Oil Company (ARAMCO). The delegation argued that the establishment of an Economic Research Institute at AUB would benefit Lebanon and the broader region. Indeed, the proposal for an institute was supported by economists from the Point IV program as well as the United Nations Relief and Works Agency (UNRWA), which was created to assist Palestinian refugees.[53]

However, the Ford Foundation's efforts were not entirely altruistic. In discussing the rationale for funding AUC's Social Research Institute, the report stated there was a "fundamental need of the West to understand and appraise the mind and the mores as well as motivations of the Arab world." "For we cannot deal successfully with that world, as our unhappy experiences to date already indicate," the delegation wrote, "until we at least know more about the impact which the stream of Western ideas makes not only upon the already existing structure of Moslem concepts and convictions, but on Arab society itself." "We must get behind the life of the area to find the underlying motivations in their various disguises," the report added. AUC's experience in the region was essential to achieving this goal, as "it is not only established in, but accepted by the Arab world."[54]

Within two years, this determination was communicated to AUC. Ward Madison, the university's executive director, informed acting president Wendell Cleland that the Ford Foundation identified the university as one of five institutions in the region "to be strengthened." After Cleland returned to Washington in 1955, he wrote Professor John Provinse, director of AUC's new Social Research Center (SRC). Cleland explained that he hoped to send the SRC basic research topics that represented "the interests of the State Department." Indeed, early drafts of the SRC proposal identified OIR as a liaison agency along with different American universities and Egyptian governmental bodies.[55]

While the Ford Foundation was preparing to enter the Middle East, the Rockefeller Foundation began reassessing its support for programs in the region. In June 1950, John Marshall, associate director of the Foundation's Division of the Humanities, visited the region. Over five weeks, he traveled to Iran, Iraq, and Egypt. Marshall reported that it was "in many ways the most formative visits I have ever made in my work for the Foundation, particularly in the fact that they posed rather sharply the problem of how the people of one culture can come to an understanding of peoples of other cultures." A Harvard-trained medievalist, Marshall joined the foundation in 1933. Although he had visited the region before, Marshall explained, this was his "first opportunity to really get any grasp of the thought and tradition of these people." He expected to find Islam was the main influence on the different populations, but Marshall reported that it was secondary to "the process of westernization which they are undergoing." He was careful to differentiate westernization from modernization, because the latter implied "development rooted in their cultures, an evolution by which those cultures accommodated themselves to the demands of the present-day world." Evolution, however, "was not discernible." "Wherever change can be noted," Marshall wrote, "it involves the adoption, hardly even the adaptation, of practices and ways of thinking that have developed in the west." Use of the term "westernization," he added, "should be a constant reminder that what is 'modern' in the Near East is essentially alien to its practices and thinking. It seems modern to us of the west, because in origin it is essentially western."[56]

Marshall acknowledged that his observations were limited. He did not speak any of the local languages nor did he interact with "the less westernized mass of the population." Instead, his main contacts were Western-educated academics and political elites. Marshall promoted these intellectuals in his report. "They seem to me less ready than were their elders, by and large, simply to adopt what the west has taught them," he wrote, "and far more inclined to be concerned with its adaptation to their psychology and their culture." To encourage and support this new generation, Marshall proposed that the Rockefeller Foundation attempt to copy the success of AUB in the region's "Moslem universities." Although AUB was the "seed bed of the Arab awakening" and the source of leadership in different countries throughout the Middle East, Marshall asserted that "one grave and inevitable defect" was that it "developed in the framework of Christianity rather than Islam." He added that "many of the ablest leaders the AUB produced were themselves Christian, and hence without much personal influence in and on Islam." If a similar cohort of Muslim leaders could be developed with the Rockefeller Foundation's support, Marshall wrote that "the consequences might be similarly incalculable."[57]

Marshall's report was well received at the foundation and found support from a leading scholar. Hamilton Gibb agreed with Marshall's assessment that Western influence and Westernization were the "salient problems" faced by the region. However, Gibb cautioned that observers should not confuse "public life" with "social order and cultural values." He explained that the public sphere, which included government, professionals, and the press, centered on "the degree of emulation, and capacity for adoption, of western practices." In contrast, Islam and its relationship to the West defined social order and values. Gibb agreed that the new states had weak social and political structures that contributed to the lack of nationalist sentiment. In addition, he argued that the young intellectuals Marshall promoted had yet to determine how to resolve these issues while accommodating Muslim values. Gibb asserted that this failure contributed to the popularity of groups like the Muslim Brotherhood. Because of these issues, he reported, the young intellectuals were "beginning to realize the necessity for deep and realistic thinking."[58]

Within a year, however, Marshall offered a more somber and negative assessment. The Iranian government's nationalization of the oil industry and the assassinations of Lebanese prime minister Riad al-Sohl, Pakistani prime minister Liaquat Ali Khan, and Jordan's King Abdullah influenced Marshall's 1951 report on the region. Marshall wrote that the events were "merely symptomatic of deep unrest and of the possibility of radical and even revolutionary change throughout the Muslem [sic] World." Although the events had little to do with religious identification and each occurred within different historical and political contexts, Marshall believed the culprit was Islam. Referencing McGill's William Cantwell Smith, Marshall asserted that "Islam remains a world that is to an extraordinary degree self-contained and impregnable to outside influence." He warned against the influence of religious leaders on the "illiterate opinion" of the majority and of the "virtually unreachable reservoir of Muslem [sic] fanaticism" present in the tribes of Syria, Iran, Iraq, and North Africa. Marshall stated:

> In short, the West knows little and understands less of a force in Near Eastern life which is, unless I am completely misled, *the* governing influence in the lives of a great majority of its Muslem [sic] population, and *a* governing influence, though less apparent as such, in the lives of even its educated minority. Without a better understanding of contemporary Islam, the West will continue to misunderstand the Near East and to miscalculate its actions. Even worse, by misunderstanding and miscalculation, the West will continue to be misunderstood even in its most disinterested and benevolent actions in the Near East.[59]

Marshall feared that the Soviet Union would benefit from and seek to aggravate this misunderstanding. He warned that without a "better understanding of the Near Eastern mind," the Western nations would lose the "minds of the great mass of men and women of the Near East." Turkey was the only country, Marshall found, which had definitively sided with the West. The "battle for minds" was ongoing throughout the region, he wrote, with direct and dire implications for military and diplomatic relations. While

Marshall conceded that there may be other factors influencing the actions of those in the region, the risk of Islam as a mobilized political force was too great to ignore. "As a virtually impregnable and self-perpetuating community, Islam in the grip of ignorant leadership could prove to be an anti-Western force of incalculable proportions throughout the Muslem [*sic*] world," he wrote. Marshall added, "Its potentialities as a force in an area of critical importance for the peace of the world are certainly no longer to be disregarded."[60]

Since Islam could not be influenced from the outside, Marshall questioned if internal reforms were possible. He still found hope among Western-educated intellectuals who were not only subject to outside influence but could form a secular leadership. He advocated for the Rockefeller Foundation's continued support of Near Eastern institutions and the strengthening of research programs in the region. "I am convinced," he wrote, "that the relatively small [Rockefeller Foundation] grants for work in the social sciences and the humanities at the American University of Beirut have led to contributions to the solution of Near Eastern problems out of all proportion to the amounts involved." He believed that grants to other institutions would have similar benefits. Marshall also recommended that the Rockefeller Foundation prioritize studies of the "current thinking and movements of Islam," including by scholars in the region. He identified Turkey and Iran as the most promising countries for the Rockefeller Foundation's efforts. Marshall also viewed Lebanon, Iraq, and Syria favorably but was concerned about their political volatility.[61]

Although Marshall's assessment was well received, the Rockefeller Foundation was concerned how it would be viewed by a non-American audience. Charles Fahs, director of humanities at the Rockefeller Foundation, wrote that it was a "stimulating paper" and considered distributing it to the trustees. However, he did not want it circulated outside the Rockefeller Foundation's U.S. offices. In the accompanying cover memorandum, Marshall noted, "I should be in serious difficulties in Islam if some of the statements this report contains ever got into unfriendly hands."[62] Within seven months, however, a military coup in Egypt would challenge a number of Marshall's claims about the role of religion.

The Ties That Bind

Throughout the 1950s, Harold Hoskins was at the center of American educational efforts related to the Middle East. He served as president of the

NECA, was chairman of AUB's Board of Trustees, and was named director of the State Department's Foreign Service Institute (FSI) in 1955. As president of the NECA, Hoskins traveled to the region in 1953 and visited all of the organization's member institutions. He discussed the trip with AUB's Board and reported that each NECA member institution had problems, mainly involving personnel and funds. However, the trip left him with a "deeper feeling of the soundness and importance of our educational work as one of the most consistent factors of U.S. Foreign Policy, often more effective than what is contributed by many of our diplomats." In particular, Hoskins referenced the rapidly increasing number of AUB graduates who were prominent in government and business and referred specifically to the new prime ministers of Lebanon and Jordan.[63]

Hoskins also emphasized these points to the State Department. In a June 1953 presentation to the FSI, he stressed the important role played by AUB and the other NECA institutions in the region. "As character and leadership builders," Hoskins explained, the American educational institutions played an important and unique role beyond education. He focused on AUB and noted that eighteen of its graduates attended the founding of the UN and more recent alumni were leaders in government and business positions throughout the region. AUB's role, Hoskins stated, was not to replace local institutions but "to serve as an example and gadfly." This required that AUB remain "private and independent for its own sake and for its continuing influence."[64]

Two years later, however, AUB's financial difficulties threatened its continued viability. John Case, chairman of AUB's Board of Trustees and vice president of Socony Mobil Oil Company (later Mobil), contacted the State Department. Although AUB had a $7,000,000 endowment, it was facing a $500,000 deficit for the year. This was due to the growth of several schools and departments to serve the U.S. Technical Assistance Program for the region. Case warned that the deficit would lead to "drastic cuts" that would have an impact on the program. Case explained that AUB "did not wish [for] long term subsidization by the Government nor did it for generally similar reasons wish to become known as a creature of the oil companies." Instead, it sought short-term assistance from Washington, while it discussed long-term support with the Rockefeller and Ford Foundations. Under Secretary of State Herbert Hoover Jr. reassured Case that "the University's problem is currently being given the most careful and sympathetic study." Indeed, AUB's problem initiated four years of discussions between the university and the highest levels of the State Department and the CIA over the university's future.[65]

Support from State Department partisans continued with Eisenhower's secretary of state, John Foster Dulles. John Foster and his brother Allen had long-standing ties to the missionary movement and the halls of power in Washington and Wall Street. Although C. Wright Mills only mentioned the Dulles brothers in passing, they embodied the "power elite." The sons of a Presbyterian minister, their grandfather, John Welsh Dulles, directed missionary campaigns for the American Sunday School Union. Evenings were spent reading religious stories, including missionary tracts. The Dulles brothers were also the grandsons of Secretary of State John W. Foster and attended the Paris Peace Conference with their uncle, Secretary of State Robert Lansing. Graduates of Princeton, the brothers worked in and maintained extensive connections to Wall Street firms. During World War II, Allen Dulles served in the OSS as William Donovan's European deputy and oversaw operations in Switzerland and occupied Germany. Their shared perspective on America's place in the postwar world ensured an unprecedented level of cooperation and coordination between the State Department and CIA in the 1950s. John Foster and Allen Dulles were actively involved in the State Department's attempts to resolve AUB's financial problems.[66]

On May 25, 1956, President Eisenhower gave a commencement address at Baylor University. "The whole free world would be stronger if there existed adequate institutions of modern techniques and sciences in areas of the world where the hunger for knowledge and the ability to use knowledge are unsatisfied because educational facilities are often not equal to the need," Eisenhower told the audience. "I firmly believe that if some or all of our great universities, strongly supported by private foundations that exist in number throughout this land, sparked by the zeal and fire of educated Americans, would devote themselves to this task, the prospects for a peaceful and prosperous world would be mightily enhanced," he added.[67]

The U.S. Embassy in Beirut and the State Department attempted to apply the sentiments expressed in Eisenhower's speech to AUB. Donald Heath, U.S. ambassador to Lebanon, wrote to Secretary of State Dulles that the university presented "one of [the] greatest opportunities for [the] achievement [of the] objectives [the] President mentioned [in] his Baylor University speech." The university already received funds through the International Cooperation Agency (ICA) and sought an additional $20 million over several years to assist with capital improvements and to fund its endowment. Although Democratic Senator William Fulbright supported providing the university with the necessary funds through the Mutual Security Act, the effort was stymied by other members of Congress.[68]

In late October 1956, Britain, France, and Israel invaded Egypt in an attempt to overthrow Gamal Abdel Nasser's regime. Nasser came to power through the July 1952 coup that ousted Egypt's King Farouk. Although relations with Washington were cordial, the Eisenhower administration viewed Nasser's neutrality in the Cold War with skepticism. The Suez War was rooted in the simmering Arab-Israeli conflict and the decline of British and French power in the region. Britain was reluctant to withdraw from its military bases in Egypt, a key demand of Nasser's government. Israel sought to delay, if not scuttle, the Eisenhower administration's attempts to resolve the Arab-Israeli conflict and undermine relations between Washington and Cairo. Meanwhile, France struggled to defeat the Algerian revolution, which Nasser openly supported. Israel's February 1955 raid on the Egyptian-controlled Gaza Strip killed over forty Egyptian soldiers and Palestinian civilians. In response, an angry and embarrassed Nasser requested American weaponry. After Secretary of State Dulles refused the request, Egypt purchased weapons from Czechoslovakia. The weapons deal, likely approved at the highest levels of the Kremlin, led to a rift between Cairo and Washington. Tensions increased further after Dulles rejected Egypt's request for development loans to expand the Aswan Dam. On July 26, Nasser nationalized the Suez Canal Company in response to the public rejection. Three months later, the tripartite invasion was launched without Washington's approval. The invasion infuriated Eisenhower and the United States pressured Britain, France, and Israel publicly and privately to withdraw. Nasser emerged from the war politically triumphant with increased prestige across the region and the "Third World."

After the 1956 Suez War, AUB's leadership attempted to demonstrate its support of America's goals in the region. In January 1957, President Eisenhower addressed a joint session of Congress and unveiled what would become known as the Eisenhower Doctrine. The doctrine's goal was to contain Egyptian president Gamal Abdel Nasser's growing influence. Shortly after Eisenhower's speech, AUB's Case met with Under Secretary of State Robert Murphy in Washington. He emphasized the need for teachers in Saudi Arabia and Kuwait fluent in Arabic and explained that the majority of teachers were trained in Egypt. Case warned that there were "inevitable political implications" to Egypt's predominant role in education and argued that AUB "should serve as the training ground for teachers who would be oriented for a more favorable attitude toward the West, especially the United States." Although sympathetic, Foggy Bottom was unable to overcome congressional resistance. Nor were the major foundations willing to provide the necessary funds.[69]

Six months later, Case explained the university's dire situation in two letters to CIA director Allen Dulles. He approached Dulles "for advice and support because of your knowledge of the importance of the [AUB] to Western civilization and your old interest in the Near East colleges." Case noted that AUB had received increased support from the ICA, oil companies, and foundations, but its endowment was insufficient, and its costs remained high. "Recent developments have strengthened our conviction that the University is exerting an influence in the Arab world and the contiguous areas which is of the utmost importance to the United States and to the Western world," Case wrote. He added, "We believe that this influence can be far greater in the future if the University can obtain adequate financial backing." Case admitted that in the past AUB was reluctant to accept direct support from the U.S. government, but due to the financial situation it believed that "an outright grant without conditions would not endanger the status and reputation of the University as a free private institution." After a series of meetings in the United States with the Rockefeller and Ford Foundations and testimony before the Senate, Case sent a second letter to Allen Dulles. He informed the CIA director that the Ford Foundation "did not intend to adopt the AUB nor was it willing to pour money down the drain by supporting something which would not survive." Case reiterated the need for a grant from the U.S. government and argued that it "would carry less implication of interference than the ICA training contracts or even grants by the large Foundations for specific projects." He added, "I can think of no expenditure of Government funds which can be expected to yield comparable benefits to our position and policy in the Middle East." It is unclear if Dulles responded to Case or attempted to influence Congress. Over the next twelve months, however, the State Department maintained an active interest in AUB's financial standing. A combination of grants from the Rockefeller and Ford Foundations as well as increased funds from the ICA resolved AUB's short-term budget crisis. However, it still needed at least $10 million for an expansion of the campus, including a new medical center.[70]

By the end of the decade, Senator Fulbright and the State Department were able to overcome congressional opponents and provide AUB with some of the needed funds for capital projects. However, the State Department admitted that increased support from Washington exacerbated AUB's long-term financial problems due to the need to create and sustain programs. As a result, the U.S. government needed to consider contributions to operating and capital costs. Although the State Department acknowledged the "tremendous contribution" of American educational institutions in the region, it also conceded that "their future as American institutions in the area depends in great part on the degree to which they remain clearly private." Foggy Bottom feared that large-scale support would "seriously dilute their private character and thus threaten their security" as nationalist sentiments in the region increased. The State Department continued to advocate for funding the institutions "in an unspectacular and unpublicized manner."[71]

While it sought financial support from Washington, AUB conducted an examination of its educational mission regionally and internationally. Led by Constantine Zurayk, a professor of history and vice president of the university, the internal study argued that AUB had certain advantages over other universities in the region. This included freedom from government control and the ability to establish its own standards and encourage freedom of thought. However, these freedoms were not absolute. Zurayk explained that the Lebanese government and others exercised a certain amount of indirect control by deciding whether or not to recognize AUB's degrees. AUB, Zurayk explained, also enjoyed the advantage of strong cultural ties and contacts with Western countries as well as its traditions and former graduates.[72]

The university's position also had disadvantages, which, according to Zurayk, included being a foreign institution in a "nationalization-conscious" society and the moniker "American" university. As AUB did not enjoy government support, its ability to grow was limited and it was comparatively more expensive than other regional universities. He noted that the university's future was dependent on different factors, some of which it could not control, including the impact of nationalism in the region and the future of America's relationship with the Arab world. However, he argued that AUB could control its performance and that it needed to become "stronger and broader" by emphasizing "intellectual pioneering, moral and spiritual values, and quality of achievement."[73]

By the mid-1950s, AUC also had chronic budget problems. However, it stood to benefit from the 1954 Agricultural Trade Development and Assistance Act, Public Law 480 (PL 480), which authorized the sale of surplus wheat and other agricultural commodities to developing nations. The commodities were paid for in local currency, which was deposited in local U.S.

government bank accounts and could be withdrawn for aid projects in the country. Unlike Lebanon, Egypt was a PL 480 recipient. Indeed, AUB's ineligibility for PL 480 funds was a source of frustration to State Department and congressional supporters. Within two years, the Egyptian total alone equaled 6.7 million Egyptian pounds. The State Department in conjunction with the U.S. Embassy in Cairo developed a proposal for a portion of the PL 480 funds to be distributed to American educational institutions in the region, including AUC. However, regional and international politics intervened to delay the proposal.[74]

AUC became a point of contention between Washington and Cairo. Although the State Department was unwilling to "reduce or fuzzy" its hard-line policy toward Egypt by allowing funds to be distributed to AUC, Senator Fulbright came to the rescue. Fulbright's amendment to the Mutual Security Act of 1957 provided the mechanism to fund overseas schools founded by American citizens. By 1959, $500,000 was available to the university from PL 480 funds and the same amount a year later. The influx of funds was roughly five times AUC's annual budget and enabled the university to embark on new construction and projects.[75]

The university faced another crisis due to the passage of Egyptian Law 160, which also reflected tensions between Nasser and the Eisenhower administration. The law required Egyptian ownership of the country's educational institutions and that Arabs comprise the majority of administrative and teaching personnel. In addition, the schools were required to adhere to the Ministry of Education's curriculum and exams. AUC president Raymond McClain reached out to Mohamed Hassanein Heikal, Nasser's confidant and editor of the newspaper *Al-Ahram*. After discussing the issue with the Egyptian president, Heikal informed McClain that Nasser "fully appreciated" the university's contribution and it had "nothing to worry about." Nasser also reassured U.S. Ambassador to Egypt Raymond Hare in a separate meeting "that everything would be all right with regard to [AUC] and that it was not necessary to pursue the matter further." However, the issue lingered for another year and was not fully resolved until relations with Washington improved at the end of the Eisenhower administration. Minister of Education Kamal el-Din Hussein later revealed that the university was exempted from Law 160 because Nasser believed it was important to "maintain cultural ties with the United States through AUC."[76]

Two years later, the ICA conducted an evaluation of American universities in the region. The commission was initially led by William Stevenson, the former president of Oberlin College, and included former AUC president John Badeau. Badeau became ambassador to Egypt while the report was finalized. Produced in April 1961, the ICA report explained that even though foreign educational institutions were welcome in the region before World War II, they were now coming under the authority of new ministries of education. In addition, while the American universities were the leading institutions prior to the war, they were "only a few of the growing number of educational influences serving the area."[77]

The ICA report stated that AUC was the "least" American of the universities under review. It added that it was "just this fact that makes it an effective American influence and should enable it to continue serving within a strongly nationalistic cultural situation." Moreover, it found that AUC's "particular significance" was its location "from which presently emanates many of the strongest forces of the Arab world." The report asserted that AUC's reputation and "the contacts it establishes with significant Egyptian groups is a major source of American influence in the [United Arab Republic]." Without the university, the report said, "The foreign cultural field in Egypt would be left largely to neutralists and Soviet bloc influences, which would be both a loss to the Egyptian community and to the Western world." "It is precisely because conditions are changing rapidly in Cairo and traditional bonds of friendship with the West are weakened that the American University faces a new, more significant and exacting role," the report added.[78]

The Stevenson Commission also evaluated AUB, but the university was less receptive to its findings. This was due largely to Zurayk's internal assessment, which had the support of AUB's Board. John Case, chairman of AUB's Board of Trustees, remarked that he believed the ICA report "was thinking about the type of university program which would appeal to the U.S. government." In particular, this was evident in the emphasis on technical education. Instead, Case asserted that Zurayk's program, which recommended that AUB remain a private university and strengthen its relationships in the region, was "far more apt to gain real support."[79]

However, it was uncertain how AUB could remain a private institution. Emile Bustani, a prominent businessman and AUB board member, argued that while outreach to graduates was necessary it would not be sufficient to meet the university's future financial needs. Bustani, who was also a member of the Lebanese Parliament, asserted that "every effort should be made to acquaint the U.S. government with the value of an American University in Beirut and to recognize its responsibility toward such a university."[80]

The passage of the Foreign Assistance Act in 1961 and the creation of the U.S. Agency for International Development (USAID) were initially greeted with relief in Beirut and Cairo. However, at AUB it sparked an internal debate about accepting governmental support and the degree of coordination that was required between the university and the State Department. Yet by 1963, the university faced a large deficit and the continued support of the Rockefeller and Ford Foundations was uncertain. The Ford Foundation was again reluctant to provide AUB with long-term grants unless it received similar funding from Washington.[81]

Meanwhile, attempts to raise money from Arab countries demonstrated AUB's uncertain position. In late 1962, Case traveled to Saudi Arabia hoping for an audience with King Saud bin 'Abd al-'Aziz al-Sa'ud. The State Department encouraged AUB's outreach to Saudi Arabia for political and financial reasons. Case hoped King Saud would help fund a new medical center and carried a letter of support from President Kennedy. Saud, however, was ill and Case met with Crown Prince Faisal, who was reluctant to offer immediate support. Instead, Faisal requested that AUB detail the advantages and benefits to Saudi Arabia of a new medical center in Beirut. He also inquired why Washington, "which was going to spend a great deal of money in Israel, could not provide the small sum required for the operation of the medical center?" Saudi Arabia eventually approved a $500,000 contribution to the medical center. Case also received support from Kuwait for the hospital and the university. Yet the support came with the expectation that AUB would assist with Kuwait's expanding educational and health care sectors.[82]

While Washington recognized AUB's importance to the region, the implications of U.S. government funding on the university remained a concern. During the May 22, 1963, meeting of the AUB Board, Harold Hoskins asked "whether or not the time had come when the University should admit that it was receiving substantial assistance from the U.S. government?" If not, he suggested that the "word 'American' should be dropped from the university's name." Hoskins's statement came after considerable discussion over the previous year about fundraising difficulties and debate over government support. In the ensuing discussion, AUB's Board decided that "the dangers" of continued reliance on government financing were understood. An alternative source of financing was not available, however. The meeting minutes noted that Washington "recognized the need to retain the university's independent character" and that to date AUB had been "successful in avoiding governmental interference." With support from Washington, AUB was able to secure additional funding from American philanthropic foundations. It also embarked on an active campaign over the next decade to secure funding from states, corporations, and wealthy donors in the region.[83]

Before his death in 1972, former AUB president Bayard Dodge reflected on his stewardship of the university. AUB experienced a dramatic transformation during his twenty-five year tenure. It actively courted closer ties to Washington and was promoted by American officials as well as the officers of leading philanthropic foundations. Dodge, however, expressed relief that his term was over before the U.S. government began providing large-scale support to AUB. Yet he still promoted the university's mission in the region and its missionary heritage. Echoing Harold Hoskins, Dodge stated, "Through the good schools we founded we got to many people when they were young and trained not only minds but characters."[84]

During and after World War II, AUB and AUC supported Washington's goals but sought to maintain their appearance of independence and freedom of action. However, U.S. government officials saw the universities not just as key outposts representing American ideals but potential sources of recruitment for anti-Axis sabotage activities during the war and supporters of the United States after the conflict. As demonstrated by Washington's recognition of Israel and the 1948 Palestine War, AUB and AUC sought to maintain their transnational identities at least publicly. Privately, however, the university officials conceded that their public opposition to U.S. government policies was partially for local consumption.

The universities attempted to balance between their American, regional, and local identities. They drew on the State Department partisans, directly and indirectly, to find support for their universities and programs. Philanthropic foundations—in particular the Ford and Rockefeller Foundations—and private donors served to underwrite the university's programs and initiatives. While it would be an exaggeration to suggest that this funding was at the behest of the U.S. government, the foundations and Washington found common purpose in promoting AUB and AUC as vanguards of American values and ideals in a region considered vital to U.S. national security interests.[85] Moreover, the patronizing language used by university administrators to describe the region's inhabitants reflected not only their own cultural and religious biases and stereotypes but their attempts to promote the value of their institutions to Washington.

With the emergence of the Cold War, Washington believed AUB and AUC were vital to winning the battle for hearts and minds in the Middle East. Well before the term was coined, American educational institutions in the Middle East were examples of American "soft power" in the Cold War competition with Moscow. But the universities were not passive entities, as their respective administrations actively promoted their unique positions and prestigious reputations within the region to Washington and local political elites. Indeed, they fully embraced their status as America's sheet anchors in the Middle East. However, like Cold War universities in the United States, they also sought to guard their independence—or the appearance of it—even when accepting government funds. In addition, funding either directly by the government or indirectly through foundations did not always guarantee that the knowledge produced would align with America's national security interests.[86]

CHAPTER **5**

(In)Visible Government

The National Defense Education Act
and the Establishment of Middle
East Studies, 1950–1967

> Area studies have a special meaning for the new diplomacy, going
> well beyond their practical importance for men who have to make
> decisions affecting little-known parts of the world. Area studies
> constitute the first explicit recognition, in the main-stream of
> American intellectual history, of the simple proposition that
> people are different.
>
> —MCGEORGE BUNDY

Hurtling through space at 15,000 miles per hour, a small silver orb emitted a simple pulsating signal from its twin radio transmitters. Composed of an aluminum shell and weighing less than 200 pounds, the sphere raced across the October evening sky oblivious to its historic mission or the commotion that would ensue as listening stations began to hear its unique voice. The transmissions continued for three weeks and were heard by scientists, intelligence analysts, and ham radio operators around the globe. Although silent and unobservable without special equipment, the tiny satellite continued circling the planet for ninety-two days before losing orbit and descending back to earth. Its official name was *Iskustvenniy Sputnik Zemli,* or artificial satellite of the earth, but it would become known to the world as Sputnik.[1]

Although the American press and public were shocked by Sputnik, the Eisenhower administration initially dismissed it as a "propaganda stunt" and a "silly bauble." After a larger satellite was launched into an even higher orbit less than a month later carrying a small dog named Laika, the White House was forced to act. Within a year, Congress passed the National Defense Education Act (NDEA), which authorized federal funding for the study of languages needed for "strategic areas," the creation of university-based, multidisciplinary centers, and a dramatic increase in spending on science and math.[2]

The Sputnik crisis succeeded in securing federal funding for area studies where previous efforts failed. Originally intended as a temporary measure, the legislation formally established area studies in the United States and became integral, if not essential, to the study of foreign areas in American higher education. Yet the NDEA has often been overlooked in discussions of the Sputnik crisis and its effect on area studies has received less attention than its impact on math and the sciences. The NDEA was also a culmination of the close and mutually beneficial relationship between the national security establishment and academia. Within a decade of its passage, however, that relationship became strained. Meanwhile, the foreign policy and national security establishments improved their training facilities and enhanced their analytical capabilities.[3]

The Princeton Consultants

A decade before Sputnik, the State Department and the Central Intelligence Agency (CIA) attempted to identify sources within major universities for foreign area intelligence and training in analytical methods. This was reflected in the creation of the External Research Staff (ERS), which served as a coordinating body to identify, collect, and contract research on foreign areas. Due to budget constraints, the CIA and Department of Defense subsidized the group's activities, but it remained within the State Department. After the Eisenhower administration took office, the State Department again faced budgetary pressures and proposed cutting ERS. However, the ERS benefited from the close relationship between Secretary of State John Foster Dulles and his brother, Director of Central Intelligence (DCI) Allen Dulles. The CIA continued funding the ERS but kept it in the State Department. A CIA assessment stated that this decision was based "mainly on the belief that private external and in particular academic researchers in the social sciences preferred to deal with the Department of State in the functions carried out by [the] ERS." The assessment explained that while the Pentagon could replicate the clearinghouse functions of the

ERS, "it is believed that the academic community would not be as inclined to work with Defense as with State." Similarly, it reported that the administrative benefits gained by moving the ERS into the CIA were outweighed by the potential that "we might have trouble working with the academic world because of the nature of this Agency." Yet the ERS was only one aspect of Washington's relationship with academia.[4]

The creation of the National Intelligence Estimate (NIE) dramatically expanded and enhanced the national security establishment's intelligence collection and analysis requirements and capabilities. Produced by the CIA's Office of National Estimates (ONE), the NIE provided the president with a summary of key issues based on available intelligence. In October 1950, then DCI general Bedell Smith oversaw the creation of ONE. Smith later described it as the "heart of the Central Intelligence Agency and of the national intelligence machinery." To oversee ONE, Smith selected Harvard's William Langer as assistant director for National Estimates. Langer was recommended by William Donovan, and Smith reportedly pressured Harvard into allowing the former Research and Analysis (R&A) head to take a leave of absence for the post. Eleven estimates were initially ordered and over a 100 were produced within four years.[5]

Smith served as Eisenhower's chief of staff during World War II. As tensions increased between the former wartime allies in early 1946, he was ordered to Moscow to meet with Stalin. Prior to the meeting, Smith was briefed by George Kennan, then the U.S. embassy's chargé d'affaires. As discussed in Chapter 3, Kennan was later selected by Secretary of State George Marshall to lead the State Department's Policy Planning Staff (PPS). After he returned to Princeton, Kennan was frequently called on by the State Department and the CIA for analysis, including for the newly established ONE.[6]

To support ONE, Smith proposed the creation of an outside panel of experts and asked General Donovan for recommendations. Donovan remained involved in intelligence activities after he returned to his legal practice in New York. He suggested that Smith create an "Evaluation Group" comprised of "men of experience and imagination and constructive intellects." Donovan wrote, "It might include a scholar, a strategist, familiar with the uses and capabilities of the different services—[a] scientist with knowledge and experience in current inventions, and two to three broad gauged men of affairs." Donovan advised Smith to establish a research and analysis branch similar to that of the Office of Strategic Services (OSS), which would be "the intellectual base of the organization." "Such a concept," he explained, "together with the putting under one tent the various essential functions of Secret Intelligence and Operations, place intelligence on a different plane." Donovan added that since the CIA "must be set for a long pull," the agency should retain "certain outstanding older and representative economists, scientists and linguistic and other specialists" as consultants. A week later, Donovan wrote Smith with a "survey" of scholars to be considered. He listed several OSS veterans, including E. A. Speiser and John Wilson as experts on the Near East. Donovan identified Yale's William T. R. Fox, Frederick Dunn, and Gabriel Almond as well as Columbia's Philip Mosely, and Charles B. Fahs of the Rockefeller Foundation. He emphasized that "the men listed in these pages represent an extremely careful selection," but cautioned that "security inquiry has not been attempted."[7]

Smith followed Donovan's advice and established the expert panel. Comprised of "five or six outstanding men," the panel developed into the Board of National Estimates (BNE). According to Deputy Director of Central Intelligence William Harding Jackson, BNE's goal was to obtain "independent judgment, free of department bias" in evaluating the NIEs. Smith and Jackson did not believe such assessments were possible from a joint intelligence committee. Jackson also thought the process would produce a "more authoritative judgment" than would be available from the ONE staff. "All intelligence personnel," he later explained, "departmental as well as central, were bureaucrats isolated from reality." The BNE, Jackson argued, would be "composed of men of great prestige with practical experience in the conduct of affairs." These outside experts "would subject the findings of the intelligence bureaucrats to the test of practical realism."[8]

Langer also served as the BNE's first chairman. Apparently attempting to re-create his experience as head of R&A, Langer recruited academics to the BNE. However, he did not conduct the BNE as a panel of equals. Langer believed he was personally responsible for the NIEs the panel reviewed. Yet Jackson was less enamored with the BNE's performance. He later recalled that "these professors were as uncomprehending of practical considerations as were the intelligence bureaucrats." As a result, Jackson moved to establish an external panel of consultants dubbed the "Princeton Consultants." The Princeton Consultants were originally intended to provide "practical realism" when evaluating the NIE, versus the "ivory tower" expertise of the BNE and the myopia of the ONE.[9]

DCI Allen Dulles expanded the role of the Princeton Consultants. At least four times a year, the Consultants met at the Nassau Inn near the Princeton University campus in the "Gun Room." Held over two days, the meetings often coincided with those of the Princeton Board of Trustees, which included Dulles. Former ONE staff member Ludwell Lee Montague later explained that "the basic idea was to get away from the bureaucratic atmosphere of Washington." Since the majority of consultants lived and worked in the northeastern United States and Jackson had a home in Princeton, it was a "convenient midpoint" and a "pleasant place" to meet. In addition to Kennan, the initial consultants included Vannevar Bush, the president of the Carnegie Institution; Hamilton Fish Armstrong of the Council on Foreign Relations; and Charles Fahs, the Rockefeller Foundation's director of humanities.[10]

Langer's replacement at ONE, Sherman Kent, was an OSS R&A alum and former Yale professor. Kent returned to Yale after the war and published *Strategic Intelligence for American World Policy,* one of the earliest and most influential works on the subject. Although Jackson was skeptical of academics, especially OSS veterans, he was impressed by Kent's book and recruited him to serve as assistant director of National Estimates.[11]

Unlike Jackson, Allen Dulles viewed Langer's tenure favorably. In a letter from July 1956, Dulles wrote to persuade Langer to continue serving as a consultant. He explained that the "Princeton consultants group is a part of our organization on which I rely highly for all sorts of purposes." The National Intelligence Estimates "profit enormously from the opportunity that [Sherman Kent's] people have to sit down several times a year and review our current estimative problems with a wise and experienced group like yours," Dulles wrote. "I also value this opportunity of keeping leaders in the academic world aware of our estimative work," he stated. Dulles added, "You continuously suggest new and rewarding lines of inquiry, you have sent us (and I hope will continue to do so) valuable recruits from among your students, and the consultants panel itself has proved a most useful proving ground for prospective members of the Board of National Estimates." Langer remained active with the Princeton Consultants for the rest of the Eisenhower administration.[12]

Other consultants from academia included Columbia's Philip Mosely, Princeton's T. Cuyler Young and Joseph Strayer, and MIT's Max Millikan and Lucian Pye. Mosely maintained extensive connections to the intelligence community as the head of Columbia's Russian Institute. An OSS and State

Department veteran, T. Cuyler Young replaced Philip Hitti as head of Princeton's Near East studies program. Before joining Princeton's faculty, Young served as the public affairs officer in the U.S. Embassy in Tehran. Millikan led MIT's Center for International Studies (CENIS) after briefly serving as assistant director of the CIA. Lucian Pye was a political scientist whose work on modernization theory will be discussed in Chapter 6. Strayer, however, had a different background. According to medieval historian Norman F. Cantor—and Strayer's former graduate student—his advisor's involvement with the CIA went beyond the consultant's board. Cantor explained that Strayer was recruited by Allen Dulles. "For at least five summers Strayer spent five days a week at CIA headquarters in Langley, Virginia, and during the year he would go down whenever there was a crisis somewhere in the world." Cantor recounted that on these occasions he was asked to fill in for Strayer's lectures. "I once had the temerity to ask him what he was doing for the CIA and why it found the services of a medievalist so important. The response was that Allen Dulles knew medievalists were used to drawing conclusions from fragmentary evidence, and that is just what the CIA did," Cantor wrote.[13]

Duke economist Calvin Hoover also served on the Consultants' Board and briefly discussed it in his memoir. A veteran of the OSS's Secret Intelligence (SI) branch in Europe, Hoover was recruited to the board by Bedell Smith after Chinese forces entered the Korean conflict. "It was a pleasure to find myself associated once more with Allen Dulles and with other friends of OSS days," he wrote. Hoover explained that the NIEs covered particular countries or situations and were largely focused on the "threat of Soviet aggression." Yet he focused almost exclusively on the Kremlin's perceived influence in Iran:

> How explosive was the political, social, and economic situation in Iran? When Mossadegh came to power, to what extent was he under the domination of the Communist party and was the Communist party effectively controlled by Moscow? If the oil resources of Iran were nationalized, would they be made available to the Soviet government and could they effectively be utilized? How serious would be the loss of these resources to the West?[14]

In spite of the eclectic approach, there were limitations to the expertise provided by the consultants. Sherman Kent recalled that under DCI Dulles the group dealt with issues beyond the Soviet Union and Eastern Europe.

However, they "suffered from the fact that only one or two of the consultants had any specialized knowledge of the Middle East or Latin America, and none, for example, of black Africa." In addition, few of the consultants had code-word clearance, so the most sensitive material could not be shared with the group. Kent stated that over time ONE's staff did not believe the consultants offered useful advice or analysis. Although their concerns were raised to Allen Dulles and his replacement John McCone, neither director was willing to disband the group, but the number of meetings per year was reduced.[15]

By April 1962, a number of consultants were based in the Cambridge, Massachusetts area. This created a logistical problem for the CIA's couriers, who could not visit all of the consultants individually in a single day. As there were more consultants from Harvard than MIT, the CIA asked Langer to secure a room on campus where they could review the classified materials. Langer accommodated the request and reserved a room on Widener Library's top floor. He resigned from the Consultants' Board the following year in order to join President Kennedy's Foreign Intelligence Advisory Board. Dulles also remained active with the consultants after he was replaced as DCI, and he continued attending meetings until his death in 1969.[16]

Much of the Princeton Consultants' work is still shrouded in secrecy, but it remained active until ONE was disbanded in November 1973. The BNE was eventually dominated by professional intelligence officers, while the consultants were generally academics. By 1971, Montague notes, "the intelligence professionalism of the CIA" was "far superior to anything known in 1950."[17]

Drowning in Oil

While the national security establishment attempted to enhance its foreign area analysis, American oil companies already had success in this arena. Indeed, a 1950 internal assessment by the State Department on Middle East oil found that the operations of American oil companies "familiarizes large numbers of U.S. technicians with strategic materials in a strategic area; area intelligence is consequently excellent." It added that "oil companies are instrumental and can be more instrumental in contributing to the attainment of overall U.S. policy objectives for the area, e.g. economic and political stability, increased standard of living, Western orientation, development of democratic processes, expansion of international trade, etc."[18]

Washington's failure to produce a government-funded program for area studies during the Korean conflict led the universities to pursue other sources for support. The combination of oil wealth, experience in the region, affinity with the goals of the U.S. government, and the need for trained American personnel made oil companies a natural sponsor for university programs. By 1951, several oil companies were contributing to Princeton's Near East program. They were also instrumental in the creation of a program at Harvard.

In March 1953, a meeting was held on the Harvard campus to discuss establishing a Middle East studies program. Attendees included representatives from Standard Oil of New Jersey (later Exxon) and New York (Socony, later Mobil), ARAMCO, U.S. Army Intelligence, the State Department, and the CIA. The program proposal declared that America's "international commitment to counter the Soviet threat in the Middle East, the fundamental importance of Middle-eastern [*sic*] oil to our economy, and the continuing crisis in the area make it imperative that American universities turn their attention to this vitally important but hitherto relatively neglected region." In fields ranging from economics to social psychology, the proposal stated there was a need for "a graduate program designed both to train selected men for service in private industry and in government, and at the same time to encourage scholarly basic research on the modern Middle East."[19]

Chaired by Dean Edward Mason of the School of Public Administration, the meeting's morning session evaluated the prospects of establishing a Middle East studies program. An OSS veteran and former economic advisor to Secretary of State George Marshall, Mason argued that the "market" for graduates should determine the "whole curriculum, the whole training program." He carefully defined the market as "the principal American companies operating in the Near East, plus the State Department, the CIA and other government agencies."[20]

Mason's suggestion was supported by the different attendees. While they agreed that the region was neglected, the participants disagreed on whether a program was needed. Although there were already several Middle East programs, the consensus was that none covered the modern era well or at all. Compared to Britain, Harvard's Richard Frye asserted that America was "tremendously behind the times and we are not really training people." The director of the State Department's Foreign Service Institute (FSI), Harry Smith, added that the potential existed to increase government personnel in the region by "at least 100%."[21]

Kermit "Kim" Roosevelt Jr. attended the meeting on behalf of the Harvard Foundation, but he was also there as a representative of the CIA. One of the key figures involved in the 1953 coup to overthrow Iranian prime minister Mohammed Mossadegh, Roosevelt explained that based on his experience as "a consultant for a number of government agencies," if Harvard was "satisfied with a pure government market, the government could take care of all the products for the next ten years." He added, "From the point of view of the research that would be done, the government would regard that as of tremendous value."[22]

At least one participant was skeptical of Harvard's intent. Writing afterward to Philip Hitti at Princeton, FSI's Harry Smith explained, "Many of us had the impression that Harvard was inviting us and entertaining us in order to get our stamp of approval on a *fait accompli*." He added that while the university had an advantage because of the number of foreign nationals that attend its professional schools, "I still think they are trying to get on a gravy train and are definitely after oil money." In spite of his criticisms, Smith conceded that it was a "very good conference" and that the representatives from Harvard "show themselves 'against sin' in many respects, and, I suppose in the long run the thing will work out as contributing to our relations with the area rather than the other way around."[23]

Smith's skepticism was not unfounded. Later that summer, Frye sent a copy of the Center for Middle East Studies' (CMES) preliminary announcement to British scholar Bernard Lewis, then at the University of London's School of Oriental and African Studies (SOAS). Frye admitted in the accompanying letter, "As you will see the great emphasis is upon oil, and I, frankly, am beginning to drown in oil."[24]

What Frye disclosed privately, William Langer admitted publicly over three decades later. In his autobiography, Langer wrote that he was asked by university administration to examine the possibility of creating a center for studying the Middle East similar to Harvard's Russian Research Center. He explained that the impetus behind the request was "several American oil companies, in need of trained personnel," who were "prepared to supply financial support."[25]

CMES was formally established in 1954. It offered a two-year master's degree in Regional Studies and a joint doctoral program with other departments. After returning from Washington and his duties as assistant director of National Estimates, Langer served as the first director of CMES. Fellow historian and OSS veteran Richard Frye was appointed associate director.

Frye was also a member of both the Social Science Research Council (SSRC) Committee on Near and Middle Eastern Studies and the American Council of Learned Societies (ACLS) Committee on Near Eastern Studies. Echoing the earlier proposal, the Center's program announcement declared that its purpose was "to train specialists for academic and non-academic work in an area which has become increasingly important in world affairs and in which the interests and responsibilities of the United States have grown steadily since the Second World War."[26]

Langer was one of several national security academics to emerge during the early Cold War period. Like Pendleton Herring, his former Harvard colleague, Langer was comfortable in the halls of government as well as academia, and he influenced both over the next decade. He was the son of German immigrants. When his father died at a young age, Langer and his brothers were raised by their mother in South Boston. He was fortunate to attend Harvard on scholarship and after serving in the U.S. Army during World War I, Langer returned for graduate school. He studied under Archibald Cary Coolidge, a European historian and member of the Inquiry. Trained as a diplomatic historian, Langer was not a Middle East scholar. Instead, his goal at CMES was to establish the program and recruit top faculty.[27]

By the end of the year, Harvard announced that Oxford's Hamilton Gibb was joining CMES. The preeminent Orientalist scholar at the time, Gibb was recruited after a contentious competition with rival Princeton. Gibb's transition from Oxford to Harvard was emblematic of the broader postwar shift in hegemony from Britain to America. It also demonstrated, as historian Zachary Lockman notes, that American universities were challenging their European equivalents in the study of the region.[28] Gibb's appointment at Harvard not only validated the emerging field of Middle East studies, it also represented the continuity between Orientalist thought and writings and the production of knowledge in American Middle East studies. Indeed, Gibb later hailed the central role of Orientalists to area studies. In a 1963 speech at London's SOAS, he explained:

> The orientalist's function is to furnish that core out of his knowledge and understanding of the invisibles—the values, attitudes and mental processes characteristic of the "great culture" that underlie the application even today of the social and economic data—to explain the why, rather than the what and the how, and this precisely because he is or should be able to see the

data not simply as isolated facts, explicable in and by themselves, but in the broad context and longer perspective of cultural habit and tradition.[29]

Gibb succeeded Langer as director of the CMES, which also recruited the FSI's Charles Ferguson. Ferguson was considered the leading American linguist for the region. Before joining the Harvard faculty, Ferguson led the FSI's Arabic Language training school based in Beirut. Anthropologist Derwood "Ted" W. Lockard, former director of the CIA's Middle East Division, joined the Center in the fall. Lockard replaced Frye as associate director and served until 1972.[30]

CMES initially shared space with the Russian Research Center. In its first year, six students enrolled in the program. In spite of its stellar reputation and respected faculty, CMES experienced the usual growing pains of any new academic program, including internal disputes over curriculum and problematic students. It also sought closer relations with corporations and the U.S. government.[31]

Middle East Oil and Middle Eastern Studies

After taking office, the Eisenhower administration increasingly viewed nationalist governments in the Middle East and the broader decolonizing world with suspicion and hostility. Six months before Eisenhower's inauguration, a nationalist coup in Egypt overthrew the monarchy of King Farouk, potentially threatening the Anglo-American position in the region. Although the Eisenhower administration initially attempted to reach an accommodation with the new Egyptian government, especially after Gamal Abdel Nasser consolidated power, it adopted a more confrontational approach with Iran. The Anglo-American–orchestrated coup that removed Mossadegh reaffirmed Washington's willingness to defend its perceived interests in the Middle East.

Oil interests were a central factor in the August 1953 coup. Iran's oil reserves and facilities, especially the Abadan refinery, were essential to Britain's economy and military. The lengthy oil concession negotiations between Tehran and London that culminated in the 1951 nationalization of the Anglo-Iranian Oil Company (AIOC) also troubled Washington. Although the Truman administration initially rejected British plans to overthrow Mossadegh, it was increasingly concerned about the regional and the global implications of turmoil in Iran. By March 1953, the situation in Washington and

Tehran had changed. Mossadegh's National Front coalition was splintering and U.S. Ambassador to Iran Loy Henderson received queries from elements in the Iranian military about support for a coup. Over the next five months, the Eisenhower administration implemented TPAJAX, a public and covert effort to undermine Mossadegh's government. The successful August 19 coup—after the initial attempt failed four days earlier—reinstalled Mohammad Reza Shah Pahlavi. Mossadegh was placed under house arrest and died fourteen years later. A new oil agreement was signed in 1954. Britain and the United States agreed to fifty-fifty profit sharing with Iran, the same percentage London rejected a few years earlier, setting the crisis in motion. Yet one major difference was that the consortium of American oil companies and independents received 60 percent of the Anglo-American share of profits.[32]

Two events held in 1956 demonstrated the importance of oil companies to the nascent field of Middle East studies. In May, Princeton hosted its Eighth Annual Near East Conference, a two-day affair whose topic was "Economic Development of the Near East." Executives from ARAMCO, Gulf Oil, Socony, Continental Oil, Cal-Tex, Atlantic Refining, and Standard Oil of New Jersey attended the conference. In addition, ARAMCO's representatives made a presentation. The other attendees included representatives of the State Department, the UN, the Rockefeller and Ford Foundations, and the Carnegie Corporation.[33]

Six months later, during the 1956 Suez War, a meeting of the "Visiting Committee" for Harvard's CMES was held. Unlike the Princeton conference, the committee was comprised overwhelmingly of oil company executives and there were no attendees from government agencies, embassies, or the UN. The meeting was attended by the same oil companies that attended Princeton's conference, and they were joined by representatives of the Ford and Rockefeller Foundations. Howard Page of Standard Oil of New Jersey and William Langer, CMES's former director, served as cochairs.[34]

The initial discussion focused on the job market for Harvard graduates. Even though Gibb attended the meeting, Langer dominated the discussion and reported that there was a "dearth of top-notch Americans applying to the program." This was due to the availability of other job opportunities, which did not require the extensive time commitment for a degree. Except for ARAMCO, the other oil companies reported that they filled their positions either with individuals trained in British schools or through the State Department's FSI. ARAMCO's Terry Duce explained that the company would require employees for the next ten to fifteen years until "a sufficient number of Arabs could be trained." The attendees agreed that government service offered the best market for Harvard's graduates. As the region's commercial development improved over time, they anticipated that nonoil companies would require trained personnel.[35]

Langer emphasized that CMES was not created "to develop Arab philosophers." He added that it was important to encourage "able, young American students into the program." Langer requested assistance from the attendees to determine if "the program was adequate and useful." If not, Harvard was "prepared to shift it to meet [their] requirements." He reassured the oil company representatives that ad hoc programs could be developed in conjunction with other departments and programs to meet their training needs and interests. Langer concluded the meeting with a plea for cooperation between CMES and the companies, stating that Harvard did not want to "find students, support them, and then find that the companies did not want them." Although it was not part of the main discussion, the Harvard meeting coincided with the 1956 Suez War.[36]

Constructing a Problem Area

As discussed in Chapter 4, following the 1956 Suez War, the Eisenhower administration sought to contain Nasser's influence regionally and globally. After the conflict, Nasser emerged as one of the leaders of the "non-aligned movement" with Yugoslavia's Josip Broz Tito, Kwame Nkrumah of Ghana, and Indonesia's Sukarno.[37] Washington viewed Nasser as either an active Soviet client or an unwitting supporter of Moscow's goals in the region and the broader Third World. Through a combination of military and economic aid, the Eisenhower Doctrine sought to buttress conservative Arab regimes aligned with Washington.[38]

The Middle East's increasing importance in America's Cold War planning was the subject of several books published before and after the Suez War. George Lenczowski's *The Middle East in World Affairs* was arguably the most influential work produced during this period. An émigré from Poland and former Polish Foreign Service officer in British Mandate Palestine, Lenczowski established an early reputation within policy circles and a relationship with the Ford Foundation. In May 1951, the public relations firm Earl Newsom and Company met with Lenczowski, then at Hamilton College, on behalf of Standard Oil of New Jersey. The meeting occurred shortly after the AIOC was nationalized. Lenczowski recommended that the Western states "pursue a policy of firmness with persuasion, use skillful manipulation of personalities and indicate a willingness, at least, to make a show of force." He asserted that this was preferable to the alternative approach of "accommodate the Asiatics, treat them as equals, never use force." Lenczowski stated Lebanon was the center of communist activity in the region and warned Standard against contact with Israel "so as not to alienate the Arabs." He also described Syrians as "diseased," Egyptians as "effeminate," and said the Saudis were "real fighters." In spite of these dubious assertions, Newsom recommended that the Ford Foundation retain Lenczowski as a consultant for Middle East–related programs.[39]

Lenczowski's meeting with Newton coincided with the completion of *The Middle East in World Affairs.* The derogatory descriptions he expressed about the region's inhabitants were generally absent from the book. Instead, Lenczowski offered a sweeping analysis of great power politics in the region from the late Ottoman period to the early Cold War. Echoing George Kennan's "Long Telegram," Lenczowski portrayed Soviet actions in the region as inherited from tsarist policy. With British primacy contested, Lenczowski concluded that Anglo-American cooperation combined with "respect for the legitimate aspirations of the native peoples, would secure this vital area for the Free World."[40]

Lenczowski's analysis influenced two other scholars with ties to the foreign policy establishment. Halford Hoskins, a former director of the School of Advanced International Studies (SAIS) and a State Department consultant during World War II, published *The Middle East: Problem Area in World Politics* two years before the Suez crisis. Hoskins argued that the region was strategic due to its geography and resources, but that the newly independent nations were vulnerable to communist influence. This combination, Hoskins wrote, made the Middle East "an area whose attitudes and outlook may well exercise a decisive influence on the shape of things to come." Hoskins acknowledged that his prior government service and conversations with policymakers and diplomats influenced his analysis. The Middle East, he argued, offered the ideal "laboratory conditions for the study of international relations." With Britain's ability to protect the region in doubt, Hoskins asserted that only the United States had the financial and military means to continue London's policies. Two years later, the Suez crisis accelerated London's declining regional influence and Washington attempted to expand its containment policy with the Eisenhower Doctrine.[41]

John Campbell's *Defense of the Middle East: Problems of American Policy* also drew on Lenczowski's analysis. Campbell was director of political studies at the Council on Foreign Relations and the book grew out of a study group convened to discuss how the Middle East could be defended against the Soviet Union. Although the study group first met before the 1956 Suez War, the crisis shaped the book's analysis and conclusions.[42] Campbell presented the defense of the Middle East as integral to America's survival. He stated that "we need assume no inconsistency between what serves our own national interests broadly conceived, and what serves those of other nations." Yet Campbell's recommendations reflected the Eisenhower Doctrine as well as its limitations, which were already apparent by the time *Defense of the Middle East* was published. Campbell wrote that Washington needed to "find policies which help the nations of the Middle East to develop the will and the strength to meet the challenges of the modern world and to maintain their freedom without menacing that of others." However, he conceded "that is a tall order."[43]

As the Eisenhower Doctrine was under development, a group of scholars met at Johns Hopkins University to discuss the implications of the Suez crisis. The conference produced an edited volume, *Tensions in the Middle East*, which was published as revolutions swept across the region. Inspired by Nasser's call for Arab unity, the nationalist movements threatened to unseat the conservative regimes with ties to Washington and London. The conference participants and contributors to the volume included OSS veterans J. C. Hurewitz, Robert Strausz-Hupé, and Robert Sethian. British scholar and former intelligence official Bernard Lewis also attended, as did Paul Nitze, the former State Department official who oversaw the development of National Security Council (NSC) report number 68 and cofounded SAIS. Of the conference participants, Lewis would have the most lasting impact on Middle East studies. Indeed, the themes of his presentation were repeated in his work over the next half century and eventually adopted by other scholars in the post–Cold War era.[44]

Lewis examined the region as a Cold War battleground after the Suez crisis. He argued that the region should be viewed as a "civilization" rather than as individual nation-states. The root cause of the "present discontents," Lewis wrote, was a "clash between civilizations." He believed that this conflict had begun with the emergence of Islam and its eventual expansion into North Africa and Spain and had continued with the failed "Christian counteroffensive" of the Crusades. The century and a half of Western domination after Ottoman rule "shattered traditional patterns of thought and behavior, of political and social loyalty and organization, beyond repair, and has posed to the peoples of the Middle East an immense problem of readjustment, both in their dealings with the outside world and in their own internal affairs," Lewis asserted.[45] He claimed that the people of the region were experiencing a "crisis of transition" that the West initiated, but which they must resolve alone. Although this phrase reflected the thinking of modernization theorists, Lewis suggested a very different policy approach. He called for a policy of "masterly inactivity" in which neither the West nor the Soviet bloc interfered in the region. Johns Hopkins University's C. Grove Haines argued that the policy approach suggested by Lewis would expose the region to Soviet "penetration and dominance." The United States, Haines wrote, must "shoulder the greatest part of the burden, for alone among the Western powers it enjoys at least a measure of respect in the area and the power and prestige that are essential to the exertion of influence."[46]

The National Defense Education Act

While the Middle East was increasing in importance, the field of Middle East studies was still underdeveloped. The early efforts to establish university-based area studies and language training programs were hindered by congressional resistance to government funding. Although he was the president of Columbia University before becoming the thirty-fourth president of the United States, Eisenhower did not favor federal funding for education. Meanwhile, the issue of racial segregation hung over the education debate. Opponents feared that government support would be an avenue to force desegregation of schools. Yet like school desegregation, which Eisenhower opposed but begrudgingly enforced, the NDEA authorized federal funding for education in spite of the White House's timid endorsement.

The Sputnik launch coincided with a crisis in American public education. The 1956–1957 school year witnessed the largest number of students in American history, resulting in a shortage of classrooms and instructors from elementary schools to colleges. Nor was this an acute shortage. Because of the postwar "baby boom," increased school enrollment was projected for the next decade. Although both Republicans and Democrats viewed education as a priority, they disagreed on Washington's role. Six months before Sputnik, the Eisenhower administration supported an emergency spending bill for school construction. Yet the White House did not exert much effort in

Congress and the legislation died in a roll-call vote. Afterward, Eisenhower pledged to back a new bill when the second session of the 85th Congress convened. Sputnik, however, intervened.[47]

Eisenhower's national security credentials were earned in World War II, but Sputnik provided Democrats with an opportunity to challenge his reputation and policies. Senate Majority Leader Lyndon Johnson called Sputnik a "second Pearl Harbor" and announced subcommittee hearings to investigate the state of the U.S. missile program. Johnson's aide, George Reedy, insisted that Sputnik, "if properly handled, would blast the Republicans out of the water, unify the Democratic party, and elect you president." Although Eisenhower dismissed Sputnik's military significance, the successful launch of a second Soviet satellite compounded American fears and criticism of the administration.[48]

Eisenhower's political vulnerability was exacerbated by the conclusions of the Gaither Report, which was finalized during the Sputnik crisis. Led by H. Rowan Gaither of the RAND Corporation, the report examined America's military preparedness in the nuclear age. Although he was not chairman of the committee, Paul Nitze was the driving force behind the report's near-apocalyptic assessment of Soviet missile superiority. The White House rejected the report's conclusions, but after it was leaked to the press and to select Democrats, including Senator John F. Kennedy, criticism mounted. The public failure of an American missile launch a month after Sputnik appeared to validate the Gaither Report's conclusions and further emboldened Democrats. Arthur Larson, Eisenhower's advisor and speechwriter, informed other staff members that the president's "prestige in his special area is slipping."[49]

Like the Korean War, the Sputnik crisis created another opportunity to fund foreign language programs. Over the previous year, there were efforts by the Commissioner of Education to identify the language needs of government agencies. Two weeks after the second Sputnik launch, Secretary of Health, Education, and Welfare (HEW) Marion B. Folsom presented the cabinet with a proposal for improvements in education. Instead of focusing on school construction, Folsom's proposal was framed around "Strengthening and Improvement in the Teaching of Foreign Language." It also included provisions for improving math and science instruction.[50]

HEW's proposal was developed into legislation by the end of the year. Folsom briefed Eisenhower while he was celebrating the holidays in Gettysburg. The proposals, Folsom explained, reflected "some plain truths." He wrote, "Education is now more crucially important to long-term national security than ever before." Folsom added that "there are deficiencies in education, which if allowed to continue, could seriously weaken our national security effort." However, this did not mean that the federal government should exert greater control and authority over education. HEW recommended that the main sources of support remain state, local, and private agencies, but strengthened by Washington. Formalized as the "Education Development Act of 1958," the administration's program was submitted to Congress in January.[51]

Education became an important part of Eisenhower's domestic agenda, but it was linked to national security. Eisenhower scheduled four "science and security" speeches, which emphasized the latter. Yet he was initially unwilling to pursue more than temporary funding to the states. Meanwhile, Democrats led by Alabama's Senator Lister Hill and his protégé, Representative Carl Elliott, sought more sweeping support for education while maintaining control at the state and local levels.[52]

In Congress, federal funding for education was increasingly tied to national defense. Speaking on the floor of the Senate in January, Senator Hill made this connection clear. "A severe blow—some would say a disastrous blow—has been struck at America's self-confidence and at her prestige in the world," he declared. American technological supremacy, Hill stated, was threatened by a country "which only 40 years ago was a nation of peasants." From basic scientific research to the instruction of foreign languages, he asserted, "We Americans know we must mobilize our nation's brainpower in the struggle for survival. The path we choose to pursue may well determine the future not only of western civilization but freedom and peace for all the peoples of the world," Hill warned.[53]

As the legislation was debated on Capitol Hill, the Office of Education (OE) hosted a conference on the U.S. government's language needs. Held on March 22, 1958, the meeting was attended by thirty-six officials from twenty-nine different agencies, including representatives from the Department of Defense, the military services, the State Department, CIA, and the National Security Agency (NSA). The discussion was informed by a 1954 study produced by William R. Parker, a professor of English at New York University. Parker also served as the executive secretary of the Modern Language Association and was secretary of the ACLS's Board of Directors. Parker's report, "The National Interest and Foreign Languages," did not make any explicit recommendations. However, it placed the issue of language training and area studies squarely in the realm of national security. "For America to fulfill her present role of world leadership," he wrote, *"we clearly need many more persons adequately trained in languages other than those of Western Europe."*[54]

The conference attendees identified a need for language training across the different government agencies. Improved language training was also supported by influential figures inside and outside the administration. James Bryant Conant, former Harvard president and ambassador to West Germany, pressed the issue with Secretary Folsom. Milton Eisenhower, the president's brother and president of Johns Hopkins University, also recommended expanding the proposed legislation to include foreign languages.[55]

Following the State Department conference, the OE proposed funding for university-based area studies centers. The centers would prepare students for employment overseas in the government and business sectors, as well as careers in education, by providing them with a "basic understanding of the aspirations, customs, and traditions of the countries in which they live and work." Proposed funding for area studies centers also received support from Secretary of State Dulles. However, one threat to finalizing negotiations for the education bill was that the panic over Sputnik was abating.[56]

Allies in the press attempted to maintain the crisis atmosphere and sway public opinion. *Life* magazine published a series of articles on the "Crisis of Education," which compared the United States unfavorably to the Soviet Union and advocated for fundamental reforms. *Life*'s recommendations for improvements were similar to the administration's proposals. Eisenhower even referenced the magazine's coverage in his March 28 cabinet meeting and in private discussions. Secretary Folsom also wrote a letter of thanks to *Life*'s editors for the series. The support from *Life* magazine was not coincidental. *Time-Life* publisher Henry Luce was a close supporter of Eisenhower and the most influential media owner at the time. During Eisenhower's presidency, *Time* and *Life* provided consistently favorable coverage of the administration.[57]

Events in the Middle East were also linked to education reform. Writing in the *Washington Post*, Malvina Lindsay argued that the lack of Arabic-language skills among American diplomats in Baghdad was partially to blame for the lack of intelligence on the recent Free Officers' Coup in Iraq. Lindsay wrote that a survey conducted by the University of Wisconsin demonstrated "the frightening unpreparedness of this country in linguistics for the Middle East cold war." In spite of warnings a decade earlier, Lindsey reported that the Wisconsin survey found only twenty-three out of roughly

1,800 higher education institutions offered one or more Arabic courses. In addition, only twelve offered Middle East studies classes. In spite of recent language training efforts by the State and Defense Departments, "a small proportion of diplomats and officials sent overseas" had the necessary language proficiency. This contrasted with the Soviet Union, where "Russian technicians are trained in the languages and cultures of areas to which they are sent." Lindsay concluded that if Congress passed the educational legislation under debate it could improve America's ability to train more language specialists.[58]

In late July, HR 13247 was finally brought to the House floor. Carl Elliott, the Alabama Democrat who coauthored the bill and pushed it through the Education and Labor committee, proclaimed that it was "America's answer to the Soviet challenge." This was reinforced by the bill's final language. "The present emergency demands that additional and more adequate educational opportunities be made available," it declared. Although the states still maintained primary responsibility for education, the bill stated that "the national interest requires, however, that the Federal Government give assistance to education for programs which are important to our defense." In spite of the national security overtones and substantial efforts of Elliott and Hill, passing the legislation required an unlikely alliance of the Eisenhower administration and organized labor. After nearly a month of negotiations and last-minute attempts to scuttle the bill, it was passed on August 24 and signed by Eisenhower nine days later. In the accompanying signing statement, Eisenhower wrote that it was only a temporary four-year measure that would "do much to strengthen our American system of education so that it can meet the broad and increasing demands imposed upon it by considerations of basic national security."[59]

Implementing the NDEA

National security and language training became even more intertwined with the NDEA's implementation. The legislation authorized the Commissioner of Education to determine which foreign languages were "needed by the Federal Government or by business, industry or education." To assist with the assessment, Washington turned to the American Council of Learned Societies. The ACLS was directly involved in efforts to improve and expand foreign language training and area studies in the United States prior to Sputnik. Indeed, it was these efforts that led the OE to determine that the

ACLS was the "logical non-governmental agency" to oversee a survey of which language centers should be established. The OE recommended the creation of a steering panel mostly drawn from current and former ACLS officials to oversee the survey. Harold B. Hoskins, the director of the State Department's FSI and the ACLS treasurer, and Mortimer Graves, the former executive secretary of the ACLS, were among those recommended for the steering panel. Although Graves retired from the ACLS before the Sputnik launch, he was called on after the NDEA became law.[60]

The ACLS findings were released to the public in March 1959. It recommended establishing centers for language training in Arabic, Chinese, Hindustani, Japanese, Portuguese, and Russian. The OE explained that these "critically needed foreign languages" were "spoken by more than 1 billion people, or about 35 percent of the world's population yet very few people in the United States have studied any of them." Secretary of Health, Education, and Welfare Arthur S. Flemming explained that the initial languages were just the beginning. "This nation, however, cannot in the long run meet its already gigantic commercial and diplomatic commitments around the globe without adequate instruction for its citizens in more than 50 other official and unofficial modern foreign languages," he said. "Many of these languages are not taught at all in any American university or college, and priorities will need to be established in this area," Flemming added.[61]

In the first four years, $61 million was allocated for NDEA's Title VI programs. Of which, $8 million per year was designated for language development (or Part A of Title VI), with funding of area centers, stipends, and research. An additional $7.25 million per year was allocated for language institutes and stipends (designated Part B of Title VI). Although Eisenhower intended for the NDEA to be temporary, Title VI funding was renewed in 1961 and 1963 at the same levels. In 1964, the NDEA was reauthorized for an additional four years. Title VI funding was increased to $13 million per year and authorized to increase to $18 million by 1968. In addition, Part B of Title VI was eliminated in favor of Title XI institutes that were to cover a range of topics for different audiences.[62] What Amy Newhall has described as the "devil's bargain" between academia and the national security state for area studies served to justify continued funding over the next five decades. However, as will be demonstrated, national security would also be used by opponents to argue for cutting funding to Title VI or ending it altogether.[63]

Four years after the NDEA was signed, the American Association for Middle East Studies (AAMES) organized a study of the field. The first professional organization for Middle East studies, AAMES was established in 1959. Unlike other scholarly organization, AAMES was primarily focused on undergraduate education. This was reinforced by a study the organization commissioned to determine the "overall problems to which the rapid spread of Middle East studies has given rise" as well as to formulate measures for improvement. Led by Columbia's J. C. Hurewitz, the study focused on undergraduate instruction. In the report's preface, Hurewitz explained that the emergence of Middle East studies was part of a larger postwar trend of "broadening the liberal arts education" in American universities and colleges. He noted that the traditional curriculum focused heavily on Western civilization and the increase in non-Western studies was "intended to redress the balance." He conceded that "the intimate connection between such area studies and politics could not be denied." "Although the present survey did not set out to answer the question, it has indirectly helped illuminate the relationship between the unprecedented problems of American security and the growth of undergraduate instruction on one foreign area," Hurewitz wrote. He added, "To admit the original political stimulus is not to denigrate the value of such studies. It is merely to put them into proper perspective."[64]

The study found that there were 330 faculty members and 180 colleges and universities offering courses related to the Middle East.[65] Administrators were asked to select four reasons for adding Middle East courses to the curriculum. The largest percentage of respondents, 78 percent, identified "American security" as the main rationale. This was even more pronounced among universities at the "Top" schools, where it was selected by 91 percent of administrators. In addition, 53 percent of all administrators and 68 percent at the "Top" programs identified "cultural enrichment" as a major reason for adding Middle East courses.[66] Whether the rationale was national security or cultural enrichment (or both), fifteen Title VI centers were established for Arabic language instruction by 1965. In addition, Turkish was taught at nine centers, Hebrew at seven, and Persian at six university-based centers. A total of 1,084 students were studying Middle Eastern languages by 1964, a dramatic increase from only 286 students in 1958.[67]

Perhaps the longest-lasting impact of the NDEA was an increase in the number of doctoral students trained in the different areas. The Middle East, however, lagged behind other areas. In 1951, there were a total of 181 international studies PhDs, of which 24 were related to the Middle East. By 1960, 241 doctorates were awarded in international studies, including 28 for the Middle East. Six years later, a total of 379 international studies PhDs were awarded, of which 40 were in Middle East studies.[68]

Institution Building

Three years before Sputnik, the Rockefeller Foundation began discussing a long-term strategy for funding area studies. Led by Charles H. Fahs, the Foundation's director of humanities, it considered offering sizable institution-building grants to select programs. After the grants were dispersed, the Rockefeller Foundation would no longer fund area studies programs on a regular basis. The proposal was shelved but then revisited after the NDEA's passage when the Rockefeller Foundation was approached by Harvard's CMES. As part of an ambitious fundraising campaign, CMES asked for a $500,000 grant that would help it meet its $2 million goal. During the negotiations, the Rockefeller Foundation also encouraged the Ford Foundation to provide Harvard with a similar institution-building grant. CMES eventually received a $500,000 grant from Rockefeller and $950,000 from Ford.[69]

The discussions between Harvard and the Rockefeller Foundation also revealed the perception of area studies specialists inside and outside of academia. Dean Rusk, future U.S. secretary of state and Rockefeller Foundation president, informed Harvard president Nathan Pusey that the university's Middle East studies program had made "remarkable progress over the past few years." Rusk noted that the Rockefeller Foundation was encouraged by Harvard's fundraising campaign and its potential to solidify CMES. He also offered advice for recruiting area studies personnel. Rusk reported that the Rockefeller Foundation had observed that there were varying standards for area studies appointments. "There have been instances where appointments were tolerated, rather than made with enthusiasm," he wrote, "possibly on the assumption that one cannot expect too much from men in area studies." The successful fundraising campaign, Rusk explained, would allow Harvard to secure and tenure the best area studies scholars. He suggested that this could be achieved by identifying scholars who were highly qualified in a particular discipline and who also had competence in their particular area, like Harvard's recruitment of Hamilton Gibb. Rusk conceded, however, "I realize that it is a bit rough to suggest a unique man as a standard."[70]

Gibb remained at the helm when CMES celebrated its tenth anniversary. Although the program was originally intended to produce candidates for the oil industry and government service, by the mid-1960s Harvard declared that its focus had shifted to providing graduate training and promoting research into the "less explored areas" of the history and culture of the region. In addition, the university asserted that the program was "impartial" toward the "contending factions" in the region "torn by bitter disputes and infested by angry unscrupulous propaganda." It explained that these factions were "sharply sensitive to their image as presented in America, both in content and in tone." CMES acknowledged that the majority of students in the Master of Arts (AM) program were still geared toward the government and business sectors, but that a significant number also pursued doctoral degrees.[71]

The Harvard program experienced dramatic growth in its first decade. From 1954 to 1958, CMES had a total of fifty-five students, of which forty were in the master's program. During this period, eleven AM and two PhD degrees were awarded. In 1959, the program increased the number of master's and doctoral students admitted to the programs. From 1959 to 1964, 245 students were admitted, of which 156 were master's students. The rise in admissions was matched by an increased number of degrees conferred, with sixty-three AM degrees awarded during the later period. Of the seventy-four total AM degrees awarded in the program's first decade, fourteen (19 percent) of the graduates worked for the government and five (7 percent) in the business sector, while twenty-eight (38 percent) continued their graduate studies, including Fulbright scholars. Although the program's growth continued, it experienced a major setback when Hamilton Gibb suffered a stroke in 1963 and was unable to resume his duties after an extended recuperation. Gibb died in 1971 and CMES struggled to find an academic leader that could replace him.[72]

Princeton's program also expanded prior to the NDEA. Under the leadership of T. Cuyler Young, the Near East studies program maintained its ties to the foreign policy and national security establishments. By 1959, the Near East program produced twenty-six PhDs and awarded forty-three master's and twenty-seven BA degrees. During this period, it also trained eighteen FSOs and fifty-four officers from the Department of Defense.[73]

Like Harvard, Princeton also sought additional funding for its Near East program at the end of the 1950s. In 1954, it received a $500,000 capital grant from the Rockefeller Foundation. Six years later, Princeton received a $2.5 million institution-building grant from the Ford Foundation, a portion of which was for the Near East program.[74] The combination of federal funding through the NDEA and support from the foundations ensured the long-term viability of both programs. Over the next two decades, however, Princeton maintained a more prestigious faculty, especially after Hamilton Gibb's illness. In addition to Young and Morroe Berger, the faculty included Manfred Halpern, a State Department veteran and modernization theorist. Yet the program still struggled to shift its focus toward the modern era and the Department of Oriental Studies was not split into separate Near Eastern Studies and East Asian Studies departments until 1969.[75]

Foundation support was not limited to Harvard and Princeton. After the NDEA was passed, the Ford Foundation initiated a new program to award large, multiyear institution-building grants to public and private universities for area and language studies. Columbia and the University of California at Berkeley and Los Angeles joined Harvard as the first recipients. By 1963, the Ford Foundation awarded $26 million to fifteen institutions, including Boston University, Cornell, Northwestern, Princeton, Yale, and the Universities of Chicago and Pennsylvania. Public universities receiving the awards included Indiana, Michigan, Washington, and Wisconsin. The funds went to forty-four area studies programs, including seven for the Middle East. However, the boom times would not last. The foundations abandoned area studies by the end of the decade. Much like the federal government, the Ford Foundation under the leadership of McGeorge Bundy shifted its focus to modernization and development. The former dean of Harvard College, Bundy also served as national security advisor under Kennedy and Johnson. In a foreshadowing of the Nixon administration's decision to cut funding to area studies, the Ford Foundation argued that a sufficient number of area studies scholars had been trained and the programs no longer needed large-scale support. At the same time, the Ford Foundation's embrace of modernization was not coincidental and reflected Washington's foreign policy goals.[76]

The Foreign Service Institute

University-based area studies programs were viewed by the foreign policy and national security establishments as the initial stage of training for scholars as well as future government officials. Those graduates hired by the State Department or the CIA were eventually trained at the State Department's FSI. As discussed in Chapter 3, the FSI was first established in 1946 and the outbreak of the Korean War found the Institute with excess classroom capacity and an insufficient number of instructors. Moreover, language and area instruction for certain geographic areas, including the Near and Middle East, was not viewed by many Foreign Service Officers (FSOs) as beneficial to their careers. By 1952, the FSI was also beginning to evaluate how to improve its training programs for the Middle East, which were conducted in conjunction with Princeton and other universities. The FSI determined that the university programs "though quite adequate for certain aspects of instruction not given up to now at the Institute, are by and large not satisfactory for the special needs and requirements of Government language-and-area specialists." To address the gap, the FSI proposed a pilot program that would be based in the Middle East. The region was chosen because the FSI's staff had more "academic and field experience in the Near East than in any other area."[77]

The new effort was also justified based on America's increasing interests in the area. Although the Middle East was considered of "great strategic importance" to the United States and there were twenty-one posts and 262 FSOs in Arabic-speaking countries, the State Department conceded that "very few can presently be classed as experts on the area." In addition, only twelve FSOs had intensive Arabic training. Attempting to obtain the necessary budgetary approval, FSI drew sharp comparisons to the Soviet Union, which it reported had three training centers focused on the Middle East. Repeating a familiar argument, FSI stated that "our national interest makes it imperative that the Department take immediate steps to increase the number of trained specialists in the Near East and South Asia." The Beirut program was intended to train current and future FSOs based on the belief that "Arabic language and culture can be studied and understood much better within the area itself than from outside." FSI added that it was not possible to duplicate this environment at the Institute or an American university.[78]

The FSI's Arabic training included two parts. Initial instruction was conducted over five months in Washington. For two hours a day, students received language training and instruction on the politics, history, and culture of the area as well as U.S. policy in the region. The instructors were State Department personnel and outside scholars, including OSS veterans Harold Glidden, Richard Sanger, Robert Sethian, and Carleton Coon. Other notable instructors included SAIS's Majid Khadduri and the State Department's W. Wendell Cleland. After the initial training was completed, FSOs spent ten weeks in Lebanon.[79]

Launched in March 1953, the FSI's Language-and-Area School, Near East was based at the U.S. Embassy in Beirut and was led by Charles Ferguson, who left a year later for Harvard's fledgling Middle East program. The FSI coordinated with the American University of Beirut (AUB) to provide intermediate and advanced training in Arabic. Area studies in Beirut provided the trainees with the geographic, historical, economic, and social background of the region. Foggy Bottom continued to rely on Princeton for intermediate and advanced training in Persian and Turkish.[80]

Lebanon was also the site of Britain's Middle East Center for Arab Studies (MECAS). Originally based in Jerusalem, MECAS was established in the mountain village of Shimlan outside Beirut. MECAS provided language training for the U.K. Foreign Office, intelligence and military services, as well as private businesses. Led by a career foreign service officer, MECAS relied on native Arabic instructors. Unlike FSI, MECAS did not emphasize area studies and it stressed instruction in Modern Standard Arabic over colloquial dialects. MECAS drew largely on AUB faculty members for lectures on the history and politics of the region.[81]

In 1955, Harold Hoskins was named director of the FSI. Hoskins inherited an FSI that was underutilized and understaffed, but under his leadership the Institute expanded and improved its services. During his tenure it became known as "Hoskins University." Hoskins was charged with implementing a training program for State Department personnel. He also created an advisory board with representatives from academia and business, including Harvard's William Langer. The FSI's shortcomings were compounded by the Sputnik launch and criticisms in the press of America's deficiencies in science and languages. In response to press reports in March 1958 that roughly 50 percent of FSOs did not possess any foreign language skills, the FSI instituted mandatory training and testing program. The goal of the program was that all FSOs would obtain proficiency in a "world language" (French, German, and Spanish) and have "useful" knowledge of the principal language of the country where they were assigned. By the end of 1959, it reported that the number of FSOs without any foreign language skills had been reduced to 16.5 percent. In addition, the FSI benefited from a dramatic increase in its training budget. For example, the budget for foreign language training in 1960 exceeded the FSI's entire training budget for the 1955 fiscal year.[82]

In September 1959, the Senate Foreign Relations Committee considered creating a Foreign Service Academy. However, an internal State Department assessment ruled out this possibility. Writing to Senator Mike Mansfield of Montana, Loy Henderson, then deputy under secretary of state for administration, explained that the review "strengthened the Department's confidence in the current practice of drawing [FSOs] directly from the universities, public and private, of this country as the best means of obtaining qualified people with a wide range of geographic and educational backgrounds." Henderson added that the State Department determined that the creation of an academy "would not improve the caliber of the young people now becoming available to the [Foreign] Service."[83]

The internal assessment confirmed the State Department's reluctance to establish an academy for either undergraduate or graduate training. Foggy Bottom argued that an academy could not compete with the faculty and resources of a major university, whose graduates could already be found in the Foreign Service. The combination of continued recruitment of university graduates and government-financed student loans was considered superior to establishing a stand-alone institution. In addition, the State Department believed that FSOs derived greater benefit from additional training during their careers, particularly in language training, which was available through the FSI. It conceded, however, that the FSI's training program needed to be expanded. Finally, the State Department explained that FSOs were drawn from across the country and from different socioeconomic backgrounds and that establishing an academy would reverse this trend.[84]

In spite of the reliance on the FSI, an internal review identified problems with the language training program. Led by Cornell's J. Milton Cowen, the review found that retaining staff members was a major concern as they were often recruited by leading universities. This was compounded by the lack of materials for instruction as well as inconsistent and unpredictable class sizes. However, the Cowen report acknowledged that because of the specialized nature of the FSI's language training, the review committee could not identify a more economical or effective alternative.[85]

Academia and the Invisible Government

Although national security interests drove the creation of area studies centers and the expansion of the State Department's FSI, less than a decade after the NDEA was passed the U.S. government's relationship with academia was increasingly strained. In July 1965, embarrassing revelations about "Project Camelot" led the State Department to institute changes in government support of foreign area research. Project Camelot was funded by the U.S. Army's Office of Research and Development and involved an interdisciplinary research group from several universities, including Brooklyn College and the University of Pittsburgh. The project examined potential causes of instability in Latin America. Chilean scholars were informed of the army's involvement in the project by a Norwegian sociologist. Although Chile was not one of the countries to be examined, the revelations created a scandal that reverberated in Washington.[86] In response, Secretary of State Dean Rusk established the Foreign Affairs Research Council to "formulate policy, determine Department needs, and examine all government-sponsored research projects in terms of foreign policy risks they may entail and consider means for reducing such risks." The Council was chaired by the director of the State Department's Bureau of Intelligence and Research (INR) and staffed by the ERS. Gene Lyons described the Council's role as determining "what research should *not*, rather than what should, be sponsored by the government."[87]

Meanwhile, the CIA's attempts to strengthen relations with academia encountered resistance. Three months after Project Camelot was exposed, Ray Cline, deputy director of the CIA, informed Director William Raborn that scholars in the social sciences were reluctant to engage openly with government agencies, in particular the CIA. Cline detailed the reactions of the Consultants' Board to a proposal for the establishment of area and functional panels. The Consultants' Board warned that the proposal would be "coldly received" and "arouse suspicion and antagonism." Scholars in the social sciences, he stated, "have come increasingly to fear that association with the U.S. military and intelligence agencies—above all with the CIA—will jeopardize their opportunities for investigations and research abroad." "In short we are in a period of poor relations between the Government (CIA) and the scholars as far as social science is concerned. It may last for some time. This does not apply to the natural and physical sciences," Cline explained.[88]

The main issue dividing the social sciences, Cline reported, was a "moral one." He explained that "counterinsurgency has brought the issue to a head viz. do we put down the good insurgents with the bad?" "Social science is *not* a science and mountains of research do not yield political wisdom, though they provide platforms for debate over foreign policy," he wrote. As Chapter 6 details, counterinsurgency was an important aspect of the implementation of modernization theory in the developing world.[89]

Instead of creating formal panels in conjunction with the SSRC, the CIA decided to continue informal relations with individual scholars holding security clearances. Cline explained that "we are increasing our list of cleared consultants, with due care, concentrating on our substantive task—and not on the 'CIA image.'" He added that the Consultants' Board would continue to provide input on national estimates, and that "for military and economic research we will draw from an increased list of specialists according to the problem." Cline cautioned that "we have a more difficult problem in political matters where the emphasis is on current intelligence and not on research."[90]

Cline's memo argued that the publication and success of *The Invisible Government* by journalists David Wise and Thomas Ross served to undermine relations between the CIA and academia. In their discussion of the postwar expansion of the national security bureaucracy, Wise and Ross asserted, "There are two governments in the United States today. One is visible. The other is invisible." They explained that "the first is the government that citizens read about," while the second was "the interlocking, hidden machinery that carries out the policies of the United States in the Cold War." "This second, invisible government gathers intelligence, conducts espionage, and plans and executes secret operations all over the world," they wrote.[91] Published in 1964, *The Invisible Government* found a welcome audience in an America still struggling to understand the assassination of President Kennedy. It offered readers insights into the activities and excesses of the myriad government and military agencies, in particular the CIA, from the Bay of Pigs to the "secret war" in Vietnam.

The Invisible Government also revealed the "two-way" relationship between academic institutions and the CIA. Wise and Ross explained that the agency covertly funded research programs at some institutions while the universities assisted with recruiting personnel and provided "a pool of expert knowledge about foreign countries upon which the intelligence agency can, and does, draw." They wrote, "Despite the possible loss of academic freedom, most universities and professors have shown little reluctance to work for the CIA. The agency has been able to obtain the services of almost all of the academic institutions and individuals it has approached." *The Invisible Government* concluded with a warning: "There is a real danger that the academic community may find itself so closely allied with the Invisible Government that it will have lost its ability to function as an independent critic of our government and society."[92]

Within a year, the CIA found that the seemingly cozy relationship described by *The Invisible Government* was strained. In his memorandum from

November 1965, Cline observed "there is a growing tendency in certain quarters to look for CIA behind the Government front in foreign affairs and in the foundations and universities." "Some of our consultants," he wrote, "expressed alarm at the way in which their colleagues have accepted 'The Invisible Government' as a factual description of the CIA's role and serious concern [*sic*] over the lack of understanding their colleagues show for the problems of our Government." A relationship with the CIA was no longer seen positively among academics. Instead, "there is an insinuation that he is being used." Cline added that the Consultants' Board "reminded us in no uncertain terms of the current strain in Government-academic relations."[93]

While the CIA's leadership complained internally about its portrayal in *The Invisible Government*, they also sought to undermine the book. Wise and Ross later revealed that before publication they were pressured by DCI John McCone. When they refused not to publish *The Invisible Government*, the CIA attempted to place negative reviews in major media outlets in order to discredit its claims. McCone also requested that President Johnson publicly criticize the book in a press conference. Johnson, however, demurred.[94]

Revelations about the relationship between academia and the CIA were further exposed by *Ramparts* magazine in April 1966. The cover story, "The University on the Make," was ostensibly an exposé of a mid-1950s training program in South Vietnam overseen by Michigan State University. However, Stanley K. Sheinbaum, a former Michigan State economics professor, explained in the introduction that the real targets were the "automatic cold warriors" that could be found on "every university campus," particularly in the social sciences. The article raised questions about the extent of cooperation between university departments and the intelligence community. It also had an impact beyond the critics of U.S. policy in Vietnam. Coupled with the publication of *The Invisible Government* and a five-part series in the *New York Times* in April 1966 on the Michigan State controversy, the U.S. intelligence community was interested and concerned about the coverage. At a meeting of the President's Foreign Intelligence Advisory Board held at the end of May 1966, media coverage of the intelligence community, in particular the articles published by *Ramparts* and the *New York Times*, were distributed to Board members and placed on the agenda for discussion.[95]

Hiwar and the Congress for Cultural Freedom

The revelations in *Ramparts* magazine and the *New York Times* also exposed another secret relationship. The Congress for Cultural Freedom (CCF) was officially established in 1950 by the CIA. Historian Frances Stonor Saunders describes the CCF as a massive and long-running Cold War propaganda effort to promote American values among the intelligentsia in thirty-five countries. The CCF funded over twenty publications, including the anticommunist monthly magazine *Encounter* and *Hiwar* ("Dialogue"), a Beirut-based bimonthly journal.[96]

Tawfiq Sayigh founded *Hiwar* in November 1962. A Palestinian refugee from Lebanon, Sayigh was an Arabic lecturer at London's School of Oriental and African Studies. He was initially approached by translator Denys Johnson-Davies on behalf of the CCF, which wanted to publish an Arabic-language magazine. Although Sayigh's political affiliations were not public, his later writings for *Hiwar* revealed an alignment with the CCF's leftist anticommunism. Sayigh traveled to France to meet with John Hunt, who was a member of the CCF's Secretariat and managed its Paris office. An American novelist, Hunt was also a CIA agent and served as the main intermediary between the CCF and the agency. Sayigh recorded in his diary that he demanded complete editorial freedom, including the journal's name, and Hunt agreed.[97]

Hiwar was attacked before the first volume was published. The Lebanese magazine *Sayad* criticized *Hiwar*'s connection to the CCF. Sayigh, however, ignored the criticism. The inaugural volume contained an editorial describing *Hiwar*'s mission. The journal, Sayigh wrote, would be unique. Unlike other journals in the Arab world, he explained, *Hiwar* was a "public cultural magazine" that covered different types of literature, art, and ideas but was written in a manner that was accessible by a general readership and moderate in its approach. Drawing on writers and intellectuals from across the Arab world, the magazine would focus on important causes and issues from an Arab perspective. Although it was not a "foreign magazine" published in an Arab country, he stated that it shared the objectives of the CCF in defending the freedom of intellectual inquiry. As such, *Hiwar* would publish debates on different topics and focus on freedom, especially "the freedom of culture, the freedom of thought, expression, speech and reading, around the world." Sayigh's editorial reflected his private thoughts and concerns about the limits placed on intellectual freedom by communist regimes.[98]

The journal continued to attract attention over the next few years. This was due to its U.S.-based funding and professional production as well as its low price and sizable reimbursements for contributors. Meanwhile, leading figures in Beirut's intellectual scene argued with Sayigh about his relationship with the CCF. In particular, they found the CCF's anticommunist stance problematic and predicted that it would interfere in editorial matters. The intellectuals also warned of the CCF's real or imagined ties to Zionist groups and cautioned that a larger backlash against the magazine was coming that would ruin his reputation. Sayigh consistently dismissed their concerns and promised to protect *Hiwar*'s independence.[99]

In spite of the criticism, *Hiwar* published articles and poetry by leading Arab intellectuals over the next five years. Contributors included historian Albert Hourani and the poets Ghada al-Samman, Badr Shakir al-Sayyab, and Muhammad al-Maghut. *Hiwar* also published translations of interviews with American intellectuals, including playwright T. S. Eliot and authors Henry Miller and James Baldwin. In its last year, the journal reproduced Tayeb Salih's classic *Season of Migration to the North* in full. Although it was supposed to focus on culture, *Hiwar* delved into regional and international politics. It translated an interview with Algeria's first president, Ahmed Ben Bella, that was originally published in the CCF-backed French magazine *Preuves*. There were also articles critical of the Egyptian revolution and Nasser's government, including by the University of London's Panayiotis Jerasimof (P. J.) Vatikiotis. It could be argued that these articles represented editorial decisions that reflected U.S. foreign policy, particularly the criticism of Nasser and favorable coverage of Ben Bella. However, when *Encounter* editor Melvin Lasky also published in *Hiwar*, the article was not related to Cold War politics.[100]

Controversy followed *Hiwar* during its brief run. It was banned in Iraq less than a year after it was founded. Sayigh asked the Iraqi Ministry of Information for an explanation, but his inquiries were ignored. In addition, leftist Lebanese magazines and intellectual journals continued to criticize *Hiwar* over the next few years. The negative attention reached a new height in 1965 after Egyptian short story writer Yousef Idris first accepted and then publicly rejected an award from *Hiwar*. This was only a preview of what was to come.[101]

In April 1966, the *New York Times* reported that the CIA was supporting "anti-Communist but liberal organizations of intellectuals," in particular the CCF. It added that *Encounter* was an indirect recipient of CIA funds through the CCF. Both *Encounter* and the CCF challenged the story in letters to the editor. A month later, the Egyptian daily *Rose al-Yusuf* published an article detailing the *New York Times* revelations about the CCF and its links to *Hiwar. Hiwar* was quickly banned in Egypt.[102]

Sayigh denied the accusations of CIA funding. He published a statement in *Hiwar's* August 1966 edition as well as in regional newspapers. CCF officials reassured him that they did not have a relationship with the agency, Sayigh explained. He took the opportunity to criticize the Arab newspapers, which reprinted the *New York Times'* claims but not his denials, and reasserted *Hiwar's* independence as well as the CCF's from Washington. Later that month, Sayigh wrote to friends in England. He described the attacks on the journal and expressed relief that no other governments followed Cairo's lead in banning *Hiwar*. He was mistaken. Over the next month, a "Stop *Hiwar*" campaign quickly followed in regional newspapers from Lebanon to Kuwait.[103]

Determined to keep *Hiwar* running, Sayigh traveled to Paris in the fall to meet with CCF officials. He was reassured by Hunt that the organization had not received CIA funding. Less than a year later, however, the CCF publicly admitted that the accusations were true. The confirmation about CIA support spelled the end of *Hiwar* and its last volume was published in April 1967. A month later, Sayigh issued a statement announcing the magazine's closure and appealed for support from Arab funders. There was no response. Sayigh eventually joined the faculty at the University of California, Berkeley but died of a heart attack in January 1971.[104]

Institutionalizing Middle East Studies

Suspect funding was not limited to *Hiwar*. Three years earlier, the journal *Middle Eastern Affairs* ceased publication after thirteen years. Backed by the New York–based Council for Middle Eastern Affairs and edited by Benjamin Shwadran, the journal focused on the contemporary Middle East. That same year, AAMES also ceased operations and its journal, *Middle Eastern Studies,* was discontinued. Senator William Fulbright's 1963 investigation into lobbying agents of foreign governments revealed that the American Zionist Council funded AAMES and the Council for Middle Eastern Affairs. Funding to both organizations was apparently discontinued after the Senate hearings.[105]

With the closure of AAMES, the field lacked a major scholarly association. Although the American Oriental Society was still active, it was considered too narrowly focused. With funding from the Ford Foundation, the Middle East Studies Association (MESA) was formed in 1966. MESA grew out of the SSRC-ACLS Joint Committee, led by Princeton sociologist Morroe Berger. The organization defined the Middle East as stretching from North Africa to parts of Central Asia and focused on contemporary history and politics.

As MESA was launched, Berger also conducted an assessment of the field for the HEW. Berger was a veteran of army intelligence during World War II and completed language training at Princeton's Army Specialized Training Program (ASTP). After the war, he received his PhD at Columbia and maintained contact with the intelligence community, performing research for General Donovan on issues related to the Soviet Union.[106] Berger reported that there was an increase in the number of Middle East centers after the NDEA was passed, however, the region was still not considered a priority for funding or research. He offered several explanations for this trend. "The modern Middle East and North Africa is not a center of great cultural achievement," Berger wrote, "nor is it likely to become one in the near future." This compounded the difficulty of language acquisition, which was also made more challenging because the study of regional languages did not begin until undergraduate or graduate studies. "The study of the region or its languages, therefore, does not constitute its own reward so far as modern culture is concerned," he added. Moreover, Berger asserted that the region was "not a center of great political power nor does it have the potential to become one." In addition, it was "receding in immediate political importance to the U.S. (and even in 'headline' or 'nuisance' value) relative to Africa, Latin America, and the Far East." Because of these factors, Berger concluded that the contemporary Middle East had "only in small degree the kinds of traits that seem to be important in attracting scholarly attention." While this did not "diminish the validity and intellectual value" of scholarship and study of the region, he claimed that it did limit the "field's capacity for growth in the numbers who study and teach." Less than a month later, the June 1967 Arab-Israeli War broke out. In its aftermath, contrary to Berger's analysis, there was increased government and scholarly interest in the Middle East.[107]

Held in December 1967, MESA's first annual conference had only modest attendance. The association also founded several journals, including the *Middle East Studies Association Bulletin* and the *International Journal of Middle East Studies*. MESA experienced internal controversies and growing pains over the next two decades. Meanwhile, America's increased interests and involvement in the region served to exacerbate tensions in the field.[108]

Reflecting on area studies five years after the NDEA was passed, Hamilton Gibb doubted whether the programs provided sufficient training for future scholars. However, he argued that the programs were valuable to current and future government employees. Universities, Gibb explained, were the most effective option for such training.[109]

Berger's 1967 assessment also discussed the connection to government service. "In the past," Berger explained, "it was doubted that this nation would support the scholarly study of other nations except as part of a program of national security." Yet Berger cautioned that "in the future it may be difficult to study other nations under an educational program that has to be called the National Defense Education Act." Although President Eisenhower declared that the NDEA was temporary, more than five decades later it remains the foundation for the study of foreign areas in American universities and colleges.[110]

Building on prior efforts, the NDEA firmly established area studies in the United States. The initial allocation of $15.25 million per year for four years demonstrated the federal government's ability to immediately impact higher education. Critics of the NDEA, particularly those at universities like Princeton with existing programs, argued that it was a "shotgun" approach to deal with an issue that required a more surgical response. Yet within a decade after passage, the impact of the legislation was quantifiable from the growth in the number of centers to the number of students educated, as well as the development of textbooks and related course materials. In addition, federal funding benefited new and existing programs as the NDEA supported fellowships and course development tools. However, support for Middle East studies consistently lagged behind the rest of Asia, a condition that persisted even after the NDEA.

Mirroring the growth spurred by the NDEA, the national security establishment experienced a similar expansion during this period. This included the further development of its internal training facilities, like the FSI, as well as collaboration with academia. Meanwhile, the Princeton Consultants were another example of the growing and powerful "invisible government" and the permeable line between academia and the national security state. Yet the CIA's internal discussions over funding the ERS revealed that the national security establishment deliberately misled academics that it sought to retain for contract research as well as for collection of their publications. The CIA claimed that academics would be less cooperative if the ERS was not housed within the State Department. Yet there was hardly a dearth of scholars willing to collaborate openly or secretly with the intelligence community. Moreover, if the subterfuge was revealed at the time, it would have heightened suspicions about the expanding "invisible government." Although open contacts between academia and government agencies became more difficult to sustain by the mid-1960s, they continued and in some respects expanded.

CHAPTER 6

Modernizing the Middle East

Constructing Traditional Society
and Expertise, 1950–1973

> How can a branch of social science be produced which takes upon
> itself a responsible concern for national security matters, and how
> can talented individuals from within social science be drawn into
> this area?
>
> —ITHIEL DE SOLA POOL, 1963

G eorge Kennan looked to the East and was troubled. Although he was
recently nominated to serve as ambassador to the Soviet Union, relations with the Kremlin were not the source of his consternation. Instead, it
was Iran's decision in October 1951 to sever diplomatic relations with Britain
and expel its diplomatic staff. Iranian prime minister Mohammad Mossadegh's announcement followed tense oil concession negotiations with
London that resulted in the nationalization of the Anglo-Iranian Oil Company (AIOC). Kennan wrote Secretary of State Dean Acheson in January
1952 and placed the recent events in a broader perspective. There was a
"sweeping and fateful misunderstanding underlying our approach to the
peoples of Asia and the Middle East," he explained. Kennan acknowledged
that he was not an area expert, but stated that "surely one of the reasons for
our continued failures throughout these areas has been our inability to understand how profound, how irrational, and how erratic has been the reaction
generally of the respective peoples to the ideas and impulses that have come
to them from the West in recent decades." Nor could Washington expect
that the situation would improve by providing aid. "The fanatical local
chauvinisms of the Middle East," Kennan asserted, could not be made

"friendly or dependable." Instead, he recommended that Washington take a firm stance to curb the "appetites of local potentates." Although hardly as influential as his "Long Telegram," Kennan's letter reflected discussions and concerns within the State Department over rising nationalist movements in the developing world. Washington's attempts to comprehend, guide, and contain those movements contributed to the development of modernization theory.[1]

The intellectual origins of modernization theory can be traced to research surveys conducted by Columbia University's Bureau for Applied Social Research (BASR) for the U.S. State Department and Voice of America (VOA) in the Middle East. Modernization theory was informed by ideas about race that were widely held in the social sciences and the halls of government. These notions were reproduced in claims about "traditional society" in the developing world and reflected U.S. foreign policy toward Iran and Egypt during the 1950s and 1960s. Although modernization theory was ultimately abandoned, its underlying assertions about the irrationality and hostility of populations in the developing world continued to influence policymakers after the Cold War was over.[2]

Race, the Social Sciences, and Policy

Modernization theory drew on notions of racial and cultural hierarchy rooted in Western intellectual discourse. Prior to World War II, the social sciences were directly involved in American and European colonial expansion. Imperialism and race shaped the disciplinary foundations of international relations. Similarly, anthropology's origins were influenced by British imperial expansion and the maintenance of colonies. In addition, studies of racial hierarchy were essential features of imperial management and knowledge production.[3]

The aftermath of World War II and revelations of the Holocaust led to a change in intellectual perceptions of race. While notions of racial supremacy were no longer embraced among American intellectual and political elites, they were not abandoned. Instead, intellectuals emphasized "cultural differences," especially between Western nations and their former colonial possessions and territories. American intellectuals did not hesitate to describe the newly independent states and their populations as "traditional," "primitive," and "backward." Modernization, they believed, would enable these societies to join the universal norm.[4]

The Truman administration's Point IV program, which offered scientific and technical assistance to developing countries, reflected Washington's concern about political instability in the former colonial territories. Yet the barely concealed disdain for these areas was apparent in Kennan's January 1952 letter to Acheson and other internal correspondence within the State Department. Development policy linked the notions of racial hierarchy and superiority to containment policy. The State Department believed—or hoped—that development would prevent Soviet influence and shape the emerging societies in America's image. The paternalism inherent in modernization theory can ultimately be traced back to long-standing ideas of American exceptionalism, manifest destiny, and the "white man's burden."[5]

To explain the backwardness of other societies, modernization theorists drew on the works of Orientalist scholars. The depictions of the Orient as inherently deficient, static, and driven by emotion and tradition were reproduced in the analysis of the developing world. In addition, Orientalist scholarship provided the supposed area knowledge and language skills that many theorists lacked. Modernization theorists also relied on psychosocial analysis of the different areas and their populations. Orientalist scholarship reinforced the perception that the failure of the newly emerging states to adopt American-defined modernization was evidence of their long-standing pathological flaws. Diagnosing the pathology of the different populations, especially those enamored with charismatic nationalist leaders at odds with Washington, was one of the subtle but important tasks that modernization theorists believed they were performing.[6]

These sentiments were not limited to Europeans and Americans and demonstrate their prevalence in policy circles and the social sciences. Elie Salem, a native of Lebanon, also relied on Orientalist explanations to explain political events. Salem, like his fellow countryman Charles Malik, believed that the Arab states needed to align with the West. Egyptian president Gamal Abdel Nasser's popularity and antagonistic relationship with Washington and its European allies threatened their notions of Arab nationalism as well as the position of conservative Arab elites. Salem, then an assistant professor at Johns Hopkins, provided an analysis of the "Arab mind" and its inherent limitations at a conference hosted by the university after the 1956 Suez War. Arab political behavior, Salem argued, was immature and stunted. This was not due to colonialism, he explained, but was historically rooted in Arab culture and society. Seven years earlier, Columbia's BASR initiated a project on behalf of the State Department and VOA in the Middle East to provide an understanding of the "Oriental mind."[7]

The Bureau of Applied Social Research

Like other scholars of his generation, Daniel Lerner's experience and activities during World War II had a lasting impact. Based in Paris, Lerner served in the Allies' Psychological Warfare Division (PWD) and oversaw the development of weekly intelligence summaries. His PWD experience and access to relevant policy documents and officials served as the basis for his doctoral dissertation, which examined the effectiveness of Allied propaganda efforts against Nazi Germany. Lerner's PWD service as well as his dissertation and the subsequent book, *Sykewar,* helped to shape a number of the ideas that appeared in his most influential work, *The Passing of Traditional Society.*[8]

One consistent theme of Lerner's scholarship was the role of social scientists in shaping policy. Indeed, *Sykewar*'s final chapter offered recommendations for the development of a propaganda policy informed by social scientists. Lerner argued that in the ideological war with the Soviet Union, the United States relied largely on its economic and technological prowess. He warned that in the global competition with Moscow "a predominantly economic strategy may not be adequate against a predominantly ideological strategy." If America's approach proved insufficient, he wrote, "We shall need to consult the intelligence specialist (the social scientist) and the communication specialist (the propagandist)—rather than or in addition to, the diplomat, the economist, and the soldier." Because policymakers were often reactive, rather than strategic and analytical, it was incumbent on policy scientists to "clarify issues and specify needs before they begin to be felt by politicians." "Even if political leadership is not particularly insensitive," Lerner argued, "needs may be *felt* too late."[9]

Lerner returned to this argument in the edited volume, *The Policy Sciences.* The concluding chapter, cowritten with Columbia's Robert Merton, examined the possibilities and limitations of scholars working in the academic, business, and government sectors. Merton, a preeminent sociologist, also served as the associate director of BASR. Although Merton and Lerner advocated for scholars to inform policy, they cautioned that "in a world where the threat of the 'garrison-prison state' hangs heavy in the political atmosphere," it was essential to retain freedom of choice. The stakes were very high, not just for the social sciences but for Western democracies. Merton and Lerner wrote that "developing policy sciences of democracy" was perhaps "the most promising alternative to involuntary suicide." Lerner brought this perspective and research philosophy to BASR.[10]

BASR was initially based at Princeton and moved to Columbia in 1944. It was led by Paul Lazarsfeld, a native of Austria who fled the Nazis and became an influential figure in the early study of mass communications. Lazarsfeld was also effective at securing commercial and governmental grants to pursue research. BASR benefited from ties to the burgeoning postwar national security establishment. Roughly 75 percent of its revenue was through government contracts, in particular to evaluate VOA for the State Department. Lerner joined BASR in 1951 to work on the VOA surveys. The data collected and reports produced by BASR served as the basis for *The Passing of Traditional Society*.[11]

VOA was integral to American propaganda efforts during and after World War II. The service began broadcasting in April 1942 and three months later became part of the newly established Office of War Information (OWI). Although OWI was disbanded by President Truman, VOA survived. In July 1945, a State Department commission called for maintaining the service to further America's postwar foreign policy goals. Led by Columbia's Arthur McMahon, the commission asserted that the wartime experience demonstrated the importance of public diplomacy. America, they wrote, could not be "indifferent to the ways in which our society is portrayed in other countries." The VOA continued with a drastically reduced budget and profile until January 1948, when the Cold War offered a new rationale for continuing and expanding the service.[12]

With a new mission, VOA turned to overcoming Soviet jamming of its signal. In 1950, the State Department asked the Massachusetts Institute of Technology (MIT) for assistance. An interdisciplinary group examined the technical aspect and also performed an evaluation of VOA programming. Dubbed "Project TROY," it led to the establishment of MIT's Center for International Studies (CENIS) two years later with funding from the CIA and the Ford Foundation.[13]

While MIT focused on VOA broadcasts to the Soviet bloc, BASR evaluated the service in Western Europe, Latin America, and the Middle East. The original contract with VOA was signed in May 1949, but was renegotiated a year later to focus on the Middle East. VOA began broadcasting to the region in 1950, in response to Radio Moscow's new Middle East service. The new BASR studies were to incorporate other forms of mass media beyond the VOA broadcasts.[14]

In preparation for an April 1950 meeting with VOA, BASR's Lazarsfeld and Charles Glock wrote an overview of the communication studies and discussed some initial observations. They acknowledged that the impetus for the research was "perhaps more from needs deriving from the world political situation than from purely scholarly interests." "The whole program of such comparative communications really reflects a rather general trend in American operations abroad," Lazarsfeld and Glock wrote, "While it is inappropriate to talk about an American empire, it is entirely in place to discuss the large and growing sphere of American influence." Mass communication, they explained, could serve a purpose akin to that of anthropology during the British Empire. Unlike Britain's direct rule, however, America's interactions with its sphere of influence were "largely by remote control" through propaganda and information services. "International communications research will be a natural concomitant of the current American situation in world politics," they predicted.[15]

However, Lazarsfeld and Glock argued there were different approaches to mass media. While Western media emphasized a "diffusion of opinion rather than information," they asserted that in Muslim countries, "it is not as obvious as with us that each person should have an opinion on public affairs." They also observed that opinions on public affairs in Western industrialized countries were considered "part of the 'rights and duties' of a fully developed personality." In contrast, in "countries which are closer to their own medieval past, opinions are likely to be much more a matter of loyalties." What they called the "feudal perspective" was not the sole factor, and they claimed that it could be compounded by religious views. Lazarsfeld and Glock stated that fatalism in Muslim countries was "very strong" and "might be reflected in the narrow range of topics on which it is considered appropriate to have an opinion." Although VOA sought to influence public opinion around the globe, the initial survey results indicated that "many people in underdeveloped areas have great difficulty in understanding what they are told about the rest of the world." Yet Lazarsfeld and Glock concluded that it was important to determine international attitudes toward the United States and what influenced those perceptions. "In many parts of the world it is quite likely that political attitudes and general images are closely connected," they wrote.[16]

Evaluating Mass Media in the Middle East

BASR initially conducted surveys in Greece and Turkey. The study originally focused on the "opinion leaders" and their responses to different types
of media, including VOA broadcasts. However, BASR encountered problems with this approach and changed the focus before conducting surveys
in the Arab states and Iran. These changes were detailed in a memorandum
likely authored by Lazarsfeld and Glock. "Since there is no known proce-
dure for the study of communications media and of foreign radio in backward countries, and furthermore, since no trained research personnel was
available in these countries, it became necessary to devise methods and to
depend on a local and supervisory personnel which was engaged at long
distance," the memo explained. The new focus emphasized "the study of the
culturally backward segments of the population rather than on the opinion
leaders." Instead of assuming the presence of opinion leaders, the new questionnaire attempted to identify if they actually existed. In addition, it sought
information about the "political attitudes of the respondents" based on their
views of foreign radio broadcasts. Even with the revised study parameters
and government sponsorship, BASR still claimed that it sought "objectivity." However, the search for objectivity was balanced with the VOA's
needs. BASR included specific questions to provide the broadcaster with
information and recommendations. Some of the survey questions were modified versions of those submitted by VOA. In addition, BASR agreed to
notify the broadcaster of any "affirmative or negative comments or suggestions" related to programming.[17]

Yet even these new parameters were revised. BASR shifted to a psychological and political examination of the different countries. A study of public
opinion in Egypt, authored by sociologists Patricia Kendall and Benjamin
Ringer, explained that instead of examining how interviewees interacted
with mass media, the final reports emphasized "*what* they would be most
likely to take from the media and *what* they would be most likely to communicate to others." Drawing on 331 interviews, Kendall and Ringer justified
the change with the observation that "most of the major findings regarding
communications habits in any one Middle Eastern country can be duplicated
in any other." They added that "behavior of any type can best be evaluated
and understood when it is viewed in a context of political and psychological
realities, without this perspective the behavior is likely to seem abstract and
may actually lead to misleading conclusions."[18]

The survey found that different segments of the Egyptian population agreed "foreign interference" and "British occupation" were major concerns. However, Kendall and Ringer cautioned that uniformity of opinion existed only superficially and the "character of Egyptian nationalism" differed. Egyptian professionals, they explained, had conflicted attitudes toward the West. They were "drawn to the West and usually want to identify with Western culture and peoples." Egyptian professionals also recognized their dependence on the West and need for assistance to solve their economic and social problems. However, these sentiments were complicated by feelings of Western paternalism and racism. The continued presence of British troops at Suez, Kendall and Ringer wrote, was a "declaration, implicitly if not explicitly, that Britain does not consider Egypt capable of defending the Canal against possible aggression." As Egyptian professionals considered themselves to be the intellectual and cultural leaders of the region, the lack of Western confidence led them to develop "a sense of doubt about themselves." "They are not at all sure how they measure up to Western standards," Kendall and Ringer added.[19]

Egyptian hostility toward Britain and America was discounted. Their anger was not due to mistreatment, Kendall and Ringer wrote, but because London and Washington "did not fulfill their promises to Egypt." One implication of these sentiments was a "retaliatory friendliness" toward Moscow. They explained that these contradictory sentiments resulted in an "impotent nationalism," as few Egyptian professionals could suggest how to resolve the issue of British occupation.[20]

In contrast, Kendall and Ringer claimed that the hostility of Egyptian peasants toward Britain was due to their religious devotion. "Farmers derive major satisfaction from their religion, pointing to their faith as a source of happiness and contentment," Kendall and Ringer wrote. "It is not hard to understand, then, that a powerful non-Muslim country is looked on as a personal threat."[21]

In a summary of the different reports, sociologist Siegfried Kracauer applied similar assertions to the entire region. Kracauer's *From Caligari to Hitler*, published five years earlier, offered a psychological analysis of interwar German cinema and its influence on Nazi films. *From Caligari to Hitler* was initially written for the State Department as an analysis of "the fascist mind set." Kracauer adapted this approach in a summary of the BASR reports and relied heavily on Orientalist notions and arguments about the region.[22]

Kracauer reported that the masses of the region, from rural Turkey to Egyptian peasants, were "in a stage of transition." "It is as if inertia were slowly receding," he wrote. "Broad Middle Eastern populations are about to enter into the political arena," Kracauer explained, "And since an opinion vacuum is as dangerous as a power vacuum, their appearance on the scene alone would account for the necessity of establishing contacts with them." The United States needed to "immunize the masses against the potential impact of Communist propaganda," he explained. While Islam could serve as a barrier to communist influence, Kracauer added that "it is always advisable to try to mold a mind as long as it is still malleable."[23]

Kracauer's report detailed "Oriental values" for VOA. He explained that they were "a compound of traits and attitudes palpably at variance with Western attitudes and preferences." These values persisted, Kracauer asserted, among Greeks, Turks, Arabs, and even the elites of the different societies that were surveyed. Yet he recommended that VOA target these populations differently. Although Greece and Turkey were generally supportive of Washington, the surveys revealed most Arabs were hostile to U.S. foreign policy. Even those who were sympathetic to the United States, Kracauer reported, were opposed to U.S. policy, in particular toward Palestine and the creation of Israel. He suggested that audiences in Greece and Turkey would be more receptive to VOA broadcasts that promoted "good will toward Americans." While he recommended producing documentary films that demonstrated the lives of Greek and Arab Americans, Kracauer warned that the movies "should not be expected to improve the Arabs' political moods." "In communicating with the influential Arabic [sic] elite, adequate political reasoning is the thing that counts most," he explained. "The Arabs might prove sensitive to Communist intolerance if they get the impression that it is a variant of their own fanaticism," Kracauer wrote. "Tolerance is a virtue of civilization which they are hardly in a position to appreciate—at least for the time being."[24]

These notions of Oriental values also pervaded Lerner's study of Turkish media. Drawing on 300 surveys, it was the first report produced by BASR. The report contained a number of assertions about Turkish society that Lerner adapted in *The Passing of Traditional Society*. He argued that Turkey was neither modern nor feudal, but "a changing society, in transition from old to new ways." As a part of that transition, Lerner hypothesized—and claimed that the surveys confirmed—that mass communication was embedded in Turkey's "deeper processes of economic, social and psychological change." He stratified Turkish society into three parts based on their media habits: "The Modern Turk," "The Transitional Turk," and "The Traditional Turk."

While the modern Turk was already Westernized and did not pose a problem for foreign broadcasters, reaching the traditional Turk was a "major long range challenge." Lerner argued that VOA should focus on the transitional Turks, who were increasing in influence and political activity and were "in a position to carry information from the mass media to the inaccessible peasantry."[25]

Once the VOA surveys were completed, Lerner was faced with a choice. In an exchange with Columbia's William T. Fox, he explained that there were two possible book projects. The first was a "pretty straight forward account" of the survey findings related to media with a "quite uninspired framework." A second option was to recode the survey data to provide a comparative analysis of the different countries. Lerner set his sights higher and chose the latter. While the new study would not appeal to VOA, it aligned with America's larger Cold War goals and interests. Lerner left Columbia and joined CENIS. Hemant Shah details how Lerner recoded the BASR survey data to fit his theory of the relationship between mass media and modernization. This included a highly selective methodology that relied on omission of questions and responses, subjective scoring, and the creation of indices to measure "empathy" and "happiness." Armed with a recoded data set and an ideologically driven analytical framework, Lerner wrote *The Passing of Traditional Society*.[26]

Instability in the Near East

As BASR finalized the VOA reports, the State Department assessed the causes of instability in the region. Conducted by the State Department's Office of Intelligence and Research (OIR) and the Division of Research and Analysis for the Near East, South Asia, and Africa (DRN), the assessment's goal was to determine the best approach for U.S. economic and technical assistance. While the Point IV program targeted the peasantry in underdeveloped countries, Intelligence Estimate (IE) 36 released in January 1952 argued that in the Middle East, this approach might be misguided. It described the peasantry as "still largely a passive element in Near Eastern political life." Instead, IE 36 claimed that the source of instability was the challenge to the traditional leadership of the different states in the region by "emerging groups," in particular the "urban middle sector."[27]

Over a decade later, DRN's Manfred Halpern referenced IE 36 in *The Politics of Social Change in the Middle East and North Africa*. He stated that it was a "prototype for a series of such studies of other underdeveloped areas." Halpern noted that the report's emphasis on the urban middle sector influenced other scholars who were in government service at the time, including his Princeton colleague T. Cuyler Young, and John J. Johnson, a Latin American historian at Stanford.[28]

The Egyptian Free Officers Coup in July 1952 appeared to validate IE 36. Led by middle-tier officers drawn from working-class and professional backgrounds, the Revolutionary Command Council (RCC) was initially dominated by Mohammad Naguib and Gamal Abdel Nasser. Both men were the sons of civil servants and fought in the 1948 Palestine War. Within two years, Naguib was pushed aside and Nasser emerged as the leader of the RCC and Egypt.

In October 1952, a follow-up study reinforced the original findings. IE 45 reported that U.S. policy objectives in the Middle East were threatened by the "basic social and political instability of most of the area." This instability not only threatened local governments but U.S. interests in the region. Echoing George Kennan's assessment ten months earlier, IE 45 argued that it was "reflected in extreme nationalism," which compounded the area's "traditional distrust of Western aims and policies." The report stated that instability was caused by the conflict between traditional elites and the "emerging urban middle sector." Improvements in education led to the expansion of the middle sector "far beyond the numbers whose aspirations can be satisfied under the area's existing social, political, and economic organization." IE 45 added that "this urban sector is motivated not only by the consequent frustration of its aspirations but also by a concept of 'popular' and 'national' control in political and economic fields, which is based on Western ideals." In spite of Western influence, the urban middle sector was motivated by "anti-foreignism," which was "a potent weapon for present use against the holders of political or economic power."[29]

The report argued that the Egyptian Free Officers' Coup and Mossadegh's nationalist policies were manifestations of the instability in the region caused by the emerging middle sector. While the peasantry across the region was not politically active, IE 45 warned that they could be "increasingly aroused" by urban leaders. It also cautioned that if the new regimes were unable to satisfy the aspirations of their populations they would adopt "increasingly neutralist or extremist positions abroad" and "more radical and authoritarian policies at home." As a result, there was "the continual danger of disorder and of increasing Communist influence," and Islam could not be relied on "as a lasting barrier" to communism. Moreover, the report asserted that the new regimes would likely maintain anti-Western attitudes in the near future.[30]

IE 45 was incorporated into National Intelligence Estimate (NIE) number 73, which shared the same title and was finalized three months later. However, there were several major differences. The emphasis on the "urban middle sector" was replaced by a warning of "rising discontent among nearly all social groups." It also emphasized Moscow's role in fomenting instability and anti-Western sentiment. Although the State Department's emphasis on the "middle sector" was not immediately adopted, it dovetailed with Lerner's discussion of the "transitional" populations presented in the BASR reports. Lerner expanded on this idea in *The Passing of Traditional Society*.[31]

The Passing of Traditional Society

A profoundly political work, *The Passing of Traditional Society* was informed by and reflected American national security interests at the height of the Cold War. Published six years after the VOA studies were completed, the ensuing period witnessed Nasser's emergence and the rise of pan-Arab sentiments and movements. As previously discussed, Nasser's stature in the region and the broader Third World increased after the 1956 Suez War. After the war, revolutions swept across the region inspired by Egypt's example and Washington attempted to contain Nasser with the Eisenhower Doctrine. These events should have challenged the assertions in the BASR surveys. Instead, drawing on the recoded data, they reaffirmed Lerner's notions about the region and the broader developing world, with an important caveat. Instead of impotent nationalism, the Middle East was characterized by radical and ultimately doomed nationalism and revolutionary fervor. These themes were adopted by other modernization theorists and Orientalist scholars in their assessments of the region.

Mass communication indicated a society's level of modernization. *The Passing of Traditional Society* examined the role of media in Turkey, Egypt, Syria, Jordan, Lebanon, and Iran. While Lerner acknowledged the role of the BASR surveys in providing his underlying data, VOA was not mentioned. The division between "traditional" and "modern" societies that were introduced in the BASR reports served as the theoretical foundations of *The Passing of Traditional Society*. Indeed, they would be the *sine qua non* of modernization theory. The United States served as the model for modernization, and Lerner claimed that "the sequence of current events in the

Middle East can be understood as a deviation, in some measure a deliberate deformation, of the Western model." The Western model could be applied in the Middle East and globally. "From the West came the stimuli which undermined traditional society in the Middle East," he wrote. Lerner argued, "What the West is, in this sense, the Middle East seeks to become." Turkey and Lebanon were presented as successful examples of modernization. In contrast, Egypt, Syria, Jordan, and Iran demonstrated the tensions evident in "transitional" societies.[32]

Lerner recast the finding and arguments of the BASR reports to offer a biting critique of Nasser's rule. Although he acknowledged that Nasser had successfully harnessed the "symbols of Arab nationalism," Lerner doubted it would be sufficient to resolve Egypt's problems. He stated that "by raising expectations among Egyptians, Nasser has also raised the standards of performance by which his regime will be judged." Nasser's use of mass media was not an indicator of the transition to modernity, but was a tool for more nefarious intentions. "Nasser has gone the way of total politization [*sic*]—the distinctive mark of totalitarianism in our century," Lerner wrote. In order to obscure his failings, Nasser appealed to Arabs, Africans, and Muslims. "Wielding inadequate power to enact rapidly their grand designs, such leaders have yoked all values to their quest for power," he explained.[33]

Nasser's aspirations for regional, if not global, hegemony were merely a façade to obscure the "shame" of colonial rule. "To persist in shaping the world to the ambivalent imagery of youth, among ex-colonials as among ex-imperialists, may in the long run serve pathology better than policy," Lerner claimed. He labeled this pathology the "Nasser syndrome," which compensated "the fantasy life for damages inflicted in a no longer relevant past" and obscured the path to "a realistic political future." The nationalization of the Suez Canal was one manifestation of this syndrome and Lerner asserted that it was intended to exalt "the Self by humiliating the West." Lerner concluded that Nasser's reliance on charisma, while powerful, might ultimately lead to his ruin. He wrote, "[Nasser] has shaped and diffused a new image of self-and-society in Egypt and the area. If he cannot satisfy its requirement, this image may prove his undoing. But the image itself will remain."[34]

Lerner compared Nasser to the founder of the Turkish Republic, Mustafa Kemal Atatürk, and Iran's Mossadegh. In contrast to the portrayal of Nasser, Atatürk was discussed in near glowing terms. Lerner praised Atatürk's efforts to "undermine the 'oriental mentality' which interdicted republican development." This included his use of mass communication, promotion of literacy and education, adoption of Latin script, and the establishment of "People's Houses."[35]

Mossadegh, however, was another example of the "Nasser syndrome." Drawing on the BASR research conducted at the height of tensions over the nationalization of the AIOC, Lerner recounted Mossadegh's flirtations with the left as well as his supposed vanity and unpredictability. "Mossadegh rode high to a fall," Lerner wrote, "Nasser may do the same." Like Nasser, Mossadegh also suffered from the shame of colonial domination, which influenced his policies. The differing approaches of the regional leaders brought into relief that "the crux of the matter has been, not whether, but *how* one should move from traditional ways toward modern life-styles." For modernization to be successful, Lerner implied that the "right kind" of leadership was required.[36]

Events in the region undermined Lerner's assertions. The outbreak of civil strife in Lebanon due largely to President Camille Chamoun's attempts to stay in power, rather than communist or Nasserist subversion, led to the intervention of American forces. Two years later, the Turkish military launched a coup that ousted the democratically elected government of Adnan Menderes. Lerner's faith in modernization theory, however, was unshaken and *The Passing of Traditional Society* was one of the most influential modernization theory texts.[37]

Over the next decade, modernization theory was embraced in academia and in Washington. American policymakers were eager to contain revolutionary movements and challenge Moscow's influence in the newly independent nations with an alternative to the Marxist model of development. Washington was receptive to the claim by modernization theorists that the transition from traditional to modern societies was linear and the United States was the example for developing countries to emulate. In the Middle East, the United States deemed some revolutions appropriate while others were to be opposed. Atatürk and the Shah of Iran were moderate leaders worthy of support, while Nasser and Mossadegh were undermined.[38]

MIT's CENIS was the hub of modernization theory. Led by economist Max Millikan and economic historian Walt Whitman Rostow, CENIS had an interdisciplinary, policy-driven research agenda. Millikan explained that CENIS's goal was to "apply social science to problems bearing on the peace and development of the world community." One area of focus was mass communication. Lerner joined the center in 1953 and BASR's Lazarsfeld served on CENIS's Planning Committee.[39]

Although their shared institutional connection was brief, Lerner and Rostow were linked intellectually. The same year *The Passing of Traditional Society* was published, Rostow wrote *The Stages of Economic Growth*. While Lerner offered a behavioral approach to understanding modernization, Rostow provided a descriptive model of the process. *The Stages of Economic Growth* drew on the works of Lerner and other scholars as well as Rostow's own contributions. This included the notion of "take off," which Rostow asserted was the pivotal stage of development. Rostow's reputation rose above other modernization theorists when he was selected by President Kennedy to serve as deputy national security advisor.[40]

Modernization and Militarization

As the junior senator from Massachusetts, John Kennedy was a vocal critic of the Eisenhower administration's approach to the decolonizing world. Although he supported the administration's efforts in South Vietnam, Kennedy warned that Eisenhower and Secretary of State John Foster Dulles were unnecessarily, if not foolishly, driving a wedge between the United States and newly independent neutral countries. By 1960, the United Nations admitted forty-eight new member states with a combined population of almost a billion people. The majority were former British, French, and Dutch colonies. Kennedy argued that through its policies the Eisenhower administration was pushing the new states toward Moscow. Soviet Premier Nikita Khrushchev added to Kennedy's concerns when he declared that national liberation struggles in the decolonizing world were "sacred." As president, Kennedy attempted to engage with the nonaligned nations through public diplomacy and foreign aid.[41]

A month after taking office, Rostow sent Kennedy a proposal detailing changes in U.S. foreign aid policy. He explained that previous administrations focused almost exclusively on military aid. Rostow described it as "the Old Look" and noted that the Eisenhower administration's last budget only requested $500 million for "development purposes" out of $2.2 billion for nonmilitary assistance. "We begin with a program that is almost wholly defensive in character and one which commands neither the resources, the administration, nor the criteria designed to move the underdeveloped countries towards sustained economic growth," Rostow wrote. "The New Look" he proposed was a "coordinated Free World effort with enough resources to move forward those nations prepared to mobilize their own resources for development purposes." Rostow stated that "the goal is to help other countries learn how to grow."[42]

Rostow advocated for short- and long-term policies. He argued that the administration should maintain military aid for countries in need of "shoring up," including "rickety partners" like Jordan, Laos, and South Vietnam. Rostow explained that the administration could "shift rapidly out of defense support and special assistance into long-term development lending in places where there appears to be a basis for turn-around." He identified Turkey, Greece, and Iran as potential candidates.[43]

Rostow's policy suggestions were implemented over the next eight months. Using a phrase coined by speechwriter Richard Goodwin, Rostow declared in March that it was time to launch an "economic development decade" in Latin America. After the Alliance for Progress was launched later that month, Rostow turned toward Asia and Africa. In an October 1961 memorandum, Rostow argued that aid should be tied to long-term U.S. strategic objectives, which included the viability and independence of the recipient states, their increased attention to domestic issues, and "long-term dependence on the West." Rostow stated that it was possible "to use aid for serious long-run American objectives with respect to neutrals and, also, occasionally and sparingly to yield a minor tactical gain." He warned against focusing on "short-term tactics" as "long-term dependence on American or Communist aid may be one significant factor in determining how neutrals align themselves on the major world issues."[44]

Counterinsurgency was intertwined with the new focus on development and became increasingly important over time. In his February 28, 1961 memorandum to President Kennedy outlining the "New Look" approach, Rostow argued that "both the scale and the type of forces we support under the military aid program should be put under fresh scrutiny, notably in the light of the guerrilla problem." In addition, renewed efforts were needed to ensure that recipients of U.S. military aid were using it "for constructive purposes." Rostow explained that "we have stirred great hopes in Asia, the Middle East, Africa and Latin America and acquired very serious commitments to development, notably in the Indian Peninsula and in Latin America." He continued, "We must back our play or these hopes will fade. Foreign aid will not solve the guerrilla problem; but a program like this may be the necessary backdrop to a solution."[45]

Counterinsurgency and support for the military in developing nations eventually trumped the focus on development. Modernization theorists argued that the military was an essential force for modernizing the Third World. MIT's Lucian Pye was a leading advocate for this approach. While Lerner used the Middle East as the template for his theories about traditional society, Pye focused on Burma. Unlike Lerner, Pye was careful to note that he did not claim "universal applicability" for his study of Burma. "The great variety represented by the traditional societies cannot be denied," he wrote. However, Pye abandoned these limitations in other discussions of development and non-Western societies.[46]

In 1963, Pye participated in the Smithsonian Institute's Research Group in Psychology and the Social Sciences. Organized and led by his MIT colleague, Ithiel de Sola Pool, the group produced a report for the Office of Naval Research. Pye focused on the military's role in the developing world and challenged the notion that development should focus solely on social and economic conditions. He argued that military assistance was integral to the overall welfare of developing nations, particularly those with active insurgencies. "The military problems of maintaining law and order and of insuring civilian cooperation in case of war justify the expenditure of resources to reduce social and economic discontent," Pye stated.[47]

Like Lerner's analysis of mass media, Pye promoted the military based on psychosocial analysis. He asserted that it had a "most fundamental role to play in the developmental process." "This role is essentially psychological. It involves giving to a people a sense of identity and of national pride," Pye explained. He claimed that the leadership of the newly independent countries suffered from "a constellation of insecurities and inhibitions." "The sense of inferiority and the lack of assertiveness of a people who have once been dominated by foreigners cannot be easily eradicated," he wrote. Improved economic status would not be sufficient. Instead, Pye argued that military competence was a preliminary indicator of industrial development. In addition, the military's "fundamental function" was to "assist a people to gain a sense of self-respect." "Military development may thus be crucial in assisting former colonial peoples to overcome their profound sense of inferiority," Pye asserted. He added that "this is in part because any people who feel that their national army is ludicrous and ineffectual must also feel that their collective national identity is incapable of great things."[48]

Self-respect played an important role in modernization. Pye claimed that the leaders of the newly independent countries were often ineffectual as demonstrated by their "profound psychological inhibitions toward making complete and enthusiastic commitments to modernize their societies." Military competence, Pye argued, would allow these societies to regain their self-respect. Otherwise, their attempts to modernize served "only to remind them of their inferiority" relative to the West.[49]

For modernization and democratization to succeed in the developing world, Pye asserted that the military needed to play a nation-building role. This role included ensuring a loyal citizenry, improving bureaucratic inefficiencies, and introducing tradition-bound societies to technological advances. While political leaders were often preoccupied with symbolism and unwilling to demand the necessary sacrifice of the citizenry for modernization, military commanders had to instill loyalty and duty in their troops. "Armies in transitional societies may have obligations in the political sphere which extend far beyond those assumed by armies in more developed and politically stable societies," Pye wrote. "In some situations," he explained, "it is clearly apparent that the military must assume a more direct political role if democratic development is to occur." Although Pye acknowledged the potential for the military to impede democratization, he argued that Washington could stress the importance of "a strong sense of responsibility and of pride in profession" to the new military leaders.[50]

In promoting the military, Pye resolved one issue that undermined Lerner's *The Passing of Traditional Society*—namely, the role of the Turkish military's 1960 coup in interrupting the country's transition to modernity. Instead, Pye identified the effectiveness of Turkey's military establishment as an example to other non-Western countries. Like Lerner, he found Atatürk to be the ideal military and political leader for the developing nations to emulate. The explicit connection between modernization, the military, and counterinsurgency was not limited to Pye. Indeed, it was repeated in policy circles, including by Rostow who oversaw a January 1963 policy paper by the State Department's Policy Planning Staff (PPS) entitled, "Role of the Military in Underdeveloped Areas." The study recommended the United States support military-led development, especially in countries with active insurgencies.[51]

Washington and the military leaders it allied with preferred the certainty of authoritarianism over the risk of democracy. This also reflected the Orientalist roots of modernization theory. While the United States may have been the model for development, democracy was deemed too uncertain for the irrational and politically unsophisticated populations of the developing world. A strong guiding hand was required to ensure that development proceeded according to the "right" path. Invariably, military leaders with anticommunist credentials were favored regardless of their abuses at home.[52]

Not all militaries were viewed favorably. Writing in 1961, P. J. Vatikiotis was skeptical of the Egyptian military's involvement in politics. Unlike other postcolonial nations, he argued, Egypt's military was created by the previous dynasty rather than in a war of independence. This contributed to the centralization of power under one individual and the paucity of robust and independent political institutions. Vatikiotis also questioned whether the military was capable of leading Egypt's modernization. Although he conceded that they "may be better equipped than other groups," Vatikiotis added a caveat: "but how much better, only time will tell." From the regime's slim ideological foundations to its use of mass media, Vatikiotis found evidence of Lerner's "Nasser syndrome." By co-opting different sectors of Egyptian society, Vatikiotis claimed that Nasser "has been able to rule the passive masses, whose relative inertia made it easy to coerce them." Yet many of the same criticisms could be—and eventually were—made of the military regimes backed by Washington.[53]

The Middle East as Laboratory

Before he accepted a faculty position at Princeton in 1958, Manfred Halpern was a member of the State Department's DRN. A native of Germany who fled the Nazis, Halpern completed his PhD at Johns Hopkins University while working at the State Department. Like other DRN personnel, his intelligence experience dated to World War II. Halpern's classified analysis revealed a number of preconceived notions about Islam, the Middle East, and its inhabitants that were reproduced in his scholarship, including in an August 1958 assessment of Arab nationalism and its implications for U.S. policy in the region. The brief memorandum demonstrated the influence of Lerner's *The Passing of Traditional Society* as well as the outlines of Halpern's argument in *The Politics of Social Change in the Middle East and North Africa*, published five years later. "The Arab world is in the throes of change and the chief political manifestation of that change is nationalism," Halpern wrote. While Arab nationalism threatened the existing social order in the Arab states, Halpern argued that this was predictable. "There has never been any real chance of preserving traditional loyalties," he explained, "Islam cannot sustain them." Halpern asserted that nationalism was "only one symptom of the transformation of Arab society" and reflected its "transitional and hence still unstable character." He warned that "if the Arab transformation is frustrated and becomes a transition to nowhere, the Arabs may well turn against their traditional enemy—the Christian West."[54]

The Politics of Social Change in the Middle East and North Africa was based on Halpern's doctoral dissertation. He conducted additional research while at Princeton and as a consultant for the RAND Corporation. In addition to visiting the region for the first time, Halpern was given access to unclassified State Department reports and dispatches. In return, the Department reviewed and approved the manuscript for publication. Halpern, however, did not acknowledge this arrangement in the book.[55]

Halpern regarded the Middle East as a "laboratory" to examine modernization. Building on the arguments in his 1958 DRN memorandum, he asserted in *The Politics of Social Change* that the region's nationalist revolutions were only one symptom of "a more profound and yet unfinished social transformation." This transformation, he explained, would change "what men believe, how men act, and how men relate to each other." "The nationalist revolution has put Africans and Asians themselves in charge of the fire that is now melting and transmuting the form and substance of their faith and society," he wrote. Halpern questioned, however, whether they were prepared for the difficulties of the transformation and their vulnerability to greater powers.[56]

Covering the area from Morocco to Pakistan, Halpern's characterizations of the region and its inhabitants were dominated by essentializations and stereotypes. Drawing on the work of Orientalist scholars like Hamilton Gibb, he declared that the lack of a secular tradition combined with inherent irrationality made the population of the region susceptible to extremist leaders. From secular nationalists to communists and what he called neo-Islamic totalitarian movements, Halpern saw danger and instability throughout the modernizing Middle East. While leaders like Nasser could use "modern, secular language" in order to reach a larger audience, they also had to rely on knowledge of the Qur'an. "In such a communication, there can be no complete rationality, no complete honesty," Halpern wrote. Presaging Samuel Huntington's critique of modernization theory, he argued that the essential task for regional leaders was the establishment of political institutions and that it was necessary to differentiate between moderate, radical, and extremist leaders. Halpern warned that "without help, the non-totalitarian leaders in the Middle East are almost certain to find their tasks beyond their strength." As will be demonstrated, Halpern's recommendations reflected State Department assessments about reaching an accommodation with Nasser and the vulnerability of the conservative Arab regimes.[57]

The reaction to Halpern's scholarship revealed a split between modernization theorists and area specialists. Halpern's colleagues at Princeton, sociologist Morroe Berger and anthropologist T. Cuyler Young, were critical of his work. Their objections were supported by Columbia's J. C. Hurewitz, but not by Berkeley's George Lenczowski. In contrast, modernization theorists Lucian Pye and Columbia's Dankwart Rustow supported Halpern's research. In spite of the objection from area scholars, Princeton's Department of Politics also viewed Halpern favorably. His interest in modernization and comparative politics, the department argued, made him "far more attractive" than a "narrow area studies specialist with whom most of us could not communicate on a meaningful professional level."[58]

Modernization and the Cold War Middle East

Like its development, the implementation of modernization theory in the Middle East was tied to U.S. foreign policy interests. This was reflected in Washington's determinations of which countries were "in transition" and those that still required assistance, as well as its preference for loyal authoritarian regimes. It was perhaps best demonstrated by the evolving relationship between successive presidential administrations and Iran's Mohammad Reza Shah Pahlavi. As Mark Gasiorowski details, after Mossadegh was overthrown the Eisenhower administration strengthened the shah's domestic base of support and ability to repress opposition. In addition, the shah was presented to American and European audiences as a moderate ally in a troubled and unstable region. The Kennedy administration, however, pressured the shah to reform, leading to tensions between Tehran and Washington. In response to these calls, the shah launched the "White Revolution," a halfhearted and generally unsuccessful attempt at social and economic reform. The most notable aspects of the White Revolution were land reform and women's right to vote. Calls for land reform in Iran dated to the Mossadegh era, but in the hands of the shah the policy was used to reward political allies and reduce the wealth and holdings of potential competitors.[59]

The Kennedy administration eventually embraced the shah's "revolution from above." As Roland Popp demonstrates, Washington overlooked political repression in Iran as well as a fraudulent referendum on the shah's reform program. In response to the over 99 percent favorable vote, Kennedy wrote a letter to the shah commending him on the outcome. Within Iran, one of the main opponents of the White Revolution was a young cleric, Ayatollah Ruhollah Khomeini. Khomeini was initially placed under house arrest for six months. After he continued to speak out, the shah had Khomeini exiled in 1964. Khomeini maintained his vocal opposition over the next fifteen years, culminating in his triumphant return to Tehran after the shah was overthrown.[60]

Relations with Tehran were strengthened during the Johnson administration. As president, Lyndon Johnson was determined to reward the shah's loyalty and support for Washington's policies in the Middle East and Southeast Asia. Almost four months after assuming office, Johnson addressed Congress on foreign aid. Iran was listed as one of fourteen countries "in transition" to "self-support." However, the State Department's Near Eastern Affairs (NEA) division was not consulted on the decision and was surprised by LBJ's announcement. After NEA was assured that Iran would continue to receive assistance for the next several years, it concurred in the assessment. Two years later, the U.S. Embassy in Tehran declared that the shah was "making Iran a show-case of modernization in this part of the world." The office of the United States Agency for International Development (USAID) in Iran was closed the following November. Johnson praised the shah in a letter marking the occasion. "Many times—as I face frustrating and difficult problems in various parts of the world—I am heartened to remember what Iran has accomplished under your great leadership," he wrote. Over the next decade, American officials balanced their optimistic assessments of Iran's economic development and the shah's enlightened rule with his desire for increasing quantities of military hardware. At the same time, warnings from within the State Department bureaucracy about the prospects for instability, including from Harvard's William Polk, were ignored.[61]

In contrast, Nasser was deemed a threat to Washington's interests in the region and globally. The Eisenhower administration's efforts to contain his influence were public and private. When the Eisenhower Doctrine was shelved, the administration attempted to use foreign aid to improve relations with Cairo. Under Public Law (PL) 480, the United States provided Egypt with $239 million in aid from 1959 to 1961. This program was expanded by Kennedy in an attempt to reach an accommodation with Nasser and was part of a broader policy of engagement with the nonaligned nations.[62]

NIE 36–61 offered a rationale for this approach. The NIE reported that "militant nationalism will continue to be the most dynamic force in Arab political affairs, and Nasser is very likely to remain its foremost leader and symbol for the foreseeable future." It added, "The long-term outlook for the conservative and Western-aligned regimes is bleak." However, the NIE was not entirely negative. It stated that a "fundamental breach" between Moscow and Cairo was probable in the future due to the "inherent incompatibility between ultimate Soviet ambitions in the Middle East and the aspirations of Nasser and the Arab nationalists to preserve and strengthen their independent position."[63]

National Security Council (NSC) staff member Robert Komer wrote Deputy National Security Advisor Rostow in support of the NIE's conclusions. "As you have pointed out, one of the key things we have to offer is assistance in economic development," he stated. Komer, whose nickname was "Blowtorch" due to his temperament, was uncharacteristically reasonable in his assessment. "In turn, however, we must let Nasser know that we expect a compensatory quid pro quo in a less antagonistic policy on his part," Komer added, "A rapprochement along these lines may take years and involve numerous zigs and zags."[64]

Relations between Washington and Cairo would zig and zag for the next decade. After Syria abandoned its union with Egypt in September 1961, Komer recommended that the administration approve a broad aid package. He argued that the combination of Nasser's weakened political position and Egypt's deteriorating economy created an opportunity for Washington. The Kennedy administration moved forward on Komer's proposal, albeit cautiously, and PL 480 assistance was increased through 1965. In addition, economic and political advisors were dispatched to Cairo for meetings with Nasser. In Egypt, they were joined by Ambassador John Badeau, who was the former president of the American University in Cairo (AUC). Although Nasser was leery of State Department Arabists, he welcomed Badeau's appointment. The two men got off to an awkward start, however, after Badeau insisted on speaking Arabic in their initial meeting. When Badeau began speaking classical Arabic, Nasser interjected and requested he speak English. Even though Badeau was crestfallen, he managed a brief improvement in relations with Egypt. Meanwhile, U.S. aid led to tensions between Cairo and Moscow.[65]

The accommodation was short-lived. In September 1962, the Arab Cold War, which had simmered during the late 1950s, erupted into open hostilities with the civil war in Yemen. Backed by Nasser, elements of the Yemeni military overthrew the new monarch, Imam Muhammad al-Badr. However, al-Badr survived the coup d'état and reemerged in northern Yemen. Although Washington and Cairo signed a three-year aid package a month later, improved relations did not last. The ensuing Yemeni civil war became a regional conflict as America's conservative Arab allies, in particular Saudi Arabia, supported al-Badr against Egypt and the republican forces. In addition, the Johnson administration was less willing to accommodate Nasser, especially after Egypt openly supported rebels in the Congolese civil war. Renewed tensions emerged in the negotiations over a new aid package and the U.S. Congress pressured the Johnson administration to cut aid to Egypt. Angered by the negotiations and threats from Washington, Nasser lashed out in a December 23, 1964 speech. "Whoever does not like our conduct can go drink from the sea," he declared. American food aid was only renewed for six months and then canceled altogether.[66]

In *Philosophy of the Revolution*, Nasser asserted that "every nation on earth" experienced a political and social revolution. Egypt, he explained, was experiencing both simultaneously. "Between the millstone we are now living in two revolutions," Nasser wrote, "one demanding that we should unite together, love one another and committed to reaching our goal; the other forces us, in spite of ourselves, to disperse and give way to hatred, everyone thinking only of himself." Badeau and Rostow recognized later that Yemen was Egypt's millstone. Both offered similar explanations for Nasser's commitment to the conflict. Writing in 1968, Badeau explained that for Egypt "the struggle in Yemen was viewed in terms of its effect on the modernizing of the Arab world, the success of the revolutionary regime and system, and the credibility of a [United Arab Republic] commitment to a sister revolutionary state." Four years later, Rostow offered a similar assessment. But drawing on Lerner, he added that "Nasser's image of himself and what he stood for in the Arab world was at stake."[67]

The Arab-Israeli conflict, Egypt's other millstone, reemerged in the midst of the Yemeni civil war. Tensions were heightened after Israel's unilateral decision to divert water resources from the Jordan River in August 1963. A series of cross-border raids by Palestinian guerrilla fighters, or *fedayeen*, based in Syria in late 1966 and early 1967 led to punishing reprisals by Israel that escalated into an international crisis. Although the Johnson administration hoped to avoid an outbreak of war, it did not actively prevent a conflict. Nor was President Johnson displeased by Israel's swift victory in the

June 1967 War. In a crushing military and political defeat for Nasser and pan-Arabism, Israel captured and occupied the West Bank, including East Jerusalem, the Gaza Strip, Syria's Golan Heights, and Egypt's Sinai Peninsula.[68]

Deciphering the Arab Mind

Washington's policies in the Middle East and the broader Cold War appeared to be validated by Israel's victory in the June 1967 war. A humiliated Nasser was easier to contain and undermine and Moscow's regional ambitions were dealt a severe blow. The brief conflict also coincided with the escalating war in Vietnam. America's difficulties in Vietnam inspired a broader debate among policymakers and social scientists over if and how the United States could achieve victory. While modernization theorists advocated for a combination of development and counterinsurgency, Harvard's Samuel Huntington disagreed. Published at the height of the Vietnam War, Huntington's *Political Order and Changing Societies* critiqued modernization theory.[69]

Huntington argued that modernization was misguided. He asserted that Westernization was not guaranteed and that Washington should pursue stability in the Third World instead. Although modernization theory emphasized social and economic conditions, Huntington wrote that political institutions were underdeveloped and largely ignored. In part, this was due to the theory's false logic that improvements in social and economic conditions would naturally translate into political stability. He countered that economic development and political stability were independent and not interrelated. Huntington also warned that depending on the situation, reforms could promote instability and serve as a "catalyst rather than a substitute for revolution." The imperative for modernizing societies, Huntington explained, was the establishment of robust political parties and institutions. He warned that if elites did not "organize the masses through the existing political system," they risked being overthrown by dissidents. "In the modernizing world he controls the future who organizes its politics," Huntington wrote.[70]

Huntington's elite-driven political process dovetailed neatly with America's support for authoritarian rulers. If stability was the main goal, as Huntington claimed, those leaders with established anticommunist credentials, military training, and existing ties to Washington were the perfect candidates. In the Middle East, this meant a continued reliance on the conservative Arab monarchies—rebranded as "moderates"—and the non-Arab "modern" states of Israel, Turkey, and Iran. As in 1967, radical leaders or "romantic revolutionaries" like Nasser that could not be contained would be confronted and defeated. Although it still maintained rhetorical power, "modernization" as a policy goal was abandoned. Indeed, a 1969 OIR report explained that modernization of the Arab states required "de-Arabization." It claimed that the failure of the Arab states to modernize according to the Western model "was at the very core of the Arab system of social relations and values." This emphasis on the incurable pathology of Arabs became more pronounced, and one of its main proponents was a veteran of State Department intelligence, Harold Glidden.[71]

Glidden served in the State Department for over two decades, including with Manfred Halpern in DRN. As discussed in Chapter 3, Glidden was also a member of the Research and Analysis (R&A) division of the Office of Strategic Services (OSS) and was stationed in Cairo at the end of the war. His analysis was well regarded within DRN and his assertions about the appeal of communism to Arab society were favorably compared to Lucian Pye's observations about other non-Western societies. Although Glidden would have been considered a State Department "Arabist," which implied favoritism toward the Arab states, his disparaging remarks about Arabs demonstrated a different bias. In an August 1958 memorandum on propaganda in the Arab world, Glidden stated that "abusive and intemperate language toward the U.S. or its representatives is not unusual. Neither is it out of line with accepted Arab propaganda or cultural traditions." "It is rather characteristic of Arabs, when confronted with embarrassing evidence of their misdeeds, to seek refuge in lame excuses of various kinds," he added.[72]

Five years later, Glidden was stationed in the U.S. Embassy in Baghdad during the first Ba'th Party coup that overthrew the government of 'Abd al-Karim Qasim. Discussing the postcoup consolidation of power with a *Washington Post* reporter, Glidden claimed that "if Arabs ever took over [the] world, they would start instantly to tear it down." He explained that "Arab values of vengeance, prestige, and obsession with feuding" made them "absolutists rather than relativists."[73]

After his retirement, Glidden articulated these sentiments in a different forum. He presented an assessment of the Arab world and the Arab-Israeli conflict at the 1971 American Psychiatric Association's annual meeting. Published in the *American Journal of Psychiatry* nine months later, Glidden argued that Arab behavior toward Israel was driven by "shame" and "vengeance." These characteristics were the "by-product of Arab values brought into play by any conflict with an external non-Arab adversary." Glidden cautioned that while in the West this was viewed as aberrant behavior, for the Arabs it was "normative." "The Arabs are accustomed to masking their motivations and drives," he wrote, "and it is up to us to try to discover the face behind the mask."[74]

Glidden traced these emotions to Arab tribal values. He argued that these values required conformity and contributed to the "strong authoritarian tone to Arab culture and society." Failure to conform, he claimed, produced shame. In contrast to the "guilt-oriented" Judeo-Christian Western society, he claimed that Arab society was "shame-oriented." According to Glidden, it was discovery of the act by outsiders rather than its performance that defined shame for Arabs. Echoing an OSS report on Egypt three decades earlier, he wrote that "there is an intense concern with and catering to outward appearances and public opinion that many observers have noted as being characteristic of the Arabs."[75]

Glidden's assertions were based on little if any evidence and supporting scholarship. The article had few sources and none for the major claims about Arab society and culture or the role of shame and vengeance. Nevertheless, he built on the assertions of Lerner and Pye about the role of shame in non-Western societies. Glidden stated that the structure of Arab society made it particularly susceptible to shame. "In the Arab value system," he wrote, "one of the major attributes of prestige is the ability to dominate others."[76]

Shame and vengeance were directly related to the inability to resolve the Arab-Israeli conflict. As Arab society was group-based, Glidden argued that the Arab states could not openly break with the Palestinian cause. Even though Israel had repeatedly demonstrated its superiority on the battlefield, "for the Arabs defeat does not generate a desire for peace; instead, it produces an emotional need for revenge, and this need is deepened rather than attenuated by each successive defeat." Glidden added that the Arab states not only feared Israel but each other. These fears, he reported, were at the heart of inter-Arab relations and were responsible for "generalized suspicion and distrust" between them. "The art of subterfuge is well developed in Arab life, as well as in Islam itself," Glidden wrote, "and no Arab underestimates its possibilities." He asserted that these emotions were "expressed in various ways throughout the whole of Arab society, and they spring from Arab values that lie at the innermost core of that society's identity." Thus, hostilities between Israel and the Arab states were "a classic case of culture conflict." Although Glidden's claims were easily refuted by the political events of the previous decade as well as intelligence that he would have had access to at DNR—and were undermined further after the 1978 Camp David Accords between Egypt and Israel—the notions of Arab society and the Arab mind persisted.[77]

Anthropologist Raphael Patai made similar claims in *The Arab Mind*. Originally from Budapest, Patai grew up in a Zionist family that migrated to British Mandate Palestine. He received his doctorate from Hebrew University and eventually accepted a position at Philadelphia's Dropsie College. Although Patai claimed to have an "incurable romanticism" and "life-long attachment to Araby," he drew on a variety of sources to provide a stereotypical and derogatory portrayal of Arabs and Islam. Like *The Passing of the Traditional Society*, *The Arab Mind* was also a critique of Nasserism, albeit published after the Egyptian leader's death.[78]

In analyzing Arab identity and national character, Patai focused on notions of honor and shame as well as sexual mores and hostility. He traced the behavioral deficiencies in Arab character and society to child-rearing practices and inherited "Bedouin values." Virility, Patai argued, was of paramount importance for Arabs and was to be upheld even to the detriment of other values. Shame was not only connected to these notions of honor, but Patai echoed Glidden and argued that in Arab society it was more powerful than guilt. "What pressures the Arab to behave in an honorable manner is not guilt but shame, or, more precisely, the psychological drive to escape or prevent negative judgment by others," he wrote.[79]

The Arab Mind devoted considerable discussion to sexual mores and prohibitions. Sex was a "prime mental preoccupation in the Arab world," he claimed, and Arabs were more lascivious than Westerners. This was demonstrated by practices like segregation of the sexes and the *hijab*. Patai argued that these differences were even more pronounced in the wake of the sexual revolution. However, he was optimistic that there would be a change. "Ultimately the Arab mind will have no choice but to accept Western sexual mores," Patai wrote, "and its innate ingenuity will find a way to modify and mold them until it will create, after the example of 'Arab socialism', a special subvariety of the new sexuality."[80]

Patai reported that Arabs were generally more tolerant of homosexuality than Westerners. He explained that this was tied to notions of male virility, but "as with all other expressions of sexuality is never given any publicity."

"These are private affairs and remain in private," Patai wrote. In contrast, masturbation was viewed as "shameful," as it was not a "masculine act." These theories of shame related to homosexuality, masturbation, and sexual mores were tested three decades later in Iraq.[81]

Yet even before the 2003 invasion of Iraq, *The Arab Mind* found and maintained an audience. Receptiveness to Patai's arguments reflected a particular political and ideological agenda. Interest in *The Arab Mind* has also been tied to larger geopolitical events. It was revised in 1983, after Israel's invasion of Lebanon the previous year, and reissued in 2002 after the September 11 attacks.[82]

The Arab Mind Reborn

In early October 2003, Kasim Mehaddi Hilas was transferred to Abu Ghraib prison outside of Baghdad. He described his ordeal to U.S. Army investigators three months later. At Abu Ghraib, Hilas was stripped of his clothes, forced to wear women's underwear, and a bag was placed over his head. He was threatened and taunted by the army translator and was beaten and tortured by the guards. "[Specialist Charles Graner] cuffed my hands with irons behind my back to the metal of the window, to the point my feet were off the ground and I was hanging there, for about 5 hours just because I asked about the time, because I wanted to pray," he testified. "And then they took all my clothes and he took the female underwear and he put it over my head. After he released me from the window, he tied me to my bed until dawn," Hilas added. He also recounted the abuse he witnessed of other prisoners, including rape, sodomy, and forced sexual acts. These acts were photographed by the prison guards and the pictures, which were shared between the soldiers, eventually led to revelations of the abuse.[83] Major General Antonio Taguba's final report on the Abu Ghraib scandal found that military intelligence and CIA personnel requested the military police guards "set physical and mental conditions for favorable interrogation of witnesses." Journalist Seymour Hersh later wrote that the rationale for the humiliation and degradation of prisoners was based on Patai's *The Arab Mind*. A key reference source for neoconservative advocates of the 2003 invasion of Iraq, American interrogators drew on Patai's discussion of sexual mores and prohibitions in Arab culture and society. Hersh reported that the pictures were taken in order to instill "fear of exposure" among the prisoners and force them to become informants.[84]

The 2002 edition of *The Arab Mind* contained a new foreword by Colonel Norvell De Atkine. An instructor at the John F. Kennedy Special Warfare School in Fort Bragg, North Carolina, De Atkine argued that it was important to understand the "social and cultural environment" that led to the September 11 attacks. *The Arab Mind*, he explained, contributed to this understanding and formed the basis of his "cultural instruction" of military officers. De Atkine asserted that the positive response to his training from military personnel validated Patai's work. In contrast, he claimed that recent scholarship on the Middle East, especially in political science, was "jargon- and agenda-laden, bordering on the indecipherable." "A fixation on race, class, and gender has had a destructive effect on Middle East scholarship," he declared. De Atkine is not alone in his view of the changes in Middle East scholarship. Indeed, it is part of a broader political and ideological split between academia and the national security establishment that impacted how Middle East studies were viewed in Washington and was reflected in the 2003 invasion and occupation of Iraq.[85]

U.S. national security interests influenced the development of modernization theory, its application in the Cold War Middle East, and eventual abandonment. Like the Inquiry, modernization theorists constructed their own categories to define the region and its inhabitants and relied on Orientalist scholarship to justify and validate their claims. Even though Hamilton Gibb eventually abandoned some of his earlier assertions in an attempt to analyze contemporary events, these changes were not reflected in the analysis of modernization theorists.[86]

The intersection between the U.S. State Department and intelligence agencies with the development of modernization theory influenced the claims made by the different scholars. For over a decade, modernization theorists attempted to understand and explain the motivations of those living in the developing world. By the end of the 1960s, however, this approach was largely abandoned. Instead, failure to side with Washington was indicative of a larger pathology that could be rectified by force. Internal State Department assessments as well as the writings of Harold Glidden and Raphael Patai demonstrated the persistence of the notions underlying modernization theory and Orientalist scholarship. Although the arguments presented by Glidden and Patai were not unique and there were other attempts to examine the "Arab mind," acceptance of the dated and error-laden text by the U.S. military and intelligence agencies after September 11 indicates its importance to and relationship with American national security interests.

Although Lerner's *The Passing of Traditional Society* was published the same year that the National Defense Education Act (NDEA) was passed, area knowledge was not a prerequisite for modernization theorists. Ideological predispositions and alignment with America's Cold War interests predominated over regional expertise. As the remainder of the book demonstrates, the decline of modernization theory did not lead to a resurgence of area studies expertise. Instead, think tanks emerged mirroring the close ties of modernization theorists to the U.S. national security establishment and occasionally reproducing their claims about Arab society and Islam.[87]

CHAPTER **7**

Privatizing Knowledge

Think Tanks, Middle East Expertise,
and the Decline of Area Studies, 1973–1988

If you did not exist, we would have to ask someone to create you.

—PRESIDENT LYNDON B. JOHNSON, September 29, 1966

It was a bright, cold March morning on the White House's north lawn. As the flags of their respective nations flapped behind them in the brisk wind, Jimmy Carter, Anwar Sadat, and Menachem Begin sat at a nineteenth-century walnut table and read from prepared texts. Sixteen months of intense and at times acrimonious negotiations brokered by Washington led to the Camp David Accords. Compared to the surprise announcement six months earlier that a framework agreement was reached, the signing ceremony was brief and perfunctory. The Camp David Accords not only marked the end of the conflict between Egypt and Israel, but the beginning of the end of the Cold War in the Middle East. They also demonstrated Washington's greater involvement in the region. Ironically, heightened American interests in the Middle East exacerbated a growing rift with academia. A little over a decade after the National Defense Education Act (NDEA) was passed, Washington already considered area studies a failure. This determination contributed in part to the increased prominence of think tanks and the privatization of knowledge related to the Middle East over the next two decades.

Washington's negative perception of area studies was the result of the growing split between academia and the U.S. government, with relations reaching their nadir as campus protests erupted over the Vietnam War. This split was exacerbated by a new generation of scholars who were more skeptical of America's role in the world and previous support within academia for U.S. national security interests. Well-funded think tanks emerged at the expense of academia and benefited from its strained relationship with Washington by aligning with America's goals and interests in the Middle East.[1]

The Era of Limits

Although the Vietnam War and the tensions between academia and Washington predated Richard Nixon's presidency, his administration presided over and contributed to an even greater deterioration in relations. Over the previous three years, campus protests against the war increased in frequency and ferocity. A freeze on protests was enacted following the November 1968 election, but they resumed six months later. In his memoirs, Henry Kissinger, who served as national security advisor during Nixon's first term, expressed sympathy and frustration with the protestors and blamed them for extending the conflict. "They were, in my view, as wrong as they were passionate," Kissinger wrote. "Emotion was not a policy. We had to end the war, but in conditions that did not undermine America's power to help build the new international order upon which the future of even the most enraged depended," he argued.[2]

The new international order that Nixon and Kissinger sought to construct was a reflection of America's diminished influence due to Vietnam. Kissinger claimed that when the administration came into office "the intellectual capital of U.S. postwar policy had been used up and when the conditions of determining postwar U.S. policy had been altered, we had to adjust our foreign policy to the new facts of life." One adjustment was the policy of "Vietnamization." Initiated by President Johnson and accelerated by Nixon, it called for South Vietnamese forces to assume greater responsibility for the fighting. The policy also served as a model for the Nixon Doctrine, in which local allies secured and ensured American interests around the globe. "It is beyond the physical and psychological capacity of the U.S. to make itself responsible for every part of the world," Kissinger explained.[3]

In the Middle East, the Nixon Doctrine relied on three countries: Iran, Saudi Arabia, and Israel. Although Washington's alliance with Tehran and Riyadh was known as the "Twin Pillars" policy, America's "special relationship" with Israel served as the third pillar. The U.S.-Israeli relationship expanded dramatically after the June 1967 Arab-Israeli War, including large quantities of military aid. While Israel contained and countered "radical" states and political movements in the Eastern Mediterranean, Iran's military was the new guarantor of security in the Persian Gulf. Meanwhile, Saudi Arabia relied on its oil wealth to co-opt or counter radical movements in the region.[4]

The antiwar protests also had implications for higher education. Student protests reached their apogee with the invasion of Cambodia in April 1970 and a month later were marked by the shooting deaths of four students by Ohio national guardsmen at Kent State University. Nor was the antiwar movement limited to students. Kissinger returned to the Harvard campus, where he was a professor of government, and was confronted by former colleagues over the war. Yet even before the invasion of Cambodia, area studies funding was in jeopardy. Although the NDEA was intended to be a temporary measure, Congress continued its funding through 1968. The Higher Education Amendments of 1968 extended and increased NDEA funding for the next three fiscal years. However, the Nixon administration threatened to end support for Title VI. After the deaths at Kent State, the *Washington Post* reported that an omnibus bill to fund higher education was unlikely to pass due to the ongoing campus protests. Conservative members of Congress also threatened to add antiprotest measures to any legislation over the White House's objections.[5]

A centerpiece of the Nixon administration's education policy was the creation of the National Foundation for Higher Education. Originally proposed by the Carnegie Commission on Higher Education in December 1968, it would be a vehicle for reform and institutional development. Adopted by Nixon, Congress expanded the National Foundation's mandate to include the operation of existing programs, including Title VI.[6]

Meanwhile, the Nixon administration proposed reductions in area studies funding. The budget for the 1971 fiscal year reduced federal support from $18 million to $15.3 million. A further reduction to $6 million was scheduled for the following year. In response, academic institutions argued that government funding was essential for Asian and Middle Eastern languages because they were "unproductive" for academic institutions to support. They claimed that this was due to the extra costs for faculty and equipment compared to other disciplines. In addition to the economic argument, the universities asserted that "it is in the national interest that there be a trained corps of scholars in the languages, the politics and the economics of areas of the world central to United States foreign policy." The universities argued that they were unable to support the programs independently and government funding was essential for their continued operation. However, anonymous administration officials told the *New York Times* that area studies were "outmoded" and "unproductive" and that Washington should not support "elitist programs." The White House sought to mollify the universities by claiming that the National Foundation for Higher Education would support area studies once it was established with an initial funding of $200 million in the 1972 fiscal year.[7]

Funding was restored thanks to lobbying by advocates inside and outside of government. Advocates included Harvard president Nathan Pusey, Kissinger, and then White House staff member Daniel Patrick Moynihan. Support was maintained at $15.3 million for the 1971 and 1972 fiscal years. Although the administration still hoped that the National Foundation for Higher Education would assume responsibility for area studies, it agreed to maintain funding until the foundation was established.[8]

The threat to area studies returned three years later. Funding was eliminated from the proposed 1973 fiscal year budget, which Nixon deemed his "peacetime" budget after the Paris Peace Accords were signed in January 1973 ending the Vietnam War. To justify the reductions, the Office of Education (OE) argued that federal support only accounted for 10 percent of the annual budgets of area studies centers. It claimed that the centers "were now established and should be able to continue their studies of the non-Western world without direct Federal institutional assistance." The OE also sought to reassure the universities that federal funds would still "flow to the centers" in the form of expanded financial assistance to students. This reflected the administration's increasing emphasis on shifting support from academic institutions to students. The OE also offered other conflicting claims to justify its decision. It stated that "an adequate cadre of specialists" had been created to ensure a "self-sustaining supply of future generations of similar specialists," while also acknowledging that Title VI did not provide "a necessary incentive to draw graduate students to the subject fields."[9]

In April 1973, Secretary of Health, Education, and Welfare Caspar Weinberger testified before Congress and reiterated these points. Before becoming HEW secretary, Weinberger served as Nixon's deputy director of the Office of Management and Budget, which replaced the Bureau of the Budget (BOB). He earned the nickname "Cap the Knife" for his budget-cutting acumen, which he continued at HEW. Addressing Congress, Weinberger emphasized Title VI's gains over the previous fifteen years and stated that "significant capacity for teaching non-Western languages and cultures has been established in the nation's colleges and universities." He explained that the administration believed "these efforts are now strong enough to make it on their own."[10]

Academic institutions again lobbied the administration. Marshall Shulman, director of Columbia's Russian Institute, wrote in the *New York Times* that the lessons of Vietnam demonstrated the need for area and language experts. He explained that the cuts to Title VI amounted to less than the cost of one fighter-bomber. Shulman asserted that the Nixon Doctrine and détente with Moscow did not justify ending federal support. "Even under the most optimistic of assumptions," he wrote, "our nation will be called upon to make judgments about the Soviet Union, China, Africa, Asia, and Latin America, for which we as a people are wholly unprepared." Shulman argued that language training programs represented "a national necessity" and needed financial support from America's governmental, business, philanthropic, and academic sectors. The next day, the *Times* published an editorial that criticized the administration's proposal as "penny wise but pound foolish" and warned that the cuts would "cripple or destroy" existing efforts to train area specialists.[11]

The Nixon administration persisted in its efforts even after the House of Representative restored Title VI funding. In a letter to Senator John McClellan, chairman of the Senate Committee on Appropriations, Weinberger criticized the actions by the House as "ill advised" and asked the Senate to make the administration's requested cuts. He reiterated that Title VI had achieved its goals and academic institutions were now self-sufficient. However, Weinberger's claims were not supported by the universities or an evaluation of area studies that had been sponsored by the Social Science Research Council (SSRC).[12]

The Lambert Report

A decade after the NDEA was passed, the OE and the SSRC initiated an assessment of area studies. Led by sociologist Richard Lambert, the review was the first major survey since the legislation was signed and the most comprehensive since the series of reports produced in the early Cold War period, as discussed in Chapter 3. In the report's preface, SSRC president Pendleton Herring hailed the progress to date. "Area studies have been innovative, experimental, and resilient. They have met a challenge, and they fulfill a need," he declared. Hanging over the report was the Nixon administration's threat to cut funding. In spite of the progress made because of Title VI, Herring explained that "financial support is uncertain, and the nature and status of area competence is a matter for some academic debate." He added that "public policy with respect to area studies is not strongly supportive. Employment and research opportunities are not as favorable as they have been. The period immediately ahead does not seem propitious." However, Herring argued that the "necessities of the age" made area specialists essential and that "there can be no surplus, no over-supply of persons" with the requisite skills and competence.[13]

Contrary to the administration's claims, Lambert found that significant shortcomings still existed after fifteen years of federal support. He argued that there were not a sufficient number of Americans trained in the areas outside the United States and Western Europe. This was compounded by the Eurocentric focus of American education, which he claimed was "stunting the growth" and limiting the perspectives of students and the general public. Like Herring, Lambert cautioned that there was no way to determine if a sufficient number of specialists had been achieved or if it was even possible to identify the appropriate number. In addition, job prospects for area specialists outside of academia were uncertain. Although businesses supported the creation of different regional programs, including for the Middle East, they had not hired a large number of the graduates. Even though the State Department had dispatched personnel for training at the different area centers, it was not a major employer.[14]

Lambert also cautioned that foreign policy interests should not be the key factor in determining the appropriate priority for training specialists. He argued that rapidly shifting interests could lead to shortages of specialists for particular areas. Lambert added that an approach that placed a priority on areas where the United States had longer-term interests could lead to a repeat of the experience in Vietnam, where America had little contemporary knowledge and even fewer trained specialists, an issue that persisted even after the war was over. However, Lambert's warnings were ignored.[15]

The Peace Process

The lack of area specialists was particularly pronounced for the Middle East. Yet the June 1967 War marked the beginning of greater American involvement in the region through the Arab-Israeli peace process and increased military aid and coordination with Israel. While Nixon and Kissinger focused on Vietnam after taking office, Secretary of State William Rogers was responsible for the Middle East. Rogers sought to build on UN Security Council Resolution (UNSCR) 242 and conduct bilateral negotiations between Israel and the combatant Arab states mediated by the superpowers. UNSCR 242 contained the framework for the "land for peace" formula that defined the Arab-Israeli peace process, whereby Israel would withdraw from the territories it occupied during the June War in exchange for a peaceful settlement. However, Kissinger was hostile to Rogers's efforts. The Israelis and the Kremlin were also reluctant to support the Rogers Plan. Although Nasser eventually accepted the Rogers Plan, Nixon and Kissinger were determined not to reward Syria and Egypt until they abandoned their ties to Moscow. In the first volume of his memoirs, Kissinger wrote that the goal was "to demonstrate even to radical Arabs that we were indispensable to *any* progress and that it could not be extorted from us by Soviet pressure." While the State Department wanted to include the Soviet Union in negotiations, Kissinger "wanted to frustrate the radicals—who were in any event hostile to us—by demonstrating that in the Middle East friendship with the United States was the precondition to diplomatic progress." Over the next two years, Kissinger obtained Nixon's support and they scuttled the Rogers Plan. After Nasser's death, the Nixon administration disregarded Egyptian president Anwar Sadat's signals that he was ready to engage in meaningful negotiations with Israel and repair relations with Washington.[16]

After Nixon's landslide victory in the 1972 presidential election, Kissinger served as both secretary of state and national security advisor. Less than a year later, Nixon was mired in the Watergate scandal and Kissinger had authority over foreign policy. In response to the October 1973 Arab-Israeli War, Kissinger conducted high-profile "shuttle diplomacy" aimed at achieving a cease fire. However, his private actions served to heighten the crisis. While meeting with Israeli prime minister Golda Meir, Kissinger encouraged Israel to continue pressing its counteroffensive against Egypt, leading to a near nuclear showdown between the superpowers. Yet publicly he struck a more conciliatory tone. After a cease fire was implemented, Kissinger explained in a State Department press conference that "the conditions that produced this war were clearly intolerable to the Arab nations and that in the process of negotiations it will be necessary to make substantial concessions." In December, Washington and Moscow convened a multilateral peace conference in Geneva. However, it only met once.[17]

Kissinger abandoned the Geneva process and concentrated on negotiations between Egypt and Israel. This was a deliberate choice. Kissinger hoped to rupture relations between Moscow and Cairo. Like the Israelis, Kissinger also hoped to break the unified Arab negotiating position. Meanwhile, Sadat was ready to abandon relations with the Soviet Union and sought peace with Israel. In contrast to the multiple meetings Kissinger held between Egypt and Israel, the Syrian-Israeli track was less explored.[18]

In Beirut, the leadership of the Palestine Liberation Organization (PLO) recognized an opportunity. Established in 1964, the PLO was an umbrella organization for different Palestinian groups whose political beliefs covered the broad spectrum from Marxist-Leninist factions to conservative Arab nationalists. The PLO was expelled from Jordan three years earlier during the country's brief civil war and created a para-state in Lebanon. Led by Yasir Arafat, the organization's leadership was concerned that Jordan's King Hussein would regain the Israeli-occupied West Bank through the Geneva process and it would be left on the sidelines of any comprehensive agreement. Arafat also believed that Washington held the key to an eventual settlement with Israel. The United States, however, viewed the PLO with suspicion and hostility due to its support from the Soviet Union, China, Cuba, and Vietnam, as well as its alignment with "radical" Arab states. As will be discussed, the adoption of high profile-terrorist attacks by some PLO factions increased the organization's profile at the cost of its international legitimacy. Another complication was the PLO's rejection of UNSCR 242 because it did not recognize Palestinian national rights. Nevertheless, Arafat pursued relations with the United States through a combination of personal envoys, sympathetic world leaders, and public statements. In response to Arafat's efforts, some American diplomats and policymakers advocated for official contacts with the PLO as a way to promote moderates within the organization. By 1974, the PLO was recognized by the UN and the Arab League as the representative of the Palestinian people. Among the leading proponents of developing relations with the PLO was William Quandt, a National Security Council (NSC) staff member and expert on the Algerian revolution and national movement. Quandt later joined the faculty at the University of Pennsylvania and eventually served in the Carter administration. Kissinger, however, ignored the PLO's overtures.[19]

Kissinger's autonomy as secretary of state continued during the brief Ford presidency. His diplomatic efforts resulted in initial disengagement agreements between the combatant states. The negotiations also led to increased cooperation and tensions between the United States and Israel. Kissinger and President Gerald Ford blamed Israel for the failure to complete a second Sinai disengagement agreement with Egypt. Although Ford announced a reappraisal of relations with Israel, it was quickly abandoned after a sharp response from Capitol Hill. The Sinai II agreement between Egypt and Israel was signed in September 1975. It was accompanied by secret agreements, including a memorandum of understanding (MOU) between Israel and the United States that limited Washington's ability to engage with the PLO. In addition, the United Stated agreed to coordinate with Israel on future peace proposals. These aspects of the MOU established precedents that shaped Washington's approach to the Arab-Israeli peace process for the next four decades.[20]

Meanwhile, Lebanon descended into civil war. The PLO attempted to demonstrate its value to Washington by guarding the U.S. Embassy in Beirut and the private residences of American officials. It also assisted with the June 1976 evacuation of embassy personnel from Lebanon. Although President Ford and Kissinger thanked the PLO for their assistance with the evacuation, there was no change in Washington's stance toward the organization. Instead, further negotiations between Israel and the Arab states were placed on hold until after the November presidential election. Kissinger informed his deputies and ambassadors in the region that he intended to push for a comprehensive settlement after the election. He explained that the PLO would be included only after progress was made with Egypt, Jordan, and Syria. Kissinger's realization of the need for a comprehensive settlement that included the Palestinians was also shared by a number of experts who participated in a study group sponsored by the Brookings Institution.[21]

Think Tanks and the Middle East

The term "think tank" was used by the U.S. military during World War II to refer to a secure room or location where strategy and plans could be discussed. It was first applied to the RAND Corporation in the 1950s. Originally a subsidiary of Douglas Aircraft, RAND was spun off into an autonomous unit after the war. However, it relied on the U.S. government for funding and its research was focused on the military. With offices in Washington and Santa Monica, California, RAND's funding and research diversified and expanded over time. RAND became the model for think tanks to emulate. As the number of think tanks expanded in the late Cold War era, so did their influence on policy. However, the external experts were never completely impartial as future contracts remained an ongoing concern. In addition, think tank staffers were recruited to serve in different presidential administrations and members of the foreign policy and national security establishments increasingly found positions in think tanks after leaving government.[22]

Like RAND, the Brookings Institution is another established and prestigious think tank. Founded in 1916 as the Institute for Government Research (IGR), funding was initially provided by several prominent individuals, including John D. Rockefeller, Cleveland Dodge, banker J. P. Morgan, and businessman Robert S. Brookings. IGR's mission was to provide nonpartisan analysis of the government with a focus on administrative efficiency. Robert Brookings served as the IGR's major fundraiser, eventually securing a major grant from the Rockefeller Foundation. In 1927, the IGR merged with two other institutions (one focused on economic research and the other a graduate school in public policy) and was renamed the Brookings Institution. In his speech marking the fiftieth anniversary of Brookings, President Lyndon Johnson called it a "national institution" whose work was important to the White House, the Congress, and the country.[23] His successor, however, was less enamored with Brookings. Nixon and his advisors considered Brookings a "threat."[24]

Although Brookings has generally been regarded as a liberal think tank, its policy positions have historically been more nuanced. For example, it initially supported and then opposed the New Deal. Yet it also assisted with the formation of the UN and the development of the Marshall Plan. Unlike RAND, Brookings did not conduct contract research, nor is it a federally funded research and development center. Its revenues were limited to individual contributions and grants from philanthropic foundations, including the Ford and Rockefeller Foundations. In addition, government-related research did not account for a large percentage of the Brookings Institution's budget. RAND and Brookings also benefited from corporate contributions. During the Cold War, Brookings foreign policy analysis largely focused on the Soviet Union. In 1975, however, it expanded to the Middle East and the Arab-Israeli peace process.[25]

The new focus on the Middle East grew out of the Trilateral Commission. Formed in 1972 by David Rockefeller, chairman of Chase Manhattan Bank, and Henry Owens of Brookings, the Trilateral Commission was an attempt by business, academic, and political elites to strengthen ties between America, Europe, and Japan. Columbia's Zbigniew Brzezinski was another Commission cofounder and staunch critic of the Nixon-Ford-Kissinger foreign policy approach. Brzezinski served as the Trilateral Commission's first director. The Commission sponsored a number of meetings and reports on issues related to the world economy. It was also concerned with the shared "security challenges" related to the Middle East. One attendee was Georgia governor and Democratic presidential candidate Jimmy Carter. Brzezinski later wrote that Carter attended a Commission meeting held in Kyoto, Japan, and spoke "forcefully and clearly on behalf of a fair Middle East settlement as very much in the U.S. national interest." Carter's connections to the Trilateral Commission continued after the election, when several members were chosen for prominent Cabinet positions.[26]

The Brookings Institution examined prospects for a new American strategy toward the peace process. According to William Quandt, by 1975 the prevailing belief was that high-level shuttle diplomacy had "exhausted itself." Henry Owen, director of Foreign Policy at Brookings, asked former U.S. ambassador Charles Yost and Princeton's Morroe Berger to assemble a group of academics to develop the strategy. Owen mischievously described the effort to Brookings president Kermit Gordon as "What Could Be Our Most Important Study Yet—or How to Prevent the World from Being Blown Up!" In addition to Brzezinski and Quandt, the study group included Malcolm Kerr and Stephen Spiegel of the University of California at Los Angeles (UCLA) and Harvard's Nadav Safran.[27]

The study group's final report, *Toward Peace in the Middle East,* called for Washington to pursue a comprehensive settlement to the Arab-Israeli conflict. It reaffirmed that the United States had "a vital interest in the establishment of peace" in the region. However, the report cautioned that the Sinai disengagement agreements did not address the underlying causes of the conflict and advocated that any settlement address and integrate several key elements. This included security for all of the parties and Israel's staged withdrawal to the June 1967 borders. The report's most progressive and controversial recommendation was for Palestinian self-determination. This would be achieved as part of a larger agreement in which Israel was recognized and an independent Palestinian state would be created or through the formation of a Palestinian-Jordanian confederation. The Brookings group did not offer a recommendation on Jerusalem, but called for open access to the city's holy sites. *Toward Peace in the Middle*

East argued that the United States should offer a negotiating framework and substantive proposals as well as any economic and military assistance needed to conclude a settlement. It also recommended that Washington involve the Soviet Union in negotiations if the Kremlin could provide constructive support. Although the report proposed a comprehensive solution, it advocated for a phased implementation. This caveat would be a recurring feature of peace proposals to resolve the Israeli-Palestinian conflict over the next three decades.[28]

The Brookings report was shared with Carter and Cyrus Vance, a Trilateral Commission member who became secretary of state. In his memoir, Brzezinski explained that the recommendations were "timely and realistic" as they "protected Israeli security while enhancing the prospects for a constructive U.S. relationship with the Arab world, something clearly in the U.S. interest." Based on Carter's comments at the Trilateral Commission meeting in Kyoto, Brzezinski added that he knew the governor would be "sympathetic" to the report. Although Carter and Vance read the report, Quandt cautions that "it would be an exaggeration to say that the report served as a blueprint for the policies of the first year."[29]

While it may not have been a blueprint, *Toward Peace in the Middle East* appeared to set the parameters for the Carter administration's attempts to resolve the Arab-Israeli conflict. Brzezinski was named national security advisor and Quandt returned to the NSC. Shortly after taking office, the Carter administration identified the Middle East as an "urgent priority" and pursued a comprehensive resolution to the conflict, including outreach to the PLO. Secretary of State Vance visited the region and Carter hosted Israeli prime minister Yitzhak Rabin in Washington. A week later, Carter laid out principles for resolving the Arab-Israeli conflict at a town hall meeting in Clinton, Massachusetts. Quandt writes that Carter deliberately pursued public diplomacy to contrast with Kissinger's penchant for secrecy. Carter also sought to counter leaks to the press by Rabin and his advisors. Instead, there was an immediate backlash from members of Congress and skepticism in the press. In particular, Carter's public statements about the need for a solution to the Palestinian problem, including his use of the term "Palestinian homeland," attracted positive and negative attention.[30]

The administration's plan brought renewed attention to the Brookings report.[31] In Israel, Carter's initiative and the Brookings report were linked to and criticized for their similarity to the defunct Rogers Plan. The U.S. Embassy in Tel Aviv reported that the origins of Carter's proposal were "seen as lying in the Rogers Plan and the Brookings report. The first of which is totally rejected here and the latter regarded with grave suspicion."[32] These criticisms were repeated by leaders of the American Jewish community, in particular Rabbi Arthur Hertzberg of the American Jewish Congress (AJC). A former colleague of Brzezinski at Columbia, Hertzberg criticized the Brookings report in an interview with the Israeli newspaper *Maariv*. "I object to it vigorously, and argue with the administration leaders most vehemently in this respect, in order to make them see that it is a negative way, which cannot lead to peace," Hertzberg said. "I tell them at every opportunity that the setting up of a Palestinian state, or a 'national home' for the Palestinians not only will not guarantee the U.S. the oil it requires, but will definitely jeopardize U.S. interests since it will permanently undermine—withhold from the Middle East—the stability it needs," he added.[33]

Several Arab states also expressed interest in the Brookings report after Carter's public statements. In Damascus, Syria's Foreign Ministry requested information about the Trilateral Commission and copies of the Brookings report. The Tunisian Foreign Ministry was "impressed" by the Brookings report and informed U.S. Ambassador Edward Mulcahy that it was "very close in spirit to Tunisian proposals for settling [the] Arab/Israeli conflict put forth many years ago and still adhered to."[34] In spite of the optimism, the Carter administration faced a number of hurdles, in particular Egyptian president Sadat's reluctance to accept full normalization of relations with Israel and the PLO's rejection of UNSCR 242.[35]

Carter's difficulties were compounded by the May 1977 Israeli elections, which brought the Likud Party to power. Within a month, Chief of Staff Hamilton Jordan warned Carter of the domestic political implications of his foreign policy approach. Jordan emphasized the need to consult Congress and suggested that the American Jewish community could play a "special and potentially constructive role." Carter's hopes for a comprehensive settlement, however, were scuttled, in part due to the resistance of the new Israeli government led by Menachem Begin. Although Begin eventually signed the Camp David Accords with Egypt, a broader agreement remained unfulfilled. In addition, the provision for limited autonomy for Palestinians in the West Bank and Gaza was never implemented. Nor did subsequent administrations follow Carter's example. Yet, as will be demonstrated, other think tanks sought to replicate the perceived influence of the Brookings Institution.[36]

The Rise of Terror Studies

Think tanks influenced America's policy toward the Arab-Israeli peace process, and they were integral to the emergence of terror studies. The study of terrorism was one consequence of the unresolved issues from the 1948 and 1967 Arab-Israeli Wars, in particular the Palestinian national movement. Political violence and acts of terrorism were not unique to the Arab-Israeli conflict or the PLO. Indeed, political violence was a hallmark of postwar anticolonial struggles and national liberation movements. Yet how "terrorism" was defined and studied was inextricably linked to U.S. foreign policy goals and interests in the Middle East and beyond.

Beginning in 1969, members of the Popular Front for the Liberation of Palestine (PFLP), conducted high-profile airplane hijackings. A leftist faction of the PLO, the PFLP's goal was primarily propaganda and recruitment as it competed with other factions for financial and political support. It also sought to confront and embarrass the Arab states, Israel, the United States, and the broader international community over the Palestinian issue. The actions of the PFLP and other PLO factions increased the international profile of the Palestinians. However, they also raised the ire of the United States, Israel, and Jordan, which initially served as the organization's main military and political base. On September 6, 1970, the PFLP successfully hijacked three airplanes from different international airliners. A fourth hijacking was prevented by Israeli security. Two of the planes landed at Jordan's Dawson Field, a former British air base outside Amman. The third hijacked airliner was brought to Cairo, where it was destroyed after the crew and passengers were forced to disembark. Three days later, another hijacked plane landed in Jordan. The three aircraft at Dawson Field were destroyed and the PFLP demanded the release of Palestinian prisoners held by Israel and several European states in exchange for the crew members and passengers. Although a rift developed within the PLO over the hijackings, King Hussein launched a bloody confrontation with the organization.[37]

The September 1970 Jordanian Civil War, also known as "Black September," contributed to increased militancy by Palestinian groups. This culminated in the 1972 Munich Olympics attack orchestrated by the Black September Organization (BSO), an offshoot of the PLO's mainstream Fatah faction. In response, the Nixon administration launched a new counterterrorism policy. The Cabinet Committee to Combat Terrorism (CCCT) was established and led by Secretary of State Rogers. Its goals were to prevent terrorism domestically and internationally and to coordinate a response to any successful attacks. The Nixon administration also sought improved coordination and counterterrorism actions with European allies, Israel, and friendly Arab states while pursuing a UN resolution condemning terrorism. In New York, the UN General Assembly was reluctant to support American and Israeli efforts. Instead, the majority of states voted for Resolution 3034, which supported national liberation movements while also expressing concern over terrorism. Domestically, the administration launched a controversial program codenamed "Operation Boulder," which targeted Arab visa applicants and initiated surveillance of Arab-American students and organizations. Once the surveillance program was revealed, however, Operation Boulder was quickly shut down.[38]

After the Munich attack, the State Department sponsored two conferences on terrorism in four years. In addition, the Office of External Research initiated and oversaw a $250,000 research and analysis program on the subject. Meanwhile, the BSO began targeting diplomats, including the March 1973 assassination of U.S. ambassador to Sudan, Cleo Noel. Following Noel's assassination, the State Department ordered its embassies in the region to emphasize to the different Arab governments that Washington took "a serious view" of their "support for or toleration of" the BSO. Yet the Nixon administration's attempt to obtain a blanket condemnation of terrorism was challenged by the U.S. Embassies in Beirut and Tel Aviv. Through CIA deputy director General Vernon Walters, Kissinger also warned the PLO against further attacks on American diplomats, which aligned with Arafat's goal of establishing relations with Washington.[39]

In spite of the Nixon administration's encouragement, terror studies had limited visibility. There were few scholars in the field and the academics who were active often specialized in a particular discipline. Five years after Munich, historian J. Bowyer Bell explained that "there were still no satisfactory answers. No one had a definition of terrorism." He wrote, "In academia, the various concerned disciplines could not even define 'terror'. There was no agreement as to the effectiveness of 'terror', or the basic causes of the phenomenon, or the best means of approach to analyze it." Yet the combination of government interest and independent efforts led to the exponential expansion of terrorism expertise.[40]

These efforts were reflected in the terrorism conferences sponsored by the State Department. The first conference, held in 1972, found general agreement that terrorism was "the product of frustration induced by unresolved grievances." However, four years later most attendees were skeptical that terrorism could be stopped by removing its root causes. Several months before the 1976 State Department conference, the PFLP conducted another high-profile hijacking and brought the airliner to Entebbe, Uganda. Israeli forces conducted a surprise raid that freed the hostages, killed the hijackers, and embarrassed the government of Ugandan president Idi Amin. The only Israeli casualty was Yonatan (Jonathan) Netanyahu, the older brother of the future Israeli prime minister Benyamin (Benjamin) Netanyahu. The success of the Entebbe operation stood in sharp contrast to America's failure in Vietnam, a point that was reiterated by political observers and commentators. That failure was compounded only a few years later when U.S. Special Forces were unable to rescue American hostages held in Iran.[41]

Washington's burgeoning counterterrorism relationship with Israel was on display at the Jonathan Institute's July 1979 conference on terrorism. Based in Jerusalem, the Jonathan Institute was an Israeli think tank established by Benjamin Netanyahu and named after his brother. The institute maintained close ties to the Israeli political and military establishments. Among those affiliated with the institute were current and former Israeli prime ministers and foreign ministers, including Golda Meir, Yitzhak Rabin, Menachem Begin, Moshe Dayan, and Shimon Peres. The purpose of the July 1979 conference was "to focus public attention on the grave threat that international terrorism poses to all democratic societies, to study the real nature of today's terrorism, and to propose measures for combating and defeating international terror movements." Among the conference participants were former CIA director and future president George H. W. Bush, Democratic Senator Henry "Scoop" Jackson, and Republican congressman and future vice presidential candidate Jack Kemp.[42]

The organizers hoped the conference would be the beginning of an "anti-terror alliance" of Western democracies. This was reflected in the presented papers that emphasized the role of the Arab states and the Soviet Union in supporting terrorism while ignoring or dismissing the context for political violence. While terrorism was presented as a threat to the West, the disparity in power between state and nonstate actors was not discussed or was understated.[43] The Jonathan Institute conferences were successful in aligning Israel's definition of terrorism with U.S. Cold War goals.[44] After the Cold War, the emphasis on the Soviet Union was abandoned but the claim that terrorism was a threat to Western civilization persisted.[45]

Oil and Middle East Studies

The emergence of the Organization of the Petroleum Exporting Countries (OPEC), the nationalization of oil resources by producing states, and increased global demand contributed to rising oil prices in the early 1970s. Prices spiked even further after the October 1973 War and the oil boycott imposed by OPEC's Arab members. Ostensibly targeted at the United States in an attempt to force a change in American policy toward the Arab-Israeli conflict, the Arab states differed on whether to include Europe and Japan. Over four decades later, the ultimate effect of the boycott remains unclear. Several OPEC members increased production to profit from rising prices, making it difficult to determine if the global oil supply actually decreased. One of the member states that ignored the boycott was Iran. Mohammad Reza Shah Pahlavi used the newfound wealth to embark on a military spending spree. By 1978, Iran's military expenditures were $9.5 billion, an astonishing 765 percent increase in six years.[46]

Iran's profligacy was not limited to weapons sales. The shah, members of his extended family, and inner circle made contributions to fifty-five educational institutions. Some also served on university boards. The shah also had influential supporters among members of the academy, most notably Harvard's Richard Frye and George Lenczowski of the University of California, Berkeley. Frye was instrumental in the shah receiving an honorary degree from Harvard in 1968. Harvard president Nathan Pusey presented the shah as a modern and progressive leader and declared that he was a "twentieth century ruler who has found in power a constructive instrument to advance social and economic revolution in an ancient world."

Twelve years later, with the shah's regime overthrown and his progressive image in tatters, Pusey still defended the discredited leader. Pusey explained to the *Harvard Crimson* that the shah "seemed sincerely interested in how to promote modernization in backward parts of the world and he seemed to be doing it pretty well. But I guess he was doing it too well. That was his problem."[47]

George Lenczowski provided another uncritical view of the Pahlavi regime. As discussed in Chapter 5, Lenczowski was a Hamilton College professor with ties to American oil companies and the U.S. foreign policy establishment. By the early 1970s, he was a Berkeley faculty member and was affiliated with the American Enterprise Institute (AEI), a conservative think tank. Originally founded as the American Enterprise Association in 1938, AEI focused largely on domestic policy issues, especially criticizing the New Deal. AEI benefited from the conservative turn in American politics beginning with Nixon's 1968 victory. By 1977, the organization's annual budget was $5 million, which was provided by corporations. Executives from Mobil Oil, Standard Oil of California, and other large corporations joined AEI's board. These ties increased during the Carter presidency. According to Norm Ornstein, an AEI Fellow, corporations wanted a conservative "center for ideas" outside of a university setting because academia was deemed "more liberal."[48]

Lenczowski served as the director of AEI's Middle East Research Project and authored eleven studies. The analysis generally reflected AEI's ties to business interests. This was on display in Lenczowski's *Middle East Oil in a Revolutionary Age,* in which he argued that consuming nations needed to reach an accommodation with oil-producing states rather than pursuing autarky.[49]

In 1975, Lenczowski joined Stanford's Hoover Institution. Three years later he published the edited volume *Iran under the Pahlavis.* The volume's tone and content were sharply different from the AEI studies. *Iran under the Pahlavis* sought to demonstrate how the enlightened rule of Reza Shah and Mohammad Reza Shah guided Iran into modernity. Lenczowski asserted that the Pahlavi regime was responsible for Iran's noncommunist transformation, which he claimed had surpassed that of Japan and Turkey. Under the rule of Mohammad Reza Shah, Lenczowski claimed that Iran's "ancient legacy was being revived in its full dimensions." The shah was overthrown within a year.[50]

As the Iranian revolution reached its crescendo in December 1978, National Security Advisor Brzezinski informed Carter that an "arc of crisis" stretching from the Horn of Africa to South Asia threatened U.S. interests. Lenczowski borrowed the term for a *Foreign Affairs* article published a few months later and offered a critique of the shah's rule that was absent from *Iran under the Pahlavis.* The shah's collapse exposed America's limited military capabilities in the Persian Gulf. Building on the "arc of crisis" thesis, Brzezinski called for the creation of a "regional security framework" to replace the fallen Iranian pillar. The Soviet invasion of Afghanistan in December expedited the planning and led to a formal declaration of U.S. interest in the Persian Gulf with the Carter Doctrine. Deliberately framed like the Truman Doctrine, Carter issued the blunt warning to the Kremlin in his 1980 State of the Union address. Three months after Carter's declaration, the Rapid Deployment Joint Task Force (RDJTF) was created and dispatched to the region. The RDJTF evolved into the U.S. military's Central Command.[51]

In spite of the public animosity between Tehran and Washington, secret contacts and relations continued. Most prominently with the Reagan administration's attempt to trade weapons for American hostages held in Lebanon. Israel assisted with the negotiations and maintained secret relations with Tehran for more than a decade after the revolution.[52]

Iran was not the only oil-rich country to pursue relations with American academia. Reflecting America's expanded involvement in the region and the increasing coffers of oil-producing nations, Georgetown established the Center for Contemporary Arab Studies (CCAS) in 1975. CCAS received funding from the U.S. government as well as donations from Saudi Arabia, Oman, and the United Arab Emirates (UAE). Two years later, Libya provided CCAS with a $750,000 gift to endow a chair. Saudi Arabia also provided $1 million to the University of Southern California to establish the King Faisal Chair of Islamic and Arab Studies. The gift was part of a broader arrangement to create a Middle East Studies Center at USC with donations from Riyadh as well as major corporations. Over the next two decades, Saudi Arabia expanded the size and number of gifts it provided to elite American universities. Major donations were provided by individuals and state-based foundations to Harvard, Berkeley, Princeton, Georgetown, Duke, and Cornell. Donations from Arab countries have been a source of contention in the United States. Opponents assert that they have contributed to, if not directly influenced, anti-Israeli and anti-American attitudes in Middle East studies scholarship. Yet the criticism often conflates opposition to Israel's policies with antagonism toward the United States. While Muammar el-Qaddafi's Libya was clearly opposed to Washington's policies and allies in the region, the same could not easily be said for the Arab Gulf monarchies. Saudi Arabia and other donors from oil-rich Arab countries were primarily interested in influencing American perceptions about their countries and ruling families, especially after the 1973–1974 oil embargo. In addition, the Soviet invasion of Afghanistan provided the United States, Israel, Saudi Arabia, and Egypt with an opportunity to ally against a common foe. Nor were similar criticisms raised about donations and ties by Mohammad Reza Shah Pahlavi's regime. Moreover, America's military presence in the Persian Gulf region increased after the Cold War, as did donations to elite American universities, which suggests reinforcing rather than opposing U.S. foreign policy and national security interests.[53]

The Family Jewels

Washington's increased involvement in the Middle East coincided with a controversy that had implications on foreign policy as well as the relationship between the government and academia. Revelations about decision making during the Vietnam War contained in the "Pentagon Papers," combined with the Watergate scandal, undermined the faith of Americans in the political establishment. In December 1974, a new series of revelations about the actions of the CIA published in the *New York Times* appeared to affirm the worst suspicions about the national security establishment. Seymour Hersh's front-page story described the CIA's illegal surveillance of 10,000 American antiwar protesters as well as members of Congress at the behest of the Nixon administration. Hersh reported that the agency had performed a number of actions dating to the Eisenhower administration that were prohibited by U.S. law. In a confidential speech to the Council on Foreign Relations, Director of Central Intelligence (DCI) William Colby explained that he had already ordered an internal review that identified some improprieties. He added, however, "I think family skeletons are best left where they are—in the closet."[54]

The Ford administration scrambled to respond to Hersh's claims. Colby drafted a lengthy memorandum to Secretary of State Kissinger detailing the CIA's actions, which included wiretapping reporters, monitoring antiwar protestors, opening mail, and conducting illegal searches. In a conversation with Kissinger, Colby revealed other CIA operations, such as medical and psychological experiments and the attempted assassinations of foreign leaders. The information was summarized in a memorandum to a vacationing President Ford on Christmas Day. "I have discussed these activities with [Colby], and must tell you that some few of [the CIA's activities] clearly were illegal, while others—though not technically illegal—raise profound moral questions. A number, while neither illegal nor morally unsound, demonstrated very poor judgment," Kissinger wrote.[55]

After the New Year, Ford returned to Washington and attempted to contain the crisis. On January 4, he met with Richard Helms, former DCI and ambassador to Iran. Helms served as DCI for Presidents Johnson and

Nixon and was directly implicated in the emerging scandal. President Ford was friendly but blunt: "Frankly, we are in a mess." Ford informed Helms that he planned to create a "Blue Ribbon Panel" to investigate the accusations. However, Ford was concerned that the investigation might go too far. Although Helms welcomed the inquiry, he cautioned that "a lot of dead cats will come out." "I don't know everything that went on in the Agency," he added, "maybe no one really does. But I know enough to say that if the dead cats come out, I will participate." One of the "dead cats" was that during the Kennedy administration, Attorney General Robert Kennedy managed "Operation Mongoose," the assassination plot directed against Cuba's Fidel Castro.[56]

Later that day, Ford convened a meeting of his chief advisors. The attendees included Kissinger, Vice President Nelson Rockefeller, Chief of Staff Donald Rumsfeld, and the recently appointed National Security Advisor Brent Scowcroft. During the meeting, Kissinger described the "horrors" book of CIA actions. If the public learned the details, Ford explained, "We are concerned that the CIA would be destroyed." Rockefeller added, "And we become the laughingstock around the world." Ford asked the vice president to lead the investigation.[57] Released six months later, the Rockefeller Commission offered a number of modest criticisms of the CIA and recommendations for reform. It also justified a number of the agency's operations due to the need for intelligence on foreign areas. Yet the Rockefeller Commission was not the only, or most prominent, investigation.[58]

One consequence of the Watergate scandal was the sweeping Democratic Party victory in the 1974 elections and a new Congress determined to contain executive power. Hersh's article resulted in the formation of a Senate investigative committee led by Idaho Democrat Frank Church in January 1975. Church, who had presidential ambitions, held an unprecedented series of hearings into the CIA's activities, culminating in a scathing report. Among the Church Committee's findings were the interactions between the CIA and academia. The report stated bluntly that the agency has "long-developed clandestine relationships with the American academic community, which range from academics making introductions for intelligence purposes to intelligence collection while abroad, to academic research and writing where CIA sponsorship is hidden." It added that the agency provided funds to private American organizations operating overseas whose activities were in support of "or could be conceived to support" U.S. foreign policy goals. The report also confirmed that the CIA had maintained relationships with

American philanthropic foundations until 1967, in order to funnel funds to private organizations whose work the agency supported.[59]

The Church Committee detailed the CIA's "massive" funding of private foundations in the 1960s. From 1963 to 1966, the CIA provided partial or full funding for 108 of 700 grants over $10,000 that were awarded by 164 foundations, excluding the Rockefeller and Ford Foundations and the Carnegie Corporation. These foundations were legitimate organizations and not front operations for distributing CIA funds. CIA funding accounted for almost half of the grants for international activities and a third of the grants in the physical, life, and social sciences. Activities funded by the CIA included the creation of a research institute at a major research university in 1951—presumably the Massachusetts Institute of Technology (MIT)—and its continued financial support for over a decade, as well as an international education exchange program operated by American universities.[60]

The CIA also maintained covert relationships with individual academics. It used several hundred scholars, including administrators, faculty, and graduate students, to make "introductions for intelligence purposes, [and] occasionally write books and other material to be used for propaganda purposes abroad." While the CIA was affiliated with over 100 American colleges, universities, and institutes, the relationships between the scholars and the agency varied. In some cases, the Committee found, only the individual involved was aware of the relationship, while at other institutions a university official also knew of the "operational use made of academics on his campus." The Committee reported that American scholars overseas collected intelligence for the agency. Indeed, the CIA viewed its relationships with the American academic community as "perhaps its most sensitive domestic area" and had "strict controls governing these operations." For example, it could not recruit recipients of the Fulbright-Hays Fellowship and did not recruit individuals who received funds from the Ford and Rockefeller Foundations, the Carnegie Corporation, or the employees of these foundations. However, the Church Committee did not comment on the briefing and debriefing of fellowship recipients by the CIA and other national security agencies prior to the 1960s.[61]

The Church Committee chastised the CIA for its recruitment of American academics. It objected to the CIA's claim that the agency hesitated expanding the program due to the "risks of exposure." The Church Committee stated that the CIA needed to appreciate the "dangers to the integrity of individuals and institutions." It also admonished the agency for recruiting academics who received funding through government-sponsored programs. "It is unacceptable that Americans would go overseas under a cultural or academic exchange program funded openly by the United States Congress and at the same time serve an operational purpose directed by the Central Intelligence Agency," the report stated. Although the Church Committee report led to greater oversight of the intelligence community, that did not extend to academia. Instead, the academic community was left to police itself and set the appropriate standards.[62]

The Church Committee investigation led to a shake-up in the Ford administration. In October 1975, Ford fired Secretary of Defense James Schlesinger and DCI Colby. Donald Rumsfeld, Ford's chief of staff, replaced Schlesinger at the Defense Department. Richard "Dick" Cheney was named chief of staff and George H. W. Bush, then the U.S. ambassador to China, was tapped for the CIA post. Bush accepted the position reluctantly as he feared it would limit his presidential ambitions. Instead, it enhanced his political prospects, and the scandal provided the CIA with an opportunity to clean house.[63]

Bush's defense of the agency was on display after the Church Committee report was released. William Van Alstyne, a Duke law professor and the president of the American Association of University Professors (AAUP), rebuked the CIA in a May 4, 1976 letter addressed to Bush. "A government which corrupts the colleges and universities by making political fronts of them has betrayed academic freedom and compromised all who teach," he wrote. Van Alstyne asked Bush to "take steps to end the exploitation of the academic community and to disengage the Agency from covert activities which induce academics to betray their professional trust."[64]

Bush, however, rejected Van Alstyne's argument. He explained that the CIA's relations with academia ranged from contract research for the sciences and social sciences to paid and unpaid consultations and interviews with individuals returning from travel abroad. The goal of this research, he explained, was to fulfill the CIA's "primary responsibility; i.e., to provide the policy makers of our government with information and assessments of foreign developments." Bush added that the CIA sought "voluntary and willing cooperation of individuals" and said these relationships remained covert because some scholars feared that they would be "badgered" by those who feel they "should not be free to make this particular choice." He invited Van Alstyne to meet with senior CIA officials in order to "find a way toward a better understanding."[65]

Former CIA officials also offered advice on reforming the agency. William Bundy, the brother of former national security advisor McGeorge Bundy and a CIA veteran from the Kennedy and Johnson administrations, suggested that the agency separate its analysis and operations divisions. Bundy, who was also the editor of *Foreign Affairs*, argued that the separation would help restore links between the CIA and academia. Bush countered that "we have never been isolated from academia even during the worst of the recent period." He reiterated that many of the academics who maintained relations with the CIA preferred it was secret in order to avoid being "hounded by the emotional and the trendy among their colleagues." "For this reason you and many others are probably unaware just how deep and extensive these relationships are," Bush wrote. Unlike his letter to Van Alstyne, Bush offered Bundy some specifics about the existing relationships. He explained that the CIA's Office of Political Research, which was created after the Office of National Estimates was disbanded in 1973, maintained relations with at least eighty senior faculty members at Harvard, Princeton, Stanford, MIT, and the Universities of Chicago, California, and Michigan. Bush added that CIA analysts were welcome at a number of universities for sabbaticals and openly attended professional meetings, and that the controversy had not hindered the recruitment of top candidates. He conceded that the CIA was not a destination for liberal arts graduates from the top universities, but explained that "these people simply do not appear to be interested in federal service of any kind." However, he noted that the quality of the CIA's professional force had improved and roughly 45 percent had graduate degrees from leading programs. "The mass and often indiscriminate intake of professionals in the 50's will not be repeated," Bush said. He added that "it provided many first rate people, but it also saddled the Agency with a large number of third-raters. Virtually all of these have been eased out in the last few years."[66]

The attempts to improve relations between the CIA and academia continued during the Carter administration. Bush's replacement, Admiral Stansfield Turner, was briefed on the subject by B. Vincent Davis, a professor of political science at the University of Kentucky. Davis also served as president of the International Studies Association and was retained by Turner to serve as a special advisor. Writing in May 1977, Davis warned Turner that the cynicism toward government by academics and the general public was also shared by policymakers toward university scholars. Davis recounted a conversation he had a decade earlier with Thomas Hughes, then director of the State Department's Bureau of Intelligence and Research (INR) and the future president of the Carnegie Endowment for International Peace. After dismissing college texts on U.S. foreign policy as inaccurate, Hughes declared, "I don't really care what you teach college kids." Davis proposed that the CIA fund seminars on topical issues in which academics would be invited to participate. However, he recommended that the CIA's central role remain secret. Instead, CIA personnel would attend as merely one of several government agencies participating in the seminars. Although the idea of the seminars appealed to Turner, he was wary of the proposed $100,000 budget and the suggestion that a front organization was needed. "This is simply going backwards and asking for the same kinds of problems that the CIA has come a cropper on in days past," Turner wrote, "Either we are honest, or we are not." Instead, Turner informed Davis that the CIA would attempt to organize seminars without obscuring its role. Yet this attempt at transparency would not last.[67]

The New Left and Middle East Studies

Middle East studies were not immune from the post-Vietnam schisms in American society and academia reflected in the Church Commission report. Reduced federal funding combined with decreased support from the foundations placed severe constraints on the growth of area studies. Although NDEA funding was targeted at strategic areas, there was no mechanism to ensure that the types of research conducted by graduate students would further U.S. national security interests other than obtaining competence in a particular foreign language. Scholars who completed their doctoral degrees during and after the Vietnam War were generally more reluctant to conduct research on behalf of the U.S. government. The new generation of scholars also sought to distance themselves from, if not challenge outright, the prevailing orthodoxy within the field as represented by Orientalist scholars.

The intellectual shift in Middle East studies owed much to the "New Left" movement in academia. Emerging out of the political activism of the 1960s, the New Left scholars built on the political critique of America's role in the world and analyzed the structural factors underlying developments in the Middle East. The initial wave of scholarship focused on the political economy of the region.[68] Over the next decade, Middle East studies and scholarship in general shifted from focusing on elites to examining the influence of race, class, and gender across different disciplines.[69]

The New Left's connection to the antiwar movement was also demonstrated by the creation of the Middle East Research and Information Project (MERIP). MERIP was founded by a collective of scholars affiliated with the Committee of Returned Volunteers, which organized Peace Corps veterans against the Vietnam War. They sought to link U.S. foreign policy in Southeast Asia with the Middle East, focusing on Israel/Palestine as well as the Persian Gulf region. Originally based in Boston and Washington, MERIP published the first issue of its *MERIP Reports* in May 1971, but subsequent editions were released infrequently for the next four years. MERIP struggled in its first decade to become an established journal with stable financing, content produced by writers from inside and outside the collective, and reliable distribution. However, the combination of increased interest in the region due to the Iranian Revolution and a professional editorial staff contributed to greater circulation. By the end of the decade, scholars affiliated with MERIP had faculty appointments at leading universities and were active members of MESA.[70]

The intelligence community monitored the emergence of the New Left. Deputy Director of the CIA Vernon Walters, speaking at the Institute for American Strategy (later the American Security Council Foundation) in January 1976, claimed that the New Left was unwittingly supporting the Kremlin. "Everything the New Left fights against benefits the Soviet Union," he said.[71]

Perhaps the most influential challenge to the prevailing orthodoxy in Middle East studies was offered by Edward Said's *Orientalism*. Intellectual critiques of Orientalism were not new, but none of the prior efforts had Said's immediate or long-term impact. However, *Orientalism* was not without its flaws or detractors, and the book received mixed reviews initially. While some scholars welcomed it, others objected to Said's dense writing style as well as to his monolithic treatment of the Occident. A number of reviews chastised Said for ignoring Orientalist scholarship from before the British and French imperial periods as well as the extensive works of German Orientalist scholars who did not have colonial holdings in the Middle East.[72]

The sharpest criticism was authored by Princeton's Bernard Lewis, albeit four years after *Orientalism* was published. Arguably the leading Orientalist scholar in the United States, Lewis wrote a critique that appeared in the *New York Review of Books,* which also published an exchange between the two scholars. This debate continued for the next two decades, with the Arab-Israeli conflict heavily influencing both antagonists and their supporters. A professor of Comparative Literature at Columbia, Said was an outspoken advocate for the Palestinian cause. He also had a seat on the Palestinian National Council, the PLO's "parliament in exile." Lewis, however, was a supporter of Israel's policies in the Middle East and increasingly an advocate for a robust American Cold War policy. Although Said arguably won the contest of ideas within academia, Lewis's influence was far more pronounced within policy circles.[73]

While the new generation of scholars represented a shift in Middle East studies, an incident at Harvard served as a reminder of the relationship between the intelligence community and academia. After Hamilton Gibb's death in 1971, Harvard's CMES suffered from a lack of leadership. Harvard's History Department unsuccessfully pursued several leading scholars who could also lead CMES as Gibb's replacement, including Gustave von Grunebaum, Albert Hourani, and Bernard Lewis. By the early 1980s, it appeared that the university found a scholar who could return CMES to prominence. Nadav Safran, a Harvard-trained political scientist and professor of government, became CMES's director in 1983. Safran served as a consultant to the State Department, participated in the 1975 Brookings Institution study group, and advocated for CMES to be relevant in policy circles as well as in academia. In addition, he sought an expansion of course offerings, with a particular focus on the modern era and contemporary issues.[74]

Two years later, however, CMES was mired in scandal. In October 1985, the *Harvard Crimson* reported that a planned conference on "Islam and Politics in the Contemporary Muslim World" received $45,700 in funding from the CIA. Conference participants were unaware of the agency's support and more than half withdrew in protest when it was exposed. Safran also received a $107,430 grant from the CIA to support research for a book on Saudi Arabia. As part of the grant contract, the agency required final approval of the manuscript and nondisclosure of its funding. While the preface to Safran's *Saudi Arabia: The Ceaseless Quest for Security* acknowledged the support of the RAND Corporation and the Rockefeller Foundation, the CIA was not mentioned.[75]

Harvard launched an investigation in response to the revelations and subsequent uproar in the academic community. Three members of the CMES Executive Committee, including Richard Frye—despite his previous connections to the intelligence community—called for Safran's resignation. MESA also issued a statement that criticized Safran for not abiding by its resolution on disclosure of funding sources. Harvard's investigation found Safran at fault for failing to reveal CIA funding for the conference. In the case of the grant for the book, however, the report blamed Dean of Faculty Henry Rosovsky. The investigation found that Safran followed the university's procedures and notified Rosovsky of the grant and its unusual terms, but the Dean did not conduct the appropriate review. After the report was released Safran resigned his position as director and the CMES Executive Committee was disbanded due to internal splits over the controversy. The Safran scandal also led to revelations that two political science professors, Samuel Huntington and Richard Betts, were conducting research for the CIA.[76]

Robert Gates, then the CIA's deputy director of intelligence, spoke at Harvard's John F. Kennedy School of Government a month later. The talk was limited to professors and reporters and Gates sought to quell anger over the Safran scandal. "Working with your government to bring about a better foreign policy is not shameful; it is consistent with a scholar's highest duty," Gates told the audience. He announced new policies that the agency hoped would allow it to maintain relations with academia. This included advance notice to participants of CIA funding for conferences as well as permission for scholars to acknowledge the agency's support of research and publications. However, Harvard president Derek Bok did not believe the changes to CIA policy were sufficient and the university adopted new restrictions on outside funding of research.[77]

"All That Is Best in the American Way of Life"

Like universities in the United States and Europe, the American University of Beirut (AUB) was the site of protests and strikes as the student body became increasingly politicized. A large number of AUB's students identified with the PLO and the leftist Lebanese National Movement, which led to critical coverage of the university in American media. An October 1970 *Newsweek* article branded it "Guerilla U." and depicted AUB's students as benefiting from an American-style education while condemning Washington's policies. Negative coverage in other media outlets, including an NBC News program, forced the AUB Board to embark on a spirited defense. However, university officials were privately assured by State Department contacts that the negative media coverage was not as serious as they feared.[78]

Foggy Bottom also defended the university against domestic critics. Following the negative press coverage, Senator Abraham Ribicoff of Connecticut inquired about U.S. government support for AUB. David Abshire, assistant secretary for congressional relations, explained that "most reporting on the AUB painted a distorted and inaccurate picture of the University." Although some students were active with the PLO, Abshire stated that "AUB is one of the finest educational institutions in the Middle East or Asia." He wrote, "It is a cultural 'window' to the United States. It has introduced American ideas and values to the area. Its graduates have played a vital role in the development of their respective countries." Abshire added that through its different programs "AUB has helped to bring a 'quiet revolution' to the Middle East, the effects of which will endure long after political slogans and nationalistic antipathies have lost their hold on the minds of men." He argued that AUB's situation was similar that of universities in the United States with students who belonged to the Black Panther Party or the Weathermen. "In our view, it would be wrong to suspend American aid to the AUB because of the actions of a small minority of the student body who engage in actions inimicable to American interests," Abshire said.[79]

However, there were limits to the State Department's support. After the March 1973 assassination of Ambassador Noel (discussed previously), a front-page article in the AUB student newspaper, *Outlook*, expressed support for the Khartoum attack. In response, U.S. Ambassador to Lebanon William Buffum warned university officials that "expressions of radical sentiment such as approval of [the] Khartoum killing could have [a] serious, negative effect on future American support for AUB." Buffum added that the university "should be aware of [the] implications for both private and public support from [the] United States should it appear that [the] student body has been taken over by those advocating extremist tactics." AUB's administration responded quickly to Buffum's concerns and reassured him that they would not allow *Outlook* to become a "political organ."[80]

AUB's political and financial problems were exacerbated by the outbreak of the Lebanese civil war in 1975. The university's woes were compounded further by the 1982 Israeli invasion. Rival Lebanese militias emerged after the PLO was exiled from Beirut, including the Lebanese Shia militia, Hizbullah. Armed groups, including Hizbullah, began attacking American and Israeli targets and members of the AUB faculty and administration were kidnapped and assassinated, as were other Westerners. The university was forced to reduce its operations and did not reemerge from forced stagnation until the 1989 Taif Accord ended the civil war.[81]

Regional conflicts also had an impact on the American University in Cairo (AUC). In spite of tensions with the United States, Nasser recognized AUC's importance to maintaining ties to Washington and his daughter, Mona, attended the university. In 1967, the Center for Arabic Study Abroad (CASA) was established at AUC and eventually became the leading regional program for Arabic-language instruction.[82] Meanwhile, the State Department recommended a $57.5 million grant to AUC from Public Law (PL) 480 funds. The proposal stated that "Congress is familiar with the American University in Cairo's important role as a representative of all that is best in the American way of life." It explained that AUC's principal objectives included "to serve as an intellectual and cultural meeting place for the Arab world and the West" and "to help educate American specialists in the language and culture of the Arab world."[83] However, AUC's operations and plans were hindered by the June 1967 Arab-Israeli War. The Egyptian government sequestered AUC and broke off relations with Washington. In addition to public calls in the Egyptian press for AUC to be nationalized, there were protests and threats to university property. Although the sequestration remained in place, Nasser ignored the calls to nationalize the university.[84]

The U.S. Embassy was shuttered during the interwar period. A small contingent, including Ambassador Hermann Eilts, operated an Interests Section out of the Spanish Embassy. Tensions between Washington and Cairo led Assistant Secretary for Near East and South Asian Affairs Joseph Sisco to remark after a brief visit to the university that it was "a definite asset in our efforts to maintain a U.S. presence in Egypt."[85] Due in part to its precarious position under sequestration, an AUC professor working on research for the U.S. Air Force sought to end his participation in the project as it moved toward a more advanced phase. The university informed the air force that it was "concerned that disclosure of this research by parties hostile to AUC's and/or [the U.S. government's] presence in Egypt might jeopardize its relationship with the [government of Egypt] and its position in Egypt."[86]

The sequestration of AUC was not lifted until after the October 1973 War and relations between Washington and Cairo improved. AUC attempted to benefit from the decreased tensions and sought another large grant from PL 480 funds for investment projects around Cairo. In response to the request, Ambassador Eilts explained that he favored continued support of AUC even though "it had shown a somewhat ambivalent attitude" toward the U.S.

government "except when it comes to wanting money." Eilts added that the university should maintain its independence but "on matters where there is a direct [U.S. government] interest which could be furthered by AUC cooperation I would have no hesitation in expecting a *quid pro quo* for our help."[87]

In 1975, Egypt officially recognized bachelor's degrees from the AUC, which enabled graduates to work in Egyptian universities as well as the foreign and civil services. AUC also established an intensive English and two-year master's program for recent graduates of Egyptian universities. Sadat's new economic policy, *al-infitah* ("the opening up") benefited AUC graduates as they found employment with American and European corporations. In addition, the need for English-speaking employees led companies to raid AUC staff. Egypt's ties to the United States increased after Sadat's assassination and the country became a key regional ally under Husni Mubarak's rule.[88]

Toward Peace?

The Brookings Institution's perceived influence on the Carter administration inspired other think tanks. William Simon, President Ford's secretary of the treasury, told the *Washington Post* that AEI could play a key role for the Republican Party in the 1980 election. While the Democratic Party "had Brookings," Simon asserted that the Republicans "ought to use AEI—and we will over the next four years." President Ford joined AEI after leaving office and was joined by members of his administration as the institute's staff swelled.[89] In California, the Hoover Institution experienced similar growth in size and influence. A glowing February 1978 profile of the Hoover Institution in the *New York Times Magazine* described it as "the brightest star in a small constellation of conservative think tanks" aligned with the Republican Party.[90] After Ronald Reagan's sweeping 1980 victory over Carter, staffers from the conservative think tanks were welcomed into the new administration. Within a few years Brookings was competing with AEI and the Heritage Foundation for the attention of the press and policymakers.[91]

While the conservative think tanks attempted to copy Brookings, the Reagan administration did not follow Carter's example of extensive involvement in the Arab-Israeli peace process. In addition, key members of Carter's foreign policy and national security staff remained outside of government for the next three decades, including Brzezinski and Quandt. While Quandt remained active with the Brookings Institution, Harold Saunders, the former assistant secretary of state for Near East and South Asian Affairs, joined AEI. Saunders worked with Kissinger on the post–October War disengagement agreements and assisted with the Camp David Accords. As the director of INR at the State Department, Saunders asked AEI and the Brookings Institution for an assessment of the Palestinian issue. After the Camp David Accords were signed, AEI developed a proposal for autonomy elections in the West Bank and Gaza Strip. Although Quandt and Saunders advocated for continued American engagement with the peace process, U.S. foreign policy toward the Arab-Israeli conflict during the Reagan administration was dominated by conservative elements with close ties to Israel. As Chapter 8 discusses, there was a pronounced shift at AEI as the institute became aligned with the neoconservative agenda.[92]

Less than a year after Reagan took office, Israel and the United States signed a strategic cooperation MOU. The agreement was designed to counter Soviet ambitions in the region and involved greater military and intelligence coordination and collaboration between the United States and Israel. Six months later, Israel invaded Lebanon after receiving approval from Secretary of State Alexander Haig for a limited operation. However, a larger offensive was always planned.[93] Israel's 1982 invasion of Lebanon and siege of Beirut tested the improved relations with the Reagan administration. In addition, the heavy civilian casualties led to widespread condemnation of Israel and testy exchanges between Reagan and Israeli prime minister Begin that contributed to a cease fire. The Reagan administration attempted to restart the Arab-Israeli peace process after the PLO left Beirut. But the Reagan Plan, which called for autonomy for the West Bank and Gaza, was undermined by the assassination of newly elected Lebanese president Bashir Gemayel and the subsequent massacre of Palestinian civilians in the Sabra and Shatila refugee camps. Reagan's peace initiative was eventually shelved and strategic cooperation with Israel continued.[94]

The establishment and influence of the Washington Institute for Near East Policy (WINEP) also reflected the burgeoning strategic relationship between the United States and Israel. Funded by the influential pro-Israel lobby, the American Israel Public Affairs Committee (AIPAC), WINEP was formed in February 1985. The overlap between AIPAC and WINEP was not superficial. Martyn Indyk, a former deputy director for research at AIPAC, served as WINEP's first executive director. Other AIPAC officials were among WINEP's founders. While WINEP alternately billed itself as an organization focused on "public policy" and "research and education," it did little to mask its pro-Israel orientation. The attempt to align American and Israeli interests even extended to the organization's name and the deliberate choice of "Near East," which corresponded to the State Department's designation.[95]

WINEP grew rapidly and developed strong links to Washington policy circles. Within four years it had a permanent staff of ten, including five Israeli and American fellows. Its initial annual operating budget of $750,000 was funded largely by contributions from the American Jewish community.[96] WINEP's ties to policymakers were increasingly apparent. In September 1988, Secretary of State George Shultz appeared at a WINEP-sponsored conference. The conference was held ten months into the first Palestinian *intifada*, or uprising, in the occupied West Bank and Gaza Strip and corresponded with a period of unprecedented international criticism of Israel. As pictures of Israeli soldiers shooting at or beating unarmed Palestinian youths were broadcast around the world, the PLO's leadership renewed its attempt to obtain recognition from Washington. However, those efforts were initially rebuffed by the Reagan administration. In his WINEP speech, Shultz asserted that peace could not be achieved through the creation of a Palestinian state. Shultz stated that if the PLO renounced terrorism, recognized Israel, and accepted UN Security Council Resolutions 242 and 338, Washington would consider it for participation in the peace process. The PLO met Washington's conditions two months later, and Reagan announced that the United States would begin discussions with the organization.[97]

Coinciding with Shultz's speech, WINEP published *Building for Peace: An American Strategy for the Middle East*. The report was based on a study group established by WINEP and comprised of the Middle East policy advisors from the presidential campaigns of both Vice President George H. W. Bush and Massachusetts Governor Michael Dukakis. WINEP deliberately attempted to copy the perceived success of the Brookings Institution's 1975 study group and final report. "The Brookings plan was precisely what we were trying to replicate," Indyk explained. He added, "The key was that the people engaged in the report went into the administration and had a common idea of what they wanted to do." Cochaired by Under Secretary of State for Political Affairs Lawrence Eagleburger and former vice president Walter Mondale, the WINEP study group was comprised largely of former policymakers rather than scholars. There was also little overlap in participants and UCLA's Stephen Spiegel was the only individual to serve on both study groups. Other notable members included former (and future) defense secretary Donald Rumsfeld, Harvard's Joseph Nye Jr., conservative columnist Charles Krauthammer, and Daniel Pipes, the director of the Foreign Policy Institute.[98]

Building for Peace offered recommendations on U.S. policy toward the Arab-Israeli conflict and the Persian Gulf. It argued that the Middle East was a "dangerous place" for the United States and the next administration faced a region in transition. The report advocated for Washington to "reshape the political environment" of the Arab-Israeli conflict. In what would become a common refrain over the next two decades, *Building for Peace* asserted that "the U.S. cannot make peace for these parties; it can only assist them once they are willing to do so." This recommendation reflected WINEP's first policy paper, "Acting with Caution: Middle East Policy Planning for the Second Reagan Administration," authored by Dennis Ross. Ross argued that the Reagan administration needed to revive the approach adopted by Kissinger before the October 1973 War of "patiently awaiting real movement from the local parties."[99]

While the PLO sought recognition from Washington, *Building for Peace* recommended that the next presidential administration cultivate a new Palestinian leadership drawn from the occupied Palestinian territories. In addition, it asserted that any negotiations between Israel, Jordan, and the Palestinians would require a "prolonged transition period" so that "the intentions of the Palestinians to live in peace with Israel and Jordan could be tested." Before either negotiations or the transition period, the study group advocated "confidence-building measures" between Israeli and Palestinians. These recommendations were accepted in part by the Bush and Clinton administrations and the emphasis on confidence-building measures became a hallmark of the Oslo Accords.[100]

After George H. W. Bush's victory in the 1988 presidential election, some of the individuals involved in the WINEP study group became key figures in his administration. Eagleburger was promoted to deputy secretary of state, Richard Haas was named the NSC's senior director for Near East and South Asian Affairs, and Dennis Ross was selected to head the State Department's Policy Planning Staff (PPS). Other members included Francis Fukuyama, Haas's aide on the NSC; Ross's aide Aaron David Miller; and Secretary of State James Baker's speechwriter, Harvey Sicherman.[101]

The Brookings Institution also launched a study group in preparation for the 1988 election. Coordinated by William Quandt, the study group was cochaired by former U.S. ambassadors Samuel Lewis and Hermann

Eilts. The final report, *Toward Arab-Israeli Peace*, revealed sharp disagreements among the study group members over the role of the United States in facilitating negotiations and the participation of the PLO. However, consensus was reached on several major points. The Brookings study group warned that continued stalemate threatened U.S. national interests. In contrast to WINEP's *Building Peace*, the Brookings study group recommended that the next administration should provide "a steady, high-level commitment" to the peace process. This included formulating a strategy based on UNSCR 242 and direct negotiations between Israelis and Palestinians. *Toward Arab-Israeli Peace* recommended that the Palestinians should select their own representatives to participate in negotiations, but conceded that the representatives would likely need the PLO's "implicit or explicit endorsement." Like the 1975 Brookings report and WINEP's *Building Peace*, the 1988 study group also called for "transitional steps" between Israel and the Palestinians, including halting Israeli settlements.[102]

Although the AJC's Executive Chairman Henry Siegman participated in the Brookings study group, he had concerns about the report. After reviewing a second draft of the report, AJC president Theodore Mann informed Siegman that "a kind of chill went through me" because of the recommendation that the next administration adopt an active role. "It brought to mind the new Carter administration in early 1977," Mann wrote. He added that Carter's assertiveness frightened the Israelis and contributed to the Likud Party's electoral victory. While he praised Carter's tenacity in pursuing peace between Egypt and Israel, Mann argued that it was Sadat's efforts, not "American assertiveness," that was responsible for the breakthrough.[103]

In addition to the Brookings study group, Quandt published an edited volume to commemorate the ten-year anniversary of the Camp David Accords. *The Middle East: Ten Years after Camp David* featured essays by several scholars and policymakers who participated in the study group. In the volume's introduction, Quandt argued that the Egyptian-Israeli peace treaty offered an example of what was possible between Israelis and Palestinians with support from Washington and Moscow. The edited volume and the Brookings study group were largely ignored, however. Instead, WINEP's recommendations and staff would predominate in Washington. As Chapter 8 demonstrates, WINEP succeeded not only in copying the Brookings Institution, but the two organizations eventually shared leadership and policy recommendations.[104]

The New Cold War and Area Studies

Heightened tensions with Moscow during Ronald Reagan's first term led to renewed interest in area studies. This was reflected in a 1981 study by the RAND Corporation that examined Title VI programs two decades after the NDEA was passed. The RAND study found that the combination of declining enrollment and funding and decreased demand for area experts threatened the long-term viability of Title VI programs. It acknowledged that the hiring of area specialists in the academic and nonacademic sectors was insufficient. To respond to the changing environment, RAND recommended that area studies centers shift their focus from the humanities, which had high levels of unemployment, to policy-oriented positions, which included preparing students for nonacademic positions. By failing to do so, RAND explained, there was a "disjunction between center focus and national need as defined by academic, governmental, and business employers." For instance, despite the need for Soviet experts, languages other than Russian were prioritized for the Soviet Union-Eastern Europe area. The RAND study concluded on a positive note, however, and suggested Title VI could adapt to the new environment through a combination of renewed public interest and new legislation.[105]

Over the next two years, other examinations of language and area studies built on the RAND study. In 1983, the Stanford Research Institute (SRI) assessed the Pentagon's foreign language requirements and capabilities on behalf of the Association of American Universities (AAU). The SRI report stated that the Department of Defense (DOD) was the "nation's largest consumer of foreign area research and foreign language expertise." It added that the "indirect support" the intelligence community received from academic institutions and individual scholars was "of vital importance to analysts and area specialists." However, it found that the Pentagon believed academia was "out of sync" with its "highly specialized needs." In addition, DOD did not share the concerns of the academic community about a dearth in the quality and quantity of area and language specialists. Nor did SRI find support in Washington for greater expenditures on area and language programs. Yet the SRI report cautioned that there was a "strong correlation between the health and rigor of language and area study programs within the academic community and the quality of area and language specialists within the Defense Intelligence community." Due to the ties between the Pentagon and academia, the report warned, any deterioration threatened national interests. Although it acknowledged that the combination of government and foundation support post-Sputnik had impressive results, by 1983 the boom was over. Moreover, the decline in funding had implications for the different government agencies as they were unable to replace retired personnel.[106]

The SRI report found a gap between the production of knowledge in academia and the needs of the intelligence community. Analysts often required specific information to assist with the completion of certain tasks. In contrast, academic research offered contextual knowledge about countries and societies that was either not directly related to policy questions and issues or of limited value. Analysts were first introduced to scholarly literature during their formal education, which was reinforced through maintaining personal or professional contacts as well as references in popular literature. Thus, academic scholarship provided "the broad basis and background for analysts preparing for more specific, classified studies." The report noted that analysts tended toward periodicals that covered contemporary issues, in particular *Foreign Affairs*, as well as technical publications. Scholarly journals, monographs, and other academic publications were typically drawn on for "deeper research where time and analytical requirements permit or demand them." However, the use of scholarly monographs and publications was generally limited to providing specific background material for assessments, which were typically based on classified intelligence data.[107]

The report found that the Pentagon no longer viewed academia with suspicion. However, it found that "academic fears about the intelligence connections have not been entirely alleviated." It noted that scholars and centers of African and Middle East studies were still reluctant to embrace an open relationship with the intelligence community. For example, Middle East scholars were concerned that participating in a program sponsored by the Defense Intelligence Agency (DIA) "might make them appear to be 'handmaidens' of American strategy and intelligence interests."[108]

These observations were repeated and reinforced by an AAU assessment of area studies the following year. Again led by Richard Lambert, the new report confirmed that the era of rapid growth in area studies was over. Lambert found that reduced federal support in the 1970s led to a decline in the number of Title VI National Resource Centers from 107 to 46. After funding was restored in the early 1980s, the number of National Resource Centers increased to 76. However, federal funding alone was insufficient. Indeed, a survey by the Rockefeller Foundation warned that area studies centers anticipated a "disaster" due to cuts in the types of funding available to the universities. In addition, Lambert reported that there was a decline in the number of foreign area experts in the United States.[109]

Lambert's new report drew heavily on the 1983 SRI assessment for the Pentagon. Indeed, the impetus for the new report was the renewed interest by the DOD in language training. Less than a decade after he declared that university centers were ready to stand on their own, Caspar Weinberger, now Reagan's secretary of defense, stated that language and area studies as well as mathematics and science were the subjects most important to the DOD and the most at risk. As he oversaw a dramatic increase in defense spending, Weinberger's reputation as "Cap the Knife" was abandoned. Yet Weinberger's concerns were echoed by other government agencies, Congress, and academic institutions and societies.[110]

The 1984 Lambert report recommended a number of modifications to area studies funding and programs. This included supplemental funding from the Pentagon for language instruction, especially for areas where it had identified a critical need. Lambert also called for a long-term strategy and plan for language and area studies. For the Middle East, Lambert asserted that more university-based centers were needed with additional government support, especially to focus on language training in local Arabic dialects. However, the Cold War ended before the recommendations could be implemented and the peace dividend from American hegemony proved illusory.[111]

The thirtieth anniversary of the NDEA found area studies in general, and Middle East studies in particular, at a crossroads. A year later, the Cold War competition that instigated the NDEA's passage was over. Middle East studies expanded and diversified during a period of funding constraints. In addition, a new generation of scholars influenced by the civil rights and anti-war movements emerged. Many, but not all, were less inclined to produce knowledge deemed useful by the foreign policy and national security establishments. Although the rift between academia and the U.S. government appeared to widen, especially in the wake of the Church Committee's investigation and report, the national security establishment was able to maintain relations with scholars and institutions for research and training. Thus, debates over new research paradigms within Middle East studies or in the academic disciplines had little impact on the foreign policy and national security establishments. Moreover, studies conducted during a period of heightened Cold War tensions recommended that area studies scholarship align more closely with the requirements of government agencies. Even though the New Left scholars seized the commanding heights of academia, their hopes of transforming academic institutions, American society, and U.S. foreign policy were stymied by more entrenched and powerful forces.

The Middle East, and in particular the Arab-Israeli conflict, was a focal point for debates over the future of U.S. foreign policy and America's international standing. While Nixon, Ford, and Kissinger promoted détente with Moscow, the Trilateral Commission sought to renew relations with America's allies. Neoconservatives, as Chapter 8 discuss, were opposed to both strands of U.S. foreign policy and instead sought to reassert American primacy.

Private policy-related think tanks rose to prominence in the late Cold War period at the expense of university-based area studies centers. Well-funded and actively embracing the U.S. foreign policy and national security establishments, think tanks like the Brookings Institution, AEI, and WINEP offered the seemingly impartial expertise Washington desired. They also reflected the closer ties between the United States and Israel after the June 1967 Arab-Israeli War. This was demonstrated in the recommendations related to the peace process as well as the creation of terror studies. The think tanks also resembled the Inquiry discussed in Chapter 1. Think tank-based experts were often ideologically predisposed to ensure an alignment with U.S. foreign policy goals and interests. This alignment was even more pronounced after the Cold War.

CHAPTER 8

Empire and Its Limitations

Neoconservatism, the Bush Doctrine, and the Global War on Terror, 1989–2009

> History. We don't know. We'll all be dead.
>
> —GEORGE W. BUSH

It was a warm June morning on the West Point campus. Nine months after the terrorist attacks on New York City and Washington stunned the nation and the world, President George W. Bush addressed the graduating class in Michie Stadium. In response to the attacks by al-Qaʻida ("the base"), a shadowy transnational organization led by Saudi exile Osama bin Laden, the United States launched a "Global War on Terror." At West Point, Bush signaled a new phase in the war and an expanding rationale for American intervention abroad. He outlined a strategy of "preemptive action" and ensuring unrivaled American military supremacy, which he claimed was needed to counter "new threats." Bush asserted that deterrence and containment were "not possible when unbalanced dictators with weapons of mass destruction can deliver those weapons on missiles or secretly provide them to terrorist allies." In what would be a consistent refrain by the administration to justify invading Iraq, Bush proclaimed "if we wait for threats to materialize, we will have waited too long." Although he stated that the United States could not impose democracy on other countries, the "Freedom Agenda" became a key pillar of the Bush Doctrine and Iraq was its test case. Over the next nine months, military forces in the Persian Gulf were steadily increased in preparation for the invasion while the administration presented its case to the American public and the international community.[1]

The Bush Doctrine and the invasion and occupation of Iraq were the culmination of several postwar trends that converged and were reaffirmed by the end of the Cold War and the First Persian Gulf War. First was American involvement in and hegemony over the Middle East. Second were the notions of American exceptionalism and the United States as a benevolent empire that in the aftermath of September 11 would reshape the Middle East. The third trend was the rise of the neoconservative movement and its increasing influence on U.S. foreign policy. This was further evidenced in America's expanded relationship with Israel and their shared strategic interests in the region. These trends were reproduced in the increasing privatization and militarization of the production of knowledge related to the Middle East.[2]

Whither Middle East Studies?

Iraq's August 1990 invasion of Kuwait challenged the post–Cold War euphoria. The slow buildup of U.S. and coalition forces in Saudi Arabia contributed to exhaustive media coverage and analysis that drew heavily on expert commentary from former military and administration officials. For regional expertise, the media relied largely on think tanks. Among the most quoted experts were the Brookings Institution's Judith Kipper and William Quandt, Anthony Cordesman of the Center for Strategic and International Studies (CSIS), and Martin Indyk of the Washington Institute for Near East Policy (WINEP). University-based scholars were also sought, including Columbia's Richard Bulliet, Fouad Ajami of Johns Hopkins, and Georgetown's Edward Luttwak.[3] One implication of the media's reliance on think tanks for expertise was that the analysis overwhelmingly supported the administration's position and ignored the antiwar opposition.[4]

The end of the Cold War coupled with the triumph of the U.S.-led coalition in the First Persian Gulf War confirmed American hegemony in the Middle East. In addition, the surprise agreement in September 1993 between Israel and the Palestine Liberation Organization (PLO) reflected the changing regional and international landscapes. Yet America's expanding interests and involvement in the region were not reflected in increased support for Middle East studies. Instead, there was a reassessment of the need for area studies and their future.

Almost three years after the Soviet Union collapsed, Stanley Heginbotham, vice president of the Social Science Research Council (SSRC), discussed the implications for area studies. He reported that the major governmental and private funders of international studies were beginning to reassess their priorities and redirect resources accordingly. Heginbotham warned that programs that sought to maintain their Cold War focus rather than adapt to the new funding realities were at risk. He acknowledged that over the previous four decades the "underlying concern" of funding area studies programs was to "strengthen our capacity to mount programs that would undermine Soviet ability to infiltrate and capture those countries in [sic] behalf of the Soviet bloc." It was also part of "a more proactive effort to gain the adherence of such countries to the foreign and international security policy goals of the United States." Heginbotham explained that because there was a dearth of knowledge on different world regions, funders were willing to support a variety of programs even if they "had no identifiable relationship to Cold War concerns." However, American scholars were now expected to take the lead "in promoting international scholarship that has shared norms, standards, problem solving, and methodologies." In short, the Cold War contest of ideas was over and American scholars were expected to represent American predominance.[5]

The role and future of area studies led to a debate within the disciplines. Yet the arguments over the merits of area studies were not new and echoed earlier discussions dating to the 1940s. Critics of area studies often ignored the evolution in the type and range of scholarship produced over the previous five decades. Nevertheless, the funding pressures facing universities in the mid-1990s gave the discussions an added urgency and contributed to their contentious nature, especially in political science. The decade and the century ended with the future of Middle East studies still unresolved. However, these debates paled in comparison to the criticism and threats levied at Middle East studies after September 11.[6]

The Oslo Accords and the Peace Process

President George H. W. Bush and Secretary of State James Baker launched a diplomatic initiative to resolve the Arab-Israeli conflict after the First Persian Gulf War. However, they encountered resistance from Israeli prime minister Yitzhak Shamir (1986–1992). Hanging over the conference was the question of whether the Palestinians would participate and what role, if any, there would be for the PLO. The first Palestinian *intifada* was flagging and the PLO was damaged by Arafat's support of Saddam Hussein during the

First Persian Gulf War. In addition, the relationship between the organization and Washington was put on hold after two years of low-level discussions. Shamir was unwilling to attend the conference if the PLO was invited. However, the PLO still had international legitimacy. Baker resolved the issue with the creation of a joint Palestinian-Jordanian delegation that did not contain PLO members from outside the occupied Palestinian territories. The 1991 Madrid Peace Conference and the subsequent direct negotiations between Israelis and Palestinians inspired optimism that a peace treaty was achievable. Although WINEP shared in this optimism, it maintained that the United States "should not be any more anxious to reach an agreement than the parties themselves."[7]

The Bush foreign policy team contained several figures associated with WINEP and the institute had an active media presence during the First Persian Gulf War. During the Madrid Conference, WINEP's executive director Martin Indyk served as an expert commentator for CNN. In preparation for the 1992 presidential campaign, the institute assembled another bipartisan study group. Comprised of the Middle East experts from the Bush and Clinton campaigns as well as participants from its earlier study group, WINEP produced a new report entitled *Pursuing Peace*.[8]

Pursuing Peace argued that the end of the Cold War and the Gulf War had "broken the back" of the rejectionists and discredited the PLO. With a new Israeli government led by Prime Minister Yitzhak Rabin (1992–1995) committed to peace negotiations, the report found that the regional and international landscapes were promising. However, it did not recommend that the next administration pursue a comprehensive solution. Instead, it argued that Washington should focus on achieving interim solutions between Israel and the Arab states. Echoing Israel's position, *Pursuing Peace* advocated for Palestinian self-government rather than a Palestinian state. While the report acknowledged that Israel's occupation was "unwanted and unwelcome," the caveats to ending it repeatedly undermined negotiations over the next two decades.[9]

Pursuing Peace reaffirmed America's special relationship with Israel. It stated that even after the Cold War, the United States had a continuing need for "powerful and reliable local military allies." The report cautioned that Washington needed to clarify that its goal was not "a U.S. deal imposed on Israel," but "an Arab-Israeli deal underwritten by a confident U.S.-Israeli relationship." This proposed linkage between American and Israeli interests in the region became even more pronounced after September 11.

When George H. W. Bush lost the 1992 presidential election it appeared that President Bill Clinton would select a new team to focus on the Middle East. However, Clinton and Secretary of State Warren Christopher surprisingly appointed a holdover from the Bush administration, Dennis Ross, to serve as special Middle East coordinator. Before the post was announced, Ross was due to return to WINEP and replace Indyk as executive director. Meanwhile, Indyk was selected by National Security Advisor Anthony Lake to serve as head of the Middle East office of the National Security Council (NSC)—the post Ross held during the Reagan administration. Indyk later wrote that the appointment of Ross was a "quiet coup." He added that it reflected Ross's "political skills and the wisdom of Clinton and Christopher in understanding the importance of continuity."[10]

Yet Ross was not responsible for the breakthrough between Israel and the PLO. Rather than embracing the Madrid process, the Clinton administration adopted WINEP's language, in particular the familiar refrain that Washington "could not want peace more than the parties." Instead, secret negotiations brokered by Norway led to the 1993 Declaration of Principles between Israel and the PLO and a five-year interim agreement for limited Palestinian self-rule in the Gaza Strip and the West Bank city of Jericho. The Clinton administration was heavily involved in subsequent negotiations over the next seven years to achieve a final agreement, which was undermined in part by the 1995 assassination of Rabin and Benjamin Netanyahu's emergence as leader of the Likud Party. When talks stalled, the Clinton administration deferred to WINEP's approach and insisted that the parties had to want peace for negotiations to succeed. This approach contrasted with the recommendations of those outside WINEP and the administration who argued for a more active American role to break the deadlock.[11]

Privately, the Clinton administration sided more closely with Israel. A November 1998 memorandum from Secretary of State Madeline Albright to Israeli prime minister Benjamin Netanyahu (1996–1999) explained that the United States would "conduct a thorough consultation process with Israel in advance with respect to any ideas the U.S. may wish to offer to the parties for their consideration." Two years later Netanyahu's successor, Ehud Barak (1999–2001), relied on this pledge to scuttle American suggestions at the Camp David summit. Before the summit, Clinton convinced a reluctant Arafat to attend the talks and promised not to blame him if they failed. After the summit failed, Clinton blamed Arafat—as did Dennis Ross—even though negotiations continued until January 2001.[12]

WINEP's influence during the Clinton presidency was not limited to the Israeli-Palestinian conflict. Most prominently, the Clinton administration's policy of "dual containment" of Iraq and Iran was detailed in a speech by Indyk to the institute. In his memoirs, Indyk writes that the term emerged after a conversation with a *New York Times* reporter in which he explained the Clinton administration's policy of "aggressive containment" of Iraq and "active containment" of Iran.[13]

With the collapse of the peace process and outbreak of the second Palestinian *intifada* in September 2000, WINEP continued to expand its presence in media and policy circles. Indyk joined the Brookings Institution after serving as U.S. ambassador to Israel and assistant secretary of state for Near East Affairs. At Brookings, he received a call from media mogul Haim Saban, a wealthy donor to the Democratic Party. Saban wanted to establish a think tank specifically focused on the Middle East and securing Israel's future. Saban rejected Indyk's suggestion that he donate to WINEP, preferring instead to form his own think tank. The Saban Center for Middle East Policy was established after its namesake made a $13 million donation to the Brookings Institution. As Saban later explained his interest in politics and foreign policy, "I am a one-issue guy and my issue is Israel."[14]

Saban was not alone. The attachment to Israel and protecting and promoting its relationship with America united Democrats and Republicans. It also paralleled a tightening of the "special relationship" between the United States and Israel in the post–Cold War era. During the Clinton administration it evolved into a "strategic relationship." After September 11, it was transformed into a "strategic alliance" with increased military and intelligence assistance and collaboration. While the relationship with Israel was enhanced, the George W. Bush administration disengaged from the peace process and adopted a policy of conflict management rather than conflict resolution, which was in line with WINEP's recommendations. Bush also relied on Israel and newly elected prime minister Ariel Sharon (2001–2006) to suppress the second *intifada*, believing it would force the Palestinians to make the necessary concessions for a final peace deal. Arafat was sidelined by the Bush administration, who argued that a new Palestinian leadership untainted by terror was required to achieve peace. With the invasions of Afghanistan and Iraq, the peace process was no longer a priority for Washington. High-profile diplomacy continued, including the 2007 Annapolis Summit, but with no tangible results.[15]

Neoconservatives and U.S. Foreign Policy

Although it was not immediately apparent at the time he was elected, neo-conservatives would have a profound influence on the administration of George W. Bush. Indeed, Bush presided over the most conservative adminis-tration in the postwar era. Already emboldened by American military and economic dominance after the Cold War, the September 11 attacks provided neoconservatives with the opportunity and the pretext to implement their vision of American foreign and domestic policies. The major tenets of neo-conservative ideology include staunch anticommunism, a predominant U.S. military, selective advocacy for human rights, unwavering support for the state of Israel, and promotion of a neoliberal economic agenda. Once con-sidered on the fringes of the Democratic and Republican parties, the presence of neoconservatives in key national security and advisory positions in the Bush administration ensured their influence on policymaking.[16]

The intellectual origins of neoconservatism are traced to two professors at the University of Chicago: Leo Strauss and Arnold Wohlstetter. A pro-fessor of political science, Strauss was born in Germany and immigrated to the United States in 1938. He was also a follower of Vladimir Jabotinsky the founder of revisionist Zionism and progenitor of Israel's right wing Likud Party. Strauss's attitudes toward Israel and the United States were shaped by his flight from Nazi Germany and by Jabotinsky's worldview. Although some neoconservatives reject claims of Strauss's importance, Jacob Heilb-runn argues that he helped to "midwife the neoconservative movement." Strauss's influence reached across two generations of neoconservatives as he or one of his students taught leading figures in the movement, including Alan Bloom, Irving and William Kristol, Paul Wolfowitz, and Francis Fukuyama.[17]

While Strauss focused on political philosophy and the classics, Wohl-stetter specialized in Cold War nuclear strategy. Born in New York to German émigré parents, Wohlstetter served as a consultant to the RAND Corporation in the 1950s and advised the Pentagon on nuclear policy. At Chicago, he mentored Wolfowitz, Richard Perle, and Zalmay Khalilzad. Wohlstetter also influenced Senator "Scoop" Jackson, an ardent supporter of Israel and critic of détente with Moscow. Perle worked as an aide for Jackson and then joined the Reagan administration, where he served as as-sistant secretary of defense. Meanwhile, Wolfowitz worked in the Defense Department during the Carter administration. He stayed in Washington after Reagan was elected and served as the head of the State Department's Policy Planning Staff (PPS). At PPS, Wolfowitz hired Fukuyama, Khalilzad, I. Lewis "Scooter" Libby, and Alan Keyes.[18]

The neoconservative movement and the New Left shared an origin point with the Vietnam War. A number of leading neoconservatives were Democrats and active in the New Left. George McGovern's failed 1972 presidential campaign was a watershed moment for neoconservatives, including Norman Podhoretz, a former Trotskyist who split with the New Left movement over criticism of Israel. In the pages of *Commentary* and through the Coalition for a Democratic Majority (CDM), which he cofounded in 1972, Podhoretz sought to change the Democratic Party. However, the Coalition was ignored by the Carter administration. Instead, the organization found support from Republicans and conservative Democrats, including Senator Jackson, who was defeated by Carter in the 1976 Democratic Party presidential primaries.[19]

The CDM was one of three organizations launched by neoconservatives in the 1970s that shared policy positions and key members. Established in 1976, the Committee on the Present Danger (CPD) was cochaired by Paul Nitze and Yale law professor Eugene Rostow. Like his brother, Walt Whitman, Rostow also served in the Johnson administration. The CPD was opposed to détente and the policy proposals of the Trilateral Commission. It grew out of several earlier efforts, including "Team B," which argued that the Central Intelligence Agency (CIA) had underestimated Soviet military capabilities. Like National Security Council Report number 68 (NSC-68) and the Gaither Report, Nitze's influence on Team B was obvious. As with those earlier efforts, Team B also exaggerated the Soviet threat. At the CPD's first press conference, held after Carter was elected, the organization boasted 141 founding members drawn from both parties. Over the next four years, it was highly critical of the Carter administration's foreign policy, especially the Strategic Arms Limitation Treaty negotiations with Moscow.[20]

The Jewish Institute for National Security Affairs (JINSA) was also established in 1976. While the CDM and CDP sought to directly influence policymakers, JINSA initially targeted the base of the Democratic Party. It emphasized the need for strengthening ties between the United States and Israel as well as a hard-line approach toward Moscow. Like the CDM and the CDP, JINSA also advocated for greater defense spending. With support from the American Jewish Committee, JINSA initially aligned with Israel's Labor Party. Over the next decade, however, its policy positions moved to the right. By the late 1990s, its board members consisted of several figures that reemerged in prominent positions in the Bush administration including Perle, Dick Cheney, John Bolton, and Douglas Feith.[21]

In 1980, neoconservatives flocked to the Republican Party and embraced Ronald Reagan. Irving Kristol, Podhoretz's colleague at *Commentary*, took credit for the exodus from the Democratic Party. Kristol's connections to conservatives in government, business, and academia were essential to the movement. During the 1950s, he served as the executive director of the Congress for Cultural Freedom (CCF) and as coeditor of the journal *Encounter*, discussed in Chapter 5. Two decades later, Kristol became affiliated with the American Enterprise Institute (AEI) and recruited other neoconservatives to join the think tank.[22]

AEI emerged as a conservative competitor to the Brookings Institution after the 1976 presidential election. At first, AEI's policy analysis reflected the bipartisan support for the Arab-Israeli peace process and the Camp David Accords. In public statements and op-eds, research fellows Harold Saunders and Judith Kipper (later of the Brookings Institution) advocated for a resolution of the Palestinian issue, including contact with the PLO.[23] By the mid-1980s, however, AEI shifted further to the right. This was due in part to Kristol's influence and the new leadership of Christopher De-Muth, a veteran of the Nixon and Reagan administrations. AEI's previous director, William Baroody Jr., was ousted for mismanagement as well as for criticism of Israel at events sponsored by the institute during his tenure. Saunders and Kipper also left AEI.[24]

In 1985, Kristol founded *The National Interest*. The journal became a bastion of the neoconservative movement. For neoconservatives, the end of the Cold War was an affirmation of their hard-line stance. This was reflected in the triumphalism of Fukuyama's 1989 article, "The End of History," published by the journal. Three years later, it was reproduced in the formation of the 1992 Defense Planning Guidance (DPG). Developed by the Wolfowitz-led Office for Defense Policy, the initial draft laid out a vision of American military supremacy and preventing the emergence of a new superpower rival. Although the DPG has often been attributed to Wolfowitz, Libby and Khalilzad drafted the initial version with advice from Perle and Wohlstetter. Wolfowitz did not review the document before it was leaked to the *New York Times* and attempted to distance himself from the contents—because he did not believe the proposed strategy was aggressive enough. Although the language of the DPG was eventually modified, the strategy of ensuring American dominance from potential rivals—particularly over strategic areas like the Middle East—remained. After September 11, it was recrafted as the Bush Doctrine.[25]

During the Clinton presidency, Wolfowitz and former members of the Ford, Reagan, and George H. W. Bush administrations advocated for a tougher American policy toward Iraq. Embraced and emboldened by allies at well-funded think tanks, including AEI and WINEP, neoconservatives launched the Project for the New American Century (PNAC). Irving Kristol's son, William, cofounded PNAC in 1997. A former speechwriter for Vice President Dan Quayle, William Kristol also founded the *Weekly Standard*. PNAC was similar to previous and existing neoconservative organizations like the CDM, the CPD, and JINSA. Further reinforcing the connections between the conservative organizations, AEI, PNAC, and the *Weekly Standard* were all located in the same building. A year after it was established, PNAC published an open letter calling on the Clinton administration to overthrow Saddam Hussein. The letter was signed by leading neoconservatives, as well as Clinton's former Director of Central Intelligence (DCI), James Woolsey, and former (and future) secretary of defense Donald Rumsfeld.[26]

The PNAC letter was similar to a 1996 policy document cowritten by Perle and David Wurmser. Entitled "A Clean Break: A New Strategy for Securing the Realm," the document was published by the Institute for Advanced Strategic and Political Studies, a think tank with offices in the United States and Israel. "A Clean Break" recommended that Prime Minister Netanyahu adopt a different approach to the Arab-Israeli peace process. This included abandoning the "land for peace" formula embodied in UN Security Council Resolutions 242 and 338 and reaffirmed by the Camp David Accords and the Oslo Accords. Instead, "A Clean Break" argued that Israel should pursue a policy of "peace for peace" toward Syria, Lebanon, and the Palestinians and called for the overthrow of Saddam Hussein's regime. Three years later, Wurmser reintroduced these proposals in *Tyranny's Ally*.[27]

Tyranny's Ally laid out many of the arguments for the eventual invasion of Iraq. Wurmser, a research fellow at AEI and director of its Middle East Studies Program, argued that Saddam Hussein's power was increasing. He criticized the Clinton administration and the CIA for failing to overthrow the Iraqi regime through covert action. Saddam Hussein, he asserted, was still determined to be the regional hegemon and neither sanctions nor limited military actions would successfully deter him. Wurmser advocated for the exile-based opposition group, the Iraqi National Congress (INC), and promoted Jordan as a regional power broker. He also suggested that Iraq's Shi'a population could assist in challenging, if not overthrowing, Iran's revolutionary regime. Wurmser's overly optimistic claims and questionable analysis were welcomed in neoconservative policy circles and he later served as Vice President Dick Cheney's Middle East advisor.[28]

The Bush Doctrine and 9/11

Reflecting on September 11, Bush claimed that he was determined to break with previous policy. "The United States would consider any nation that harbored terrorists to be responsible for the acts of those terrorists," Bush wrote. He added, "This new doctrine overturned the approach of the past, which treated terrorist groups as distinct from the sponsors. We had to force nations to choose whether they would fight the terrorists or share in their fate." Four days later at Camp David, Bush and his national security team discussed preparations for the invasion of Afghanistan. Deputy Secretary of Defense Wolfowitz raised the possibility of attacking Iraq as well as the Taliban and al-Qa'ida. Although Wolfowitz's suggestion was not approved, less than two weeks later Bush ordered Secretary of Defense Donald Rumsfeld to begin secretly planning for the invasion of Iraq.[29]

The White House released the 2002 National Security Strategy (NSS) a year later. While the NSS expanded on the key points of Bush's June 2002 West Point address, the major change was a new emphasis on promoting democracy. The core of the strategy remained the shift from a policy of deterrence and containment to preemption against terrorist organizations and their state sponsors, in particular those who sought or planned to use weapons of mass destruction (WMD). It was aimed primarily at Iraq, one of the countries Bush identified as part of the "axis of evil" in his first State of the Union address. Over the previous decade, the NSS stated, "rogue states" emerged that "reject basic human values and hate the United States and everything for which it stands." It established the rationale for invasion by asserting that the United States "must be prepared to stop rogue states and their terrorist clients before they are able to threaten or use weapons of mass destruction against the United States and our allies and friends."[30]

Implicit in the Bush Doctrine was the notion of America as a benevolent empire. Unlike previous empires, the United States sought no territory to conquer or even resources, but to make the world safe for democracy.

Neoconservatives endorsing military action touted its benefits and the altruism of American empire. Among the leading proponents of this argument were Robert Kagan, William Kristol, and Max Boot. Although not necessarily a neoconservative, Harvard's Niall Ferguson also called on the United States to accept the mantle of empire relinquished by Britain. Inside and outside the administration, leading neoconservatives offered assurances that empire would be inexpensive in terms of lives lost and cost to the treasury. Compared to the despotism of the "axis of evil," the invasion of Iraq was presented as a humanitarian intervention that would safeguard the United States, its allies, and Iraqis. It would also serve as a catalyst for change across the region and reshape the Middle East in America's image while sending a clear message to other rogue states: you are next.[31]

Constructing a Threat

The 2002 NSS was part of the Bush administration's broader campaign to convince the American public and allies of the threat posed by Iraq. Over the next nine months, the administration and its neoconservative allies in academia and think tanks built the case for war in the media and on the world stage. However, this was a bipartisan effort and the administration received support from Democratic Party hawks, including Kenneth Pollack, director of research at the Brookings Saban Center. A former CIA analyst and member of Clinton's NSC staff, Pollack's *The Threatening Storm* was one of the earliest and most influential books to support the invasion of Iraq. Pollack drew on his prior experience in government and the book was vetted by the CIA and NSC before publication. *The Threatening Storm* argued that Saddam Hussein was attempting to reconstitute his WMD program dismantled after the First Persian Gulf War, including nuclear weapons. Pollack concluded that the "sooner we undertake the invasion of Iraq the better."[32]

Pollack painted an even starker picture in the press. Writing in the *New York Times,* he argued that Saddam Hussein could not be deterred and a future war with Iraq was inevitable: "There is every reason to believe that the question is not one of war or no war, but rather war now or war later—a war without nuclear weapons or a war with them." He repeated this argument five months later and added that "we must weigh the costs of a war with Iraq today, but on the other side of the balance we must place the cost of a war with a nuclear-armed Iraq tomorrow." Pollack's assertions resembled the statements of Bush administration officials, including then National Security Advisor Condoleezza Rice, who explained that there would "always be some uncertainty about how quickly [Saddam Hussein] can acquire nuclear weapons. But we don't want the smoking gun to be a mushroom cloud."[33]

The Bush administration also drew on a small but influential group of Middle East scholars, including Princeton's Bernard Lewis and Fouad Ajami of Johns Hopkins University's School of Advanced International Studies (SAIS). Both men had access to the highest levels of the administration, in particular Vice President Cheney. Their expertise was cited as evidence that the United States would be greeted as liberators in Iraq and regime change would catalyze a democratic transformation of the region. After the 1956 Suez War, Lewis claimed that a "clash of civilizations" between the West and the Muslim world explained Nasser's popularity. Over the next six decades, he would retain faith in the explanatory power of the "clash" and argue that it was at the root of the region's political problems. The phrase reappeared in a September 1990 article in *The Atlantic* following Iraq's invasion of Kuwait entitled "The Roots of Muslim Rage." Three years later, it was adopted and popularized by Samuel Huntington in a 1993 article from *Foreign Affairs* and a subsequent book.[34]

Huntington's "Clash of Civilizations" thesis was hotly debated and challenged. With the Soviet Union dismantled, Huntington claimed that future conflict would occur along the "cultural fault lines" separating the different civilizations. He identified eight major civilizations, including "Western" and "Islamic." Islam was portrayed as monolithic and "civilization" as static and isolated. Although his assessment was deemed prophetic after September 11, Huntington was skeptical about the invasion of Iraq. In contrast, Lewis embraced intervention.[35]

Lewis maintained close ties to key neoconservatives. He was an advisor to Senator "Scoop" Jackson and mentor to Richard Perle. After September 11, he was invited to formal and informal briefings by the Bush administration. Lewis's argument that the United States had to adopt a firm stance in the Middle East found a welcome audience. He met and briefed President Bush, Vice President Cheney, and National Security Advisor Rice. According to David Frum, Bush's former speechwriter, among the president's briefing materials was a "marked up article" by Lewis. He gave a talk to the Pentagon's Defense Advisory Board, chaired by Perle, and was also invited by Bush's chief political strategist Karl Rove to brief White House and NSC staffers. Lewis was a guest at a White House state dinner and at the vice president's residence. Although Lewis later downplayed his influence, Cheney promoted his expertise. In a March 2003 interview on NBC's *Meet the Press*, Cheney referenced the retired Princeton professor and stated that a "strong, firm U.S. response to terror and to threats to the United States would go a long way, frankly, towards calming things in that part of the world."[36]

Although it did not address September 11 directly, Lewis's *What Went Wrong?* benefited from the increased attention and focus on Islam and the Middle East. The book remained on the *New York Times* best-seller list for several months. Lewis traced Islam's long decline to the sixteenth century and the Ottoman defeat at Vienna. The subsequent military defeats, he explained, were symptomatic of the broader political, economic, and cultural failures of Muslim societies to embrace modernity. Attempts to overcome Western dominance in these areas were also unsuccessful and left the Muslim world even further behind and looking to assign blame. Historically, Lewis stated, blame was assigned to the Mongols and the Turks. But it shifted—with encouragement from the increasingly autocratic and repressive leaders of Arab and Muslim states—to the European Imperial powers, the United States, and Israel. Meanwhile, the rise of Islamic fundamentalism sought answers in "a real or imagined past." However, Lewis understated the impact of colonialism and America's support for autocratic leaders in the region and elsewhere as well as its promotion of religious movements to counter secular nationalist and communist groups. Lewis's solution aligned with the Bush administration's "Freedom Agenda." "It is precisely the lack of freedom—freedom of the mind from constraint and indoctrination, to question and inquire and speak; freedom of the economy from corrupt and pervasive mismanagement; freedom of women from male oppression; freedom of citizens from tyranny—that underlies so many of the troubles of the Muslim world," he wrote. Lewis cautioned that the "road to democracy" was not easy, but it was preferable to the alternative.[37]

Less than nine months after *What Went Wrong?* was published, Lewis penned a *Wall Street Journal* op-ed promoting the invasion of Iraq. Entitled "Time for Toppling," Lewis affirmed the president's "axis of evil" claim and argued that regime change in Iraq would assist efforts to resolve the Israeli-Palestinian conflict. His assertions were echoed by supporters of the invasion who claimed that the road to peace in Jerusalem was through Baghdad.[38]

The administration's case for war was strengthened by the Iraqi National Congress, which provided experts to government agencies and the press.

Among the experts was the now infamous defector codenamed "Curveball" who provided information on Iraq's WMD program to German intelligence, the CIA, and the press. Meanwhile, Kanan Makiya publicly advocated for the war. A professor of Middle East studies at Brandeis, Makiya was one of several bridges between the INC and the Bush administration. Like other neoconservatives, he was a former leftist. In 1989, Makiya published *Republic of Fear* under the pseudonym Samir al-Khalil. An indictment of Saddam Hussein's regime, the book detailed the abuses by Iraq's Ba'th Party. *Republic of Fear* became a best-seller after Iraq's 1990 invasion and occupation of Kuwait. Over the next decade, it was frequently cited by advocates for regime change. In the buildup to the Second Persian Gulf War, Makiya was a frequent media commentator and contributor on both sides of the Atlantic. Although his promotion of the U.S.-led invasion drew the ire of other prominent intellectuals, including Edward Said, Makiya was undeterred. In April 2003, he accompanied American and INC forces entering Baghdad.[39]

Drawing on faulty intelligence and misinformation, the Bush administration depicted Iraq as an imminent threat to U.S. national security that could be quickly neutralized. Three weeks before the invasion, President Bush spoke at AEI. Twenty AEI alumni were members of the Bush administration and the speech reinforced the role of neoconservatives in shaping the Freedom Agenda. Liberating Iraq, Bush stated, would demonstrate "the power of freedom to transform that vital region." "America's interests in security, and America's belief in liberty, both lead in the same direction: to a free and peaceful Iraq," Bush declared.[40] The optimistic scenarios for a post-Saddam Iraq pervaded the Bush administration and the American press. Decision making was consolidated at the Pentagon and the office of Vice President Cheney. Alternative voices within Washington, particularly the State Department, were excluded. In addition, prior planning for postwar reconstruction of Iraq was deliberately ignored.[41]

The rapid collapse of Saddam Hussein's regime appeared to validate the claims of the Bush administration and neoconservatives. However, the failure to find an active WMD program and the emergence of a stubborn insurgency that metastasized into a sectarian civil war exposed the arguments for invasion and the optimistic assessments of a short, cheap occupation. The White House and the Pentagon were criticized for the lack of postwar planning and the corruption and incompetence of the Coalition Provisional Authority. Revelations of human rights abuses, including at Abu

Ghraib prison, further exposed the arguments of neoconservatives in favor of the war and contributed to the insurgency. Rather than weakening the other "rogue states" in the region, Washington faced an emboldened Iran and Syria and a resurgent Taliban in Afghanistan. These factors contributed to an overstretched U.S. military and decline in America's global standing. In short, the opposite of what advocates predicted.[42]

America's floundering occupation of Iraq also led to splits in the neoconservative movement. A few neoconservatives, like Francis Fukuyama, renounced their support for the war and the movement. Others, like Fouad Ajami, placed the blame on Iraqis for failing to embrace the "American gift" of liberty. Ajami also claimed that continued strife in Iraq proved Huntington's "clash of civilizations" thesis was correct.[43]

Like Ajami, Lewis was unrepentant. His next book, *The Crisis of Islam*, was published after the invasion and expanded on the arguments in *What Went Wrong?* and his November 2001 article "The Revolt of Islam," published by the *New Yorker*. Lewis offered a sweeping but selective history of terrorism dating to the eleventh century. He also focused on the possibility of regime change in Iran and argued that as in Iraq, "there are democratic oppositions capable of taking over and forming governments."[44]

The focus on Iran reflected an attempt by neoconservatives to expand and win the war in Iraq. As he did four years earlier, Lewis published an op-ed in the *Wall Street Journal* warning of the dangers of Iran's nuclear program. Deterrence and mutual assured destruction, he argued, could not work against an enemy gripped by messianic and suicidal leaders. The essay was published near the end of Israel's 2006 invasion of Lebanon, in which neoconservatives again sought to depict the conflict in stark Manichean terms. Defeating and dismantling Hizbullah, they argued, would not only weaken Syria and Iran but would assist America's floundering effort in Iraq. This connection to Washington's broader policies was expressed by Secretary of State Condoleezza Rice, who claimed that "what we are seeing here, in a sense, is the birth pangs of a new Middle East." Hizbullah's influence inside and outside Lebanon only increased after the conflict, and elements within the Bush administration led by Vice President Cheney continued to press for a confrontation with Tehran.[45]

Kenneth Pollack, however, demurred. Chastened by the experience in Iraq, he argued against invading Iran and for a more flexible policy of engagement and containment. Pollack wrote that deterrence was possible even with a nuclear-armed Iran. Two years later, he supported the "surge" in Iraq.[46]

Resurrecting Lawrence

The persistence of the Iraqi insurgency led to an examination of past coun-terinsurgency efforts and a shift in American military strategy. Building on successes by local commanders in Ramadi and Tal Afar, General David Petraeus lobbied for the development of a new counterinsurgency doctrine while serving as commander of Fort Leavenworth in Kansas. At Fort Leavenworth, Petraeus was responsible for the Army's Combined Arms Center, which develops training doctrines and produces the journal *Military Review*. Under Petraeus and editor Colonel William Daley, the journal became an outlet for criticism of military practices in Iraq and the promotion of counterinsurgency methods. In February 2006, Petraeus organized a meeting of 135 experts to discuss counterinsurgency efforts. The meeting marked the beginning of a shift in U.S. military practices in Iraq and Afghanistan.[47]

Some of the counterinsurgency experts were inspired by T. E. Lawrence's example. During World War II, Lawrence's *Seven Pillars of Wisdom* inspired American scholars assigned to the Middle East. In the twenty-first century, it was rebranded as a counterinsurgency manual. That *Seven Pillars* was loosely based on the truth was conveniently disregarded and its Orientalist sentiments were embraced as cultural insights. One expert was Lieutenant Colonel John Nagl, who received his PhD from Oxford and served in both Gulf Wars. His doctoral dissertation and eventual book focused on guerrilla warfare in Vietnam and British Malaya and its title—*Learning to Eat Soup with a Knife*—was borrowed from a passage in *Seven Pillars*.[48]

A year after the Fort Leavenworth meeting, a World War II Army manual on Iraq was reissued with a new introduction by Nagl. The booklet shared a number of similarities with other World War II–era manuals produced by the Office of Strategic Services (OSS) for American soldiers including the same—now discredited—Orientalist depictions and illustrations. Nagl explained that he wished he had read the manual before his own deployment to Iraq. "Some of the guidance in this little book is eerie to anyone who has fought in Iraq recently," he wrote. Nagl quoted a lengthy passage from the manual describing the fighting prowess of Iraqis and lamented, "Would that we had listened to the warning that the Arabs are skilled guerilla fighters."[49]

Nagl was critical of the U.S. Army's oversights before invading Iraq. Yet he also claimed that based on his experience the book's practical, "timeless" advice and simple Arabic phrases could assist America's counterinsurgency efforts. Nagl stated that successful counterinsurgency required a deep understanding of "the local history and the people's culture, their customs and their language." However, the manual's oversimplifications of Iraqi society and history—even more glaring after sixty years—belied this argument.[50]

Lieutenant Colonel David Kilcullen is another counterinsurgency theorist inspired by Lawrence. In 2006, *Military Review* published Kilcullen's "Twenty-Eight Articles" of counterinsurgency. The article was modeled after a memo written by Lawrence for Britain's Arab Bureau almost a century earlier. Based in Cairo, the Arab Bureau was composed of intelligence officers whose expert advice informed British policymakers. Lawrence explained that his "Twenty-Seven Articles" were a reflection of his "personal conclusions" based on his experience in the Hijaz and intended as "stalking horses for beginners in the Arab armies." He cautioned that the advice was only for dealing with Bedouins, since "townspeople or Syrians require totally different treatment." Yet this qualifier was modified even further by Lawrence, who wrote, "Handling Hejaz [*sic*] Arabs is an art, not a science, with exceptions and no obvious rules." Building on the "counterinsurgency theory" of Lawrence's memo, Kilcullen stated that his article was intended to provide practical advice to soldiers in the field based on the "collective experience, the distilled essence of what those who went before you have learned." He advised that the suggestions were "expressed as commandments, for clarity, but really are more like folklore" and should be applied "judiciously and skeptically." The folklore did not end there, however.[51]

Four years later in *Counterinsurgency*, Kilcullen again valorized Lawrence. He argued that the British officer was a model of "cultural leverage" in an insurgency. Kilcullen asserted that bilingual and bicultural individuals could "exploit cultural norms and expectations to generate operational norms and effects." He stated that "Lawrence's comment [in *Seven Pillars*] that 'Arabs could be swung on an idea as on a cord' reflects this level of cultural competence." It is telling that Kilcullen chose to promote Lawrence's statement as a reflection of cultural understanding but only offered an abridged version. In *Seven Pillars of Wisdom*, Lawrence wrote that Arabs were easily persuaded "for the unpledged allegiance of their minds made them obedient servants."[52]

The army's new counterinsurgency strategy was a key element of the "surge." Promoted by General Petraeus and AEI's Frederick Kagan, a former military history professor at West Point and member of PNAC, the surge also involved the infusion of additional troops and the co-optation of leading tribal families in Iraq's Anbar province. The new strategy succeeded in decreasing violence and reduced the number of American and Iraqi casualties. Hailed as a "success," the surge appeared to provide the United States with the opportunity to declare a semblance of a victory by the end of the Bush administration.[53]

Middle East Studies and 9/11

Shortly after September 11, the American Council of Trustees and Alumni (ACTA) published a report entitled *Defending Civilization*. Founded in 1995 by Lynne Cheney, wife of former Vice President Cheney, ACTA's ties to the Bush administration's agenda were reproduced in *Defending Civilization*. The report claimed that academia was the only part of American society that did not respond in a patriotic manner to the attacks. Instead, it stated that "professors from across the country sponsored teach-ins that typically ranged from moral equivocation to explicit condemnation of America." While American politicians and media figures stood with President Bush in "calling evil by its rightful name," the report asserted that professors "demurred" and "refused to make judgments." Some members of the academy "invoked tolerance and diversity as antidotes to evil," while others "pointed accusatory fingers, not at the terrorists, but at America itself."[54]

ACTA declared that the insufficient expressions of patriotism and criticism of U.S. foreign policy were part of a larger problem at American universities. Indeed, the report's subtitle claimed that academia was "failing America." ACTA criticized universities for adding courses on Islam and Asia and asserted that instead universities needed to ensure that students understood the "unique contributions of America and Western civilization." *Defending Civilization* claimed that the urgency with which courses were added immediately after the attacks "reinforced the mindset that it was America—and America's failure to understand Islam—that were to blame." "America's first line of defense is a confident understanding of how and why this nation was founded, and of the continuing relevance and urgency of its first principles," it stated.[55]

The most controversial aspect of *Defending Civilization* was the selective quotes critical of the United States and U.S. foreign policy attributed to over a hundred faculty, staff, and students. ACTA's attempt to blacklist the professors led to an outcry, and the report was reissued in February 2002. Although the names of the individuals were removed, their titles and institutional affiliations remained, thereby implicating the entire university department or student body in the remarks that ACTA deemed objectionable. The revised version added new statements of support and derision, including those directed at ACTA or the *Defending Civilization* report.[56]

Defending Civilization was followed by an online monitoring effort that specifically targeted Middle East studies scholars. Established by Daniel Pipes, a Harvard PhD in medieval Middle Eastern history, the effort was linked to his Middle East Forum think tank. The "Campus Watch" website monitored statements by faculty members and students deemed anti-Israel or anti-American. Like the ACTA report, the attempted blacklisting led to a backlash. A number of Middle East scholars who were not initially named by Campus Watch requested that Pipes add them to the list. The site eventually adopted ACTA's approach and began providing a "survey of institutions" rather than naming individuals.[57]

More sophisticated efforts to target Middle East studies were to come. WINEP published *Ivory Towers on Sand*, written by former research fellow Martin Kramer. *Ivory Towers on Sand* argued that Middle East studies scholars were culpable for the September 11 attacks because they failed to predict the rise of Islamic political movements. This failure, Kramer claimed, was due to the field's wholesale adoption of Said's *Orientalism* and related intellectual and political perspectives. Said's influence on the field was compounded by that of Georgetown's John Esposito and John Voll. Kramer asserted that Esposito and Voll presented overly optimistic and fundamentally flawed portrayals of Islam. Preoccupied by their criticism of the United States and Israel, Middle East studies scholars had a "blind spot" on political Islam.[58]

Ivory Towers on Sand was part of a larger concerted effort to target Title VI funding of Middle East studies centers. Kramer laid out a series of "modest reforms" of Middle East studies that could serve as a "prototype" for other Title VI programs, such as revising how Middle East centers were evaluated to enhance the weight given to outreach and including nonacademics in the Title VI review process. Kramer also suggested that congressional hearings should be held to determine the "contribution of Middle Eastern studies to American public policy," in which academics and nonacademics could present testimony. The hearings, he wrote, "could sensitize the academic recipients of taxpayer dollars to the concerns of the American people, expressed through their elected representatives." The goal of these reforms, Kramer claimed, was to remove the "culture of irrelevance" that pervaded the field. Although he suggested that a subcommittee hearing would also provide the representatives from academia with the opportunity to address their concerns to members of Congress, the obvious imbalance in power was ignored.[59]

The changes advocated in *Ivory Towers on Sand* served as a blueprint for conservative commentators and groups to attack Title VI funding. Following a congressional subcommittee hearing in June 2003, in which Kramer's allies testified, a bill was attached to the reauthorization of Title VI funding. Essentially mirroring Kramer's recommendation, House Resolution 3077 (H.R. 3077) called for the creation of an advisory board to ensure that government-funded academic programs related to international affairs would reflect "diverse perspectives and represent the full range of views." Of the three advisory board members appointed by the secretary of education, two were required to be representatives of a U.S. national security agency. Two additional board members were to be appointed by the majority leaders of the House and Senate. The intent of H.R. 3077 was in sharp contrast to the original language of the National Defense Education Act (NDEA), which restricted the intervention of government agencies on issues of curriculum, instruction, administration, or personnel of the institutions receiving funds. Ironically, the language was added to the bill to mollify the criticism of states' rights advocates, whose ideological brethren supported H.R. 3077 nearly five decades later.[60]

Although the House passed H.R. 3077, it did not make it out of committee in the Senate. A similar attempt the following year was also unsuccessful. While the attempts to impose a politicized oversight board failed, the combined impact of high-profile efforts to police and intimidate Middle East scholars had a chilling effect on the field.[61]

Following the failure of H.R. 3077 to become law, a new academic society was established for Middle East studies. Arguing that the Middle East Studies Association (MESA) had become "too overtly politicized," Lewis and Ajami formed the Association for the Study of the Middle East and Africa (ASMEA) in 2007. Five years later, Lewis claimed that ASMEA was created "to maintain an independent academic integrity in Middle Eastern studies." Other prominent figures included former secretary of state George Shultz and former president of the Council on Foreign Relations Leslie Gelb, both prominent supporters of the Iraq war. ASMEA also launched a scholarly publication, the *Journal of the Middle East and Africa*, and hosts an annual conference. At its first annual conference ASMEA claimed it had 500 members from forty countries.[62]

The scrutiny and criticism of Middle East studies scholars and centers coincided with a dramatic increase in enrollment for Arabic classes as well as courses on the history and politics of the region. A 2002 survey by the Modern Language Association reported that 10,596 university and college students were enrolled in Arabic courses that year—almost double the number in 1998. Within four years, enrollments more than doubled. By 2013, over 32,000 students were enrolled in Arabic classes.[63] Although the number of Title VI National Resource Centers increased from fourteen to seventeen, the boost in federal funding after September 11 was insufficient to compensate for the increased demand and years of underfunding.[64] In addition, the dramatic spike in student enrollment was exacerbated by a distinct shortage in the number of qualified Arabic instructors.[65]

Meanwhile, a controversial program established after the Cold War found new support inside and outside of Washington. In 1991, Senator David Boren of Oklahoma sponsored the creation of the National Security Education Program (NSEP). The NSEP provides funding for language study to institutions and individuals. Individual recipients agree to work for a U.S. national security agency for at least one year.[66] The NSEP is administered by the Pentagon, with the secretary of defense and the National Security Education Board overseeing the programs and policies. Comprised of thirteen members, the National Security Education Board is chaired by the president of the National Defense University and includes the CIA director. Although the program was greeted with hostility by major academic associations, a significant number of Boren Fellows receive language training through Title VI centers. Similar fellowship programs were created after September 11, including the Pat Roberts Intelligence Scholarship Program and the Critical Languages Scholarship Program.[67]

There were attempts to challenge the prevailing zeitgeist. Scholars not tied to the Bush administration or the neoconservative movement contested how the region was portrayed and the calls for an American empire.[68] Another source of alternate viewpoints was Al Jazeera, the pan-Arab satellite television station based in Qatar. Launched in 1996, Al Jazeera established a reputation for high quality and professional production, probing questions, and heated debates that stood in sharp contrast to traditional state-run Arab media. This initially led to favorable coverage in the *New York Times* and the *New Yorker*. After September 11, however, Bush administration officials refused to appear on the network and portrayed Al Jazeera as sympathetic to, if not affiliated with, al-Qaʻida. Al Jazeera's offices in Kabul and Baghdad were bombed, and a journalist was killed during the invasion of Iraq. A cameraman, Sami al-Hajj, was also arrested and spent seven years in prison at the Guantanamo Bay Naval Base in Cuba without charge. Even more troubling was a 2004 memorandum of conversation between Bush and British prime minister Tony Blair that was leaked to the press, in which they discussed bombing Al Jazeera's Qatar headquarters. The Bush administration also attempted to directly challenge Al Jazeera with an Iraq-based satellite television channel, Al-Hurra, and a radio station, Radio Sawa. Both, however, were widely panned and considered failures. In spite of these efforts, Al Jazeera's influence continued to expand, including in the United States and Europe after its English-language channel and website were launched.[69]

The National Security State 2.0

The CIA and the Pentagon were faced with sharp budget cuts after the Cold War. This was compounded by a series of embarrassing revelations, including the arrests of high-level spies and a sexual discrimination lawsuit. After American troops were killed in Somalia in October 1993, the Clinton administration proposed reforms of the intelligence agencies. The CIA's budget was eventually reduced, especially for the Directorate of Operations and counterterrorism efforts.[70]

Middle East studies scholars were not the only Americans who missed or discounted the threat of terrorism. After the August 1998 attacks on the U.S. embassies in Kenya and Tanzania, the CIA ranked bin Laden and al-Qaʻida at the highest threat level, but the agency was still forced to fight for resources. Although DCI George Tenet "declared war" on bin Laden in December 1998, he was not willing to redirect personnel or funding from the other parts of the agency in order to confront al-Qaʻida as there were too many competing priorities and limited resources. In addition, Tenet's decision was not communicated to other intelligence agencies in the U.S. government. Moreover, the CIA's request for additional funding was ignored by the Clinton White House and the Republican-controlled Congress, who were locked in a bitter impeachment effort. Nor did the Bush administration initially view terrorism and al-Qaʻida as a mortal threat. That changed after September 11.[71]

As discussed in Chapter 7, reforms instituted after the 1975 Church Committee report placed limitations on the intelligence community's domestic and foreign actions. Less than a week after September 11, however, those restrictions were abandoned. Bush signed an Executive Order authorizing the CIA to use lethal force against al-Qa'ida.[72] With the "gloves off," a series of controversial programs were implemented. Legal justifications were provided either by Executive Order or under the mandate of the "Uniting and Strengthening America by Providing Appropriate Tools Required to Intercept and Obstruct Terrorism" (USA PATRIOT) Act. This included the expanded use of "extraordinary rendition," in which suspected terrorists were interrogated or tortured by the CIA or foreign governments. Bush also authorized the creation of "Camp X-ray" at the Guantanamo Bay Naval Base to hold captured "enemy combatants." Meanwhile, the CIA introduced armed drones for the targeted assassination of "high value targets" that were deemed too difficult to capture. The National Security Agency (NSA) implemented a massive domestic and foreign surveillance program in support of these efforts. In addition, a wide-scale sweep of Muslims in the United States with expired visas was conducted, and over 5,000 people were arrested and deported.[73]

Prior to September 11, the U.S. intelligence community was comprised of fourteen agencies with tens of thousands of employees. The size of the community expanded dramatically after the attacks. According to the *Washington Post*, roughly 1,270 government organizations and 1,930 private companies worked on programs related to terrorism, homeland security, and intelligence across the country. To support the burgeoning growth, the public U.S. intelligence budget more than doubled to $75 billion, while the figure for military and counterterrorism activities was much higher. The unrestrained growth resulted in redundancies, lack of coordination, and information overload as the different agencies competed for attention for their voluminous reports and analysis.[74]

In contrast to the postwar growth of the national security establishment discussed in Chapter 3, the post–September 11 expansion relied heavily on the private sector. Existing corporations expanded operations and a plethora of new firms were established. A decade after the attacks, roughly 265,000 of the estimated 854,000 individuals with top-secret security clearances were contractors. In addition, contractors comprised nearly 30 percent of the employees in the different intelligence agencies and were involved in activities ranging from training personnel and analyzing data to conducting rendition operations and interrogations at secret prisons. Privatization was not limited to the intelligence community, however, as a notable feature of the Global War on Terror was the reliance on private military contractors. Military contractors performed a range of duties, from laundry and food services for the U.S. military to serving as guards for elected leaders and dignitaries, including Afghanistan's president Hamid Karzai. They were also casualties. For example, contractors comprised roughly one-third of the CIA's casualties since September 11. Although contractors were supposed to save money, the Pentagon eventually determined that they were at least 25 percent more expensive than government employees. By 2010, the Obama administration attempted to reduce the number of contractors, but it was limited to only a 7 percent reduction over two years.[75]

Although a Global War on Terror was launched, Arabic language skills were not prioritized. Indeed, the U.S. armed forces continued to purge gay and lesbian Arabic translators despite the obvious need for their skills. A General Accounting Office report found that the U.S. Army did not fill 44 percent of authorized positions for translators and interpreters for critical languages, including Arabic. In addition, 6 percent of positions with the needed language skills were vacant. To cope with the sustained insurgency in Iraq, Washington outsourced Arabic translation and intelligence gathering to regional allies, in particular Jordan. Jordan's support for American efforts in Iraq was part of a broader policy of intelligence coordination between Amman and Washington after September 11, which included the interrogation, imprisonment, and torture of individuals brought to different countries in the region under the extraordinary rendition program.[76]

Human Terrain Systems

The Bush administration's reliance on privatization and outsourcing was demonstrated in another controversial program to collect local knowledge about Afghanistan and Iraq. Although the use of American social scientists for intelligence gathering resembled the OSS, the Human Terrain System (HTS) brought social scientists together with military contractors. Initiated in 2006, the goal of HTS was to assist the American military with obtaining a better understanding of the social and cultural issues of the different combat areas. Within a year, six Human Terrain Teams (HTTs) were deployed in Afghanistan and Iraq and the Pentagon was anxious for more. Each HTT was comprised of five individuals, including a team leader with military experience, cultural and regional studies analysts, and data researchers. Although a majority of team members had degrees in political science and international relations, they were dubbed "anthropologists" by the media and military leaders. Yet they described themselves as "cultural advisors" to the U.S. military and "cultural brokers" to Iraqis and Afghans.[77]

In spite of the ambitious goals for the program and its large budget, the implementation was rushed and ultimately fell short. Few, if any, of the "anthropologists" had regional experience. Former team members accused the military contractor, BAE Systems, of gross mismanagement, including the failure to hire trained instructors or recruit individuals with the requisite regional and language knowledge and qualifications. A U.S. Army investigation confirmed these complaints and identified other problems, including fraud, sexual harassment, racism, and poor government oversight. Although BAE Systems was replaced by a new military contractor, the lack of regional knowledge and language expertise among HTTs persisted.[78]

Poor implementation, however, was not the only issue. Within academia, the program was criticized for the link between the information collected by team members and American counterinsurgency and combat operations. Each HTT compiled ethnographic data on particular areas, including the local political leadership and socioeconomic information, which was shared with other government agencies. Adding to the uncertain status of the social scientists, some were armed. In addition, the U.S. military acknowledged the similarity between the HTS and controversial Vietnam-era counterinsurgency programs.[79]

After articles about the HTS appeared in the press, the Executive Board of the American Anthropological Association (AAA) issued a formal statement declaring that the program violated the organization's code of ethics. The AAA stated that anthropologists in the HTS were placed in situations where they were indistinguishable from military personnel and restricted from adhering to their ethical obligation to reveal their identity and role as well as to obtain voluntary informed consent from subjects in war zones. While advocates for the HTS argued that the program was intended to improve relations between the military and civilian populations, team members acknowledged that information gathered by the anthropologists assisted with combat operations (or "kinetic engagements").[80]

Criticisms of HTS within academia were reinforced by the insider accounts of former trainees and team members. They described the lack of substantive training, lowered standards for recruitment (due to the dearth of qualified social scientists willing to join the program), and the pseudo-scientific research methods. Insider accounts also revealed the increasingly blurred line between the HTS scholars and soldiers, and the pressure on team members to conform to the military's definition and expectations of the program.[81]

Organizational problems with the HTS were compounded by the deaths of team members. By 2009, three HTT members were killed in Afghanistan and Iraq. A fourth was indicted on murder charges after he executed a handcuffed Afghan prisoner who attacked and severely burned a female team member. The team member later died of her injuries. While few in number, the deaths demonstrated that insurgents in Afghanistan and Iraq did not distinguish HTS members from military personnel or they were unable to do so. The Pentagon canceled the HTS in 2015, having spent at least $726 million on the program.[82]

Terror Studies and 9/11

Terror studies emerged in the 1970s but were largely marginalized within American academia. During the late Cold War period, terror experts relied heavily on the narrative of Soviet sponsorship. After the Cold War, however, the focus shifted to an emphasis on religion, in particular "Islamic terrorism." Scholars with ties to the neoconservative movement were the main proponents of the notion that Islam and Islamic terrorism were new threats. This included Bernard Lewis, Martin Kramer, and Daniel Pipes, who were joined by former journalist Steve Emerson. Their arguments about Islamic terrorism aligned with Samuel Huntington's "Clash of Civilizations" thesis and the increasing popularity of Hizbullah in Lebanon and the Islamic Resistance Movement (Hamas) in the occupied Palestinian territories. Hizbullah targeted Israeli forces in occupied southern Lebanon, eventually forcing a unilateral withdrawal in May 2000. Meanwhile, Hamas opposed the Oslo Accords, and its suicide attacks on Israeli military and civilian targets were initially opposed by the Arafat-led Palestinian National Authority. During the second *intifada*, however, they were emulated by other Palestinian groups.[83]

Although largely ignored at the time, bin Laden's 1996 and 1998 declarations of *jihad* signaled al-Qa'ida's emergence. Al-Qa'ida's focus and aims are different from those of Hizbullah and Hamas, but after September 11 the groups were often conflated by Washington and terrorism experts. Terrorism experts benefited from and exploited greater media coverage and the interest of the general public. Meanwhile, terror studies were infused with new sources of funding from the federal government.[84]

Higher education rushed to focus on terrorism. By 2004, 100 private and state universities and colleges launched programs in terrorism and emergency management. The programs tended to expand on existing criminal justice and emergency management programs at these institutions. Terrorism, the *New York Times* explained, was regarded as "the flashy side of disaster studies." In addition, a number of for-profit and online colleges provided courses and degrees in terror studies and homeland security.[85]

As part of the expanding national security budget, the federal government began funding terrorism-related research centers. The Department of Homeland Security (DHS) established twelve university-based "centers of excellence." In 2003, DHS awarded the University of Southern California $15.3 million to create the first interdisciplinary homeland security center. Two years later, the University of Maryland established the National Consortium for the Study of Terrorism and Response to Terrorism (START) with a $12 million DHS grant. Other centers were also funded to focus on border security, protecting the food supply chain, animal diseases, and microbial hazards. Meanwhile, National Science Foundation (NSF) research grants focused on terrorism skyrocketed. By 2005, the NSF awarded 135 grants for over $47 million. In comparison, from 1996 to 2000 only eight grants were awarded for a total of $1.5 million.[86]

Washington also funded research in the social sciences. In 2008, Project Minerva was established to fund university-based, interdisciplinary, social science research projects. In announcing Project Minerva, named after the Roman goddess of war and wisdom, Secretary of Defense Robert Gates noted that it was the fiftieth anniversary of the NDEA. As in the aftermath of Sputnik, Gates explained, the United States was "again trying to come to terms with new threats to national security." He acknowledged that the relationship between academia and the U.S. government had changed since the time of the NDEA and ranged from friendly to antagonistic. "Too many mistakes have been made over the years because our government and military did not understand—or even seek to understand—the countries or cultures we were dealing with," Gates conceded. He concluded with a call for finding "new ways" for academia, "this pillar of American society to serve our citizens, our nation, and the world."[87]

Like the NDEA, Project Minerva focused on "areas of strategic importance to U.S. national security policy." The majority of grants, totaling $17 million, are administered by the NSF. In the first two years, Minerva funded a number of studies and workshops focused on terrorism and civil strife in the Middle East. By 2014, however, the impact of the Arab revolutions and counterrevolutions was apparent, and the Pentagon sought a better understanding of social movements in the region and the impact of social media platforms like Twitter.[88]

In *Known and Unknown,* Donald Rumsfeld conceded that the Bush administration "could have engaged and asked more of the American public in the war effort." He added that President Bush should have "pushed for more education and scholarship on Islam and more training in languages like Arabic, Pashtu, and Farsi." While hardly a mea culpa for the attitude of the Bush administration and its allies toward academia and Middle East studies, Rumsfeld's admission demonstrates in part that the reality of the Global War on Terror fell far short of the hopes and plans of its architects. More than a decade later, those plans remain in tatters.[89]

The Bush Doctrine and the invasion of Iraq reflected the neoconservative's vision of America and the Middle East. To promote that vision, neoconservatives in the administration, academia, think tanks, and the media presented an optimistic view of the benefits of an aggressive and robust foreign policy. Within the government, dissenting voices were dismissed or squelched. In academia, the September 11 attacks provided an opportunity to settle old scores dating to the Vietnam War and levy unfounded accusations of bias and insufficient patriotism.

The late and post–Cold War periods witnessed the increased influence of the privatized knowledge of think tanks on U.S. foreign policy in the Middle East. Indeed, relations with the U.S. national security establishment were a key aspect of their raison d'être. The profound impact of Brookings, WINEP, and AEI on U.S. foreign policy formation and implementation contributed to the emergence of new think tanks.[90] Yet a decade after September 11, university-based Middle East studies centers and programs still struggled with increased enrollment and reduced federal funding, and continued to operate under a cloud of suspicion. In comparison, the generous funding toward HTS and Project Minerva demonstrates the value placed on education aligned with national security interests.

Similarly, the massive expansion of the national security state since September 11 and the overwhelming reliance on contractors calls into question the priorities of the U.S. government. More than a decade later, there is still a dearth of qualified personnel with the requisite language skills. Yet, as the leaks by former NSA contractor Edward Snowden reveal, long after bin Laden's death the agency maintains a pervasive global spying effort. But it still lacks the analysts to quickly and efficiently assess the enormous troves of data collected. The collection, however, continues unabated.

Epilogue

America and the Arab Spring

> In a global and totalitarian war, intelligence must be global and totalitarian.
>
> —WILLIAM DONOVAN

Cairo's Tahrir Square was the scene of yet another mass protest. The crowd chanted "the army, the people, and the police are one hand" and roared in approval as military helicopters flew overhead. Although the scene from Tahrir resembled the 2011 protests that unseated the thirty-year rule of Husni Mubarak, the target was his elected successor, Mohamed Morsi. Organizers claimed that the June 30 protests were the largest in human history. The Egyptian military used the apparent popular mandate to justify overthrowing and arresting Morsi after only a year in office and launched a harsh crackdown on his party, the Muslim Brotherhood.[1]

After the coup, the Obama administration avoided criticizing the Egyptian military. An anonymous administration official informed the *New York Times* that "the law does not require us to make a formal determination as to whether a coup took place, and it is not in our national interest to make such a determination. We will not say it was a coup, we will not say it was not a coup, we will just not say." Less than two months later, Secretary of State John Kerry claimed that the Egyptian military was "restoring democracy" by removing Morsi from office. Kerry's statement still hung in the air when Egyptian security forces killed over 1,000 protesters at Rabi'a al-'Adawiya and al-Nahda Squares on August 14. The preordained succession to power of Defense Minister Field Marshal Abdel Fattah el-Sisi completed the counterrevolution.[2]

Over the previous two years, popular movements for change across the Middle East encountered a lukewarm reception from Washington, especially when they challenged America's strategic interests and allies in the region. While the Obama administration offered occasional rhetorical support for some of the Arab revolutions and intervened directly in Libya and covertly in Syria, it also aligned more firmly and openly with the conservative regimes in the Persian Gulf. The administration's policies were matched by the analysis and recommendations of national security academics, in particular neoconservatives, who generally viewed the revolutions with skepticism and hostility.

America's Arab Spring

Six months after taking office, President Barack Obama gave a major address at Cairo University. The speech was part of a broader effort to improve relations with the Muslim world. Contrary to the rhetoric of a "new beginning," Obama continued, and in some cases expanded, the Bush administration's policies or reverted to the emphasis on stability. This was demonstrated by Washington's response to the Arab revolutions, beginning with Tunisia.

Tunisia's revolution began with Tarek Mohamad Bouazizi's self-immolation on December 17, 2010. The incident occurred after police seized the twenty-six-year-old fruit vendor's goods. Wide-scale protests followed, which were met with a harsh response by Tunisian security forces that inspired further demonstrations. Washington deemed Tunisian president Zine el-Abidine Ben Ali a "moderate" ally, in spite of his regime's rampant corruption and brutality. As the protests unfolded in Tunisia, the Obama administration did not embrace the revolution until Ben Ali was in exile. The rest of the region, however, took notice and protests around the theme of "the people want to bring down the regime" spread from Morocco to Yemen. When Husni Mubarak's regime in Egypt was threatened, the United States was faced with a choice between its interests and its values. The Obama administration tried to split the difference. After internal debate, the White House openly called for Mubarak to leave office. Yet Washington's favored replacement was Omar Suleiman, the vice president of Egypt and former head of Egyptian intelligence, who was rejected by the protestors. After Mubarak stepped down on February 11, he was replaced by the Supreme Council of the Armed Forces.[3]

The United States was reluctant to part with Mubarak. Former secretary of state Hillary Clinton wrote that Mubarak's Egypt "served as a linchpin of peace in a volatile region." Although some of President Obama's advisors identified with the young protestors in Egypt, there were concerns that it could be a repeat of the 1979 Iranian Revolution. "Extremists hijacked the broad-based popular revolution against the Shah and established a brutal theocracy," Clinton explained. She added that "if something similar happened in Egypt, it would be a catastrophe, for the people of Egypt as well as for Israeli and U.S. interests." Clinton was also concerned about the Muslim Brotherhood, the organization in the best position to win a post-Mubarak election. While the Brotherhood was more "moderate" than before, Clinton stated that "it was impossible to know how it would behave and what would happen if it gained control."[4]

Outside the administration, influential national security academics and foreign policy specialists echoed the internal discussions. This was particularly pronounced among advocates for the invasion of Iraq. Less than a decade later, Bernard Lewis, Niall Ferguson, and Leslie Gelb warned of the dangers that the revolutions posed to U.S. interests in the region. Their arguments ranged from economic to ideological and were generally dismissive of the protestors and their aims.[5] In his memoir, former secretary of defense Robert Gates echoed their concerns as well as those expressed by former secretary of state Clinton. "The history of revolutions is not a happy one," Gates explained, "Power ends up in the hands not of moderate reformers but of better-organized and far more ruthless extremists."[6]

In the region, however, the uprisings were generally viewed with enthusiasm. Al Jazeera, the pan-Arab satellite television channel, was on the frontlines of the mass protests in Tunisia, Egypt, Yemen, Syria, and Libya. The network's coverage again stood in sharp contrast to state-run media, which attempted to discount the size and scale of the unfolding demonstrations. Arabic-language newspapers like the London-based *Al-Quds al-Arabi*, Egypt's *Al-Masry Al-Youm*, and *Al-Akhbar* in Lebanon were similarly effusive in their support of the uprisings.[7] Egypt's *Al-Ahram*, which had ties to the former regime, embraced the revolutions after Mubarak's fall from power.[8]

In spite of its public rhetoric, the Obama administration evaluated the different revolutions based on how they corresponded to perceived U.S. interests. In May 2011, President Obama declared that it "will be the policy of the United States to promote reform across the region, and to support transitions to democracy." Actual policies fell far short of that goal, however. In Libya, the United States and the North Atlantic Treaty Organization (NATO) engaged in regime change disguised as a humanitarian intervention. There was considerable pressure for a similar intervention in Syria, including from American allies in the region. Instead, the Obama administration attempted to fund and train an opposition force, but had little success. In contrast, American officials largely ignored the protests in Bahrain, Jordan, Yemen, Algeria, and Morocco. Saudi Arabia's March 2011 invasion of Bahrain, under the aegis of the Gulf Cooperation Council (GCC), drew only a halfhearted response from Washington. Within a year, the same repressive Gulf monarchies were embraced by the Obama administration.[9]

America's Gulf

Nearly fifteen months after the Arab Spring began, Secretary of State Hillary Clinton attended the first U.S.-GCC Strategic Cooperation Forum in Riyadh, Saudi Arabia. Comprised of the conservative Arab monarchies in the Persian Gulf, the GCC was established in the wake of the Iranian revolution. Twenty years later, the GCC was a key component of Washington's attempts to contain Tehran. The symbolism of Clinton meeting and posing for pictures with the foreign ministers of the GCC states could not have been a more striking refutation of the aims of the Arab revolutions— or more at odds with Washington's proclaimed support for the spread of freedom, democracy, and equal rights in the Arab world and beyond. Prior to the Forum, the United Arab Emirates (UAE) closed the offices of the National Democratic Institute (NDI). An American nongovernmental organization with ties to the Democratic Party, the NDI's mission is to improve governmental accountability. Yet the State Department only offered a muted response to the closure.[10]

In her memoir, Clinton confirmed the administration's reluctance to embrace the Arab revolutions. Recounting her November 2011 speech at the NDI, Clinton explained that "America has many important national interests in the region, and they will not always align perfectly, despite our best efforts." The United States, she added, "will always have imperfect partners who doubtless view us as imperfect too, and we'll always face imperatives that drive us to make imperfect compromises." Among those imperfect compromises are relations with the GCC, which Clinton referenced only cryptically. Instead, *Hard Choices* revealed her sympathy with conservative forces in the region, as Clinton effectively adopted the positions of the regimes in Bahrain and Egypt.[11]

In the midst of the Arab Spring, American forces withdrew from Iraq and were redeployed around the region. The Obama administration sought to create a new "security architecture" for the Persian Gulf in order to contain Iran. Washington's plans drew on the U.S. military's previous deployments in the region and expanded relations with the GCC. One aspect of this relationship has been unprecedented weapons sales by the George W. Bush and Obama administrations, especially to Saudi Arabia and the UAE. Since 2008, GCC members have agreed to purchase over $90 billion in weapons systems.[12]

The withdrawal of American forces from Iraq was temporary. In September 2014, Obama announced a new campaign against the Islamic State in Iraq and *as-Sham* (ISIS). Obama's speech drew on notions of American exceptionalism. "Abroad, American leadership is the one constant in an uncertain world. It is America that has the capacity and the will to mobilize the world against terrorists," he declared. A product of the Syrian civil war and sectarian discord in Iraq, ISIS has received support from America's allies in the region, including Saudi Arabia, Turkey, and the UAE. In spite of Washington's embrace of the GCC, Obama claimed that "it is America that is helping Muslim communities around the world not just in the fight against terrorism, but in the fight for opportunity, and tolerance, and a more hopeful future."[13] It is uncertain whether the 2015 nuclear agreement between Washington and Tehran is a sign of a more hopeful future or if the United States will continue to rely on the GCC and other autocratic regimes to extend its military presence in the region.

An Era of Persistent War

America's large military footprint in the Middle East is extended by a lighter one. Since September 11, 2001, a constellation of drone bases have been established from Afghanistan to East Africa. More than a decade after the attacks, however, the *Washington Post* reported that the United States may only be halfway through the Global War on Terror, or Overseas Contingency Operations as it was dubbed by the Obama administration. Instead of reducing or eliminating the kill and detain lists, known as "the disposition matrix," it is constantly being updated by the Pentagon and the Central Intelligence Agency (CIA). Meanwhile, U.S. officials have conceded that the individuals now targeted are not the same level of status, importance, or threat as their predecessors. Yet the lists remain.[14]

The Obama administration's surveillance efforts are equally robust. During the Obama presidency, the number of suspects added to the U.S. government's "Terrorism Screening Database" increased tenfold. Yet only 40 percent of the roughly 680,000 individuals added to the database had ties to known organizations. One reason for the dramatic growth of the watch list is that government officials only need "reasonable suspicion" to add an individual to the database.[15]

The expansion of the Terrorism Screening Database is only one aspect of America's unprecedented spying program led by the National Security Agency (NSA). After September 11, the NSA embarked on a massive data collection effort targeted at foreign and domestic sources. These activities were conducted in coordination with leading technology companies and sometimes without their knowledge. Contrary to the public statements of NSA and administration officials, including President Obama, the data collection was not limited to suspected terrorists and included American citizens. NSA surveillance was coordinated with America's English-speaking allies— Britain, Canada, Australia, and New Zealand—which with the United States are known as the "Five Eyes." Surveillance data was also shared with Israel. In addition, the NSA expanded its relationship with Saudi Arabia's Ministry of the Interior in spite of Riyadh's poor human rights record and crackdown on internal dissent. Yet as discussed in Chapter 8, the NSA is still hamstrung by a lack of analysts with the requisite language skills. But the collection continues.[16]

While the NSA uses the latest technology to gather signals intelligence, other agencies within the intelligence community continue to rely on traditional methods. In late 2012, the Pentagon confirmed that an expansion and transformation of the Defense Intelligence Agency (DIA) was underway. The *Washington Post* reported that "U.S. officials said the DIA needed to be repositioned as the wars in Iraq and Afghanistan give way to what many expect will be a period of sporadic conflicts and simmering threats requiring close-in intelligence work." Among the top priorities for intelligence gathering were Islamist militant groups, "weapons transfers by North Korea and Iran, and military modernization underway in China." When the transformation is complete, DIA operatives will be "deployed across North Africa and other trouble spots" and coordinate with the CIA and the U.S. Joint Special Operations Command. The DIA is reportedly constructing elaborate cover stories for the operatives, including posing as academics or business executives.[17]

Middle East Studies after the Arab Spring

As observed in the response to the invasion and occupation of Iraq, there was a discernible ideological and political split over the Arab Spring. While some national security academics framed events within and consistently warned of the threat to U.S. interests in the region, most Middle East scholars generally welcomed the revolutions and attempted to put them in the broader perspective of regional and international history. Although numerous articles, monographs, and edited volumes have been published attempting to examine and explain the Arab revolutions, events in the region remain fluid and dynamic. The coup in Egypt and civil wars or strife in Syria, Libya, Iraq, Yemen, and Lebanon demonstrate that it is far too early to provide a final judgment on the Arab Spring.[18]

In spite of Washington's continued involvement in the region, there are renewed attempts to target Middle East studies funding. In March 2014, "reforms" to Title VI were proposed. Building on the failed attempts after September 11, a similar coalition of organizations and individuals has again charged that Middle East studies are dominated by anti-Israel and anti-American scholars whose politics stifle debate and discussion and are not aligned with U.S. interests in the region. These efforts coincided with attempts by Republican lawmakers to cut National Science Foundation (NSF) grants for social and behavioral research that are not related to national security or economics.[19] In response to the accusations, representatives of the Middle East Studies Association (MESA) defended the field by reasserting its importance to policymakers and American national security interests.[20]

Meanwhile, American universities are flocking to the Persian Gulf to establish branch campuses. Nearly a century and a half after the Syrian Protestant College (SPC) was founded in Beirut, a different spirit and mission is driving these endeavors. Which raises the questions: Can American universities play a positive role in countries where there is little or no political freedom and human rights and labor abuses are rampant? Or will they also adopt Washington's "imperfect compromises" on issues of academic freedom and freedom of inquiry?[21]

At the same time, several Persian Gulf states are funding Washington-based think tanks. In 2013, Qatar provided $14.8 million to the Brookings

Institution to fund a center in Doha and a program on U.S. relations with Muslim countries. Similarly, the UAE donated to the Washington-based Center for Strategic and International Studies (CSIS). Criticism of the funding has focused on the apparent attempts by Qatar and the UAE to buy influence in Washington. However, the close ties and shared interests between the United States and its Persian Gulf allies have been ignored.[22]

Reflecting on the twenty-fifth anniversary of the NDEA in 1983, Stewart McClure lamented his role in naming the legislation. McClure served as the chief clerk for the Senate Committee on Labor, Education, and Public Welfare for over two decades. "I invented that god-awful title: The National Defense Education Act," McClure explained, "If there are any words less compatible really, intellectually, with the purposes of education—it's not to defend the country; it's to defend the mind and develop the human spirit, not to develop cannons and battleships." He added, "It was a horrible title, but it worked. It worked. How could you attack it?" Yet as this book has demonstrated, knowledge and expertise about foreign areas were viewed as essential to America's defense and security.[23]

America's engagement with the Middle East has corresponded to its evolution as a superpower. Over the past century, the United States was transformed from a regional power with limited interests in the Middle East to a hyperpower with hegemony over the region. U.S. foreign policy interests have had a predominant influence on the production of knowledge about the Middle East. Those interests were informed by material and ideological factors, including Orientalist perceptions and notions of American exceptionalism, which were reproduced in the development of regional expertise. Yet this was not simply a one-way relationship between center and periphery. Rather, the interactions between the United States and the Middle East also influenced the production of knowledge and the actions of governmental and nongovernmental institutions.

Washington sought and cultivated the development of expertise that reflected its interests and goals. This was evidenced in the transition from private to privatized knowledge. The foreign policy and national security establishments initially relied on the privately held knowledge of missionaries, Orientalist scholars, and representatives of business interests. As American interests in the region expanded during the Second World War, Washington broadened its base of sources. The United States not only relied on the intelligence of its allies, but developed its own network of spies and informants. In response to its postwar global commitments, the U.S. government sought to formalize the education, training, and recruitment of area specialists. It was joined in this effort by universities, academic societies, and foundations. However, the national security establishment of the late Cold War period was dramatically different in size, scope, and requirements from two decades earlier. The need for trained personnel and research and analysis methods were less pronounced as government agencies developed their own internal training programs and techniques for data collection and analysis. Although university-based programs and centers were still important sources of recruitment and basic language training, academic studies and monographs were deemed less relevant to the daily needs of government agencies. The increased reliance and emphasis on classified information appeared to mitigate the need for academic expertise. Meanwhile, the privatized knowledge and expertise of think tanks, which drew on and benefited from close ties to the U.S. foreign policy and national security establishments, predominated in policy circles and the press.

Orientalist perceptions and scholarship influenced U.S. foreign policy in the Middle East. The Inquiry's recommendations for the postwar disposition of the territories of the Ottoman Empire relied on analysis of the region and its inhabitants that were steeped in notions of racial and religious supremacy. Orientalist representations were incorporated into the intelligence produced by the Office of Strategic Services (OSS) and influenced the actions of the Allies during and after the Second World War. In the early Cold War period, these notions influenced support for American educational institutions in the region by the State Department and philanthropic foundations. They were also reflected in Washington's fears of nationalist movements and leaders and incorporated into modernization theory. After the Cold War, Orientalist preconceptions and representations were reproduced in the justifications of U.S. policies in the Global War on Terror and response to the Arab uprisings. Nor were they limited to Americans, as "native informants" often relied on and reinforced these same characterizations for ideological and political reasons.

Knowledge and expertise were constructed to match national security interests and ideology. In the era before American hegemony, this was reflected in Alfred Thayer Mahan's invention of the region as well as the creation of racial and religious categories by the Inquiry during World War I. It continued during the Cold War with attempts to decipher the Oriental mind or segmentation of populations by modernization theorists. In the late and post–Cold War eras, these characterizations persisted in discussions of terrorism and sectarian identities.

U.S. foreign policy interests were also reproduced by the national security academics that alternated between government service and prominent universities. Some, like William Langer, were influential in both spheres. The foreign policy and national security establishments considered prior government service as a major qualification, which included serving in the Inquiry as well as the State Department or the intelligence agencies. At the height of the Cold War, the external opinions of academics with intelligence experience and credentials were also important to the expanding government agencies. The once close and mutually beneficial relationships between university scholars and government agencies were eventually replicated with think tanks. Moreover, prominent figures alternating between the U.S. government and influential think tanks has become the norm.

A consistent theme across these different time periods was the supposed immaturity of the region's population. This rationale was used during World War I to promote the creation of British and French mandates. It was repeated at the height of the Cold War by the Eisenhower administration to justify overthrowing the Mossadegh government in Iran and was a key component of modernization theory. Similar claims were made by neoconservatives as the occupation of Iraq floundered and in response to the Arab revolutions.

A related notion was that non-Western leaders and populations only understand force and power. Experts repeated these sentiments when advising President Roosevelt and the OSS's William Donovan during World War II and in response to nationalist leaders during the Cold War. Similarly, as part of the Global War on Terror, it was argued that a firm demonstration of force would punish America's enemies and deter future acts of terrorism. This was not limited to the Middle East, however. President Harry Truman applied a similar logic to the Soviet Union, remarking that the only language Stalin understood was "how many divisions have you?" Therefore, such assertions are more revealing about the United States and elite sentiments of power than about the Middle East or other regions.[24]

Area studies were tied to the expansion of the national security establishment. Although Cold War policies drove the creation of area studies, federal funding had predictable results as well as unintended consequences. Area studies initially appeared to provide the expertise needed by the foreign policy and national security establishments. However, less than a decade after the NDEA was passed, scholars were increasingly reluctant to openly collaborate with the government. The expansion of area studies and federal support for language study, coupled with the social movements of the 1960s and 1970s, led to a diversification of the field. Meanwhile, U.S. government agencies developed, expanded, and enhanced their own research, analysis, and training capabilities that benefited from but were independent of university-based scholarship. In the wake of campus protests and a failing war, the Nixon administration was ready to abandon area studies. Paradoxically, as U.S. interests and involvement in the Middle East increased over the next two decades, government funding of area studies plateaued or decreased. The emergence of well-funded, private think tanks in the late and post–Cold War periods contributed to the reduced influence of university-based Middle East studies programs. In addition, the field struggled with reduced funding, an uncertain mission, and attacks from inside and outside academia. After September 11, there was open hostility toward Middle East studies and scholars, particularly those critical of U.S. foreign policy in the region.

The NDEA was the culmination of earlier efforts to establish area studies in the United States. While the law did not create area studies, it is unlikely that the programs would have thrived without Washington's intervention and funding. Instead, they would have remained starved for resources and isolated to a few elite institutions. The NDEA was successful in dramatically increasing the number of Americans trained in foreign languages for strategic areas, a key part of its original mandate. However, there was never a guarantee that the individuals receiving fellowships would pursue the type of research or careers in government service intended by the legislation. In addition, the connection between national security and education that was essential to the bill's passage made them inseparable. Over the next six decades, education leaders relied on the national security justification to maintain funding for area studies, while politicians emphasized the importance of knowledge for and service to the state.

The emphasis on "useful knowledge" over academic knowledge has persisted. A common refrain in the press and among political leaders is that academic knowledge is only valuable if its benefits can be understood and applied outside the university or peer-reviewed publications. A related claim and criticism is that scholars should be able to predict future events based on their knowledge and expertise. Middle East scholars have been criticized for their failure to foresee the September 11 attacks and the Arab revolutions. Such claims confuse the role of scholarship and scholars with that of intelligence agencies or diplomats. Nor have American intelligence agencies demonstrated a consistent ability to forecast events even with far greater resources and attention on these issues. Instead, numerous foreign policy failures, including the Vietnam War and the invasion of Iraq, have repeatedly revealed the dangers of groupthink within the U.S. national security establishment. By embracing think tanks and funding national security scholarships and research, Washington is intent on promoting further alignment with state interests, rather than encouraging alternative perspectives.[25]

Within academia, area studies were viewed with skepticism. This was evident in the early discussions of adapting wartime programs during World War II and fears about producing "superficial" scholars. Although these concerns were overlooked by government agencies eager for qualified candidates, they persisted long after the NDEA was passed. The embrace of modernization theory by academia and the U.S. government revealed the limitations of area expertise and the predominance of ideology. Nor were area experts embraced after modernization theory was abandoned. Instead, Washington deemed area studies a failure and sought to reduce or eliminate federal funding. Criticisms of area studies by the disciplines reemerged after the Cold War with a renewed vigor, in spite of significant changes in the quality, diversity, and breadth of scholarship.

The relationship between academic institutions and the federal government were dynamic. Universities were not passive institutions bending to the dictates of an all-powerful state. Rather, they shared and sought to benefit from Washington's Cold War goals. Universities and scholars welcomed relations with the foreign policy and intelligence establishments during the early Cold War period. Yet over time and in response to changing domestic and international conditions, open collaboration became more difficult to maintain. The Middle East studies programs at Harvard and Princeton were launched before the NDEA to produce candidates for employment by government agencies and multinational corporations. However, both institutions had difficulty meeting their original mandates. Harvard drew on a strong funding base, but the program suffered from inconsistent leadership. In contrast, Princeton benefited from strong leadership, but struggled with gearing its program to meet the needs of the government agencies for contemporary knowledge of the Middle East. Modernization theorists were active at both Princeton and Harvard and often had or maintained ties to the U.S. national security establishment. These ties continued in the late and post–Cold War periods, contributing in part to a scandal at Harvard.

A similar relationship existed between the U.S. government and American educational institutions in the Middle East. The American University of Beirut (AUB) and the American University in Cairo (AUC) maintained transnational identities that reinforced and competed with their educational missions. Washington sought to create Cold War universities that would represent American ideals and policies in the Middle East. The universities were also highly regarded by and benefited from the support of governmental and business elites across the region. Washington's support for AUB and AUC reflected and was at times hindered by its policies. Yet like their counterparts in the United States, both universities had agency. This was evidenced in their development of local bases of support and their attempts to affect and occasionally contest Washington's policies.

Foundations played an integral role in the development of area studies and support of American academic institutions in the Middle East. Their actions were in line with Washington's interests as well as their own missions. Prior to the NDEA, the Rockefeller and Ford Foundations funded the Middle East programs at Princeton and Harvard. The Ford Foundation also backed the Social Science Research Council's (SSRC) Committee on Near and Middle East Studies and MESA. In addition, both the Rockefeller and Ford Foundations provided essential support to AUB and AUC when funding from the U.S. government was not available.

During the late Cold War period, think tanks became integral to policymaking toward the Middle East. While university-based scholars were increasingly viewed with skepticism in policy circles, the influence of think tanks was reinforced by generous funding and access to policymakers and the media. Although the Brookings Institution was primarily focused on domestic policy issues, its recommendations for the Arab-Israeli peace process influenced the Carter administration as well as the actions of other think tanks. Meanwhile, regional analysis by the American Enterprise Institute (AEI) shifted from reflecting corporate interests to adopting the agenda of the neoconservative movement. The emergence of the Washington Institute for Near East Policy (WINEP) during the Reagan administration reflected the closer ties and shared interests of the United States and Israel. In addition, WINEP alumni have held key roles in multiple administrations as well as at other influential think tanks, including Brookings.

This story continues to evolve. Although I conducted a significant amount of archival research, some institutions were not examined. Future studies should focus on the programs established before the NDEA at Columbia, the University of Pennsylvania, and University of Michigan, as well as those that benefited from the legislation, like Berkeley, UCLA, and Georgetown. There are also significant gaps in the historical record that are likely to remain. More than seven years after I completed preliminary research at the U.S. National Archives, a number of Freedom of Information Act (FOIA) requests are still unprocessed. In addition, the records of key agencies are either partially declassified or remain closed to researchers, including the CIA and the DIA. Even when an archive is open and accessible to researchers, the question of what is and what is *not* in the historical record persists and a number of troubling gaps in national, university, and foundation archives remain. It is unclear what, if anything, to make of these omissions as the information contained in documents declassified under FOIA can be frustratingly unremarkable. Nor can scholars or the general public expect this situation to improve as the George W. Bush and Obama administrations have taken secrecy to new levels. Meanwhile, the staff of the CIA's FOIA office has been reduced and the agency has become more stringent in the information it is willing to declassify, much to the chagrin of scholars.[26]

Yet the need for transparency has arguably never been greater. As of this writing, American drones and fighter jets patrol the skies from Pakistan to Somalia. Operations are authorized in over a dozen countries and global surveillance persists. To support these efforts, there is an increased emphasis on knowledge and expertise aligned with national security interests. As America's involvement with the Middle East deepens, it appears that the dream palace will remain.

Notes

Introduction

Epigraph: Kermit Roosevelt, *Arabs, Oil, and History: The Story of the Middle East* (Port Washington, NY: Kennikat Press, 1969): 9.

1. Alfred Thayer Mahan, *From Sail to Steam: Recollections of Naval Life* (New York: Harper & Brothers, 1906): 200, 220–224.
2. Ibid., 222–223; Richard S. West Jr., *Admirals of American Empire* (New York: Bobbs-Merrill, 1948): 133–134.
3. West, *Admirals of American Empire*, 147–161; Richard Immerman, *Empire for Liberty: A History of American Imperialism from Benjamin Franklin to Paul Wolfowitz* (Princeton, NJ: Princeton University Press, 2010): 142–143.
4. As I note in "The Crossroads of the World: U.S. and British Foreign Policy Doctrines and the Construct of the Middle East, 1902–2007," *Diplomatic History* 38, no. 2 (2014): 299–344, while Mahan is credited with coining the term the "Middle East," it may already have been in use by British military officials stationed in the region. In addition, it is unlikely that the term would have gained acceptance without adoption by the British press, which promoted Mahan's expertise and impartiality as an American. See also Clayton R. Koppes, "Captain Mahan, General Gordon, and the Origins of the Term 'Middle East,'" *Middle Eastern Studies* 12 (January 1976): 95–98; Roger Adelson, *London and the Invention of the Middle East: Money, Power, and War, 1902–1922* (New Haven, CT: Yale University Press, 1995); Roderic Davison, "Where Is the Middle East?" *Foreign Affairs* 38 (1960): 669.
5. T. E. Lawrence, *Seven Pillars of Wisdom: A Triumph* (New York: Acorn Books, 1991): 24–25. On Lawrence's constructed image, see Fred D. Crawford and

Joseph A. Berton, "How Well Did Lawrence of Arabia Know Lawrence of Arabia?" *English Literature in Transition, 1880–1930* 39, no. 3 (1996): 299–318. Questioning Lawrence's role and claims, see George Antonius, *The Arab Awakening: The Story of the Arab National Movement* (New York: Capricorn Book, 1965): 319–326. Michael Korda, *Hero: The Life and Legend of Lawrence of Arabia* (New York: HarperCollins, 2010): 592–593, is a favorable biography that briefly discusses some of the criticism of *Seven Pillars* by Lawrence's peers and rivals.

6. See Khalil, "The Crossroads of the World." For national security interests as social constructions, see David Campbell, *Writing Security: United States Foreign Policy and the Politics of Identity* (Minneapolis: University of Minnesota Press, 1998); Alexander Wendt, *Social Theory of International Politics* (Cambridge: Cambridge University Press, 1999); Jutta Weldes, *Constructing National Interests: The United States and the Cuban Missile Crisis* (Minneapolis: University of Minnesota Press, 1999); Christian G. Appy, ed., *Cold War Constructions: The Political Culture of United States Imperialism, 1945–1966* (Amherst: University of Massachusetts Press, 2000). For the relationship of geographic constructions to U.S. foreign policy during the Cold War, see Matthew Farish, *The Contours of America's Cold War* (Minneapolis: University of Minnesota Press, 2010); Timothy Barney, *Mapping the Cold War: Cartography and the Framing of America's International Power* (Chapel Hill: University of North Carolina Press, 2015). For geographic constructs see Martin W. Lewis and Karen Wigen, *The Myth of Continents: A Critique of Metageography* (Berkeley: University of California Press, 1997).

7. Zachary Lockman, *Contending Visions of the Middle East: The History and Politics of Orientalism*, 2nd ed. (Cambridge: Cambridge University Press, 2010): 66–69. See also Albert Hourani, *Islam in European Thought* (Cambridge: Cambridge University Press, 1991). For a history of Orientalism and a critique of Edward Said, see Robert Irwin, *Dangerous Knowledge: Orientalism and Its Discontents* (Woodstock, NY: Overlook Press, 2006); for European study of non-Islamic Asian religions, see Urs App, *The Birth of Orientalism* (Philadelphia: University of Pennsylvania Press, 2010).

8. Lockman, *Contending Visions of the Middle East*, 68, 101–104; Irwin, *Dangerous Knowledge*, 213–214. On perceptions of Asia and Asian Americans, see Robert G. Lee, *Orientals: Asian Americans in Popular Culture* (Philadelphia: Temple University Press, 1999); John Kuo Wei Tchen, *New York before Chinatown: Orientalism and the Shaping of America Culture, 1776–1882* (Baltimore: Johns Hopkins University Press, 1999); Henry Yu, *Thinking Orientals: Migration, Contact, and Exoticism in Modern America* (New York: Oxford University Press, 2001); Christina Klein, *Cold War Orientalism: Asia in the Middlebrow Imagination, 1945–1961* (Berkeley: University of California Press, 2003). For American conceptions of Arabs and Islam, see Michael Suleiman, *The Arabs in the Mind of America* (Brattleboro, VT: Amana Books,

1988); Fuad Sha'ban. *Islam and Arabs in Early American Thought: Roots of Orientalism in America* (Durham, NC: Acorn Press, 1991); Timothy Marr, *The Cultural Roots of American Islamicism* (Cambridge: Cambridge University Press, 2006); Karine Walther, *Sacred Interests: The United States and the Islamic World, 1821–1921* (Chapel Hill: University of North Carolina Press, 2015).

9. Edward Said, *Orientalism* (New York: Vintage, 1979): 2–5, 201–328.

10. For the relationship between popular culture and U.S. foreign policy, see Douglas Little, *American Orientalism: The United States and the Middle East since 1945* (Chapel Hill: University of North Carolina Press, 2004); Matthew F. Jacobs, *Imagining the Middle East: The Building of an American Foreign Policy, 1918–1967* (Chapel Hill: University of North Carolina Press, 2011), examines an "informal network" of scholars and experts that influenced the development of U.S. foreign policy during the early Cold War period; Mary Ann Heiss, "Real Men Don't Wear Pajamas: Anglo-American Cultural Perceptions of Mohammad Mossadeq and the Iranian Oil Nationalization Dispute," in *Empire and Revolution: The United States and the Third World since 1945,* ed. Peter Hahn and Mary Ann Heiss (Columbus: Ohio State University Press, 2001), demonstrates that Orientalist perceptions influenced the Eisenhower administration's policy toward Iranian prime minister Mohammad Mossadegh. For popular culture as a reflection of U.S. foreign policy, see Melani McAlister, *Epic Encounters: Culture, Media, and U.S. Interests in the Middle East, 1945–2000.* 2nd ed. (Berkeley: University of California Press, 2005). For Orientalism and U.S. foreign policy in the developing world, see Matthew Connelly, "Taking Off the Cold War Lens: Visions of North-South Conflict during the Algerian War for Independence," *American Historical Review* 105, no. 3 (June 2000): 739–769; Salim Yaqub, *Containing Arab Nationalism: The Eisenhower Doctrine and the Middle East* (Chapel Hill: University of North Carolina Press, 2004), argues that the links between disparaging and racist remarks by American officials and policy formation and implementation are tenuous. For Said's limited influence on diplomatic historians, see Andrew Rotter, "Saidism without Said: Orientalism and U.S. Diplomatic History," *American Historical Review* 104, no. 4 (October 2000): 1205–1217.

11. Several scholars have argued for a post-Orientalism analysis when discussing U.S.-Middle East relations. However, as will be demonstrated, American policymakers and the expertise they promoted and relied on over the past century drew heavily on the Orientalist tradition. In addition, the link between area studies and Orientalism that Said traced is explored further in the pages that follow. See McAlister, *Epic Encounters,* and Hamid Dabashi, *Post-Orientalism: Knowledge and Power in Time of Terror* (Piscataway, NJ: Transaction Publishers, 2008). See also Ussama Makdisi, "After Said: The Limits and Possibilities of a Critical Scholarship of U.S.-Arab Relations," *Diplomatic History* 38, no. 3 (June 2014). For Said's own contribution, see *Culture and Imperialism* (New York: Vintage, 1994).

12. See Walter A. McDougall, *Promised Land, Crusader State: The American Encounter with the World Since 1776* (New York: Houghton Mifflin, 1997): 5, 18; Walter L. Hixson, *American Settler Colonialism: A History* (New York: Palgrave Macmillan, 2013); Eran Shalev, *American Zion: The Old Testament as a Political Text from the Revolution to the Civil War* (New Haven, CT: Yale University Press, 2013).

13. Meghana V. Nayak and Christopher Malone, "American Orientalism and American Exceptionalism: A Critical Rethinking of U.S. Hegemony," *International Studies Review* 11 (2009): 253–276; Jack P. Greene, *The Intellectual Construction of America: Exceptionalism and Identity from 1492 to 1800* (Chapel Hill: University of North Carolina Press, 1993); Bernard Bailyn, *The Ideological Origins of the American Revolution* (Cambridge, MA: Belknap Press of Harvard University Press, 1967): 140–143; Loren Baritz, "The Idea of the West," *American Historical Review* 66, no. 3 (April 1961): 618–640.

14. Michael Adas, "From Settler Colony to Global Hegemon: Integrating the Exceptionalist Narrative of the American Experience into World History," *American Historical Review* 106, no. 5 (December 2001): 1692–1720; Paul Kramer, "Power and Connection: Imperial Histories of the United States in the World," *American Historical Review* 116, no. 5 (December 2011): 1348–1391; Anders Stephanson, *Manifest Destiny: American Expansion and the Empire of Right* (New York: Hill and Wang, 1996): 124; Andrew Preston, *Sword of the Spirit, Shield of Faith: Religion in American War and Diplomacy* (New York: Alfred A. Knopf, 2012).

15. See Elizabeth Borgwardt, *A New Deal for the World: America's Vision for Human Rights* (Cambridge, MA: Harvard University Press, 2007); G. John Ikenberry, *Liberal Leviathan: The Origins, Crisis, and Transformation of the American World Order* (Princeton, NJ: Princeton University Press, 2011); Melvyn Leffler, *A Preponderance of Power: National Security, the Truman Administration, and the Cold War* (Stanford, CA: Stanford University Press, 1993).

16. On ideology and national security interests, see Anders Stephanson, "Ideology and Neorealist Mirrors," *Diplomatic History* (April 1993): 285–295; Michael Hunt, *Ideology and U.S. Foreign Policy* (New Haven, CT: Yale University Press, 1987). On economic interests and foreign policy, see Gabriel Kolko, *The Roots of American Foreign Policy* (Boston: Beacon Press, 1969); Kolko, *Confronting the Third World: United States Foreign Policy, 1945–1980* (New York: Pantheon, 1988); William Appleman Williams, *The Tragedy of American Diplomacy* (New York: W. W. Norton, 1959). There are a number of works that emphasize America's strategic interests in the Middle East, including H. W. Brands, *Into the Labyrinth: The United States and the Middle East, 1945–1993* (New York: McGraw-Hill, 1994); John Lewis Gaddis, *We Now Know: Rethinking Cold War History* (New York: Oxford University Press, 1997); Fawaz A. Gerges, *The Superpowers and the Middle East: Regional and International Politics, 1955–1967* (Boulder, CO: Westview Press, 1994);

Peter L. Hahn, *Crisis and Crossfire: The United States and the Middle East since 1945* (Washington, DC: Potomac Books, 2005); Bruce R. Kuniholm, *The Origins of the Cold War in the Near East: Great Power Conflict and Diplomacy in Iran, Turkey, and Greece* (Princeton, NJ: Princeton University Press, 1980); William Roger Louis, *The British Empire in the Middle East, 1945–1951: Arab Nationalism, the United States, and Postwar Imperialism* (New York: Oxford University Press, 1984); Yaqub, *Containing Arab Nationalism*. For provocative essays examining all these factors, see Perry Anderson, "Imperium," *New Left Review* 83 (September–October 2013): 5–111, and "Consilium," *New Left Review* 83 (September–October 2013): 116–157; see also Anderson, *American Foreign Policy and Its Thinkers* (London: Verso, 2015), and the forum in *Diplomatic History* 39, no. 2 (April 2015): 359–409.

17. Dorothy Ross, *The Origins of American Social Science* (Cambridge: Cambridge University Press, 1991): 22–50, 471–472.

18. For studies on the relationship between the U.S. national security state and academia not related to Middle East studies, see Gene M. Lyons, *The Uneasy Partnership: Social Science and the Federal Government in the Twentieth Century* (New York: Russell Sage Foundation, 1969); Sigmund Diamond, *Compromised Campus: The Collaboration of Universities with the Intelligence Community* (New York: Oxford University Press, 1992); Frances Stonor Saunders, *The Cultural Cold War: The CIA and the World of Arts and Letters* (New York: The New Press, 1999); Christopher Simpson, ed. *Universities and Empire: Money and Politics in the Social Sciences during the Cold War* (New York: The New Press, 1999); Joy Rohde, *Armed with Expertise: The Militarization of American Social Research during the Cold War* (Ithaca, NY: Cornell University Press, 2013); Ron Robin, *The Making of the Cold War Enemy: Culture and Politics in the Military-Industrial Complex* (Princeton, NJ: Princeton University Press, 2001); Ido Oren, *Our Enemies and US: America's Rivalries and the Making of Political Science* (Ithaca, NY: Cornell University Press, 2003); Bruce Kuklick, *Blind Oracles: Intellectuals and War from Kennan and Kissinger* (Princeton, NJ: Princeton University Press, 2006); Andrew Abbott and James T. Sparrow, "Hot War, Cold War: The Structures of Sociological Action, 1940–1955," in *Sociology in America*, ed. Craig Calhoun (Chicago: University of Chicago Press, 2007); David C. Engerman, *Know Your Enemy: The Rise and Fall of America's Soviet Experts* (New York: Oxford University Press, 2009); Robin Winks, *Cloak and Gown: Scholars in the Secret War, 1939–1961* (New York: William Morrow, 1987); David Price, *Anthropological Intelligence: The Deployment and Neglect of American Anthropology in the Second World War* (Durham, NC: Duke University Press, 2008); Susan H. Allen, *Classical Spies: American Archaeologists with the OSS in World War II Greece* (Ann Arbor: University of Michigan Press, 2011); Hugh Wilford, *The Mighty Wurlitzer: How the CIA Played America* (Cambridge, MA: Harvard University Press, 2009); Wilford, *America's Great Game: The CIA's Secret Arabists and the Shaping of the Modern Middle East* (New York: Basic Books, 2013).

19. For the rise of the postwar national security establishment, see Michael Sherry, *In the Shadow of War: The United States since the 1930s* (New Haven, CT: Yale University Press, 1995); Michael J. Hogan, *A Cross of Iron: Harry S. Truman and the Origins of the National Security State, 1945–1954* (Cambridge: Cambridge University Press, 1998); Aaron L. Friedberg, *In the Shadow of the Garrison State: America's Anti-Statism and its Cold War Grand Strategy* (Princeton, NJ: Princeton University Press, 2000); Amy Zegart, *Flawed by Design: The Evolution of the CIA, JCS, and NSC* (Stanford, CA: Stanford University Press, 1999); Douglas T. Stuart, *Creating the National Security State: A History of the Law That Transformed America* (Princeton, NJ: Princeton University Press, 2008). For the wartime activities of the Office of Strategic Services (OSS) and the Cold War operations of the Central Intelligence Agency (CIA), including in the Middle East, see Winks, *Cloak and Gown*; Price, *Anthropological Intelligence*; Allen, *Classical Spies*; Wilford, *America's Great Game*.

20. On the emergence of the Cold War university with an emphasis on science and technology, see Roger Geiger, *Research and Relevant Knowledge: American Research Universities since World War II* (New York: Oxford University Press, 1993); Christopher Simpson, *Science of Coercion: Communication Research and Psychological Warfare, 1945–1960* (New York: Oxford University Press, 1994); Stuart W. Leslie, *The Cold War and American Science: The Military-Industrial-Academic Complex at MIT and Stanford* (New York: Columbia University Press, 1993); Noam Chomsky et al., ed. *The Cold War and the University* (New York: The New Press, 1997); Rebecca S. Lowen, *Creating the Cold War University: The Transformation of Stanford* (Berkeley: University of California Press, 1997).

21. Several works have examined different aspects of the emergence of Middle East expertise, however, they only briefly discuss the interactions and influence of the U.S. government on the production and professionalization of knowledge about the region; see Zachary Lockman, *Contending Visions of the Middle East*; Lockman, *Field Notes: The Making of Middle East Studies in the United States* (Stanford, CA: Stanford University Press, 2016); Jacobs, *Imagining the Middle East*; Timothy Mitchell, "The Middle East in the Past and Future of Social Science," in *The Politics of Knowledge: Area Studies and the Disciplines,* ed. David Szanton (Berkeley: University of California Press, 2004); Lara Deeb and Jessica Winegar, *Anthropology's Politics: Disciplining the Middle East* (Stanford, CA: Stanford University Press, 2016); Peter Johnson and Judith Tucker, "Middle East Studies Network in the United States," *MERIP Reports* 38 (1974): 3–20, 26; Lisa Hajjar and Steve Niva, "(Re)Made in the USA: Middle East Studies in the Global Era," *Middle East Report* 205 (October–December 1997): 2–9.

22. Mitchell, "The Middle East in the Past and Future of Social Science," 2; Vicente Rafael, "The Culture of Area Studies in the United States," *Social Text* 41 (Winter 1994): 91–111.

1. Private Knowledge

Epigraph: Wilson quoted in Lawrence Gelfand, *The Inquiry: American Preparations for Peace, 1917–1919* (New Haven, CT: Yale University Press, 1963): 174.

1. Personal Diary of William Linn Westermann (hereafter Westermann Diary), December 4, 1918, 1, Columbia University Archives (hereafter CUA); "Nation Awaits Peace Plan," *New York Times,* December 1, 1918; "Transport Ready for the President," *New York Times,* December 2, 1918; "President Starts Abroad," *New York Times,* December 5, 1918.

2. The most exhaustive study is Gelfand's *The Inquiry.* Matthew Jacobs's *Imagining the Middle East: The Building of an American Foreign Policy, 1918–1967* (Chapel Hill: University of North Carolina Press, 2011) briefly discusses the Inquiry but not how its recommendations were adopted or ignored by Wilson. Michael Oren, *Power, Faith, and Fantasy: America in the Middle East, 1776 to the Present* (New York: W. W. Norton, 2007), has an abbreviated but favorable discussion of the group's activities. The Inquiry is most often discussed as part of broader studies on the Wilson presidency and the Paris Peace Conference; see John Milton Cooper, *Woodrow Wilson: A Biography* (New York: Alfred A. Knopf, 2009); Inga Floto, *Colonel House in Paris* (Princeton, NJ: Princeton University Press, 1980); Alexander L. George and Juliette L. George, *Woodrow Wilson and Colonel House: A Personality Study* (New York: John Day Company, 1956); Godfrey Hodgson, *Woodrow Wilson's Right Hand: The Life of Colonel Edward M. House* (New Haven, CT: Yale University Press, 2006); Thomas Knock, *To End All Wars: Woodrow Wilson and the Quest for a New World Order* (New York: Oxford University Press, 1992); Margaret MacMillan, *Paris 1919: Six Months That Changed the World* (New York: Random House, 2001); Charles E. Neu, *Colonel House: A Biography of Woodrow Wilson's Silent Partner* (New York: Oxford University Press, 2015).

3. For the State Department before and during World War II, see Phillip J. Baram, *The Department of State in the Middle East, 1919–1945* (Philadelphia: University of Pennsylvania Press, 1978); Bruce Kuklick, *Puritans in Babylon, The Ancient Near East and American Intellectual Life, 1880–1930* (Princeton, NJ: Princeton University Press, 1996). For interactions between the United States and the region prior to the mid-nineteenth century, see Oren, *Power, Faith, and Fantasy;* James A. Field, *America and the Mediterranean World, 1776–1882* (Princeton, NJ: Princeton University Press, 1969); Robert J. Allison, *The Crescent Obscured: The United States and the Muslim World, 1776–1816* (New York: Oxford University Press, 1995).

4. See Robert Kaplan, *The Arabists: The Romance of an American Elite* (New York: Free Press, 1993). For a critique of Kaplan's argument, see John Solecki, "Arabists and the Myth," *Middle East Journal* 44, no. 3 (Summer 1990): 446–457.

5. See Mehmet Ali Dögan and Heather Sharkey, eds. *American Missionaries and the Middle East: Foundational Encounters* (Salt Lake City: University of Utah Press, 2011) and Ussama Makdisi, *Artillery of Heaven: American Missionaries and the Failed Conversion of the Middle East* (Ithaca, NY: Cornell University Press, 2008).

6. Carleton S. Coon Jr., ed., *Daniel Bliss and the Founding of the American University of Beirut* (Washington, DC: Middle East Institute, 1989): 71–74; Joseph L. Grabill, *Protestant Diplomacy and the Near East: Missionary Influence on American Policy, 1810–1927* (Minneapolis: University of Minnesota Press, 1971): 24–34; Makdisi, *Artillery of Heaven*, 211–212; Ussama Makdisi, *Faith Misplaced: The Broken Promise of U.S.-Arab Relations, 1820–2001* (New York: Public Affairs, 2010): 61–67.

7. Makdisi, *Faith Misplaced*, 65–72. In addition to George Antonius's classic *The Arab Awakening,* see Abdulrazzak Patel, *The Arab Nahdah: The Making of the Intellectual and Humanist Movement* (Edinburgh: Edinburgh University Press, 2013), and Rashid Khalidi, Lisa Anderson, Muhammad Muslih, and Reeva Simon, eds., *The Origins of Arab Nationalism* (New York: Columbia University Press, 1991).

8. Grabill, *Protestant Diplomacy and the Near East,* 81–89; Karine V. Walther, *Sacred Interests: The United States and the Islamic World, 1821–1921* (Chapel Hill: University of North Carolina Press, 2015): 273.

9. John Milton Cooper Jr. *Woodrow Wilson: A Biography* (New York: Alfred A. Knopf, 2009): 420–421; Robert T. Handy, "Protestant Theological Tensions and Political Styles in the Progressive Period," in *Religion and American Politics,* ed. Mark A. Noll and Luke E. Harlow, 2nd ed. (New York: Oxford University Press, 2007): 227–240.

10. Cooper, *Woodrow Wilson,* 174–182

11. Ibid., 180–276.

12. Ibid., 285–295.

13. Woodrow Wilson, *The Papers of Woodrow Wilson* (hereafter *PWW*), Vol. 41, "An Address to a Joint Session of Congress," February 11, 1918, 519–527; Cooper, *Woodrow Wilson,* 385–386, 417–420. Wilson quoted in Cooper.

14. Cooper, *Woodrow Wilson,* 163; Gelfand, *The Inquiry,* 37–39. Wilson quoted in Cooper.

15. George Herring, *From Colony to Superpower: U.S. Foreign Relations since 1776* (New York: Oxford University Press, 2008): 381.

16. Ibid., 40–44; Ronald Steel, *Walter Lippmann and the American Century* (Boston: Little, Brown, 1980): 128–129. Shotwell's quote originally cited in Gelfand.

17. Steel, *Walter Lippmann,* 133–134; Cooper, *Woodrow Wilson,* 420–421. According to Cooper, an earlier version of the memorandum was delivered on Christmas Day, which Wilson did not review due to the holiday. The revised version served as the basis for the Fourteen Points speech.

18. Cooper, *Woodrow Wilson,* 421–424; Woodrow Wilson, *PWW,* Vol. 45, "An Address to a Joint Session of Congress," January 8, 1918, 534–539.

19. Cooper, *Woodrow Wilson*, 421–423.

20. Wilson, *PWW,* Vol. 46, "An Address to a Joint Session of Congress," February 11, 1918, 318–324.

21. Trygve Throntveit, "The Fable of the Fourteen Points: Woodrow Wilson and National Self-Determination," *Diplomatic History* 35, no. 3 (June 2011): 445–481. Throntveit asserts that Wilson's language in the "Four Points" speech was "irresponsible." He adds, "Wilson's nice distinctions between self-government and self-determination were known only to his closest advisors—and even they saw but dimly into his mind."

22. *PWW,* Vol. 5, "The Modern Democratic State," December 1885, 71–76. See also Ronald J. Pestritto, *Woodrow Wilson and the Roots of Modern Liberalism* (New York: Rowman & Littlefield, 2005): 68–69.

23. See Erez Manela, *The Wilsonian Moment: Self-Determination and the International Origins of Anticolonial Nationalism* (New York: Oxford University Press, 2007).

24. See Gary Gerstle, "Race and Nation in the Thought and Politics of Woodrow Wilson," in *Reconsidering Woodrow Wilson: Progressivism, Internationalism, War and Peace,* ed. John Milton Cooper Jr. (Baltimore: Johns Hopkins University Press, 2008): 93–94.

25. "Report on the Inquiry: Its Scope and Method," March 20, 1918, Document 883, Inquiry Records, Entry M1107, Roll 43, United States National Archives and Records Administration, College Park, Maryland (hereafter NARACP). The memorandum explained that for each disputed area the Inquiry needed to collect the following data: "what resources human and material it contains, what is the concrete interest of each power in the area, what political group or groups within each power are concerned in that interest." In addition, it would be "necessary also to know the place of that area in the general plan of each power's foreign policy."

26. Gelfand, *The Inquiry,* 47–48; *Foreign Relations of the United States (hereafter FRUS), The Paris Peace Conference, 1919, Vol. I,* 97–98.

27. See Gelfand, *The Inquiry,* 47–51, 60–63, 76–77, 227. Coolidge quoted in Gelfand. For a similar assessment of the Western Asia division's experts by William Yale, the State Department's "special agent" in the region, see Scott Anderson, *Lawrence in Arabia: War, Deceit, Imperial Folly, and the Making of the Modern Middle East* (New York: Doubleday, 2013): 488. Also see R. Bayly Winder, "Four Decades of Middle Eastern Study," *Middle East Journal* 41, no. 1 (Winter 1987): 40–41.

28. *FRUS, The Paris Peace Conference, 1919, Vol. I,* 20.

29. Gelfand, *The Inquiry,* 60. Gelfand notes that the scholars in the Balkans group fell into two categories. The first he described as Americans from different disciplines that traveled in the region at one time. The second were immigrants from southeastern Europe living in the United States, which included Dominian. One characteristic of the latter group, he explained,

was that their "training and experience had not provided any professional competency for handling or criticizing the source materials."

30. Leo Dominian, "The Mohammedan World," May 20, 1918, Document 137, 1, Inquiry Records, Entry M1107, NARACP.

31. Dominian, "The Mohammedan World," 71.

32. Leo Dominian, "The Arab Problem in Relation to Syria, Palestine, and Mesopotamia," April 15, 1918, Document 1016, Inquiry Records, Entry M1107, NARACP.

33. Ibid.

34. Leo Dominian, "Arabia," March 31, 1918, Document 1018, Inquiry Records, Entry M1107, Roll 47, NARACP.

35. Westermann Diary, March 23, 1919, 46–47. William Westermann recorded in his diary that Dominian was mistakenly invited (or invited himself) to meet with Secretary of State Robert Lansing in order to participate in the Inter-Allied Commission to Syria (later known as the King-Crane Commission). Westermann raised his objections to Isaiah Bowman, writing that "[I] told him my mind about Dominian and any connection of his with this inter-allied commission, which was to the effect that Dominian did not do and must not have any connection with it. Bowman saw the point and was willing to fix it."

36. E. H. Byrne, "Report on the Desires of Syrians," October 7, 1918, Document 82, Inquiry Records, Entry M1107, NARACP.

37. Ibid.

38. Howard Crosby Butler, "Report on the Proposals for an Independent Arab State of States," undated, Document 79, 36, Entry M1107, NARACP.

39. Ibid.

40. William Westermann and Others, "Report upon the Just and Practical Boundaries for subdivisions of the Turkish Empire," undated, 1–2, Document 606, Inquiry Records, Entry M1107, NARACP. On Westermann's background, see John Allen, "Inventing the Middle East," *On Wisconsin* (Winter 2004): 36–39.

41. Westermann and Others, "Report upon the Just and Practical Boundaries for subdivisions of the Turkish Empire," 3.

42. Ibid., 3–4

43. Ibid., 35–37.

44. Ibid., 37–38.

45. Ibid., 55–56.

46. On the Eastern Question, see Huseyin Yilmaz, "The Eastern Question and the Ottoman Empire: The Genesis of the Near and Middle East in the Nineteenth Century," in *Is There a Middle East? The Evolution of a Geopolitical Concept*, ed. Michael Bonine, Abbas Amanat, and Michael Gasper (Stanford, CA: Stanford University Press, 2011): 11–35; also Osamah Khalil, "The Crossroads of the World: U.S. and British Foreign Policy Doctrines and the Construct of the Middle East, 1902–2007," *Diplomatic History* 38, no. 2 (April 2014): 299–344.

47. Ali A. Allawi, *Faisal I of Iraq* (New Haven, CT: Yale University Press, 2014): 5–6, 60–62. See also MacMillan, *Paris 1919*, 387–388; Makdisi, *Faith Misplaced*, 127–128;

48. MacMillan, *Paris 1919*, 374; Makdisi, *Faith Misplaced*, 128.

49. Charles Smith, *Palestine and the Arab-Israeli Conflict*, 4th ed. (Boston: Bedford/St. Martins, 2001): 35–36. See also Walter Laqueur, *A History of Zionism: From the French Revolution to the Establishment of the State of Israel* (New York: Shocken Books, 1976).

50. Tom Segev, *One Palestine, Complete* (New York: Henry Holt, 1999): 39–49, 70–76; Rashid Khalidi, *The Iron Cage: The Story of the Palestinian Struggle for Statehood* (Boston: Beacon Press, 2006): 32–33. Segev notes that at the time of the Balfour Declaration the Zionist movement was "highly fragmented, with activists working independently in different capitals."

51. Segev, *One Palestine*, 36–39. Lloyd George quoted in Segev.

52. Wilson quoted in Lawrence Davidson, *America's Palestine: Popular and Official Perceptions from Balfour to Israeli Statehood* (Gainesville: University Press of Florida, 2001): 15–17.

53. Segev, *One Palestine*, 13, 50–54; MacMillan, *Paris 1919*, 415. Lloyd George quoted in MacMillan.

54. Segev, *One Palestine*, 50–55.

55. "Palestine," David Magie, undated, Document 364, Inquiry Records, Entry M1107, NARACP. Emphasis in original. For discussions of official and popular perceptions of Palestine, see Davidson, *America's Palestine*, and Kathleen Christison, *Perceptions of Palestine: Their Influence on U.S. Middle East Policy* (Berkeley: University of California Press, 2001). On the Ottoman parliament, see Michelle U. Campos, *Ottoman Brothers: Muslims, Christians, and Jews in Early Twentieth-Century Palestine* (Stanford, CA: Stanford University Press, 2011).

56. Westermann Diary, February 4, 1919, 32. It is unclear which report Westermann was referring to, although it may be the aforementioned "Report upon the Just and Practical Boundaries for subdivisions of the Turkish Empire," which was authored by Westermann "and others." The notation "and others" was handwritten on the report's cover page.

57. Macmillan, *Paris 1919*, 53.

58. Robert Lansing, *Peace Negotiations: A Personal Narrative* (New York: Houghton Mifflin, 1921): 97–98.

59. Neil Smith, *American Empire: Roosevelt's Geographer and the Prelude to Globalization* (Berkeley: University of California Press, 2003): 143–147.

60. Westermann Diary, January 16, 1919, 20.

61. Allawi, *Faisal I of Iraq*, 70–173, 197; Rustum Haidar, *Mudhakkirāt Rustum Haidar* (Beirut: Dar al-Arabiya al-Mawsou'at, 1988): 220.

62. Westermann Diary, January 20, 1919, 24–25.

63. Allawi, *Faisal I of Iraq*, 197; Haidar, *Mudhakkirāt Rustum Haidar*, 220.

64. Allawi, *Faisal I of Iraq*, 197; Haidar, *Mudhakkirāt Rustum Haidar*, 220; Westermann Diary, January 27, 1919, 29; Ernest Hamlin Abbott, "An Interview with Prince Feisal," *Outlook*, April 2, 1919.

65. Cooper, *Woodrow Wilson*, 467–471.

66. Allawi, *Faisal I of Iraq*, 183–184, 197–203; Zeine N. Zeine, *The Struggle for Arab Independence: Western Diplomacy and the Rise and Fall of Faisal's Kingdom in Syria* (New York: Caravan Books, 1977): 62–67; FRUS, *The Paris Peace Conference, 1919, Vol. III*, 889–891.

67. FRUS, *The Paris Peace Conference, 1919, Vol. III*, 892.

68. Ibid., 1016–1018.

69. Ibid., 1019–1020.

70. Westermann Diary, February 12, 1919, 35.

71. Makdisi, *Faith Misplaced*, 134–135.

72. Westermann Diary, March 23, 1919, 46–48; April 4, 1919, 54–55.

73. See Priya Satia, *Spies in Arabia: The Great War and the Cultural Foundations of Britain's Covert Empire in the Middle East* (New York: Oxford University Press, 2008): 35–38.

74. Westermann Diary, March 23, 1919, 46–48. Bell's assessment matched her own report to London on "Self Determination in Mesopotamia"; see Georgina Howell, *Gertrude Bell: Queen of the Desert, Shaper of Nations* (New York: Farrar, Straus and Giroux, 2006): 307–309.

75. Westermann Diary, April 15, May 13, and May 16, 1919, 60, 73–74; Westermann apparently objected to Lybyer's appointment and informed his former colleague that "he did not know much about Syria." On Lybyer's role, see Harry N. Howard, *An American Inquiry in the Middle East: The King-Crane Commission* (Beirut: Khayats, 1963), and Andrew Patrick, *America's Forgotten Middle East Initiative: The King-Crane Commission of 1919* (London: I. B. Tauris, 2015).

76. Westerman Diary, May 17, 1919, 74.

77. Ibid., June 20 and 30, 1919, 91–94. Maalouf also admitted that the British were paying a monthly stipend of £150,000 to Faysal until the peace treaty was declared. A portion of those funds were used to attend the conference.

78. See John Milton Cooper, *Breaking the Heart of the World: Woodrow Wilson and the Fight for the League of Nations* (Cambridge: Cambridge University Press, 2010).

79. Neil Smith, *American Empire*, 81–88, 106–108. On the Mandate system, see Susan Pedersen, *The Guardians: The League of Nations and the Crisis of Empire* (New York: Oxford University Press, 2015).

80. Neil Smith, *American Empire*, 84; MacMillan, *Paris 1919*, 406, 423.

81. MacMillan, *Paris 1919*, 406; Edward M. House, "The Versailles Peace in Retrospect," in *What Really Happened at Paris: The Story of the Peace Conference, 1918–1919*, ed. Edward Mandell House and Charles Seymour (New York: Charles Scribner's Sons, 1921): 432; Allawi records similar sentiments by Lloyd George and Lansing; see Allawi, *Faisal I of Iraq*, 203–205.

82. Mary C. Wilson, *King Abdullah, Britain, and the Making of Jordan* (Cambridge: Cambridge University Press, 1990): 36–45.

83. See Eugene Rogan, *The Fall of the Ottomans: The Great War in the Middle East* (New York: Basic Books, 2015): 393–395; MacMillan, *Paris 1919*, 442–455;

84. Westermann Diary, May 17, 1919, 78.

85. Gelfand disputed Lansing's claim and argued that the Inquiry's recommendations served as a baseline for the negotiations; see *The Inquiry*, 321–323.

86. Sidney E. Mezes, "Preparations for Peace" in House and Seymour, *What Really Happened at Paris*, 5.

87. Ibid., 3, 14.

88. Isaiah Bowman, "Constantinople and the Balkans," in House and Seymour, *What Really Happened at Paris*, 154–155.

89. Neil Smith, *American Empire*, 172.

90. Ibid., 156–162; Neu, *Colonel House*, 405–406, 422.

91. Edward M. House, "The Versailles Peace in Retrospect," 425–426, 437.

92. William Westermann, "The Armenian Problem and the disruption of Turkey," in House and Seymour, *What Really Happened at Paris*, 177.

93. Allen, "Inventing the Middle East." See also, Baram, *The Department of State in the Middle East*, 132–133.

94. Neil Smith, *American Empire*, 192–196. Bowman quoted in Smith. See Inderjeet Parmar, *Think Tanks and Power in Foreign Policy: A Comparative Study of the Role and Influence of the Council on Foreign Relations and the Royal Institute of International Affairs* (New York: Palgrave MacMillan, 2004), for the growing post–World War I relationship between the two institutions. For the CFR's early history, see Michael Wala, *The Council on Foreign Relations and American Foreign Policy in the Early Cold War* (Providence: Berghahn Books, 1994): 1–56.

95. Lippmann to Donovan, July 31, 1941, OSS Director's Office Files, M1642, Roll 66, NARACP.

2. Wartime Expertise

Epigraph: "Adventures in the Arab World, 1896–1961," unpublished autobiography manuscript, William A. Eddy Personal Papers, Box 1, Princeton University Archives (hereafter PUA).

1. "Yale 'News' Poll Reveals Bulldogs Swing to War," "Harvard, Yale Glee Clubs to Sing Tonight," *Harvard Crimson*, November 21, 1941; United Press, "Over the Wire: Nazis Bombard Russians," *Harvard Crimson*, November 21, 1941; "Gala Activities Highlight Weekend," *Yale Daily News*, November 22, 1941.

2. Thomas F. Troy, *Donovan and the CIA: A History of the Establishment of the Central Intelligence Agency* (Frederick, MD: University Publications of America, 1981): 106–107. Troy explains that the Special Information Services was a forerunner of the Secret Intelligence (SI) branch of the Office of

Strategic Services (OSS) and Phillips was tasked with recruiting agents for overseas assignments.

3. For prior efforts, including naval and military intelligence, see Rhodri Jeffreys-Jones, "The Role of British Intelligence in the Mythologies Underpinning the OSS and Early CIA," *Intelligence and National Security* 15, no. 2 (Summer 2000): 5–19; Rhodri Jeffreys-Jones, "Antecedents and Memory as Factors in the Creation of the CIA," *Diplomatic History* 40, no. 1 (2016): 140–154; Richard Immerman, *The Hidden Hand: A Brief History of the CIA* (Malden, MA : John Wiley & Sons, 2014): 9–10.

4. Carleton Coon, *Adventures and Discoveries: The Autobiography of Carleton Coon* (Englewood Cliffs, NJ: Prentice Hall, 1981): 162; Carleton Coon, "Torch Anthology," 4, RG 226, Entry 99, Box 49, United States National Archives and Records Administration, College Park, Maryland (hereafter NARACP); Coon, *A North Africa Story: The Anthropologist as OSS Agent, 1941–1943* (Ipswich, MA: Gambit, 1980): 5–6. There is a discrepancy in Coon's different accounts of the meeting with Phillips. In *Adventures and Discoveries,* he states that the meeting occurred the day before the game in his office. However, in "Torch Anthology" and *A North Africa Story,* Coon reports that the meeting occurred the day of the game.

5. Coon, *Adventures and Discoveries,* 162; Coon, *A North Africa Story,* 6.

6. Burton Hersh, *The Old Boys: The American Elite and the Origins of the CIA* (New York: Maxwell Macmillan International, 1992): 1–35, 54–55; Rhodri Jeffreys-Jones, *In Spies We Trust: The Story of Western Intelligence* (New York: Oxford University Press, 2013): 68–94.

7. "History of OSS-Cairo," undated, RG 226, Entry 99, Box 54, OSS, NARACP; Barry Katz, *Foreign Intelligence: Research and Analysis in the Office of Strategic Services, 1942–1945* (Cambridge, MA: Harvard University Press, 1989): 1–3.

8. Troy, *Donovan and the CIA,* 419–420.

9. Archibald MacLeish to William Donovan, June 29, 1941, Box 1, William J. Donovan Papers, U.S. Army Heritage and Education Center (hereafter WJD, USAHEC).

10. Katz, *Foreign Intelligence,* 5.

11. Ibid.; William L. Langer, *In and Out of the Ivory Tower: The Autobiography of William L. Langer* (New York: N. Watson Academic Publications, 1977): 181–187.

12. Langer, *In and Out of the Ivory Tower,* 182.

13. Troy, *Foreign Intelligence,* 427.

14. Walter Wright to William Langer, January 14, 1942; John Wilson to Langer, December 14, 1942, RG 226, Entry 146, Box 135, OSS, NARACP; Robin Winks, *Cloak and Gown: Scholars in the Secret War, 1939–1961* (New York: William Morrow, 1987): 84–85.

15. J. C. Hurewitz, "The Education of J. C. Hurewitz," in *Paths to the Middle East: Ten Scholars Look Back,* ed. Thomas Naff (Albany: State University of

New York Press, 1993): 69–73. For a discussion of the different missionary organizations, see Joseph L. Grabill, *Protestant Diplomacy and the Near East: Missionary Influence on American Policy, 1810–1927* (Minneapolis: University of Minnesota Press, 1971): 3–34.

16. Hurewitz, "The Education of J. C. Hurewitz."

17. E. A. Speiser, "Near Eastern Studies in America, 1939–1945," *Archiv Orientalni* 1–2, December 1947: 87.

18. Philip K. Hitti Personal Papers, Box 1, American University of Beirut Jafet Library Archive and Special Collection (hereafter AUBA); John R. Starkey, "A Talk with Philip Hitti," *ARAMCO World*, July/August 1971.

19. Harold Dodds to Dana Munro, May 26, 1942, AC 129, Box 13, PUA. The School for Public and International Affairs at Princeton was renamed the Woodrow Wilson School of Public and International Affairs in 1948.

20. Dana G. Munro, "School of Public and International Affairs Memorandum," June 30, 1942, PUA; "Princeton University Army Specialized Training Program, Area and Language, Arabic and Turkish," undated, AC 129, Box 13, PUA.

21. "Plan for Training Program for Military Government Work in Near Eastern Area," undated, AC 129, Box 13, PUA.

22. "Strictly Confidential," undated, AC 129, Box 13, PUA.

23. Wright to Langer, "Conversations with Professor Philip K. Hitti," November 11, 1941, RG 226, Entry 146, Box 135, OSS, NARACP.

24. Donovan to Roosevelt, February 10, 1942, RG 226, Entry M1642, Roll 22, OSS, NARACP. Donovan provided President Roosevelt with copies and informed him that 250 copies of each guide were produced and provided to the War Department to be distributed to servicemen.

25. "Life in Egypt," "Life in the Persian Gulf," and "Life in Eritrea," all undated, RG 226, Entry 146, Box 135, OSS, NARACP. Although no author is listed, based on his responsibilities at the time, Harold Glidden was likely responsible for producing (or at least contributing to) the Egypt travel guide.

26. "Short Guide to Syria," April 22, 1942, R&A 624, RG 226, Entry M1221, OSS, NARACP. "Syria" encompassed Syria and Lebanon, both under French Mandates and were governed by Free French forces.

27. In contrast, the North Africa guide warned, "*Never strike them. They do not know how to box; one right on the jaw would knock a Moslem down*" (emphasis in original). "A Pocket Guide to North Africa," 1943, War and Navy Department: 38. An electronic version is available at https://archive.org /details/PocketGuideToNorthAfrica (last accessed June 21, 2015).

28. Ibid. The original draft offered even more explicit (and questionable) advice considering that "common sense" was to be used at all times, including, "Shake hands with Arabs; otherwise, don't touch them. Don't strike Arabs. Urinate and defecate in private. Don't expose your genitals in the presence of Arabs. Don't break wind noticeably in their presence."

29. "A Short Guide to Iraq," War and Navy Departments, 1943: 4. The final version is available at https://archive.org/details/AShortGuideToIraq_175 (last accessed June 21, 2015); "Short Guide to Iraq, R&A No. 633/Report No. 45," May 13, 1942, Box 42A, WJD, USAHEC. Like the Syria guide, the draft Iraq guide produced by the OSS offered advice that was excised or modified from the final version. For example, the reference to Lawrence was absent. The draft Iraq guide also warned that "the Occidental skull isn't adapted to the penetrating Oriental sun." However, this sentence did not appear in the final version. Instead, the guide warned about the dangers of extended exposure to the sun and extreme heat.

30. Donovan to Joint Chiefs of Staff (JCS), July 27, 1942, RG 226, Entry 1642, Roll 18; "History of OSS-Cairo," undated, RG 226, Entry 99, Box 54, OSS, NARACP.

31. "Subcommittee of Joint Psychological Warfare Committee, Verbatim Report, July 29, 1942," RG 226, M1642, Roll 8, OSS, NARACP. The initial officers assigned to Cairo were Lieutenant Turner McBaine and Lieutenant Commander Joseph Leete, a former instructor at the American University in Cairo (AUC) who was fluent in Arabic.

32. "History of OSS-Cairo," undated, RG 226, Entry 99, Box 54, OSS, NARACP. The History of OSS-Cairo notes, "So far as is known this was the first time that the United States was given British SIS reports directly and with no restrictions on their official use in the United States. It had been the invariable insistence of the British that our agencies, such as State, War, and Navy, obtain British SIS reports only after they had passed through the Foreign Office, War Office and Admiralty, thus subjecting them to possible British policy control. Even reports obtained from the London headquarters of British SIS were marked 'For the attention of Colonel Donovan and one other high ranking officer only,' and it was forbidden for COI to disseminate them to other United States officials."

33. Ibid. According to the official history, the Near East section "did not at the time realize the advantages to be gained by having a field coordinator in close contact with its agents, and in many cases it did not even notify Lieutenant McBaine when a representative was sent to his post." It added that in some cases the inability to obtain clearance "proved to be a source of embarrassment" for McBaine and the Near East section.

34. Nelson Glueck to Walter Wright, Glueck to Wallace Phillips, December 12, 1941, RG 226, Entry 210, Box 383, OSS, NARACP.

35. "Curriculum Vitae of Nelson Glueck," December 24, 1941, RG 226, Entry 210, Box 383, OSS, NARACP.

36. Ibid.

37. Ibid.

38. Ibid.; "Memorandum on the Strategic importance of Palestine and Transjordan," February 3, 1942, RG 226, Entry 210, Box 383, OSS, NARACP.

39. Glueck to Henry Field, February 10, 1942, RG 226, Entry 210, Box 383, OSS, NARACP.

40. David Williamson to David Bruce, February 28, 1942, RG 226, Entry 210, Box 383, OSS, NARACP.

41. William Hicks to Caleb, May 24, 1943 and August 20, 1943, RG 226, Entry 210, Box 383, OSS, NARACP.

42. "Archeology after the War," RG 226, Entry 210, Box 383, OSS, NARACP.

43. William Hicks to Caleb, May 24, 1943, RG 226, Entry 210, Box 383, OSS, NARACP.

44. George Marshall to William Donovan, December 23, 1942, WJD, US-AHEC; Winks, *Cloak and Gown*, 84–85. Donovan quoted in Winks. The full reports for Morocco, Tunisia, and Algeria can be found in Donovan's papers at USAHEC.

45. "Psychological Warfare in North Africa," July 20, 1942, RG 226, M1642, Roll 34, OSS, NARACP.

46. Ibid.

47. Coon, *Adventures and Discoveries*, 162; Coon, *A North Africa Story*, 6.

48. "Torch Anthology," RG 226, Entry 99, Box 49, OSS, NARACP. Apparently this was not Coon's first issue with the State Department. In the Torch Anthology, Coon reported that because of a 1933 incident in Ethiopia (which he did not describe further), he was on the State Department's blacklist and the OSS had difficulty obtaining a diplomatic cover for him.

49. "Job Description in the Case of Carleton Steven Coon," July 10, 1943, "Halliwell to Guenther," August 4, 1943, RG 226, Entry 1568, and "Torch Anthology," RG 226, Entry 99, Box 49, NARACP.

50. "Torch Anthology," 14; Coon, *Adventures and Discoveries*, 164.

51. The full translation of the text is quoted in David Price, *Anthropological Intelligence: The Deployment and Neglect of American Anthropology in the Second World War* (Durham, NC: Duke University Press, 2008): 250.

52. "Torch Anthology," 14–15. Coon wrote that this was the OSS's sole print propaganda success. He explained that the British experienced similar frustrations, "They had bales of funny books and cartoons which the Arabs could not understand or did not consider funny." Britain had apparent success with an ornately decorated card for the Muslim holy month of Ramadan, which they provided to the OSS agents to distribute and were in turn given copies of the modified Roosevelt speech.

53. William Hicks to Caleb, August 20, 1943, RG 226, Entry 210, Box 383, OSS, NARACP.

54. William Hicks to Caleb, March 15, 1944, RG 226, Entry 210, Box 383, OSS, NARACP.

55. Gordon Loud to Shepardson, November 2, 1943 and November 3, 1943, RG 226, Entry 210, Box 383, OSS, NARACP.

56. "Deleted from Hicks newsletter #3," May 15, 1944. RG 226, Entry 210, Box 383, OSS, NARACP.

57. *Foreign Relations of the United States (hereafter FRUS), The Near East, South Asia, and Africa, the Far East, 1944, Vol. V,* 1.

58. *FRUS, The Near East and Africa, 1943, Vol. IV,* 859–860, 921. At the end of 1944, then secretary of the navy James Forrestal detailed the United States' strategic interest in developing and protecting Persian Gulf oil in a memo to Secretary of State Edward Stettinius. Forrestal stated that "it is patently in the Navy's interest that no part of the national wealth, as represented by the present holdings of foreign oil reserves by American nationals, be lost at this time. Indeed, the active expansion of such holdings is very much to be desired." See *FRUS, The Near East, South Asia, and Africa, the Far East, 1944, Vol. V,* 755–756.

59. *FRUS, The British Commonwealth and Europe, 1944, Vol. III,* 15–18. In their memorandum of conversation, the State Department representatives stated that the legal questions regarding the disposition of the different territories were "complicated and novel." While Iraq was already independent and Syria and Lebanon were to become independent after the war, the British political leadership asserted that "Palestine must under any circumstance have special treatment."

60. E. A. Speiser to William Langer, April 19, 1944, RG 226, Entry 1, Box 6, OSS, NARACP.

61. Ibid.

62. Speiser to Sherman Kent, October 20, 1944, RG 226, Entry 1, Box 6, OSS, NARACP.

63. Ibid.

64. Ibid.

65. Langer to Aldrich, October 23, 1944, RG 226, Entry 1, Box 23, OSS, NARACP.

66. Richard Frye, *Greater Iran: A 20th Century Odyssey* (Costa Mesa, CA.: Mazda Publishers, 2005): 1–15.

67. Ibid., 47–56.

68. "OSS Cairo to American Legation, Kabul," March 18, 1944, RG 226, Entry 215, Box 1, OSS, NARACP. The letter noted that in the past, Afghanistan had been the responsibility of the OSS's India Office, but "for some reason" was now included in the Near East and under the purview of OSS Cairo.

69. "Position of American Teachers in Afghanistan," August 19, 1944, RG 226, Entry 215, Box 1, OSS, NARACP.

70. Richard Frye to Caleb, June 28, 1944, Richard Frye to Caleb, January 29, 1945, RG 226, Entry 215, Box 1, OSS, NARACP.

71. Frye, *Greater Iran,* 66–81.

72. "Survey of Iranian Oil Concessions, R&A No. 1981.1," April 8, 1944; "Iranian Oil as a Potential Source of Political Conflict, R&A No. 1981.2," May 9, 1944; "The Three Power Problem in Iran, R&A No. 2201," July 13, 1944; Box 42A, WJD, USAHEC.

73. Carleton Coon to William Donovan, "Intelligence Work in Arab Countries," September 22, 1944, RG 226, Entry 210, Box 354, OSS, NARACP.

74. Ibid.

75. Ibid.

76. Price, *Anthropological Intelligence*, 255–259.

77. Thomas W. Lippmann, *Arabian Knight: Colonel Bill Eddy USMC and the Rise of American Power in the Middle East* (Vista, CA: Selwa Press, 2008): 112–113.

78. "JCS to Roosevelt, Subject: Oil Reserves," June 8, 1943, *FRUS, The Near East and Africa, 1943, Vol. IV*, 921. Roosevelt quoted in Lloyd C. Gardner, *Three Kings: The Rise of an American Empire in the Middle East after World War II* (New York: The New Press, 2009): 26–27.

79. Stettinius to Roosevelt, December 22, 1944, *FRUS, The Near East, South Asia, and Africa, the Far East, 1944, Vol. V*, 757–758.

80. Lippmann, *Arabian Knight*, 112–125.

81. William A. Eddy, *FDR Meets Ibn Saud* (New York: American Friends of the Middle East, 1954): 14, 23.

82. Ibid., 33–37.

83. Langer, *In and Out of the Ivory Tower*, 230–231; David C. Engerman, *Know Your Enemy: The Rise and Fall of America's Soviet Experts* (New York: Oxford University Press, 2009): 45–48.

84. Crane to Lange, "World Regions in the Social Sciences: Report of a Committee of the Social Science Research Council," June 2, 1943, RG 226, Entry 146, Box 121, OSS, NARACP. In addition to Mortimer Graves (ACLS) and Philip Hitti (Princeton), other attendees included Elizabeth Bacon and W. Duncan Strong (Ethnogeographic Board), J. M. Cowan (ACLS), Donald Young (SSRC), Marvin Niehuss (University of Michigan), Miller D. Steever (Lafayette), William C. De Vane (Yale), John Dodds (Stanford), Cornelius W. deKiewiet (Cornell), W. Freeman Twaddell (University of Wisconsin), John Fogg Jr. (University of Pennsylvania), William N. Fenton (Bureau of American Ethnology, Smithsonian Institute), Charles Hyneman (U.S. Army Training Branch), David Stevens, Joseph Willits, John Marshall, and Roger Evans (Rockefeller Foundation).

85. Crane to Langer, "World Regions in the Social Sciences."

86. "The Conference on Area and Language Programs in American Universities," March 15–16, 1944, RG 1.1, Series 1.1, Sub-Series Area and Language Studies, Box 210, Rockefeller Foundation Archives (hereafter RFA).

87. Ibid.

88. Ibid.

89. Ibid.

90. Ibid.

91. Bradley Smith, *The Shadow Warriors: O.S.S. and the Origins of the C.I.A.* (New York: Basic Books, 1983): 206–207. After the war, the SSU was transferred to the War Department and a year later was transferred again to the Central Intelligence Group's Office of Special Operation.

92. S1297, "Hearings on Science Legislation," October 31, 1945, Record Group 286, National Archives and Records Administration, Washington, DC (hereafter NARADC).

93. Ibid.

94. Testimony of Wesley C. Mitchell, October 29, 1945, S1297, Record Group 286, NARADC.

95. Ibid.

96. Suzanne Mettler, *Soldiers to Citizens: The G.I. Bill and the Making of the Greatest Generation* (New York: Oxford University Press, 2005): 42. By 1947 over one million veterans enrolled in college, a fivefold increase from the previous year. Two years later, the number of veterans in college doubled. When eligibility ended for World War II veterans, 7.8 million (51 percent of all who severed in the military) had attended school or training, of which 2.2 million veterans attended college or university.

97. Douglas Waller, *Wild Bill Donovan: The Spymaster Who Created the OSS and Modern American Espionage* (New York: Free Press, 2011): 304–318.

98. Katz, *Foreign Intelligence*, 17–18; Hugh Wilford, *America's Great Game: The CIA's Secret Arabists and the Shaping of the Modern Middle East* (New York: Basic Books, 2013): 55.

99. Gordon Merriam to Loy Henderson, November 2, 1945, RG59, Entry 1434, Box 1, NARACP.

100. See Robert Vitalis, *America's Kingdom: Mythmaking on the Saudi Oil Frontier* (Stanford, CA: Stanford University Press, 2007).

101. McGeorge Bundy, "The Battlefields of Power and the Searchlights of the Academy," in *The Dimensions of Diplomacy*, ed. E. A. J. Johnson (Baltimore: Johns Hopkins University Press, 1964): 2–3; Immanuel Wallerstein, "The Unintended Consequences of Cold War Area Studies," in *The Cold War and the University*, ed. Noam Chomsky et al. (New York: The New Press, 1997): 195–232; Peter Novick, *That Noble Dream: The "Objectivity Question" and the American Historical Profession* (Cambridge: Cambridge University Press, 1988).

3. A Time of National Emergency

Epigraph: "Address before the Commission on Colleges and Universities, North Central Association of Colleges and Secondary Schools, Chicago, Illinois," March 29, 1951, Record Group (RG) 59, Entry 5091, Box 556, United States National Archives and Records Administration, College Park, Maryland (hereafter NARACP).

1. David McCullough, *Truman* (New York: Simon & Schuster, 1992): 546–548.

2. Scholars have given the origins of the Truman Doctrine and its relationship to the Middle East significant attention, see Melvyn Leffler, *A Preponderance of Power: National Security, the Truman Administration, and the Cold War* (Stanford, CA: Stanford University Press, 1993); John Lewis Gaddis, *Strategies of Containment: A Critical Appraisal of American National Security*

Policy during the Cold War (New York: Oxford University Press, 1982); Arnold Offner, *Another Such Victory: President Truman and the Cold War, 1945–1953* (Stanford, CA: Stanford University Press, 2002); Bruce R. Kuniholm, *The Origins of the Cold War in the Near East: Great Power Conflict and Diplomacy in Iran, Turkey, and Greece* (Princeton, NJ: Princeton University Press, 1980); Lloyd C. Gardner, *Three Kings: The Rise of an American Empire in the Middle East after World War II* (New York: The New Press, 2009).

3. Thomas McCormick uses the term "ins-and-outers" to describe members of the "foreign policy elite" that alternated between the public and private sectors. See McCormick, *America's Half-Century: United States Foreign Policy in the Cold War and After,* 2nd ed. (Baltimore: Johns Hopkins University Press, 1995): 12–16.

4. See Thomas Etzold, "American Organization for National Security, 1945–50," in *Containment: Documents on American Policy and Strategy 1945–1950,* ed. Thomas Etzold and John Lewis Gaddis (New York: Columbia University Press, 1978): 10–11; Anna Kasten Nelson, "President Truman and the Evolution of the National Security Council," *Journal of American History* 72 (1985): 369–374. See Amy Zegart's *Flawed by Design: The Evolution of the CIA, JCS, and NSC* (Stanford, CA: Stanford University Press, 1999) and Douglas Stuart's *Creating the National Security State: A History of the Law That Transformed America* (Princeton, NJ: Princeton University Press, 2008) for the creation of the NSC and its role in policy formation. See Arthur Darling, *The Central Intelligence Agency: An Instrument of Government to 1950* (University Park: Pennsylvania State University Press, 1990): 183–184, for a discussion on the creation of the position of Director of Central Intelligence (DCI) and the creation of the Central Intelligence Group (CIG) after the OSS was dissolved.

5. Timothy Weiner, *Legacy of Ashes: The History of the CIA* (New York: Doubleday, 2007): 28–29; Finance Division to Executive, Office of Policy Coordination (OPC), "CIA Responsibility and Accountability for ECA Counterpart Funds Expended by OPC," October 17, 1949, in *The CIA under Harry Truman: CIA Cold War Records,* ed. Michael Warner (Honolulu: University Press of the Pacific, 2005): 321–322. The Economic Cooperation Administration (ECA), the agency that managed the Marshall Plan funds, had "no specific policies or regulations to govern the expenditures of the funds by the CIA." Funds were used to "purchase a newspaper for a labor group, the underwriting of a peace conference, direct propaganda and other miscellaneous activities."

6. "National Security Council Intelligence Directive No. 2," January 13, 1948, *Foreign Relations of the United States (hereafter FRUS), Emergence of the Intelligence Establishment, 1945–1950, Retrospective Volume,* http://history.state .gov/historicaldocuments/frus1945-50Intel/d425 (last accessed January 4, 2013); "National Security Council Intelligence Directive No. 4," December 12, 1947, *FRUS, Emergence of the Intelligence Establishment,* http://

history.state.gov/historicaldocuments/frus1945-50Intel/d422 (last accessed January 4, 2014); "National Security Council Intelligence Directive No. 7," February 12, 1948, *FRUS, Emergence of the Intelligence Establishment,* http://history.state.gov/historicaldocuments/frus1945-50Intel/d427. See also Hugh Wilford, *The Mighty Wurlitzer: How the CIA Played America* (Cambridge, MA: Harvard University Press, 2008): 25–28.

7. For example, the discussions and negotiations between academic societies, foundations, and the nascent national security establishment are either overlooked or only briefly mentioned in Lyons, *The Uneasy Partnership* (New York: Russell Sage Foundation, 1969); Diamond, *Compromised Campus* (New York: Oxford University Press, 1992); Engerman, *Know Your Enemy* (New York: Oxford University Press, 2009); Inderjeet Parmar, *Foundations of the American Century: The Ford, Carnegie, and Rockefeller Foundations in the Rise of American Power* (New York: Columbia University Press, 2012); Immanuel Wallerstein, "The Unintended Consequences of Cold War Area Studies," in *The Cold War and the University: Toward an Intellectual History of the Postwar Years,* ed. Noam Chomsky et al. (New York: The New Press, 1997): 195–232; Laura Nader, "The Phantom Factor: Impact of the Cold War on Anthropology," in Chomsky et al., *The Cold War and the University*; Bruce Cumings, "Boundary Displacement: Area Studies and International Studies During and After the Cold War," in *Universities and Empire: Money and Politics in the Social Sciences During the Cold War,* ed. Christopher Simpson (New York: The New Press, 1998): 159–187; Robin, *The Making of the Cold War Enemy* (Princeton, NJ: Princeton University Press, 2001); and Jacobs, *Imagining the Middle East* (Chapel Hill: University of North Carolina Press, 2011).

8. See *FRUS, The Near East and Africa, 1947, Vol. V*: 623, and Khalil, "The Crossroads of the World: U.S. and British Foreign Policy Doctrines and the Construct of the Middle East, 1902–2007," *Diplomatic History* 38, no. 2 (April 2014): 299–344.

9. "Princeton University Press Release," April 21, 1947, RG 59, Entry 5091, Box 555, NARACP.

10. Harry Lee Smith Jr. to Philip Hitti, April 14, 1947 and May 12, 1947; Smith to William Maddox, May 1, 1947, RG 59, Entry 5091, Box 555, NARACP; Gordon Merriam to NEA, March 28, 1947, RG59, Entry 1434, Box 1, NARACP.

11. Christian Ravandal to Harold Dodds, May 26, 1947, RG 59, Entry 5091, Box 555, NARACP.

12. Merriam to Loy Henderson, July 1, 1947, RG59, Entry 1434, Box 1, NARACP.

13. Dept. of Oriental Studies, 1933–1966, Box 9, January 29, 1951, AC 164, Princeton University Archives (hereafter PUA). The Rockefeller Foundation and the Carnegie Corporation provided five-year grants of $42,500 and $61,000, respectively. ARAMCO and Cal-Tex provided $11,500 and $10,000 per year for five years, respectively, while Gulf Oil made a $10,000 contribu-

tion over two years. Other initial contributors included the Grant and Dodge Foundations, at $8,000 per year and $5,000 per year, respectively.

14. "Princeton University Bicentennial Conference, Near Eastern Culture and Society, The Arab and Moslem World: Studies and Problems, 25 April 1947," RG 59, Entry 5091, Box 555, NARACP.

15. Khalil, "The Crossroads of the World," 317–318; Jacobs, *Imagining the Middle East,* 48–49; R. Bayly Winder, "Four Decades of Middle Eastern Study," *Middle East Journal* 41, no. 1 (Winter 1987): 40, 44. It should be noted that MEI did not respond to my request for access to its archives.

16. "Report to the Carnegie Corporation, 1948–1949," AC 164, Dept. of Oriental Studies, 1933–1966, Box 9, PUA. In its 1948–1949 annual report to the Carnegie Corporation, Princeton stated that 51 students enrolled in area and language study in the first term and 69 students were enrolled in the second term. The following year, the program boasted a dramatic increase of 172 students enrolled in the first term and 129 in the second. In addition, the program had 10 full-time graduate students, including 2 from the Department of State in the 1948/1949 academic year, and added another 10 graduate students the following year. In the special language program, 20 Army and Air Force officers attended courses in Arabic, Persian, Turkish, and Greek. By 1950, this number dropped to 3 Army officers and an FSO.

17. "Program in Near Eastern Studies: A Descriptive Statement, Princeton University Department of Oriental Languages and Literature, 1951," RG 59, Entry 5091, Box 555, NARACP.

18. William Nelson Fenton, *Area Studies in American Universities* (Washington, DC: American Council on Education, 1947): 82.

19. Ibid., 83. Fenton's top three priorities in order were: "The Americas," "Western Europe and its margins," and "The Slavonic World, the Far East." It should be noted that he never defined the geographic area for the Near East or the "Arabic World" but used the terms synonymously.

20. Ibid., 47–50, 84–85.

21. David Price, *Anthropological Intelligence: The Deployment and Neglect of American Anthropology in the Second World War* (Durham, NC: Duke University Press, 2008): 97–101.

22. Robert Hall, *Area Studies: With Special Reference to Their Implications for Research in the Social Sciences* (New York: Social Science Research Council, May 1947): 12, 17–18.

23. Ibid., 17–18.

24. Ibid., 18–19.

25. Ibid., 19, 45.

26. Ibid., 82–83.

27. Ibid., 50–68, 81–84.

28. Ibid., 85.

29. W. Park Armstrong to Walter B. Smith, April 1, 1953, RG 59, Entry 1494, Box 68, NARACP.

30. W. Park Armstrong to Walter B. Smith, October 31, 1952, CIA CREST, NARACP. A slightly different version of the ERS's goals are detailed in "Bureau of Intelligence and Research Semi-Annual Report to the President's Board of Consultants on Foreign Intelligence Activities, Final Draft," April 23, 1959, RG59, Entry 1595, Box 1, NARACP.

31. Penniman to Gladdieux, "Department of State Facilities, Available to Educational and Research Institutions," January 24, 1951, Ford Foundation Archives (hereafter FFA), General File 1951, State Department. It should be noted that a Freedom of Information Act request, now over six years old, is still pending.

32. By 1952, ERS's staff increased to ten, three of which were classified as "secretaries." The State Department contributed $60,000 annually in salary, travel and other operating expenses. It acknowledged that the staffing levels were insufficient and that there was a significant backlog of work. Armstrong to Smith, 31 October 1952.

33. E. M. Kirkpatrick, "Report of the Joint State-CIA External Research Staff for the period August 1–November 30, 1948," January 4, 1949, RG 59, Entry 1434, Box 2, NARACP. In his first six weeks as chief of ERS, Evron Kirkpatrick contacted departments within State Department Intelligence and the CIA, the Social Science Division of the Office of Education, Army and Air Force intelligence, the Board of Foreign Scholarships, the National Security Resources Board, and the Research and Development Board of the National Military Establishment (later the Department of Defense), and the Library of Congress' Foreign Area Committee and the Legislative Reference Service. For Kirkpatrick's post-ERS activities, see Ido Oren, *Our Enemies and US: America's Rivalries and the Making of Political Science* (Ithaca, NY: Cornell University Press, 2003): 154–163.

34. Kirkpatrick, "Report of the Joint State-CIA External Research Staff"; Penniman to Gladdieux, January 24, 1951.

35. Kirkpatrick, "Report of the Joint State-CIA External Research Staff"; Penniman also met with professors Gabriel Almond, Bernard Brodie, Cecil Driver, Andrew Gyorgy, and Klauss Knorr.

36. Robin Winks, *Cloak and Gown* (New York: William Morrow, 1987): 40–41; Bruce Kuklick, *Blind Oracles* (Princeton, NJ: Princeton University Press, 2006): 84–85. It should be noted that Yale's William Fox and Gabriel Almond, a former political science professor at Yale and Stanford, objected to Winks's characterization of Yale's Institute of International Studies. See Gabriel Almond and William T. R. Fox, "Yale at War," *New York Times,* September 20, 1987.

37. Kirkpatrick, "Report of the Joint State-CIA External Research Staff."

38. Ibid. The report stated that "continuing contact has been maintained with SAIS under the agreement negotiated some time ago." Although the report notes that the agreement was attached, it was apparently not declassified by the State Department, and I was unable to find a copy at the U.S. archives or

the Johns Hopkins University archives. SAIS became part of Johns Hopkins University in 1950. See Kuklick, *Blind Oracles,* 44, 79.

39. Kirkpatrick, "Report of the Joint State-CIA External Research Staff." On the FBI and Kluckhohn, see Diamond, *Compromised Campus,* 58–59. For more on the Russian Research Center, see Engerman, *Know Your Enemy,* 43–70. Kirkpatrick cited six reports collected from the Russian Research Center on topics related to the Soviet Union, including economic and resource issues.

40. Nader, "The Phantom Factor," 112–113; Peter Mandler, "Deconstructing 'Cold War Anthropology,'" in *Uncertain Empire: American History and the Idea of the Cold War,* ed. Joel Isaac and Duncan Bell (New York: Oxford University Press): 250.

41. Kirkpatrick, "Report of the Joint State-CIA External Research Staff."

42. Ibid.

43. Christopher Simpson, *Blowback: America's Recruitment of Nazis and Its Effect on the Cold War* (New York: Weidenfeld & Nicolson, 1988): 109–112.

44. "Memorandum on Eurasian Research Institute—Draft," July 7, 1948, Evron Kirkpatrick to William Donovan, July 12, 1948; Phillip Moseley to Donovan, October 23, 1948; Bernard to Donovan, December 28, 1948; William J. Donovan Papers, Box 73a, U.S. Army Heritage and Education Center (hereafter USAHEC). Engerman, *Know Your Enemy,* 40. Kirkpatrick, "Report of the Joint State-CIA External Research Staff." The Institute is also discussed by Bruce Cumings, "Boundary Displacement," 164–165; and Engerman, *Know Your Enemy,* 39–40.

45. "Publications of the Bureau of Intelligence and Research," April 9, 1959, RG59, Entry 1595, Box 3; "Bureau of Intelligence and Research Semi-Annual Report to the President's Board of Consultants on Foreign Intelligence Activities, Final Draft," April 23, 1959, RG59, Entry 1595, Box 1, NARACP. For P-Source, see Wilford, *The Mighty Wurlitzer,* 128.

46. Mortimer Graves to John Marshall, April 15, 1949, Record Group 1.2, Series 200 R, Box 263, Rockefeller Foundation Archives (hereafter RFA).

47. "Committee on Problems and Policy Agenda and Minutes," September 13–14, 1948, SSRC, Accession 2, Series 1, Sub-Series 20, RFA. On ACLS activities in the 1930s, see Records of the Committee on Mediterranean and Near Eastern Studies, ACLS, Box 83, Library of Congress (hereafter LOC).

48. American Council of Learned Societies, *A Program for Near Eastern Studies in the United States* (ACLS: Washington, DC, 1949). Sidney Glazer served as acting chief of the State Department's International Broadcasting Division-Near East Section; Harold Glidden was a researcher for the Near East and Africa Division of the State Department's OIR; Halford Hoskins was a former consultant to the State Department for the Middle East during World War II and future director of SAIS. He also served on the editorial board of the *Middle East Journal.* Edwin Wright was special assistant to the

assistant secretary for Near Eastern and African Affairs and the acting director of the Middle East Institute.

49. American Council of Learned Societies, *A Program for Near Eastern Studies*, 1–7.

50. Ibid., 6–10.

51. Ibid., 33–38.

52. Ibid, 1–4, 18–20, 23–24.

53. Mortimer Graves, "A Cultural Relations Policy in the Near East," in *The Near East and the Great Powers*, ed. Richard Frye (Cambridge, MA: Harvard University Press, 1951): 74–76.

54. William Steuck, *Rethinking the Korean War* (Princeton, NJ: Princeton University Press, 2002): 61–119. For the origins of the Korean civil war, see Bruce Cumings, *Origins of the Korean War*, Vol. 1: *Liberation and the Emergence of Separate Regimes, 1945–1947* (Princeton, NJ: Princeton University Press, 1981) and *Origins of the Korean War*, Vol. 2: *The Roaring of the Cataract, 1947–1950* (Princeton, NJ: Princeton University Press, 1990).

55. Harry Hawkins to Haywood Martin, September 27, 1950, RG59, Entry 5091, Box 556, NARACP.

56. Steuck, *Rethinking the Korean War*, 61–119; Leffler, *A Preponderance of Power*, 355–360.

57. Harry S. Truman, "Proclamation 2914: Proclaiming the Existence of a National Emergency," December 16, 1950, Harry S. Truman Library and Museum (hereafter HSTL), http://www.trumanlibrary.org/publicpapers /index.php?pid=994&st=&st1=(last accessed August 9, 2013); "Language and Area Training Conference," December 27, 1950, RG59, Entry 5091, Box 556, NARACP. A number of government departments were to attend, including the State Department, Department of Defense, CIA, NSRB, Labor, Commerce, and the Office of Education. Other proposed attendees included the ACLS, the Ford Foundation, the Library of Congress, and the American Council on Education.

58. Special Report of the External Research Staff, December 26, 1950, RG 59, Entry 558B, Box 10, NARACP. This document was declassified (and partially redacted) in December 2014. It lists twenty-six contracts in progress and at least six completed. Two studies on Iraq, classified as "restricted," were completed by Dorothy Van Ess, a former missionary in Iraq and administrator of a girls' school in Basra. Her studies examined "Religion of the People of Iraq" and the "Cultural Characteristics the People of Iraq." Van Ess later published *Fatima and Her Sisters* (New York: John Day, 1961), which was based on her time in Iraq. Donald N. Wilber completed another study on Iranian politics, classified "confidential." Three years later, Wilber was involved in planning the overthrow of Iranian prime minister Mossadegh and authored the CIA's internal history of the coup. See the National Security Archive's "The Secret History of the Iranian Coup, 1953," http:// nsarchive.gwu.edu/NSAEBB/NSAEBB28/ (last accessed May 28, 2015). The

studies were prepared for the State Department's Research and Intelligence division, and Wilber is identified as "Donald N. Wilbur [*sic*]."

59. Hitti to McGhee, December 19, 1950, RG59, Central Decimal File, 880.412/12–1950, NARACP. Hitti is also quoted in Jacobs, *Imagining the Middle East* (43); however, the larger context of the national emergency declaration as well as the preexisting relationship between Princeton and Washington are not discussed.

60. James Adams to Henry Lee Smith Jr., February 5, 1951, RG 59, Entry 5091, Box 555, NARACP.

61. Elmer Staats to Henry Lee Smith Jr., "Informal Meeting to Discuss Program Training of Area Specialists," March 1951, "SSRC Proposal: A Project for Training Area Specialists," January 19, 1951, RG59, Entry 5091, Box 556, NARACP.

62. Ibid. The cost of the three-year program was estimated to be $15.5 million, including instruction costs, living stipends, and travel. Coverage was to be provided for all world areas, with the majority of positions assigned to "critical regions." Of the 1,000 trainees, 250 were designated for the Soviet Union, 200 for the "Far East," and 150 for "Central and Western Europe." A hundred trainees each were assigned to "South Asia," "Southeast Asia," and the "Middle East," 60 for "Latin America," and 40 for "Africa." Each region would have a subdivision where some students would be assigned based on academic discipline, including sociology, political science, economics, anthropology, psychology, history, and linguistics. For training for the Middle East region, the SSRC identified the centers at Princeton, University of Pennsylvania, Michigan, Columbia, and Johns Hopkins.

63. Staats to Smith, "Informal Meeting to Discuss Program Training of Area Specialists," March 1951; James Webb to Staats, March 6, 1951; "Department of State Staff Study," undated, RG59, Entry 5091, Box 556, NARACP.

64. "Department of State Staff Study," n.d.

65. Webb to Staats, March 6, 1951. Webb authorized the FSI's Frank Hopkins and Henry Smith to represent the State Department in discussions with other agencies.

66. "Department of State Staff Study," n.d.

67. Ibid. On the loyalty review board from 1946–1948, see Arthur S. Flemming Oral History, June 19, 1989, HSTL, http://www.trumanlibrary.org/oralhist /flemming.htm (last accessed August 9, 2013).

68. Robert Clark to Arthur Flemming, "Shortage of Language and Area Specialists," March 12, 1951, RG59, Entry 5091, Box 556, NARACP.

69. Ibid. Graves's figures ranged from country-specific estimates to those for broader and vaguely defined areas. For example, he estimated Iran and Turkey required ten and fifteen specialists, respectively. Meanwhile, the "Western Mediterranean" and "Eastern Mediterranean" regions required twenty and thirty specialists, respectively. For the even vaguer, "Moslem World," thirty specialists were needed.

70. Ibid.
71. Hopkins to Martin, Rowe, Jean, Dubrow, "Proposal to Employ Young College Graduates and Enroll Them in University-Language-and-Area Programs," March 23, 1951, RG 59, Entry 5091, Box 556, NARACP.
72. Ibid.
73. Wood to Members of the World Area Research Committee, "Second Progress Report on a Project for Training Area Specialists," March 2c, 1951, RG 59, Entry 5091, Box 556, NARACP. Attendees included Frank S. Hopkins (chairman, Department of State), Henry Lee Smith Jr. (FSI, Department of State), Captain J. J. O'Donnell (U.S. Navy), Major Gordon D. Buckley (U.S. Army), Luther Evans (Library of Congress), Donald Stone (ECA), Robert Clark (NSRB), Colonel Matthew Baird (director of training, CIA), Dr. James C. O'Brien (assistant commissioner, Office of Education, FSA), Elmer Staats (BOB), Charles Odegaard (director, ACLS), and E. Pendleton Herring, Wendell Bennett, Bryce Wood (SSRC).
74. E. Pendleton Herring, *The Impact of War: Our American Democracy under Arms* (New York: Farrar & Rinehart, 1941); see also Jeffery M. Dorwart, *Eberstadt and Forrestal: A National Security Partnership, 1909–1949* (College Station: Texas A&M University Press, 1991): 3, 95–98.
75. On Bennett's wartime service, see Price, *Anthropological Intelligence,* 98–c9; Wood to Members of the World Area Research Committee, "Second Progress Report on a Project for Training Area Specialists."
76. Wood to Members of the World Area Research Committee, "Second Progress Report on a Project for Training Area Specialists."
77. Ibid.
78. Ibid.
79. Ibid.
80. "Ad Hoc Committee on University Language-and-Area Training, Meeting Minutes," March 22, 1951, RG 59, Entry 5091, Box 556, NARACP.
81. Ibid.
82. "World Area Research Committee Meeting Minutes," March 30, 1951, RG 59, Entry 5091, Box 556, NARACP. Present at the meeting were members of the SSRC's Committee on World Area Research: Robert B. Hall (chairman, University of Michigan), Ralph L. Beals (University of California, Los Angeles), Wendell Bennett (Yale), W. Norman Brown (University of Pennsylvania), Donald C. McKay (Harvard), George Taylor (University of Washington), and Bryce Wood (SSRC). Also present were Harold Deutsch (University of Minnesota); Philip Mosely (Columbia); David Mandelbaum (University of California, Berkeley); Lauriston Sharp, J. Milton Cowan, and L. Gray Cowan (Cornell University); Frank Hopkins and Harry Smith (FSI).
83. "World Area Research Committee Meeting Minutes," March 30, 1951; Hopkins to Staats, March 29, 1951, RG 59, Entry 5091, Box 556, NARACP.

84. "World Area Research Committee Meeting Minutes," March 30, 1951; Kirkpatrick to Meloy, June 11, 1951, RG 59, Entry 5091, Box 556, NARACP.
85. "World Area Research Committee Meeting Minutes," March 30, 1951.
86. Cumings, "Boundary Displacement," 167–171; Engerman, *Know Your Enemy*, 5, 14–15. Mosely was director of studies for the Council on Foreign Relations (1955–1963) and an active member of the American Political Science Association and served on several of the Ford Foundation's boards and committees.
87. "World Area Research Committee Meeting Minutes," March 30, 1951.
88. Ibid.; "Social Science Research Council Survey of Area Centers," May 15, 1951, RG 59, Entry 5091, Box 556, NARACP.
89. Wendell C. Bennett, *Area Studies in American Universities* (New York: SSRC, June 1951): vi, 15, 20; "Social Science Research Council Survey of Area Centers," May 15, 1951. The data that was not published included detailed information collected on the citizenship status, gender, and military service status of graduate students by area of study. Similarly absent was an addendum listing the universities that reported their ability and capacity to expand their existing programs.
90. Bennett, *Area Studies in American Universities*, v–3. Bennett noted that the SSRC's Committee on World Area Research determined that new data was needed "as a basis for a sound national policy." He added that "aside from the traditional function of research training, the universities may be called upon to meet the increasing government needs" for area specialists.
91. "Area Specialists," n.d., RG 59, Entry 5091, Box 556, NARACP.
92. Bennett, *Area Studies in American Universities*, 7–9.
93. Ibid., 10–15, 24, 46, 68–69.
94. Ibid., 24–25, 33–37. The SSRC defined the Near East as North Africa, Egypt, Arabia, Israel, Turkey, Syria, Iran, and Iraq. Bennett reported that only two universities offered Advanced Arabic and Turkish. Although Persian was offered at five universities, it was not taught at the advanced level.
95. Report of the (Ad Hoc) Committee on Area and Language Specialists on 'The Shortage of Area and Language Specialists,'" August 20, 1951, RG 59, Entry 5091, Box 556, NARACP. Including Ramspeck, the committee was comprised of representatives from the State Department, CIA, Department of Defense (DOD), the NSRB, the ECA, the Office of Education, and the Library of Congress. Of the 1,500, it was estimated that DOD would require fewer than 200 specialists, particularly those with language proficiency. The projected number of specialists needed for these areas was 215 (Western Europe), 182 (Eastern Europe), 139 (Near East), and 131 (Southeast Asia).
96. Ibid. A minority report was issued by the U.S. Navy's representative on the committee. It disputed claims of a shortage of language and area specialists. Referring to data from the Bennett report, the U.S. Navy argued a sufficient quantity of specialists would be ready within three years.
97. Ibid.

98. Smith to Earl Sohm, "Establishment of a Departmental Committee on Language and Area Specialists," April 29, 1952, RG 59, Entry 5091, Box 556, NARACP.

99. "Departmental Committee on Language and Area Specialists, Minutes of February 19, 1952 Meeting of the Special Survey Committee," RG 59, Entry 5091, Box 556, NARACP.

100. "Summary Minutes of Conference on Near Eastern Studies, 11 January 1951," SSRC, Accession 1, Series 1, Sub-Series 20, RFA. Although the conference was chaired by Michigan's Robert Hall, the Near Eastern Studies Committee was considered separate from the Council's World Area Research Committee, which he also led and served on as the main interface with government agencies on area studies. It was not until the following year that the Committee defined the Near East as Afghanistan, Iran, Israel, Turkey, and the "Arab world," including North Africa. "The Social Sciences and the Near East: Proposals for Research and Development," February 28, 1952, SSRC, Accession 1, Series 1, Sub-Series 20, RFA.

101. "Summary Minutes of Conference on Near Eastern Studies, 11 January 1951." Among the committee's initial actions was a survey of existing facilities to determine the types of courses, research materials, and funding available for students. In addition, the committee was to examine how to organize and fund fieldwork and develop curriculum standards. Finally, the attendees identified a number of areas where scholarship and information were lacking. These included statistical data for the entire region; shortage of studies on most countries in the area except for Palestine; and insufficient coverage of Soviet Central Asia and Afghanistan.

102. "Minutes Committee on the Near and Middle East," February 7, 1951, SSRC, Accession 1, Series 1, Sub-Series 20, RFA. Like the ACLS committee, a significant number of the SSRC's committee members were OSS veterans, including Hurewitz, Frye, as well as the University of Pennsylvania's E. A. Speiser, who sat in for Carleton Coon. Robert Hall served as acting chair of the meeting, as his Michigan colleague George Cameron was on a research trip abroad. SSRC President Pendleton Herring and Afif Tannous of the Department of Agriculture's Office of Foreign Agricultural Relations also attended the meeting. Although Princeton's C. C. Pratt attended the January conference, neither he nor his colleagues joined the SSRC committee.

103. Ibid.; "Minutes Committee on the Near and Middle East," April 28, 1951, SSRC, Accession 1, Series 1, Sub-Series 20, RFA. Sydney Fisher's edited volume, *Social Forces in the Middle East* (Ithaca, NY: Cornell University Press, 1955), was the published product from the initial meeting. A reprinted edition was published by Greenwood Press in 1968.

104. "Minutes Committee on the Near and Middle East," June 7, 1951, SSRC, Accession 1, Series 1, Sub-Series 20, RFA. The topics ranged from "Opposition to Westernization in the Near East," by Raphael Patai of Dropsie

College, to SAIS's Majid Khadduri's "Political Forces Operating in the Arab League," and Columbia's J. C. Hurewitz's "Anglo-American Relations in the Near East in the Past Decade."

105. "Area Studies a Reexamination," September 22, 1948, Rockefeller Foundation, RG 3.2, Series 900, Area Studies, RFA; Parmar, *Foundations of the American Century*, 2

106. "The Rockefeller Foundation Over-All Support for Area Studies," January 20, 1955, Rockefeller Foundation, RG 3.2, Series 900, Area Studies, RFA; Waldemar A. Nielsen, *The Big Foundations* (New York: Columbia University Press, 1972): 50–56. Funding decreased from 1950 to 1953, averaging $624,000 per year. Although 1954 witnessed a dramatic spike in funding by the Rockefeller Foundation—increasing from $337,545 in 1953 to nearly $2.3 million—it coincided with the internal debate over area studies.

107. The Ford Foundation, "Report of the Study for the Ford Foundation on Policy and Program," October 1950; Ford Foundation Annual Report for 1952, 31, December 1952, FFA.; Nielsen, *The Big Foundations*, 78–79.

108. E. Pendleton Herring to Bernard Gladieux, "Area Training Program of the Social Science Research Council-Preliminary Draft," March 5, 1951, SSRC, Accession 2, Series 1, Sub-Series 39, RFA.

109. Ibid.

110. "Program for the Near East, July 1952," Near East General File 1952, FFA.

111. McGhee to Hoffman, February 9, 1951, FFA, General File, State Department, 1951.

112. Russell to Davis, "Transcript of Secretary of State Dean Acheson's Remarks," May 7, 1951, FFA, General File 1951, State Department, April–May 1951.

113. "Minutes Committee on the Near and Middle East," January 26, 1952, SSRC, Accession 1, Series 1, Sub-Series 20, RFA. Neither the SSRC's proposal for expanding area studies nor the research program of the Committee on Near and Middle East Studies was funded. However, the meeting minutes note that the Ford Foundation did express an interest in the "general subject of Near Eastern studies." The committee resubmitted its research program the following year. Although not all projects were funded two committee members, J. C. Hurewitz and Majid Khadduri, were awarded Ford fellowships in 1953 and 1954, respectively. Moreover, the Columbia Near East program was awarded a three-year grant in 1953 for $150,000. Ford Foundation Annual Report for 1953, Ford Foundation Annual Report for 1954.

114. Ford Foundation Annual Report for 1952. Of the initial fellows, forty-seven were to conduct research in sixteen countries in 1952 and eighteen were to conduct research in the second year. Funding for Academic Year (AY) 1952–1953 was $480,000 and $500,000 for AY 1953–1954. The Ford Foundation also provided a $100,000 grant to the University of Michigan's Near East program.

115. Pelcovits and Fina to Evans, "Weekly Roundup," September 23, 1957, RG59, Entry 1498, Box 7, NARACP. The report noted the orientation and subsequent debriefing of William Klausner, a Ford Fellow returning to the United States after two years in Thailand, where he conducted research on village culture. It added that the ERS was "arranging a number of interviews for Ford Fellows who are departing for their areas of study."

116. Charles Fahs to Dean Rusk, "Long-Range Policy with Regard to Area Studies," April 5, 1954; Rockefeller Foundation, "A Reexamination of Rockefeller Foundation Program in Area Studies," October 24, 1954, RG 3.2, Series 900, Sub-Series Area Studies, RFA.

117. Smith to Norman Burns, July 1, 1953; Burns to Smith, July 3, 1953, RG 59, Entry 5091, Box 555, NARACP.

118. Smith to Hitti, May 28, 1953; T. Cuyler Young to Smith, June 1, 1953; Smith to Young, June 8, 1953, RG 59, Entry 5091, Box 555, NARACP.

119. "National Intelligence Survey Program," September 9, 1948, RG 59, Entry 1595, Box 9, NARACP. The report noted that because of the administrative burden on OIR, the CIA agreed to provide funds to the State Department to employ six NIS analysts by fiscal year 1949.

120. Cyrus Peake to Allan Evans, June 16, 1954, RG59, Entry 1498, Box 4, NARACP.

121. Ibid.

4. America's Sheet Anchors

Epigraph: Elizabeth R. Starkey and John R. Starkey, "A Talk with Bayard Dodge," *ARAMCO World,* July/August 1972, http://www.saudiaramcoworld.com /issue/197204/a.talk.with.bayard.dodge.htm (last accessed December 27, 2013).

1. Donovan to JCS, July 27, 1942, RG 226, Entry M1642, Roll 18; "History of OSS-Cairo," undated, RG 226, Entry 99, Box 54, OSS, United States National Archives and Records Administration, College Park, Maryland (hereafter NARACP). It should be noted that Donovan's assertions were drawn from Harold Hoskins's assessment of the region and reported to the State Department. They would also be reiterated by Secretary of State Cordell Hull in a telegram to London, see *Foreign Relations of the United States (hereafter FRUS), The Near East and Africa, 1942, Vol. IV,* 26–29.

2. Ibid.

3. Although several books have been written about AUB and AUC, they do not focus on the relationship between the U.S. foreign policy and national security establishments and educational institutions in the Middle East. This includes Betty Anderson, *The American University of Beirut: Arab Nationalism and Liberal Education* (Austin: University of Texas Press, 2011); Brian VanDeMark, *American Sheikhs: Two Families, Four Generations, and the Story of America's Influence in the Middle East* (Amherst, NY:

Prometheus Books, 2012). For official histories, see Bayard Dodge, *The American University of Beirut: A Brief History of the University and the Land Which It Serves* (Beirut: Khayats, 1958); Lawrence R. Murphy, *The American University in Cairo: 1919–1987* (Cairo: American University in Cairo Press, 1987). Suhayr Ḥusayn Aḥmad al-Biyali, *Aḥdāf al-Jāmiʿah al-Amrīkīyah bi-al-Qāhirah: dirāsah watnā'iqīyah mundhu al-nash'ah ḥattá ʿām 1980 M* (Al-Miniyā: Dār Farḥah lil-Nashr wa-al-Tawzīʿ, 2002) relies on the AUC archives and published works. On AUB and AUC as examples of American "soft power," see Rasmus Bertelsen, "Private Foreign-Affiliated Universities, the State, and Soft Power: The American University of Beirut and the American University in Cairo," *Foreign Policy Analysis*, 2012, 293–311.

4. Murphy, *The American University in Cairo*, 1–20, 150. The university changed its name to "in" Cairo in 1961. For more on Presbyterian activities in Egypt, see Beth Baron, "Comparing Missions: Pentecostal and Presbyterian Orphanages on the Nile," in *American Missionaries and the Middle East*, ed. Mehmet Ali Dŏgan and Heather J. Sharkey (Salt Lake City: University of Utah Press, 2011): 260–284.

5. Murphy, *The American University in Cairo*, 2–3, 20–22.

6. Ibid., 34.

7. Ibid., 32–35.

8. Ussama Makdisi, *Artillery of Heaven: American Missionaries and the Failed Conversion of the Middle East* (Ithaca, NY: Cornell University Press, 2008): 214.

9. AUB Board of Trustees Reports, Book III, 1908–1929, American University of Beirut Jafet Library Archives and Special Collections (hereafter AUBA); Starkey, "A Talk with Bayard Dodge." Funding from the Rockefeller Foundation began with a modest donation of $5,000 annual gift in 1917. In 1923, the foundation provided $22,000–$25,000 to underwrite the salaries of adjunct professors of anatomy, histology, and pharmacology. Four years later, the Foundation made a five-year donation of $1 million for AUB's medical school, including $250,000 for building and equipment and $750,000 as an endowment for teaching medical sciences. Support continued into the 1930s, including funds for construction of AUB's hospital. In 1938, the Foundation promised a $1 million grant if AUB could raise $500,000.

10. "History of OSS Cairo," undated, RG 226, Entry 99, Box 54, OSS, NARACP; Wendell Cleland Presidential Papers, American University in Cairo Archives (hereafter AUCA); John Badeau Oral History, February 25, 1969, John F. Kennedy Presidential Library.

11. Badeau to Halsey, September 22, 1942, RG 226, Entry M1642, Roll 73, OSS, NARACP. Emphasis in original.

12. "American Cultural Activities in Arab Lands," undated, RG 59, Entry 1434, Box 2, NARACP.

13. Ibid.

14. *FRUS, Near East and Africa, 1942, Vol. IV,* 26–29; Bayard Dodge's Diary 78, AUBA.

15. "Cultural Relations Policy for the Near East," March 9, 1943, RG 226, Entry 146, Box 256, OSS, NARACP.

16. Ibid.

17. Ibid.

18. Bayard Dodge's Diary, 82. Two years later, the State Department provided an additional $80,000 to AUB (99).

19. "Post-War Cultural Development in the Near East," February 17, 1945, Document 114661, RG 226, Entry 16, Box 1299, OSS, NARACP.

20. Ibid.

21. Ibid.

22. Memorandum by Chief of the Division of Near Eastern Affairs (Merriam) to the Under Secretary of State (Acheson), May 8, 1946, *FRUS, The Near East and Africa, 1946, Vol. VII,* 597–598.

23. David Hackett Fischer, *Liberty and Freedom: A Visual History of America's Founding Ideas* (New York: Oxford University Press, 2005): 35.

24. *FRUS, The Near East and Africa, 1946, Vol. VII,* 597–598, 615–616, 645–646, 708–709; Louis, *The British Empire in the Middle East, 1948–1951,* 386; Maurice M. Labelle Jr., "'The Only Thorn': Early Saudi-American Relations and the Question of Palestine, 1945–1949," *Diplomatic History* 35, no. 2 (April 2011): 257–281.

25. Badeau to Dodge, October 15, 1946, John Badeau Presidential Papers, AUCA. Badeau explained that the letter would be delivered to the American ambassador to Egypt and published in the local press, likely through the United States Information Service. Emphasis in original.

26. Dodge to Badeau, October 21, 1946, Badeau Presidential Papers, AUCA.

27. Badeau to Dodge, October 29, 1946, Badeau Presidential Papers, AUCA.

28. Badeau to Azzam, October 29, 1946, Badeau Presidential Papers, AUCA

29. Of the different works by the Israeli "new historians," Avi Shlaim, *Collusion across the Jordan: King Abdullah, the Zionist Movement, and the Partition of Palestine* (New York: Columbia University Press, 1988), offers the most detailed examination of inter-Arab rivalries and secret agreements between Transjordan's King Abdullah, the British government, and the Zionist leadership in Palestine.

30. Bayard Dodge's Diary, 107.

31. Badeau to Truman, May 17, 1948, Badeau Presidential Papers, AUCA.

32. S. Pinckney Tuck to George Marshall, May 24, 1948, Box 7165, Central Decimal Files (hereafter CDF), NARACP.

33. Badeau to Azzam, May 21, 1948, Badeau Presidential Papers, AUCA.

34. Paterson to Acheson, June 11, 1949, Box 7165, CDF, NARACP.

35. AUB Board of Trustees Reports, Book V, 1947–1952, January 6, 1948, AUBA. On campus protests, Tuck to Marshall, December 16, 1947; Lowell C. Pinkerton to Marshall, May 12, 1948, CDF, NARACP. On at least one

occasion, the embassy also reported on the distribution of AUB faculty by nationality and religion. See Robert McClintock to Christian Herter, 12 June 1959, Box 2938, CDF, NARACP.

36. "Minutes of Informal Meetings between British and American Officials Held at the Department of State, October 23 to 28, Inclusive concerning the Raising of Living Standards in the Middle East," 1947, RG 59, Entry 1436, Box 16, Folder U.S.-U.K. Discussions, NARACP. See also Foreign Office (FO) 371/68041 AN 1197, "Washington Talks on the Middle East," United Kingdom Public Records Office (hereafter UK PRO). A Summary of the "Pentagon Talks" is available in *FRUS, The Near East and Africa, 1947, Vol. V*, 485–626.

37. "Minutes of Informal Meetings between British and American Officials Held at the Department of State, October 23 to 28, Inclusive Concerning the Raising of Living Standards in the Middle East."

38. Ibid.

39. CIA, "The Break-Up of the Colonial Empires and Its Implications for American Security," September 3, 1948, http://www.foia.cia.gov/sites/default /files/document_conversions/89801/DOC_0001166383.pdf (last accessed January 7, 2014).

40. Harry S. Truman's Inaugural Address, January 20, 1949, http://www .trumanlibrary.org/whistlestop/50yr_archive/inagural20jan1949.htm; Jason Scott Smith, *Building New Deal Liberalism: The Political Economy of Public Works, 1933–1956* (Cambridge: Cambridge Press, 2009): 249.

41. McGhee to Penrose, October 6, 1949, RG59, Entry 1422, Box 4, NARACP. McGhee was responding to two letters from Penrose. The partisans included Wendell Cleland, Harold Glidden, and Edwin Wright.

42. Joseph Satterthwaite to George Allen, February 4, 1949; Satterthwaite to Willard Thorp, February 4, 1949, RG 59, Entry 1434, Box 2, NARACP.

43. Satterthwaite to Thorp, February 4, 1949.

44. Although AUB graduates served as government ministers in other countries, they encountered discrimination within the Lebanese government, especially the Foreign Ministry, which favored the alumni of French institutions. The U.S. Embassy in Beirut actively lobbied the Lebanese government to end this practice. See Harold B. Minor to Acheson, September 10, 1951, March 4, 1952, RG 59, Box 5448; McClintock to John Foster Dulles, February 12, 1958, Box 4927, CDF, NARACP.

45. Wendell Cleland to Chartrand, February 21, 1949, RG59, Entry 1434, Box 2, NARACP.

46. "Memorandum of Conversation by the Officer in Charge of Lebanon-Syria-Iraq Affairs," *FRUS, The Near East, South Asia, and Africa, 1950, Vol. V*, 852–855.

47. George McGhee to Paul Hoffman, February 9, 1951. Ford Foundation Archives, General File 1951, State Department.

48. Ibid.

49. AUB Board of Trustees Reports, Book V 1947–1952, "October 17, 1951 Meeting Minutes," AUBA.

50. "Near East Program Report and Recommendations," July 1952, 1, General File, Near East, 1952, Ford Foundation Archives (hereafter FFA); Edward H. Berman, *The Influence of the Carnegie, Ford, and Rockefeller Foundations on American Foreign Policy: The Ideology of Philanthropy* (Albany: State University of New York Press, 1983): 56–57.

51. "Near East Program Report and Recommendations," July 1952.

52. Ibid.

53. Ibid. The delegation proposed $200,000 for three years to support the institute. On Marshall, see Brett Gary, *The Nervous Liberals: Propaganda Anxieties from World War I to the Cold War* (New York: Columbia University Press, 2011): 85.

54. "Near East Program Report and Recommendations," July 1952. The initial grant for the SRC was $85,000 for three years.

55. Ward Madison to Wendell Cleland, October 19, 1953, W. Wendell Cleland Personal Papers, AUCA; Cleland to Provinse, January 24, 1955, Raymond McLain Personal Papers, AUCA.

56. John Marshall to Charles Fahs, "Area Studies in the Near East," June 27, 1950, RG 3.2, Series 900, Sub-Series Area Studies, Box 31, Folder 165, Rockefeller Foundation Archives (hereafter RFA).

57. Ibid.; Gary, *The Nervous Liberals*, 91.

58. Hamilton Gibb to John Marshall, August 11, 1950, RG 3.2, Series 900, Sub-Series Area Studies, Box 31, Folder 165, RFA. Marshall's assessment was also shared with Matta Akrawi, an Iraqi member of the United Nations Educational, Scientific, and Cultural Organization (UNESCO) Secretariat, who agreed with his findings. Akrawi would later author several book on education in the Arab states.

59. John Marshall, "The Near East, 1951," November 13, 1951, RG 3, Series 911, Sub-Series Program and Policy Report, Box 2, Folder 15, RFA. Emphasis in original. For more on Smith, see Zachary Lockman, *Field Notes: The Making of Middle East Studies in the United States* (Stanford, CA: Stanford University Press, 2016): 89, 136–137.

60. Marshall, "The Near East, 1951."

61. Ibid.

62. John Marshall to Charles Fahs, "JM's General Report on the Near East, 1951," December 7, 1951. RG 3, Series 911, Sub-Series Programs and Policy 1951–1954, Box 1, Folder 6, RFA.

63. AUB Board of Trustees Reports, Book VI January 1952–June 2, 1955, May 25, 1953, AUBA.

64. Harold Hoskins, "Talk to Special FSI Group in Washington, D.C.: American Education in the Near East," June 25, 1953, Hoskins Personal Papers, Box 1, Princeton University Archives (hereafter PUA).

65. Memorandum of Conversation, July 21, 1955, Box 4927, 1955–1959, CDF, NARACP.

66. Richard Immerman, *Empire for Liberty: A History of American Imperialism from Benjamin Franklin to Paul Wolfowitz* (Princeton, NJ: Princeton University Press, 2010): 163–195; Hugh Wilford, *America's Great Game: The CIA's Secret Arabists and the Shaping of the Modern Middle East* (New York: Basic Books, 2013): 55. For background on the Dulles family, see Stephen Kinzer, *The Brothers: John Foster Dulles, Allen Dulles, and Their Secret World War* (New York: Henry Holt, 2013): 7–36; C. Wright Mills, *The Power Elite* (New York: Oxford University Press, 1956); Allen Dulles Profile and Recommendation (for CIA), William J. Donovan Papers, Box 1, U.S. Army Heritage and Education Center (hereafter USAHEC).

67. Dwight D. Eisenhower, "Address and Remarks at the Baylor University Commencement Ceremonies, Waco, Texas," May 25, 1956, http://www.presidency.ucsb.edu/ws/?pid=10499e (last accessed May 14, 2015).

68. Donald Heath to John Foster Dulles, June 3, 1956, Box 4927, 1955–1959, CDF, NARACP. The Mutual Security Act of 1951 authorized foreign and military aid to American allies. It was renewed annually until 1961, when it was replaced by the Foreign Assistance Act signed by President Kennedy.

69. Memorandum of Conversation, January 10, 1957, Box 4927, 1955–1959, CDF, NARACP.

70. John Case to Allen Dulles, June 4, 1957 and June 11, 1957, Box 4927, 1955–1959, CDF, NARACP. This included reporting on the hiring and performance of AUB's new president, J. Paul Leonard, as well as National Science Foundation grants awarded to the university.

71. Armin H. Meyer to Parker T. Hart, July 20, 1959, RG 59, Entry 3131, Box 1, NARACP. At the end of fiscal year 1959, AUB was awarded $2.5 million in grants under the Mutual Security Act for capital projects. In addition, AUB's contract with the ICA was roughly $2 million including tuition and travel costs.

72. Ibid.

73. Ibid.

74. Murphy, *The American University in Cairo*, 145.

75. Ibid., 147–149. AUC was also awarded a $500,000 ICA contract in fiscal year 1959. Meyer to Hart, July 20, 1959.

76. Meyer to Hart, April 28, 1959, Box 4927, 1955–1959, CDF; Stuart D. Rockwell to Edgar, May 15, 1959, RG 59, Entry 3131, Box 1, NARACP; Murphy, *The American University in Cairo*, 149–152. Heikal and Hussein quoted in Murphy.

77. Report of the Middle East Survey Commission, 1961, AUCA.

78. Ibid., 3–4.

79. AUB Board of Trustees Reports, November 14–15, 1961, Book IX February 1961–December 1963, Box 5, Sec. AA2, AUBA.

80. Ibid.

81. AUB Board of Trustees Reports, September 12, 1962; December 19, 1962; January 2, 1963; May 22, 1963, Book IX February 1961–December 1963, Box 5, Sec. AA2, AUBA.

82. AUB Board of Trustees Reports, November 28, 1962; June 25–28, 1963; Book IX February 1961–December 1963, Box 5, Sec. AA2, AUBA; Parker T. Hart to Dean Rusk, June 25, 1962, RG 59, Box 2798, Rusk to U.S. Embassy Kuwait, December 12, 1963, CDF, NARACP.

83. AUB Board of Trustees Reports, January 2, 1963; May 22, 1963, Book IX February 1961–December 1963, Box 5, Sec. AA2; Book X February 1964–December 1965, Box 6, Sec AA2, AUBA.

84. Starkey, "A Talk with Bayard Dodge."

85. For a similar dynamic involving the support of philanthropic foundations for public diplomacy efforts that involved the promotion of American music and the arts during the Cold War, see Penny Von Eschen, *Satchmo Blows Up the World: Jazz Ambassadors Play the World* (Cambridge, MA: Harvard University Press, 2006); Michael Krenn, *Fall-Out Shelters for the Human Spirit: American Art and the Cold War* (Chapel Hill: University of North Carolina Press, 2005).

86. For example, see Anderson, *The American University of Beirut*, and Cyrus Schayegh, "The Man in the Middle: Developmentalism at the Beirut Economic Research Institute in-between the U.S. and the Middle East, 1952–1967," (paper presented at the "AUB: 150th Anniversary Conference," Beirut, Lebanon, May 2013).

5. (In)Visible Government

Epigraph: McGeorge Bundy, "The Battlefields of Power and the Searchlights of the Academy," in *The Dimensions of Diplomacy*, ed. E. A. J. Johnson (Baltimore: Johns Hopkins University Press, 1964): 3.

1. Michael Brzezinski, *Red Moon Rising* (New York: Times Books, 2007): 167, 176, 197; Robert Divine, *The Sputnik Challenge* (New York: Oxford University Press, 1993): xiii–xiv; National Aeronautics and Space Administration (NASA) National Space Science Data Center, "Sputnik I," http://nssdc.gsfc.nasa.gov/nmc/spacecraftDisplay.do?id=1957-001B (last accessed August 2, 2014).

2. Brzezinski, *Red Moon Rising*, 171, 213–216; Divine, *Sputnik Challenge*, 164–165; David Szanton, "The Origins, Nature, and Challenges of Area Studies in the United States," in *The Politics of Knowledge: Area Studies and the Disciplines*, ed. David Szanton (Berkeley: University of California Press, 2003): 8–9.

3. Barbara Barksdale Clowse, *Brainpower for the Cold War: The Sputnik Crisis and National Defense Education Act of 1958* (Westport, CT: Greenwood Press, 1981), focuses on the legislative aspect of the NDEA. Nancy Ruther, *Barely There, Powerfully Present: Thirty Years of U.S. Policy on International Higher Education* (New York: Routledge, 2002), examines the legislative history of federal support for higher education. Wayne J. Urban, *More Than Science and Sputnik: The National Defense Education Act of 1958* (Tuscaloosa: University of Alabama Press, 2010), discusses the key individuals and debates guiding the

passage of the NDEA with a focus on the sciences. Roger Geiger's *Research and Relevant Knowledge: American Research Universities since World War II* (New York: Oxford University Press, 1993), details the emergence of the research universities with a focus on the sciences before and after Sputnik. Yanek Mieczkowski, *Eisenhower's Sputnik Moment: The Race for Space and World Prestige* (Ithaca, NY: Cornell University Press, 2013), examines the Eisenhower administration's post-Sputnik science and technology policies. Szanton, *The Politics of Knowledge,* and Zachary Lockman, *Contending Visions of the Middle East: The History and Politics of Orientalism,* 2nd ed. (Cambridge: Cambridge University Press, 2010), emphasize the NDEA as the beginning of government-funded, university-based area studies programs, but overlook the U.S. national security establishment's relationship with existing Middle East studies centers and programs. Lockman, *Field Notes: The Making of Middle East Studies in the United States* (Stanford, CA: Stanford University Press, 2016) discusses the NDEA's impact on Middle East studies and emphasizes the importance of prior funding by philanthropic foundations to the field. However, he understates the role of U.S. government agencies in coordinating with the foundations and existing academic programs prior to the NDEA. Matthew Jacobs, *Imagining the Middle East: The Building of an American Foreign Policy, 1918–1967* (Chapel Hill: University of North Carolina Press, 2011); Ussama Makdisi, *Faith Misplaced: The Broken Promise of U.S.-Arab Relations, 1820–2001* (New York: Public Affairs, 2010); and Hugh Wilford, *America's Great Game: The CIA's Secret Arabists and the Shaping of the Modern Middle East* (New York: Basic Books, 2013) do not discuss the NDEA and its influence on Middle East studies and expertise.

4. "Financing the External Research Staff (ERS) in the Department of State, January 1, 1955, CIA CREST, United States National Archives and Records Administration, College Park, Maryland (hereafter NARACP).

5. Ludwell Lee Montague, *General Walter Bedell Smith as Director of Central Intelligence, October 1950–February 1953* (University Park: Pennsylvania State University Press, 1992): 129–130; Donald P. Steury, ed. *Sherman Kent and the Board of National Estimates* (Washington, DC: Central Intelligence Agency, 1994): 56, 151. On the number of NIEs produced, see the CIA's declassified discussion, "The Making of an NIE," https://www.cia.gov /library/center-for-the-study-of-intelligence/csi-publications/books-and -monographs/sherman-kent-and-the-board-of-national-estimates-collected -essays/making.html#rtoc12 (last accessed June 22, 2012).

6. Tim Weiner, *Legacy of Ashes: The History of the CIA* (New York: Doubleday, 2007): 14–16. On Kennan and the "Long Telegram," see Melvyn Leffler, *A Preponderance of Power: National Security, the Truman Administration, and the Cold War* (Stanford, CA: Stanford University Press, 1993): 108–109, 142; Anders Stephanson, *Kennan and the Art of Foreign Policy* (Cambridge, MA: Harvard University Press, 1989): 45–53.

7. William Donovan to W. Bedell Smith, October 13, 1950, and October 20, 1950; William J. Donovan Papers, Box 1A, U.S. Army Heritage and Education Center (hereafter USAHEC). Donovan's list favored elite East Coast universities, especially Harvard, Columbia, Yale, and Cornell. He also recommended Dartmouth president John Dickey, a State Department veteran, and acting Cornell president Cornelis de Kiewiet. A number of economists were listed, including John Kenneth Galbraith.

8. "Interview with William Harding Jackson," December 8–9, 1969, RG 263, Entry NN3–263–91–004, Box 2, NARACP.

9. Ibid. On Langer's tenure, see Steury, *Sherman Kent and the Board of National Estimates*, 143–155; Ray Cline, *Secrets, Spies, and Scholars* (Washington, DC: Acropolis Books, 1976): 111; John Cavanagh, "Dulles Papers Reveal CIA Consulting Network," *Forerunner*, April 29, 1980.

10. Montague, *General Walter Bedell Smith*, 135–136; Cavanagh, "Dulles Papers Reveal CIA Consulting Network." The CIA's "The Making of an NIE" also has a section on the Princeton consultants.

11. "Interview with William Harding Jackson." For more information on Kent's BNE service and influence, see Robert McNamara, *In Retrospect: The Tragedy and Lessons of Vietnam* (New York: Vintage, 1996): 154–155.

12. Dulles to Langer, July 2, 1956, William Langer Personal Papers, Box 1, Harvard University Archives (hereafter HUA).

13. Cavanagh, "Dulles Papers Reveal CIA Consulting Network"; Allen Dulles Personal Papers, Box 45, Folder 10, Princeton Consultants, Seeley G. Mudd Manuscript Library, Princeton University Archives (hereafter PUA); T. Cuyler Young Faculty File, PUA; Norman F. Cantor, *Inventing the Middle Ages: The Lives, Works, and Ideas of the Great Medievalists of the Twentieth Century* (New York: William Morrow, 1991): 261–262.

14. Calvin Hoover, *Memoirs of Capitalism, Communism, and Nazism* (Durham, NC: Duke University Press, 1965): 269–270; Cavanagh, "Dulles Papers Reveal CIA Consulting Network." Like Hoover, Richard Bissell briefly discussed his role in the Princeton Consultants in *Reflections of a Cold Warrior: From Yalta to the Bay of Pigs* (New Haven, CT: Yale University Press, 1996): 75–76. Although Young served on the Consultants' Board, he reportedly disagreed with the decision to overthrow Mossadegh. See Lockman, *Field Notes*, 131–133.

15. CIA, "The Making of an NIE."

16. Smith to Langer, April 10, 1962; Langer to Smith, April 18, 1962; McCone to Langer, January 24, 1963, Langer Personal Papers (HUFP 19.46), Box 1, HUA; Allen Dulles Personal Papers, Box 45, Folder 10, Seeley G. Mudd Manuscript Library, PUA.

17. Montague, *General Walter Bedell Smith*, 136; CIA, "The Making of an NIE." I have an outstanding Freedom of Information Act request for additional records on the activities and membership of the Princeton Consultants.

18. *Foreign Relations of the United States (hereafter FRUS), The Near East, South Asia, and Africa, 1950, Vol. V,* 80.

19. "Proposal for a Program in Middle Eastern Studies," March 26, 1953, HUFP 19.9, Box 12, HUA.

20. "Middle Eastern Studies Conference Minutes," May 11, 1953, HUFP 19.9, Box 12, HUA.

21. Ibid., 4, 10.

22. Ibid., 24.

23. Smith to Hitti, May 12, 1953, RG59, Entry 5091, Box 555, NARACP.

24. Frye to Lewis, July 2, 1954, HUF 569.5, Box 1, HUA.

25. William Langer, *In and Out of the Ivory Tower* (New York: N. Watson Academic Publications, 1977): 231–232.

26. "Harvard University, Center for Middle East Studies, 1954–1955," RG59, Entry 5091, Box 555, NARACP.

27. Langer, *In and Out of the Ivory Tower,* 1–45, 106–144, 162–168.

28. Lockman, *Contending Visions of the Middle East,* 111.

29. Hamilton Gibb, *Area Studies Reconsidered* (London: University of London, 1963): 15.

30. Don Babai, ed. *Reflections on the Past, Visions of the Future: The Center for Middle East Studies, Harvard University* (Cambridge, MA: Harvard University Press, 2004): 9; David Price, *Anthropological Intelligence: The Deployment and Neglect of American Anthropology in the Second World War* (Durham, NC: Duke University Press, 2008): 221–222.

31. Lockard to Langer, October 5, 1955; Langer to Lockard, October 7, 1955, HUF 569.5, Box 1, HUA; Babai, *Reflections on the Past, Visions of the Future,* 6.

32. The 1953 coup has received extensive coverage. See Ervand Abrahamian, *The Coup: 1953, The CIA, and the Roots of Modern U.S.-Iranian Relations* (New York: The New Press, 2013); Hugh Wilford, *America's Great Game: The CIA's Secret Arabists and the Shaping of the Modern Middle East* (New York: Basic Books, 2013); Stephen Kinzer, *The Brothers: John Foster Dulles, Allen Dulles, and Their Secret World War* (New York: Henry Holt, 2013); Mary Ann Heiss, *Empire and Nationhood: The United States, Great Britain, and Iranian Oil, 1950–1954* (New York: Columbia University Press, 1997); Kermit Roosevelt, *Countercoup: The Struggle for the Control of Iran* (New York: McGraw-Hill, 1979); James Bill, *The Eagle and the Lion: the Tragedy of American-Iranian Relations* (New Haven, CT: Yale University Press, 1988), to name a few. See also the CIA's internal history of the coup, Dr. Donald N. Wilber, "Overthrow of Premier Mossadeq of Iran: November 1952–August 1953," March 1954, National Security Archive, http://www2.gwu.edu/~nsarchiv/NSAEBB/NSAEBB435/ (last accessed September 15, 2014).

33. "Princeton University, Eighth Annual Near East Conference, May 18 and 19, 1956," HUF 569.5, Box 1, HUA. J. Terry Duce, vice president of ARAMCO and a member of the Near East program's Advisory Council, and his

colleague Joseph Ellender, ARAMCO's chief economist, discussed "The Economic Resources of the Near East: Present and Future."

34. "Harvard Foundation, Center for Middle Eastern Studies, Pre-Dinner Meeting," November 11, 1956, HUF 569, Box 1, HUA.

35. Ibid.

36. Ibid.

37. The Suez War has received significant attention by scholars and journalists; see William Roger Louis and Roger Owen, eds., *Suez 1956: The Crisis and Its Consequences* (New York: Oxford University Press, 1989); Keith Kyle, *Suez 1956: Britain's End of Empire in the Middle East* (New York: St. Martin's Press, 1991); Wilford, *America's Great Game.* For Anglo-American coordination, see Peter Hahn, *The United States, Great Britain, and Egypt, 1945–1956* (Chapel Hill: University of North Carolina Press, 1991). For Israel's decision making, see Avi Shlaim, *The Iron Wall: Israel and the Arab World* (New York: Norton, 2001). For France's goals and actions, see Irwin M. Wall, *France, the United States, and the Algerian War* (Berkeley: University of California Press, 2001). For view of C. Douglas Dillon, U.S. Ambassador to France, see *FRUS, Suez Crisis, 1955–1957, Vol. XVI,* 858.

38. For the Eisenhower Doctrine, see Salim Yaqub, *Containing Arab Nationalism* (Chapel Hill: University of North Carolina Press, 2004); Osamah Khalil, "The Crossroads of the World: U.S. and British Foreign Policy Doctrines and the Construct of the Middle East, 1902–2007," *Diplomatic History* 38, no. 2 (April 2014): 299–344.

39. Ferry to Davis, May 23, 1951, "Comments of Professor George Lenczowski on Iran and the Middle East," Near East General File 1951, Ford Foundation Archives (hereafter FFA); Peter J. Chelkowski and Robert J. Pranger, eds. *Ideology and Power in the Middle East* (Durham, NC: Duke University Press, 1988): 1–4.

40. George Lenczowski, *The Middle East in World Affairs* (Ithaca, NY: Cornell University Press, 1952): 412–428. Subsequent editions were published after periods of increased regional tension and reflected U.S. national security interests. In the wake of the Suez War, the third edition proclaimed that "the Middle East is in a state of revolutionary change." Lenczowski warned against continued European colonial involvement in the region and said the United States was "better placed to set a new style of relations between the West and the Middle East" that would reconcile "local national aspirations with vital Western interests." See Lenczowski, *The Middle East in World Affairs,* 3rd ed. (Ithaca, NY: Cornell University, 1962): ix, 680.

41. Halford L. Hoskins, *The Middle East: Problem Area in World Politics* (New York: Macmillan, 1954): 2, 255, 276, 278–288.

42. John Campbell, *Defense of the Middle East: Problems of American Policy* (New York: Council on Foreign Relations and Harper & Brothers, 1958): viii–ix. The study group members included Princeton's T. Cuyler Young and

Dankwart Rustow, Philip Mosely, and J. C. Hurewitz of Columbia, and former AUC president John Badeau.

43. Ibid., 4, 203, 345–359.

44. For more on the upheavals in the region and Washington's response, see William Roger Louis and Roger Owen, eds., *A Revolutionary Year: The Middle East in 1958* (London: I. B. Tauris, 2002); Juan Romero, *The Iraqi Revolution of 1958: A Revolutionary Quest for Unity and Security* (Lanham, MD.: University Press of America, 2011); and Yaqub, *Containing Arab Nationalism.*

45. Bernard Lewis, "The Middle East in World Affairs," in *Tensions in the Middle East,* ed. Philip W. Thayer (Baltimore: Johns Hopkins University Press, 1958): 55–57.

46. Lewis, "The Middle East in World Affairs," 51, 54–55, 59; C. Grove Haines, "Commentary," in *Tensions in the Middle East,* ed. Philip W. Thayer (Baltimore: Johns Hopkins University Press, 1958): 60–61, 66–67.

47. Stephen Ambrose, *Eisenhower: Soldier and President* (New York: Simon & Schuster, 1991): 417; William Stanley Hoole, "The National Defense Education Act of 1958: A Brief Chronology," December 1–27, 1960, RG 12, Entry 126, Box 48, NARACP.

48. Johnson quoted in Geiger, *Research and Relevant Knowledge,* 162; Julian E. Zelizer, *Arsenal of Democracy: The Politics of National Security from World War II to the War on Terrorism* (New York: Basic Books, 2010): 138–140. Reedy quoted in Zelizer.

49. James Ledbetter, *Unwarranted Influence: Dwight D. Eisenhower and the Military-Industrial Complex* (New Haven, CT: Yale University Press, 2011): 88–90; Larson quoted in Ledbetter. For the propaganda implications of Sputnik, see Kenneth Osgood, *Total Cold War: Eisenhower's Secret Propaganda Battle at Home and Abroad* (Lawrence: University of Kansas Press, 2006).

50. Hoole, "The National Defense Education Act of 1958," 28–68.

51. Ibid., 68–85.

52. Clowse, *Brainpower for the Cold War,* 55–56, 66–67; Hoole, "The National Defense Education Act of 1958," 85–107.

53. Clowse, *Brainpower for the Cold War,* 66–67; Hoole, "The National Defense Education Act of 1958," 101–102. For more on Elliott and Hill, see Urban, *More Than Science and Sputnik* 10–72.

54. Hoole, "The National Defense Education Act of 1958," 101–102; William Parker, *The National Interest and Foreign Languages* (Washington, DC: Government Printing Office, April 1954): 4. Emphasis in original.

55. Marion Folsom Oral History, February 27, 1968, 75–76, Dwight D. Eisenhower Presidential Library (hereafter DDEL); Dwight D. Eisenhower, *Waging Peace, 1956–1961* (New York: Doubleday, 1965): 242–243.

56. Clowse, *Brainpower for the Cold War,* 88–104; Hoole, "The National Defense Education Act of 1958," 111; Johnston to Hoole, November 7, 1960, RG 12, Entry 122, Box 122, NARACP.

57. Minutes of Cabinet Meeting, March 28, 1958, DDEL; "Crisis in Education—Part 1," *Life*, March 24, 1958; "Crisis in Education—Part 2,' *Life*, March 31, 1958; Clowse, *Brainpower for the Cold War*, 106–107; David Halberstam, *The Powers That Be* (New York: Knopf, 1975): 91–93, 355.

58. Malvina Lindsay, "Language Curtain Shrouds Mideast," *Washington Post*, July 31, 1958.

59. Clowse, *Brainpower for the Cold War*, 115–138; Hoole, "The National Defense Education Act of 1958," 153; Amy Newhall, "The Unraveling of the Devil's Bargain: The History and Politics of Language Acquisition," in *Academic Freedom after September 11*, ed. Beshara Doumani (New York: Zone Books, 2006): 210; Public Law 85–864, National Defense Education Act of 1958, September 2, 1958.

60. Mildenberger to Babbidge, September 17, 1958, RG 12, Entry 17, Box 75, NDEA Files, NARACP.

61. "Statement by Arthur S. Flemming, Secretary of Health, Education, and Welfare," March 23, 1959, RG 12, Entry 17, Box 74, Budget Justification Files, NARACP; L. G. Derthick, "A Statement of Policy: Language Development Program Centers and Research and Studies," March 10, 1959, RG 59, Entry 1595, Box 1, NARACP. It should be noted that the ACLS only focused on language needs, not area studies programs, which were to be examined in a separate study.

62. "Defense Educational Activities, Office of Education: Advanced Training in Foreign Languages and Areas, Fiscal Year 1959," January 5, 1959, RG 12, Entry 17, Box 73, NDEA Files, NARACP; Ruther, *Barely There*, 66–70; Jeffrey Bale, "Language Education and Imperialism: The Case of Title VI and Arabic, 1958–1991," *Journal for Critical Education Policy Studies* 9, no. 1 (May 2011): 376–408. Bale notes that from 1959 to 1967, 13 percent of Title VI funds ($4.34 million) were designated for twelve Middle East centers. During this period, the Middle East ranked fifth out of the eight funded regions. He notes that after 1973, the Middle East was one of only four regions to have an average of more than twelve centers (390–391).

63. See Newhall, "The Unraveling of the Devil's Bargain."

64. J. C. Hurewitz, *Undergraduate Instruction on the Middle East in American Colleges and Universities*, Provisional Draft (New York: American Association for Middle East Studies, May 1, 1962): iii–iv. Hurewitz explained that unlike graduate education that was intended for professional training, undergraduate instruction on non-Western areas "is normally designed to impart to the student a comprehensive understanding of his own civilization in global perspective and thus hopefully to convey to him a sense of responsibility as a citizen in a land that has suddenly and not too happily taken over duties of world leadership." On AAMES focus, see J. C. Hurewitz, "The Education of J. C. Hurewitz," in *Paths to the Middle East: Ten Scholars Look Back*, ed. Thomas Naff (Albany: State University of New York Press, 1993): 90. For the founding of AAMES, see Lockman, *Field Notes*, 160–170.

65. Hurewitz, *Undergraduate Instruction*, 12. The survey was initially sent to the faculty and administrators on the AAMES list. It was then expanded to other faculty and administrators who were identified through the survey. In total, 201 institutions and 393 faculty members completed the questionnaire. Language classes without a social science component or that focused on the ancient history of the region were deemed Oriental studies and excluded from the study.

66. Ibid., 36–37.

67. Morroe Berger, "Middle Eastern and North African Studies: Development and Needs," May 15, 1967, RG Accession 1, Series 1, Sub-Series 20, Box 242, Folder 1456, Social Science Research Council Archives (hereafter SSRCA).

68. Robert McCaughey, *International Studies and Academic Enterprise: A Chapter in the Enclosure of American Learning* (New York: Columbia University Press, 1984): 200.

69. Rockefeller Foundation Annual Report 1961; Ford Foundation Annual Report 1962; Babai, *Reflections on the Past, Visions of the Future*, 9.

70. Rusk to Pusey, April 15, 1959, Box 3, Rockefeller Foundation Archives (hereafter RFA); CMES Director and Assistant Director's Files (UAV 569.12), HUA.

71. "Harvard University, Center for Middle Eastern Studies, The First Ten Years, 1954–1964," December 1964, HUF 571, HUA.

72. Ibid. It should be noted that ten (13.5 percent) of the graduates were "unaccounted for" by the time the report was published.

73. "Report to the President, for the year July 1, 1958–June 30, 1959, Department of Oriental Studies and Program in Near Eastern Studies," Department of Oriental Studies, AC 164, Box 12, Presidential Reports Folder, PUA.

74. McCaughey, *International Studies and Academic Enterprise*, 192; Lockman, *Field Notes*, 211–212.

75. For more on Princeton's attempts to focus on the modern era, see Lockman, *Field Notes*, 210–211.

76. McCaughey, *International Studies and Academic Enterprise*, 239–242; Ruther, *Barely There*, 91; George M. Beckmann, "The Role of the Foundations," *Annals of the American Academy of Political and Social Science* 356 (November 1964): 16; Lockman, *Field Notes*, 206–207. According to Beckmann, the largest number of area studies programs were focused on East Asia (twelve) followed by Slavic or East European (ten), and South and Southeast Asia (eight).

77. Smith to Burns, "Task Force report on Near East language-and-area program," March 31, 1952, RG59, Entry 5091, Box 557, Language and Area General (1951–1955) Folder, NARACP.

78. Burns to Humelsine, "Proposed FSI Training Installation in Beirut," December 8, 1952; Montague to Humelsine, "Proposed FSI Training Instruction at Beirut," January 6, 1953, RG 59, Entry 5091, Box 557, NARACP.

79. Burns to Humelsine, December 8, 1952. For an insider's view of the FSI's training during this period, see Brooks Wrampelmeier Oral History, March 22, 2000, The Association for Diplomatic Studies and Training Foreign Affairs Oral History Project, http://www.adst.org/OH%20TOCs /Wrampelmeier,%20Brooks.toc.pdf (last accessed April 24, 2016).

80. Sollenberger to Oechsner, "Language-and-area specialization programs conducted by the Foreign Service Institute," November 12, 1953, RG 59, Entry 5091, Box 557, NARACP.

81. Beirut to Washington, January 25, 1959, Central Decimal File, Box 4927; FO 366/2938, 366/3403, 366/3539, UK PRO. For a favorable view of MECAS, see Leslie McLoughlin, *A Nest of Spies?* (London: Alhani, 1993).

82. "Department of State, Foreign Service Institute, Language Training and Skills," November 15, 1959, Hoskins Papers, Box 4, Folder 2, PUA; "Principal Witness Statement," January 17, 1961, Hoskins Papers, Box 4, Folder 5, PUA; Dulles to Langer, February 29, 1956, Langer Papers, Box 1, HUA.

83. Henderson to Mansfield, March 3, 1960, Harold Hoskins Personal Papers, Box 4, Folder 3, PUA.

84. "Recruitment and Training in the Foreign Service: Position of the Department of State on a Foreign Service Academy and Related Questions," undated, Hoskins Papers, Box 4, Folder 3, PUA. FSOs were graduates of over 200 different American universities and colleges and roughly 60 percent had graduate degrees. The report noted that a survey of lower-level FSOs revealed that 5 percent were from high-income families. In contrast, middle-income and lower-income families accounted for 79 percent and 16 percent, respectively.

85. "A Report on Language Training in the Foreign Service Institute," February 1960, Hoskins Papers, Box 4, Folder 3, PUA.

86. Ellen Herman, "Project Camelot and the Career of Cold War Psychology," in *Universities and Empire: Money and Politics in the Social Sciences during the Cold War*, ed. Christopher Simpson (New York: The New Press, 1998): 101–104.

87. Foreign Affairs Manual Circular, No. 352, August 24, 1965, CIA CREST, NARACP; Gene M. Lyons, *The Uneasy Partnership: Social Science and the Federal Government in the Twentieth Century* (New York: Russell Sage Foundation, 1969): 211. The Council was separate from the interagency Foreign Affairs Research Coordination Group (FAR) created in December 1964. FAR was chaired by the director of ERS and was comprised of ten agencies, including State, Defense, CIA, USAID, HEW, and the NSF. See Foreign Affairs Manual Circular, No. 261, December 10, 1965.

88. Cline to Raborn, "Organization of Panels of Social Scientists," November 18, 1965, RG 263, Entry History Source Collection (NN3–263–94–010), Box 9, NARACP.

89. Ibid. Emphasis in original. Although source text is deleted in the declassified document, there is little doubt from the description of the consultants

that the recommendations presented to DCI Raborn were from "The Princeton Consultants." Describing the group, Cline explained, "They are a group of distinguished scholars and social scientists in both regional and functional fields who have met with us periodically as friends since December 1950. We owe much to them. In [the] early days they helped us define the form and content appropriate to a national estimate. (The meeting of 28 October was their fifty-second.) The membership has changed with the years, but the group has maintained continuity of service and devotion to national intelligence and CIA. Although referred to as [source text deleted] as you know, the members of the group come from all over the country." Although the memorandum listed the professors and their institutional affiliations, the source text was deleted in the declassified copy. One name that was not deleted was that of former DCI Allen Dulles. Cline explained that Dulles was a "member" of the board and had participated in the discussion of outreach to social scientists.

90. Ibid. Cline noted that the CIA was "encouraging analysts to attend meetings of scholarly and professional associations. (During FY 1965 our records show that more than 300 [Deputy Director of Intelligence (DDI)] employees attended meetings of this kind.) We are requiring written reports of any matters which were helpful to them or of potential use to others in the Agency, which we will send to all interested divisions in the Agency."

91. David Wise and Thomas Ross, *The Invisible Government* (New York: Random House, 1964): 3.

92. Ibid., 243, 355.

93. Cline to Raborn, "Organization of Panels of Social Scientists," November 18, 1965.

94. See Wise and Ross, *The Invisible Government* (New York: Vintage Books, 1974): viii; John Prados, *The Family Jewels: The CIA, Secrecy, and Presidential Power* (Austin: University of Texas Press, 2013): 203–205.

95. Warren Hinckle, Robert Scheer, Sol Stern, and Stanley K. Sheinbaum, "The University on the Make," *Ramparts*, April 1966; "Electronic Prying Grows," *New York Times*, April 27, 1966; "Memorandum for the Members of the Board," May 19, 1966, William Langer Personal Papers, HUGFP 19.46, Box 1, Folder CIA 1960–1971, HUA.

96. Frances Stonor Saunders, *The Cultural Cold War: The CIA and the World of Arts and Letters* (New York: The New Press, 1999): 1, 86–87, 334; Issa J. Boulatta, "The Beleaguered Unicorn: A Study of Tawfiq Sayigh," *Journal of Arabic Literature* 4 (1973): 69–70.

97. Tawfiq Sayigh, *Mudhakkirāt Tawfiq Sayigh*, ed. Mahmud Chreih (Beirut: Dar Nelson, 2011): 42–43; Denys Johnson-Davies, *Memories in Translation: A Life between the Lines of Arabic Literature* (Cairo: American University of Cairo Press, 2006): 70; On Hunt's background see Saunders, *The Cultural Cold War*, 241–243; Peter Coleman, *The Liberal Conspiracy: The Congress for Cultural Freedom and the Struggle for the Mind of Postwar Europe* (New York:

Free Press, 1989): 173–174. Sami Mahdi, *Tajribat Tawfiq Sayigh al-Shiʻriyah wa-Marjiʻiyātuhā al-Fikrīyah wa-al-Fannīyah* (Beirut: Riyad al-Rayyis, 2009), argues that Sayigh's poetry revealed an affinity with the policies of the Syrian Social Nationalist Party.

98. Sayigh, *Hiwar* 1 (November 1962): 1; Sayigh, *Mudhakkirāt*, 42–43; Boulatta, "The Beleaguered Unicorn," 81.

99. Sayigh, *Mudhakkirāt*, 17, 23.

100. For Ben Bella interview, see *Hiwar* 8 (February 1964): 5–16; P. J. Vatikiotis, "Al-Muthaqqaf al-ʻArabī waʾl-mujtamaʻ al-ḥadīth," *Hiwar* 4 (May 1963): 41–51; Melvin Lasky, "Fī Intiẓār Ghādā," *Hiwar* 5 (August 1963): 125. On the Kennedy administration's courtship of Algeria, see Philip Muehlenbeck, *Betting on the Africans: John F. Kennedy's Courting of African Nationalist Leaders* (New York: Oxford University Press, 2012).

101. Mahmud Shurayh, *Tawfiq Sayigh: Sīrat Shaʻir wa-Manfī* (London: Riad el-Rayyes Books, 1989), 137.

102. Shurayh, *Tawfiq Sayigh*, 138–140; "Electronic Prying Grows," "Letters to the Editor of the Times: Freedom of Encounter Magazine," *New York Times*, May 10, 1966; "Arab Magazine Banned in Cairo," *New York Times*, July 22, 1966;

103. Shurayh, *Tawfiq Sayigh*, 155–164; Sayigh, *Hiwar* 23 (August 1966): 139–141

104. Boulatta, "The Beleaguered Unicorn," 69–71; Shurayh, *Tawfiq Sayigh*, 161–163.

105. See Lockman, *Field Notes*, 166–170; Timothy Mitchell, "The Middle East in the Past and Future of Social Science," in *The Politics of Knowledge: Area Studies and the Disciplines*, ed. David Szanton (Berkeley: University of California Press, 2004): 10–11.

106. The September 1947 correspondences between Berger and Donovan can be found in William J. Donovan Papers, Box 1A, USAHEC.

107. Morroe Berger, "Middle Eastern and North African Studies: Development and Needs," May 15, 1967, SSRC Archives Accession 1, Series 1, Subseries 20, Box 242, Rockefeller Foundation Archives (RFA); Berger's 1967 assessment of the field was republished in the second *Middle East Studies Association Bulletin* (vol. 1, no. 2, November 1967: 1–18) and noted that it was submitted before the June 1967 war.

108. For more on MESA's founding and contentious politics after 1967, see Lockman, *Field Notes*, 176–191.

109. Gibb, *Area Studies Reconsidered*, 4–5.

110. Berger, "Middle Eastern and North African Studies: Development and Needs," May 15, 1967.

6. Modernizing the Middle East

Epigraph: Ithiel de Sola Pool, "Some Implications of This Volume," in *Social Science Research and National Security*, ed. Ithiel de Sola Pool (Washington, DC: Smithsonian Institute, March 1963): 10.

1. George Kennan to Dean Acheson, January 22, 1952, 1, RG 59, Entry 1494, Box 68, United States National Archives and Records Administration, College Park, Maryland (hereafter NARACP). Although written to Acheson, Kennan's letter was copied and shared with other divisions, including the Division of Research and Analysis for Near East, South Asia, and Africa Affairs (DRN). See also Anders Stephanson, *Kennan and the Art of Foreign Policy* (Cambridge, MA: Harvard University Press, 1989): 168–171, for a discussion of Kennan's racial views; George Kennan, *The Kennan Diaries,* edited by Frank Costigliola (New York: W. W. Norton, 2014): 301, 304–308. For Anglo-American relations and Iran, see Ervand Abrahamian, *The Coup* (New York: The New Press, 2013), and Mary Ann Heiss, *Empire and Nationhood* (New York: Columbia University Press, 1997).

2. Scholars have often overlooked the influential role played by the BASR reports and the State Department in the development of modernization theory. Christopher Simpson, *Science and Coercion* (New York: Oxford University Press, 1994), examines the relationship between mass communication and psychological warfare, covering Daniel Lerner and the BASR reports. Mass communication scholars have discussed the BASR reports and their relationship to VOA. See Timothy Glander, *Origins of Mass Communications Research during the American Cold War: Educational Effects and Contemporary Implications* (Mahwah, NJ: LEA Publishers, 2000), and Hemant Shah, *The Production of Modernization: Daniel Lerner, Mass Media, and the Passing of Traditional Society* (Philadelphia: Temple University Press, 2011); Rohan Samarajiwa, "The Murky Beginnings of the Communication and Development Field: Voice of America and 'The Passing of Traditional Society,'" in *Rethinking Development Communication,* edited by Neville Jayweera and Sarath Amunugama (Singapore: Asian Mass Communication Research and Information Center, 1987): 3–19. Irene Gendzier, *Managing Political Change: Social Scientists in the Third World* (Boulder, CO: Westview Press, 1985), and Matthew F. Jacobs, *Imagining the Middle East* (Chapel Hill: University of North Carolina Press, 2011), rely on Lerner's admission that *The Passing of Traditional Society: Modernizing the Middle East* (New York: Free Press, 1958) used the BASR surveys. However, they do not examine the reports, their influence on Lerner's scholarship, or their relationship to VOA. Similarly, Douglas Little's *American Orientalism* (Chapel Hill: University of North Carolina Press, 2004) notes that Manfred Halpern was a State Department veteran, but does not discuss how his scholarship reflected his DRN service. In addition, Lerner and Halpern are not discussed at length in the works of David Engerman, Nils Gilman, and Michael Latham. See Engerman, *Know Your Enemy* (New York: Oxford University Press, 2009); Gilman, *Mandarins of the Future: Modernization in Cold War America* (Baltimore: Johns Hopkins University Press, 2003); and Latham, *Modernization as Ideology: American Social Science and "Nation Building" in the Kennedy Era* (Chapel Hill: University of North Carolina Press, 2000) and

The Right Kind of Revolution: Modernization, Development and U.S. Foreign Policy from Cold War to the Present (Ithaca, NY: Cornell University Press, 2011).

3. For racism and international relations, see David Long, "Paternalism and the Internationalization of Imperialism: J. A. Hobson on the International Government of the 'Lower Races,'" in *Imperialism and Internationalism in the Discipline of International Relations,* ed. David Long and Brian Schmidt (Albany: State University of New York Press, 2005): 71–92; Robert Vitalis, "Birth of a Discipline," 159–182, in *Imperialism and Internationalism in the Discipline of International Relations,* ed. David Long and Brian Schmidt (Albany: State University of New York Press, 2005); Vitalis, "The Noble American Science of Imperial Relations and Its Laws of Race Development," *Comparative Studies in Society and History* 52, no. 4 (2010): 909–938. On British imperial knowledge production, see Nicholas Dirks, *Castes of Mind: Colonialism and the Making of Modern India* (Princeton, NJ: Princeton University Press, 2001); James Hevia, *The Imperial Security State: British Colonial Knowledge and Empire-Building in Asia* (Cambridge: Cambridge University Press, 2012). On racism and American imperialism, see Paul Kramer, *The Blood of Government: Race, Empire, the United States, and the Philippines* (Chapel Hill: University of North Carolina Press, 2006); Eric T. Love, *Race over Empire: Racism and U.S. Imperialism, 1865–1900* (Chapel Hill: University of North Carolina Press, 2004).

4. See Richard King, *Race, Culture, and the Intellectuals, 1940–1970* (Baltimore: Johns Hopkins University Press, 2004): 2–6.

5. Michael Hunt, *Ideology and U.S. Foreign Policy* (New Haven, CT: Yale University Press, 1987): 159–162; Latham, *Modernization as Ideology,* 6, 14; Thomas Borstelmann, *The Cold War and the Color Line: American Race Relations in the Global Arena* (Cambridge, MA: Harvard University Press 2001): 10–44. For the Point IV program and modernization, see David Ekbladh, *The Great American Mission: Modernization and the Construction of an American World Order* (Princeton, NJ: Princeton University Press, 2010).

6. See Edward Said, *Orientalism* (New York: Vintage, 1979): 285–296, and Zachary Lockman, *Contending Visions of the Middle East: The History and Politics of Orientalism,* 2nd ed. (Cambridge: Cambridge University Press, 2010): 133–139.

7. Elie Salem, "Problems of Arab Political Behavior," in *Tensions in the Middle East,* ed. Philip W. Thayer (Baltimore: Johns Hopkins University Press, 1958): 68–80. For example, see Malik's introduction in *Tensions in the Middle East* and his work "The Near East: The Search for Truth," *Foreign Affairs* 30, no. 2 (January 1952): 231–264.

8. See Shah, *The Production of Modernization,* 31–38.

9. Daniel Lerner, *Psychological Warfare against Nazi Germany: The Sykewar Campaign, D-Day to VE-Day* (Cambridge, MA: MIT Press, 1971): 318. Emphasis in original. Lerner's *Sykewar,* originally published in 1949, was reissued in 1971 with the modified title. See discussions of *Sykewar* in

Gendzier, *Managing Political Change,* 53; Shah, *The Production of Moderniza-tion,* 41–45; Samarajiwa, "The Murky Beginnings," 6–7.

10. Robert Merton and Daniel Lerner, "Social Scientists and Research Policy," in *The Policy Sciences: Recent Developments in Scope and Method,* ed. Daniel Lerner and Harold Lasswell (Stanford, CA: Stanford University Press, 1951): 306–307.

11. Glander, *Origins of Mass Communications Research,* 105–125; Shah, *The Production of Modernization,* 79–80. BASR was originally known as the Office of Radio Research at Princeton. With funding from the Rockefeller Foundation, the Lazarsfeld-led Office of Radio Research became the leading (if not only) center in the United States conducting research on mass communications in the late 1930s and early 1940s. During the war, Lazarsfeld conducted propaganda assessments for the Office of War Information.

12. Alan Heil Jr., *Voice of America: A History* (New York: Columbia University Press, 2003): 32–47; Nicholas Cull, *The Cold War and the United States Information Agency: American Propaganda and Public Diplomacy, 1945–1989* (Cambridge: Cambridge University Press, 2008): 12–24. McMahon report quoted in Heil.

13. Cull, *The Cold War and the United States Information Agency,* 60–61; Latham, *Modernization as Ideology,* 54–55.

14. Shah, *The Production of Modernization,* 83–84. Under the new agreement, BASR conducted assessments of VOA broadcasts in Egypt, Israel, Turkey, Lebanon, Syria, Iraq, Iran, Jordan, Greece, and Germany. However, the surveys of Israel and Iraq were not completed.

15. Paul T. Lazarsfeld and Charles Y. Glock, "The Comparative Study of Communications Systems," April 28, 1950, BASR, Box 23. See also Shah, *The Production of Modernization,* 87–88.

16. Shah, *The Production of Modernization,* 12–17. Shah notes that Lazarsfeld was challenged by an Indonesian scholar when he made similar statements about the lack of opinion on public affairs in Muslim-majority countries. However, he apparently ignored those objections (94–95).

17. "Policy Memorandum," undated, BASR, Box 23, Confidential Policy Memorandum Folder, Columbia University Archives (hereafter CUA). The memorandum also recommended that BASR rely on VOA or other government agencies for nonclassified background information on the different countries. See Samarajiwa, "The Murky Beginnings," 8–9, for the similarity of VOA's questions with those Lerner published in *The Passing of Traditional Society.*

18. "Climates of Opinion in Egypt," BASR, January 1952, RG 59, P311, Box 3, NARACP. Emphasis in original.

19. Ibid., xiii–xiv.

20. Ibid., xv.

21. Ibid., xix.

22. Shah, *The Production of Modernization,* 92.

23. Siegfried Kracauer, "Appeals to the Near and Middle East," 5–6, May 1952, RG59, Entry P311, Box 2, NARACP. See also Kracauer, *From Caligari to Hitler* (Princeton, NJ: Princeton University Press, 1947).

24. Kracauer, "Appeals to the Near and Middle East," 30–31, 39–40.

25. Daniel Lerner, George Schueller, and Mary Stycos, "Mass Communications Audiences in Turkey," October 1952, i–vi, RG 59, Entry P311, Box 3, NARACP; See also Shah, *The Production of Modernization*, 88–91.

26. Shah, *The Production of Modernization*, 102–112. Lerner quoted in Shah.

27. "Confidential Memorandum (Regarding Intelligence Estimate 36)," undated, 1–3, RG 59, Entry 1494, Box 65, NARACP. The memorandum defined political instability as "circumstances where (i) pressures for political change are strong and growing; (ii) procedures for orderly change are enfeebled, frustrated, or absent." Additional studies were requested from different geographic regions to test the assessment's conclusions. These studies were to examine several factors, including the traditional structure of power within a given society and the centers of political power, and evaluate any significant political and economic changes in the society and their causes. In addition, the studies were to determine if the source for dissatisfaction among different classes was communist inspired and assess the political impact of American technical and economic assistance.

28. See Manfred Halpern, *The Politics of Social Change in the Middle East and North Africa* (Princeton, NJ: Princeton University Press, 1963): 54–55n4.

29. "Intelligence Estimate 45: Conditions and Trends in the Middle East Affecting US Security," October 15, 1952, RG 59, Entry 1494, Box 65, NARACP.

30. Ibid., 2–4.

31. "National Intelligence Estimate 73: Conditions and Trends in the Middle East Affecting U.S. Security," January 15, 1953, http://www.foia.cia.gov/sites/default/files/document_conversions/89801/DOC_0000119704.pdf, (last accessed April 24, 2016).

32. Lerner, *The Passing of Traditional Society*, 44, 79–82; see also Osamah Khalil, "The Crossroads of the World: U.S. and British Foreign Policy Doctrines and the Construct of the Middle East, 1902–2007," *Diplomatic History* 38, no. 2 (April 2014): 327–328.

33. Ibid., 216–248. David Riesman echoed this assessment in his introduction to *The Passing of Traditional Society* (9).

34. Ibid., 249–263.

35. Ibid., 112.

36. Ibid., 389–390, 405–406. Emphasis in original.

37. For Lerner's analysis of the Turkish military postcoup, see Daniel Lerner and Richard D. Robinson "Swords and Ploughshares: The Turkish Army as a Modernizing Force," in *The Military and Modernization*, ed. Henry Bienen (Chicago: Aldine Atherton, 1971): 117–148. See Salim Yaqub, *Containing Arab*

Nationalism (Chapel Hill: University of North Carolina Press, 2004), for a discussion of the Eisenhower Doctrine and U.S. intervention in Lebanon.

38. See Latham, *Modernization as Ideology*, and Latham, *The Right Kind of Revolution*; Gilman, *Mandarins of the Future*.

39. Shah, *The Production of Modernization*, 102; Gilman, *Mandarins of the Future*, 158–159, 190–194. Millikan quoted in Gilman.

40. Shah, *The Production of Modernization*, 112–113; Gilman, *Mandarins of the Future*, 190–194.

41. Latham, *Modernization as Ideology*, 2–3; Robert Rakove, *Kennedy, Johnson, and the Nonaligned World* (Cambridge: Cambridge University Press, 2013): xxi–xxii, 33–36.

42. Walt Whitman Rostow to President Kennedy, "Crucial Issues in Foreign Aid," February 28, 1961, Document 94, *Foreign Relations of the United States (hereafter FRUS), Foreign Economic Policy, 1961–1963, Vol. IX*, http://history .state.gov/historicaldocuments/frus1961-63v09/d94.

43. Ibid.

44. Latham, *Modernization as Ideology*, 69–70; Mark Haefele, "Rostow's Stages of Economic Growth: Ideas and Action," in *Staging Growth: Modernization, Development, and the Global Cold War*, ed. David C. Engerman, Nils Gilman, Mark Haefele, and Michael Latham (Amherst: University of Massachusetts Press, 2003): 94–96n 91; Rostow to Kennedy, "Neutralism and Foreign Aid," October 4, 1961, Document 118, *FRUS, Foreign Economic Policy, 1961–1963, Vol. IX*, http://history.state.gov/historicaldocuments /frus1961-63v09/d118.

45. Rostow to Kennedy, "Crucial Issues in Foreign Aid."

46. Lucian Pye, *Politics, Personality, and Nation Building: Burma's Search for Identity* (New Haven, CT: Yale University Press, 1962): 286.

47. Pye, "Military Development in the New Countries," in Pool, *Social Science Research and National Security*, 150. For more on the relationship between counterinsurgency and modernization, see Latham's *Modernization as Ideology* and *The Right Kind of Revolution*; Gilman's *Mandarins of the Future*; and Jeremy Kuzmarov, *Modernizing Repression: Police Training and Nation-Building in the American Century* (Boston: University of Massachusetts Press, 2012).

48. Pye, "Military Development," 152–153.

49. Ibid.

50. Ibid., 157–164.

51. Ibid., 153, 158; Bradley R. Simpson, *Economists with Guns: Authoritarian Development and U.S.-Indonesian Relations, 1960–1968* (Stanford, CA: Stanford University Press, 2008): 72–73.

52. See Gilman, *Mandarins of the Future*, 11, 50–51.

53. P. J. Vatikiotis, *The Egyptian Army in Politics: Pattern for New Nations?* (Westport, CT: Greenwood Press, 1975): 251–257. Vatikiotis expanded on his critique of the Egyptian revolution and lack of intellectual contribution in

"Al-Muthaqqaf al-'Arabī wa-al-mujtama' al-ḥadīth," *Hiwar,* no. 4 (May 1963): 41–51. A similar critique was advanced after Nasser's death by Tawfiq al-Hakim, *'Awdat al-Wa'ī* (Beirut: Dar al-Shurūq, 1974), or *The Return of Consciousness,* translated by R. Bayly Winder (New York: New York University Press, 1985).

54. Manfred Halpern to Elbert Mathews, "Arab Nationalism as a Problem for US Policy," August 5, 1959 RG 59, Entry 1498, Box 11, NARACP.

55. Richard Sanger to Allan Evans, "Access to RME Files by Manfred Halpern and Other Visiting Scholars," December 21, 1959; Sanger to Evans, "Additional Comment regarding Access to RME Files by Manfred Halpern," December 28, 1969 RG 59, Entry 1595, Box 2, NARACP; Manfred Halpern Faculty Files, Seeley G. Mudd Library Princeton University.

56. Manfred Halpern Faculty Files, memorandum by Professor Harry Eckstein, Department of Politics, 1966, Seeley G. Mudd Library Princeton University; Halpern, *The Politics of Social Change*: 3–4; and Khalil, "The Crossroads of the World," 328–329.

57. Halpern, *The Politics of Social Change,* xiii–xiv, 351–352, 361–364. See also, Khalil, "The Crossroads of the World," 328–329.

58. Department of Politics, undated memorandum; "Berger to Beaney," February 11, 1966; "Lenczowski to Eckstein," February 18, 1966; "Pye to Eckstein," March 1, 1966; and "Rustow to Eckstein," February 28, 1966, Halpern Faculty File, Seeley G. Mudd Library Princeton University.

59. See Mark Gasiorowski, *U.S. Foreign Policy and the Shah: Building a Client State in Iran* (Ithaca, NY: Cornell University Press, 1991); Ali Ansari, *Modern Iran since 1921: The Pahlavis and After* (London: Pearson Education, 2003): 147–165. A more favorable analysis of the White Revolution can be found in Odd Arne Westad, *The Global Cold War: Third World Interventions and the Making of Our Times* (Cambridge: Cambridge University Press, 2005).

60. Roland Popp, "An Application of Modernization Theory during the Cold War? The Case of Pahlavi Iran," *International History Review* 30, no. 1 (March 2008): 91–92.

61. Jernegan to Rusk, "Iran as a Country in Transition from Aid to Self-support," March 20, 1964, Document 9; Rostow to Johnson, "Iran Military Purchase Loan: Information," May 23, 1966, Document 143; President Johnson to Shah Pahlavi, November 28, 1967, Document 250, *FRUS, Iran, 1964–1968, Vol. XXII*; Lyndon B. Johnson, "Special Message to the Congress on Foreign Aid," March 19, 1964, http://www.presidency.ucsb.edu/ws/index .php?pid=26118&st=&st1=(last accessed June 14, 2014); Ansari, *Modern Iran since 1921,* 160–162; Popp, "An Application of Modernization Theory," 93–95.

62. Jacobs, *Imagining the Middle East,* 175; Rakove, *Kennedy, Johnson, and the Nonaligned World,* 89. For more on Washington's attempts to undermine Nasser, see Hugh Wilford, *America's Great Game: The CIA's Secret Arabists and the Shaping of the Modern Middle East* (New York: Basic Books, 2013); Miles Copeland, *The Game of Nations: The Amorality of Power Politics*

(London: Weidenfeld and Nicolson, 1969); Yaqub, *Containing Arab Nationalism*.

63. "NIE 36–61: Nasser and the Future of Arab Nationalism," June 27, 1961, Document 68, *FRUS, Near East, 1961–1962, Vol. XVII*.

64. Robert Komer to Walt Whitman Rostow, June 30, 1961, Doc. 74, *FRUS, Near East, 1961–1962, Vol. XVII*. For more on Komer, see Frank Leith Jones, *Blowtorch: Robert Komer, Vietnam, and American Cold War Strategy* (Annapolis, MD: Naval Institute Press, 2014).

65. See Rakove, *Kennedy, Johnson, and the Nonaligned World*, 194–201; Jacobs, *Imagining the Middle East*, 176–177. On Badeau and Nasser, see Mohamed Hassanein Heikel, *The Cairo Documents: The Inside Story of Nasser and His Relationship with World Leaders, Rebels, and Statesmen* (New York: Doubleday, 1973): 201. Komer to Bundy, "Memorandum to the President: A Shift in Policy toward Nasser," December 8, 1961, Document 149, *FRUS, Near East, 1961–1962, Vol. XVII*. For an insider account of Egyptian-Soviet relations, see Heikel, *Sphinx and Commissar: The Rise and Fall of Soviet Influence in the Arab World* (London: St. James's Place, 1978).

66. Jesse Ferris, *Nasser's Gamble: How Intervention in Yemen Caused the Six Day War and the Decline of Egyptian Power* (Princeton, NJ: Princeton University Press, 2013): 29–31, 107–108; Jacobs, *Imagining the Middle East*, 177–178; Malcolm Kerr, *The Arab Cold War: Gamal 'Abd al-Nasir and his Rivals, 1958–1970* (New York: Oxford University Press, 1971). Nasser quoted in John S. Badeau, *The American Approach to the Arab World* (New York: Harper & Row, 1968): 87, and Malik Mufti, "The United States and Nasserist Pan-Arabism," in *The Middle East and the United States: A Historical and Political Reassessment*, 4th ed., ed. David Lesch (Boulder, CO: Westview Press, 2007): 154–155.

67. Gamal Abdel Nasser, *Falsafat al-Thawra* (Cairo: Dār wa-Matabi' al-Sha'b, 1966): 23–24. A slightly different translation can be found in Nasser, *The Philosophy of the Revolution* (Buffalo, NY: Smith, Keynes and Marshall, 1959): 36–37; Badeau, *The American Approach to the Arab World*, 66; Walt Whitman Rostow, *The Diffusion of Power: An Essay in Recent History* (New York: Macmillan, 1972): 199; Lerner's claims also influenced Copeland's analysis of Egypt and Nasser (96, 110).

68. For discussions of the errors and miscalculations that led to the June 1967 war, see William Quandt, *Peace Process: American Diplomacy and the Arab-Israeli Conflict since 1967*, 3rd ed. (Berkeley and Washington, DC: University of California Press and Brookings Institution, 2005); Avi Shlaim, *The Iron Wall: Israel and the Arab World* (New York: Norton, 2001); Tom Segev, *1967: Israel, the War, and the Year That Transformed the Middle East* (New York: Metropolitan Books, 2007).

69. Samuel Huntington, *Political Order in Changing Societies* (New Haven, CT: Yale University Press, 1968). See also Nils Gilman, "Modernization Theory, the Highest Stage of American Intellectual History," in Engerman,

Gilman, Haefele, and Latham, *Staging Growth*, 62–66. Huntington made a similar argument and critique in "The Change to Change: Modernization, Development, and Politics," in *Comparative Modernization: A Reader*, ed. C. E. Black (New York: Free Press, 1970).

70. Huntington, *Political Order in Changing Societies*, 7, 397–461.

71. The OIR report, "The Roots of Arab Resistance to Modernization," is quoted in Jacobs, *Imagining the Middle East*, 140. See Rostow, *The Diffusion of Power*, 199.

72. Glidden to Cuming, "Propaganda Terms of Abuse in Arabic," August 18, 1958, RG 59, Entry 1561, Box 24 NARACP; Keyser to Evans, "Attached Glidden Paper on Arab Society," November 4, 1959, Keyser to Evans, "Pye's Paper on Social Change in Non-Western Societies," November 20, 1959, RG 59, Entry 1595, Box 1. The Pye paper discussed by DNR officials was "The Policy Implications of Social Change in Non-Western Societies," written in April 1957, but it remains unpublished.

73. Little, *American Orientalism*, 30–31. Glidden quoted in Little. For the involvement of the United States in the 1963 Ba'th Party coup, see Brandon Wolfe-Hunnicutt, "Embracing Regime Change in Iraq: The American Foreign Policy and the 1963 Coup d'état in Baghdad," *Diplomatic History* 39, no. 1 (January 2015): 98–125.

74. Harold J. Glidden, "The Arab World," *American Journal of Psychiatry* 128, no. 8 (February 1972): 984; Said, *Orientalism*, 48–49. See also Said's May 1, 1974 letter to *Commentary* magazine in which he discusses and dismisses Glidden's article; http://www.commentarymagazine.com/article/the-arab-mind /(last accessed June 8, 2014).

75. Glidden, "The Arab World," 984–985. As I note in Chapter 2, it is unclear who authored the OSS report on Egypt. However, it was in line with Glidden's responsibilities at the time.

76. Ibid., 985–986.

77. Ibid., 986–988.

78. Raphael Patai, *The Arab Mind* (New York: Charles Scribner's Sons, 1973): 1. Patai briefly discussed *The Philosophy of the Revolution* and dismissed it as Nasser's "little book." He also devoted considerable attention to challenging Nasser's assertion that Egypt stood at the intersection of Africa and the Arab and Islamic worlds. For biographical details, see Robert McG. Thomas Jr., "Raphael Patai, 85, Scholar of Jewish and Arab Cultures," *New York Times* July 25, 1996, http://www.nytimes.com/1996/07/25/arts/raphael-patai -85-a-scholar-of-jewish-and-arab-cultures.html (last accessed June 11, 2014).

79. Patai, *The Arab Mind*, 90–92, 106.

80. Ibid., 118, 140–142.

81. Ibid., 134–135.

82. Ibid., 134–135.

83. "Translation of Statement Provided by Kasim Mehaddi Hilas," in Mark Danner, *Torture and Truth: America, Abu Ghraib, and the War on Terror* (New York: New York Review of Books, 2004): 242–243.

84. Antonio Taguba, "Article 15–6 Investigation of the 800th Military Police Brigade," May 2004, 18, in Danner, *Torture and Truth;* Seymour M. Hersh, *Chain of Command: The Road from 9/11 to Abu Ghraib* (New York: Harper-Collins, 2004): 1–39.

85. See Norvell B. De Atkine, "Foreword," in Patai, *The Arab Mind* (New York: Hatherleigh Press, 2002): i–iii. De Atkine's foreword was reprinted as "The Arab Mind Revisited," *Middle East Quarterly,* Summer 2004, 47–55. The editors' note also had a staunch defense of Patai and criticism of Hersh's reporting.

86. See Hamilton Gibb, *Area Studies Reconsidered* (London: University of London, 1963).

87. See Lucian W. Pye, ed. *Political Science and Area Studies: Rivals or Partners?* (Bloomington: Indiana University Press, 1975), for an attempt by some modernization theorists to analyze and bridge the gap between the disciplines and area studies.

7. Privatizing Knowledge

Epigraph: Lyndon Baines Johnson, "Government and the Critical Intelligence: An Address by President Lyndon B. Johnson Marking the Fiftieth Anniversary of the Brookings Institution" (Washington, DC: Brookings Institution, 1966), http://www.brookings.edu/~/media/About/Content/History/critical_intelligence _lbj.pdf (last accessed March 12, 2014).

1. These trends have been treated separately by scholars and unrelated to the perceived decline of area studies. The role and influence of think tanks on the policymaking process has focused almost exclusively on domestic policies and politics. See James Allen Smith, *The Idea Brokers: Think Tanks and the Rise of the New Policy Elite* (New York: The New Press, 1991); Andrew Rich, *Think Tanks, Public Policy, and the Politics of Expertise* (Cambridge: Cambridge University Press, 2004); Thomas Medvetz, *Think Tanks in America* (Chicago: University of Chicago Press, 2012). Donald E. Abelson, *A Capitol Idea: Think Tanks and U.S. Foreign Policy* (Montreal: McGill-Queen's University Press, 2006), examines the influence of think tanks on U.S. foreign policy after September 11, including the American Enterprise Institute (AEI) and Brookings. Zachary Lockman, *Contending Visions of the Middle East: The History and Politics of Orientalism,* 2nd ed. (Cambridge: Cambridge University Press, 2010): 224–230, 247–249, briefly discusses the relationship between the Brookings Institution and the Washington Institute for Near East Policy and the Arab-Israeli peace process, as well as the emergence of terror studies. The most detailed discussion of the 1975 Brookings Institution report and its relationship to the Carter administration's policies is Jorgen Jensehaugen, "Blueprint for Arab-Israeli Peace? President Carter and the Brookings Report," *Diplomacy and Statecraft* 25 (August 2014): 492–508. The Brookings report is also briefly discussed in

William Quandt, *Peace Process: American Diplomacy and the Arab-Israeli Conflict since 1967,* 3rd ed. (Berkeley and Washington, DC: University of California Press and Brookings Institution, 2005); Steven Spiegel, *The Other Arab Israeli Conflict: Making America's Middle East Policy from Truman to Reagan* (Chicago: University of Chicago Press, 1985): 323; and Douglas Little, *American Orientalism: The United States and the Middle East since 1945* (Chapel Hill: University of North Carolina Press, 2004): 288–289. On post-1960s intellectual debates, see Daniel Rodgers, *Age of Fracture* (Cambridge, MA: Harvard University Press, 2011).

2. Henry Kissinger, *White House Years* (Boston: Little, Brown, 1979): 510. On global protests in 1968, see Jeremi Suri, *Power and Protest: Global Revolution and the Rise of Détente* (Cambridge, MA: Harvard University Press, 2003): 164–212.

3. Kissinger quoted in Jeremi Suri, "Henry Kissinger and American Grand Strategy," in *Nixon in the World: American Foreign Relations, 1969–1977,* ec. Fredrik Logevall and Andrew Preston (New York: Oxford University Press, 2008): 68–69.

4. Quandt, *Peace Process,* 103–104. On the formulation of the Nixon Doctrine, see Daniel Sargent, *A Superpower Transformed: The Remaking of American Foreign Relations in the 1970s* (New York: Oxford University Press, 2015): 42–43, 53–58. For application of the doctrine, see William Stivers, *America's Confrontation with Revolutionary Change in the Middle East* (New York: St. Martin's Press, 1986): 60–76. On relations between the U.S. and Israel, see David Schoenbaum, *The United States and the State of Israel* (New York: Oxford University Press, 1993); Michelle Mart, *Eye on Israel: How America Came to View the Jewish State as an Ally* (Albany: State University of New York Press, 2006); Douglas Little, "The Making of a Special Relationship: The United States and Israel, 1957–1968," *International Journal of Middle East Studies* 25 (1993): 563–585; Yaacov Bar-Simon-Tov, "The United States and Israel since 1948: A 'Special Relationship'?" *Diplomatic History* 22, no. 2 (April 1998): 231–262. On Iran, see Roham Alvandi, *Nixon, Kissinger, and the Shah: The United States and Iran in the Cold War* (New York: Oxford University Press, 2014); Andrew Scott Cooper, *Oil Kings: How the U.S., Iran, and Saudi Arabia Changed the Balance of Power in the Middle East* (New York: Simon & Schuster, 2011). On Saudi Arabia, see Fred Halliday, "A Curious and Close Liaison: Saudi Arabia's Relations with the United States," in *State, Society, and Economy in Saudi Arabia,* ed. Tim Niblock (London: Croom Helm, 1982).

5. Eric Wentworth, "Campus Unrest May Kill Higher Education Bill," *Washington Post,* May 9, 1970; Kissinger, *White House Years,* 515; Nancy Ruther, *Barely There, Powerfully Present: Thirty Years of U.S. Policy on International Higher Education* (New York: Routledge, 2002): 100–101. For Kissinger's background and relationship with Nixon, see Robert Dallek, *Nixon and Kissinger: Partners in Power* (New York: HarperCollins, 2007): 3–59,

89–103. For Kissinger's activities as an FBI informant at Harvard, see Sigmund Diamond, *Compromised Campus: The Collaboration of Universities with the Intelligence Community* (New York: Oxford University Press, 1992): 138–150.

6. Clark Kerr, "Washington: National Foundation for Higher Education," *Change* 3 (May–June 1970): 8–9, 69.

7. David Rosenbaum, "Scholars Upset by Fund Cutback," *New York Times*, April 25, 1970; Richard Semple, "Nixon Asks More for College Fund," *New York Times*, April 29, 1970.

8. Semple, "Nixon Asks More for College Fund"; Amy Newhall, "The Unraveling of the Devil's Bargain: The History and Politics of Language Acquisition," in *Academic Freedom after September 11*, ed. Beshara Doumani (New York: Zone Books, 2006): 211.

9. "NDEA Title VI Area Studies Program," undated, RG12, Entry A1–91, Box 27, United States National Archives and Records Administration, College Park, Maryland (hereafter NARACP).

10. Frank Ching, "Foreign Language and Area Studies in Colleges, Faced with End of U.S. Aid, Have Uncertain Future," *New York Times*, April 2, 1973. See Caspar Weinberger with Gretchen Roberts, *In the Arena: A Memoir of the 20th Century* (Washington, DC: Regnery Publishing, 2001): 191–252.

11. Marshall Shulman, "Lament for the Language Training Centers," *New York Times*, April 6, 1973; "The Language Programs," *New York Times*, April 7, 1973.

12. Weinberger to McClellan, May 8, 1973, RG12, Entry A1–91, Box 27, NARACP.

13. Pendleton Herring, preface to Richard Lambert, *Language and Area Studies Review* (Philadelphia: The American Academy of Political and Social Sciences, October 1973): xvii.

14. Lambert, *Language and Area Studies Review*, 366–367.

15. Ibid., 367–373.

16. Kissinger, *White House Years*, 354. Emphasis in original. See also Salim Yaqub, "The Weight of Conquest: Henry Kissinger and the Arab-Israeli Conflict," in Logevall and Preston, *Nixon and the World*, 227–248. On the consolidation of foreign-policy decision making by Nixon and Kissinger, see William Bundy, *A Tangled Web: The Making of Foreign Policy in the Nixon Presidency* (New York: Hill and Wang, 1998), and Sargent, *A Superpower Transformed*, 45–46. For a critical assessment of Kissinger's influence on foreign policy, see Jussi M. Hahnhimäki, *The Flawed Architect: Henry Kissinger and American Foreign Policy* (New York: Oxford University, 2004). For a discussion of how Kissinger's intellectual development shaped his diplomacy, see Bruce Kuklick, *Blind Oracles: Intellectuals and War from Kennan to Kissinger* (Princeton, NJ: Princeton University Press, 2006): 182–203.

17. Quandt, *Peace Process*, 98–124. Kissinger quoted in Quandt. For the relevant Kissinger discussions see "U.S. Embassy Soviet Union Cable 13148 to

Department of State," October 21, 1973, http://www2.gwu.edu/~nsarchiv /NSAEBB/NSAEBB98/octwar-51.pdf, and "Memcon between Meir and Kissinger," October 22, 1973, 1:35–2:15 P.M., http://www2.gwu.edu/~nsarchiv /NSAEBB/NSAEBB98/octwar-54.pdf. See also Craig Daigle, *The Limits of Détente: The United States, the Soviet Union, and the Arab-Israeli Conflict, 1969–1973* (New Haven, CT: Yale University Press, 2010). For a more critical view of Kissinger's role, see Yigal Kipnis, *1973: The Road to War* (Charlottesville, VA: Just World Books, 2013).

18. Quandt, *Peace Process*, 141–159.

19. Paul Thomas Chamberlin, *The Global Offensive: The United States, the Palestine Liberation Organization, and the Making of the Post–Cold War Order* (Oxford: Oxford University Press, 2012): 231–256. For a detailed discussion of the history of the PLO and its factions, see Yezid Sayigh, *Armed Struggle and the Search for State: The Palestinian National Movement, 1949–1993* (New York: Oxford University Press, 2000); On the emergence of a Palestinian-led PLO, see Osamah Khalil, "Pax Americana: The United States, the Palestinians, and the Peace Process, 1948–2008," *New Centennial Review* 8, no. 1 (2008): 1–41. See Abu Iyad with Eric Rouleau, *My Home, My Land: A Narrative of the Palestinian Struggle* (New York: Times Books, 1981): 121–133, for the PLO leadership's view of the post-October 1973 political environment.

20. Quandt, *Peace Process*, 159–172. For the precise language of the MOU, see the Israeli Ministry of Foreign Affairs, "Israel-United States Memorandum of Understanding," September 1, 1975, http://mfa.gov.il/MFA/ForeignPolicy /MFADocuments/Yearbook2/Pages/112%20Israel-United%20States%20 Memorandum%20of%20Understandi.aspx (last accessed May 9, 2016); see also Gerald R. Ford, *A Time to Heal: The Autobiography of Gerald R. Ford* (New York: Harper & Row, 1979): 287, and Yitzhak Rabin, *The Rabin Memoirs* (Boston: Little, Brown, 1979): 261–263. For the MOU's implications on U.S.-PLO relations, see Osamah Khalil, "The Radical Crescent: The United States, the Palestine Liberation Organisation, and the Lebanese Civil War, 1973–1978," *Diplomacy and Statecraft* 27 (September 2016): 1–27.

21. *Foreign Relations of the United States (hereafter FRUS), Arab-Israeli Dispute 1974–1976, Vol. XXVI*, "Minutes of National Security Council Meeting," April 7, 1976: 1017, and "Memorandum of Conversation," August 7, 1976: 1059–1060. See also Kissinger's *Years of Renewal* (New York: Simon & Schuster, 1999): 1042. For more on U.S.-PLO relations during the first phase of the Lebanese civil war, see Khalil, "The Radical Crescent," and David Wight, "Kissinger's Levantine Dilemma: The Ford Administration and the Syrian Occupation of Lebanon," *Diplomatic History* 37, no. 1 (2013): 144–177.

22. See Abelson, *A Capitol Idea*, 43–46; Alex Abella, *Soldiers of Reason: The RAND Corporation and the Rise of American Empire* (New York: Harcourt, 2008); James Allen Smith, *The Idea Brokers*, xiii–xiv, 115–116; Andrew Rich, *Think Tanks, Public Policy, and the Politics of Expertise* (Cambridge: Cam-

bridge University Press, 2004): 42; U.S. Congress, Office of Technology Assessment, *A History of the Department of Defense Federally Funded Research and Development Centers* (Washington, DC: Government Printing Office, June 1995).

23. Rich, *Think Tanks, Public Policy, and the Politics of Expertise*, 40; Charles H. Saunders, *The Brookings Institution: A Fifty Year History* (Washington, DC: Brookings Institution, 1966): 12–13; Johnson, "Government and the Critical Intelligence."

24. Stephen Klaidman, "Think Tank Helps Shape U.S. Policy," *Washington Post*, October 31, 1976.

25. James Allen Smith, *The Idea Brokers*, 78–79, 271–272; Rich, *Think Tanks, Public Policy, and the Politics of Expertise*, 65–66. For an insider account of the Brookings Institution, see Alice M. Rivlin, "Policy Analysis at the Brookings Institution," in *Organizations for Policy Analysis: Helping Government Think*, ed. Carol H. Weiss (London: Sage Publications, 1991).

26. See Sargent, *A Superpower Transformed*, 170–173; Gaddis Smith, *Morality, Reason, and Power: American Diplomacy in the Carter Years* (New York: Hill and Wang, 1985): 37–38; Zbigniew Brzezinski, *Power and Principle: Memoirs of the National Security Advisor, 1977–1981* (New York: Farrar, Straus and Giroux, 1983): 5–6, 288–289; Georges Berthoin, David Rockefeller, and Takeshi Watanabe, "Foreword," in *Trilateral Commission Task Force Reports, 15–19* (New York: New York University Press, 1981): vii.

27. Author interview with William Quandt, June 4, 2013; Owen to Gordon, November 12, 1974; and Stifel to Gordon, April 29, 1975, Brookings Institution Archive, Foreign Policy Studies Program, Director Henry Owen's Project Files, 1970–1980. The study group was funded through a grant from the Rockefeller Foundation.

28. Brookings Institution, *Toward Peace in the Middle East* (Washington, DC: Brookings Institution, 1975): 1–3.

29. Quandt, *Peace Process*, 178, 436n1; Brzezinski, *Power and Principle*, 84–86; Spiegel, *The Other Arab Israeli Conflict*, 323. Steven Spiegel, another member of the Brookings study group and political science professor at UCLA, concurred with Quandt's assessment.

30. Quandt, *Peace Process*, 180–182; H. D. S. Greenway, "Israel Has Mixed View of Carter Policy," *Washington Post*, March 12, 1977; Bernard Gwertzman, "Carter's 'Plan' for Mideast Peace Creates Shock Waves," *New York Times*, March 21, 1977.

31. Gwertzman, "Carter's 'Plan' for Mideast Peace Creates Shock Waves"; Greenway, "Israel Has Mixed View"; William E. Farrell, "Rabin Now Favoring Full Mideast Pact," *New York Times*, March 16, 1977; James Reston, "How to Save Israel," *New York Times*, March 18, 1977. One of the earliest mentions of the Brookings report and its connection to the Carter administration was Rowland Evans and Robert Novak, "Arafat at the Table?" *Washington Post*, December 18, 1976.

32. Greenway, "Israel Has Mixed View"; Thomas Dunnigan to Vance, March 10, 1977, and March 15, 1977, Access Archival Database, National Archives and Records Administration (hereafter AAD). According to Dunnigan's cable, Israeli prime minister Rabin sought to play down criticism of the Carter administration after returning from Washington. Rabin stated that "the Rogers Plan was meant to be imposed while Carter had expressed an opinion but wants the two parties to decide the issues themselves."

33. Brzezinski to Carter, undated, *FRUS, 1977–1980, Vol. VIII, Arab-Israeli Dispute, January 1977–August 1978*, 328; Lewis to Vance, July 2, 1977, AAD. Another critic of Carter's approach was Theodore Mann, later president of the American Jewish Congress. Mann met frequently with administration officials and expressed his displeasure with their approach in the press. See Theodore R. Mann, *"If I Am Only for Myself . . .": The American Jewish Community's Pursuit of Social Justice, A Memoir* (West Conshohocken, PA: Infinity, 2012): 100, 190.

34. Murphy to Vance, March 31, 1977; Mulcahy to Vance, March 24, 1977, AAD.

35. For example, see Memorandum of Conversation, April 4, 1977, *FRUS, 1977–1980, Vol. VIII, Arab-Israeli Dispute, January 1977–August 1978*, 167–176. On the PLO, see Khalil, "The Radical Crescent."

36. Memorandum of Conversation, April 4, 1977, *FRUS, 1977–1980, Vol. VIII*, 184–189; Jordan to Carter, "Foreign Policy and Domestic Politics," June 1977, Jimmy Carter Presidential Library (hereafter JCPL).

37. For the PFLP hijackings and the Nixon administration's policy toward the PLO and the Jordanian Civil War, see Chamberlin, *The Global Offensive*, 100–131. See also Kai Bird, *The Good Spy: The Life and Death of Robert Ames* (New York: Crown Publishers, 2014): 99–100.

38. Lisa Stampnitzky, *Disciplining Terror: How Experts Invented "Terrorism,"* (Cambridge: Cambridge University Press, 2013): 27–28; Chamberlin, *The Global Offensive*, 178–192; Hoffacker to Kissinger, "Major Problems in Combating Terrorism," October 4, 1973, Digital National Security Archive (hereafter DNSA). For Operation Boulder, see Mustafa Bayoumi, *How Does It Feel to Be a Problem? Being Young and Arab in America* (New York: Penguin, 2008): 264–265; Sarah M. A. Gualtieri, *Between Arab and White: Race and Ethnicity in the Early Syrian American Diaspora* (Berkeley: University of California, Berkeley, 2009): 177–178.

39. Chamberlin, *The Global Offensive*, 193–196; DOS Outgoing Telegram, "Arab Governments Ongoing Support for Black September Organization, March 8, 1973, and Zurhellen to Kissinger, "Campaign against Terrorism," March 23, 1973, DNSA. On warnings to the PLO, see "Talking Points for Meeting with General Walters," undated, NSC Files, Henry A. Kissinger Office Files, Box 139, Richard M. Nixon Presidential Library (hereafter RMNPL); see also Kissinger, *Years of Upheaval* (Boston: Little, Brown, 1982): 627–628.

40. See Stampnitzky, *Disciplining Terror*, 29–30; J. Bowyer Bell, "Trends on Terror," *World Politics* 29, no. 3 (April 1977): 476–488.

41. Stampnitzky, *Disciplining Terror*, 49; On Entebbe's impact, see Melani McAlister, *Epic Encounters: Culture, Media, and U.S. Interests in the Middle East since 1945* (Berkeley: University of California Press, 2005): 182–186.

42. Stampnitzky, *Disciplining Terror*, 111–114; Benjamin Netanyahu, ed., *International Terrorism: Challenge and Response* (New Brunswick, NJ: Transaction Publishers, 1981): i.

43. For example, see Benjamin Netanyahu, ed., *Terrorism: How the West Can Win* (New York: Farrar, Straus and Giroux, 1986). In "Defining Terrorism," Netanyahu writes that terrorism is "not a sporadic phenomenon born of social misery and frustration. It is rooted in the political ambitions and designs of expansionist states and the groups that serve them. Without the support of such states, *international* terrorism would be impossible." Emphasis in original.

44. This was further demonstrated at an April 1980 conference sponsored by the Coalition for a Democratic Majority (CDM). The Coalition was a neoconservative organization and several prominent members attended the Jonathan Institute's conference, including Norman Podhoretz, editor of *Commentary* magazine. Held in Washington, the CDM conference's theme was "Totalitarianism, Terrorism, and American Foreign Policy." The conference was organized at the behest of the Netanyahu family and also honored Soviet dissident Andrei Sakharov. See Justin Vaïsse, *Neoconservatism: The Biography of a Movement* (Cambridge, MA: Belknap Press of Harvard University Press, 2010): 146.

45. Stampnitzky, *Disciplining Terror*, 111–122.

46. For a discussion of the boycott and the manufactured oil embargo crisis, see Timothy Mitchell, *Carbon Democracy: Political Power in the Age of Oil* (New York: Verso Books, 2013): 173–199; On OPEC's origins see Nathan Citino, *From Arab Nationalism to OPEC: Eisenhower, King Sa'ūd, and the Making of U.S.-Saudi Relations* (Bloomington: Indiana University Press, 2002), and Francisco Parra, *Oil Politics: A Modern History of Petroleum* (London: I. B. Tauris, 2004). For Iran's military spending during the 1970s see Mark Gasiorowski, *U.S. Foreign Policy and the Shah: Building a Client State* (Ithaca, NY: Cornell University Press, 1991): 112; James Bill, *The Eagle and the Lion: The Tragedy of American-Iranian Relations* (New Haven, CT: Yale University Press, 1988): 200–202.

47. See Bill, *The Eagle and the Lion*, 373–374; Pusey quoted in Suzanne R. Spring, "Year of the Shah," *Harvard Crimson*, June 5, 1980.

48. Steven Klaidman, "A Look at Former President Ford's Think Tank Institution," *Washington Post*, February 20, 1977; Thomas Medvetz, *Think Tanks in America* (Chicago: University of Chicago Press, 2012): 68, 106–107. Ornstein quoted in Medvetz.

49. George Lenczowski, *Middle East Oil in a Revolutionary Age* (Washington, DC: American Enterprise Institute, 1976): 36. See also Lenczowski, *United States Interests in the Middle East* (Washington, DC: American Enterprise Institute, 1968).

50. George Lenczowski, ed. *Iran under the Pahlavis* (Stanford, CA: Hoover Institution Press, 1978): x, 433, 475. For an examination of the different forces in Iran contributing to the revolution, see Ervand Abrahamian, *Iran between Two Revolutions* (Princeton, NJ: Princeton University Press, 1982), and Ali M. Ansari, *Modern Iran since 1921: The Pahlavis and After* (London: Pearson Education, 2003): 192–249. For U.S. policy and the Iranian revolution, see Bill, *The Eagle and the Lion,* 216–316, and Gary Sick, *All Fall Down: America's Fateful Encounter with Iran* (London: I. B. Tauris, 1985).

51. Brzezinski to Carter, "Consultative Security Framework on the Middle East" February 28, 1979, Box 15, JCPL; Lenczowski, "The Arc of Crisis: Its Central Sector," *Foreign Affairs* 57, no. 4 (Spring 1979): 796–820; for the "arc of crisis" and the Carter Doctrine, see Sargent, 261–262, 286–289. See also Zbigniew Brzezinski, *Power and Principle,* 443–456, and Khalil, "The Crossroads of the World."

52. See Trita Parsi, *Treacherous Alliance: The Secret Dealings of Israel, Iran, and the United States* (New Haven, CT: Yale University Press, 2007), and Mahmood Mamdani, *Good Muslim, Bad Muslim: America, the Cold War, and the Roots of Terror* (New York: Pantheon Books, 2004): 110–114. For the regional and historical implications of the Iranian revolution, see David W. Lesch, *1979: The Year That Shaped the Modern Middle East* (Boulder, CO: Westview Press, 2001), and Hamit Bozarslan, "Revisiting the Middle East's 1979," *Economy and Society* 41, no. 4 (November 2012): 558–567; Toby Craig Jones, "America, Oil, and War in the Middle East," *Journal of American History* 99, no. 1 (2012): 208–218. For a critique of U.S. press coverage of the Iranian revolution and aftermath, see Edward Said, *Covering Islam: How the Media and the Experts Determine How We See the World,* rev. ed. (New York: Vintage, 1997).

53. See Seth Cropsey, "Arab Money and the Universities," *Commentary,* April 1979: 72–74; Mitchell Bard, *The Arab Lobby: The Invisible Alliance That Undermines America's Interests in the Middle East* (New York: HarperCollins, 2010): 300–313. See Zachary Lockman, *Field Notes: The Making of Middle East Studies in the United States* (Stanford, CA: Stanford University Press, 2016): 233–235, for a discussion of Iranian funding of a program at Princeton and an SSRC conference to be held in Iran.

54. Seymour Hersh, "Huge C.I.A. Operation Reported in U.S. against Antiwar Forces, Other Dissidents in Nixon Years," *New York Times,* December 22, 1974. Hersh's revelations about the CIA emerged after a separate investigation and report by the Senate Armed Services Committee into spying by the Pentagon on Nixon's NSC. Anonymous CIA sources quoted by Hersh suggested that the operation was conducted by the CIA's counterintelligence division led by James Jesus Angleton, a veteran official whose work in

the clandestine services dated to the Office of Strategic Services (OSS). The sources believed that the domestic spying effort grew out of Angleton's attempts to identify foreign sources of support for the antiwar movement. Angleton resigned shortly after Hersh's article was published. For more on Angleton's background and career, see Robin Winks, *Cloak and Gown: Scholars in the Secret War, 1939–1961* (New York: William Morrow, 1987): 322–438.

55. Kissinger to Ford, "Colby Report," December 25, 1974, Richard B. Cheney Files, Box 5 (http://www.fordlibrarymuseum.gov/library/document/0005 /1561477.pdf), and Memorandum of Conversation, Gerald R. Ford Presidential Library (hereafter GFPL).

56. "Memorandum of Conversation," January 4, 1975, 1, Brent Scowcroft Memoranda of Conversation Collection, Box 8, GFPL; Tim Weiner, *Legacy of Ashes: The History of the CIA* (New York: Doubleday, 2007): 336–339.

57. "Allegations of CIA Domestic Activities," January 4, 1975, 2, Brent Scowcroft Memoranda of Conversation Collection, Box 8, GFPL.

58. Nelson Rockefeller, *Report to the President by the Commission on CIA Activities within the United States* (New York: Manor Books, 1975).

59. United States Senate, *Final Report of the Select Committee to Study Governmental Operations with Respect to Intelligence Activities, Book 1* (Washington, DC: Government Printing Office, 1976): 181. For a detailed discussion of the Church Commission, see Loch K. Johnson, *A Season of Inquiry: The Senate Intelligence Investigation* (Lexington: University of Kentucky Press, 1985).

60. U.S. Senate, *Final Report of the Select Committee*, 182–183.

61. Ibid., 189–190. Operational use of individuals was defined as "recruitment, use, or training, on either a witting or unwitting basis, for intelligence purposes. That is, the individual is directed or 'tasked' to do something for the CIA—as opposed to volunteering information. Such purposes include covert action, clandestine intelligence collection (espionage) and various kinds of support functions" (184n5).

62. Ibid., 191.

63. Weiner, *Legacy of Ashes*, 346–348.

64. Van Alstyne to Bush, May 4, 1976, CIA CREST.

65. Bush to Van Alstyne, May 11, 1976, CIA CREST. In a detailed follow-up letter on May 24, 1976, Van Alstyne accepted the invitation to meet with senior officials. He also listed the Church Committee's findings on the overt and covert use of academics and reiterated his request that the CIA no longer use academics for covert operations. Van Alstyne to Bush, May 24, 1976, CIA CREST.

66. Bush to Bundy, May 28, 1976, CIA CREST.

67. Davis to Turner, May 3, 1977 and Turner to Davis, May 12, 1977, CIA CREST.

68. Zachary Lockman, *Contending of the Middle East: The History and Politics of Orientalism*, 2nd ed. (Cambridge: Cambridge University Press, 2010): 151–153,

178–182; Lisa Hajjar and Steve Niva, "(Re)Made in the USA: Middle East Studies in the Global Era," *Middle East Report* 205 (October–December 1997): 2–9. The most influential studies were Peter Gran, *Islamic Roots of Capitalism* (Syracuse, NY: Syracuse University Press, 1978); Roger Owen, *The Middle East in the World Economy, 1800–1914* (London: Metheun, 1981); and Joe Stork, *Middle East Oil and the Energy Crisis* (New York: Monthly Review Press, 1975). For an overview of the New Left, see Van Gosse, "A Movement of Movements: The Definition and Periodization of the New Left," in *A Companion to Post-1945 America,* ed. Jean-Christophe Agnew and Roy Rosenzweig (Malden, MA: Blackwell, 2002): 277–302; for a critical view of the New Left, see William O'Neill, *Coming Apart: An Informal History of America in the 1960s* (Chicago: Ivan R. Dee, 2005): 275–306.

69. Among the most prominent works related to the Middle East were Abrahamian, *Iran between Two Revolutions*; Hanna Batatu, *The Old Social Classes and the Revolutionary Movements of Iraq: A Study of Iraq's Old Landed and Commercial Classes and of Its Communists, Ba'thists, and Free Officers* (Princeton, NJ: Princeton University Press, 1978); Joel Beinin and Zachary Lockman, *Workers on the Nile: Nationalism, Communism, Islam, and the Egyptian working class, 1882–1954* (Princeton, NJ: Princeton University Press, 1987);

70. Author interview with Joel Beinin, April 16, 2014; Peter Johnson and Joe Stork, "MERIP: The First Decade," *MERIP Reports* 100/101 (October–December 1981): 50–55.

71. Text of Address, Lieutenant General Vernon Walters, January 26, 27, 1976, CIA CREST. Among the New Left activities that the CIA monitored was the attempt to remove Evron Kirkpatrick as executive director of the American Political Science Association after revelations that a corporation he co-founded received funding from the agency. See Memorandum for the Record, "Projected Rampart's Issue 'CIA and the Universities,'" January 31, 1968, CIA CREST. For the controversy, see Ido Oren, *Our Enemies and US: America's Rivalries and the Making of Political Science* (Ithaca, NY: Cornell University Press, 2003): 161–162.

72. Edward Said, *Orientalism* (New York: Vintage, 1979): 2–5; Lockman, *Contending Visions of the Middle East,* 193–200.

73. Lockman, *Contending Visions,* 190–192; Bernard Lewis, "The Question of Orientalism," *New York Review of Books,* June 24, 1982; Edward W. Said and Oleg Grabar, reply by Bernard Lewis, "Orientalism: An Exchange," *New York Review of Books,* August 12, 1982.

74. Don Babai, ed., *Reflections on the Past, Visions of the Future: The Center for Middle East Studies, Harvard University* (Cambridge, MA: Harvard University Press, 2004): 16–17. Safran served on the State Department's Near East Affairs (NEA) Advisory Board; "Meeting of NEA Advisors," February 10–11, 1967, RG 59, Entry 5657, Box 1, NARACP.

75. Kristin A. Goss, "Safran to Leave Top Post after Inquiry into CIA Funding," *Harvard Crimson* 6 (January 1986); Lockman, *Contending Visions,* 244–245.

76. Goss, "Safran to Leave Top Post"; Fox Butterfield, "Scholar to Quit Post at Harvard over CIA Tie," *New York Times,* January 2, 1986; Chris Mooney, "For Your Eyes Only," *Lingua Franca* (November 2000): 37.

77. Mooney, "For Your Eyes Only," 38; "Code Breaking," *Harvard Crimson,* February 22, 1986; David S. Hilzenrath, "Spooked," *Harvard Crimson,* June 5, 1986. Gates quoted by Hilzenrath.

78. Betty Anderson, *The American University of Beirut: Arab Nationalism and Liberal Education* (Austin: University of Texas Press, 2011): 151–158; AUB Board of Trustees Reports, Book XIII–Book XIX (January 1969–November 1981); President's Annual Report to the Board of Trustees, 1970–1991, American University of Beirut Jafet Library Archive and Special Collection (hereafter AUBA).

79. Abshire to Ribicoff, March 15, 1971, RG 59, Entry 5624, Box 3, NARACP.

80. Buffum to Kissinger, March 12, 1973, AAD.

81. AUBA, President's Annual Report to the Board of Trustees, 1970–1991. For the PLO's para-state in Lebanon and decision making during the 1982 war, see Rashid Khalidi's *Under Siege: PLO Decisionmaking during the 1982 War* (New York: Columbia University Press, 1986) and *The Iron Cage: The Story of the Palestinian Struggle for Statehood* (Boston: Beacon Press, 2006). For Israel's invasion, see Avi Shlaim, *The Iron Wall: Israel and the Arab World* (New York: Norton, 2001). On the Lebanese Shi'a militia's origins and the kidnappings, see Augustus Richard Norton, *Hezbollah: A Short History* (Princeton, NJ: Princeton University Press, 2007), and Amal Saad-Ghorayeb, *Hizbullah: Politics and Religion* (London: Pluto Books, 2002). Hizbullah held AUB's acting president David Dodge hostage for a year and was responsible for the 1984 assassination of noted scholar and AUB president Malcolm Kerr. See Susan Kerr van de Ven, *One Family's Response to Terrorism: A Daughter's Memoir* (Syracuse, NY: Syracuse University Press, 2008).

82. Lawrence R. Murphy, *The American University in Cairo: 1919–1987* (Cairo: American University in Cairo Press, 1987): 171–178; Ernest McCarus, "History of Arabic Study in the United States," in *The Arabic Language in America,* ed. Aleya Rouchdy (Detroit: Wayne State University Press, 1992): 214–215.

83. Christie to Bovis, March 27, 1967, RG 59, Entry 5657, Box 1, NARACP. Part of the endowment grant was intended to cover AUC's short-term debts from large capital projects, while the remainder was to be spent over twenty years and ensure the university's continued operation. Although it was a large grant amount, the State Department explained that the United States held $285 million in inconvertible Egyptian currency. It added that the United Arab Republic's annual loan repayments exceeded the U.S. government's expenditures in Egyptian currency.

84. Murphy, *The American University in Cairo*, 171–178; Suhayr Husayn Ahmad al-Biyali, *Ahdāf al-Jāmi'ah al-Amrīkīyah bi-al-Qāhirah: dirāsah wathā'iqīyah mundhu al-nash'ah ḥattá 'ām 1980 M* (Al-Miniyā: Dār Farḥah lil-Nashr wa-al-Tawzī', 2002): 256.

85. Hermann Eilts Oral History, August 12, 1988, Association for Diplomatic Studies and Training, http://www.adst.org/OH%20TOCs/Eilts,%20 Herman.toc.pdf (last accessed May 27, 2015); Sisco to Barco, June 19, 1970; RG 59, Entry 5657, Box 6, NARACP.

86. Greene to Sterner, April 10, 1973; RG 59, Entry 5657, Box 11, NARACP.

87. Eilts to Sterner, February 15, 1974, RG 59, Entry 5657, Box 12, NARACP. Emphasis in original.

88. Murphy, *The American University in Cairo*, 200–203; AUC President's Annual Reports 1973–1974 and 1974–1975, Byrd Presidential Papers, Box 2, AUCA. For the shift from Nasser to Sadat, see Tarek Osman, *Egypt on the Brink: From Nasser to the Muslim Brotherhood* (New Haven, CT: Yale University Press, 2010). See Steve Coll, *Ghost Wars: The Secret History of the CIA, Afghanistan, and Bin Laden from the Soviet Invasion to September 10* (New York: Penguin, 2004), on Egypt's support for Afghanistan's *mujahidin*.

89. Klaidman, "A Look at Former President Ford's Think Tank Institution."

90. Kenneth Lamott, "Right Thinking Think-Tank," *New York Times Magazine*, July 23, 1978. Stanford provided roughly 30 percent of Hoover's annual $2 million budget, and 40 percent was through donations and corporate gifts. Hoover's press also published or reprinted a significant number of academic works.

91. Martin Tolchin, "Brookings Thinks about Its Future," *New York Times*, December 14, 1983; Clyde H. Farnsworth, "No Recession in Ideas at Capital Think Tanks," *New York Times*, November 10, 1982.

92. Harold Saunders Oral History, The Association for Diplomatic Studies and Training Foreign Affairs Oral History Project, November 24, 1993, http://www.adst.org/OH%20TOCs/Saunders,%20Harold%20H.toc.pdf (last accessed December 30, 2015).

93. Shlaim, *The Iron Wall*, 391–392; Seth Anziska, "Israel, the United States, and the War in Lebanon" (paper presented at the MESA 2014 Annual Meeting, Washington, DC): 3–6, 9–13.

94. See Quandt, *Peace Process*, 254–260; Shlaim, *The Iron Wall*, 415–423. For recent revelations on Israel's role in the Sabra and Shatila massacres, see Seth Anziska, "A Preventable Massacre," *New York Times*, September 6, 2012, and Anziska, "Camp David's Shadow: The United States, Lebanon, and the Israeli-Palestinian Conflict, 1977–1988" (PhD dissertation, Columbia University, 2015).

95. Martin Indyk, *Innocent Abroad: An Intimate Account of American Peace Diplomacy in the Middle East* (New York: Simon & Schuster, 2009): 15. See also the Washington Institute, "Mission and History," www.washingtoninstitute .org/about/mission-and-history (last accessed May 2, 2014).

96. David B. Ottoway, "Mideast Institute's Experts and Ideas Ascendant," *Washington Post*, March 24, 1989. A review of the op-ed articles in the *New York Times, Washington Post*, the *Wall Street Journal*, and the *Los Angeles Times* from January 1, 1985 to December 31, 1988 revealed an average of one op-ed and one letter to the editor per year by research fellows affiliated with WINEP.

97. Robert Pear, "Shultz Says U.S. Opposes P.L.O. Statehood Plans," *New York Times*, September 17, 1988. For more on U.S.-Palestinian relations and the machinations behind the decision to open a dialogue with the PLO, see Quandt, *Peace Process*, 278–285, and Khalil, "Pax Americana."

98. Ottoway, "Mideast Institute's Experts and Ideas Ascendant"; Washington Institute for Near East Policy, *Building for Peace: American Strategy in the Middle East* (Washington, DC: WINEP, 1988).

99. Ottoway, "Mideast Institute's Experts and Ideas Ascendant."

100. Washington Institute for Near East Policy, *Building for Peace*, vii–xviii.

101. Ottoway, "Mideast Institute's Experts and Ideas Ascendant"; Washington Institute for Near East Policy, *Building for Peace*, vii–xviii.

102. Brookings Institution, *Toward Arab-Israeli Peace: Report of a Study Group* (Washington, DC: Brookings Institution, 1988): xi–xiv, 3–7. Other than Quandt, the only member to serve on both Brookings study groups was Rita Hauser. A prominent attorney, Hauser was also selected by President Nixon to serve as U.S. ambassador to the UN Commission on Human Rights.

103. Mann to Siegman, December 29, 1987, American Jewish Congress Archives, Series VII, Sub-Series B, Box 629. Siegman was also the executive director of the American Association for Middle East Studies (AAMES) discussed in Chapter 5; see Lockman, *Field Notes*, 160–170

104. William Quandt, ed., *The Middle East: Ten Years after Camp David* (Washington, DC: Brookings Institution, 1988): 16; author interview with William Quandt.

105. Lorraine M. McDonnell, Sue E. Berryman, and Douglas Scott, *Federal Support for International Studies: The Role of NDEA Title VI* (Santa Monica, CA: RAND Corporation, May 1981): i–xiii. See also Hajjar and Niva, "(Re) Made in the USA."

106. SRI International, *Defense Intelligence: Foreign Area/Language Needs and Academe* (Washington, DC: SRI, October 1983): 4–7; Joy Rohde, *Armed with Expertise: The Militarization of American Social Research during the Cold War* (Ithaca, NY: Cornell University Press, 2013): 121. SRI was established in 1946 to oversee Stanford's research projects and maintained extensive ties to the Pentagon. Stanford eventually privatized SRI after protests and it became a leading federal contractor.

107. SRI International, *Defense Intelligence*, 31–33.

108. Ibid., 37–38.

109. Richard Lambert, *Beyond Growth: The Next Stage in Language and Area Studies* (Washington, DC: Association of American Universities, 1984): 10–13.

110. Ibid., 22–23. See Weinberger, *In the Arena*, 287–323; Julian E. Zelizer, *Arsenal of Democracy: The Politics of National Security from World War II to the War on Terrorism* (New York: Basic Books, 2010): 306.

111. Lambert, *Beyond Growth*, 17–19, 412–414.

8. Empire and Its Limitations

Epigraph: Bob Woodward, *Plan of Attack* (New York: Simon & Schuster, 2004): 443. Bush's statement was in response to a question by Woodward on how history would judge the war in Iraq.

1. President Bush Delivers Graduation Speech at West Point, June 1, 2002, http://georgewbush-whitehouse.archives.gov/news/releases/2002/06 /20020601-3.html (last accessed May 5, 2015).

2. A number of works have examined the neoconservative movement, however, the relationship to Middle East studies is discussed either in passing or not at all. These works include Jacob Heilbrunn, *They Knew They Were Right: The Rise of the Neocons* (New York: Doubleday, 2008); Anne Norton, *Leo Strauss and the Politics of American Empire* (New Haven, CT: Yale University Press, 2004); James Mann, *Rise of the Vulcans: The History of Bush's War Cabinet* (New York: Viking, 2004); Justin Vaïsse, *Neoconservatism: The Biography of a Movement* (Cambridge, MA: Belknap Press of Harvard University Press, 2010); Michael MacDonald, *Overreach: Delusions of Regime Change in Iraq* (Cambridge, MA: Harvard University Press, 2010); Zachary Lockman, *Contending Visions of the Middle East: The History and Politics of Orientalism*, 2nd ed. (Cambridge: Cambridge University Press, 2010): 253–273, discusses the attack on Middle East studies but only briefly examines its relationship to U.S. foreign policy in the region.

3. Craig LaMay, Martha FitzSimon, and Jeanne Sahadi, eds. *The Media at War: The Press and the Persian Gulf Conflict, A Report of the Gannett Foundation* (New York: Gannett Foundation Media Center, June 1991): 3, 43; Phil McCombs, "Siege of the Mideast Experts," *Washington Post,* August 21, 1990. See also Joel Beinin, "Money, Media, and Policy Consensus: The Washington Institute for Near East Policy," *Middle East Report* 180 (January–February 1993): 10–15.

4. See Douglas Kellner, *The Persian Gulf and TV War* (Boulder, CO: Westview Press, 1992): 79–80; Ella Shohat, "The Media's War," in *Seeing through the Media: The Persian Gulf War,* ed. Susan Jeffords and Lauren Rabinovitcz (New Brunswick, NJ: Rutgers University Press, 1994): 147–154.

5. Stanley Heginbotham, "Rethinking International Scholarship: The Transition from the Cold War Era," *Items: Newsletter of the SSRC* 48, no. 2/3 (1994): 34–35.

6. See Robert H. Bates, "Area Studies and Political Science: Rupture and Possible Synthesis," *Africa Today* 44, no. 2 (1997): 123–131; Bates, "Area Studies and the Discipline: A Useful Controversy?" *PS: Political Science and Politics* 30, no. 2 (1997): 166–169; Peter A. Hall and Sidney Tarrow, "Global-

ization and Area Studies: When Is Too Broad Too Narrow?" *Chronicle of Higher Education*, January 23, 1988; Mark Tessler, Jodi Nachtaway, and Anne Banda, eds., *Area Studies and Social Science: Strategies for Understanding Middle East Politics* (Bloomington: Indiana University Press, 1999): vii–xx, and Lisa Anderson, "Politics in the Middle East: Opportunities and Limits in the Quest for Theory," in Tessler, Nachtaway, and Banda, *Area Studies and Social Science*, 1–10; Rashid Khalidi, "Is There a Future for Middle East Studies? 1994 MESA Presidential Address," *Middle East Studies Association Bulletin* 29, no. 1 (July 1995): 1–6.

7. William Quandt, *Peace Process: American Diplomacy and the Arab-Israeli Conflict since 1967*, 3rd ed. (Berkeley and Washington, D.C.: University of California Press and Brookings Institution, 2005): 303–313; Washington Institute for Near East Policy, *Pursuing Peace: An American Strategy for the Arab-Israeli Peace Process* (Washington, DC: WINEP, 1992): vii.

8. See Beinin, "Money, Media, and Policy Consensus."

9. Washington Institute for Near East Policy, *Pursuing Peace*, iii–vi. New participants in the 1992 study group included Les Aspin, William Cohen, Madeline Albright, Alexander Haig, Sam Nunn, and Jeane Kirkpatrick.

10. Martin Indyk, *Innocent Abroad: An Intimate Account of American Peace Diplomacy in the Middle East* (New York: Simon & Schuster, 2009): 23–24.

11. Quandt, *Peace Process*, 322–323, describes Ross and Indyk as the "intellectual architects" of the Clinton administration's approach to the peace process. For example, see Alison Mitchell, "The Puzzle for the U.S.: How to Play Peacemaker," *New York Times*, July 31, 1997, in which White House spokesman Michael McCurry stated, "We cannot do for the parties what they must do themselves, which is reconcile their differences." In contrast, Richard Haas of the Brookings Institution, who was a former member of the Bush administration, argued that "a high U.S. profile is a necessity" to break the deadlocked negotiations.

12. For Albright's memorandum, see Ahron Bregman, *Cursed Victory: A History of Israel and the Occupied Territories* (London: Penguin, 2014): 228–239. On blaming Arafat, see Dennis Ross, *The Missing Peace: The Inside Story of the Fight for Middle East Peace* (New York: Farrar, Straus and Giroux, 2004).

13. Indyk, *Innocent Abroad*, 41–43.

14. Connie Bruck, "The Influencer," *New Yorker*, May 10, 2010; Aaron Ross Sorkin, "Schlepping to Moguldom," *New York Times*, September 5, 2004. In the *New Yorker* profile, Saban stated that donations to political parties, establishing think tanks, and controlling media outlets were the "three ways to be influential in American politics."

15. Quandt, *Peace Process*, 386–412; George W. Bush, *Decision Points* (New York: Crown Publishers, 2010): 400–407. See also Osamah Khalil, "Pax Americana," *New Centennial Review* 8, no. 1 (2008): 1–41, in which I examine the shift to conflict management and the post-Arafat period. Ross's support of conflict management continues over a decade later; see Dennis Ross, "Open

a Middle Road to Mideast Peace," *New York Times,* May 23, 2014. See also Elliott Abrams, *Tested by Zion: The Bush Administration and the Israeli-Palestinian Conflict* (Cambridge: Cambridge University Press, 2013).

16. Vaïsse, *Neoconservatism,* 6–13.

17. Heilbrunn, *They Knew They Were Right,* 78–79, 114, 142–143. For Jabotinksy's influence on Israeli politics and foreign policy, see Avi Shlaim's *The Iron Wall: Israel and the Arab World* (New York: Norton, 2001).

18. Heilbrunn, *They Knew They Were Right,* 101–105, 184–186; Vaïsse, *Neoconservatism,* 119–121. For Wohlstetter's influence at RAND, see Fred Kaplan, *The Wizards of Armageddon* (New York: Simon & Schuster, 1983); Alex Abella, *Soldiers of Reason: The RAND Corporation and the Rise of American Empire* (New York: Harcourt, 2008); Bruce Kuklick, *Blind Oracles: Intellectuals and War from Kennan to Kissinger* (Princeton, NJ: Princeton University Press, 2006): 60–64.

19. Heilbrunn, *They Knew They Were Right,* 78–79, 114, 142–143; Vaïsse, *Neoconservatism,* 6–13.

20. Vaïsse, *Neoconservatism,* 153–179; Campbell Craig and Fredrik Logevall, *America's Cold War: The Politics of Insecurity* (Cambridge, MA: Harvard University Press, 2009): 306–308.

21. Vaïsse, *Neoconservatism,* 147; Joel Beinin, "The Israelization of American Middle East Policy Discourse," *Social Text* 21, no. 2 (Summer 2003): 132; Jason Vest, "The Men from JINSA and CSP," *The Nation,* August 15, 2002.

22. Heilbrunn, *They Knew They Were Right,* 154–159; Frances Stonor Saunders, *The Cultural Cold War: The CIA and the World of Arts and Letters* (New York: The New Press, 1999): 157, 170, 419; Vaïsse, *Neoconservatism,* 204–208.

23. Harold Saunders Oral History, The Association for Diplomatic Studies and Training Foreign Affairs Oral History Project, November 24, 1993, http://www.adst.org/OH%20TOCs/Saunders,%20Harold%20H.toc.pdf (last accessed December 30, 2015); Harold H. Saunders, *Conversations with Harold H. Saunders: U.S. Policy in the Middle East in the 1980s* (Washington, DC: American Enterprise Institute, 1982); Harold Saunders, "Don't Fear Palestinian Talks," *New York Times,* March 4, 1984; Judith Kipper, "PLO, Take the Step," *New York Times,* February 24, 1982.

24. Heilbrunn, *They Knew They Were Right,* 158–159; Vaïsse, *Neoconservatism,* 204–208.

25. Heilbrunn, *They Knew They Were Right,* 195–197; Mann, *Rise of the Vulcans,* 209–210. For a counterview of the DPG, see Eric S. Edelman, "Strange Career of the 1992 Defense Planning Guidance," in *In Uncertain Times: American Foreign Policy after the Berlin Wall and 9/11,* ed. Melvyn P. Leffler and Jeffrey W. Legro (Ithaca, NY: Cornell University Press, 2011).

26. Vaïsse, *Neoconservatism,* 206, 226–227; Heilbrunn, *They Knew They Were Right,* 221–225, 237–238. For a full list of signatories to the PNAC letter sent to President Bill Clinton, see http://www.informationclearinghouse.info /article5527.htm (last accessed July 8, 2014).

27. The text of "A Clean Break: A New Strategy for Securing the Realm" can be found at http://www.informationclearinghouse.info/article1438.htm (last

accessed July 8, 2014). See also Joel Beinin, "The Israelization of American Middle East Policy Discourse." Although Douglas Feith is often credited as the author or coauthor of "A Clean Break," he has publicly denied it. See his letter to the *Washington Post,* September 16, 2004. Heilbrunn, however, describes Feith's letter as a "weaselly" attempt to distance himself from the document (*They Knew They Were Right,* 237–238).

28. David Wurmser, *Tyranny's Ally: America's Failure to Defeat Saddam Hussein* (Washington, DC: AEI Press, 1999); Heilbrunn, *They Knew They Were Right,* 224. Prior to AEI and the Institute for Advanced and Strategic Political Studies, Wurmser was employed by WINEP.

29. Bush, *Decision Points,* 136–137, 185–190; Woodward, *Plan of Attack,* 24–26; Mark Danner, "Rumsfeld's War and Its Consequences Now," *New York Review of Books,* December 19, 2013. Rumsfeld writes in *Known and Unknown: A Memoir* (New York: Sentinel, 2011): 425, that Bush "wanted the options to be 'creative,' which I took to mean that he wanted something different from the massive land force assembled during the 1991 Gulf War. I certainly did not get the impression the President had made up his mind on the merits of toppling Saddam Hussein's regime. In fact, at the September 15 NSC meeting at Camp David days earlier when Iraq had been raised, he had specifically kept the focus on Afghanistan."

30. George W. Bush, *The National Security Strategy of the United States of America,* September 2002.

31. Vaïsse, *Neoconservatism,* 234–235. For example see Niall Ferguson's *Empire: The Rise and Demise of the British World Order and the Lessons for Global Power* (New York: Basic Books, 2002) and *Colossus: The Rise and Fall of the American Empire* (New York: Penguin, 2004). See also William Kristol and Robert Kagan, "Toward a Neo-Reaganite Foreign Policy," *Foreign Affairs,* July/August 1996, for a preview of this line of argument.

32. Kenneth M. Pollack, *The Threatening Storm: The Case for Invading Iraq* (New York: Random House, 2002): 418, 426.

33. See Kenneth M. Pollack, "Why Iraq Can't Be Deterred," *New York Times,* September 26, 2002; Pollack, "A Last Chance to Stop Iraq," *New York Times,* February 21, 2003; Condoleezza Rice, interview with CNN, September 8, 2002.

34. Bernard Lewis, "The Roots of Muslim Rage," *The Atlantic,* September 1990; Lewis, "The Revolt of Islam," *New Yorker,* November 19, 2001.

35. Samuel Huntington's "Clash of Civilizations," *Foreign Affairs* 72 (1993); Huntington, *The Clash of Civilizations and the Remaking of the World Order* (New York: Touchstone, 1996).

36. See Peter Waldman, "A Historian's Take on Islam Steers U.S. in Terrorism Fight," *Wall Street Journal,* February 3, 2004; Evan R. Goldstein, "Osama bin Laden Made Me Famous," *Chronicle of Higher Education,* April 22, 2012; Bernard Lewis and Buntzie Ellis Churchill, *Notes on a Century: Reflections of a Middle East Historian* (New York: Viking, 2012): 328–335; Dick Cheney, *In*

My Time: A Personal and Political Memoir (New York: Simon & Schuster, 2011): 327; Vice President Dick Cheney, interview by Tim Russert, NBC, *Meet the Press,* March 16, 2003.

37. Lewis, *What Went Wrong? Western Impact and Middle Eastern Response* (New York: Oxford University Press, 2002): 3, 151–159.

38. Lewis, "Time for Toppling," *Wall Street Journal,* September 23, 2002; Jeffrey Donovan, "U.S.: Mideast Policy—Does the Road to Jerusalem Run through Baghdad?" Radio Free Europe/Radio Liberty, June 26, 2002.

39. Bob Woodward, *State of Denial* (New York: Simon & Schuster, 2007): 128, 216–217; Kanan Makiya, *Republic of Fear: The Politics of Modern Iraq* (Berkeley: University of California, 1989); Makiya, "Free Iraq Starts to Take Form" *National Post,* April 17, 2003; Laura Secor, "The Dissident," *Boston Globe,* November 3, 2002; Edward Said, "Misinformation about Iraq," *Al-Ahram Weekly,* November 28–December 4, 2002. Although Makiya never responded to Said, other INC members did; see Abdel Khaliq Hussein "Mawqif al-Muthaqqafīn al-'Arab min al-qadīyah al-'Irāqīya—radd 'alā Edward Said," *Al-Hiwar,* December 12, 2002, http://www.ahewar.org/debat /show.art.asp?aid=4336 (last accessed November 12, 2014).

40. "President discusses the Future of Iraq," White House Office of the Press Secretary news release, February 26, 2003, http://georgewbush-whitehouse .archives.gov/news/releases/2003/02/20030226-11.html (last accessed December 18, 2015).

41. See Woodward, *Plan of Attack* and *State of Denial.*

42. In addition to the memoirs of the different members of the Bush administration, the Iraq war has spawned numerous books by journalists offering different perspectives, from the White House to the U.S. military and the Coalition Provisional Authority, as well as the Iraqi insurgency. See Thomas Ricks, *Fiasco: The American Military Adventure in Iraq* (New York: Penguin Press, 2006); Rajiv Chandrasekaran, *Imperial Life in the Emerald City: Inside Iraq's Green Zone* (New York: Alfred A. Knopf, 2006); and Woodward's *State of Denial.* For the impact of the war on Iraqis, see Anthony Shadid, *Night Draws Near: Iraq's People in the Shadow of America's War* (New York: Henry Holt, 2005); and Nir Rosen's *In the Belly of the Green Bird: The Triumph of the Martyrs in Iraq* (New York: Free Press, 2006); and *Aftermath: Following the Bloodshed of America's Wars in the Muslim World* (New York: Nation Books, 2010). See also Ali A. Allawi, *The Occupation of Iraq: Winning the War, Losing the Peace* (New Haven, CT: Yale University Press, 2007); Peter Hahn, *Mission Accomplished? The United States and Iraq since World War I* (New York: Oxford University Press, 2012): 136–201.

43. Francis Fukuyama, "After Neoconservatism," *New York Times,* February 19, 2006; Fouad Ajami, "Iraq May Survive, but the Dream Is Dead," *New York Times,* May 26, 2004; Ajami, "The Clash," *New York Times,* January 6, 2008; Ajami, "Samuel Huntington's Warning," *Wall Street Journal,* December 30, 2008.

44. Lewis, *The Crisis of Islam: Holy War and Unholy Terror* (New York: Modern Library, 2003): 137–164. In *Notes on a Century* (New York: Viking, 2012): 331–334, Lewis attempted to distance himself from the invasion of Iraq, including reprinted emails to National Security Advisor Stephen Hadley. However, the emails were from 2006—well into the occupation of Iraq—rather than the period preceding the invasion. For a more nuanced treatment of the history of terrorism and suicide attacks, see Robert Pape, *Dying to Win: The Strategic Logic of Suicide Terrorism* (New York: Random House, 2005).

45. "Secretary Rice Holds a News Conference," *Washington Post,* July 21, 2006; Bernard Lewis, "August 22," *Wall Street Journal,* August 8, 2006. The op-ed's title was a reference to a statement by then Iranian president Mahmoud Ahmadinejad in which he promised a response to U.S. questions about Iran's nuclear program "by the end of August" 2006. Lewis explained that August 22, 2006 "corresponds, in the Islamic calendar, to the 27th day of the month of Rajab of the year 1427. This, by tradition, is the night when many Muslims commemorate the night flight of the prophet Muhammad on the winged horse Buraq, first to 'the farthest mosque', usually identified with Jerusalem, and then to heaven and back (c.f., Koran XVII.1). This might well be deemed an appropriate date for the apocalyptic ending of Israel and if necessary of the world. It is far from certain that Mr. Ahmadinejad plans any such cataclysmic events precisely for Aug. 22. But it would be wise to bear the possibility in mind." It is worth noting that the date passed without incident.

46. Kenneth M. Pollack, *The Persian Puzzle: The Conflict between Iran and America* (New York: Random House, 2005): 382–386, and Pollack, "A Switch in Time: A New Strategy for America in Iraq" (Washington, DC: Brookings Institution, February 2006); Pollack and Michael O'Hanlon, "A War We Just Might Win," *New York Times,* July 30, 2007.

47. See Thomas Ricks, *The Gamble: General David Petraeus and the American Military Adventure in Iraq, 2006–2008* (New York: Penguin Press, 2010): 18–19, 24–31. For a critique of U.S. counterinsurgency doctrine, see Laleh Khalili, *Time in the Shadows: Confinement in Counterinsurgencies* (Stanford, CA: Stanford University Press, 2012).

48. Peter Maas, "Professor Nagl's War," *New York Times Magazine,* January 11. 2004.

49. John Nagl, foreword to U.S. Army's *Instructions for American Servicemen in Iraq during World War II* (Chicago: University of Chicago Press, 2007): v–vi. xii.

50. Ibid., vi–xii.

51. Bruce Westrate, *The Arab Bureau: British Policy in the Middle East, 1916–1920* (University Park: Pennsylvania State University Press, 1992): 3–4; T. E. Lawrence, "Twenty Seven Articles," *Arab Bulletin,* August 20, 1917, http://www.telstudies.org/writings/works/articles_essays/1917_twenty-seven _articles.shtml (last accessed September 12, 2014); David Kilcullen,

"'Twenty-Eight Articles': Fundamentals of Company-level Counterinsurgency," *Military Review,* May/June 2006: 103.

52. David Kilcullen, *Counterinsurgency* (New York: Oxford University Press, 2010): 224; T. E. Lawrence, *Seven Pillars of Wisdom: A Triumph* (New York: Acorn Books, 1991): 42. This perception of Lawrence has also been adopted by U.S. law enforcement; see Mark G. Stainbrook, "Policing with Muslim Communities in the Age of Terrorism," *Police Chief* LXXVII, no. 4 (April 2010), http://www.policechiefmagazine.org/magazine/index.cfm?fuseaction =display_arch&article_id=2050&issue_id=42010 (last accessed September 14, 2014).

53. See also Frederick W. Kagan, "Choosing Victory: A Plan for Success in Iraq," AEI Online, January 5, 2007, http://www.aei.org/publication/choosing -victory-a-plan-for-success-in-iraq (last accessed May 5, 2015); Bob Woodward, *The War Within: A Secret White House History, 2006–2008* (New York: Simon & Schuster, 2008); Ricks, *The Gamble,* 94–97, 106–272. For a critique of counterinsurgency doctrine and Petraeus, see Daniel Bolger, *Why We Lost: A General's Inside Account of the Iraq and Afghanistan Wars* (New York: Houghton Mifflin Harcourt, 2014): 237–276.

54. American Council of Trustees and Alumni, *Defending Civilization: How Our Universities Are Failing America and What Can Be Done about It* (Washington, DC: American Council of Trustees and Alumni, 2001): 1. Although Lynne Cheney was ACTA's founding chairman, she was not serving in that capacity when the report was published. However, she was repeatedly quoted throughout *Defending Civilization* to reinforce the report's claims. In an October 5, 2001 speech, Cheney stated, "To say that it is more important now [to study Islam] implies that the events of September 11 were our fault, that it was our failure . . . that led to so many deaths and so much destruction." Former vice presidential candidate and then Democratic senator Joe Lieberman was also affiliated with ACTA and served on its National Council.

55. American Council of Trustees and Alumni, *Defending Civilization,* 7.

56. Ibid., 13–43.

57. Joel Beinin, "The New McCarthyism: Policing Thought about the Middle East," in *Academic Freedom after September 11,* ed. Beshara Doumani (New York: Zone Books, 2006): 244–245; Lockman, *Contending Visions,* 255–256.

58. Martin Kramer, *Ivory Towers on Sand: The Failure of Middle Eastern Studies in America* (Washington, DC: Washington Institute for Near East Policy, 2001): 39–48, 55–57. Kramer was serving as the editor of the *Middle East Quarterly* when *Ivory Towers on Sand* was published. Kramer's accusations in the book were not limited to September 11. For example, he suggested that a 1974 article from the Middle East Research and Information Project (MERIP) entitled "Middle East Studies Network in the United States," written by Peter Johnson and Judith Tucker, which discussed the connections between the U.S. government and the American University of Beirut

(AUB) may have inspired the 1984 assassination of university president Malcolm Kerr (46).

59. Martin Kramer, *Ivory Towers on Sand*, 127–129.

60. Beinin, "The New McCarthyism," 253–254; Newhall, "The Unraveling of the Devil's Bargain: The History and Politics of Language Acquisition," in *Academic Freedom after September 11*, ed. Beshara Doumani (New York: Zone Books, 2006): 219–221. See testimony by Hoover Institution Fellow Stanley Kurtz before the House of Representatives Subcommittee on Select Education, June 21, 2003, http://www.gpo.gov/fdsys/pkg/CHRG-108hhrg88815 /html/CHRG-108hhrg88815.htm (last accessed August 21, 2014); see Public Law 85–864 (NDEA), Title I, Sec. 102, for general provisions and prohibitions on the federal control of education.

61. See Newhall, "The Unraveling of the Devil's Bargain," 221; Lockman, *Contending Visions* 266–273; Lara Deeb and Jessica Winegar, *Anthropology's Politics: Disciplining the Middle East* (Stanford, CA: Stanford University Press, 2016): 81–114.

62. Richard Byrne, "First Meeting for New Group on Middle East and African Studies Places Islamic Extremism at Center of Its Agenda," *Chronicle of Higher Education*, April 28, 2008; Goldstein, "Osama bin Laden Made me Famous"; Lockman, *Contending Visions*, 271–272.

63. See David Goldberg, Dennis Looney, and Natalia Lusin, *Enrollments in Languages Other Than English in United States Institutions of Higher Education, Fall 2013* (New York: Modern Language Association, February 2015). In comparison, Chinese courses maintained higher enrollments from 2002 (34,153) to 2013 (61,055). However, the percentage increase was far less (79%) than for Arabic courses (205%). From 2009 to 2013, Arabic courses experienced a 7.5 percent decline in enrollment, while Chinese enrollment increased by 2 percent. The percentage decrease in enrollment during this period was less pronounced, 4.8 percent, when all variants of Arabic instruction are included.

64. For example, Title VI funding during fiscal years 1991 to 1998 ranged from $16.5 million to $19.49 million per year. Funding increased from $23 million (FY 2001) to $27.1 million (FY 2002) and $30 million (FY 2003) before dropping to an average of $28.9 million per year during the 2004–2008 period. Data courtesy of the U.S. Department of Education and Charles Kurzman (http://kurzman.unc.edu/international-education/crippling -international-education-sources/).

65. Newhall, "The Unraveling of the Devil's Bargain," 205; Seteny Shami and Marcial Godoy-Anativia, "Pensée 2: Between the Hammer and the Anvil: Middle East Studies in the Aftermath of 9/11," *International Journal of Middle East Studies* 39 (2007): 346–349; Jennifer Jacobson, "The Clash over Middle East Studies," *Chronicle of Higher Education*, February 6, 2004. Newhall reports that twelve PhDs in Arabic were awarded in 1999, fifteen in 2000, and six in 2001. Shami and Godoy-Anativia note that in spite of

the discussions, an increase in funds had not materialized by fiscal year 2008.

66. The NSEP identifies the "Departments of Defense, Homeland Security, and State, or any element of the Intelligence Community" as the "priority agencies" to fulfill the service requirement. See "NSEP Service Requirement for Boren Scholars," https://www.borenawards.org/boren_scholars_service .html.

67. Newhall, "The Unraveling of the Devil's Bargain," 213–219.

68. See Mahmood Mamdani, *Good Muslim, Bad Muslim: America, the Cold War, and the Roots of Terror* (New York: Pantheon Books, 2004); Chalmers Johnson, *The Sorrows of Empire: Militarism, Secrecy, and the End of the Republic* (New York: Metropolitan Books, 2004); Lloyd C. Gardner and Marilyn B. Young, eds., *The New American Empire: A 21st Century Teach-In on U.S. Foreign Policy* (New York: The New Press, 2005); Andrew Bacevich, *American Empire: The Realities and Consequences of U.S. Diplomacy* (Cambridge, MA: Harvard University Press, 2002). For the perspective of Middle East historians, see Rashid Khalidi, *Resurrecting Empire: Western Footprints and America's Perilous Path in the Middle East* (Boston: Beacon Press, 2004); Mark Levine, *Why They Don't Hate Us: Lifting the Veil on the Axis of Evil* (Oxford: One World, 2005); Juan Cole's *Napoleon's Egypt: Invading the Middle East* (New York: Palgrave Macmillan, 2007) and his *Informed Comment* blog (www.juancole.com). See also Edward Said's collected essays, *From Oslo to Iraq and the Road Map* (New York: Vintage, 2004).

69. For positive coverage, see John Burns, "Arab TV Gets a New Slant: Newscasts without Censorship," *New York Times*, July 4, 1999, and Mary Anne Weaver, "Democracy by Decree," *New Yorker*, November 20, 2000. Negative coverage after 9/11 included Fouad Ajami, "What the Muslim World Is Watching," *New York Times*, November 18, 2001. On the leaked memorandum, see David Leigh and Richard Norton Taylor, "Labour MPs leaked Bush's proposal to bomb al-Jazeera," *The Guardian*, January 8, 2006, and Wadah Khanfar, "Why Did You Want to Bomb Me, Mr. Bush and Mr. Blair," *The Guardian*, November 30, 2005. See also Gwladys Fouché, "Sami al-Haj: 'I Lived Inside Guantánamo as a Journalist,'" *The Guardian*, July 17, 2009. For more on Al Jazeera's influence, see Marc Lynch, *Voices of the New Arab Public: Iraq, Al Jazeera, and Middle East Politics Today* (New York: Columbia University Press, 2006); Philip Seib, *The Al Jazeera Effect: How the New Global Media Are Reshaping World Politics* (Dulles, VA: Potomac Book, 2008).

70. See Loch K. Johnson, *The Threat on the Horizon: An Inside Account of America's Search for Security after the Cold War* (New York: Oxford University Press, 2011), for a detailed discussion of intelligence community reforms after the Cold War and before September 11. Amy Zegart, *Spying Blind: The CIA, the FBI, and the Origins of 9/11* (Princeton, NJ: Princeton University Press, 2009), examines intelligence failures that contributed to the attacks.

71. Steve Coll, *Ghost Wars: The Secret History of the CIA, Afghanistan, and Bin Laden from the Soviet Invasion to September 10* (New York: Penguin, 2004): 436–437; "Joint Inquiry into Intelligence Community Activities before and after the Terrorist Attacks of September 11, 2001," Report of the U.S. Senate Select Committee on Intelligence and U.S. House Permanent Select Committee on Intelligence, December 2002, http://www.intelligence.senate .gov/sites/default/files/publications/CRPT-107srpt351.pdf (last accessed May 5, 2015). For the Bush administration's pre-9/11 attitude toward terrorism and al-Qaʻida, see Richard A. Clarke, *Against All Enemies: Inside America's War on Terror* (New York: Free Press, 2004).

72. See Bob Woodward, *Bush at War* (New York: Simon & Schuster, 2002): 139–140; Jeremy Scahill, *Blackwater: The Rise of the World's Most Powerful Mercenary Army* (New York: Nation Books, 2007): 337.

73. Woodward, *State of Denial*, 275–276. On deportations see Mustafa Bayoumi, *How Does It Feel to Be a Problem? Being Young and Arab in America* (New York: Penguin, 2008): 266–267. On the USA PATRIOT Act, see David Cole and James X. Dempsey, *Terrorism and the Constitution: Sacrificing Civil Liberties in the Name of National Security* (New York: The New Press, 2002). For torture, see David Cole, ed., *The Torture Memos: Rationalizing the Unthinkable* (New York: The New Press, 2009). For a defense of the Bush administration from one of the drafters of its policies, see John Yoo, *War by Other Means: An Insider's Account of the War on Terror* (New York: Atlantic Monthly Press, 2006); On the NSA, see Glenn Greenwald, *No Place to Hide: Edward Snowden, the NSA, and the U.S. Surveillance State* (New York: Metropolitan Books, 2014). The Justice Department released redacted versions of the internal discussions in support of the domestic surveillance program; see Ellen Nakashima, "Legal Memos Released on Bush-era Justification for Warrantless Wiretapping," *Washington Post*, September 6, 2014, http://apps.washingtonpost.com/g/documents/national/a-memo-for -the-attorney-general-may-2004/1226/ and http://apps.washingtonpost.com /g/documents/national/a-memo-for-the-attorney-general-july-2004/1224/ (last accessed September 10, 2014).

74. "Joint Inquiry into Intelligence Community Activities before and after the Terrorist Attacks of September 11, 2001"; Dana Priest and William M. Arkin, "A Hidden World, Growing beyond Control," *Washington Post*, July 19, 2010; Priest and Arkin, *Top Secret America: The Rise of the New American Security State* (New York: Little, Brown, 2011): 4–6.

75. Dana Priest and William M. Arkin, "National Security, Inc.," *Washington Post*, July 20, 2011; Priest and Arkin, *Top Secret America*, 181–184.

76. Sara Hebel, "National-Security Concerns Spur Congressional Interest in Language Programs," *Chronicle of Higher Education*, March 15, 2002; George Packer, "Betrayed," *New Yorker*, March 26, 2007. For more on the CIA's rendition program, including Jordan's role, see Open Society Justice Initia- tive, *Globalizing Torture: CIA Secret Detention and Extraordinary Rendition*

(New York: Open Society Foundations, 2013); Max Fisher, "A Staggering Map of the 54 Countries That Reportedly Participated in the CIA's Rendition Program," *Washington Post*, February 5, 2013; Ian Cobain and Ben Quinn, "How U.S. Firms Profited from Torture Flights," *The Guardian*, August 31, 2011; Joanne Mariner, "We'll Make You See Death," *Salon.com*, April 10, 2008.

77. See Roberto J. Gonzalez, "Indirect Rule and Embedded Anthropologists: Practical, Theoretical and Ethical Concerns," in *Anthropology and Global Counterinsurgency*, ed. John D. Kelly, Beatrice Jauregui, Sean T. Mitchell, and Jeremy Walton (Chicago: University of Chicago Press, 2010): 232–235.

78. Gonzalez, "Indirect Rule and Embedded Anthropologists"; Vanessa M. Gezari, *The Tender Soldier: A True Story of War and Sacrifice* (New York: Simon & Schuster, 2013): 173, 197–198; Tom Vanden Brook, "Army Plows Ahead with Troubled War-zone Program," *USA Today*, February 28, 2013.

79. See Jacob Kipp, Lester Grau, Karl Prinslow, and Don Smith, "The Human Terrain System: A CORDS for the 21st Century," *Military Review* (September–October 2006): 8–14; Fred Renzi, "Networks: Terra Incognita and the Case for Ethnographic Intelligence," *Military Review* (September–October 2006): 180–186; Gonzalez, "Indirect Rule and Embedded Anthropologists," 234–235. For a defense of the HTS by a Human Terrain Team member, see Marcus B. Griffin, "An Anthropologist among Soldiers: Notes from the Field," in Kelly et al., *Anthropology and Global Counterinsurgency*: 215–299.

80. David Glenn, "Program to Embed Anthropologists with Military Lacks Ethical Standards, Report Says," *Chronicle of Higher Education*, December 3, 2009; David Glenn, "Anthropologists in a War Zone: Scholars Debate Their Role," *Chronicle of Higher Education*, November 30, 2007; David Price, "Counterinsurgency's Free Ride," *Counterpunch*, April 7, 2009; David Vine, "Enabling the Kill Chain," *Chronicle of Higher Education*, November 30, 2007. Jim Landers, "Anthropologist from Plano Maps Afghanistan's Human Terrain for Army," *Dallas Morning News*, March 8, 2009. The AAA's statement on the HTS can be found at http://www.aaanet.org/about/Policies/statements/Human-Terrain-System-Statement.cfm (last accessed July 14, 2014).

81. Gezari, *The Tender Soldier*, 163–198; Gonzalez, "Indirect Rule and Embedded Anthropologists," 234; David Glenn, "Former Human Terrain System Participant Describes Program in Disarray," *Chronicle of Higher Education*, December 5, 2007; John Stanton, "Human Terrain Systems and Military Intelligence," *Counterpunch*, April 15, 2010.

82. Gonzalez, "Indirect Rule and Embedded Anthropologists," 244; Gezari, *The Tender Soldier*, 127–162; Matthew Barakat, "Contractor Dies from Afghanistan Burn Injuries," *Associated Press*, January 9, 2009; Tom Vanden Brook, "Army Kills Controversial Social Science Program," *USA Today*, June 29, 2015.

83. Augustus Richard Norton, *Hezbollah: A Short History* (Princeton, NJ: Princeton University Press, 2007): 90; Rashid Khalidi, *The Iron Cage: The Story of the Palestinian Struggle for Statehood* (Boston: Beacon Press, 2006): 179. For a discussion of Hamas's political activities and social services, see Sara Roy, *Hamas and Civil Society in Gaza: Engaging the Islamist Social Sector* (Princeton, NJ: Princeton University Press, 2013).

84. Lisa Stampnitzky, *Disciplining Terror: How Experts Invented "Terrorism"* (Cambridge: Cambridge University Press, 2013): 139–164; See also Pape, *Dying to Win*. On bin Laden's declarations and al-Qa'ida's formation, see Fawaz Gerges, *The Rise and Fall of Al-Qaeda* (New York: Oxford University Press, 2011): 34–68.

85. Claire Hoffman, "As Anxiety Grows, So Does Field of Terror Study," *New York Times*, September 1, 2004. Thomas Bartlett, "Degrees of Security," *Chronicle of Higher Education*, April 11, 2003.

86. See Stampnitzky, *Disciplining Terror*, 196–197; Anne Marie Borrego, "U. of Southern California Wins Federal Grant for Terrorism-Research Center," *Chronicle of Higher Education*, December 5, 2003; Kelly Field, "Texas A&M and U. of Minnesota Win Federal Grants for Terrorism Research Centers," *Chronicle of Higher Education*, April 28, 2004. For a listing of the different "centers of excellence," see http://www.dhs.gov/st-centers-excellence. For information on Maryland's START program, see http://www.start.umd.edu/about/about-start.

87. David Glenn, "New Details of 'Minerva' Project Emerge, as Social Scientists Weigh Pentagon Ties," *Chronicle of Higher Education*, May 12, 2008; Evan R. Goldstein, "Enlisting Social Scientists," *Chronicle of Higher Education*, July 4, 2008; Sharon Weinberger, "Pentagon's Project Minerva Sparks New Anthro Concerns," *Wired* 1 (May 2008); Robert Gates, "Speech to the Association of American Universities," April 14, 2008, http://www.defense.gov/speeches/speech.aspx?speechid=1228 (last accessed July 25, 2014);

88. Nafeez Ahmed, "Pentagon Preparing for Mass Civil Breakdown," *The Guardian*, June 12, 2014. For a listing of Minerva-funded research projects and aims, see http://minerva.dtic.mil/funded.html (last accessed July 25, 2014), and for a detailed report produced by the Pentagon of Minerva-funded projects, see "Minerva Research Summaries and Resources, Fall 2013," http://minerva.dtic.mil/doc/2013_MinervaResearchSummaries_0905.pdf (last accessed July 25, 2014). For thoughtful historical reflections on Minerva, see Ron Robin, "The Minerva Controversy; a Cautionary Tale," December 11, 2008, http://essays.ssrc.org/minerva/2008/12/11/robin/ (last accessed December 27, 2015) and David Engerman, "Knowing the Enemy," January 23, 2009, http://essays.ssrc.org/minerva/2009/01/23/engerman/ (last accessed December 27, 2015).

89. Rumsfeld, *Known and Unknown*, 360.

90. For example, see Kevin Baron, "Revenge of the Liberal Foreign Policy Wonks," *National Journal*, June 7, 2014. On the growth in think tanks

globally, see James G. McGann with Richard Sabatini, *Global Think Tanks: Policy Networks and Governance* (New York: Routledge, 2011).

Epilogue

Epigraph: Donovan quoted in Tim Weiner, *Legacy of Ashes: The History of the CIA* (New York: Doubleday, 2007): 3.

1. David D. Kirkpatrick, Kareem Fahim, and Ben Hubbard, "By the Millions, Egyptians Seek Morsi's Ouster," *New York Times,* June 30, 2013; Jahd Khalil, "'The Army, People and Police Are One Hand,' Egyptian protesters say," *The National.AE,* July 2, 2013, http://www.thenational.ae/news/world/middle-east/the-army-people-and-police-are-one-hand-egyptian-protesters-say#ixzz3AljzOfLV. There are numerous videos available of the 2013 protests, some professionally produced relying on footage from Egypt's CBC television station.

2. David Jackson, "Obama to Morsi: Democracy is more than Elections," *USA Today,* July 2, 2012; Mark Landler, "Aid to Egypt Can Keep Flowing, Despite Overthrow, White House Decides," *New York Times,* July 25, 2013; Michael Gordon and Kareem Fahim, "Kerry Says Egypt's Military Was 'Restoring Democracy' in Ousting Morsi," *New York Times,* August 1, 2013. For a detailed investigation of the Rabi'a al-'Adawiya and al-Nahda attacks, see Human Rights Watch, "All According to Plan," August 12, 2014, http://www.hrw.org/reports/2014/08/12/all-according-plan.

3. Juan Cole, *The New Arabs: How the Millennial Generation Is Changing the Middle East* (New York: Simon & Schuster, 2014): 125–164.

4. Hillary Rodham Clinton, *Hard Choices* (New York: Simon & Schuster, 2014): 341.

5. David Horovitz, "A mass expression of outrage against injustice," *Jerusalem Post,* February 25, 2011, http://www.jpost.com/Opinion/Columnists/Article.aspx?id=209770 (last accessed February 25, 2011); Niall Ferguson, "Un-American Revolutions," *The Daily Beast,* February 27, 2011, http://www.thedailybeast.com/newsweek/2011/02/27/un-american-revolutions.html (last accessed February 25, 2011); and "In 2021 We'll Be Amazed How Much the World Has Changed," *The Telegraph,* March 14, 2011, http://www.telegraph.co.uk/finance/financevideo/8367183/Niall-Ferguson-In-2021-well-be-amazed-how-much-the-world-has-changed.html (last accessed February 25, 2011); Leslie Gelb, "Meet the Losers," *The Daily Beast,* March 9, 2011, http://www.thedailybeast.com/articles/2011/03/09/mideast-revolution-people-lose-oil-companies-win.html (last accessed April 25, 2016). For a fuller discussion of their claims, see Osamah Khalil, "The Counterrevolutionary Year: The Arab Spring and U.S. Foreign Policy in the Middle East," in *American Studies Encounters the Middle East,* ed. Alex Lubin and Marwan Kraidy (Chapel Hill: University of North Carolina Press, 2016): 286–301.

6. Robert Gates, *Duty: Memoirs of a Secretary at War* (New York: Alfred A. Knopf, 2014): 502–523.

7. See "Matā Tanjaḥ al-Thawra," *Al-Masry al-Youm*, February 26, 2011; "13 Hizban Jadīdan Taḵaruju min Raḥam al-Tahrir," *Al-Masry al-Youm*, February 17, 2011; Abdel Bari Atwan, "Mubarak Lā Yastaḥiqq Makharajan Musharrifan," *Al-Quds al-Arabi*, February 9, 2011; Abdel Bari Atwan, "Lā Mafarr Min al-Ruḍūkh Lil-Thawra" *Al-Quds al-Arabi*, February 11, 2011.

8. See Issam Rifaat, "Ṣundūq Lil-isthmār Bi-Amwālna al-Munhūba," *Al-Ahram*, February 14, 2011; "Lā Aḥad Fawqa Al-Qanūn," *Al-Ahram*, April 13, 2011.

9. See Barack Obama, "Remarks by the President on the Middle East and North Africa," May 19, 2011, http://www.whitehouse.gov/the-press-office /2011/05/19/remarks-president-middle-east-and-north-africa%20 (last accessed October 26, 2014); Thomas Friedman, "Obama on the World, *New York Times*, August 8, 2014; Clinton, *Hard Choices*, 161–164. Clinton later criticized the administration's decision not to back the Syrian opposition earlier and with greater support; see Jeffrey Goldberg, "Hillary Clinton: 'Failure' to Help Syrian Rebels Led to the Rise of ISIS," *The Atlantic*, August 10, 2014. For a critical assessment of America's goals in Libya, see Vijay Prashad, *Arab Spring, Libyan Winter* (Oakland, CA: AK Press, 2012). On Jordan, see John Kerry, interview by Ray Suarez, *PBS NewsHour*, February 1, 2011, http://www.pbs.org/newshour/bb/politics-jan-june11-johnkerry_02-01/ (last accessed April 25, 2016).

10. "Clinton moots GCC defence shield against Iran missile," Gulfnews.com, April 1, 2014, http://gulfnews.com/clinton-moots-gcc-defence-shield -against-iran-missile-1.1002366 (last accessed August 18, 2014); Steven L. Meyers, "United Arab Emirates Shutters U.S. Backed Group," *New York Times*, March 31, 2012; "UAE Closes Dubai Office of U.S. Pro-democracy Group," *Reuters*, March 30, 2012. Founded in 1983, NDI's Board of Directors and Senior Advisory Committee boast a number of prominent American politicians largely from the Democratic Party, including former secretary of state Albright and former Senate majority leader Tom Daschle.

11. Clinton, *Hard Choices*, 341–344, 355–360.

12. Thom Shanker and Steven Lee Myers, "U.S. Planning Troop Buildup in Gulf after Exit from Iraq," *New York Times*, October 29, 2011; Meyers, "United Arab Emirates Shutters U.S. Backed Group." On weapons sales, see Sean L. Yom, "Washington's New Arms Bazaar," *Middle East Report and Information Project* (Spring 2008), http://www.merip.org/mer/mer246 /washingtons-new-arms-bazaar (last accessed October 14, 2014); "Gulf arms sales vital for U.S. companies," *United Press International*, November 15, 2011; Jim Wolf, "U.S. in $3.5 billion arms sale to UAE amid Iran tensions," *Reuters*, December 31, 2011, http://www.reuters.com/article/2011/12/31/us-usa -uae-iran-idUSTRE7BU0BF20111231.

13. Barack Obama, "Statement by the President on ISIL," September 10, 2014, http://www.whitehouse.gov/the-press-office/2014/09/10/statement-president -isil-1 (last accessed October 14, 2014).

14. Craig Whitlock and Greg Miller, "U.S. building secret drone bases in Africa, Arabian Peninsula, officials say," September 20, 2011; Greg Miller, "Under Obama, an emerging global apparatus for drone killing," *Washington Post*, December 27, 2011; Greg Miller, "Plan for Hunting Terrorists Signals U.S. Intends to Keep Adding Names to Kill Lists," *Washington Post*, October 23, 2012. On the Obama administration's drone policy, see Lloyd C. Gardner, *Killing Machine: The American Presidency in the Age of Drone Warfare* (New York: The New Press, 2013).

15. Jeremy Scahill and Ryan Deveraux, "Barack Obama's Secret Terrorist-Tracking System, by the Numbers," *The Intercept,* August 5, 2014, https://firstlook.org/theintercept/article/2014/08/05/watch-commander/.

16. See Glenn Greenwald, *No Place to Hide,* 90–169; Greenwald, Laura Poitras, and Ewen MacAskill, "NSA shares raw intelligence including Americans' data with Israel," *The Guardian,* September 11, 2013; Greenwald and Murtaza Hussein, "The NSA's New Partner in Spying: Saudi Arabia's Brutal State Police," *The Intercept,* July 25, 2014, https://firstlook.org/theintercept/2014/07/25/nsas-new-partner-spying-saudi-arabias-brutal-state-police/.

17. Greg Miller, "DIA to send hundreds more spies overseas," *Washington Post,* December 1, 2012.

18. In addition to Cole's *The New Arabs,* see also Roger Owen, *The Rise and Fall of Arab Presidents for Life* (Cambridge, MA: Harvard University Press, 2012); James Gelvin, *The Arab Uprisings: What Everyone Needs to Know* (New York: Oxford University Press, 2012); Lin Noueihed and Alex Warren, *The Battle for the Arab Spring: Revolution, Counter-Revolution, and the Making of a New Era* (New Haven, CT: Yale University Press, 2012); Marc Lynch, *The Arab Uprising: The Unfinished Revolutions of the New Middle East* (New York: Public Affairs, 2012).

19. Michael Stratford, "Battle over NSF Begins," *Inside Higher Ed,* March 14, 2014; "Pro-Israel Groups Question Federal Funds for Middle East Centers," *Inside Higher Ed,* September 18, 2014; Louis D. Brandeis Center, "The Morass of Middle East Studies: Title VI of the Higher Education Act and Federally Funded Area Studies," September 2014, http://www.brandeiscenter.com/images/uploads/practices/antisemitism_whitepaper.pdf (last accessed September 19, 2014); Lindsey Burke, "Reauthorizing the Higher Education Act—Toward Policies That Increase Access and Lower Costs," The Heritage Foundation, August 19, 2014, http://www.heritage.org/research/reports/2014/08/reauthorizing-the-higher-education-acttoward-policies-that-increase-access-and-lower-costs (last accessed February 6, 2014); Mike Gonzalez, "America Is Ill-Served by Its Government-Funded Area Studies and Foreign Policy Programs," The Heritage Foundation, August 25, 2014, http://www.heritage.org/research/reports/2014/08/america-is-ill-served-by-its-government-funded-area-studies-and-foreign-policy-programs (last accessed February 6, 2014).

20. See Nathan J. Brown, "In Defense of U.S. Funding for Area Studies," *Washington Post,* October 30, 2014.

21. See also Neema Noori, "Does Academic Freedom Globalize? The Diffusion of the American Model of Education to the Middle East and Academic Freedom," *PS: Political Science & Politics* 47, no. 3 (July 2014): 608–611.

22. Eric Lipton, Brooke Williams, and Nicholas Confessore, "Foreign Powers Buy Influence at Think Tanks," *New York Times*, September 6, 2014; Tom Hamburger and Alexander Becker, "At Fast-Growing Brookings, Donors May Have an Impact on Research Agenda," *Washington Post*, October 30, 2014. The Brookings Institution issued an official response denying the influence of foreign governments on its research; see http://www.brookings .edu/about/media-relations/news-releases/2014/0906-foreign-government -funding-us-think-tanks (last accessed September 9, 2014).

23. Stewart E. McClure Oral History, Senate Historical Office, January 28, 1983, http://www.senate.gov/artandhistory/history/resources/pdf/McClure4.pdf (last accessed September 6, 2014).

24. Truman quoted in Craig and Logevall, *America's Cold War*, 46.

25. A recent example is Nicholas Kristof, "Professors We Need You!" *New York Times*, February 15, 2014. On groupthink during the Vietnam War, see David Halberstam, *The Best and the Brightest* (New York: Ballantine Books, 1969), and Fredrik Logevall, *Choosing War: The Lost Chance for Peace and the Escalation of the War in Vietnam* (Berkeley: University of California Press, 2001). See also Noam Chomsky's classic essay "The Responsibility of Intellectuals," in *American Power and the New Mandarins* (New York: Pantheon Books, 1969): 323–366.

26. Greg Miller, "CIA Employee's Quest to Release Information 'Destroyed My Entire Career,'" *Washington Post*, July 4, 2014.

Bibliography

Archival Collections

Egypt

American University in Cairo Archives (AUCA)
    John Badeau Presidential Papers
    Thomas Bartlett Presidential Papers
    Cecil Byrd Presidential Papers
    Wendell Cleland Presidential Papers
    Raymond McLain Presidential Papers
    Richard Pedersen Presidential Papers
    Christopher Thoron Presidential Papers
    University's Annual Reports and Promotional Materials

Lebanon

American University of Beirut Jafet Library Archive and Special
    Collection (AUBA)
    AUB Board of Trustees Reports
    Bayard Dodge Papers
    Philip Hitti Personal Papers
    President's Annual Reports

United Kingdom

National Archives, Kew
    Commonwealth Office
    Foreign Office Political Correspondence

United States

American Jewish Congress Archives
    Executive Director Files

Brookings Institution Archive
    Foreign Policy Studies Program, Director Henry Owen's Project Files,
        1970–1980

Jimmy Carter Presidential Library
    Files of National Security Advisor Zbigniew Brzezinski
    Files of Chief of Staff Hamilton Jordan

Columbia University Archives (CUA)
    Bureau of Applied Social Research Files
    Middle East Institute Files
    William Westermann Papers

Dwight D. Eisenhower Presidential Library
    Cabinet Meeting Minutes
    Papers of Marion Folsom, Secretary of Health, Education, and Welfare

Gerald R. Ford Presidential Library
    Files of National Security Advisor Brent Scowcroft

Harvard University Archives (HUA)
    Center for Middle East Studies Files
    Hamilton Gibb Personal Papers
    William Langer Personal Papers

Library of Congress
    American Council of Learned Societies Archives

Richard M. Nixon Presidential Library
    Files of National Security Advisor Henry A. Kissinger
    White House Central Files, Department of Health, Education,
        and Welfare

Princeton University Archives (PUA)
    Seeley G. Mudd Manuscript Library
        Army Specialized Training Program Files
        Department of Oriental Studies Files
        Allen Dulles Personal Papers
        William Eddy Personal Papers
        Harold Hoskins Personal Papers

Rockefeller Foundation Archives (RFA)
  Ford Foundation Archives
  Rockefeller Foundation Archives
  Social Science Research Council Archives

United States National Archives, College Park and Washington, DC (NARACP)
  Central Intelligence Agency (RG 263)
    CREST Records
    History Source Collection
  Office of Education (RG 12)
    Records of the Office of the Commissioner
  Office of Strategic Services Records (RG 226)
    William Donovan, Director Files
    Research and Analysis Division
    Strategic Intelligence Division
  Records of the Inquiry (M1107)
  State Department (RG 59)
    Central Decimal and Lot Files
    External Research Staff
    Foreign Service Institute
    Near Eastern, South Asian, and African Affairs Division
    Office of Intelligence and Research
    Policy Planning Staff
    Voice of America

U.S. Army Heritage and Education Center (USAHEC)
  William J. Donovan Papers

Interviews

Joel Beinin
Rashid Khalidi
William Quandt
James Steinberg

Newspapers, Periodicals, and Webzines

Al-Ahram (Egypt)
Al-Masry Al-Youm (Egypt)
Al-Quds Al-Arabi (London)
An-Nahar (Lebanon)
Chronicle of Higher Education
Counterpunch
The Guardian
Harvard Crimson

386   Bibliography

Hiwar (Lebanon)
Inside Higher Ed
The Intercept
Life Magazine
New Yorker
New York Times
USA Today
Washington Post

Oral Histories

John Badeau, John F. Kennedy Presidential Library
Hermann Eilts, The Association for Diplomatic Studies and Training
Arthur S. Flemming, Harry S. Truman Presidential Library
Marion Folsom, Dwight D. Eisenhower Presidential Library
Stewart McClure, U.S. Senate Historical Office
Harold Saunders, The Association for Diplomatic Studies and Training
Brooks Wrampelmeier, The Association for Diplomatic Studies and Training

Published Archives

Access Archival Database
Digital National Security Archive
Foreign Relations of the United States (Government Printing Office, Washington, DC)
    The Paris Peace Conference, 1919, Vol. I and Vol. III
    The Near East and Africa, 1942, Vol. IV
    The Near East and Africa, 1943, Vol. IV
    The British Commonwealth and Europe, 1944, Vol. III
    The Near East, South Asia, and Africa, the Far East, 1944, Vol. V
    The Near East and Africa, 1946, Vol. VII
    The Near East and Africa, 1947, Vol. V
    The Near East, South Asia, and Africa, 1950, Vol. V
    Emergence of the Intelligence Establishment, 1945–1950, Retrospective Volume
    Suez Crisis, 1955–1957, Vol. XVI
    Foreign Economic Policy, 1961–1963, Vol. IX
    Near East, 1961–1962, Vol. XVII
    Iran, 1964–1968, Vol. XXII
    Arab-Israeli Dispute, 1974–1976, Vol. XXVI
    Arab-Israeli Dispute, January 1977–August 1978, Vol. VIII
The Papers of Woodrow Wilson, edited by Arthur Lisk, Vol. 5, Vol. 41, and Vol. 45. Princeton, NJ: Princeton University Press, 1966–1994.

Reports and Government Publications

American Council of Trustees and Alumni. *Defending Civilization: How Our Universities Are Failing America and What Can Be Done about It.* Washington, DC: American Council of Trustees and Alumni, 2001.

Bennett, Wendell C. *Area Studies in American Universities.* New York: Social Science Research Council, June 1951.

Brookings Institution. *Toward Peace in the Middle East.* Washington, DC: Brookings Institution, 1975.

———. *Toward Arab-Israeli Peace: Report of a Study Group.* Washington, DC: Brookings Institution, 1988.

Bush, George W. *The National Security Strategy of the United States of America.* September 2002.

Fenton, William Nelson. *Area Studies in American Universities.* Washington, DC: American Council on Education, 1947.

Goldberg, David, Dennis Looney, and Natalia Lusin. *Enrollments in Languages Other than English in United States Institutions of Higher Education, Fall 2013.* New York: Modern Language Association, February 2015.

Hall, Robert. *Area Studies: With Special Reference to Their Implications for Research in the Social Sciences.* New York: Social Science Research Council, May 1947.

Hurewitz, J. C. *Undergraduate Instruction on the Middle East in American Colleges and Universities.* Provisional Draft. New York: American Association for Middle East Studies, May 1, 1962.

LaMay, Craig, Martha FitzSimon, and Jeanne Sahadi, eds. *The Media at War: The Press and the Persian Gulf Conflict, A Report of the Gannett Foundation.* New York: Gannett Foundation Media Center, June 1991.

Lambert, Richard. *Language and Area Studies Review.* Philadelphia: American Academy of Political and Social Sciences, October 1973.

———. *Beyond Growth: The Next Stage in Language and Area Studies.* Washington, DC: Association of American Universities, 1984.

McDonnell, Lorraine M., Sue E. Berryman, and Douglas Scott. *Federal Support for International Studies: The Role of NDEA Title VI.* Santa Monica, CA: RAND Corporation, May 1981.

Open Society Justice Initiative. *Globalizing Torture: CIA Secret Detention and Extraordinary Rendition.* New York: Open Society Foundations, 2013.

Parker, William. *The National Interest and Foreign Languages.* Washington, DC: Government Printing Office, April 1954.

Pool, Ithiel de Sola, ed. *Social Science Research and National Security.* Washington, DC: Smithsonian Institute, March 1963.

SRI International. *Defense Intelligence: Foreign Area/Language Needs and Academe.* Washington, DC: SRI, October 1983.

Trilateral Commission. *Trilateral Commission Task Force Reports, 15–19.* New York: New York University Press, 1981.

U.S. Army. *Instructions for American Servicemen in Iraq during World War II.* Chicago: University of Chicago Press, 2007.

U.S. Congress. Office of Technology Assessment. *A History of the Department of Defense Federally Funded Research and Development Centers.* Washington, DC: Government Printing Office, June 1995.

U.S. Senate. *Final Report of the Select Committee to Study Governmental Operations with Respect to Intelligence Activities, Book 1.* Washington, DC: Government Printing Office, 1976.

Washington Institute for Near East Policy. *Building for Peace: American Strategy in the Middle East.* Washington, DC: WINEP, 1988.

————. *Pursuing Peace: An American Strategy for the Arab-Israeli Peace Process.* Washington, DC: WINEP, 1992.

Secondary Sources

Abbott, Ernest Hamlin. "An Interview with Prince Feisal." *Outlook.* April 2, 1919.

Abella, Alex. *Soldiers of Reason: The RAND Corporation and the Rise of American Empire.* New York: Harcourt, 2008.

Abelson, Donald E. *A Capitol Idea: Think Tanks and U.S. Foreign Policy.* Montreal: McGill-Queen's University Press, 2006.

Abrahamian, Ervand. *Iran between Two Revolutions.* Princeton, NJ: Princeton University Press, 1982.

————. *The Coup: 1953, The CIA, and the Roots of Modern U.S.-Iranian Relations* (New York: The New Press, 2013.

Abrams, Elliott. *Tested by Zion: The Bush Administration and the Israeli-Palestinian Conflict.* Cambridge: Cambridge University Press, 2013.

Abu Iyad with Eric Rouleau. *My Home, My Land: A Narrative of the Palestinian Struggle.* New York: Times Books, 1981.

Adas, Michael. "From Settler Colony to Global Hegemon: Integrating the Exceptionalist Narrative of the American Experience into World History." *American Historical Review* (December 2001): 1692–1720.

Adelson, Roger. *London and the Invention of the Middle East: Money, Power, and War, 1902–1922.* New Haven, CT: Yale University Press, 1995.

Ajami, Fouad. *The Dream Palace of the Arabs: A Generation's Odyssey.* New York: Pantheon Books, 1998.

Al-Biyali, Suhayr Ḥusayn Aḥmad. *Ahdāf al-Jāmiʿah al-Amrīkīyah bi-al-Qāhirah: dirāsah wathāʾiqīyah mundhu al-nashʾah ḥattā ʿām 1980 M.* Al-Miniyā: Dār Farḥah lil-Nashr wa-al-Tawzīʿ, 2002.

Al-Hakim, Tawfiq. *ʿAwdat al-Waʿi.* Beirut: Dar al-Shurūq, 1974.

————. *The Return of Consciousness.* Translated by R. Bayly Winder. New York: New York University Press, 1985.

Allawi, Ali A. *The Occupation of Iraq: Winning the War, Losing the Peace.* New Haven, CT: Yale University Press, 2007.

————. *Faisal I of Iraq.* New Haven, CT: Yale University Press, 2014.

Allen, John. "Inventing the Middle East." *On Wisconsin* (Winter 2004): 36–39.

Allen, Susan H. *Classical Spies: American Archaeologists with the OSS in World War II Greece.* Ann Arbor: University of Michigan Press, 2011.

Allison, Robert J. *The Crescent Obscured: The United States and the Muslim World, 1776–1816*. New York: Oxford University Press, 1995.

Alvandi, Roham. *Nixon, Kissinger, and the Shah: The United States and Iran in the Cold War*. New York: Oxford University Press, 2014.

Ambrose, Stephen. *Eisenhower: Soldier and President*. New York: Simon & Schuster, 1991.

Anderson, Betty. *The American University of Beirut: Arab Nationalism and Liberal Education*. Austin: University of Texas Press, 2011.

Anderson, Perry. "Imperium" *New Left Review* 83 (September–October 2013): 5–111.

———. "Consilium" *New Left Review* 83 (September-October 2013): 116–157.

———. *American Foreign Policy and Its Thinkers*. London: Verso, 2015.

Anderson, Scott. *Lawrence in Arabia: War, Deceit, Imperial Folly, and the Making of the Modern Middle East*. New York: Doubleday, 2013.

Ansari, Ali M. *Modern Iran since 1921: The Pahlavis and After*. London: Pearson Education, 2003.

Antonius, George. *The Arab Awakening: The Story of the Arab National Movement*. New York: Capricorn Book, 1965.

App, Urs. *The Birth of Orientalism*. Philadelphia: University of Pennsylvania Press, 2010.

Appy, Christian G., ed. *Cold War Constructions: The Political Culture of United States Imperialism, 1945–1966*. Amherst: University of Massachusetts Press, 2000.

Babai, Don, ed. *Reflections on the Past, Visions of the Future: The Center for Middle East Studies, Harvard University*. Cambridge, MA: Harvard University Press, 2004.

Bacevich, Andrew. *American Empire: The Realities and Consequences of U.S. Diplomacy*. Cambridge, MA: Harvard University Press, 2002.

Badeau, John S. *The American Approach to the Arab World*. New York: Harper & Row, 1968.

Bailyn, Bernard. *The Ideological Origins of the American Revolution*. Cambridge, MA: Belknap Press of Harvard University Press, 1967.

Bale, Jeffrey. "Language Education and Imperialism: The Case of Title VI and Arabic, 1958–1991." *Journal for Critical Education Policy Studies* 9, no. 1 (May 2011): 376–408.

Baram, Phillip J. *The Department of State in the Middle East, 1919–1945*. Philadelphia: University of Pennsylvania Press, 1978.

Bard, Mitchell. *The Arab Lobby: The Invisible Alliance That Undermines America's Interests in the Middle East*. New York: HarperCollins, 2010.

Baritz, Loren. "The Idea of the West." *American Historical Review* 66, no. 3 (April 1961): 618–640.

Barney, Timothy. *Mapping the Cold War: Cartography and the Framing of America's International Power*. Chapel Hill: University of North Carolina Press, 2015.

Bar-Simon-Tov, Yaacov. "The United States and Israel since 1948: A 'Special Relationship'?" *Diplomatic History* 22, no. 2 (April 1998): 231–262.

Batatu, Hanna. *The Old Social Classes and the Revolutionary Movements of Iraq: A Study of Iraq's Old Landed and Commercial Classes and of Its Communists, Ba'thists, and Free Officers.* Princeton, NJ: Princeton University Press, 1978.

Bates, Robert H. "Area Studies and Political Science: Rupture and Possible Synthesis." *Africa Today* 44, no. 2 (1997): 123–131.

———. "Area Studies and the Discipline: A Useful Controversy?" *PS: Political Science and Politics* 30, no. 2 (1997): 166–169.

Bayoumi, Mustafa. *How Does It Feel to Be a Problem? Being Young and Arab in America.* New York: Penguin, 2008.

Beckmann, George M. "The Role of the Foundations." *Annals of the American Academy of Political and Social Science* 356 (November 1964): 12–22.

Beinin, Joel. "Money, Media, and Policy Consensus: The Washington Institute for Near East Policy." *Middle East Report* 180 (January–February 1993): 10–15.

———. "The Israelization of American Middle East Policy Discourse." *Social Text* 21, no. 2 (Summer 2003): 125–139.

Beinin, Joel, and Zachary Lockman. *Workers on the Nile: Nationalism, Communism, Islam, and the Egyptian Working Class, 1882–1954.* Princeton, NJ: Princeton University Press, 1987.

Bell, J. Bowyer. "Trends on Terror." *World Politics* 29, no. 3 (April 1977): 476–488.

Berman, Edward H. *The Influence of the Carnegie, Ford, and Rockefeller Foundations on American Foreign Policy: The Ideology of Philanthropy.* Albany: State University of New York Press, 1983.

Bertelsen, Rasmus. "Private Foreign-Affiliated Universities, the State, and Soft Power: The American University of Beirut and the American University in Cairo." *Foreign Policy Analysis* (2012): 293–311.

Bienen, Henry, ed. *The Military and Modernization.* Chicago: Aldine Atherton, 1971.

Bill, James. *The Eagle and the Lion: The Tragedy of American-Iranian Relations.* New Haven, CT: Yale University Press, 1988.

Binder, Leonard, ed. *The Study of the Middle East: Research and Scholarship in the Humanities and the Social Sciences.* New York: John Wiley & Sons, 1976.

Bird, Kai. *The Good Spy: The Life and Death of Robert Ames.* New York: Crown Publishers, 2014.

Bissell, Richard. *Reflections of a Cold Warrior: From Yalta to the Bay of Pigs.* New Haven, CT: Yale University Press, 1996.

Black, C. E., ed. *Comparative Modernization: A Reader.* New York: Free Press, 1970.

Bolger, Daniel. *Why We Lost: A General's Inside Account of the Iraq and Afghanistan Wars.* New York: Houghton Mifflin Harcourt, 2014.

Bonine, Michael, Abbas Amanat, and Michael Gasper, eds. *Is There a Middle East? The Evolution of a Geopolitical Concept.* Stanford, CA: Stanford University Press, 2011.

Borgwardt, Elizabeth. *A New Deal for the World: America's Vision for Human Rights.* Cambridge, MA: Harvard University Press, 2007.

Borstelmann, Thomas. *The Cold War and the Color Line: American Race Relations in the Global Arena.* Cambridge, MA: Harvard University Press, 2001.

Boulatta, Issa J. "The Beleaguered Unicorn: A Study of Tawfiq Sayigh." *Journal of Arabic Literature* 4 (1973): 69–70.

Bozarslan, Hamit. "Revisiting the Middle East's 1979." *Economy and Society* 41, no. 4 (November 2012): 558–567.

Brands, H. W. *Into the Labyrinth: The United States and the Middle East, 1945–1993.* New York: McGraw-Hill, 1994.

Breckinridge, Scott D. *The C.I.A. and the U.S. Intelligence Systems.* Boulder, CO: Westview Press, 1986.

Bregman, Ahron. *Cursed Victory: A History of Israel and the Occupied Territories.* London: Penguin, 2014.

Brzezinski, Michael. *Red Moon Rising.* New York: Times Books, 2007.

Brzezinski, Zbigniew. *Power and Principle: Memoirs of the National Security Advisor, 1977–1987.* New York: Farrar, Straus and Giroux, 1983.

Bundy, William. *A Tangled Web: The Making of Foreign Policy in the Nixon Presidency.* New York: Hill and Wang, 1998.

Bush, George. *Decision Points.* New York: Crown Publishers, 2010.

Calhoun, Craig, ed. *Sociology in America.* Chicago: University of Chicago Press, 2007.

Campbell, David. *Writing Security: United States Foreign Policy and the Politics of Identity.* Minneapolis: University of Minnesota Press, 1998.

Campbell, John. *Defense of the Middle East: Problems of American Policy.* New York: Council on Foreign Relations and Harper & Brothers, 1958.

Campos, Michelle U. *Ottoman Brothers: Muslims, Christians, and Jews in Early Twentieth-Century Palestine.* Stanford, CA: Stanford University Press, 2011.

Cantor, Norman F. *Inventing the Middle Ages: The Lives, Works, and Ideas of the Great Medievalists of the Twentieth Century.* New York: William Morrow, 1991.

Cavanagh, John. "Dulles Papers Reveal CIA Consulting Network." *Forerunner.* April 29, 1980.

Chamberlin, Paul Thomas. *The Global Offensive: The United States, the Palestine Liberation Organization, and the Making of the Post–Cold War Order.* Oxford: Oxford University Press, 2012.

Chandrasekaran, Rajiv. *Imperial Life in the Emerald City: Inside Iraq's Green Zone.* New York : Alfred A. Knopf, 2006.

Chelkowski, Peter J., and Robert J. Pranger, eds. *Ideology and Power in the Middle East.* Durham, NC: Duke University Press, 1988.

Cheney, Dick. *In My Time: A Personal and Political Memoir.* New York: Simon & Schuster, 2011.

Chomsky, Noam. *American Power and the New Mandarins.* New York: Pantheon Books, 1969.

Chomsky, Noam, Ira Katznelson, R. C. Lewontin, David Montgomery, Laura Nader, Richard Ohmann, Ray Siever, Immanuel Walterst and Howa Zinn, eds. *The Cold War and the University: Toward an Intellectual History of the Postwar Years.* New York: New Press, 1997.

Christison, Kathleen. *Perceptions of Palestine: Their Influence on U.S. Middle East Policy.* Berkeley: University of California Press, 2001.

Citino, Nathan. *From Arab Nationalism to OPEC: Eisenhower, King Sa'ūd, and the Making of U.S.-Saudi Relations.* Bloomington: Indiana University Press, 2002.

Clarke, Richard A. *Against All Enemies: Inside America's War on Terror.* New York: Free Press, 2004.

Cline, Ray. *Secrets, Spies, and Scholars.* Washington, DC: Acropolis Books, 1976.

Clinton, Hillary Rodham. *Hard Choices.* New York: Simon & Schuster, 2014.

Clowse, Barbara Barksdale. *Brainpower for the Cold War: The Sputnik Crisis and National Defense Education Act of 1958.* Westport, CT: Greenwood Press, 1981.

Cole, David, ed. *The Torture Memos: Rationalizing the Unthinkable.* New York: New Press, 2009.

Cole, David, and James X. Dempsey. *Terrorism and the Constitution: Sacrificing Civil Liberties in the Name of National Security.* New York: New Press, 2002.

Cole, Juan. *Napoleon's Egypt: Invading the Middle East.* New York: Palgrave Macmillan, 2007.

——. *The New Arabs: How the Millennial Generation Is Changing the Middle East.* New York: Simon & Schuster, 2014.

Coleman, Peter. *The Liberal Conspiracy: The Congress for Cultural Freedom and the Struggle for the Mind of Postwar Europe.* New York: Free Press, 1989.

Coll, Steve. *Ghost Wars: The Secret History of the CIA, Afghanistan, and Bin Laden from the Soviet Invasion to September 10.* New York: Penguin, 2004.

Connelly, Matthew. "Taking Off the Cold War Lens: Visions of North-South Conflict during the Algerian War for Independence." *American Historical Review* 105, no. 3 (June 2000): 739–769.

Coon, Carleton. *A North Africa Story: The Anthropologist as OSS Agent.* Ipswich, MA: Gambit, 1980.

——. *Adventures and Discoveries: The Autobiography of Carleton S. Coon.* Englewood Cliffs, NJ: Prentice-Hall, 1981.

Coon, Carleton S., Jr., ed. *Daniel Bliss and the Founding of the American University of Beirut.* Washington, DC: Middle East Institute, 1989.

Cooper, Andrew Scott. *Oil Kings: How the U.S., Iran, and Saudi Arabia Changed the Balance of Power in the Middle East.* New York: Simon & Schuster, 2011.

Cooper, John Milton, Jr., ed. *Reconsidering Woodrow Wilson: Progressivism, Internationalism, War and Peace.* Baltimore: Johns Hopkins University Press, 2008.

Cooper, John Milton, Jr. *Woodrow Wilson: A Biography.* New York: Alfred A. Knopf, 2009.

——. *Breaking the Heart of the World: Woodrow Wilson and the Fight for the League of Nations.* Cambridge: Cambridge University Press, 2010.

Copeland, Miles. *The Game of Nations: The Amorality of Power Politics.* London: Weidenfeld and Nicolson, 1969.

Crawford, Fred D., and Joseph A. Berton. "How Well Did Lawrence of Arabia Know Lawrence of Arabia?" *English Literature in Transition (1880–1930)* 39, no. 3 (1996): 299–318.

Cropsey, Seth. "Arab Money and the Universities." *Commentary.* April 1979: 72–74

Cull, Nicholas. *The Cold War and the United States Information Agency: American Propaganda and Public Diplomacy, 1945–1989*. Cambridge: Cambridge University Press, 2008.

Cumings, Bruce. *Origins of the Korean War*. Vol. 1, *Liberation and the Emergence of Separate Regimes, 1945–1947*. Princeton, NJ: Princeton University Press, 1981.

———. *Origins of the Korean War*. Vol. 2, *The Roaring of the Cataract, 1947–1950*. Princeton, NJ: Princeton University Press, 1990.

Dabashi, Hamid. *Post-Orientalism: Knowledge and Power in Time of Terror*. Piscataway, NJ: Transaction Publishers, 2008.

Daigle, Craig. *The Limits of Détente: The United States, the Soviet Union, and the Arab-Israeli Conflict, 1969–1973*. New Haven, CT: Yale University Press, 2010.

Dallek, Robert. *Nixon and Kissinger: Partners in Power*. New York: HarperCollins, 2007.

Danner, Mark. *Torture and Truth: America, Abu Ghraib, and the War on Terror*. New York: New York Review of Books, 2004.

Darling, Arthur B. *The Central Intelligence Agency: An Instrument of Government to 1950*. University Park: Pennsylvania State University Press, 1990.

Davidson, Lawrence. *America's Palestine: Popular and Official Perceptions from Balfour to Israeli Statehood*. Gainesville: University Press of Florida, 2001.

Davison, Roderic. "Where Is the Middle East?" *Foreign Affairs* 38 (1960): 665–675.

Dean, Robert. *Imperial Brotherhood: Gender and the Making of Cold War Foreign Policy*. Amherst: University of Massachusetts Press, 2001.

Deeb, Lara, and Jessica Winegar. *Anthropology's Politics: Disciplining the Middle East*. Stanford, CA: Stanford University Press, 2016.

DeNovo, John. *American Interests and Politics in the Middle East, 1900–1939*. Minneapolis: University of Minnesota Press, 1963.

Diamond, Sigmund. *Compromised Campus: The Collaboration of Universities with the Intelligence Community*. New York: Oxford University Press, 1992.

Dirks, Nicholas. *Castes of Mind: Colonialism and the Making of Modern India*. Princeton, NJ: Princeton University Press, 2001.

Divine, Robert. *The Sputnik Challenge*. New York: Oxford University Press, 1993.

Dodge, Bayard. *The American University of Beirut: A Brief History of the University and the Land Which It Serves*. Beirut: Khayat, 1958.

Dögan, Mehmet Ali, and Heather Sharkey, eds. *American Missionaries and the Middle East: Foundational Encounters*. Salt Lake City: University of Utah Press, 2011.

Dorwart, Jeffery M. *Eberstadt and Forrestal: A National Security Partnership, 1909–1949*. College Station: Texas A&M University Press, 1991.

Doumani, Beshara, ed. *Academic Freedom after September 11*. New York: Zone Books, 2006.

Eddy, William A. *FDR Meets Ibn Saud*. New York: American Friends of the Middle East, 1954.

Ekbladh, David. *The Great American Mission: Modernization and the Construction of an American World Order*. Princeton, NJ: Princeton University Press, 2010.

Eisenhower, Dwight D. *Waging Peace, 1956–1961*. New York: Doubleday, 1965.

Engerman, David C. *Know Your Enemy: The Rise and Fall of America's Soviet Experts*. New York: Oxford University Press, 2009.

———. "Social Science in the Cold War." *Isis* 101, no. 2 (June 2010): 393–400.

———. "The Pedagogical Purposes of Interdisciplinary Social Science: A View from Area Studies in the United States." *Journal of the History of the Behavioral Sciences* 51, no. 1 (Winter 2015): 78–92.

Engerman, David C., Nils Gilman, Mark Haefele, and Michael Latham, eds. *Staging Growth: Modernization, Development, and the Global Cold War*. Amherst: University of Massachusetts Press, 2003.

Etzold, Thomas, and John Lewis Gaddis, eds. *Containment: Documents on American Policy and Strategy 1945–1950*. New York: Columbia University Press, 1978.

Eveland, Wilbur Crane. *Ropes of Sand: America's Failure in the Middle East*. New York: W. W. Norton, 1980.

Farish, Matthew. *The Contours of America's Cold War*. Minneapolis: University of Minnesota Press, 2010.

Ferguson, Niall. *Empire: The Rise and Demise of the British World Order and the Lessons for Global Power*. New York: Basic Books, 2002

———. *Colossus: The Rise and Fall of the American Empire*. New York: Penguin, 2004.

Ferris, Jesse. *Nasser's Gamble: How Intervention in Yemen Caused the Six Day War and the Decline of Egyptian Power*. Princeton, NJ: Princeton University Press, 2013.

Field, James A. *America and the Mediterranean World, 1776–1882*. Princeton, NJ: Princeton University Press, 1969.

Fischer, David Hackett. *Liberty and Freedom: A Visual History of America's Founding Ideas*. New York: Oxford University Press, 2005.

Fisher, Sydney N., ed. *Social Forces in the Middle East*. Ithaca, NY: Cornell University Press, 1955.

Floto, Inga. *Colonel House in Paris*. Princeton, NJ: Princeton University Press, 1980.

Ford, Gerald R. *A Time to Heal: The Autobiography of Gerald R. Ford*. New York: Harper & Row, 1979.

Friedberg, Aaron L. *In the Shadow of the Garrison State: America's Anti-Statism and Its Cold War Grand Strategy*. Princeton, NJ: Princeton University Press, 2000.

Frye, Richard, ed. *The Near East and the Great Powers*. Cambridge, MA: Harvard University Press, 1951.

———. *Greater Iran: A 20th Century Odyssey*. Costa Mesa, CA: Mazda Publishers, 2005.

Gaddis, John Lewis. *Strategies of Containment: A Critical Reappraisal of Postwar American National Security Policy*. New York: Oxford University Press, 1982.

———. *We Now Know: Rethinking Cold War History*. New York: Oxford University Press, 1997.

Gallagher, Nancy Elizabeth. *Approaches to the History of the Middle East: Interviews with Leading Middle East Historians*. Reading: Ithaca Press, 1994.

Gardner, Lloyd C. *Three Kings: The Rise of an American Empire in the Middle East after World War II*. New York: New Press, 2009.

———. *Killing Machine: The American Presidency in the Age of Drone Warfare*. New York: New Press, 2013.

Gardner, Lloyd C., and Marilyn B. Young, eds. *The New American Empire: A 21st Century Teach-In on U.S. Foreign Policy*. New York: New Press, 2005.

Gary, Brett. *The Nervous Liberals: Propaganda Anxieties from World War I to the Cold War*. New York: Columbia University Press, 2011.

Gasiorowski, Mark. *U.S. Foreign Policy and the Shah: Building a Client State in Iran*. Ithaca, NY: Cornell University Press, 1991.

Gates, Robert. *Duty: Memoirs of a Secretary at War*. New York: Alfred A. Knopf, 2014.

Geiger, Roger. *Research and Relevant Knowledge: American Research Universities since World War II*. New York: Oxford University Press, 1993.

Gelfand, Lawrence. *The Inquiry: American Preparations for Peace, 1917–1919*. New Haven, CT: Yale University Press, 1963.

Gelvin, James. *The Arab Uprisings: What Everyone Needs to Know*. New York: Oxford University Press, 2012.

Gendzier, Irene. *Managing Political Change: Social Scientists and the Third World*. Boulder, CO: Westview Press, 1985.

George, Alexander L., and Juliette L. George. *Woodrow Wilson and Colonel House: A Personality Study*. New York: John Day Company, 1956.

Gerges, Fawaz. *The Superpowers and the Middle East: Regional and International Politics, 1955–1967*. Boulder, CO: Westview Press, 1994.

———. *The Rise and Fall of Al-Qaeda*. New York: Oxford University Press, 2011.

Gezari, Vanessa M. *The Tender Soldier: A True Story of War and Sacrifice*. New York: Simon & Schuster, 2013.

Gibb, Hamilton. *Area Studies Reconsidered*. London: University of London, 1963.

Gilman, Nils. *Mandarins of the Future: Modernization Theory in Cold War America*. Baltimore: Johns Hopkins University Press, 2003.

Glander, Timothy. *Origins of Mass Communications Research during the American Cold War: Educational Effects and Contemporary Implications*. Mahwah, NJ: LEA Publishers, 2000.

Glidden, Harold J. "The Arab World." *American Journal of Psychiatry* 128, no. 8 (February 1972): 984–988.

Gosse, Van. "A Movement of Movements: The Definition and Periodization of the New Left." In *A Companion to Post-1945 America*, edited by Jean-Christophe Agnew and Roy Rosenzweig, 277–302. Malden, MA: Blackwell, 2002.

Grabill, Joseph L. *Protestant Diplomacy and the Near East: Missionary Influence on American Policy, 1810–1927*. Minneapolis: University of Minnesota Press, 1971.

Gran, Peter. *Islamic Roots of Capitalism*. Syracuse, NY: Syracuse University Press, 1978.

Greene, Jack P. *The Intellectual Construction of America: Exceptionalism and Identity from 1492 to 1800*. Chapel Hill: University of North Carolina Press, 1993.

Greenwald, Glenn. *No Place to Hide: Edward Snowden, the NSA, and the U.S. Surveillance State*. New York: Metropolitan Books, 2014.

Gruber, Carol S. *Mars and Minerva: World War I and the Uses of the Higher Learning in America.* Baton Rouge: Louisiana State University Press, 1975.

Gualtieri, Sarah. *Between Arab and White: Race and Ethnicity in the Early Syrian American Diaspora.* Berkeley: University of California, Berkeley, 2009.

Hahn, Peter. *The United States, Great Britain, and Egypt, 1945–1956: Strategy and Diplomacy in the Early Cold War.* Chapel Hill: University of North Carolina Press, 1991.

———. *Crisis and Crossfire: The United States and the Middle East since 1945.* Washington, DC: Potomac Books, 2005.

———. *Mission Accomplished? The United States and Iraq since World War I.* New York: Oxford University Press, 2012.

Hahn, Peter, and Mary Ann Heiss, eds. *Empire and Revolution: The United States and the Third World since 1945.* Columbus: Ohio State University Press, 2001.

Hahnhimäki, Jussi M. *The Flawed Architect: Henry Kissinger and American Foreign Policy.* New York: Oxford University, 2004.

Haidar, Rustum. *Mudhakkirāt Rustum Haidar.* Beirut: Dar al-Arabiya al-Mawsou'at, 1988.

Hajjar, Lisa, and Steve Niva. "(Re)Made in the USA: Middle East Studies in the Global Era." *Middle East Report* 205 (October–December 1997): 2–9.

Halberstam, David. *The Best and the Brightest.* New York: Ballantine Books, 1969.

———. *The Powers That Be.* New York: Knopf, 1975.

Halpern, Manfred. *The Politics of Social Change in the Middle East and North Africa.* Princeton, NJ: Princeton University Press, 1963.

Heginbotham, Stanley. "Rethinking International Scholarship: The Transition from the Cold War Era." *Items: Newsletter of the SSRC* 48, no. 2/3 (1994): 33–40.

Heikel, Mohamed Hassanein. *The Cairo Documents: The Inside Story of Nasser and His Relationship with World Leaders, Rebels, and Statesmen.* New York: Doubleday, 1973.

———. *Sphinx and Commissar: The Rise and Fall of Soviet Influence in the Arab World.* London: St. James's Place, 1978.

Heil, Alan, Jr., *Voice of America: A History.* New York: Columbia University Press, 2003.

Heilbrunn, Jacob. *They Knew They Were Right: The Rise of the Neocons.* New York: Doubleday, 2008.

Heiss, Mary Ann. *Empire and Nationhood: The United States, Great Britain, and Iranian Oil, 1950–1954.* New York: Columbia University Press, 1997.

Herring, E. Pendleton. *The Impact of War: Our American Democracy under Arms.* New York: Farrar & Rinehart, 1941.

Herring, George. *From Colony to Superpower: U.S. Foreign Relations since 1776.* New York: Oxford University Press, 2008.

Hersh, Burton. *The Old Boys: The American Elite and the Origins of the CIA.* New York: Maxwell Macmillan International, 1992.

Hersh, Seymour M. *Chain of Command: The Road from 9/11 to Abu Ghraib.* New York: HarperCollins, 2004.

Hevia, James. *The Imperial Security State: British Colonial Knowledge and Empire-Building in Asia*. Cambridge: Cambridge University Press, 2012.

Hinckle, Warren, Robert Scheer, Sol Stern, and Stanley K. Sheinbaum. "The University on the Make." *Ramparts*. April 1966.

Hixson, Walter L. *American Settler Colonialism: A History*. New York: Palgrave Macmillan, 2013.

Hodgson, Godfrey. *Woodrow Wilson's Right Hand: The Life of Colonel Edward M. House*. New Haven, CT: Yale University Press, 2006.

Hogan, Michael J. *A Cross of Iron: Harry S. Truman and the Origins of the National Security State, 1945–1954*. Cambridge: Cambridge University Press, 1998.

Hoover, Calvin. *Memoirs of Capitalism, Communism, and Nazism*. Durham, NC: Duke University Press, 1965.

Hoskins, Halford L. *The Middle East: Problem Area in World Politics*. New York: Macmillan, 1954.

Hourani, Albert. *Islam in European Thought*. Cambridge: Cambridge University Press, 1991.

House, Edward Mandell, and Charles Seymour, eds. *What Really Happened in Paris: The Story of the Peace Conference, 1918–1919*. New York: Charles Scribner's Sons, 1921.

Howard, Harry N. *An American Inquiry in the Middle East: The King-Crane Commission*. Beirut: Khayats, 1963.

Howell, Georgina. *Gertrude Bell: Queen of the Desert, Shaper of Nations*. New York: Farrar, Straus and Giroux, 2006.

Hunt, Michael. *Ideology and U.S. Foreign Policy*. New Haven, CT: Yale University Press, 1987.

Huntington, Samuel. *Political Order in Changing Societies*. New Haven, CT: Yale University Press, 1968.

———. "Clash of Civilizations." *Foreign Affairs* 72 (1993): 22–49.

———. *The Clash of Civilizations and the Remaking of the World Order*. New York: Touchstone, 1996.

Ikenberry, G. John. *Liberal Leviathan: The Origins, Crisis, and Transformation of the American World Order*. Princeton, NJ: Princeton University Press, 2011.

Immerman, Richard. *Empire for Liberty: A History of American Imperialism from Benjamin Franklin to Paul Wolfowitz*. Princeton, NJ: Princeton University Press, 2010.

———. *The Hidden Hand: A Brief History of the CIA*. Malden, MA : John Wiley & Sons, 2014.

Indyk, Martin. *Innocent Abroad: An Intimate Account of American Peace Diplomacy in the Middle East*. New York: Simon & Schuster, 2009.

Irwin, Robert. *Dangerous Knowledge: Orientalism and Its Discontents*. Woodstock, NY: Overlook Press, 2006.

Isaac, Joel, and Duncan Bell, eds. *Uncertain Empire: American History and the Idea of the Cold War*. New York: Oxford University Press, 2012.

Jacobs, Matthew F. *Imagining the Middle East: The Building of an American Foreign Policy, 1918–1967*. Chapel Hill: University of North Carolina Press, 2011.

Jayweera, Neville, and Sarath Amunugama, eds. *Rethinking Development Communication*. Singapore: Asian Mass Communication Research and Information Center, 1987.

Jeffreys-Jones, Rhodri. "The Role of British Intelligence in the Mythologies Underpinning the OSS and Early CIA." *Intelligence and National Security* 15, no. 2 (Summer 2000): 5–19.

———. *In Spies We Trust: The Story of Western Intelligence*. New York: Oxford University Press, 2013.

———. "Antecedents and Memory as Factors in the Creation of the CIA." *Diplomatic History* 40, no. 1 (January 2016): 140–154.

Jensehaugen, Jorgen. "Blueprint for Arab-Israeli Peace? President Carter and the Brookings Report." *Diplomacy and Statecraft* 25 (August 2014): 492–508.

Johnson, Chalmers. *The Sorrows of Empire: Militarism, Secrecy, and the End of the Republic*. New York: Metropolitan Books, 2004.

Johnson, E. A. J., ed. *The Dimensions of Diplomacy*. Baltimore: Johns Hopkins University Press, 1964.

Johnson, Loch K. *A Season of Inquiry: The Senate Intelligence Investigation*. Lexington: University of Kentucky Press, 1985.

———. *The Threat on the Horizon: An Inside Account of America's Search for Security after the Cold War*. New York: Oxford University Press, 2011.

Johnson, Peter, and Judith Tucker. "Middle East Studies Network in the United States." *MERIP Reports* 38 (1974): 3–20, 26.

Johnson-Davies, Denys. *Memories in Translation: A Life between the Lines of Arabic Literature*. Cairo: American University of Cairo Press, 2006.

Jones, Frank Leith. *Blowtorch: Robert Komer, Vietnam, and American Cold War Strategy*. Annapolis: Naval Institute Press, 2014.

Jones, Toby Craig. "America, Oil, and War in the Middle East." *Journal of American History* 99, no. 1 (June 2012): 208–218.

Kaplan, Fred. *The Wizards of Armageddon*. New York: Simon & Schuster, 1983.

Kaplan, Robert. *The Arabists: The Romance of an American Elite*. New York: The New Press, 1993.

Katz, Barry. *Foreign Intelligence: Research and Analysis in the Office of Strategic Services, 1942–1945*. Cambridge, MA: Harvard University Press, 1989.

Keefer, Louis. *Scholars in Foxholes: The Story of the Army Specialized Training Program in World War II*. Jefferson, NC: McFarland, 1988.

Kellner, Douglas. *The Persian Gulf and TV War*. Boulder, CO: Westview Press, 1992.

Kelly, John D., Beatrice Jauregui, Sean T. Mitchell, and Jeremy Walton, eds. *Anthropology and Global Counterinsurgency*. Chicago: University of Chicago Press, 2010.

Kennan, George. *The Kennan Diaries*. Edited by Frank Costigliola. New York: W. W. Norton, 2014.

Kerr, Clark. "Washington: National Foundation for Higher Education." *Change* 3 (May–June 1970): 8–9, 69.

Kerr, Malcolm. *The Arab Cold War: Gamal 'Abd al-Nasir and His Rivals, 1958–1970.* New York: Oxford University Press, 1971.

Khalidi, Rashid. *Under Siege: PLO Decisionmaking during the 1982 War.* New York: Columbia University Press, 1986.

———. "Is There a Future for Middle East Studies? 1994 MESA Presidential Address." *Middle East Studies Association Bulletin* 29, no. 1 (July 1995): 1–6.

———. *Resurrecting Empire: Western Footprints and America's Perilous Path in the Middle East.* Boston: Beacon Press, 2004.

———. *The Iron Cage: The Story of the Palestinian Struggle for Statehood.* Boston: Beacon Press, 2006.

Khalidi, Rashid, Lisa Anderson, Muhammad Muslih, and Reeva Simon, eds. *The Origins of Arab Nationalism.* New York: Columbia University Press, 1991.

Khalil, Osamah. "Pax Americana: The United States, the Palestinians, and the Peace Process, 1948–2008." *New Centennial Review* 8, no. 1 (2008): 1–41.

———. "The Crossroads of the World: U.S. and British Foreign Policy Doctrines and the Construct of the Middle East, 1902–2007." *Diplomatic History* 38, no. 2 (April 2014): 299–344.

———. "The Counterrevolutionary Year: The Arab Spring and U.S. Foreign Policy in the Middle East." In *American Studies Encounters the Middle East,* edited by Alex Lubin and Marwan Kraidy, 286–301. Chapel Hill: University of North Carolina Press, 2016.

———. "The Radical Crescent: The United States, the Palestine Liberation Organisation, and the Lebanese Civil War, 1973–1978." *Diplomacy and Statecraft* 27 (September 2016): 1–27.

Khalili, Laleh. *Time in the Shadows: Confinement in Counterinsurgencies.* Stanford, CA: Stanford University Press, 2012.

Kilcullen, David. " 'Twenty-Eight Articles': Fundamentals of Company-level Counterinsurgency." *Military Review* (May/June 2006): 103–108.

———. *Counterinsurgency.* New York: Oxford University Press, 2010.

King, Richard. *Race, Culture, and the Intellectuals, 1940–1970.* Baltimore: Johns Hopkins University Press, 2004.

Kinzer, Stephen. *The Brothers: John Foster Dulles, Allen Dulles, and Their Secret World War.* New York: Henry Holt, 2013.

Kipnis, Yigal. *1973: The Road to War.* Charlottesville, VA: Just World Books, 2013.

Kipp, Jacob, Lester Grau, Karl Prinslow, and Don Smith. "The Human Terrain System: A CORDS for the 21st Century." *Military Review* (September–October 2006): 8–14;

Kissinger, Henry. *White House Years.* Boston: Little, Brown, 1979.

———. *Years of Upheaval.* Boston: Little, Brown, 1982.

———. *Years of Renewal.* New York: Simon & Schuster, 1999.

Klein, Christina. *Cold War Orientalism: Asia in the Middlebrow Imagination, 1945–1961.* Berkeley: University of California Press, 2003.

Knock, Thomas. *To End All Wars: Woodrow Wilson and the Quest for a New World Order.* New York: Oxford University Press, 1992.

Kolko, Gabriel. *The Roots of American Foreign Policy.* Boston: Beacon Press, 1969.

———. *Confronting the Third World: United States Foreign Policy, 1945–1980.* New York: Pantheon, 1988.

Koppes, Clayton R. "Captain Mahan, General Gordon, and the Origins of the Term 'Middle East.'" *Middle Eastern Studies* 12 (January 1976): 95–98.

Korda, Michael. *Hero: The Life and Legend of Lawrence of Arabia.* New York: HarperCollins, 2010.

Kracauer, Siegfried. *From Caligari to Hitler.* Princeton, NJ: Princeton University Press, 1947.

Kramer, Martin. *Ivory Towers on Sand: The Failure of Middle Eastern Studies in America.* Washington, DC: Washington Institute for Near East Policy, 2001.

Kramer, Paul. *The Blood of Government: Race, Empire, the United States, and the Philippines.* Chapel Hill: University of North Carolina Press, 2006.

———. "Power and Connection: Imperial Histories of the United States in the World." *American Historical Review* 116, no. 5 (December 2011): 1348–1391.

Krenn, Michael. *Fall-Out Shelters for the Human Spirit: American Art and the Cold War.* Chapel Hill: University of North Carolina Press, 2005.

Kristol, William, and Robert Kagan. "Toward a Neo-Reaganite Foreign Policy." *Foreign Affairs* (July–August 1996): 18–32.

Kuklick, Bruce. *Puritans in Babylon: The Ancient Near East and American Intellectual Life, 1880–1930.* Princeton, NJ: Princeton University Press, 1996.

———. *Blind Oracles: Intellectuals and War from Kennan to Kissinger.* Princeton, NJ: Princeton University Press, 2006.

Kuniholm, Bruce R. *The Origins of the Cold War in the Near East: Great Power Conflict and Diplomacy in Iran, Turkey, and Greece.* Princeton, NJ: Princeton University Press, 1980.

Kuzmarov, Jeremy. *Modernizing Repression: Police Training and Nation-Building in the American Century.* Boston: University of Massachusetts Press, 2012.

Kyle, Keith. *Suez 1956: Britain's End of Empire in the Middle East.* New York: St. Martin's Press, 1991.

Labelle, Maurice M., Jr. "'The Only Thorn': Early Saudi-American Relations and the Question of Palestine, 1945–1949." *Diplomatic History* 35, no. 2 (April 2011): 257–281.

Langer, William. *In and Out of the Ivory Tower: The Autobiography of William L. Langer.* New York: N. Watson Academic Publications, 1977.

Lansing, Robert. *Peace Negotiations: A Personal Narrative.* New York: Houghton Mifflin, 1921.

Laqueur, Walter. *A History of Zionism: From the French Revolution to the Establishment of the State of Israel.* New York: Shocken Books, 1976.

Latham, Michael. *Modernization as Ideology: American Social Science and "Nation Building" in the Kennedy Era.* Chapel Hill: University of North Carolina Press, 2000.

———. *The Right Kind of Revolution: Modernization, Development, and U.S. Foreign Policy from Cold War to the Present.* Ithaca, NY: Cornell University Press, 2011.

Lawrence, T. E. *Seven Pillars of Wisdom: A Triumph.* New York: Acorn Books, 1991.

Ledbetter, James. *Unwarranted Influence: Dwight D. Eisenhower and the Military-Industrial Complex.* New Haven, CT: Yale University Press, 2011.

Lee, Robert G. *Orientals: Asian Americans in Popular Culture.* Philadelphia: Temple University Press, 1999.

Leffler, Melvyn. *A Preponderance of Power: National Security, the Truman Administration, and the Cold War.* Stanford, CA: Stanford University Press, 1993.

———. *For the Soul of Mankind.* New York: Hill and Wang, 2007.

Leffler, Melvyn P., and Jeffrey W. Legro, eds. *In Uncertain Times: American Foreign Policy after the Berlin Wall and 9/11.* Ithaca, NY: Cornell University Press, 2011.

Lenczowski, George. *The Middle East in World Affairs.* Ithaca, NY: Cornell University Press, 1952.

———. *The Middle East in World Affairs.* 3rd ed. Ithaca, NY: Cornell University, 1962.

———. *United States Interests in the Middle East.* Washington, DC: American Enterprise Institute, 1968.

———. *Middle East Oil in a Revolutionary Age.* Washington, DC: American Enterprise Institute, 1976.

———, ed. *Iran under the Pahlavis.* Stanford, CA: Hoover Institution Press, 1978.

———. "The Arc of Crisis: Its Central Sector." *Foreign Affairs* 57, no. 4 (Spring 1979): 796–820.

Lerner, Daniel. *The Passing of Traditional Society: Modernizing the Middle East.* New York: Free Press, 1958.

———. *Psychological Warfare against Nazi Germany: The Sykewar Campaign, D-Day to VE-Day.* Cambridge, MA: MIT Press, 1971.

Lerner, Daniel, and Harold Lasswell, eds. *The Policy Sciences: Recent Developments in Scope and Method.* Stanford, CA: Stanford University Press, 1951.

Lesch, David W. *1979: The Year That Shaped the Modern Middle East.* Boulder, CO: Westview Press, 2001.

———, ed. *The Middle East and the United States: A Historical and Political Reassessment.* 4th ed. Boulder, CO: Westview Press, 2007.

Leslie, Stuart W. *The Cold War and American Science: The Military-Industrial-Academic Complex at MIT and Stanford.* New York: Columbia University Press, 1993.

Levine, Mark. *Why They Don't Hate Us: Lifting the Veil on the Axis of Evil.* Oxford: One World, 2005.

Lewis, Bernard. "The Question of Orientalism." *New York Review of Books.* June 24, 1982.

———. "The Roots of Muslim Rage." *The Atlantic.* September 1990.

———. "The Revolt of Islam." *New Yorker.* November 19, 2001.

———. *What Went Wrong? Western Impact and Middle Eastern Response.* New York: Oxford University Press, 2002.

————. *The Crisis of Islam: Holy War and Unholy Terror.* New York: Modern Library, 2003.

Lewis, Bernard, and Buntzie Ellis Churchill. *Notes on a Century: Reflections of a Middle East Historian.* New York: Viking, 2012.

Lewis, Martin W., and Karen Wigen. *The Myth of Continents: A Critique of Metageography.* Berkeley: University of California Press, 1997.

Lippmann, Thomas W. *Arabian Knight: Colonel Bill Eddy USMC and the Rise of American Power in the Middle East.* Vista, CA: Selwa Press, 2008.

Little, Douglas. "The Making of a Special Relationship: The United States and Israel, 1957–1968," *International Journal of Middle East Studies* 25 (1993): 563–585.

————. *American Orientalism: The United States and the Middle East since 1945.* Chapel Hill: University of North Carolina Press, 2004.

Lockman, Zachary. *Contending Visions of the Middle East: The History and Politics of Orientalism.* 2nd ed. Cambridge: Cambridge University Press, 2010.

————. *Field Notes: The Making of Middle East Studies in the United States.* Stanford, CA: Stanford University Press, 2016.

Logevall, Fredrik. *Choosing War: The Lost Chance for Peace and the Escalation of the War in Vietnam.* Berkeley: University of California Press, 2001.

Logevall, Fredrik, and Andrew Preston, eds. *Nixon in the World: American Foreign Relations, 1969–1977.* New York: Oxford University Press, 2008.

Long, David, and Brian Schmidt, eds. *Imperialism and Internationalism in the Discipline of International Relations.* Albany: State University of New York Press, 2005.

Louis, William Roger. *The British Empire in the Middle East, 1948–1951.* New York: Oxford University Press, 1984.

Louis, William Roger, and Roger Owen, eds. *Suez 1956: The Crisis and Its Consequences.* New York: Oxford University Press, 1989.

————. *A Revolutionary Year: The Middle East in 1958.* London: I. B. Tauris, 2002.

Love, Eric T. *Race over Empire: Racism and U.S. Imperialism, 1865–1900.* Chapel Hill: University of North Carolina Press, 2004.

Lowen, Rebecca. *Creating the Cold War University: The Transformation of Stanford.* Berkeley: University of California Press, 1997.

Lynch, Marc. *Voices of the New Arab Public: Iraq, Al Jazeera, and Middle East Politics Today.* New York: Columbia University Press, 2006.

————. *The Arab Uprising: The Unfinished Revolutions of the New Middle East.* New York: Public Affairs, 2012.

Lyons, Gene M. *The Uneasy Partnership: Social Science and the Federal Government in the Twentieth Century.* New York: Russell Sage Foundation, 1969.

MacDonald, Michael. *Overreach: Delusions of Regime Change in Iraq.* Cambridge, MA: Harvard University Press, 2010.

MacMillan, Margaret. *Paris 1919: Six Months That Changed the World.* New York: Random House, 2001.

Mahan, Alfred Thayer. *From Sail to Steam: Recollections of Naval Life.* New York: Harper & Brothers, 1906.

Mahdi, Sami. *Tajribat Tawfīq Sayigh al-Shiʿrīyah wa-Marjiʿīyātuhā al-Fikrīyah wa-al-Fannīyah*. Beirut: Riyad al-Rayyis, 2009.

Makdisi, Ussama. *Artillery of Heaven: American Missionaries and the Failed Conversion of the Middle East*. Ithaca, NY: Cornell University Press, 2008.

———. *Faith Misplaced: The Broken Promise of U.S.-Arab Relations, 1820–2001*. New York: Public Affairs, 2010.

———. "After Said: The Limits and Possibilities of a Critical Scholarship of U.S.-Arab Relations." *Diplomatic History* 38, no. 3 (June 2014): 657–684.

Makiya, Kanan. *Republic of Fear: The Politics of Modern Iraq*. Berkeley: University of California, 1989.

Mamdani, Mahmood. *Good Muslim, Bad Muslim: America, the Cold War, and the Roots of Terror*. New York: Pantheon Books, 2004.

Manela, Erez. *The Wilsonian Moment: Self-Determination and the International Origins of Anticolonial Nationalism*. New York: Oxford University Press, 2007.

Mann, James. *Rise of the Vulcans: The History of Bush's War Cabinet*. New York: Viking, 2004.

Mann, Theodore R. *"If I Am Only for Myself . . ."*: *The American Jewish Community's Pursuit of Social Justice, A Memoir*. West Conshohocken, PA: Infinity, 2012.

Marr, Timothy. *The Cultural Roots of American Islamicism*. Cambridge: Cambridge University Press, 2006.

Mart, Michelle. *Eye on Israel: How America Came to View the Jewish State as an Ally*. Albany: State University of New York Press, 2006.

May, Ernest, ed. *American Cold War Strategy: Interpreting NSC 68*. Boston: Beacon Press, 1993.

McAlister, Melani. *Epic Encounters: Culture, Media, and U.S. Interests in the Middle East since 1945*. Berkeley: University of California Press, 2005.

McCaughey, Robert. *International Studies and Academic Enterprise: A Chapter in the Enclosure of American Learning*. New York: Columbia University Press, 1984.

McCormick, Thomas. *America's Half-Century: United States Foreign Policy in the Cold War and After*. 2nd ed. Baltimore: Johns Hopkins University Press, 1995.

McCullough, David. *Truman*. New York: Simon & Schuster, 1992.

McDougall, Walter A. *Promised Land, Crusader State: The American Encounter with the World Since 1776*. New York: Houghton Mifflin, 1997.

McGann, James G., with Richard Sabatini. *Global Think Tanks: Policy Networks and Governance*. New York: Routledge, 2011.

McLoughlin, Leslie. *A Nest of Spies?* London: Alhani, 1993.

McNamara, Robert. *In Retrospect: The Tragedy and Lessons of Vietnam*. New York: Vintage, 1996.

Medvetz, Thomas. *Think Tanks in America*. Chicago: University of Chicago Press, 2012.

Mettler, Suzanne. *Soldiers to Citizens: The G.I. Bill and the Making of the Greatest Generation*. New York: Oxford University Press, 2005.

Mieczkowski, Yanek. *Eisenhower's Sputnik Moment: The Race for Space and World Prestige*. Ithaca, NY: Cornell University Press, 2013.

Mills, C. Wright. *The Power Elite*. New York: Oxford University Press, 1956.

Mitchell, Timothy. *Colonising Egypt*. Cambridge: Cambridge University Press, 1988.

———. *Carbon Democracy: Political Power in the Age of Oil*. New York: Verso Books, 2013.

Montague, Ludwell Lee. *General Walter Bedell Smith as Director of Central Intelligence, October 1950–February 1953*. University Park: Pennsylvania State University Press, 1992.

Mooney, Chris. "For Your Eyes Only." *Lingua Franca* (November 2000): 35–43.

Muehlenbeck, Philip. *Betting on the Africans: John F. Kennedy's Courting of African Nationalist Leaders*. New York: Oxford University Press, 2012.

Murphy, Lawrence R. *The American University in Cairo: 1919–1987*. Cairo: American University in Cairo Press, 1987.

Nachtaway, Jodi, and Anne Banda, eds., *Area Studies and Social Science: Strategies for Understanding Middle East Politics*. Bloomington: Indiana University Press, 1999.

Naff, Thomas, ed. *Paths to the Middle East: Ten Scholars Look Back*. Albany: State University of New York Press, 1993.

Nasser, Gamal Abdel. *Philosophy of the Revolution*. Buffalo, NY: Smith, Keynes and Marshall, 1959.

———. *Falsafat al-Thawra*. Cairo: Dār wa-Matābi' al-Sha'b, 1966.

Nayak Meghana V., and Christopher Malone. "American Orientalism and American Exceptionalism: A Critical Rethinking of US Hegemony." *International Studies Review* 11 (2009): 253–276.

Nelson, Anna Kasten. "President Truman and the Evolution of the National Security Council." *Journal of American History* 72 (1985): 369–374.

Netanyahu, Benjamin, ed. *International Terrorism: Challenge and Response*. New Brunswick, NJ: Transaction Publishers, 1981.

———. *Terrorism: How the West Can Win*. New York: Farrar, Straus and Giroux, 1986.

Neu, Charles E. *Colonel House: A Biography of Woodrow Wilson's Silent Partner*. New York: Oxford University Press, 2015.

Niblock, Tim, ed. *State, Society, and Economy in Saudi Arabia*. London: Croom Helm, 1982.

Nielsen, Waldemar A. *The Big Foundations*. New York: Columbia University Press, 1972.

Noll, Mark A., and Luke E. Harlow, eds. *Religion and American Politics*. 2nd ed. New York: Oxford University Press, 2007.

Norton, Anne. *Leo Strauss and the Politics of American Empire*. New Haven, CT: Yale University Press, 2004.

Norton, Augustus Richard. *Hezbollah: A Short History*. Princeton, NJ: Princeton University Press, 2007.

Noueihed, Lin, and Alex Warren. *The Battle for the Arab Spring: Revolution, Counter-Revolution, and the Making of a New Era*. New Haven, CT: Yale University Press, 2012.

Novick, Peter. *That Noble Dream: The "Objectivity Question" and the American Historical Profession*. Cambridge: Cambridge University Press, 1988.

Offner, Arnold. *Another Such Victory: President Truman and the Cold War, 1945–1953*. Stanford, CA: Stanford University Press, 2002.

O'Neill, William. *Coming Apart: An Informal History of America in the 1960s*. Chicago: Ivan R. Dee, 2005.

Oren, Ido. *Our Enemies and US: America's Rivalries and the Making of Political Science*. Ithaca, NY: Cornell University Press, 2003.

Oren, Michael. *Power, Faith, and Fantasy: America in the Middle East, 1776 to the Present*. New York: W. W. Norton, 2007.

Osgood, Kenneth. *Total Cold War: Eisenhower's Secret Propaganda Battle at Home and Abroad*. Lawrence: University of Kansas Press, 2006.

Osman, Tarek. *Egypt on the Brink: From Nasser to the Muslim Brotherhood*. New Haven, CT: Yale University Press, 2010.

Owen, Roger. *The Middle East in the World Economy, 1800–1914*. London: Metheun, 1981.

———. *The Rise and Fall of Arab Presidents for Life*. Cambridge, MA: Harvard University Press, 2012.

Pape, Robert. *Dying to Win: The Strategic Logic of Suicide Terrorism*. New York: Random House, 2005.

Parmar, Inderjeet. *Think Tanks and Power in Foreign Policy: A Comparative Study of the Role and Influence of the Council on Foreign Relations and the Royal Institute of International Affairs*. New York: Palgrave MacMillan, 2004.

———. *Foundations of the American Century: The Ford, Carnegie, and Rockefeller Foundations in the Rise of American Power*. New York: Columbia University Press, 2012.

Parra, Francisco. *Oil Politics: A Modern History of Petroleum*. London: I. B. Tauris, 2004.

Parsi, Trita. *Treacherous Alliance: The Secret Dealings of Israel, Iran, and the United States*. New Haven, CT: Yale University Press, 2007.

Patai, Raphael. *The Arab Mind*. New York: Charles Scribner's Sons, 1973.

Patel, Abdulrazzak. *The Arab Nahdah: The Making of the Intellectual and Humanist Movement*. Edinburgh: Edinburgh University Press, 2013.

Patrick, Andrew. *America's Forgotten Middle East Initiative: The King-Crane Commission of 1919*. London: I. B. Tauris, 2015.

Pedersen, Susan. *The Guardians: The League of Nations and the Crisis of Empire*. New York: Oxford University Press, 2015.

Pestritto, Ronald J. *Woodrow Wilson and the Roots of Modern Liberalism*. New York: Rowman & Littlefield, 2005.

Pollack, Kenneth M. *The Threatening Storm: The Case for Invading Iraq*. New York: Random House, 2002.

———. *The Persian Puzzle: The Conflict between Iran and America*. New York: Random House, 2005.

Popp, Roland. "An Application of Modernization Theory during the Cold War? The Case of Pahlavi Iran." *The International History Review* 30, no. 1 (March 2008): 76–98.

Powell, Colin L., with Joseph E. Persico. *My American Journey.* New York: Random House, 1995.

Prados, John. *The Family Jewels: The CIA, Secrecy, and Presidential Power.* Austin: University of Texas Press, 2013.

Prashad, Vijay. *Arab Spring, Libyan Winter.* Oakland, CA: AK Press, 2012.

Preston, Andrew. *Sword of the Spirit, Shield of Faith: Religion in American War and Diplomacy.* New York: Alfred A. Knopf, 2012.

Price, David. *Anthropological Intelligence: The Deployment and Neglect of American Anthropology in the Second World War.* Durham, NC: Duke University Press, 2008.

Priest, Dana, and Arkin, William M. *Top Secret America: The Rise of the New American Security State.* New York: Little, Brown, 2011.

Pye, Lucian W. *Politics, Personality, and Nation Building: Burma's Search for Identity.* New Haven, CT: Yale University Press, 1962.

———, ed. *Political Science and Area Studies: Rivals or Partners?* Bloomington: Indiana University Press, 1975.

Quandt, William, ed. *The Middle East: Ten Years after Camp David.* Washington, DC: Brookings Institution, 1988.

———. *Peace Process: American Diplomacy and the Arab-Israeli Conflict since 1967.* 3rd ed. Berkeley and Washington, DC: University of California Press, Brookings Institution, 2005.

Rabin, Yitzhak. *The Rabin Memoirs.* Boston: Little, Brown, 1979.

Rafael, Vicente "The Culture of Area Studies in the United States." *Social Text* (Winter 1994). 91–111.

Rakove, Robert. *Kennedy, Johnson, and the Nonaligned World.* Cambridge: Cambridge University Press, 2013.

Renzi, Fred. "Networks: Terra Incognita and the Case for Ethnographic Intelligence." *Military Review* (September–October 2006): 180–186.

Rich, Andrew. *Think Tanks, Public Policy, and the Politics of Expertise.* Cambridge: Cambridge University Press, 2004.

Richelson, Jeffrey T. *The U.S. Intelligence Community.* Boulder, CO: Westview Press, 1999.

Ricks, Thomas. *Fiasco: The American Military Adventure in Iraq.* New York: Penguin Press, 2006.

———. *The Gamble: General David Petraeus and the American Military Adventure in Iraq, 2006–2008.* New York: Penguin Press, 2010.

Robin, Ron. *The Making of the Cold War Enemy: Culture and Politics in the Military-Industrial Complex.* Princeton, NJ: Princeton University Press, 2001.

Rockefeller, Nelson. *Report to the President by the Commission on CIA Activities within the United States.* New York: Manor Books, 1975.

Rodgers, Daniel. *Age of Fracture.* Cambridge, MA: Harvard University Press, 2011.

Rogan, Eugene. *The Fall of the Ottomans: The Great War in the Middle East.* New York: Basic Books, 2015.

Rohde, Joy. *Armed with Expertise: The Militarization of American Social Research during the Cold War.* Ithaca, NY: Cornell University Press, 2013.

Romero, Juan. *The Iraqi Revolution of 1958: A Revolutionary Quest for Unity and Security.* Lanham, MD: University Press of America, 2011.

Roosevelt, Kermit. *Arabs, Oil, and History: The Story of the Middle East.* Port Washington, NY: Kennikat Press, 1969.

———. *Countercoup: The Struggle for the Control of Iran.* New York: McGraw-Hill, 1979.

Rosen, Nir. *In the Belly of the Green Bird: The Triumph of the Martyrs in Iraq.* New York: Free Press, 2006.

———. *Aftermath: Following the Bloodshed of America's Wars in the Muslim World.* New York: Nation Books, 2010.

Ross, Dennis. *The Missing Peace: The Inside Story of the Fight for Middle East Peace.* New York: Farrar, Straus and Giroux, 2004.

Ross, Dorothy. *The Origins of American Social Science.* Cambridge: Cambridge University Press, 1991.

Rostow, Walt Whitman. *The Diffusion of Power: An Essay in Recent History.* New York: Macmillan, 1972.

Rotter, Andrew. "Saidism without Said: Orientalism and U.S. Diplomatic History." *American Historical Review* 104, no. 4 (October 2000): 1205–1217.

Rouchdy, Aleya. *The Arabic Language in America.* Detroit: Wayne State University Press, 1992.

Roy, Sara. *Hamas and Civil Society in Gaza: Engaging the Islamist Social Sector.* Princeton, NJ: Princeton University Press, 2013.

Rumsfeld, Donald. *Known and Unknown: A Memoir.* New York: Sentinel, 2011.

Ruther, Nancy. *Barely There, Powerfully Present: Thirty Years of U.S. Policy on International Higher Education.* New York: Routledge, 2002.

Saad-Ghorayeb, Amal. *Hizbullah: Politics and Religion.* London: Pluto Books, 2002.

Said, Edward. *Orientalism.* New York: Vintage, 1979.

———. *Culture and Imperialism.* New York: Vintage, 1994.

———. *Covering Islam: How the Media and the Experts Determine How We See the World.* Rev. ed. New York: Vintage, 1997.

———. *From Oslo to Iraq and the Road Map.* New York: Vintage, 2004.

Salahi, Yaman, and Nasrina Bargzie. "Talking Israel and Palestine on Campus: How the U.S. Department of Education Can Uphold the Civil Rights Act and the First Amendment." *Hastings Race and Poverty Law Journal* 12, no. 3 (Summer 2015): 155–190.

Sargent, Daniel. *A Superpower Transformed: The Remaking of American Foreign Relations in the 1970s.* New York: Oxford University Press, 2015.

Satia, Priya. *Spies in Arabia: The Great War and the Cultural Foundations of Britain's Covert Empire in the Middle East*. New York: Oxford University Press, 2008.

Saunders, Charles H. *The Brookings Institution: A Fifty Year History*. Washington, DC: Brookings Institution, 1966.

Saunders, Frances Stonor. *The Cultural Cold War: The CIA and the World of Arts and Letters*. New York: New Press, 1999.

Saunders, Harold H. *Conversations with Harold H. Saunders: U.S. Policy in the Middle East in the 1980s*. Washington, DC: American Enterprise Institute, 1982.

Sayigh, Tawfiq. *Mudhakkirāt Tawfiq Sayigh*. Edited by Mahmud Chreih. Beirut: Dar Nelson, 2011.

Sayigh, Yezid. *Armed Struggle and the Search for State: The Palestinian National Movement, 1949–1993*. New York: Oxford University Press, 2000.

Scahill, Jeremy. *Blackwater: The Rise of the World's Most Powerful Mercenary Army*. New York: Nation Books, 2007.

Schoenbaum, David. *The United States and the State of Israel*. New York: Oxford University Press, 1993.

Schulzinger, Robert D. *The Making of the Diplomatic Mind: The Training, Outlook, and Style of United States Foreign Service Officers, 1908–1931*. Middletown, CT: Wesleyan University Press, 1975.

Segev, Tom. *One Palestine, Complete*. New York: Henry Holt, 1999.

———. *1967: Israel, the War, and the Year That Transformed the Middle East*. New York: Metropolitan Books, 2007.

Seib, Philip. *The Al Jazeera Effect: How the New Global Media Are Reshaping World Politics*. Dulles, VA: Potomac Book, 2008.

Sha'ban, Fuad. *Islam and Arabs in Early American Thought: Roots of Orientalism in America*. Durham, NC: Acorn Press, 1991.

Shadid, Anthony. *Night Draws Near: Iraq's People in the Shadow of America's War*. New York: Henry Holt, 2005.

Shah, Hemant. *The Production of Modernization: Daniel Lerner, Mass Media, and the Passing of Traditional Society*. Philadelphia: Temple University Press, 2011.

Shalev, Eran. *American Zion: The Old Testament as a Political Text from the Revolution to the Civil War*. New Haven, CT: Yale University Press, 2013.

Shami, Seteny, and Marcial Godoy-Anativia. "Pensée 2: Between the Hammer and the Anvil: Middle East Studies in the Aftermath of 9/11." *International Journal of Middle East Studies* 39 (2007): 346–349.

Sherry, Michael S. *In the Shadow of War: The United States since the 1930s*. New Haven, CT: Yale University Press, 1995.

Shlaim, Avi. *Collusion across the Jordan: King Abdullah, the Zionist Movement, and the Partition of Palestine*. New York: Columbia University Press, 1988.

———. *The Iron Wall: Israel and the Arab World*. New York: Norton, 2001.

Shohat, Ella. "The Media's War." In *Seeing through the Media: The Persian Gulf War*, edited by Susan Jeffords and Lauren Rabinovitcz, 147–154. New Brunswick, NJ: Rutgers University Press, 1994.

Shurayh, Mahmud. *Tawfīq Sayigh: Sīrat Shaʿir wa-Manfī.* London: Riad el-Rayyes Books, 1989.

Sick, Gary. *All Fall Down: America's Fateful Encounter with Iran.* London: I. B. Tauris, 1985.

Simpson, Bradley R. *Economists with Guns: Authoritarian Development and U.S.-Indonesian Relations, 1960–1968.* Stanford, CA: Stanford University Press, 2008.

Simpson, Christopher. *Blowback: America's Recruitment of Nazis and Its Effect on the Cold War.* New York: Weidenfeld & Nicolson, 1988.

———. *Science of Coercion: Communication Research and Psychological Warfare, 1945–1960.* New York: Oxford University Press, 1994.

———, ed. *Universities and Empire: Money and Politics in the Social Sciences during the Cold War.* New York: New Press, 1998.

Smith, Bradley F. *The Shadow Warriors: O.S.S. and the Origins of the C.I.A.* New York: Basic Books, 1983.

Smith, Charles. *Palestine and the Arab-Israeli Conflict.* 4th ed. Boston: Bedford/St. Martins, 2001.

Smith, Gaddis. *Morality, Reason, and Power: American Diplomacy in the Carter Years.* New York: Hill and Wang, 1987.

Smith, James Allen. *The Idea Brokers: Think Tanks and the Rise of the New Policy Elite.* New York: New Press, 1991.

Smith, Jason Scott. *Building New Deal Liberalism: The Political Economy of Public Works, 1933–1956.* Cambridge: Cambridge Press, 2009.

Smith, Neil. *American Empire: Roosevelt's Geographer and the Prelude to Globalization.* Berkeley: University of California Press, 2003.

Solecki, John. "Arabists and the Myth." *Middle East Journal* 44, no. 3 (Summer 1990): 446–457.

Speiser, E. A. "Near Eastern Studies in America, 1939–1945." *Archiv Orientalni* 1–2 (December 1947): 76–88.

Spiegel, Steven. *The Other Arab Israeli Conflict: Making America's Middle East Policy from Truman to Reagan.* Chicago: University of Chicago Press, 1985.

Stampnitzky, Lisa. *Disciplining Terror: How Experts Invented "Terrorism."* Cambridge: Cambridge University Press, 2013.

Starkey, Elizabeth R., and John R. Starkey. "A Talk with Bayard Dodge." *ARAMCO World.* July/August 1972.

Steel, Ronald. *Walter Lippmann and the American Century.* Boston: Little, Brown, 1980.

Stephanson, Anders. *Kennan and the Art of Foreign Policy.* Cambridge, MA: Harvard University Press, 1989.

———. "Ideology and Neorealist Mirrors." *Diplomatic History* (April 1993): 285–295.

———. *Manifest Destiny: American Expansion and the Empire of Right.* New York: Hill and Wang, 1996.

Steuck, William. *Rethinking the Korean War.* Princeton, NJ: Princeton University Press, 2002.

Steury, Donald P., ed. *Sherman Kent and the Board of National Estimates.* Central Intelligence Agency: Washington, DC: 1994.

Stivers, William. *America's Confrontation with Revolutionary Change in the Middle East.* New York: St. Martin's Press, 1986.

Stork, Joe. *Middle East Oil and the Energy Crisis.* New York: Monthly Review Press, 1975.

Stuart, Douglas T. *Creating the National Security State: A History of the Law That Transformed America.* Princeton, NJ: Princeton University Press, 2008.

Suleiman, Michael. *The Arabs in the Mind of America.* Brattleboro, VT: Amana Books, 1988.

Suri, Jeremi. *Power and Protest: Global Revolution and the Rise of Détente.* Cambridge, MA: Harvard University Press, 2003.

Szanton, David, ed. *The Politics of Knowledge: Area Studies and the Disciplines.* Berkeley: University of California Press, 2004.

Tanter, Raymond, and Richard Ullman, eds. *Theory and Politics in International Relations.* Princeton, NJ: Princeton University Press, 1972.

Tchen, Jon Kuo Wei. *New York before Chinatown: Orientalism and the Shaping of America Culture, 1776–1882.* Baltimore: Johns Hopkins University Press, 1999.

Tessler, Mark, Jodi Nachtaway, and Anne Banda, eds. *Area Studies and Social Science: Strategies for Understanding Middle East Politics.* Bloomington: Indiana University Press, 1999.

Thayer, Philip W., ed. *Tensions in the Middle East.* Baltimore: Johns Hopkins University Press, 1958.

Throntveit, Trygve. "The Fable of the Fourteen Points: Woodrow Wilson and National Self-Determination." *Diplomatic History* 35, no. 3 (June 2011): 445–481.

Troy, Thomas F. *Donovan and the CIA: A History of the Establishment of the Central Intelligence Agency.* Frederick, MD: University Publications of America, 1981.

Urban, Wayne J. *More Than Science and Sputnik: The National Defense Education Act of 1958.* Tuscaloosa: University of Alabama Press, 2010.

Vaïsse, Justin. *Neoconservatism: The Biography of a Movement.* Cambridge, MA: Belknap Press of Harvard University Press, 2010.

VanDeMark, Brian. *American Sheikhs: Two Families, Four Generations, and the Story of America's Influence in the Middle East.* Amherst, NY: Prometheus Books, 2012.

Van de Ven, Susan Kerr. *One Family's Response to Terrorism: A Daughter's Memoir.* Syracuse, NY: Syracuse University Press, 2008.

Vatikiotis, P. J. *The Egyptian Army in Politics: Pattern for New Nations?* Westport, CT: Greenwood Press, 1975.

Vest, Jason. "The Men from JINSA and CSP." *The Nation.* August 15, 2002.

Vitalis, Robert. *America's Kingdom: Mythmaking on the Saudi Oil Frontier.* Stanford, CA: Stanford University Press, 2007.

———. "The Noble American Science of Imperial Relations and Its Laws of Race Development." *Comparative Studies in Society and History* 52, no. 4 (2010): 909–938.

Vogel, Lester. *To See a Promised Land.* University Park: Pennsylvania State University Press, 1993.

Von Eschen, Penny. *Satchmo Blows Up the World: Jazz Ambassadors Play the World.* Cambridge, MA: Harvard University Press, 2006.

Wala, Michael. *The Council on Foreign Relations and American Foreign Policy in the Early Cold War.* Providence: Berghahn Books, 1994.

Wall, Irwin M. *France, the United States, and the Algerian War.* Berkeley: University of California Press, 2001.

Waller, Douglas. *Wild Bill Donovan: The Spymaster Who Created the OSS and Modern American Espionage.* New York: Free Press, 2011.

Walther, Karine. *Sacred Interests: The United States and the Islamic World, 1821–1921.* Chapel Hill: University of North Carolina Press, 2015.

Warner, Michael, ed. *The CIA under Harry Truman: CIA Cold War Records.* Honolulu: University Press of the Pacific, 2005.

Weinberger, Caspar, with Gretchen Roberts. *In the Arena: A Memoir of the 20th Century.* Washington, DC: Regnery Publishing, 2001.

Weiner, Tim. *Legacy of Ashes: The History of the CIA.* New York: Doubleday, 2007.

Weiss, Carol H., ed. *Organizations for Policy Analysis: Helping Government Think.* London: Sage Publications, 1991.

Weldes, Jutta. *Constructing National Interests: The United States and the Cuban Missile Crisis.* Minneapolis: University of Minnesota Press, 1999.

Wendt, Alexander. *Social Theory of International Politics.* Cambridge: Cambridge University Press, 1999.

West, Richard, Jr. *Admirals of American Empire.* New York: Bobbs-Merrill, 1948.

Westad, Odd Arne. *The Global Cold War: Third World Interventions and the Making of Our Times.* Cambridge: Cambridge University Press, 2005.

Westrate, Bruce. *The Arab Bureau: British Policy in the Middle East, 1916–1920.* University Park: Pennsylvania State University Press, 1992.

Wight, David. "Kissinger's Levantine Dilemma: The Ford Administration and the Syrian Occupation of Lebanon." *Diplomatic History* 37, no. 1 (2013): 144–177.

Wilford, Hugh. *The Mighty Wurlitzer: How the CIA Played America.* Cambridge, MA: Harvard University Press, 2008.

———. *America's Great Game: The CIA's Secret Arabists and the Shaping of the Modern Middle East.* New York: Basic Books, 2013.

Williams, William Appleman. *The Tragedy of American Diplomacy.* New York: W. W. Norton, 1959.

Wilson, Mary C. *King Abdullah, Britain, and the Making of Jordan.* Cambridge: Cambridge University Press, 1990.

Winder, R. Bayly. "Four Decades of Middle Eastern Study." *Middle East Journal* 41, no. 1 (Winter 1987): 40–63.

Winks, Robin. *Cloak and Gown: Scholars in the Secret War, 1939–1961.* New York: William Morrow, 1987.

Wise, David, and Thomas Ross. *The Invisible Government.* New York: Random House, 1964.

Wolfe-Hunnicutt, Brandon. "Embracing Regime Change in Iraq: The American Foreign Policy and the 1963 Coup d'état in Baghdad." *Diplomatic History* 39, no. 1 (January 2015): 98–125.

Wood, Robert E. *From Marshall Plan to Debt Crisis: Foreign Aid and Development Choices in the World Economy.* Berkeley: University of California Press, 1986.

Woodward, Bob. *Bush at War.* New York: Simon & Schuster, 2002.

———. *Plan of Attack.* New York: Simon & Schuster, 2004.

———. *State of Denial.* New York: Simon & Schuster, 2007.

———. *The War Within: A Secret White House History, 2006–2008.* New York: Simon & Schuster, 2008.

Worcester, Kenton. *Social Science Research Council, 1923–1998.* New York: Social Science Research Council, 2001.

Wurmser, David. *Tyranny's Ally: America's Failure to Defeat Saddam Hussein.* Washington, DC: The AEI Press, 1999.

Yaqub, Salim. *Containing Arab Nationalism: The Eisenhower Doctrine and the Middle East.* Chapel Hill: University of North Carolina Press, 2004.

Yergin, Daniel. *The Prize: The Epic Quest for Oil, Money, and Power.* New York: Touchstone, Simon & Schuster, 1991.

Yoo, John. *War by Other Means: An Insider's Account of the War on Terror.* New York: Atlantic Monthly Press, 2006.

Yu, Henry. *Thinking Orientals: Migration, Contact, and Exoticism in Modern America.* New York: Oxford University Press, 2001.

Zegart, Amy. *Flawed by Design: The Evolution of the CIA, JCS, and NSC.* Stanford, CA: Stanford University Press, 1999.

———. *Spying Blind: The CIA, the FBI, and the Origins of 9/11.* Princeton, NJ: Princeton University Press, 2009.

Zeine, Zeine N. *The Struggle for Arab Independence: Western Diplomacy and the Rise and Fall of Faisal's Kingdom in Syria.* New York: Caravan Books, 1977.

Zelizer, Julian E. *Arsenal of Democracy: The Politics of National Security from World War II to the War on Terrorism.* New York: Basic Books, 2010.

Acknowledgments

This book began as a series of conversations and disparate research projects while I was a graduate student at the University of California, Berkeley. Beshara Doumani provided essential support and sage advice. His friendship has been invaluable. Salim Yaqub influenced this project from its inception. He continues to offer generous guidance and support, for which I am extremely grateful. Laura Nader held me to the highest standards of scholarship, and I benefited from her vast knowledge and experience. David Holloway was gracious and supportive, and I am in his debt. Daniel Sargent continues to be generous with his time and advice and was kind enough to share sources with me after I left Berkeley. Daniel's insights and counsel helped to improve this book, and it would not have been as successful without his support.

I am deeply indebted to the many archivists who assisted with my research. I spent considerable time at the U.S. National Archives in College Park, Maryland, and am grateful to the archivists and staff for their assistance. The American University in Cairo graciously opened its archives to me, and thanks to Stephen Urgola for providing some of the excellent images in this book. Thanks to Samar Mikati Kaissi and the staff of the American University of Beirut archives for accommodating my many requests. The archivists and staff members of the United Kingdom's Public Records Office, Rockefeller Foundation Archives, the Princeton University Archives and Seeley G. Mudd Library, the Harvard University Archives, the Johns Hopkins University Archives, and the Library of Congress were helpful and supportive. Thanks also to the archivists and staff of the Brookings Institution Archive and the Dwight D. Eisenhower and the Gerald R. Ford Presidential Libraries for their responsiveness to my requests.

This project would not have been completed without the generous support of the University of California, Berkeley, Department of History, the Graduate Division, and the Center for Middle East Studies. Thanks to the Society for Historians of American Foreign Relations Bennis Research Grant. My home institution, the Department of History at Syracuse University's Maxwell School of Citizenship and Public Affairs, provided generous assistance. Special thanks to Dean Jim Steinberg and Senior Associate Dean Mike Wasylenko, the Maxwell School's Appleby-Mosher Fund, and the History Department's Pigott Fund.

This book and I benefited from the generosity of fellow scholars. David Price was an early advocate of this project and was gracious with his time and advice. Joel Beinin provided important feedback as I was conceptualizing the book. Robert Vitalis offered detailed suggestions for improvement. Mayssoun Sukarieh and Lisa Stampnitzky were kind enough to share articles and sources with me in support of this project. Brandon Wolfe-Hunnicutt, Seth Anziska, and Jeremy Kuzmarov graciously agreed to review individual chapters and gave thoughtful feedback and suggestions. Zachary Lockman reviewed an initial version of the manuscript and generously shared his own manuscript with me. I am indebted to Yaman Salahi for his counsel, humor, and frequent articles, which informed parts of this book.

I presented portions of this book at conferences and invited lectures and received valuable comments and suggestions. My presentations at the annual meetings of the American Historical Association, the Society for Historians of American Foreign Relations, and the Middle East Studies Association helped to clarify my arguments and conclusions. The book also benefited from my participation in conferences hosted by the American University of Beirut. Thanks to Nadia El Cheikh, Bilal Orfali, Waleed Hazbun, John Meloy, and Cyrus Schayegh. I was fortunate to participate in Columbia University's 2012 conference on Wartime Intelligence. Thanks to the organizers, Mark Mazower and Nicholas Dirks, for their generous invitation and thoughtful feedback. I also received excellent suggestions, critiques, and advice from Priya Satia, Bruce Kuklick, Peter Mandler, and Anders Stephanson. I was thrilled to return to my undergraduate home, Temple University's History Department, and present at the Center for the Study of Force and Diplomacy. Special thanks to Richard Immerman, Beth Bailey, David Farber, and Peter Gran. I was honored to return to Berkeley and present at the Center for Middle East

Studies. Thanks to Emily Gottreich and Nezar AlSayyad for the gracious invitation.

My colleagues at Syracuse have been generous and supportive. Thanks to Carol Faulkner, Margaret Thompson, Andrew Wender Cohen, Michael Ebner, Elisabeth Lasch-Quinn, Amy Kallander, Martin Shanguhyia, and David Bennett. I am indebted to Norman Kutcher and Andrew Lipman for their help and support when it was needed most. Lydia Wasylenko and the staff of Bird Library were gracious and patient with my many requests.

Family and friends were supportive during my research excursions. They offered spare rooms, meals, and help with big and small tasks and requests. My parents and siblings were a source of inspiration. My extended family in Beirut was very helpful and gracious during and after my trips to Lebanon. Thanks to Iyad Darcazallie, Susan Hassan, Murat Dagli, Melanie Tanielian, Nadia Hijab, Silvia Pasquetti, Chris Shaw, Yves Winter, Ron Elson, Eleanore Lee, and Lubna Qureshi for their continuing friendship and encouragement. Thanks to Colleen Grogan and George Andreopoulos for their help and support when I started on this journey. I am grateful to Howard Spodek for his many years of friendship and continuing support.

When I was unable to travel, Brittany Legasey, Feride Eraip, Fatima Jaffer, Sue Strange, Khalil Issa, and Raja Abu-Hassan completed excellent research for me at archives in New York, New Jersey, California, Maryland, and Lebanon.

Andrew Kinney saw the potential in this project and shared my vision for the book. I am grateful for his guidance and support. Thanks to Katrina Vassallo and the staff of Harvard University Press for their assistance. Thanks to the staff of Westchester Publishing Services, especially Melody Negron for overseeing production and Karen Brogno for copyediting. I am grateful to the anonymous reviewers for their helpful suggestions. Any errors are my own.

Elements of the Introduction and Chapter 6 were initially examined in "The Crossroads of the World: U.S. and British Foreign Policy Doctrines and the Construct of the Middle East, 1902–2007," *Diplomatic History* 38, no. 2 (April 2014): 299–344. The Epilogue touches on some themes discussed in "The Counterrevolutionary Year: Arab Spring, the Gulf Cooperation Council, and U.S. Foreign Policy in the Middle East," in *American Studies Encounters the Middle East*, ed. Alex Lubin and Marwan Kraidy (Chapel Hill: University of North Carolina Press, 2016), 286–301. Thanks to the publishers for their consideration.

Researching and writing a book can be a solitary affair, and I am thankful that I had two companions to enrich and support this project and my life. My wife, Dalal Yassine, was a source of encouragement, inspiration, good humor, and love. My daughter, Laila, was born as I was finishing my doctorate. She developed great instincts for knowing when to let me write and when to insist that I play with her, although we both would have preferred more playing and less writing. This book is dedicated to them.

Index

www.ingramcontent.com/pod-product-compliance
Lightning Source LLC
Chambersburg PA
CBHW021830090426
42811CB00032B/2102/J